MCSE/MCSA Implementing a Windows® Server 2003 Network Infrastructure Study Guide

(Exam 70-291)

Rory McCaw
Kenneth Lind

McGraw-Hill/Osborne

New York Chicago San Francisco Lisbon London Madrid
Mexico City Milan New Delhi San Juan Seoul Singapore Sydney Toronto

The McGraw·Hill Companies

McGraw-Hill/Osborne
2100 Powell Street, 10th Floor
Emeryville, California 94608
U.S.A.

To arrange bulk purchase discounts for sales promotions, premiums, or fund-raisers, please
contact **McGraw-Hill**/Osborne at the above address. For information on translations or
book distributors outside the U.S.A., please see the International Contact Information page
immediately following the index of this book.

**MCSE/MCSA Implementing a Windows® Server 2003 Network Infrastructure Study Guide
(Exam 70-291)**

1234567890 CUS CUS 01987654

Book p/n 0-07-222567-X and CD p/n 0-07-222568-8
parts of
ISBN 0-07-222566-1

Publisher	**Acquisitions Coordinator**	**Indexer**
Brandon A. Nordin	Jessica Wilson	Valerie Perry
Vice President &	**Technical Editor**	**Composition**
Associate Publisher	Dave Field	Apollo Publishing Service
Scott Rogers		
	Copy Editor	**Series Design**
Acquisitions Editor	Brian MacDonald	Roberta Steele
Tim Green		
	Proofreader	**Cover Series Design**
Project Editor	Linda Medoff	Peter Grame
Julie M. Smith		

This book was composed with Corel VENTURA™ Publisher.

I would like to dedicate this book to my wife Dina and my daughter Emily. You two ladies bring joy and happiness into my life. Dina, you have been such a great source of strength and support for me, thank you! Thanks too for your patience and for accepting the long hours required to complete this project. Emily, even though you are too young to read, I dedicate this book to you and suggest that we put it on your list of bed time reading. ☺ Just seeing your warm smile when I emerge from my office after hours of writing cheers me up!

— Rory McCaw

I would like to dedicate this book to my lovely wife Dorette who has been my support for over 25 years, and still lets me come home. Thanks for everything Dorette.

— Kenneth S. Lind

ABOUT THE AUTHORS

Kenneth S. Lind

Kenneth Lind is the founder of No Problem Computers, a company that focuses on delivery of computer training around the Americas. Kenneth brings over 25 years of experience in computer systems and software development to his customers. He left his native Sweden 25 years ago, and lives currently in Toronto, Ontario, Canada, as well as wherever there is a Starbucks. Kenneth has developed hands-on-labs for Microsoft events such as TechEd as well as Microsoft product launches worldwide, Kenneth also develops and delivers training in Object Oriented Analysis and Design, and in database design and administration. Kenneth has authored and contributed to books on such topics as Microsoft Exchange 2000 Administration, Microsoft .NET development and Microsoft SQL Server. Kenneth has managed to gain all of Microsoft's Certifications over the years, seemingly without trying. You can reach Kenneth through his web site at www.nopcomp.com.

Rory McCaw

Rory McCaw is the founder of 1503632 Ontario Ltd, a technical training company that provides technical education resources to corporate clients worldwide. Rory's focus is on Microsoft technologies and he can be seen regularly at Microsoft district offices and events throughout North America speaking to Microsoft's customers and partners.

Rory is the author of a number of technical books, including MCSE Windows 2000 Network Infrastructure Administration, MCSA Managing a Windows 2000 Network Environment, and Migrating your Network from Windows NT 4.0 to Windows 2000.

Rory holds numerous industry designations and has been honored with the Microsoft MVP designation in the area of Windows Server technology. Rory is a humorous and accomplished consultant and presenter who has developed and delivered numerous presentations for Microsoft at events including Comdex, hands-on-lab workshops, and numerous product launch events. Throughout 2003, Rory was involved in presenting two-day Microsoft Windows Server 2003 hands-on-lab and Microsoft Security hands-on lab events to Microsoft partners at locations throughout North America. Look to Rory's personal web site at http://www.mccaw.ca to learn more about the Rory's books, training services and to find other valuable information about Microsoft technologies.

About LearnKey

LearnKey provides self-paced learning content and multimedia delivery solutions to enhance personal skills and business productivity. LearnKey claims the largest library of rich streaming-media content that engages learners in dynamic media-rich instruction complete with video clips, audio, full motion graphics, and animated illustrations. LearnKey can be found on the web at www.LearnKey.com.

CONTENTS AT A GLANCE

CONTENTS

ACKNOWLEDGMENTS

We would like to thank the following people:

- I would like to thank all the incredibly hard-working folks at Osborne/McGraw-Hill: Brandon Nordin, Scott Rogers, Gareth Hancock, Tim Green, Julie Smith, Jessica Wilson and Dave Field for their help in launching a great series and being solid team players.

- I would especially like to thank Ken Lind for the many days spent and coffees consumed discussing how we would tackle writing this book. I also want to thank you for the friendship that has resulted from the work we have done together and our shared love for technology and commitment to quality education. Thanks Ken and happy birthday!!

  —Rory McCaw

- I would like to thank the hard working staff at Osborne/McGraw-Hill for their support and team spirit throughout the production of this book. It is always hard to list names, for fear of forgetting anyone in the team. I'd like to thank: Brandon Nordin, Scott Rogers, Gareth Hancock, Tim Green, Julie Smith and Jessica Wilson for all their help.

- Great thanks to Rory McCaw for his unswerving optimism that has carried this project through a summer when we both most wanted to enjoy the weather. Thanks Rory, I'll get to Starbucks soon, if I only knew if it is Atlanta or Birmingham. ☺

- I would be remiss if I neglected to mention my support group here in Toronto. Thanks Des, John, Sunny and all the rest at the Lakeshore Restaurant.

- Thank you Nancy for your ongoing friendship and support, I enjoy those pep talks we have, and your views on the industry. Thanks for joining me for the latte at Moonpennies.

- I would like to thank my family, my wife Dorette, my daughter Inga and my son Anders, for suffering my long trips away, and long hours writing. Thank you for your understanding and support, it has meant the world to me.

  — Kenneth S. Lind

xix

The primary objective of this book is to help you prepare for and pass the 70-291 certification exam, a core requirement for the Windows Server 2003 MCSA. After completing this book you should feel confident that you have thoroughly reviewed all of the objectives that Microsoft has established for this certification exam.

In This Book

This book is organized in such a way as to serve as an in-depth review for the Implementing, Managing, and Maintaining a Microsoft Windows Server 2003 Network Infrastructure certification exam for both experienced Windows NT, Windows 2000, and Windows Server 2003professionals and newcomers to Microsoft networking technologies and operating systems. Each chapter covers a major aspect of the exam, with an emphasis on the "why" as well as the "how to" of working with and supporting Windows Server 2003 as a network administrator or system engineer.

Exam Readiness Checklist

At the end of the Introduction you will find an Exam Readiness Checklist. This table has been constructed to allow you to cross-reference the official exam objectives with the objectives as they are presented and covered in this book. The checklist also allows you to gauge your level of expertise on each objective at the outset of your studies. This should allow you to check your progress and make sure you spend the time you need on more difficult or unfamiliar sections. References have been provided for the objective exactly as the vendor presents it, the section of the study guide that covers that objective, and a chapter reference.

In Every Chapter

We've created a set of chapter components that call your attention to important items, reinforce important points, and provide helpful exam-taking hints. Take a look at what you'll find in every chapter:

■ Every chapter begins with the **Certification Objectives**—what you need to know in order to pass the section on the exam dealing with the chapter topic.

The Objective headings identify the objectives within the chapter, so you'll always know an objective when you see it!

- **Exam Watch** notes call attention to information about, and potential pitfalls in, the exam. These helpful hints are written by authors who have taken the exams and received their certification—who better to tell you what to worry about? They know what you're about to go through!

- **Practice Exercises** are interspersed throughout the chapters. These are step-by-step exercises that allow you to get the hands-on experience you need in order to pass the exams. They help you master skills that are likely to be an area of focus on the exam. Don't just read through the exercises; they are hands-on practice that you should be comfortable completing. Learning by doing is an effective way to increase your competency with a product.

- **On The Job** notes describe the issues that come up most often in real-world settings. They provide a valuable perspective on certification- and product-related topics. They point out common mistakes and address questions that have arisen from on the job discussions and experience.

- **Inside the Exam** sidebars highlight some of the most common and confusing problems that students encounter when taking a live exam. Designed to anticipate what the exam will emphasize, getting inside the exam will help ensure you know what you need to know to pass the exam. You can get a leg up on how to respond to those difficult to understand questions by focusing extra attention on these sidebars.

- **Scenario and Solutions** sections lay out potential problems and solutions in a quick-to-read format:

SCENARIO & SOLUTION

James must be available to troubleshoot the computers in any office in the four buildings of the company that he works for…	Implement a roaming profile for James so that he can access his desktop no matter what computer he is using. This is especially handy. since his roaming profile can include the mapping to a network drive that holds his diagnostic tools.

- The **Certification Summary** is a succinct review of the chapter and a restatement of salient points regarding the exam.

■ The **Two-Minute Drill** at the end of every chapter is a checklist of the main points of the chapter. It can be used for last-minute review.

■ The **Self Test** offers questions similar to those found on the certification exams. The answers to these questions, as well as explanations of the answers, can be found at the end of each chapter. By taking the Self Test after completing each chapter, you'll reinforce what you've learned from that chapter while becoming familiar with the structure of the exam questions.

■ The **Lab Question** at the end of the Self Test section offers a unique and challenging question format that requires the reader to understand multiple chapter concepts to answer correctly. These questions are more complex and more comprehensive than the other questions, as they test your ability to take all the knowledge you have gained from reading the chapter and apply it to complicated, real-world situations. These questions are aimed to be more difficult than what you will find on the exam. If you can answer these questions, you have proven that you know the subject!

Some Pointers

Once you've finished reading this book, set aside some time to do a thorough review. You might want to return to the book several times and make use of all the methods it offers for reviewing the material:

1. *Re-read all the Two-Minute Drills*, or have someone quiz you. You also can use the drills as a way to do a quick cram before the exam. You might want to make some flash cards out of 3 x 5 index cards that have the Two-Minute Drill material on them.

2. *Re-read all the Exam Watch notes*. Remember that these notes are written by authors who have taken the exam and passed. They know what you should expect—and what you should be on the lookout for.

3. *Review all the S&S sections* for quick problem solving.

4. *Re-take the Self Tests*. Taking the tests right after you've read the chapter is a good idea, because the questions help reinforce what you've just learned. However, it's an even better idea to go back later and do all the questions in the book in one sitting. Pretend that you're taking the live exam. (When you go through the questions the first time, you should mark your answers on a separate piece of paper. That way, you can run through the questions as many times as you need to until you feel comfortable with the material..)

5. *Complete the Exercises.* Did you do the exercises when you read through each chapter? If not, do them! These exercises are designed to cover exam topics, and there's no better way to get to know this material than by practicing. Be sure you understand why you are performing each step in each exercise. If there is something you are not clear on, re-read that section in the chapter.

W elcome to the MCSA Implementing a Windows Server 2003 Network Infrastructure Study Guide (Exam 70-291). The purpose of this book is to provide you with the skills and knowledge required to achieve a passing score on the Microsoft 70-291 certification exam: Implementing, Managing, and Maintaining a Microsoft Windows Server 2003 Network Infrastructure. The information in this book has been designed to explain the concepts you need to know to be successful on the certification exam. Ken and Rory are your personal technology guides and have tried to deliver to you all of the critical information, exam tips and on the job examples they could think of to help you succeed. The layout of the book as you will soon see breaks up the five key certification objectives into smaller, easier to digest sections that focus on implementing, managing and maintaining the various underlying technologies.

Ken and Rory also realize that understanding the big picture is just as important as understanding the smaller details and begin each chapter by explaining the underlying concepts necessary to establish a strong foundation from which your knowledge specific to Windows Server 2003 can be built upon.

Why the MCSA?

The Microsoft Certified Systems Administrator (MCSA) credential is one of the more recent Microsoft certifications, originally established with Windows 2000. The MCSA is the stepping stone certification to the Microsoft Certified Systems Engineer (MCSE) designation which has been around for years. The MCSE certification is designed to test a number of inter related concepts that include but are not limited to networking, administration, Active Directory, security, and monitoring. To learn more about the numerous and frequently changing Microsoft certifications look to www.microsoft.com/traincert/mcp/default.asp.

How Microsoft Defines the MCSA Audience

Microsoft defines the target audience for the MCSA on Windows Server 2003 to be for IT professionals that meet the following criteria:

- Work for a medium to large company (250 to 5000 or more users) that has a complex computing environment

■ Have 6 to 12 months experience administering client and network operating systems

■ Are experienced working in networks that have multiple physical locations with three or more domain controllers

■ Are experienced with network services are applications that include messaging, databases, file and print, proxy servers, firewalls, remote access, and that have access to the Internet

Skills Being Measured

The 70-291 exam is very broad in scope and is intended to test your knowledge and ability to administer, manage and troubleshoot multiple network services, components and features of the Windows Server 2003 operating system. The preparation guide for the 70-291 exam can be found at www.microsoft.com/traincert/exams/70-291.asp. The following is a quick summary of the certification objectives you will find within the preparation guide.

Study Strategies

A combination of theoretical and hands-on experience is always the best combination for success. We would encourage you to download a free evaluation copy of Windows Server 2003 from the Microsoft web site and walk through the exercises described in the book as well as listen to the certcams included on the CD. Once you have read the book and practiced the skills included in the exercises, try the certification exam questions included on the CD to identify areas where you could use some improvement and then review those areas.

One common obstacle or difficulty for individuals that only have the ability to learn about the features included in the Windows Server 2003 operating system at home is where and how to install the operating system without affecting their current operating system. To solve this common problem, I would encourage you to look to products like VMWare Workstation (www.vmware.com) or Connectix Virtual PC (www.connectix.com). Both of these applications allow you to install Windows Server 2003 in a virtual computer environment that runs as an application on your host operating system of your home PC. To find out more about how to do this look to my web site at **www. mccaw.ca** for detailed instructions.

One other suggestion that we might offer is to review all of the exam watch blurbs throughout the book prior to writing the exam as these are intended to give you a heads-up as to what you might expect by way of questions on the exam.

If you spend the time to learn what's being tested, you will be successful on the certification exam but don't approach this exam with the mindset that you don't have to study because this is one of the trickier exams from Microsoft.

Exam Readiness Checklist

Official Objective	Ch #	Beginner	Intermediate	Expert
Implementing, Managing and Maintaining IP Addressing	1, 2, 3			
Configure TCP/IP addressing on a server computer	1			
Manage DHCP clients and leases	2			
Manage DHCP Relay Agents	2			
Manage DHCP databases	2			
Manage DHCP scope options	2			
Manage reservations and reserved clients	2			
Diagnose and resolve issues related to Automatic Private IP Addressing (APIPA)	3			
Diagnose and resolve issues related to incorrect TCP/IP configuration	3			
Diagnose and resolve issues related to DHCP authorization	3			
Verify DHCP reservation configuration	3			
Examine the system event log and DHCP server audit logs to find related events	3			
Diagnose and resolve issues related to configuration of DHCP server and scope options	3			
Verify that the DHCP Relay Agent is working correctly	3			
Verify database integrity	3			

Exam Readiness Checklist

Official Objective	Ch #	Beginner	Intermediate	Expert
Implementing, Managing, and Maintaining Name Resolution	4, 5, 6			
Configure DNS server options	4			
Configure DNS zone options	4			
Configure DNS forwarding	4			
Manage DNS server options	5			
Manage DNS zone settings	5			
Manage DNS record settings	5			
Monitor DNS. Tools might include System Monitor, Event Viewer, Replication Monitor, and DNS debug logs	6			
Implementing, Managing, and Maintaining Network Security	7, 8			
Implement security baseline settings and audit security settings by using security templates	7			
Implement the principle of least privilege	7			
Install and configure software update services	7			
Install and configure automatic client update settings	7			
Configure software updates on earlier operating systems	8			
Monitor network protocol security. Tools might include the IP Security Monitor Microsoft Management Console (MMC) snap-in and Kerberos support tools	8			
Implementing, Managing, and Maintaining Routing and Remote Access	10, 11, 12			
Configure remote access authentication protocols	10			
Configure Internet Authentication Service (IAS) to provide authentication for Routing and Remote Access clients	10			

Exam Readiness Checklist

Official Objective	Ch #	Beginner	Intermediate	Expert
Configure Routing and Remote Access policies to permit or deny access	10			
Manage packet filters	11			
Manage Routing and Remote Access routing interfaces	11			
Manage devices and ports	11			
Manage routing protocols	11			
Manage Routing and Remote Access clients	11			
Manage routing protocols	11			
Manage routing tables	11			
Manage routing ports	11			
Implement secure access between private networks	11			
Diagnose and resolve issues related to remote access VPNs	11			
Diagnose and resolve issues related to establishing a remote access connection	12			
Diagnose and resolve user access to resources beyond the remote access server	12			
Troubleshoot demand-dial routing	12			
Troubleshoot router-to-router VPNs	12			
Maintaining a Network Infrastructure	13, 14			
Monitor network traffic. Tools might include Network Monitor and System Monitor.	13			
Troubleshoot connectivity to the Internet	14			
Diagnose and resolve issues related to service dependency	14			
Use service recovery options to diagnose and resolve	14			

Part I

Implementing, Managing, and Maintaining IP Addressing

1
IP Addressing

CERTIFICATION OBJECTIVES

1.01   Configure TCP/IP Addressing
        on a Server Computer

✓   Two-Minute Drill

Q&A   Self Test

I n this chapter, you will begin your journey to MCSA success with a look at how to configure TCP/IP on a computer running Windows Server 2003. To be successful on this certification exam, you need to have a solid grasp on the different TCP/IP options and configuration steps necessary to support computers running Windows Server 2003.

The range of topics that could fall within the single certification objective *Configure TCP/IP addressing on a server computer* could be very narrowly defined to include only how to configure a static or dynamic IP address on a server running Windows Server 2003. Or it could be very broadly defined to include the history of TCP/IP, the suite of protocols, common ports, public and private IP addresses, and much more. Entire books have been written on the topic of TCP/IP, but that is not the purpose of this book, nor the purpose of the 70-291 certification exam. In this chapter you will learn about the fundamentals of TCP/IP, how to configure a server running Windows Server 2003 with both a static and a dynamic IP address, how to subnet IP networks, and about the two IP versions supported in Windows Server 2003, versions 4 and 6.

At the end of this chapter, you should have all the knowledge you require to successfully configure TCP/IP on a server running Windows Server 2003, and to be successful on the certification exam.

CERTIFICATION OBJECTIVE 1.01

Configure TCP/IP Addressing on a Server Computer

Before you get into the meat of the chapter and learn about the different TCP/IP configuration options for a server running Windows Server 2003, you need to build a solid foundation with some background knowledge about TCP/IP. We will begin with a brief discussion about how Transmission Control Protocol/Internet Protocol (TCP/IP) enables network communications.

Any discussion about networking communications must mention the Open Systems Interconnect (OSI) architectural model. The International Standards Organization (ISO) introduced the OSI model in 1978, well before the Internet as we know it today came about. This OSI model was developed to standardize the levels of services and types of communication between computers. It separates network communications into seven layers, with each layer responsible for a specific networking function, as shown in Figure 1-1.

FIGURE 1-1

Application	The Application layer, layer seven provides access for programs to network services.
Presentation	The Presentation layer, layer six translates data between different computers on the network.
Session	The Session layer, layer five allows two applications to create a persistent connection.
Transport	The Transport layer, layer four ensures that packets are delivered in the order they are sent and monitors for loss and duplication.
Network	The Network layer, layer three determines how to send the data factoring in network conditions, and service priorities among other factors.
Data Link	The Data Link layer, layer two provides error free transfer of frames between computers over the physical layer.
Physical	The Physical layer, layer one allows for raw streams of data bits to be placed on and taken off the physical wire.

on the job

The name for a unit of data can change depending on the OSI layer at which a protocol operates. For example, frames represent data at the Data Link layer, whereas datagram is used to represent data at the Network layer. The term packet is used as the generic term that describes a unit of data at any layer.

TCP/IP is the *de facto* industry standard suite of protocols that provides communication in heterogeneous networks that include both public corporate networks and public networks such as the Internet. The TCP/IP suite of protocols is organized into a protocol *stack* that consists of four layers: link layer, Internet layer, transport layer, and application layer. Figure 1-2 shows the division of the network functions in the TCP/IP stack, the breakdown of protocols within the suite, and how the TCP/IP stack correlates to the OSI model.

Think of the OSI model as the high-level model that defines how data is to be packaged, sent, and received, and provides a definition for the role of each layer. As you can see in Figure 1-2, the application layer in the TCP/IP model corresponds to the top three OSI layers: Session, Presentation, and Application. This layer in the TCP/IP model provides applications with access to network resources through two services: Windows Sockets (WinSock) and NetBIOS. Both WinSock and NetBIOS provide standard application programming interfaces (APIs) that allow programs like Internet Explorer, Outlook, WS_FTP, and many others to access resources on the network.

The transport layer is a direct match to the Transport layer in the OSI model, and is responsible for providing guaranteed, end-to-end communication between two computers on the network using either Transmission Control Protocol (TCP) or User Datagram Protocol (UDP). The key difference between these two protocols is that UDP provides connectionless communication and doesn't guarantee the delivery

FIGURE 1-2

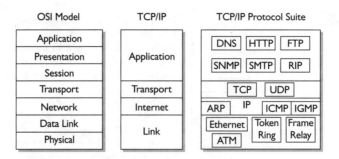

of packets, but rather places this responsibility on the application. Because UDP doesn't guarantee delivery, communication is faster. TCP, on the other hand, provides connection-based, reliable communication, and is typically the choice of most applications, particularly those that require an acknowledgement that the data has been received. Certain applications can use a combination of both TCP and UDP. FTP applications are a great example of this. FTP establishes the initial session using UDP, and then uses TCP for the transfer of data.

The Internet layer correlates to the Network layer in the OSI model, and the protocols at this level, such as IP, encapsulate data sent from the transport layer into units referred to as *packets*, address the packets, and route them to their destination.

The link layer corresponds to the Data Link and Physical layers in the OSI model. Its purpose is to specify the requirements for sending and receiving packets, and for placing the packets on the physical network, and taking them off the physical network upon receipt.

Static IP Address Configuration

Computers running Windows Server 2003 can be configured with an IP address in one of two ways: statically or dynamically. Generally speaking, most network administrators configure the servers in their organizations with static IP addresses because servers are generally configured to provide users access to applications and data, and you don't want the location of these items to change. That said, you can configure a server to obtain an IP address automatically, and set a reservation in DHCP so that address is always reserved and available for that server.

It is also quite common to have servers with multiple network interfaces, each one requiring a unique IP address. In the case of web servers, it is also quite common to bind multiple unique IP addresses to a single NIC to allow different, unique web sites to operate using unique IP addresses, but send and receive data from a server with a single NIC. Exercise 1-1 looks at the steps involved in configuring a static IP address on a server running Windows Server 2003.

MasterSim 1-1 ON THE CD

EXERCISE 1-1

Configuring a Static IP address

In this exercise you will learn how to configure a server running Windows Server 2003 with a static IP address.

1. Click **Start | Control Panel | Network Connections** and right-click **Local Area Connection**.

2. Select **Properties**.

3. Select **Internet Protocol (TCP/IP)**, and click **Properties**.

4. In the **Internet Protocol (TCP/IP) Properties** dialog box, shown in the following illustration, select **Use the following IP address**.

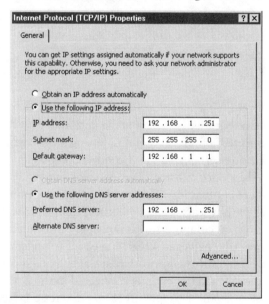

5. In the **IP address** text box, enter the static IP address that you wish to use. In the **Subnet mask** text box, enter the subnet mask you wish to use. In the **Default gateway** text box, enter the default gateway you wish to use.

6. Select **Use the following DNS server addresses**, and enter the IP address of the local DNS server in the **Preferred DNS** server text box. If the local Window Server 2003 computer is running DNS, this could be the same as the IP address you entered in the preceding step.

7. Click **OK**.

8. Click **Close**.

Local Area
Connection
Properties

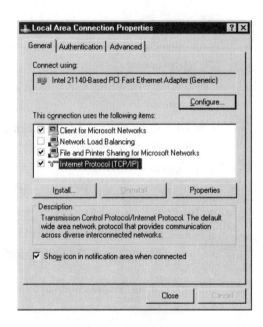

In the local area connection properties dialog box shown in Figure 1-3, another
option that I like to select is the option to **Show icon in notification area when
connected**. I find this useful in letting me see when there is network connectivity
occurring between this and another computer.

Also notice in this properties dialog box that you can see the network adapter that
you are configuring. This can be very useful when administering a computer with
multiple physical adapters. Another great way to simplify the administration of network
settings on computers with multiple physical adapters is to rename their default
connection names to something easier to understand. In simple situations where the
server has only two network adapters and one is connected to the router that connects
to the ISP and the other is connected to the LAN, I like to rename the connections
public and *private* to simplify things. Exercise 1-2 shows how to accomplish this.

EXERCISE 1-2

Renaming a Network Connection

In this exercise, you will learn how to rename a connection to make it easier to identify
by name. This can be useful on a computer with multiple physical network interfaces
to simplify the identification of the different NICs.

1. Click **Start | Control Panel | Network Connections**, right-click **Local Area Connection**, and select **Rename**. Alternatively, if you have the network connection icon in the notification area, you can right-click the network connection icon, select **Open Network Connections**, and then right-click **Local Area Connection** and select **Rename**.

2. Type the new connection name, and press ENTER.

Now that you know how to configure the basic components of a static IP address, you can take a look at the options available in the advanced properties. On the **Internet Protocol (TCP/IP) Properties** dialog box shown in Exercise 1-1, there is an **Advanced** button. Clicking this opens the Advanced TCP/IP Properties dialog box shown in Figure 1-4.

The IP Settings tab shown in Figure 1-4 allows you to add additional IP addresses and default gateways and bind them to the same single NIC. Binding additional IP addresses to a single NIC can be useful when you have multiple web sites, each bound to a unique IP address running on the local computer. This will allow you to add individual and unique host resource records for the name **www**, all bound to different IP addresses, but have all of the traffic destined to those IP addresses received by a single NIC. This can be ideal when you don't expect significant traffic to the various sites and network throughput isn't an issue.

FIGURE 1-4

Advanced TCP/IP properties

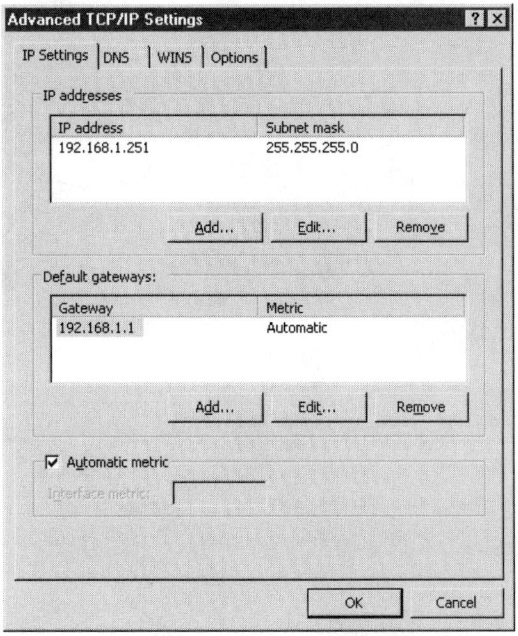

Binding multiple default gateways to the NIC is also useful for computers that are connected to a network with more than one router. A great example of this can be seen in Figure 1-5, where a company has redundant connections to the Internet. Configuring multiple default gateways allows the server to use either gateway if the metrics are the same, or it can allow you to set a preferential gateway and have the other available for fault tolerance. The second gateway would only be used if the first gateway wasn't available, thereby helping to provide an uninterruptible client experience.

On the DNS tab, shown in Figure 1-6, you can add multiple DNS servers. Every DNS client computer should be configured with both a preferred and alternate DNS server. Don't confuse the idea of a DNS client with a client and server computer; we are still talking about servers, but even servers can be configured as DNS clients. Having both a preferred and an alternate DNS server will offer the DNS client a second chance when attempting to resolve a name. The DNS tab is also where you can configure DNS suffix settings and set the order of multiple suffixes. If the computer is a member of an Active Directory domain, you can also use Group Policy to distribute DNS suffix settings. At the bottom of the DNS tab, notice the enabled option **Register this connection's addresses in DNS**. This option instructs the DHCP service on the local computer to contact the preferred DNS server and register the IP addresses to the host name of the local computer.

On the WINS tab, shown in Figure 1-7, you can enter the IP addresses of the WINS servers on your network. This allows you to configure the computer with a local WINS server address. You can see that the lmhosts lookup is enabled by default. This option allows you to create a file called lmhosts, normally saved to the

FIGURE 1-5

Binding multiple gateways

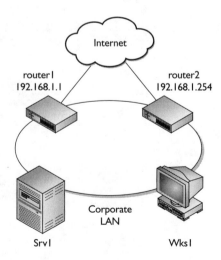

FIGURE 1-6

Advanced DNS
settings

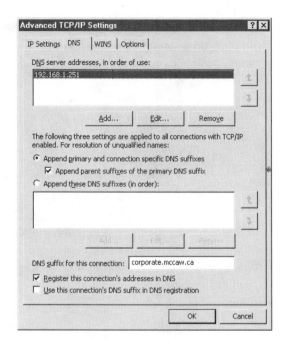

%**windir**%**system32****drivers****etc** folder, in which you can add persistent or non-persistent NetBIOS name-to-IP-address mappings. The benefit of adding persistent entries to the lmhosts file is that this file is loaded into the NetBIOS name cache when the computer initializes. Because persistent entries do not expire, this can improve the time it takes to resolve remote client NetBIOS names on the network. The potential downside to this approach is that if the name or IP address of a computer changes, an incorrect entry in the lmhosts file could result in name resolution problems until it is manually updated. Selecting the **Import LMHOSTS** button will prompt you to browse to the location of the lmhosts file you created.

FIGURE 1-7

Advanced WINS
settings

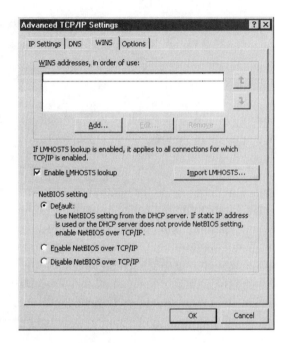

Also notice the default NetBIOS setting, which is to default to the DHCP server configuration, or in the case of a statically configured IP address, enable NetBIOS over TCP/IP.

The last tab in the Advanced TCP/IP properties dialog box is the Options tab shown in Figure 1-8. On this tab, you can edit and configure the TCP/IP Filtering settings. TCP/IP filtering allows you to restrict the incoming traffic to specific IP protocols and TCP and UDP ports. To identify what ports specific well-known services use, look to the services file in **%windir%\system32\drivers\etc**. Enabling TCP/IP filtering generally requires some testing, because you will probably configure filters that are too restrictive and prevent wanted communication from occurring successfully. For more information on TCP/IP filtering, see Chapter 11.

IP address conflicts are a common problem that often results from statically configuring an IP address. This can usually be attributed to human error caused by a typo when entering the IP address, or by entering the IP address of another computer that is currently offline. When the offline computer initializes, an error message appears during the boot process that alerts you to an IP address conflict. One of the new features included in Windows Server 2003 to alert you to static IP address configuration issues is the network error icon that appears in the notification area on the desktop of the computer that is trying to use an IP address that is already in use. This icon consists of a red question mark appearing on top on the network icon, as shown in Figure 1-9.

FIGURE 1-8

Advanced
Options

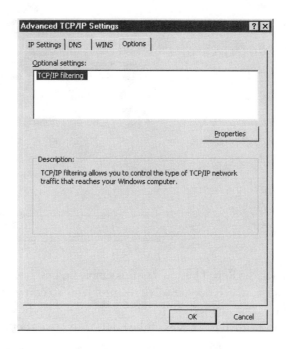

A warning message also appears on the computer that is currently using the IP address
that the initializing computer is trying to use. This message is a yellow caution icon,
which also appears in the notification area, and is shown in Figure 1-10.

Double-clicking the network configuration error icon in the notification area on
the system that is causing the IP conflict opens up the support tab of the properties
dialog box for the local area connection, as shown in Figure 1-11, and provides you
with some details of the current TCP/IP information. In this example, you can quickly
see that the computer has an IP address of 0.0.0.0 as a result of a conflict. You can

FIGURE 1-9

Network
configuration
error icon

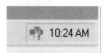

FIGURE 1-10

Warning

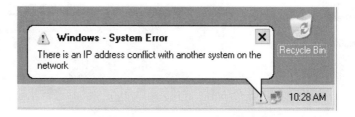

FIGURE 1-11

Local area
connection
properties

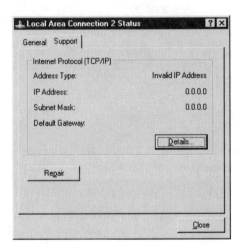

click the Repair button, but this simply flushes the address resolution protocol (ARP) cache, which doesn't solve the problem. To correct this IP address configuration problem, you need to select the General tab, click the Properties button, and edit the TCP/IP properties of the connection to either correct the spelling mistake or assign another available IP address.

Another common configuration error that often occurs while adding a static IP address is the misconfiguration of the default gateway address. Entering a default gateway address that is on a different subnet will limit the local computer to the local subnet. Windows Server 2003 polices such mistakes, and if you enter a default gateway IP address that is on a remote subnet, it will alert you to this with the message shown in Figure 1-12.

One more message that you are likely to run into at some point in your administration of TCP/IP settings on computers running Windows Server 2003 is shown in Figure 1-13. This information message alerts you to the fact that you are potentially setting yourself up for problems in the future by assigning the same static IP address to multiple NICs on the local computer. This can happen when you have disabled or removed a NIC from the local computer that had a static IP address assigned to it. If you continue and allow both NICs to have the same static IP address bound to them, and if they

FIGURE 1-12

Incorrect default
gateway
notification

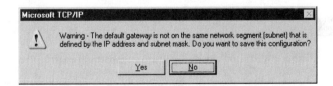

FIGURE 1-13

Potential
conflicting IP
address

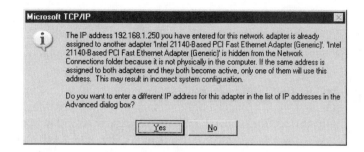

both become enabled at some point, one of them will generate an IP address conflict. The information dialog box alerts you to this and suggests that you add another IP address in the TCP/IP advanced dialog box to avoid this becoming an issue in the future. Proactive warning messages—the future is looking brighter every day!

Now that you are familiar with how to configure a static IP address, let's spend a minute looking at some other administrative tasks that you should be familiar with to assist you in resolving name resolution problems. Immediately after changing a statically configured IP address, you should open the command prompt and run the following command:

```
Ipconfig /registerdns
```

This will update the name-to-IP-address mapping on your DNS server if the zone on that DNS server is configured to allow dynamic updates. This will update and overwrite any existing name-to-IP-address mapping and allow clients to resolve the name of the host to the newly established IP address. One potential issue that you should be aware of is that old name-to-IP-address information might exist in other network client's local DNS cache, which may cause name resolution problems until the cached entries expire. For example, suppose you have a network of three servers, all with statically configured IP addresses, and all configured to use DNS1 as the local DNS server. You decide one day to change the IP address on one of the three servers, and you immediately attempt to connect to the server from one of the other servers using the server's host name. It is possible that your connection attempt will fail because the client DNS cache on the server that you are attempting to connect from contains the old name-to-IP-address mapping. To clear the client's local DNS cache, run the following command:

```
Ipconfig /flushdns
```

Now that you have learned how to configure a server running Windows Server 2003 with a static IP address, the next section will teach you how to configure the server to obtain an IP address dynamically from a DHCP server.

Dynamic IP Address Configuration

In this section, you will explore the steps involved in configuring a computer running Windows Server 2003 with a dynamically assigned IP address. The steps involved in configuring the DHCP server service will be discussed in detail in Chapter 2.

Dynamic IP address assignment allows a computer running Windows Server 2003 to obtain an IP address from a DHCP server as opposed to being configured with a static IP address. Dynamic IP address assignment is generally not used for computers running server operating systems like Windows Server 2003 in most organizations; however, it is possible and can be configured depending on the planned role of the server. The role the server will play is an important piece of the equation to consider before configuring the server to obtain an IP address automatically, as some server roles require that the computer have a static IP address, such as the DHCP and DNS server roles. Exercise 1-3 will walk you through the steps involved in configuring a computer to obtain an IP address automatically from a DHCP server.

EXERCISE 1-3

Configuring a Computer to Obtain an IP Address Dynamically

In this exercise, you will learn how to configure a server running Windows Server 2003 to obtain an IP address automatically from a DHCP server. You can do this for a server that is a member of a small network as a way of minimizing administration.

1. Click **Start** | **Control Panel** | **Network Connections**, and right-click **Local Area Connection**.

2. Select **Properties**.

3. Select **Internet Protocol (TCP/IP)**, and click **Properties**.

4. In the **Internet Protocol (TCP/IP) Properties** dialog box displayed in the following illustration, select **Obtain an IP address automatically**. Notice the difference between the Internet Protocol (TCP/IP) Properties dialog box displayed earlier in Exercise 1-1, and this one. When you select the option **Obtain an IP address automatically**, the Alternate Configuration tab appears.

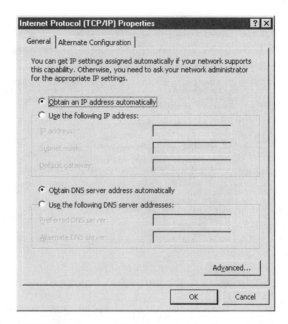

5. Select **Obtain DNS server address automatically** and click **OK**.

6. Click **OK** again to close the Local Area Connection dialog box.

To confirm that the computer was able to successfully obtain an IP address, open the command prompt and type the following command.

```
Ipconfig /all
```

This will return all of the IP configuration information for all of the network adapters installed on the local computer. The results of this command can be seen in Figure 1-14. Notice in this example that you did not successfully receive an IP address from a DHCP server, but rather you received an automatically private IP address (APIPA) on the 169.254.0.0/16 network. This will occur when the DHCP client is unable to obtain an IP address from a DHCP server on the network.

In Exercise 1-3, when you selected the option to **Obtain an IP address automatically**, you may have noticed the additional tab that appeared on the Internet Protocol (TCP/IP) Properties dialog box, known as the **Alternate Configuration** tab. The properties of the Alternate Configuration tab, shown in Figure 1-15, allow you to leave the default **Automatic private IP address** option selected, or to choose the **User configured** option. As in Windows 2000 Server, the default **Automatic private IP address** option configures a DHCP client with an IP address on the 169.254.0.0/16 network if the DHCP client service is unable to obtain an IP address from a DHCP

FIGURE 1-14

Identifying IP
address
configuration
using **ipconfig /all**

```
C:\WINDOWS\system32\cmd.exe                                          _ □ ×

C:\Documents and Settings\Administrator.WS03BASE2>ipconfig /all

Windows IP Configuration

        Host Name . . . . . . . . . . . . : WS03BASE2
        Primary Dns Suffix  . . . . . . . : corporate.mccaw.ca
        Node Type . . . . . . . . . . . . : Unknown
        IP Routing Enabled. . . . . . . . : Yes
        WINS Proxy Enabled. . . . . . . . : Yes
        DNS Suffix Search List. . . . . . : corporate.mccaw.ca
                                            mccaw.ca

Ethernet adapter Local Area Connection 2:

        Connection-specific DNS Suffix  . :
        Description . . . . . . . . . . . : Intel 21140-Based PCI Fast Ethernet Adapt
er <Generic> #2
        Physical Address. . . . . . . . . : 00-03-FF-3E-C9-72
        DHCP Enabled. . . . . . . . . . . : Yes
        Autoconfiguration Enabled . . . . : Yes
        Autoconfiguration IP Address. . . : 169.254.90.38
        Subnet Mask . . . . . . . . . . . : 255.255.0.0
        Default Gateway . . . . . . . . . :

C:\Documents and Settings\Administrator.WS03BASE2>_
```

server. In addition, it continues to attempt to lease an IP address every 5 minutes from a DHCP server.

Selecting the **User configured** option allows you to specify a static IP address, subnet mask, and default gateway as well as DNS and WINS server information. If selected, this configuration will only be used when the DHCP client fails to obtain an IP address. When the **User configured** option is selected, the DHCP client service will not continue to attempt to obtain an IP address from a DHCP server every 5 minutes as APIPA does.

FIGURE 1-15

Alternate
configuration

Internet Protocol (TCP/IP) Properties

General | Alternate Configuration

If this computer is used on more than one network, enter the alternate IP settings below.

○ Automatic private IP address

○ User configured

  IP address:
  Subnet mask:
  Default gateway:

  Preferred DNS server:
  Alternate DNS server:

  Preferred WINS server:
  Alternate WINS server:

OK   Cancel

SCENARIO & SOLUTION

What two failure options are available when you have selected to have an NIC obtain an IP address automatically?	When an NIC is set to obtain an IP address from a DHCP server and fails, the default setting is to assign an automatic private IP address (APIPA). The other option available is known as the alternate configuration, which allows you to specify an alternate static IP address to use if the DHCP client service is unable to obtain an IP address from the DHCP server.
What is the key difference between the two alternate configurations?	The APIPA option continues to attempt to obtain an IP address for the DHCP client computer every 5 minutes, but the **User configured** option does not.
What are the two properties that must be specified when statically configuring an IP address?	The IP address and subnet mask must both be specified when statically configuring an IP address.

Now that you know how to configure a server running Windows Server 2003 with a static IP or dynamic IP address, take a moment to review what you have learned.

Now we'll shift our attention to how you determine what constitutes a valid IP address, and how we design a network topology that divides a single physical network into multiple logical segments to improve performance and allow for growth.

TCP/IP Basics

An IP address is comprised of two parts: a *network ID* and a *host ID*. The network ID allows intermediary devices, such as routers or switches, to determine the destination network of the IP datagram (packet). The host ID is used to identify the host on that network. A service port is also used to define what port an incoming TCP/IP connection should establish a connection with, based on the application that is being used. For example, HTTP uses TCP port 80, whereas SMTP uses TCP port 25.

To better understand all of these different components, think about how mail is delivered. When you send a letter, you must put an address on the envelope. If you are sending an envelope to a company that is located in a ten-story building with multiple tenants, you also add a suite number. Suppose the address of this building is 40 Eglinton Ave E., and the suite number is 400. The address of 40 Eglinton Ave E., in the context of an IP address, would represent the network ID. The host ID would be represented by the suite number 400, identifying where on the network or in this case in the building, the host is located. The last part of the equation could be the port number. The port number would be equivalent to the Att: Rory McCaw portion of the address on the envelope. Once the letter is delivered to 40 Eglinton Ave E., suite 400, it would then be routed to me.

on the
Job

For a great, short video on TCP/IP and routing, execute a Google search for "Warriors of the NET."

A *subnet mask*, sometimes referred to in router lingo as a *netmask*, is used to divide an IP address into its two parts. In the case of IP v4, a subnet mask, like an IP address, is a 32-bit value that can be expressed in a couple of ways but is most commonly shown as four octets separated by periods. There are five network classes: Class A through Class E. You should be familiar with the first three classes (Class A, Class B, and Class C). The three standard IP address classes and their associated subnet masks are displayed in Table 1-1.

Each class of IP address allows for networks of various sizes. In TCP/IP networks, size is measured by two factors: the number of possible subnets and the number of hosts per subnet. All three classes of network can be identified quickly by looking at the decimal value in the first octet of an IP address. The first octet of Class A networks will have a decimal value between 1 and 126, and when converted to binary will always start with 0. Class B networks will begin with a decimal value between 128 and 191, and Class C networks will begin with a decimal value between 192 and 223. This means that in binary, Class B networks will always start with 1 and Class C networks will always start with 110. Understanding how to convert from decimal to binary and vice - versa is very important when learning to subnet. Don't worry, even if you weren't that great at math in school, you can pick this up quickly and will be converting decimal to binary in your head in no time!

The first octet of a Class A network must have a decimal value between 1 and 126; it can therefore only use the last 7 bits of the binary value in the first octet. Look to the decimal equivalents of each binary bit to see that the first (leftmost) bit has a value of 128, and therefore cannot be used in Class A networks (it must be a 0 bit as opposed to a 1 bit):

```
Decimal:      128     64    32    16     8     4     2     1

Binary:        1       1     1     1     1     1     1     1
```

TABLE 1-1	Class	Subnet Mask	Binary Value
Network Classes and Their Associated Subnet Masks	A	255.0.0.0	11111111.00000000.00000000.00000000
	B	255.255.0.0	11111111.11111111.00000000.00000000
	C	255.255.255.0	11111111.11111111.11111111.00000000

This leaves multiple combinations of the remaining seven 1 bits available to make up the value of the first octet, and brings us to the formula that can be used to determine the number of available network segments that each class of network can support. The formula to calculate this is $2^n - 2$, where n is the number of 1 bits that can be used to make up the value in the first octet (note that the -2 is used to account for the 0.0.0.0 and 255.255.255.255 networks, which are not available for use).

The 0.0.0.0 network is reserved for the default route, and the 255.255.255.255 is the broadcast address, the address that all clients on the local subnet are configured to listen for.

on the
!
()ob

The original classes did not calculate available network addresses by using $2^n - 2$; they were just understood to be 1–126, 128.–191, and 192–223. $2^n - 2$ was used when subnetting one of these networks, and the $- 2$ part was called for in RFC 950 only to be consistent with how the number of hosts was calculated. In reality, many hosts and routers can use subnets with all 0's, and all 1's (2^n).

You might have noticed from the different classes that after the Class A address space of 1–126, the 127 network is skipped, and you just move to 128–191 for the Class B address space. The 127 network is reserved for the loopback address 127.0.0.0.

Look at Table 1-2 to identify the number of available networks and the number of available hosts per network that each of the classes will support. What you will notice from Table 1-2 is that Class A networks allow for the greatest number of host addresses, and Class C networks allow for the smallest number of hosts. This is simply due to the fact that as you increase the number of available subnets, you decrease the number of hosts available on each subnet.

The formula for determining the number of available hosts is the same as that used to determine the number of available network segments: $2^n - 2$, where n is now the number of bits available to make up the host portion of the IP address. Using a Class A network again as an example, think of this network class in binary format as *nnnnnnnn.hhhhhhhh.hhhhhhhh.hhhhhhhh*, where the instances of n in the address represent the bits of the network ID, and the instances of h represent bits of the host ID. There are three octets, each 8 bits in size, for a total of 24 bits in the host ID. Using

TABLE 1-2   Breaking the Network Classes into Network Segments and Hosts per Segment

Class	Decimal Range in First Octet	# of Available Network Segments	# of Available Hosts Per Network	Subnet Mask
A	1–126	126	16,777,214	255.0.0.0
B	128–191	16,384	65534	255.255.0.0
C	192–223	2,097,151	254	255.255.255.0

the formula $2^{24} - 2$, you find that a maximum of 16,777,214 hosts can exist on a Class A network.

Note that no address range begins with 127 and that there are no addresses above 223. The 127.0.0.0 network is reserved for testing and troubleshooting purposes and is referred to as the loopback address. Addresses that begin with 224 and higher are reserved for special protocols such as IP multicasting and some are deemed unavailable and reserved for future use, therefore they are not available for use as host addresses. Additionally, host addresses that are all 0's or all 1's are not permissible because all 0's commonly denotes the network ID, and all 1's is the broadcast address for the network.

Based on Table 1-2, you can see that the number of available addresses in a given address class is fixed, with Class A networks supporting a maximum of 16,777,214 hosts and Class C networks supporting a maximum of 254. The class of network you choose for your organization will depend on a number of factors, including the current number of hosts, expected growth, existing Internet connectivity, and network architecture. Three network IDs have been reserved as private network IDs for organizations to use internally for the hosts on their networks:

- 10.0.0.0/8 (10.0.0.0 to 10.255.255.255)
- 172.16.0.0/12 (172.16.0.0 to 172.31.255.255)
- 192.168.0.0/16 (192.168.0.0 to 192.168.255.255)

If your network is not connected to the Internet, and you do not plan to connect it to the Internet (I don't know where you would be living that this would be the case, but I have to mention it), you are free to use any IP addressing scheme you like. However, if you do decide to connect to the Internet in the future, your entire network will have to be re-addressed to use one of the private network IDs or an intermediary device such as a firewall or router that performs network address translation (NAT) to hide the internal IP addresses from the Internet. Alternatively, you can contact your ISP or the Internet Assigned Numbers Authority (IANA) to apply to have a block assigned to you.

All public, Internet IP addresses are controlled by (IANA). IANA has no record of who is using the private IP ranges, but realizes that hundreds of thousands of private networks do exist. Using one of the private networks is always the best decision when you design your IP addressing scheme, so that it allows you the ability to connect to the Internet in the future with minimal configuration changes.

 on the job   **To find out more about IANA, go to** *www.iana.org.*

The preceding network address ranges are listed in Classless Interdomain Routing (CIDR) notation. CIDR notation uses the convention of listing the network address followed by a slash character (/) and then the number of bits in the subnet mask used to mask off the network. In other words, the CIDR notation of 10.0.0.0/8 refers to the network ID 10.0.0.0 with an 8-bit subnet mask, expressed in decimal as 255.0.0.0 and in binary as 11111111.00000000.00000000.00000000.

CIDR notation was adopted by Internet authorities for a couple of reasons. First was the fear that with the growth of the Internet, the number of available IP addresses would soon be depleted, and second, to help with the management of routing tables on Internet routers. With the growth of the Internet and the assignment of Class B network IDs (which allow for a maximum of 65,534 hosts per network) to companies that only require 2,000 host IPs on their networks, the number of wasted IP addresses threatened a pending depletion. One solution to this problem was to assign multiple Class C addresses to these organizations instead of Class B addresses, because each Class C block provided support for a maximum of 254 hosts. This allowed a company requiring 2,000 host IPs to receive eight Class C blocks, which would allow for 2,032 host ID's, just a little over their actual requirement.

This however led to a second problem. It complicated the administration of routers and their routing tables. Each of the Class C network IDs assigned requires its own route in the routing tables, so one of the other benefits of CIDR is that it was designed to allow for multiple Class C address spaces to be assigned, which preserved the number of available IP addresses and it also solved the problem of multiple routes by collapsing multiple network ID entries into a single entry that corresponds to all the Class C network IDs.

In this example, the eight Class C network IDs are allocated to the company beginning with the 220.78.168.0 network ID, which results in a starting network ID of 220.78.168.0 and an ending network ID of 220.78.175.0. The CIDR entry that would be added to the routing table is 220.78.168.0/21, meaning that hosts in this network would use the subnet mask 255.255.248.0.

Now that you are familiar with the obstacles that resulted in the different classes of IP addresses, you are ready to learn about subnetting.

e x a m

ⓦ a t c h

For routers to support CIDR, they must be able to support the exchange of routing information in the form of network ID/network mask pairs. The routing protocols *RIP v2, OSPF, and Border Gateway Protocol (BGP) v4 support the exchange of paired routing information. RIP v1 does not; therefore, it does not support CIDR.*

Subnetting

As organizations grow in size, their networks grow as well. To manage these networks effectively and provide acceptable levels of performance, single physical networks are divided into smaller logical networks known as *network segments* or *subnets*. Multiple network segments are used to isolate traffic to a single network and reduce overall network congestion, thereby improving performance. Subnetting is not very different from the concept of developing roads, highways, and Interstates. Using this example, each stretch of road between two stoplights could be considered a subnet, where the stoplights are routers used to route traffic from one subnet to another. A very long street or very large network could be divided into multiple segments. Subnet masks are used in TCP/IP network environments to break networks into multiple segments. This will help to improve network performance in a number of ways, one of which is limiting broadcast traffic to the local subnet from which it originated.

You will be required to know how to subnet a network into multiple logical segments on the certification exam, so this section will educate you on the basics of subnetting and show you a couple of examples.

Subnetting Example 1   As the network administrator in your organization, your local ISP has assigned your company a portion of a Class C network. The ISP uses a 27-bit subnet mask to divide the 205.219.129.0 network. You need to determine how many subnets and how many hosts per subnet the ISP can support. Then, you must determine what the available host ranges are for the ISP to use.

To solve this problem, the first step is to use the formula $2^n - 2$ to determine the number of hosts per subnet. To do this, you need to break the subnet mask into binary format. A 27-bit subnet mask is equivalent to 11111111.11111111.11111111.11100000. Converting this to decimal and arranging the numbers into octets results in the subnet mask used by the ISP of 255.255.255.224. All 1's in an octet total 255, and the third octet of 111 is equivalent to 128+64+32, which works out to 224. This leaves 5 available bits in the fourth octet for the network ID. Using the formula $2^n - 2$, where n equals 5, the maximum number of IP addresses per subnet is 30. To determine the number of subnets, use the formula $2^n - 2$, where n equals 3 (the first three bits in the fourth octet that represent the network ID 11111111.11111111.11111111.**111**00000) and you'll find that eight subnets are available. Now remember to subtract 2 subnets, those representing 000 and 111, which leaves you with 6 available subnets.

The last question is how to determine the host ranges. To do this, convert the bits in the last octet to binary and begin manipulating the different combinations as shown next with the hosts bits displayed in bold.

- ~~00000001–00011110 = 1–30~~
- 00100001–00111110 = 33–62
- 01000001–01011110 = 65–94
- 01100001–01111110 = 97–126
- 10000001–10011110 = 129–158
- 10100001–10111110 = 161–190
- 11000001–11011110 = 193–222
- ~~11100001–11111110 = 225–254~~

After you have determined the first two or three ranges, you can quickly and easily identify the pattern, and see that in this case, if you add 3 to the end of the last range, you will have the starting point of the next range. In addition, as you determined earlier, each subnet has 30 IP addresses. Be careful here not to get sloppy with your addition. A common mistake is to identify the first available host range, which in this example would be 205.219.129.1, and add 30, not thinking that 1 is a part of that block of 30 IP addresses. This can result in you miscalculating the end IP address in the range and stating it incorrectly as 205.219.129.31 when it really should be 205.219.129.30. So, don't make the mistake of adding 1+30 and coming up with an incorrect end range of 205.219.129.31 as this actually contains 31 hosts, not 30. Putting the preceding numbers together with the rest of the IP octets, you can see that the eight valid host ranges are

- ~~205.219.129.1–205.219.129.30~~
- 205.219.129.33–205.219.129.62
- 205.219.129.65–205.219.129.94
- 205.219.129.97–205.219.129.126
- 205.219.129.129–205.219.129.158
- 205.219.129.161–205.219.129.190
- 205.219.129.193–205.219.129.222
- ~~205.219.129.225–205.219.129.254~~

Subnetting Example 2   Given the subnet mask 255.255.255.192 and the network 221.41.6.0, which of the IP addresses in Table 1-3 are on the same subnet? To solve this problem, you must figure out all the valid host ranges and then analyze whether each of the IP addresses fall within those valid ranges. To accomplish this,

TABLE 1-3	221.41.6.17	221.41.6.73
	221.41.6.32	221.41.6.121
Potential IP Addresses	221.41.6.45	221.41.6.127
	221.41.6.61	221.41.6.135
	221.41.6.64	221.41.6.208

you must first determine the number of hosts per subnet. To identify the number of host bits that n will be equal to, write the subnet mask out in binary, as follows:

11111111.11111111.11111111.11000000

This tells you that n is equal to six host bits. Using the formula $2^n - 2$, where n equals 6, you find that each subnet will have 62 IP addresses. The number of available network segments will be $2^2 - 2$, which is 2. Knowing this, you can begin to draw out the valid host ranges. Do this by manipulating the options available using the network bits as shown next. The network bits are identified in bold.

- ~~00000001–00111110 = 1–62 (all 0s)~~
- 01000001–01111110 = 65–126
- 10000001–10111110 = 129–190
- ~~11000001–11111110 = 193–254 (all 1s)~~

Now you have identified the valid host ranges, which when combined with the other octets, result in the following valid host ranges:

- ~~221.41.6.1–221.41.6.62~~
- 221.41.6.65–221.41.6.126
- 221.41.6.129–221.41.6.190
- ~~221.41.6.193–221.41.6.254~~

Knowing the valid IP ranges, you are now able to see which of the preceding IP addresses fall into the valid ranges. From the list, only 221.41.6.73, 221.41.6.121, and 221.41.6.135 are valid IP addresses.

Subnetting Example 3 You are the network administrator in your organization. You have just acquired two new routers. You would like to configure the routers with an IP address at the end of the available range of IP addresses on your network. You

use the 10.10.1.0/27 network. What IP addresses are available for you to use for each of the routers?

To solve this problem, start by determining the valid host ranges and then determine the number of hosts per subnet. To identify the number of host bits that n will be equal to, write the subnet mask out in binary, as follows:

11111111.11111111.11111111.11100000

This tells you that n is equal to 5 host bits. Using the formula $2^n - 2$, where n equals 5, you find that each subnet will have 30 IP addresses. The number of available network segments will be $2^3 - 2$, which is 6. Knowing this, you can begin to draw out the valid host ranges. Do this by manipulating the options available using the network bits as shown next. The network bits are identified in bold.

- ~~**000**00001–**001**11110 = 1–30~~
- **001**00001–**001**11110 = 33–62
- **010**00001–**010**11110 = 65–94
- **011**00001–**011**11110 = 97–126
- **100**00001–**100**11110 = 129–158
- **101**00001–**101**11110 = 161–190
- **110**00001–**110**11110 = 193–222
- ~~**111**00001–**111**11110 = 225–254~~

From this list of host ranges, you can determine that depending on the network the routers will be connected to, valid IP addresses that fall at the end of the possible range include

- 10.10.1.62
- 10.10.1.94

- 10.10.1.126
- 10.10.1.158
- 10.10.1.190
- 10.10.1.222

Now that you are comfortable with the concept of subnetting, shift your attention to the new version of IP that is supported in Windows Server 2003.

IPv6

Internet Protocol version 6 support is built into Windows Server 2003, but the protocol is not installed and configured by default. Installing the IPv6 stack enables Windows Server 2003 to make use of the expanded addressing available to IPv6 enables hosts. In this section we will discuss IPv6 and explore how to install it on a computer running Windows Server 2003.

If you have a hard time remembering 32-bit IP addresses, get ready, because IPv6 addresses are 128 bits, four times the size of IPv4 addresses. The DNS service, and all other networking services included in Windows Server 2003, have been designed to support IPv6 as the standard becomes more widely adopted. As with IPv4 addresses, most people prefer to remember a host name over an IP address, and this will be even more true with IPv6.

It is highly unlikely that you will find any questions on IPv6 on the certification exam.

One important distinction to note when comparing IPv4 and IPv6 is that IPv6 is a connectionless, unreliable datagram protocol that is primarily used for addressing and routing packets between different hosts. This means that IPv6 does not establish a session prior to exchanging data, and delivery is not guaranteed. Packet delivery acknowledgment and the recovery of lost packets can be accomplished by TCP, a higher-layer protocol.

on the job *For more information on IPv6, look to http://www.microsoft.com /windowsserver2003/technologies/ipv6/default.mspx or http://www.ipv6.org, the site of the IPv6 working group.*

IP v6 isn't installed by default in Windows Server 2003, but it can be installed quite easily. Exercise 1-4 walks you through the steps involved in installing IP v6.

EXERCISE 1-4

Installing IPv6

In this exercise, you will learn how to install IPv6.

1. Click **Start | Control Panel | Network Connections**, and right-click **Local Area Connection**, and select **Properties**.

2. In the Local Area Connection Properties dialog box, click **Install**.

3. Select **Protocol** and click **Add**.

4. In the Select Network Protocol dialog box shown in the following illustration, select **Microsoft TCP/IP version 6**, and click **OK**.

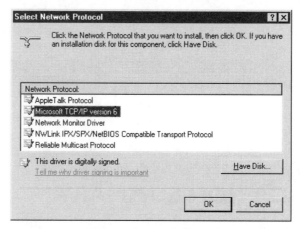

5. Once the installation is complete, you will notice Microsoft TCP/IP version 6 listed in the Local Area Connection Properties dialog box.

As you can see, when you select **Microsoft TCP/IP version 6** in the Local Area Connection Properties dialog box, the Properties button is grayed out. This is because there is nothing to configure once it is installed. To see the IP v6 address that is assigned to the computer, run the **ipconfig /all** command. The results of this command can be seen in Figure 1-16.

FIGURE 1-16

Results of
ipconfig

```
C:\WINDOWS\system32\cmd.exe                                            _ □ X
Microsoft Windows [Version 5.2.3790]
(C) Copyright 1985-2003 Microsoft Corp.

C:\Documents and Settings\Administrator.WS03BASE2>ipconfig /all

Windows IP Configuration

        Host Name . . . . . . . . . . . : WS03DC1
        Primary Dns Suffix  . . . . . . : corporate.mccaw.ca
        Node Type . . . . . . . . . . . : Unknown
        IP Routing Enabled. . . . . . . : Yes
        WINS Proxy Enabled. . . . . . . : Yes
        DNS Suffix Search List. . . . . : corporate.mccaw.ca
                                          mccaw.ca

Ethernet adapter Local Area Connection 2:

        Connection-specific DNS Suffix  . :
        Description . . . . . . . . . . : Intel 21140-Based PCI Fast Ethernet Adapt
er (Generic) #2
        Physical Address. . . . . . . . : 00-03-FF-FA-FF-FF
        DHCP Enabled. . . . . . . . . . : No
        IP Address. . . . . . . . . . . : 192.168.1.250
        Subnet Mask . . . . . . . . . . : 255.255.255.0
        IP Address. . . . . . . . . . . : fe80::203:ffff:fefa:ffff%4
        Default Gateway . . . . . . . . : 192.168.1.1
        DNS Servers . . . . . . . . . . : 192.168.1.251
                                          fec0:0:0:ffff::1%1
                                          fec0:0:0:ffff::2%1
                                          fec0:0:0:ffff::3%1


Tunnel adapter Automatic Tunneling Pseudo-Interface:

        Connection-specific DNS Suffix  . :
        Description . . . . . . . . . . : Automatic Tunneling Pseudo-Interface
        Physical Address. . . . . . . . : C0-A8-01-FA
        DHCP Enabled. . . . . . . . . . : No
        IP Address. . . . . . . . . . . : fe80::5efe:192.168.1.250%2
        Default Gateway . . . . . . . . :
        DNS Servers . . . . . . . . . . : fec0:0:0:ffff::1%1
                                          fec0:0:0:ffff::2%1
                                          fec0:0:0:ffff::3%1

        NetBIOS over Tcpip. . . . . . . : Disabled

C:\Documents and Settings\Administrator.WS03BASE2>
```

CERTIFICATION SUMMARY

In this chapter, you have learned how to install and configure a computer running Windows Server 2003 with both a static and dynamic TCP/IP address. You have also learned about some of the most common errors that you are likely to come across in your administration of TCP/IP and how to resolve them.

You have also learned how to subnet, and solve subnet-related problems, which will likely be a skill that you will be required to use on the exam. Last, we looked at IP v6 and how to install this protocol on a computer running Windows Server 2003.

The concepts discussed in this chapter are very important to understand and lay the groundwork for concepts covered in future chapters throughout this book. A solid understanding of subnetting is required to answer questions related to proper server placement and routing, as well as creating and troubleshooting VPNs.

TWO-MINUTE DRILL

Configure TCP/IP Addressing on a Server Computer

❏ Windows Server 2003 supports two versions of the Internet Protocol: versions 4 and 6.

❏ IP addresses can be statically configured or set to be dynamically assigned on computers running Windows Server 2003, although it is more common to assign static IP addresses to servers.

❏ **ipconfig** is a command that can be used to view the IP configuration of all NICs on a computer using the **/all** switch, to update DNS information using the **/registerdns** switch, and to flush the local DNS cache using the **/flushdns** switch

❏ There are three classes of networks that you can use to assign IP addresses from: Class A, B, and C. The first octet of Class A, B, and C networks have values ranging from 1–126, 128–191, and 192–223, respectively. The maximum number of available hosts on a network segment can be calculated using the formula $2^n - 2$, where n is the number of bits in the subnet used for the host ID.

❏ Four network IDs have been assigned for use in private networks: 10.0.0.0/8, 169.254.0.0/16, 172.16.0.0/12, and 192.168.0.0/16.

❏ Classless Interdomain Routing (CIDR) notation lists network IDs using the format IP address/number of network ID bits in the subnet mask. For example, 192.168.1.0/24 indicates a 24-bit subnet mask.

❏ The 127/8 network is reserved for the localhost, also known as the loopback address, which is used in troubleshooting network communications related to the network adapter.

❏ The LMHOSTS file must not have a file extension and is normally created in the **%windir%\system32\drivers\etc** folder.

❏ IP v6 is installed by selecting to add a new protocol in the Local Area Connection Properties dialog box.

SELF TEST

The following questions will help you measure your understanding of the material presented in this chapter. Read all the choices carefully because there may be more than one correct answer. Choose all correct answers for each question.

Configure TCP/IP Addressing on a Server Computer

1. You are the network administrator for your organization. You have been thinking about redesigning the IP network architecture of your organization to coincide with a planned move into a new office space. Your network must allow for 30 subnets with at least 500 hosts per subnet. You have decided to use the 10.10.1.0 network. What subnet mask will best meet your criteria?

    A. 255.255.254.0

    B. 255.255.248.0

    C. 255.255.240.0

    D. 255.255.252.0

    E. 255.255.224.0

2. You are the network administrator in your organization, and you are responsible for designing your company's IP architecture. You work for a large Internet Service Provider that owns a single Class A network ID of 24.0.0.0. You want to break the Class A network into manageable pieces, each to be used by different geographical locations where your company operates to provide access to your organization's customers. You want to design a scalable architecture that allows for growth, but limits the number of host IP addresses per network segment to no more than 950. Having fewer than 950 hosts per network segment is acceptable, but having more is not. Which subnet mask will you use to accomplish this?

    A. 255.255.248.0

    B. 255.255.254.0

    C. 255.255.252.0

    D. 255.255.240.0

3. You are the network administrator for your organization. You are new to this position and one of the first areas that you are to focus on is the setup and configuration of a new server running Windows Server 2003 with a static IP address. The company has subnetted the 192.168.1.0 network with a 26-bit subnet mask. You have been given a list of available IP addresses, but you are uncertain whether the network host ranges have be calculated correctly. Assuming that routers are in place to allow for communication between subnets, which of the following IP addresses could you use to properly configure the new server running Windows Server 2003, allowing it to communicate successfully on the network? (Choose all that apply.)

A. 192.168.1.62

B. 192.168.1.64

C. 192.168.1.121

D. 192.168.1.127

E. 192.168.1.128

4. You are the network administrator for your organization. Place the following OSI layers in the proper order from layer one to layer seven. (Choose only those that apply.)

A. Session

B. Network

C. Physical

D. Application

E. Segment

F. Transport

G. Presentation

H. Data Link

5. You are the network administrator for your company. You have two servers, VPNSRV1 and VPNSRV2, that you would like to have preload the NetBIOS-name-to-IP-address mapping of the other server in their respective NetBIOS cache upon boot. Which of the following will allow you to achieve this?

A. Create a file named hosts for each server with the other server's name-to-IP-address mapping, and store it in the **%windir%\system32\dns** directory.

B. Create a file named hosts.txt for each server with the other server's name-to-IP-address mapping, and store it in the **%windir%\system32\dns** directory.

C. Create a file named lmhosts.txt for each server with the other server's name-to-IP-address mapping, and store it in the **%windir%\system32\drivers\etc** directory.

D. Create a file named lmhosts for each server with the other server's name-to-IP-address mapping, and store it in the **%windir%\system32\drivers\etc** directory.

6. You are the network administrator for your organization. You are planning on enabling TCP/IP filtering on one of your file servers to further tighten the security configuration of the server. Before you implement TCP/IP filtering, you would like to identify the ports that you must keep open to allow wanted communication to take place. Where can you look to determine the ports used by various services?

A. **%windir%\system32\drivers\etc\ports**

B. **%windir%\system32\drivers\etc\services**

    C. %windir%\system32\drivers\etc\hosts

    D. %windir%\system32\drivers\etc\lmhosts.sam

7. You are the network administrator in your organization. You have recently changed the static IP address of a server running Windows Server 2003 on your network. After the change, some users have been reporting that they cannot connect to the server using its name. Other users have been reporting that their mapped drives have been failing. And a third group of users is experiencing no problems and is able to connect just fine. Which of the following will solve the problem?

    A. On the server, run **ipconfig /flushnds**.

    B. On the server, run **ipconfig /registerdns**.

    C. On the server, disable TCP/IP filtering.

    D. On the clients, run **ipconfig /flushdns**.

    E. On the clients, run **nbtstat –RR**.

8. You are the network administrator in your organization. You are creating a fault-tolerance and recovery strategy. Part of your strategy involves identifying ways to increase system uptime and improve overall availability. A number of your servers have been configured to obtain an IP address automatically from a DHCP server, and a reservation has been created on the DHCP server. Which of the following represents the best way to increase availability on these servers?

    A. Change their local area connection settings to be statically configured.

    B. Add a second reservation in DHCP for a second address so that they are always able to receive an IP.

    C. Configure an alternate, user-configured static IP address, subnet, gateway, DNS, and WINS server.

    D. Install IP v6 on the local area connection.

9. You are the network administrator in your organization. You have configured a server on your network to obtain an IP address from DHCP. In the DHCP scope, you have configured a reservation for the server so that it always receives the same IP address. Changes were made to the DHCP server over the weekend, and on Monday you begin hearing from users that they are unable to connect to the server. You try to ping the server by name and IP address, but you are unsuccessful. You log on to the server and in the notification area, the network connection icon appears with no indication of a problem. Which of the following strategies would you use to further diagnose the problem?

    A. On a remote computer, run **tracert** to trace the route taken to the server.

    B. On the server, open the command prompt and ping 127.0.0.1.

    C. On the domain controller for the domain, verify that the computer account for the server is enabled.

    D. On the server, open the command prompt and run **ipconfig /all**.

10. You are the network administrator in your organization. You have been tasked with the job of redesigning your corporate network's IP architecture. Your company is currently using the 192.168.1.0/24 network, but it is growing quickly and will shortly outgrow this. To accommodate growth in the future, you have suggested to change the underlying IP architecture to use the 10.10.1.0/23 network. How many subnets will this allow you to use?

    A. 510

    B. 32,766

    C. 8,190

    D. 16,382

11. You are the network administrator in your organization. You have configured a server on your network to obtain an IP address from DHCP. In the DHCP scope, you have configured a reservation for the server so that it always receives the same IP address. Changes were made to the DHCP server over the weekend, and on Monday you begin hearing from users that they are unable to connect to the server. You try to ping the server by name and IP address, but you are unsuccessful. You log on to the server and in the notification area, the network connection icon appears with no indication of a problem. You open a command prompt, and ping localhost and receive a response. You then try to ping the DHCP server, but you do not receive a response. At the command prompt, you then run **ipconfig /all**. Which of the following are you most likely to find?

    A. **ipconfig** returns an IP address of 0.0.0.0.

    B. **ipconfig** returns a User configured IP address.

    C. **ipconfig** returns an IP address on the 169.254.0.0/16 network.

    D. **ipconfig** returns an IP address with an incorrect default gateway.

12. You are the network administrator in your organization. You are planning to change your corporate IP architecture. You are currently using the 10.10.10.10 network with an 18-bit subnet mask. You would like to move to an IP addressing scheme that allows for no more than 300 hosts per subnet and provides lots of room for growth. Which of the following networks would best meet this goal?

    A. 10.10.10.0/24

    B. 10.10.10.0/23

    C. 10.10.10.0/22

    D. 10.10.10.0/25

13. You are the network administrator in your organization. You would like to subnet your 131.107.0.0, Class B network to have 120 hosts per subnet. What subnet mask do you use?

    A. 255.255.255.0

    B. 255.255.255.192

    C. 255.255.254.0

    D. 255.255.255.128

14. You are the network administrator in your organization. Your network is divided into multiple subnets. You are planning on using the 131.107.0.0 network and subnetting with a 22-bit subnet mask. Which of the following IP addresses are valid with that subnet?

    A. 131.107.4.1

    B. 131.107.5.1

    C. 131.107.248.1

    D. 131.107.7.255

15. You are the network administrator in your organization. Your organization's network uses a full Class B network with the subnet mask 255.255.224.0. How many subnets are available for you to use, and how many hosts can you have per subnet?

    A. 6 subnets and 8,190 hosts

    B. 4 subnets and 16,380 hosts

    C. 8 subnets with 1,022 hosts

    D. 2 subnets with 510 hosts

LAB QUESTION

You are the network administrator for your organization. You are tasked with the project of redesigning your organization's internal TCP/IP infrastructure. You are planning on changing from a Class C network to a Class A network that uses the 10.0.0.0 private internal network. You would like to design a network that can accommodate 12,615 hosts and that offers flexibility for future growth. You do not want any subnet to have more than 130 hosts. You also must document the first 5 valid IP ranges that will be used in the conversion. Finally, you must document the first and last IP addresses in each of the first five valid IP ranges, as these will be used by your routers. Document and explain how you arrive at your answer.

SELF TEST ANSWERS

Configure TCP/IP Addressing on a Server Computer

1. ☑ **A.** A subnet mask of 255.255.254.0 allows for 32,766 subnets, each with a maximum of 510 hosts per subnet. This would result in your lowest possible network ID being 10.10.2.0/9, and give you a first IP address range of 10.10.2.1–10.10.3.254.

☒ **B** is incorrect because a subnet mask of 255.255.248.0 would allow for 8,190 subnets and 2,046 hosts per subnet. **C** is incorrect because a subnet mask of 255.255.240.0 would allow for 4,094 subnets and 4,094 hosts per subnet. **D** is incorrect because a subnet mask of 255.255.252.0 would allow for 16,382 subnets with 1,022 hosts per subnet. **E** is incorrect because a subnet mask of 255.255.224.0 would allow for 2,046 subnets with 8,190 hosts per subnet.

2. ☑ **B.** The subnet 255.255.254.0 would allow for a maximum of 510 hosts per subnet, and a maximum 32,766 network segments allows for growth.

☒ **A** is incorrect because the subnet mask 255.255.248.0 would allow you to have 2,046 hosts per network segment and a maximum of 8,190 network segments. **C** is incorrect because the subnet mask 255.255.252.0 would allow you to have 1,022 hosts per network segment, and a maximum of 16,382 network segments. **D** is incorrect because the subnet mask 255.255.240.0 would allow you to have 4,094 hosts per network segment and a maximum of 4,094 network segments.

3. ☑ **A, and C.** A network with a network ID of 192.168.1.0/26 can have a maximum of four subnets with valid host ranges of 192.168.1.1–192.168.1.62, 192.168.1.65–192.168.1.126, 192.168.1.129–192.168.1.190, and 192.168.1.193-192.168.1.254.

☒ **B, D,** and **E** are incorrect. Because of the hosts ranges available with the network ID 192.168.1.0/26, the IP addresses 192.168.1.64, 127 and 128 are not valid.

4. ☑ **C, H, B, F, A, G,** and **D.** From layer one to layer seven, the correct order of the OSI model is Physical, Data Link, Network, Transport, Session, Presentation, and Application.

☒ **E** is incorrect because the correct order is listed above. There is no Segment layer.

5. ☑ **D.** A file named lmhosts can be created for each server with the other server's name-to-IP-address mapping, and stored in the **%windir%\system32\drivers\etc directory** to be loaded during boot. The lmhosts file must not have a file extension.

☒ **A** and **B** are incorrect because the hosts file is used for host name resolution, and can be used to preload host-name-to-IP-address mappings in the DNS client cache, but it doesn't work with NetBIOS names. **C** is incorrect because the lmhosts file must not have a file extension, and is usually saved in the **%windir%\system32\drivers\etc directory**.

6. ☑ **B.** The services file located in **%windir%\system32\drivers\etc** contains a list of the well known service ports.

   ☒ **A** is incorrect because there is no file called ports. **C** is incorrect because the hosts file is used to manually configure host name resolution. **D** is incorrect because the lmhosts.sam file is a sample lmhosts file that can be used as a reference when you create your own lmhosts file.

7. ☑ **D.** When some but not all clients are experiencing name resolution problems after the IP address of a computer has been changed, have those clients run **ipconfig /flushdns** to clear their local DNS cache of all old name-to-IP-address mappings that are likely causing the problem.

   ☒ **A** and **B** are incorrect because flushing the local DNS cache or forcing a registration of the server's new name-to-IP-address mapping on the DNS server aren't likely to resolve the problem if not all of the clients on the network are experiencing name resolution issues. **C** is incorrect because TCP/IP filtering isn't likely to be a problem because if it was enabled prior to the IP address change and clients were able to connect, then clients should still be able to connect after the name change. **E** is incorrect because the **nbtstat –RR** command is a NetBIOS command that refreshes the clients NetBIOS entry in WINS. This is not likely to be the issue.

8. ☑ **C.** The best way to improve availability is to configure an alternate, user-configured static IP address, subnet, gateway, DNS, and WINS server with the same address as that used in the DHCP server reservation. This way, if the servers are unable to contact the DHCP servers and lease or renew their IP address, they will be able to statically configure themselves with the same IP address and configuration settings, maintaining uptime and connectivity.

   ☒ **A** is incorrect because changing the computers local area connection settings to be statically configured will not increase availability. **B** is incorrect because adding a second reservation would require a new MAC address and even this wouldn't improve availability if the DHCP server went offline. **D** is incorrect because installing IP v6 on the computer wouldn't help to increase availability unless other clients and servers on the network were also using it.

9. ☑ **D.** The best way to further troubleshoot the problem is to open a command prompt and run **ipconfig /all**. This will return the IP address that the computer is currently using and help you to better diagnose and resolve the problem.

   ☒ **A** is incorrect because running **tracert** will not solve the problem, nor will it help you further diagnose what's causing the problem in this example. **B** is incorrect because pinging localhost isn't going to provide you with any information you don't already have, as there is no indication of a problem on the computer. **C** is incorrect because verifying the computer account is enabled isn't an issue that would affect IP communication.

10. ☑ **B.** This configuration will allow you to use 32,766 subnets with 510 hosts per subnet.
☒ **A, C,** and **D** are incorrect because the 10.10.1.0/23 network will allow you to have up to 32766 subnets with up to 510 hosts per subnet.

11. ☑ **C.** You are most likely to find an IP address returned that is on the 169.254.0.0/16 network, because APIPA is the default setting in Windows Server 2003 for clients that are configured to obtain an IP address automatically from a DHCP server.
☒ **A** is incorrect because you are not likely to find an IP address of 0.0.0.0 as the APIPA address would be applied by default. **B** is incorrect because a User configured IP address is a possibility only if it has been configured previously, and there was no mention of this in the question. **D** is incorrect because a statically configured IP address with an incorrect default gateway would generate an alert in the notification area.

12. ☑ **A.** The A 10.10.10.0/24 network would allow for up to 254 hosts per subnet and up to 65,536 subnets.
☒ **B** is incorrect because the 10.10.10.0/23 network would allow for up to 510 hosts per subnet and up to 32,766 subnets. **C** is incorrect because the 10.10.10.0/22 network would allow for up to 1,022 hosts per subnet and 16,382 subnets. **D** is incorrect because the 10.10.10.0/25 network would allow for up to 126 hosts per subnet and 131,070 subnets.

13. ☑ **D.** In order to have at least 120 hosts per subnet, you would have to use the 255.255.255.128 subnet mask, which would provide you with $2^6 - 2 = 126$ hosts per subnet.
☒ **A** is incorrect because the 24-bit subnet would provide you with 254 hosts per subnet, which is more than twice what you require, and is not the most efficient use of IP addresses. **B** is incorrect because the 26-bit subnet mask would only allow for 62 hosts per subnet, but up to 1,022 subnets. **C** is incorrect because the 23-bit subnet would allow up to 510 hosts per subnet and up to 126 subnets.

14. ☑ **A, B,** and **C.** 131.107.4.1, 131.107.5.1, and 131.107.248.1 are all valid IP addresses. The 131.107.4.0/22 network would allow for up to 62 subnets with up to 1,022 hosts per subnet.
☒ **D** is incorrect because the IP address 131.107.7.255 doesn't fall within any of the valid IP address ranges. This address is actually the broadcast address for the 131.107.4.0/22 network.

15. ☑ **A.** A Class B network with a 19-bit subnet mask will allow for a network with 6 subnets and up to 8,190 hosts per subnet.
☒ **B, C,** and **D** are all incorrect.

LAB ANSWER

To accommodate 12,615 hosts, without exceeding 130 hosts per subnet, you will need 25 bits in the subnet mask (255.255.255.128), which will enable you to have 126 hosts per subnet and a maximum of 131,070 subnets, providing you with lots of room for growth.

The first 5 valid IP ranges that will be used in the conversion are

- 10.0.0.129–10.0.0.254
- 10.0.1.1–10.0.1.126
- 10.0.1.129–10.0.1.254
- 10.0.2.1–10.0.2.126
- 10.0.2.129–10.0.2.254

The first and last IP addresses in each of the first five valid IP ranges are the same as the ranges listed above.

MCSE/MCSA

MICROSOFT® CERTIFIED SYSTEMS ENGINEER &
MICROSOFT® CERTIFIED SYSTEMS ADMINISTRATOR

2

Manage IP Addresses

CERTIFICATION OBJECTIVES

I n this chapter, you will learn how to manage IP addresses using the Dynamic Host Configuration Protocol (DHCP). In most corporate networks, you are likely to find a mix of both statically and dynamically assigned IP addresses. Computers running server operating systems like Windows Server 2003 will most likely be configured with one or more static IP addresses, whereas client computers running operating systems such as Windows XP, Windows 2000 Professional, Windows NT 4.0 Workstation, Windows 98, or Windows 95 are likely to have IP addresses dynamically assigned through a DHCP server. This chapter provides you with the knowledge you will require to successfully manage dynamically assigned IP addresses through DHCP using the available administrative tools.

The DHCP service is a fundamental network service used in most corporate networks, both large and small. Like a number of other network services, DHCP is an open, standards-based networking service that is not proprietary to Microsoft. Microsoft's implementation of DHCP conforms to the standards defined in the DHCP Request for Comments (RFCs), and understanding the fundamentals of the DHCP service, independent of the operating system that it runs on, will help you in your administration.

on the job

A Request for Comments (RFC) is a formal document from the Internet Engineering Task Force (IETF). RFCs are the result of a committee drafting and subsequently reviewing a formal document until a final version is agreed upon. Once that happens, this document becomes the standard and no further comments or changes are permitted except through subsequent RFCs that supersede or elaborate on all or parts of previous RFCs.

CERTIFICATION OBJECTIVE 2.01

Manage DHCP Clients and Leases

The management of DHCP clients and leases encompasses a number of different areas, but before you can manage and administer DHCP, you must first plan for the DHCP service. After you have completed the planning process, you are ready to begin deployment of DHCP through the installation of the DHCP service according to our plan. This section examines the steps and concepts involved in planning DHCP.

Planning DHCP Services

The criteria you use to make decisions when planning for DHCP within your organization will be greatly influenced by your organization's existing network architecture. The first step in the planning process should be identifying all the physical subnets in your network. This information will help you better determine the placement of your DHCP servers. It is also useful information that helps you plan for and incorporate the impact slower links can have in a WAN environment and allows you to create a strategy to address these issues. Ideally, the placement of any server running network services, such as DHCP, DNS, and WINS, should maximize response time and avoid low-speed traffic.

In large, routed networks that use subnets to divide their networks into smaller, more manageable network segments, you must identify the network segments that will use DHCP clients, and plan for a way for those clients to obtain IP addresses. In this type of multi-network segment architecture you have a couple of options.

First, you could place a DHCP server on each subnet in the routed network. This option isn't often the most feasible, however, because as the number of subnets increases, so too does the administration workload and the cost of server hardware and an operating system license for each DHCP server.

A more feasible option is to set up a single DHCP server with multiple scopes for each of the respective subnets within your organization, and then configure a single client computer running an operating system such as Windows 2000, Windows 2003, or Windows NT 4.0 Server as a DHCP relay agent. The role of a DHCP relay agent is to listen for DHCP discovery messages on their local network segment, and forward the discovery message to a specific DHCP server located on a different segment. DHCP relay agents can be necessary when you are operating in a networked environment with routers that do not allow for the forwarding of DHCP broadcast messages and therefore do not support RFC 1542, or for routers that have been configured to prevent the forwarding of DHCP broadcasts for increased network performance and management purposes. Later in this chapter we will discuss how to configure a DHCP relay agent and look at an example of how a DHCP relay agent can be used even within a small and very simple network.

A third option is to configure your RFC 1542–compliant routers to allow for the forwarding of DHCP or BOOTP traffic between subnets. This option goes against network architecture and routing best practices, however.

Service availability is another component of the planning process that should be evaluated. Having just a single DHCP server would result in availability issues if you ever need to take that server offline for hardware or software maintenance. In larger networks, it is quite common to find a single primary DHCP server and a secondary or backup DHCP server configured identically and sitting idle (from a DHCP service perspective) waiting to be enabled in case of a problem with the primary. Another common DHCP server configuration that you are likely to see in larger enterprises is two DHCP servers configured using the 80/20 design rule to balance scope distribution of IP addresses for the same scopes. This design principle will be discussed in more detail later in this chapter in the section titled "Manage DHCP Databases."

A third way to improve DHCP service availability is to implement DHCP on a cluster. If you are using either the Windows Server 2003 Enterprise Edition or the DataCenter edition of the server operating system, you can configure the Microsoft Cluster Service (MSCS) to provide high availability and failover to the DHCP service. This too is a concept that we will explore later in this chapter in the section titled "Manage DHCP Databases."

Checklist: Installing a DHCP Server

The IT industry is not generally known for having great documentation, but as a consultant, one of the real value-added services that I always provide to my clients is a detailed list of exactly what changes have been made, on what dates, and at what times to provide for better troubleshooting should a problem arise shortly after I've implemented a change. One of the simplest pieces of documentation that a number of my clients have found extremely useful is a checklist.

Table 2-1 shows a sample DHCP checklist that you can use to verify that you are ready to proceed with the installation of your first DHCP server and then continue on to configure the DHCP server.

Installing the DHCP Server Service

Now that you are familiar with the planning process, the next step is the deployment of DHCP according to your strategy. Windows Server 2003 offers you a number of different ways to accomplish many tasks such as installing the DHCP service.

When you first log on to a server running Windows Server 2003 as the administrator, or as a member of the administrators group, you are presented with the Manage Your Server wizard as shown in Figure 2-1. If you are like the majority of administrators,

TABLE 2-1	DHCP Installation Checklist

Completed	Steps
☑	Review your existing network topology and DHCP configuration. Determine the number of existing subnets and slow WAN connections.
☑	Determine the IP address range(s) on which you will require the DHCP server service.
☑	Configure the DHCP server with a static IP address.
☑	Install the DHCP server service. Optionally, disable DHCP service bindings from additional NICs on a multi-homed server.
☑	Configure the pre-determined number of scopes, their respective scope options, user and vendor classes, exclusion ranges, lease times and any other additional configurations documented in your DHCP server strategy.
☑	Configure DNS dynamic updates on the DHCP server according to your documented DHCP server strategy.
☑	Activate the scope. Optionally, authorize the DHCP server if operating in an Active Directory environment.
☑	Implement your redundancy and/ high availability plan according to your documented DHCP server strategy.

you likely simply closed that dialog box and configured it not to appear in the future. If this is the case, and you wish to see it again, Manage Your Server can be found under Start | Programs | Administrative Tools.

The Manage Your Server wizard has been significantly improved from Windows 2000 and is included to allow you to easily configure a new server running Windows Server 2003 to run one or more of the eleven available default roles. You can see in Figure 2-1 that the DHCP service isn't installed, but that the server is currently configured for both the Application Server and DNS Server roles. To configure the server for the role of DHCP server, simply select the option **Add or remove a role** found in the top right area of the Manage Your Server dialog box and run through the wizard's configuration steps.

FIGURE 2-1 Manage Your Server wizard

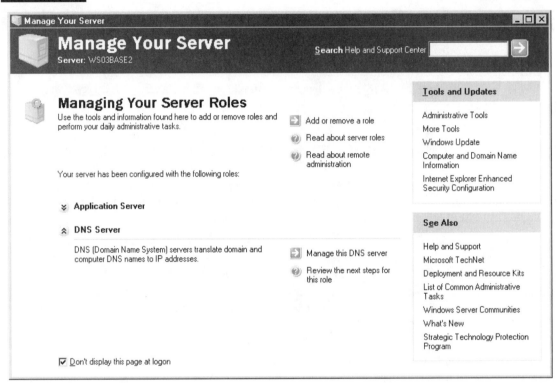

EXERCISE 2-1

CertCam 2-1 ON THE CD

Using the Manage Your Server Wizard
to Install a DHCP Server

In this exercise you will learn the steps involved in installing the DHCP server service using the Manage Your Server wizard.

1. Click Start | Programs | Administrative Tools and select Manage Your Server.

2. In the Manage Your Server dialog box, click Add or remove a role.

3. On the **Preliminary Steps** page, click Next. The wizard will briefly analyze the server's current configuration and then present you with the Server Role page.

4. On the **Server Role** page shown in the following illustration, you are presented with the results of the system scan. Select DHCP server from the list of available, default role types and click Next.

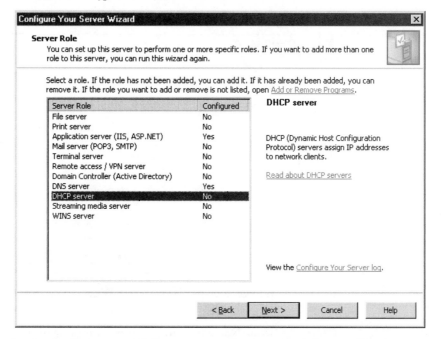

5. On the **Summary of Selections** page shown in the following illustration, verify that you have selected the DHCP server role, and click **Next**. This will start the installation of the DHCP service. After the installation, it will run the

new scope wizard to configure a new DHCP scope, as stated in the Summary dialog box.

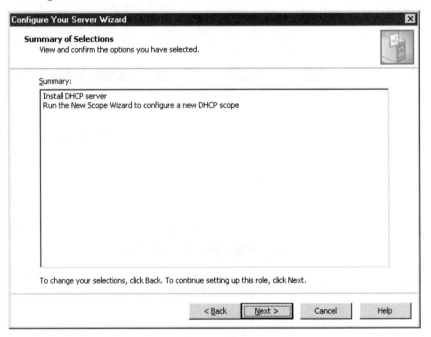

6. On the **Welcome to the New Scope Wizard** page of the New Scope Wizard dialog box, click **Next** to begin the creation of your first DHCP scope.

7. On the **Scope Name** page shown in the following illustration, type the name of the scope, and if you wish, enter an optional description, and then click **Next**.

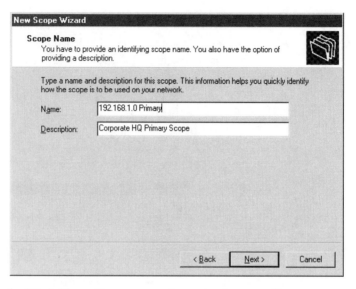

8. On the **IP Address Range** page shown in the next illustration, enter the starting and ending IP addresses and the subnet mask. The subnet mask can be configured by either entering the number of bits you wish to use for the subnet, or by entering the subnet into the **subnet mask** box. Ensure that you have planned your scopes carefully and that you enter the correct subnet mask, because the subnet mask value cannot be changed later.

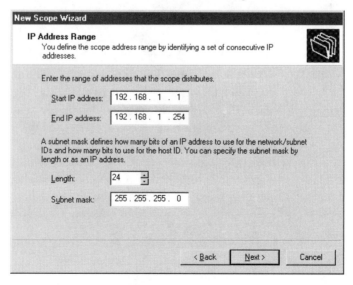

9. On the **Add Exclusions** page, shown in the following illustration, specify any IP addresses that you wish to exclude from the range of IP addresses selected by entering a start and end IP address and clicking **Add**. You can add multiple, non-contiguous exclusion ranges to meet your specific requirements. Exclusion ranges are often used to block out a number of IP addresses from a complete IP address subnet list to allow those IP addresses to be statically assigned to servers operating on that segment, such as your DHCP server or your routers and switches that require a static IP address. Once you have configured all of your required exclusion ranges, click **Next**.

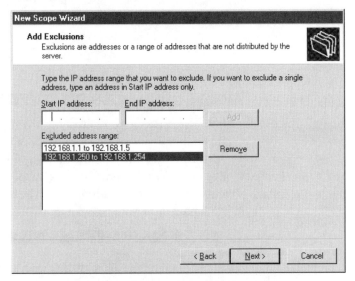

10. On the **Lease Duration** page, enter the duration in days, hours, or minutes that you wish to apply the scope to. The default is 8 days. In organizations where there are more available IP addresses than there are clients that require them, you might consider increasing the DHCP lease duration to avoid unnecessary DHCP lease and renew traffic. In organizations where mobile computers, such as notebooks or tablets, continuously connect and disconnect from the network, or where the number of clients requiring IP addresses is close to or exceeds the number of available IP addresses, you might consider reducing the lease duration to speed up the turnover and allow more IP addresses to be available more often.

11. On the **Configure DHCP Options** page, select either **Yes, I want to configure these options now** or **No, I will configure these options later**. By selecting **Yes, I want to configure these options now**, and clicking **Next**, you can define the default and most common scope options for your newly created scope.

12. On the **Router (Default Gateway)** page, enter the IP address of the routers available on the given subnet, and click **Add**. It is often considered a best practice to use the first and last available IP addresses on a give subnet as the router addresses. In the example here with the 192.168.1.0/24 network, that would mean that either or both 192.168.1.1 and 192.168.1.254 could be router addresses. When you've finished entering all of the applicable routers, click **Next**.

13. On the **Domain Name and DNS Servers** page shown in the next illustration, enter the name of the DNS Parent domain, such as corporate.mccaw.ca, and either the name or the IP address of each of the DNS servers available on your network, and click **Add**. If you choose to enter the name of the DNS server, and the computer you are installing DHCP on is configured to use DNS, you can click **Resolve** to resolve the name of the DNS server to its IP address. Click **Next**.

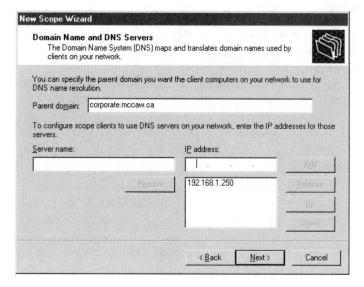

14. If your organization is still supporting older, legacy clients and servers that require NetBIOS name resolution and you are using WINS, you can enter the IP address of your WINS servers and click **Add** and **Next**.

15. The **Activate Scope** page appears next, asking you to select to activate the scope or choose to leave it deactivated and click **Next**. If you do not wish to configure any additional scope configuration options, selecting to activate the scope is fine; however, if there are other scope options you wish to configure, you should leave the scope deactivated and configure those additional settings using either **netsh** at the command line or the DHCP MMC snap-in. Click **Finish**.

16. Click **Finish** again in the **Configure Your Server Wizard** dialog box and you have now successfully installed DHCP and configured a new scope.

ⓦatch

The computer on which you are installing the DHCP server service must be configured with a static IP address and subnet mask.

One of the benefits of using the Manage Your Server wizard to configure a server for a particular role is that it will only start the services required for that role to function properly, which helps to reduce the potential attack surface on that server in an effort to make it more secure.

As previously mentioned, there are often multiple ways to accomplish the same end result with many Microsoft products, including Windows Server 2003. The installation of the DHCP service is not limited to the Configure Your Server Wizard, though that is the preferred method. Alternatively, you can use the Add/Remove Windows Components utility found within Add or Remove Programs in Control Panel to install all of your network services, including DHCP.

Whichever way you install the DHCP service, two new local groups get created upon installation: **DHCP Users** and **DHCP Administrators**. Members of the DHCP Users group are granted read-only access to the DHCP console, which can be useful for your help desk for troubleshooting and diagnosing a problem, and then escalating the trouble ticket to a member of the DHCP Administrators group to make the appropriate change. Members of the DHCP Administrators group have full administrative authority over the DHCP server service. This group can be very useful when you want to grant an individual full control over DHCP without granting full control over all of the services running on the server.

EXERCISE 2-2

Installing DHCP Using Add/Remove Programs

In this exercise you will install the Microsoft DHCP server service using Add or Remove Programs in Control Panel.

1. Click **Start | Control Panel**, and select **Add or Remove Programs**.

2. In **Add or Remove Programs**, click **Add/Remove Windows Components** and wait for the **Windows Components Wizard** dialog box to appear, as shown here:

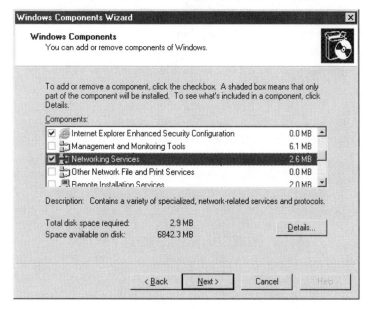

3. Scroll down the list of available components, select **Networking Services**, and click the **Details** button.

4. In the **Networking Services** dialog box, place a check mark next to **Dynamic Host Configuration Protocol (DHCP)**, and click **OK**.

5. Click **Next** in the Windows Components Wizard dialog box.

6. Click **Finish** once the installation is complete.

watch *You can administer and manage the DHCP service using either the DHCP snap-in (dhcpmgmt.msc) or the netsh command.*

Now that you are familiar with the installation of the DHCP server service, you can explore some additional management issues that you may need to address depending on the configuration of your servers, such as selecting the adapter that the DHCP service listens on, authorizing the DHCP server, as well as creating, configuring and activating scopes.

Multi-homed DHCP Servers

It is quite common to receive servers from your Original Equipment Manufacturer (OEM) with two network cards built into the servers. One benefit of this type of hardware configuration is that it allows you to bind unique IP addresses to each network adapter that are specific to two separate subnets. In a small two-subnet network, this type of configuration, shown in Figure 2-2 alleviates the need to use DHCP relay agents or to configure your routers to allow for the forwarding of DHCP or BOOTP traffic. In this example, the DHCP server is multi-homed and connected directly to both the 192.168.1.0/24 and the 192.168.2.0/24 networks, which would allow it to receive DHCP related broadcasts from both client1 and client2 on their respective subnets.

Figure 2-3 shows another common configuration, particularly for small organizations with only a few servers, and where the company is connected to the Internet by a high-speed cable or DSL connection. The issue that arises in this configuration is that your Internet Service Provider (ISP) might require that the network card used to connect to their Internet service be configured to obtain an IP address dynamically from one of their DHCP servers, and restrict you from running your own DHCP service on their network. Having rogue DHCP servers pop up and begin leasing out incorrectly configured and non-valid IP addresses on the ISP network is obviously going to be

FIGURE 2-2 Multi-homed DHCP server

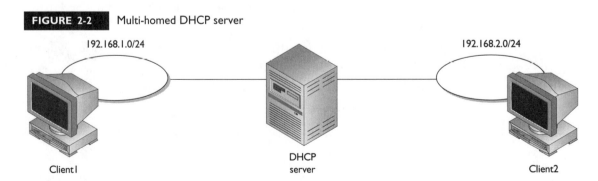

192.168.1.0/24

192.168.2.0/24

Client1

DHCP
server

Client2

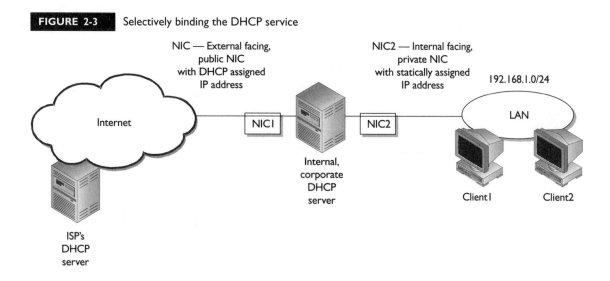

FIGURE 2-3   Selectively binding the DHCP service

frowned upon. If you have ever accidentally done this, you probably found yourself removed from the ISP network pretty quickly, as ISPs tend to be very aggressive about preventing this type of activity.

With this type of configuration, to run the DHCP service successfully on your multi-homed server that also acts as your corporate gateway to the Internet, you must unbind the DHCP service from NIC1, the externally facing, public interface. You can do this quite easily within the DHCP MMC, as you will learn in the next exercise.

EXERCISE 2-3

Binding DHCP to Specific Network Interface Cards

In this exercise you will learn how to unbind the DHCP service from a specific NIC on a multi-homed server. This allows you to specify exactly which NIC the DHCP service will listen and service requests on, and can be extremely valuable when you're configuring the DHCP server service on a server that is connected to multiple subnets or virtual local area networks (VLANs), but where you only want the DHCP service to listen on specific networks.

1. Click **Start | Programs | Administrative Tools**, and select **DHCP**.

2. In the DHCP MMC, right-click the name of your DHCP server (ws03base2. corporate.mccaw.ca) and select **Properties**.

3. In the **Properties** dialog box, shown in the following illustration, select the **Advanced** tab, and click the **Bindings** button.

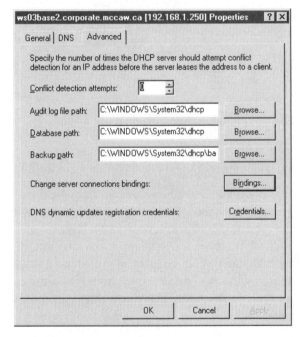

4. In the **Binding** dialog box, deselect each network interface that you do not wish to have the DHCP server service bound to, and click **OK**.

5. Click **OK** again to close the Properties dialog box.

With the DHCP server service now installed, and with a new scope created and your multi-homed server correctly configured to use only the specific network interface cards, you can shift your focus to the DHCP server authorization process.

Authorizing DHCP

Authorizing a DHCP server running on a Windows 2000 Server was a new requirement for DHCP with Windows 2000. This requirement has also been included in the Windows Server 2003 operating system, and as in Windows 2000 only applies when you're operating in an Active Directory domain environment. The DHCP server service in both Windows 2000 Server and Windows Server 2003 is configured to query Active Directory for a list of authorized DHCP servers upon initialization. If the DHCP service determines that it is not on the authorized list, the DHCP service will not initialize properly, preventing it from leasing out IP addresses to clients on your network. The authorization process was introduced to enable the detection of rogue DHCP servers, but it is limited to detecting DHCP server services running on Windows 2000 Server and Windows Server 2003. This means that anyone with a notebook computer that can gain access to your network either through a physical connection or through a wireless access point can configure a DHCP or BOOTP server running on a UNIX, Linux, or even Windows NT 4.0.

e x a m
ᙡatch

Only DHCP server services running on either Windows 2000 Server or Windows Server 2003 require authorization within the Active Directory. In the DHCP MMC, a red arrow *pointing down on the DHCP server indicates the server is not authorized. When that arrow is green and pointing upward, this signifies that it is authorized.*

Figure 2-4 displays the ws03base2.corporate.mccaw.ca DHCP server as being authorized with the green arrow (although it may be difficult to see the color in the figure) pointing up. A red arrow pointing down can also be seen at the scope level indicating that the scope is not activated. Figure 2-4 is not a true representation of an authorized DHCP service because it is a member server operating outside of an Active Directory domain, and therefore doesn't require authorization.

To authorize a DHCP server service that is running on a computer that is a member of an Active Directory domain, simply right-click the name of the DHCP server within the DHCP MMC, and select **Authorize**. To see and manage a list of all authorized servers within the Active Directory, right-click **DHCP** within the DHCP

e x a m
ᙡatch

You must be a member of the Enterprise Admins group in order to have permission to authorize a DHCP server.

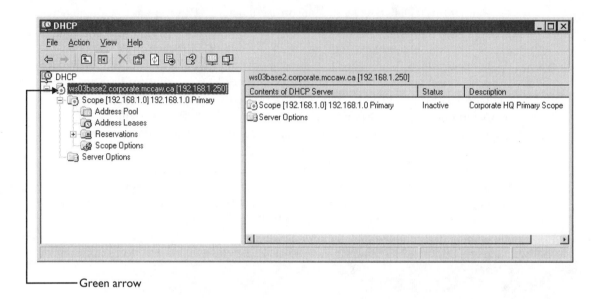

FIGURE 2-4   Determining whether DHCP is authorized

Green arrow

MMC and select **Manage authorized servers**. This will display the Manage Authorized Servers dialog box shown in Figure 2-5. To authorize a DHCP server, click **Authorize**, and in the **Authorize DHCP Server** dialog box, type the name or IP address of the DHCP server you want to authorize, and click **OK**. In the Confirm Authorization dialog box, click **OK** and then click **Close**.

FIGURE 2-5

Authorizing a
DHCP server

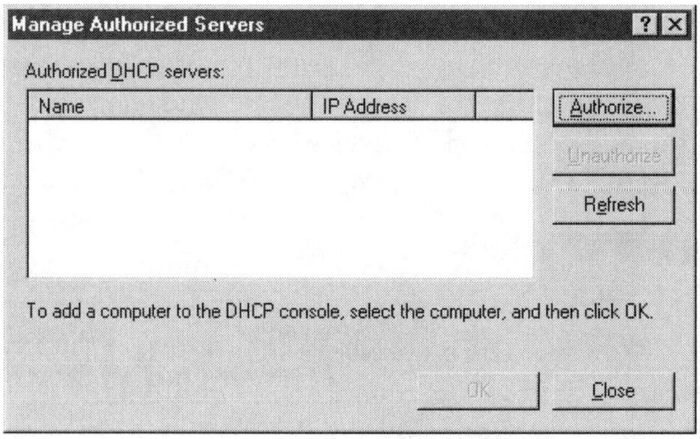

DHCP Scopes

The DHCP server service included in Windows Server 2003 offers you the ability to create three types of scopes, a regular scope, a superscope, or a multicast scope. Each of these three types of scopes can be created using either the DHCP snap-in or the **netsh** command.

A DHCP *scope* is a range of IP addresses and related configuration settings that the DHCP server uses to issue IP addresses to DHCP clients. As you learned earlier in this chapter, using the Manage Your Server wizard to install DHCP also creates a single scope through the Create a Scope wizard. Assuming that you opted to use Add or Remove Programs to install the DHCP service, and you have authorized your DHCP server within Active Directory if required, you are now at the point where you need to create a new scope. Each scope that you create on a DHCP server represents all or part of the available IP addresses on a single network segment and each scope can only include a single subnet. Once a scope is created, both the start and end IP addresses can be changed, but the subnet you originally specified cannot be changed without deleting and re-creating the scope.

<table>
<tr><td>*A scope can only include a single subnet and that subnet cannot be modified after the scope is created without*</td><td>*deleting and re-creating the scope. A minimum of one activated scope must exist for a DHCP server to lease out IP addresses.*</td></tr>
</table>

Creating a Scope

Scopes can be created either by using the DHCP snap-in or by using the **netsh** command. The DHCP snap-in scope creation process is very simple as it is all wizard driven. Being that this process was covered in Exercise 2-1 as part of the DHCP installation using Manage Your Server, we will focus our attention on using the **netsh** command to create a scope. Regardless of the tool you use to create a new scope, you should begin the scope creation process by identifying the following information that will be required:

- Name of the scope (such as **scope2**)
- Starting and ending IP address (such as 192.168.2.1 to 192.168.2.254)
- Exclusion ranges within the IP address range (such as 192.168.2.1 to 192.168.2.5 and 192.168.2.245 to 192.168.2.254)
- The lease duration (such as 15 days)

EXERCISE 2-4

Creating a New Scope Using netsh

You can administer DHCP through the graphical DHCP snap-in or via the command line, which offers you a scriptable interface that can assist in automating the administration of DHCP. This exercise will teach you how to create a scope using the **netsh** command.

1. Click **Start | Run**, type **cmd**, and click ENTER.

2. At the command prompt, type **netsh** and press ENTER.

3. Type **dhcp server \\192.168.1.250** and press ENTER.

4. Type **add scope 192.168.2.0 255.255.255.0 scope2** and press ENTER. In this example, 192.168.2.0 is the IP network of the scope, 255.255.255.0 is the subnet mask for the scope, and scope2 is the name assigned to the scope.

5. Type **scope 192.168.2.0** and press ENTER.

6. Type **set state 0** and press ENTER.

7. Type **add iprange 192.168.2.1 192.168.2.254** and press ENTER.

8. Type **add exclude range 192.168.2.1 192.168.2.5** and press ENTER.

9. Type **add exclude range 192.168.2.245 192.168.2.254** and press ENTER.

10. Type **exit** and press ENTER to exit the **netsh** utility.

11. Type **exit** and press ENTER again to exit the command prompt.

on the **Job**

netsh is a command-line shell utility that can be used to configure, manage and administer a number of network services including DHCP, WINS, and IPSec. There are a number of administrative and configuration options, such as the configuration of IPSec persistent mode, that are only available from within netsh. Spend some time getting to know this utility.

Scope Activation

With your DHCP server installed and authorized, your scopes added, and the scope options configured, you might now be ready to begin leasing out IP addresses. I say *might*, because depending on your DHCP strategy document, there might be more to do prior to activating the scope, such as configuring DNS integration, option classes, and additional scope options.

To activate a scope, you must be logged on as a member of one or more of the following groups: Administrators, DHCP Admins, or Server Operators. Unlike DHCP server authorization where you must be a member of the Enterprise Admins group to perform authorizations, activating a scope does not require as high a level of privilege.

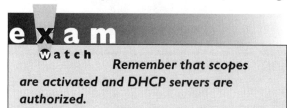

Remember that scopes are activated and DHCP servers are authorized.

Whenever you are ready to begin leasing out IP addresses, the next step is to activate the scope. Activation can be accomplished via the DHCP snap-in or using the **netsh** command.

To activate a scope from within the DHCP snap-in, right-click the scope and select **activate**. If you prefer to use the **netsh** command, type the following:

```
Dhcp server \\192.168.1.250
Scope 192.168.2.0
Set state 1
```

Superscopes

A superscope is simply an administrative grouping of scopes that can support multiple logical IP subnets on the same physical network segment. Superscopes contain one or more member scopes that can be activated together as a group. Superscopes allow a DHCP server to provide leases from more than one scope on a single physical network. Creating a superscope is also one way to get around the limitation of not being able to change the subnet mask assigned to a scope. If you originally created a small scope that you have now outgrown, you can easily create a second scope and then add both scopes to a superscope allowing you to quickly, easily, and transparently to your clients, expand your network. Exercise 2-5 looks at the process of creating a new superscope.

EXERCISE 2-5

Creating a Superscope

In this exercise you will learn how to create a superscope. Superscopes can be used to simplify DHCP administration when all of your DHCP clients are located on a single physical network segment that is divided into multiple logical IP subnets.

1. Open the DHCP snap-in and verify that one scope exists. A single scope must exist in order to create a superscope.

2. Right-click the name of your DHCP server and select **New Superscope**.

3. In the New Superscope Wizard dialog box, click **Next**.

4. On the **Superscope Name** page of the New Superscope Wizard, enter the name of the superscope and click **Next**.

5. On the **Select Scopes** page of the New Superscope Wizard, select the scope(s) that you want to include in the superscope, click **Next**.

6. Click **Finish**.

Multicast Scopes

Windows Server 2003, like Windows 2000 Server, includes support for Multicast Address Dynamic Client Allocation Protocol (MADCAP) in the form of multicast scopes that allow you to dynamically assign IP multicast addresses on TCP/IP-based networks. Unlike unicast IP addresses, which use either Class A, B, or C TCP/IP addresses, multicast addresses use Class D addresses, which allow directed communication from one point to multiple points. Multicast scopes are very easy to configure, as you will see in Exercise 2-6, but they do come with some limitations.

Multicast scopes do not support DHCP-assignable options, and any computer that wants to receive a multicast IP address must first have a valid primary computer address on a Class A, B, or C network.

The DHCP and MADCAP services are designed to function independently of one another on a server running Windows Server 2003, which enables clients to obtain an IP address and a multicast address from the DHCP service.

EXERCISE 2-6

Creating a Multicast Scope

This exercise will teach you how to create a MADCAP scope, which will allow clients on the network to obtain a Class D IP address for applications that utilize point-to-multipoint communications.

1. In the DHCP snap-in, right-click the name of the DHCP server and select **New Multicast Scope**.

2. The New Multicast Scope Wizard appears. Click **Next**.

3. On the **Multicast Scope Name** page of the New Multicast Scope Wizard, enter a name for the multicast scope and an optional description and click **Next**.

4. On the **IP Address Range** page, enter the start and end Class D addresses, and click **Next**.

5. On the **Add Exclusions** page, enter the start and end IP addresses for any exclusion ranges you wish to add, and click **Add**. When you're finished defining exclusion ranges, click **Next**.

6. On the **Lease Duration** page, the default lease period for multicast IP address leases is 30 days. Modify or leave the default setting, and click **Next**.

7. On the **Active Multicast Scope** page, select **Yes** to activate the scope or **No** to postpone activating the scope, and click **Next**.

8. Click **Finish**.

Notice that during the creation of a multicast scope, you weren't asked to specify scope configuration options. This is because multicast scopes do not allow the use of scope options. To change any of the properties that you configure for the multicast scope during its creation, simply right-click the name of the multicast scope, select Properties, and make the necessary changes on the General tab of the properties dialog box.

Integrating DDNS with DHCP

The DNS dynamic update protocol (DDNS) is a new feature that is supported only on computers running versions of the Windows 2000, Windows XP, and Windows Server 2003 operating system. Operating systems that support DDNS can dynamically update their host address record information on a Windows 2000 or Windows Server 2003 DNS server that contains a zone database file configured to allow dynamic updates. DDNS is intended to simplify administration within your network by allowing clients a way to dynamically update their DNS information as it changes.

To configure DDNS, you start on the DNS server, by configuring one or more DNS zones to allow for dynamic updates. Once the server is configured, clients supporting DDNS will be able to dynamically update their host resource record information. This is great if all of the computers in your organization are running up-to-date operating systems, but older operating systems without built-in support for DDNS aren't left out either—the answer lies with the DHCP service.

Thanks to the forethought of Microsoft's developers, DDNS can be integrated with either the Windows 2000 Server or Windows Server 2003 DHCP service to extend DDNS functionality to computers running older Microsoft operating systems. By default, computers running Windows 2000, Windows XP, and Windows Server 2003 that are configured to obtain an IP address automatically from a DHCP server will update their own Host (A) resource records on the Windows 2000 or Windows Server 2003 DNS server. The Windows Server 2003 DHCP server updates the Pointer (PTR) record for the DDNS-supporting DHCP client computers. The DHCP server can also be configured to act as a DNS proxy on behalf of older clients that do not support the dynamic update protocol. As a DNS proxy, the DHCP server can be configured to update both the Host (A) and the Pointer (PTR) resource records on behalf of the older clients as well as client operating systems that support DDNS.

e x a m
ⓦ a t c h

By default, an authorized DHCP server running on Windows Server 2003 dynamically updates all PTR resource records for Windows 2000 and Windows XP Professional clients. The options to Enable DNS dynamic updates according to the settings below *and the sub-option to* Dynamically update DNS A and PTR records only if requested *by the DHCP clients* **are the default options. This means that the DHCP server will update the DNS information only for DHCP clients that request that their DNS information be updated. Therefore no older clients such as Windows NT 4.0 or Windows 9x will have their DNS information updated, because by default they will not request that it be updated.**

The Dynamic Update Process

The ability to integrate DHCP with DNS provides you with a way of extending the dynamic registration capabilities of the DNS service to older, legacy clients such as Windows NT 4.0 and Windows 9x that do not natively support DDNS. This can greatly reduce your administration workload by allowing you to leverage DHCP, a service that is automatically dynamic and supported by all clients to perform the task of registering IP-address-to-host-name mappings in DNS on your behalf. Foregoing this option means that you will be responsible for ensuring each of your legacy clients has a correct host-name-to-IP-address mapping within DNS. Imagine the complexity and amount of time that you would need to dedicate to just this task in a large environment where client IP addresses changed regularly. This could end up being a full-time job for one or more people, or one that could be fully automated, freeing you up to focus on other more important issues.

To better understand the DNS integration and registration process, take a look at how the dynamic update process works. In this example, we assume that the default settings are enabled on the DHCP server, and on the DHCP clients running either Windows 2000 Server, Windows Server 2003, or Windows XP. Make sure you understand this process for the certification exam. You will be tested on your knowledge of DDNS and how it applies to different scenarios.

1. The client broadcasts a request for an IP address to all DHCP servers on its segment and includes in the request the client's Fully Qualified Domain Name (FQDN).

2. All DHCP servers that receive the request, and that have an available IP address to lease, broadcast an IP lease offer to the client.

3. The first IP address offer that the client receives is the one that it accepts. The client broadcasts its acceptance of the IP address so that the DHCP server that extended the offer is aware, and so that all other DHCP servers that extended offers can withdraw their offers and make those IP addresses available to other DHCP clients.

4. The DHCP server returns a DHCP acknowledgement message to the client granting an IP address lease, and sending along with the lease any additional server and scope-configured options and user and vendor option class-configured options. This concludes the normal four-step DHCP lease process. The remaining steps are a result of the integration of DHCP with DNS.

5. DHCP clients that support DDNS, and that have the option configured within their TCP/IP settings to **Register this connection's addresses in DNS**, request that DHCP send their Host (A) and Pointer (PTR) resource records to the Windows 2000 or Windows Server 2003 DNS server in the form of a DNS update message for both the forward and reverse lookup zones. Alternatively, you can configure the option to have the Windows Server 2003 DHCP server send the updates on behalf of the client. You can also select to have DHCP send A and PTR resource records to the DNS server on behalf of all clients, even those that do not natively support DDNS. To achieve this, change the default settings on the DNS tab of the DHCP server properties dialog box to those shown in the following illustration. The two changes made in the following illustration are **Always dynamically update DNS A and PTR records** and

Dynamically update DNS A and PTR records for DHCP clients that do not request updates (for example, clients running Windows NT 4.0).

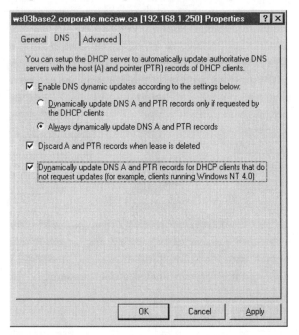

6. Making the configuration changes in Step 5 forces the Windows Server 2003 DHCP server to send an update to the Windows 2000 or Windows Server 2003 DNS server on behalf of all DHCP clients to update the client's A and PTR resource records. The FQDN that the DHCP server received in the first step of this process is used in this operation.

Only Windows 2000, Windows XP, and Windows Server 2003 clients natively support dynamic updates. To allow other Microsoft operating systems to take advantage of dynamic updates, configure the DHCP server to update the DNS records on the DNS server.

If the Windows 2000, Windows Server 2003, or Windows XP DHCP clients are statically configured, the process changes slightly from that just described. The following process occurs when the DHCP client is statically configured with an IP address.

1. The client initializes and broadcasts its statically configured IP address, allowing for any potential conflicts to be identified. If no conflicts are found, the client configures itself with the static IP address.

2. The client's DHCP client service, which is running by default on all computers running Windows 2000, Windows Server 2003, and Windows XP, sends the client's Host (A) record to the DNS server as a DNS update for the forward lookup zone on the DNS server.

3. The DHCP server sends an update to the DNS server on behalf of the client to update the client's reverse lookup record (PTR). The FQDN that the DHCP server received in the first step of this process is used in this operation.

To provide dynamic update support to all Windows clients, even those that do not natively support it, the DHCP service must be configured to handle the name registration on behalf of all clients. The extension of dynamic updates to all clients can be achieved by configuring a Windows Server 2003 DHCP server to automatically update DHCP client information in DNS. This configuration requires that all clients use the DHCP server service to obtain their IP addresses automatically through DHCP.

on the **job**

To become more familiar with the implementation and function of DHCP servers, see "Dynamic Host Configuration Protocol" in the Networking Guide of the Microsoft Windows Server 2003 Resource Kit. You can also learn more about DHCP through a number of online support webcasts available at http:// support.microsoft.com/servicedesks/Webcasts.

EXERCISE 2-7

Configuring DDNS for All clients in DHCP

To configure the DHCP server to dynamically update A and PTR resource records for all clients perform, the following steps.

1. Right-click the name of the DHCP server and select **Properties**.

2. In the Properties dialog box, select the **DNS** tab.

3. Configure the properties according to the selections made in the preceding illustration.

Best practices suggest not installing the DHCP server service and configuring it to perform dynamic DNS updates on a computer configured as a domain controller, thus avoiding having to enter credentials. Instead, the DHCP server service can be installed on a member server and the member server's computer account can be added to the DNSUpdateProxy global security group to allow that DHCP server to perform a secure dynamic update for any DNS name.

One last DHCP and DNS integration setting that we will look at is found on the Advanced tab of the DHCP server's Properties dialog box shown in the preceding illustration: the Credentials button. The credentials button is used to specify the user's credentials that you would like the DHCP service to use when performing the DNS registrations on behalf of the DHCP clients and where the DNS zone is Active Directory integrated and configured to allow only secure updates.

e x a m

ᴡatch

If all of your DHCP server's computer accounts are not members of the DNSUpdateProxy global security group,

only the DHCP server that performed the original DNS update has permission to update the name again in the future.

CERTIFICATION OBJECTIVE 2.02

Manage DHCP Relay Agent

DHCP relay agents play a specific role within a DHCP infrastructure and are one means of extending DHCP lease functionality to remote subnets that do not have a local DHCP server. Because DHCP discovery messages use broadcasts, and broadcasts are generally limited to the local subnet because of the default configuration of routers and switches, DHCP relay agents offer to extend DHCP service functionality to these remote subnets.

The DHCP Relay Agent component is a Bootstrap Protocol (BOOTP) relay agent that relays DHCP messages from DHCP clients to specific DHCP servers that the relay agent has been configured to forward to on different IP networks. The DHCP Relay Agent is compliant with RFC 1542. To support DHCP in a large, routed network, each IP network segment that contains DHCP clients requires either a DHCP server or a computer acting as a DHCP Relay Agent.

on the *Job* *The DHCP Relay Agent component cannot run on a computer running the DHCP server service, network address translation (NAT), or Internet Connection Sharing (ICS). It also must run on a computer configured with a static IP address.*

Installing and Configuring a DHCP Relay Agent

DHCP relay agents are installed and configured through the Routing and Remote Access snap-in. You must be a member of the Administrators group to install and configure a DHCP relay agent. As when you perform any administrative task, use the security best practice of using the **runas** command rather than logging on with administrative credentials.

EXERCISE 2-8

MasterSim 2-8 ON THE CD

Installing and Configuring a DHCP Relay Agent

This exercise will teach you how to install and configure a DHCP relay agent.

1. Click **Start | Administrative Tools | Routing and Remote Access**.

2. Right-click the name of the server and select **Configure and Enable Routing and Remote Access**. This will launch the Routing and Remote Access Server Setup Wizard. Click **Next** on first page of the wizard.

3. On the **Custom Configuration** page shown in the following illustration, select **Demand-dial connections (used for branch office routing)**, and **Next.**

4. Click **Finish**.

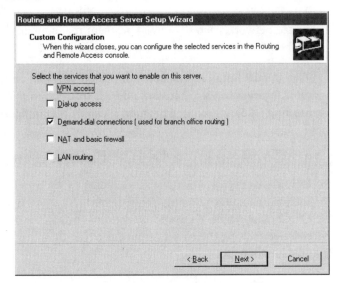

5. In the **Routing and Remote Access** warning dialog box that appears, click **Yes** to start the service.

6. In the Routing and Remote Access snap-in, expand **IP Routing** and right-click **General**. Select **New Routing Protocol**, and in the New Routing Protocol dialog box, shown here, select **DHCP Relay Agent**, and click **OK**.

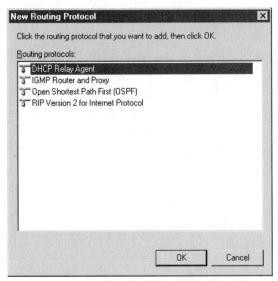

7. In the Routing and Remote Access snap-in, right-click **DHCP Relay Agent** and select **New Interface**. Select the interface on which you want the DHCP relay agent to listen, and click **OK**.

8. In the DHCP Relay Properties dialog box that appears, ensure that the **Relay DHCP packets** option is enabled, as shown here. Customize the **hop-count threshold** and **boot threshold** values to meet your specific needs, and click **OK**.

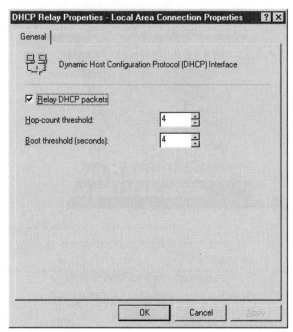

9. Right-click the DHCP Relay Agent and select **Properties**. The DHCP Relay Agent Properties dialog box will appear as shown in the following illustration. Enter the IP address of the DHCP servers one at a time, and click **Add**. When

you have finished adding all the DHCP server IP addresses that you want the DHCP relay agent to send DHCP requests to, click **OK**.

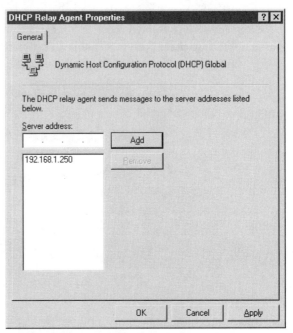

In this exercise, pay particular attention to the options in Step 7. You select whether you want to relay packets and define the hop-count and boot threshold in the properties of each individual interface that you add within the DHCP relay agent protocol. The hop-count allows you to define the number of routers between the DHCP relay agent and the DHCP server that the DHCP packets are able to traverse before the packet are dropped. The boot threshold is the length of time in seconds that the DHCP relay agent will wait before it sends the DHCPDISCOVER packet to the DHCP server.

You can also configure RRAS to lease out an IP address itself or to take advantage of an existing DHCP server on the network. If you have configured an RRAS server to obtain IP addresses through DHCP, the RRAS service will obtain a block off ten IP addresses, plus one for itself for a total of eleven, to make available to remote access clients. Once the block of ten IP addresses has been leased out, the RRAS server contacts the DHCP server to obtain another block of ten. The remote access clients never communicate directly with the DHCP server; instead, all communication with

DHCP is handled by the routing and remote access service (RRAS). By default, RRAS will not forward any additional scope information such as the address of DNS or WINS servers. For this information to be forwarded, a DHCP relay agent must be configured. RRAS clients automatically drop their leases when they disconnect, making the IP address they were using available to other remote access clients.

Troubleshooting the DHCP Relay Agent

You can troubleshoot problems with the DHCP relay agent in using the DHCP relay agent interface found within the Routing and Remote Access snap-in. As you can see in Figure 2-6, the RRAS snap-in can provide you with some initial information about the activities of the DHCP relay agent, such as whether the relay mode is enabled, the interfaces on which it is enabled, and how many requests and replies have been received or discarded, which can help you to identify areas that might require a more detailed analysis.

If requests for DHCP leased IP addresses are not getting to the DHCP servers that have been configured, confirm that network connectivity is in place and functioning properly by using the **ping** command to ping the DHCP server from the DHCP relay agent. Also confirm that the problem isn't a result of IP packet filtering being enabled on either the DHCP relay agent or DHCP server, or any router between the two that could be filtering out the forwarded requests. DHCP traffic uses the User Datagram Protocol (UDP) ports 67 and 68.

FIGURE 2-6   Troubleshooting the DHCP relay agent

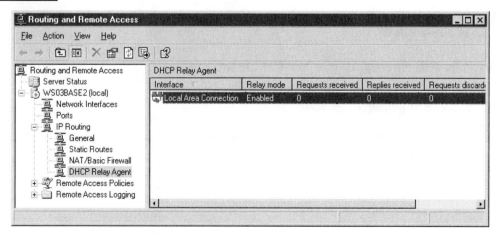

Manage DHCP Databases

Many different administrative tasks fall within the confines of managing DHCP databases. In this section we will explore some of the new features included in the Windows Server 2003 DHCP service, such as the ability to back up and restore the DHCP database from within the GUI. We will also look at the options available to achieve high availability with the DHCP service using both the 80/20 rule and the Microsoft Cluster Services (MSCS). This section will also introduce you to the steps involved in moving a DHCP database from one server to another. With all of this knowledge in hand, you will be well prepared for the certification exam and beyond.

Backing Up and Restoring the DHCP Database

One of the new features in the DHCP service in Windows Server 2003 is the ability to back up and restore your DHCP database from within the DHCP snap-in. In previous versions, the DHCP service natively provided a built-in backup feature that backed up the DHCP database to the backup subdirectory at regular intervals and during periods of low activity. In Windows Server 2003 you can perform backups when required, and specify where you want the backed-up version to be stored. Take a look at just how easy this is to accomplish in Exercise 2-9 below.

EXERCISE 2-9

Backing Up and Restoring the DHCP Database

In this exercise you will learn how to back up and restore a DHCP database running on Windows Server 2003.

1. Click **Start** | **Programs** | **Administrative Tools**, and select **DHCP**.
2. Right-click the name of your DHCP server, and select **Backup**.
3. In the **Browse For Folder** dialog box that appears, select the folder to use for the backup of your DHCP server configuration and database information The

default location is **%windir%\system32\dhcp\backup**. Click **OK** and the backup takes place.

4. Once backed up this information should be saved to backup media or a copy made and stored on the hard drive of a remote system.

5. To restore the DHCP database and configuration information, open the DHCP console, right-click the name of the DHCP server, and click **Restore**.

6. Select the directory in which the backed up DHCP information can be found and click **OK**.

7. In the DHCP dialog box that appears indicating that the DHCP service must be stopped in order for a restore to occur, click **Yes**. Once the restore process is complete, the DHCP service should start with all of your backed up DHCP configuration information restored and available.

Compacting the DHCP Database

Windows Server 2003 includes a utility named **jetpack**, which you can use to help correct problems with the DHCP database. The DHCP service stores the DHCP database in the **systemroot\system32\dhcp** directory and automatically backs up this database to the **systemroot\system32\dhcp\backup\jet\new** directory at regular intervals. The DHCP service also performs a consistency check of its database at startup and periodically thereafter to detect and correct any problems, but sometimes, even with these measures, the database can become corrupt.

You can use the **jetpack** utility to attempt to resolve DHCP database corruption problems, or to manually compact the DHCP database. To run **jetpack**, follow these steps:

1. Stop the DHCP service.

2. Open the command prompt and navigate to the **systemroot\system32\dhcp** directory.

3. Type **jetpack dhcp.mdb jetold**, where **jetold** is the name of a temporary database location that is used during the repair. Press ENTER.

4. Start the DHCP service.

Increasing Fault Tolerance for DHCP

Installing and configuring a single DHCP server in your organization presents the potential for downtime. Many organizations implement different fault tolerance strategies to ensure that their DHCP services remain available during the schedule defined within their service level agreements (SLAs) or operating level agreements (OLAs). There are a number of different ways you can achieve high DHCP service availability, all of which are discussed in this section of the chapter. The key to designing a successful high-availability strategy, independent of the service, is to identify and account for all possible points of failure. The high-availability strategies available with the DHCP server service include creating a hot standby server, distributing scopes across two DHCP servers and the use of exclusion rules and the clustering service.

Hot Standby

One method of achieving fault tolerance is through configuring a second *hot standby* DHCP server. The hot standby server is configured identically to the original and primary DHCP server, but the DHCP service is not started. When the primary DHCP server goes offline, either unexpectedly or for regular scheduled maintenance, the DHCP server service can be manually started on the hot standby, allowing for full DHCP server functionality.

There are two key drawbacks to this approach. First, a hot standby DHCP server does require manual intervention to start the DHCP service on the hot standby server. Second, and just as important, we strongly recommend that you synchronize the databases ahead of time to use different scopes. Failing to sync the databases will cause the DHCP service, both clients and server, to undergo a period of nack activity as clients attempt to renew addresses they already have but that the hot standby server has unknowingly leased out to new clients. This can cause significant disruption within a network for session-based activities such as MAPI clients like Outlook as well as client-server applications.

The 80/20 Rule

The *80/20 rule*, sometimes referred to as a *split-scope configuration*, is designed to split a single scope across multiple DHCP servers, and use exclusion ranges to make only a specific unique block of IP addresses available on each server. This fault-tolerance strategy provides availability when one server goes down by allowing the other server to service DHCP requests in addition to balancing the load on the server.

The design principle used in the split scope configuration is to assign the same scope to both DHCP servers and exclude opposite portions of the address ranges, as shown in Figure 2-7. The percentage distribution is generally 80 percent of available IP addresses on one server, and 20 percent on the second server. The second scope is reversed; hence the name "80/20 rule."

As you can see in Figure 2-7, DHCP server 1 has 80 percent of the addresses in Scope1 available to lease out, and DHCP server 2 has the remaining 20 percent of the addresses. The reverse is true for Scope2, where DHCP server 1 has 20 percent of the addresses and DHCP server 2 has 80 percent. Because both DHCP servers are separated by a router, it will take longer for the remote DHCP server to respond to DHCP clients on the remote subnet, therefore the DHCP clients will normally receive an IP address offer from their local DHCP server, because DHCP clients always accept

FIGURE 2-7   80/20 rule configuration

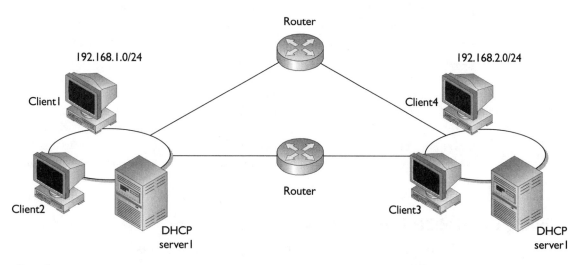

Scope1
192.168.2.1 – 192.168.2.254
Exclusion range
192.168.2.1 – 192.168.2.199
Scope2
192.168.1.1 – 192.168.1.254
Exclusion range
192.168.1.200 – 192.168.1.254

Scope1
192.168.2.1 – 192.168.2.254
Exclusion range
192.168.2.200 – 192.168.2.254
Scope2
192.168.1.1 – 192.168.1.254
Exclusion range
192.168.1.1 – 192.168.1.199

the first offer they receive. However, if either DHCP server becomes unavailable, the other DHCP server will be available to service all IP address lease requests. This example assumes that the router separating the two subnets is RFC 1542 compliant and is configured to forward DHCP broadcasts between the two subnets.

The split-scope configuration achieves high availability and redundancy through the use of multiple DHCP servers in separate subnets, with each DHCP server configured as the primary for its local subnet and the secondary for the other subnet. Multiple routers also help to ensure availability, because a single router would be considered a single point of failure.

Clustering DHCP

MSCS is another alternative for achieving high availability for your DHCP server services. A number of significant changes have been made in the cluster service included in Windows Server 2003 Enterprise and Datacenter server editions, including the ability to scale out to eight nodes.

In a simple two-node cluster configuration, the cluster service can be used to monitor and automatically detect the failure of the DHCP service, and restart the service on the node on which it failed or transfer the virtual server in which the DHCP service operates to the alternate node. This automated management and failover helps to make service failures transparent to the end user and eliminate service disruption.

A clustered DHCP server configuration achieves fault tolerance by itself but it could be further enhanced to co-exist with a split scope configuration where the cluster server is the primary DHCP server for all scopes and the non-clustered DHCP server is configured as the secondary with the remaining 20 percent of available IP addresses. A cost benefit analysis will help you to identify what mix is best for your own specific needs.

Moving the DHCP Database to Another Server

One of the issues you are likely to face in a migration to Windows Server 2003 is how to move your existing DHCP database from either a Windows NT 4.0 Server or a Windows 2000 Server. This section will introduce the steps involved in moving a DHCP database to a computer running Windows Server 2003 from both Windows NT 4.0 and Windows 2000. The good news is that if you have already invested time and energy, which also translates into money, into the creation of one or more scope with scope options, address reservations, and other customizations, this section will teach you how to leverage that existing configuration by moving it to your new Windows Server 2003 DHCP server.

Moving the DHCP Database from Windows NT 4.0 to Windows Server 2003

The process of moving your database from Windows NT 4.0 to Windows Server 2003 is not complicated, but it does require that you follow the steps carefully and perform the steps in the correct order. Exercise 2-10 teaches you how to perform the move operation successfully.

EXERCISE 2-10

Moving Your DHCP Database from Windows NT 4.0 to Windows Server 2003

This exercise will teach you how to move your DHCP database from an existing computer running Windows NT 4.0 to a computer running Windows Server 2003, allowing you to leverage the existing DHCP configuration and help you to avoid starting from scratch.

1. On the Windows NT 4.0 Server, open **Control Panel** and double-click **Services**.

2. In the **Services** dialog box, select **Microsoft DHCP Server** and click **Startup**. Under Startup Type, select **Disabled**.

3. Click **Start | Run**, type **net stop dhcpserver**, and press ENTER.

4. Click **Start | Run**, and type **regedt32**. In the Registry Editor browse to find the registry key **HKEY_LOCAL_MACHINE\SYSTEM\CurrentControlSet\ Services\DHCPServer\Configuration**. Select the **Configuration** key and select **Registry | Save As**.

5. Save the key as **c:\config.reg**.

6. On the computer running Windows Server 2003, install the DHCP server service as described earlier in the chapter through **Add/Remove Programs** in Control Panel.

7. Click **Start**, select **Run** and type **net stop dhcpserver**, and press ENTER.

8. Connect to the C: drive on the computer running Windows NT 4.0 and copy **config.reg** to the C: drive of the computer running Windows Server 2003.

9. Click **Start**, select **Run** and type **regedt32**, and press ENTER. In the Registry Editor browse to find the registry key **HKEY_LOCAL_MACHINE\ SOFTWARE\Microsoft\DhcpServer\Configuration**. Select the **Configuration** key and on the **File** menu select **Import**. Select the **c:\config.reg** file and click **Open**. Click **OK**.

10. Open Windows Explorer and delete all of the files and folders in the **%windir%\system32\dhcp** directory.

11. Copy the entire DHCP directory (all files and folders) from **%windir%\system32** on the source server to the **%windir%\system32\dhcp** directory on the computer running Windows Server 2003.

on the job

If you receive an error message: "Jet Conversion Process – The conversion was not successful...." Copy and expand the Edb500.dl_ file from the Windows Server 2003 CD to the %windir%\system32 folder and repeat Steps 10 and 11. This error message corresponds to Event ID 1008 in the Application Log.

12. Click **Start | Administrative Tools**, and select **DHCP**. In the DHCP snap-in, right-click the name of the DHCP server and select **Reconcile All Scopes**. In the **Reconcile All Scopes** dialog box, click **Verify** and click **OK**.

13. Optionally, if you are working in an Active Directory domain, authorize the DHCP server.

Moving the DHCP Database from Windows 2000 to Windows Server 2003

The DHCP database migration process from Windows 2000 to Windows Server 2003 is very similar to the process described in the previous exercise. Exercise 2-11 will walk you through the steps involved in successfully moving the DHCP database.

EXERCISE 2-11

Migrating the DHCP Database from Windows 2000 to Windows Server 2003

This exercise will provide you with the steps involved in moving your DHCP server database from a server running Windows 2000 to a server running Windows Server 2003.

1. On the server running Windows 2000, click **Start | Administrative Tools**, and select **Services**.

2. In the **Services** dialog box, double-click **Microsoft DHCP Server**, change the Startup Type to **Disabled**, and click **Stop**.

3. Click **Start | Run**, type **regedt32**, and press ENTER. In the Registry Editor, browse to the registry key **HKEY_LOCAL_MACHINE\SOFTWARE\ Microsoft\DhcpServer\Configuration**. Select the **Configuration** key, and then click **File | Export**. Select the **c: drive**, type **config.reg** as the filename, and click **Save**.

4. On the computer running Windows Server 2003, install the DHCP server service as described earlier in the chapter through **Add/Remove Programs** in Control Panel.

5. Click **Start | Run**, type **net stop dhcpserver**, and press ENTER.

6. Connect to the C: drive on the computer running Windows 2000 and copy **config.reg** to the C: drive of the computer running Windows Server 2003.

7. Click **Start | Run**, type **regedt32**, and press ENTER. In the Registry Editor, browse to the registry key **HKEY_LOCAL_MACHINE\SOFTWARE\ Microsoft\DhcpServer\Configuration**. Select the **Configuration** key, and then click **File | Import**. Select the **c:\config.reg** file, and click **Open**. Click **OK**.

8. Open Windows Explorer and delete all of the files and folders in the **%windir%\ system32\dhcp** directory.

9. Copy the entire DHCP directory (all files and folders) from **%windir%\ system32** on the source server to the **%windir%\system32\dhcp** directory on the computer running Windows Server 2003.

10. Click **Start | Run**, type **net start dhcpserver**, and press ENTER.

11. Click **Start | Administrative Tools**, and select **DHCP**. In the DHCP snap-in, right-click the name of the DHCP server and select **Reconcile All Scopes**. In the **Reconcile All Scopes** dialog box, click **Verify**, and click **OK**.

12. Optionally, if you are working in an Active Directory domain, authorize the DHCP server.

At this point, we have covered a tremendous amount of material related to the installation, configuration, and overall management of the DHCP service, but no discussion would be complete without a look at managing security issues specific to DHCP, so we'll take a look at that now.

DHCP Security

Security is at the forefront of most people's minds these days and you need to carefully plan and orchestrate security within a corporate setting. This section is designed to introduce you to some of the security issues and offer you some best practices for making your DHCP architecture more secure.

The most important thing to understand is that DHCP is not an authenticated protocol, which means that when a user or computer connects to your physical or wireless network, they are not required to provide credentials to obtain an IP address lease. Smart and savvy attackers are usually excellent researchers and spend a great deal of time collecting information that will assist them in perpetrating their attack. The DHCP service offers a wealth of valuable information to these individuals, such as the names and IP addresses of your WINS and DNS servers. If the DHCP client is a member of a user or vendor class, those options are also available to the attacker.

One common type of attack that users with access to your network can perform is a denial of service attack, where the attacker makes continuous requests for IP addresses, eventually depleting the number of available IP addresses. Obviously, good physical plant security can go a long way to preventing unauthorized users gaining access to your network and instigating such an attack, but with the growth of wireless LANs (WLANs) you need to take additional steps to limit access to only authorized personnel. Enabling auditing on each of your DHCP servers is one way to be on the lookout for malicious activity; however, only enable auditing if you are going to dedicate the appropriate amount of time to review your audit logs, because auditing does degrade performance. Once enabled, the DHCP service will begin logging to audit log files stored in **%windir%\system32\Dhcp**.

on the
Job

Client computers running Microsoft Windows XP that access 802.1x-enabled LAN switches or wireless access points (WAPs) must authenticate before DHCP will assign a leased IP address, which can help to eliminate unauthorized access.

EXERCISE 2-12

Enabling DHCP Audit Logging

This exercise will demonstrate how to configure DHCP audit logging, which you can use to provide you with the information that you need to track the source of any attacks being made against the DHCP server.

1. Click **Start** | **Administrative Tools**, and select **DHCP**.

2. In the DHCP snap-in, right-click the DHCP server, and select **Properties**.

3. On the **General** tab, shown in the following illustration, select **Enable DHCP audit logging**, and click **OK**.

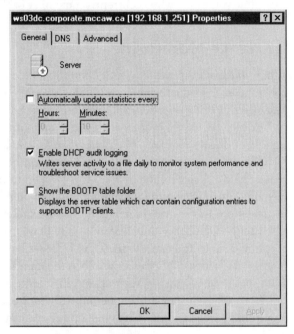

A savvy attacker might also look to wage a denial of service attack against your internal DNS infrastructure through the DHCP service if you have configured the DHCP server to act as a DNS proxy on behalf of DHCP clients by performing dynamic updates. Again, auditing can help you to detect this type of behavior if you monitor the audit logs regularly. You can also use the audit logs to allow you to track the source of the denial of service attacks using the logged IP address of the DHCP client, which is included in the audit logs.

Another security issue worth mentioning, even though it is obvious, is limiting and policing the membership of groups that have administrative privileges for network services like DHCP. In the case of DHCP, members of both the DHCP Admins and the Administrators groups have the right to administer your DHCP server service, so use technologies like Group Policy to police who is a member and who can run the administrative tools.

In an Active Directory domain, you can use software restriction policies to limit which users have the rights to run files with an .msc extension, and who can run **netsh**.

You can also use security policy to define and enforce Restricted Groups, which helps to ensure that only those individuals that you want to be able to administer DHCP can in fact administer the service. A quick look into Active Directory Users and Computers will allow you to see who is currently a member of the Administrators group.

DHCP Performance Monitoring

When you're attempting to improve performance, there are four separate categories of components to evaluate: memory, CPU, disk, and network. The primary components that affect DHCP server performance are disk speed and memory.

The DHCP service creates the greatest amount of disk activity during service initialization and backup. When you plan for the hardware that will support the DHCP service, two of the most important server components are the average time required for disk access and disk read/write operations, and the amount of physical memory. The best way to improve a DHCP serv3er's performance through hardware modifications is usually to increase the amount of RAM and to use faster hard drives.

Once the DHCP server has been installed, you can use the Performance snap-in to monitor DHCP. You can use the DHCP server Performance object to monitor the number of Offers/sec, Nacks/sec, as well as the number of Releases/sec and Requests/sec, all in real-time, as you can see in the Add Counters dialog box shown in Figure 2-8.

The key to good performance monitoring, regardless of the service you are monitoring, is realizing that no one component can be monitored in isolation. The

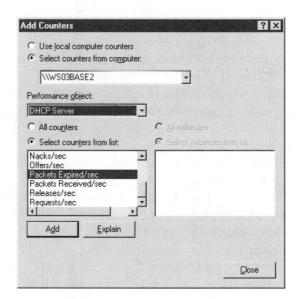

FIGURE 2-8

Monitoring DHCP using the Performance snap-in

components used by all services and applications have dependencies, and knowing how these dependencies work is critical to understanding what is really happening and how to improve performance if it isn't at an acceptable level. A great of example of this is memory. A shortage of available physical memory will affect both the CPU and disk performance because of increased reads and writes to the page file. Adding faster disks and a second CPU would be less effective than adding more physical RAM.

You can access another source of information about the performance of your DHCP server within the DHCP snap-in by right-clicking the name of the DHCP server and selecting **Display Statistics**. The information displayed in the server statistics dialog box includes the uptime of the server, and the number of specific DHCP messages such as discovers, offers, requests, acks, nacks, declines, and releases, as well as the total number of scopes and addresses in use. This information can provide you with a quick summary of what's happening on the DHCP server.

CERTIFICATION OBJECTIVE 2.04

Manage DHCP Scope Options

DHCP scope options allow you configure to numerous options through a single, centralized console that will be distributed to DHCP clients through the normal DHCP lease process, which eliminates repetitive client configuration. Scope options are defined at the individual scope level and pertain only to the specific scope, thus allowing you to configure two gateway interfaces for one particular scope and two completely different gateway interfaces that are appropriate for another scope. Think back to Figure 2-7 earlier in this chapter where you created two scopes, scope1 and scope2. The gateway addresses used for the DHCP clients on the 192.168.1.0/24 network might be 192.168.1.1 and 192.168.1.254, and would be configured within scope1, whereas the gateway addresses for clients on the 192.168.2.0/24 network would need to be different and apply only to the scope that those clients lease their IP addresses from scope2.

Scope options are very easy to configure, and allow you to provide your clients with a great deal of information along with their IP address. The Windows Server 2003 implementation of DHCP allocates 312 bytes for DHCP options. This is generally sufficient for the majority of implementations; however the Windows Server 2003 implementation of DHCP doesn't support a feature known as option overlay, meaning that if you exceed the allocated 312 bytes, some option settings will be lost.

You can configure these scope options, in addition to the standard options you are prompted to configure during the installation of the DHCP server service, either through the DHCP snap-in, or by using the **netsh** command. Exercise 2-13 walks through the steps involved in specifying scope options.

Configuring Scope Options

This exercise will teach you how to configure DHCP scope options using the DHCP snap-in. Scope options can be very useful in simplifying the end-user experience by providing name resolution information in the form of DNS and WINS server IP addresses, or by providing POP3 and SMTP server names to assist a user in configuring their mail accounts.

1. Click **Start | Administrative Tools**. In the DHCP snap-in, expand the scope you want to configure scope options for, right-click **Scope Options**, and select **Configure Options**.

2. The **Scope Options** dialog box appears, as shown in the following illustration, allowing you to scroll through the list of available options and select and configure one or more that meet your needs.

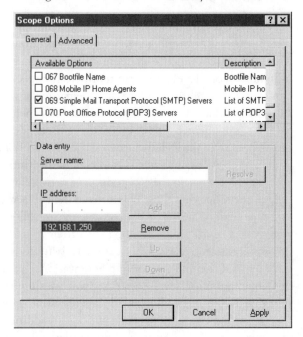

3. Select the option you wish to configure in the **Available Options** section, and enter the corresponding information in the **Data Entry** section. When you're finished adding all of your scope options, click **OK** or select the **Advanced** tab.

4. On the **Advanced** tab, you can configure both Vendor class and User class options.

Option Classes

User option classes provide one more way to group DHCP supplied configuration information for clients within a scope. There are two types of option classes available: user classes and vendor classes. You can use user classes to assign options to DHCP clients that share a common need for similar configuration settings, such as BOOTP clients, and RRAS clients. You can use vendor classes to assign vendor-specific options to clients, such as Microsoft Windows 2000, Windows 98, and all other Microsoft clients that share a common vendor type.

When option classes are not configured, you can still deliver options through the applicable server-, scope-, or client-specific options.

CERTIFICATION OBJECTIVE 2.05

Manage Reservations and Reserved Clients

DHCP address reservations are useful when you want to have more granular control over the IP address that a given DHCP client receives. DHCP client reservations are tied to a client's unique MAC address, and can be used to help guarantee the IP address that is leased out to that client.

Creating IP address reservations is very easy and can be accomplished through either the DHCP snap-in or by using **netsh**. Exercise 2-14 explores the process of creating a DHCP reservation.

EXERCISE 2-14

Creating a DHCP Client Reservation

This exercise details the steps involved in creating a DHCP client reservation. DHCP client reservations are useful when you want to help ensure that a specific client receives a specific IP address from the pool of available IP addresses.

1. In the DHCP snap-in, expand the scope that you want to create the reservation in, right-click **Reservations**, and select **New Reservation**.

2. In the **New Reservation** dialog box shown here, type the name of the workstation, the IP address you want to reserve, the MAC address of the client, and an optional description. Select the client type, click **Add**.

3. Click **Close**.

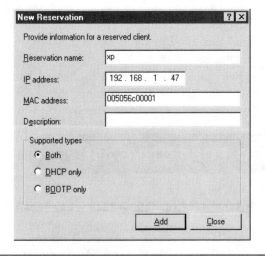

Now that the reservation has been made, select the reservation in the DHCP snap-in, and you can view all of the options that apply to that client. Right-clicking the reservation allows you to configure the options specifically for that client to provide a custom set of options that meet your specific requirements. Right-clicking the reservation and selecting properties allows you to change the MAC address associated with the reservation, and the DNS tab allows you to customize the DNS dynamic update settings for a single reservation. Normally servers are configured with static IP addresses, but in an effort to simplify administration, you could use IP address reservations to guarantee that the servers would always receive the same IP address from DHCP.

CERTIFICATION SUMMARY

This chapter has explored many different areas that fall within the larger picture of DHCP management. You have learned how to install the DHCP server service, how to configure the different types of scopes including standard scopes, multicast scopes, and superscopes, and when each type of scope can be utilized. You also learned the steps involved in activating a scope and authorizing a DHCP server within Active Directory.

In this chapter you also learned about some of the new features and functionality found in the Windows Server 2003 DHCP server service that allow you to back up the DHCP database using the DHCP snap-in. With the DHCP service installed, you learned how to configure scope options, and looked into the two different types of option classes, user classes and vendor classes.

The underlying fundamentals of the DHCP service have not changed in Windows Server 2003, but the way in which you accomplish certain administrative tasks and the number of tasks available has changed.

TWO-MINUTE DRILL

Manage DHCP Clients and Leases

❏ The DHCP service can be installed through Add or Remove Windows Components section of Add/Remove Programs, or via the Manage Your Server wizard.

❏ To install the DHCP service, you must be a member of the Administrators group. To authorize a DHCP server in Active Directory, you must be a member of the Enterprise Admins group.

❏ Two new local computer groups are added during the installation of the DHCP server service: DHCP Users and DHCP Administrators.

Manage DHCP Relay Agent

❏ DHCP relay agents can be used to allow for a single, centralized DHCP server to service DHCP clients on multiple subnets that are located across routers that either are not RFC 1542 compliant or that do not allow the forwarding of DHCP broadcasts on UCP ports 67 and 68.

❏ DHCP relay agents are configured through RRAS, and each server running RRAS that is configured to provide connectivity to incoming client connections should be configured as a DHCP relay agent to ensure that remote access clients receive all of the scope information that you want them to receive. Normally remote access clients do not receive scope information, but instead they receive the DNS and WINS server information that the server running RRAS is configured to use.

Manage DHCP Databases

❏ Event messages for DHCP are logged in the System Event Log and additional logging can be enabled through the DHCP snap-in.

❏ The DHCP snap-in allows for backing up and restoring of DHCP databases and configuration information.

❏ The **jetpack** utility can be used to compact the DHCP database.

Manage DHCP Scope Options

❑ Scope options can be defined at four levels: the DHCP server, each individual scope, the class level, and individual DHCP client reservations. Server level options are inherited by all other levels unless an option at a lower level conflicts, in which case, the lower level option takes precedence. Class level options are broken into two types: vendor and user option classes.

❑ Each scope can contain only a single subnet. IP lease durations should be kept short when available IP addresses are limited, but lease durations can be lengthened if more IP addresses are available than are required.

Manage Reservations and Reserved Clients

❑ Client reservations can be configured in DHCP to enable a client with a specific MAC address to receive a reserved IP address, and specific client options can be configured for each reservation.

SELF TEST

The following questions will help you measure your understanding of the material presented in this chapter. Read all the choices carefully, because there might be more than one correct answer. Choose all correct answers for each question.

Manage DHCP Clients and Leases

1. Which of the following command-line administration tools can you use to administer the DHCP server service?

   A. dhcpcmd

   B. ntdsutil

   C. ipconfig

   D. netsh

2. Which group or groups must you be a member of to install and configure the DHCP service on a member server running Windows Server 2003? (Choose all that apply.)

   A. Power Users

   B. Administrators

   C. DHCP Admins

   D. Schema Admins

3. As the network administrator in your organization, you have just completed the installation and configuration of the DHCP server service, and you have created multiple scopes for the different subnets used throughout your organization. The computer that you installed the DHCP server service on is a member server in your organization's Active Directory domain. What two additional steps are required to allow users in your organization to begin obtaining leased IP addresses from the DHCP server? (Choose all that apply.)

   A. Authorize the scope.

   B. Activate the server.

   C. Authorize the server.

   D. Activate the scope.

4. As the contract administrator for a number of small companies, you are responsible for handling network issues for multiple small business clients. One client has called to ask you to configure DHCP on a new computer running Windows Server 2003 that the client would like to act as a gateway to the Internet for all 15 internal employees. The new server has two network cards

and need to be connected to the high-speed cable router and the local area network to provide access to 15 other clients, but the cable provider does not allow network services like DHCP to be configured on their network. The ISP does require that the NIC connecting to the cable router be configured to obtain an IP address from DHCP, however. Which of the following is the most effective way to achieve the client's requirements?

A. Configure both NICs to obtain an IP address dynamically. Install DHCP on the new server running Windows Server 2003 and create a single scope. Bind the DHCP service to only the internal NIC.

B. Configure both NICs to obtain an IP address dynamically. Install DHCP on the new server running Windows Server 2003 and create a single scope. Bind the DHCP service to only the external NIC.

C. Configure the external NIC to obtain an IP address dynamically and statically configure the internal NIC. Install DHCP on the new server running Windows Server 2003 and create a single scope. Bind the DHCP service to only the internal NIC.

D. Configure the internal NIC to obtain an IP address dynamically and statically configure the external NIC. Install DHCP on the new server running Windows Server 2003 and create a single scope. Bind the DHCP service to only the external NIC.

E. Configure the internal NIC to obtain an IP address dynamically and statically configure the external NIC. Install DHCP on the new server running Windows Server 2003 and create a single scope. Bind the DHCP service to both the internal and external NICs and create reservations for only internal clients using their MAC addresses.

Manage DHCP Relay Agent

5. You are a member of the network administrators group in your organization. You and two of your colleagues are planning the implementation of the DHCP server service using Windows Server 2003. Currently, you have identified all of the subnets in use throughout the organization and the location and configuration of all of your servers. You would like to plan for the location of possible DHCP relay agents as an alternative to allow DHCP packets through your routers. Which of the following server configurations do not support a DHCP relay agent? (Choose all that apply.)

A. A workstation running Windows XP or Windows 2000 Professional

B. A server running Windows NT 4.0, Windows 2000 or Windows Server 2003 with a static IP address

C. A Windows 2000 Server running NAT or ICS

D. A computer running Windows Server 2003 configured as a DHCP server

E. A computer configured with multiple network cards and running IIS

6. You have installed and configured RRAS to operate as a VPN server and allow remote clients to obtain an IP address dynamically. Before you make the VPN server available to production clients, you have been testing it in the evenings from your home using your high-speed cable connection. Each time you connect, you receive an IP address, but you do not receive any of the scope options defined for the scope from the DHCP server you have configured RRAS to use. The DHCP server is configured properly and does provide the correct scope options to clients on the LAN, but not when you connect through the VPN. Establishing a VPN connection results in the computer receiving an IP address, but the WINS and DNS information is not the same as what is defined in the scope, but rather what is defined on the RRAS server. Which of the following will allow you to receive the scope information when you connect through the VPN server?

   A. Add the remote computer that you are using to establish the VPN connection to the domain.

   B. Add the DHCP server's computer account to the DNSUpdateProxy global group.

   C. Add the Everyone group to the Pre-Windows 2000 Compatible Access group.

   D. Install and configure a DHCP relay agent on the RRAS server.

7. As the administrator of your organization's network services, you have recently added a new subnet and moved DHCP client to the new subnet. The subnet does not have a DHCP server and your routers are configured to block DHCP traffic, so you have installed a DHCP relay agent on the new subnet. Clients on the new subnet are reporting that they are unable to obtain an IP address from the DHCP server. Which of the following is the most likely cause of the problem?

   A. The clients on the network have been configured to use an alternate address, which is preventing them from leasing an IP address.

   B. The computer account for the computer configured as the DHCP relay agent must be added to the DNSProxyUpdate global group.

   C. The local NIC of the DHCP relay agent must be configured to listen for requests.

   D. The DHCP relay agent is not authorized in Active Directory.

8. You are the administrator of a medium-sized company that has 100 employees and uses two subnets for its corporate network. Each subnet has both a local DHCP server and a DHCP relay agent. You have noticed that some clients on the local subnet are being served IP addresses from the DHCP server on a different subnet that the DHCP relay agent is configured to use. Which of the following options can you use to ensure that the local DHCP server services the local DHCP clients when it is available, before the DHCP relay agent?

   A. In the properties of the DHCP relay agent, increase the hop count from 4 to 6.

   B. In the properties of the DHCP relay agent, decrease the hop count from 4 to 2.

C. Increase the boot threshold to 8.

D. Decrease the boot threshold to 2.

Manage DHCP Databases

9. You are the administrator responsible for designing and implementing the DHCP infrastructure for your organization. You are in the server procurement planning stages. You are trying to configure your DHCP servers for optimal performance. Which two system components are likely to offer the greatest performance improvement for the DHCP service? (Choose all that apply.)

A. Hard disk speed

B. Number of CPUs

C. CPU speed

D. Memory

E. Number and speed of Network Interface Cards

10. As the administrator for your organization, you are involved in planning and performing the migration of the DHCP database from Windows NT 4.0 Server to Windows Server 2003. What is the first step you must take on the Windows NT 4.0 server before performing the migration?

A. Back up the DHCP database.

B. Stop the DHCP service.

C. Run **jetpack** to compact the DHCP database.

D. Reconcile the DHCP database.

Manage DHCP Scope Options

11. As a member of the network administrators group in your organization, one of your responsibilities is the configuration, management, and troubleshooting of the DHCP service. One of your colleagues has just completed some changes to the network topology and has added a new router for a second, redundant ISP connection. After testing the newly installed router, you have modified the scope options for the two scopes used on your DHCP server by adding the IP address of the new router. The lease duration for both scopes is 14 days, and both scopes are configured with a Default Routing and Remote Access Class User class option to release their DHCP lease upon shutdown. The configuration changes you and your colleague have implemented were performed on a Saturday, and the users always log off but never shut down their computers when they leave for the day. The following Monday, users report that they have no Internet connectivity. Your troubleshooting reveals that the original ISP connection is down and the DHCP clients

are not using the newly configured, alternate ISP connection. Which of the following is most likely to be the problem? (Choose all that apply.)

A.   DHCP clients only ever use the first gateway or router address assigned to them in the scope properties.

B.   Windows Server 2003–based DHCP servers allocate 312 bytes for DHCP options, and the configuration of the second router has been lost because it exceeded the amount of bytes available.

C.   The DHCP clients will not receive the updated scope information until they renew their lease.

D.   The new, alternate router must be added to DNS to allow the clients to resolve its host name and make a connection to the Internet.

12.   As the network administrator in your organization, you have just finished the installation of the DHCP service and the configuration of a single scope with multiple scope options and address reservations for specific clients. You have installed the DHCP server service on a member server within your domain. During the configuration process, you accidentally entered and confirmed the wrong subnet information. Which of the following represents the most effective way to change the incorrect subnet mask information?

A.   Delete the scope and create a new scope with the correct subnet mask.

B.   In the properties of the DHCP server, change the subnet mask affiliated with the new scope.

C.   In the properties of the scope, change the subnet mask information.

D.   Use the **netsh dhcp scope** *<scopename>* **/change subnet** *<correct subnet>* command to modify the subnet information.

13.   You have configured a DHCP server with a single scope. The IP range for the DHCP server is 192.168.1.1 to 192.168.1.254. You have also defined a number of scope options, including two DNS servers with IP addresses of 192.168.1.250 and 24.63.78.145. You set the lease duration to six days and configured an exclusion range of 192.168.1.248 to 192.168.1.254. You are about to test the DHCP configuration that is configured to obtain an IP address automatically and that has a static DNS entry of 192.168.1.251. After obtaining an IP address from the DHCP server, you run the **ipconfig /all** command. What DNS addresses will be included in the results generated by the **ipconfig /all** command?

A.   192.168.1.251

B.   192.168.1.250 and 24.63.78.145

C.   192.168.1.251, 192.168.1.250, and 24.63.78.145

D.   24.63.78.145

Manage Reservations and Reserved Clients

14. As the administrator of the DHCP services in your organization, you are considering using reservations to ensure some clients always receive the same IP address. Which of the following information must you have to create an IP address reservation? (Choose all that apply.)

A. Name of the DHCP scope

B. MAC address of the DHCP server

C. MAC address of the DHCP client

D. DHCP client's host name

15. You are the administrator of your organization's DHCP services. You have one computer that requires special options, such as a unique DNS server and a time server. You would like to use the simplest option possible to provide these options to this one computer with its IP address lease. Which of the following will most efficiently allow you to accomplish this?

A. Create a new scope of one IP address and define the unique scope options for this new scope.

B. Create an IP address reservation in the existing scope, and add the unique scope options to the scope.

C. Edit the properties of the DHCP server and define the unique scope options at the server level. Then create an IP address for the client within the scope.

D. Create an IP address reservation in the existing scope and add the unique options to the IP address reservation.

LAB QUESTION

You are the administrator of a small organization of 20 employees that is growing rapidly, and is expected to reach 100 employees within the next 12 months. The network is currently quite simple and consists of only a single subnet and a shared DSL connection that provides Internet access. All of the clients are currently using statically configured IP addresses, but you would like to implement DHCP and direct your clients to obtain an IP address from DHCP. You also want to implement a DHCP architecture that will allow you to grow and incorporate redundancy in the future. There are currently five servers on the network that you will leave statically configured and one workstation that must always receive the same IP address even though it will be dynamically configured. What steps will you take to design a scalable DHCP infrastructure that can be enhanced to provide redundancy and meet the additional criteria?

SELF TEST ANSWERS

Manage DHCP Clients and Leases

1. ☑ **D. netsh** is used to administer DHCP from the command line.

☒ **A** is incorrect because **dhcpcmd** is not a valid command-line tool. **B** is incorrect because **ntdsutil** is a tool used to administer Active Directory. **C** is incorrect because **ipconfig** is a command used to troubleshoot IP-related issues, but is not designed for DHCP administration.

2. ☑ **B** and **C**. To install the DHCP server service, you must be a member of either the Administrators or DHCP Admins groups.

☒ **A** and **D** are incorrect because membership in the Schema Admins or Power Users groups does not provide you with the rights to install the DHCP server service.

3. ☑ **C** and **D**. DHCP servers running on Windows 2000 Server or Windows Server 2003 and operating in Active Directory domains must be authorized and the scopes activated before they are able to lease out IP addresses.

☒ **A** is incorrect because scopes are activated, not authorized. **B** is incorrect because DHCP servers are authorized, not activated.

4. ☑ **C**. Configuring the external NIC to obtain an IP address dynamically will allow the computer to obtain a valid IP from the ISP. Statically configuring the internal NIC will allow you to install the DHCP service on the new server running Windows Server 2003 and create a single scope. Binding the DHCP service to only the internal NIC will allow internal clients to obtain IP addresses and prevent the DHCP service from causing problems on the ISP network.

☒ **A** and **B** are incorrect because one NIC must be configured with a static IP address in order to install the DHCP service. **D** and **E** are incorrect because the external NIC that connects to your ISP's network is the NIC that must be configured to obtain an IP address dynamically from your ISP's DHCP server.

Manage DHCP Relay Agent

5. ☑ **A**, **C**, and **D**. DHCP relay agents can only be installed on server operating systems. DHCP relay agents are not supported on computers running NAT or ICS, or on servers configured as DHCP servers.

☒ **B** is incorrect because DHCP relay agents can be installed on servers running Windows NT 4.0 or Windows 2000 Server or Windows Server 2003. **E** is incorrect because DHCP can be installed on computers configured with multiple NIC cards that also run IIS.

6. ☑ **D.** Installing and configuring a DHCP relay agent will allow you to receive all of the scope information from the DHCP server.

☒ **A** is incorrect because the remote computer does not have to be a member of the domain. **B** is incorrect because adding the computer account of the DHCP server to the DNSUpdateProxy would also have no effect on what scope options the client is receiving. **C** is incorrect because the Everyone group doesn't have anything to do with what scope information you are receiving.

7. ☑ **C.** The interface on the server running the DHCP relay agent service must be added to the DHCP relay agent IP routing protocol.

☒ **A** is incorrect because the alternate address option is only used if an IP address cannot be obtained from a DHCP server. **B** is incorrect because the computer account for the DHCP relay agent is not required to be a member of the DNSProxyUpdate global group, because the DHCP relay agent doesn't handle DNS updates. **C** is incorrect because DHCP relay agents do not require authorization in Active Directory.

8. ☑ **C.** Increasing the boot threshold will delay the forwarding of DHCP traffic from the DHCP relay agent to the remote server. The boot threshold is the length of time in seconds that the DHCP relay agent waits before sending the DHCPDiscover packet to the DHCP server.

☒ **A** and **B** are incorrect because adjusting the hop count will have no effect on whether the local DHCP server will be given more time to respond to the local DHCP client requests for an IP address. **C** is incorrect because reducing the boot threshold would actually reduce the likelihood of the local DHCP server being able to service the local DHCP client requests.

Manage DHCP Databases

9. ☑ **A** and **D.** Disk speed and physical memory are the two most important hardware components for the DHCP server service, and increasing either the speed of your drives or the amount of memory is the best way to improve the performance of the DHCP service.

☒ **B** and **C** are incorrect because CPU number and speed are not likely to have as great an impact on DHCP server performance. **E** is incorrect because the number of NICs will not have a great impact on DHCP server performance.

10. ☑ **B.** Before performing a migration of your DHCP database, the DHCP service must be stopped on the existing computer running Windows NT 4.0 and DHCP.

☒ **A** is incorrect because although backing up the DHCP database is highly recommended, it is not required. **C** is incorrect because compacting the database is not a requirement prior to migrating. **D** is incorrect because reconciling the database is also not required.

Manage DHCP Scope Options

11. ☑ **B and C.** Windows Server 2003–based DHCP servers allocate 312 bytes for DHCP options, and the configuration of the second router may have been lost because it exceeded the amount of bytes available. DHCP clients will also not receive any changes to the scope information until they renew their lease, and that is likely why they have not received the new gateway information.
☒ **A** is incorrect because DHCP clients can use multiple gateways. **D** is incorrect because gateways do not have to be added to DNS, because they are generally found via IP address.

12. ☑ **A.** One of the values that cannot be changed once a scope is created is the subnet mask. The scope must be deleted and re-created to change this value.
☒ **B, C, and D** are all incorrect because the subnet mask cannot be changed without deleting and re-creating the scope.

13. ☑ **A.** The only DNS address that will appear in the list is the IP 192.168.1.251 because the TCP/IP properties configured on the client always take precedence over any information provided by a DHCP server.
☒ **B, C, and D** are all incorrect because the TCP/IP properties configured on the client take precedence.

Manage Reservations and Reserved Clients

14. ☑ **C and D.** To create an IP address reservation, you must know the name and MAC address of the DHCP client.
☒ **A** is incorrect because the name of the DHCP scope is not required to create a client reservation. **B** is incorrect because the MAC address of the DHCP server is not required to create a client reservation.

15. ☑ **D.** The simplest and most effective way to provide a single DHCP client with specific scope options is to define them for the IP address reservation so that they only apply to that one particular client.
☒ **A** is incorrect because creating a new scope of one IP address and defining the unique scope options for the scope is not efficient. **B** is incorrect because adding the unique scope options to the existing scope would cause the options to apply to more than just the single computer. **C** is incorrect because defining the scope options at the DHCP server would cause them to apply to more than just the single computer.

LAB ANSWER

Installing Windows Server 2003 is a good starting point that will provide you with a base operating system. Once you have Windows Server 2003 installed, configure the server with a static IP address and use the Manage Your Server wizard to add the DHCP Server role to the server. During the wizard setup, select to create a new scope and define the common properties for the scope and select to exclude the IP address range that you wish to use for statically configured systems. If the DHCP server is also going to be the RRAS server that provides access to the Internet through the DSL connection, unbind the DHCP service from the external network interface card. Create an IP address reservation for the one workstation that must always receive the same IP address. If the DHCP server is going to run within an Active Directory domain, authorize the server and activate the scope. Change the TCP/IP settings for each of the clients to obtain an IP address via DHCP and monitor the DHCP snap-in to verify that the clients are obtaining an IP address.

To account for future scalability, identify another server on the network that could act as a standby DHCP server and install the DHCP service on this server, making all of the same configuration changes, but leave the DHCP server service disabled.

3

Maintain DHCP

CERTIFICATION OBJECTIVES

W ith the knowledge you have gained in Chapters 1 and 2 about the DHCP server service and the configuration of TCP/IP addressing, you can now shift your focus to maintaining and troubleshooting. Administrators tend to spend a lot of time performing maintenance and troubleshooting network services such as DHCP, because the tasks that fall within these areas tend to be repetitive, ongoing tasks as opposed to installing and configuring, which happens less often. Both skills are obviously required to provide you with a holistic skill set, but a truly savvy administrator enjoys the challenge of using their skills to diagnose and solve problems that occur once the service is in production.

In this chapter you will learn how to diagnose and resolve issues specific to Automatic Private IP Addressing, incorrect TCP/IP configurations, and DHCP server and scope options. You will also learn how to verify DHCP reservation and DHCP Relay Agent configurations as well as how to verify database integrity. The content of this chapter is intended to help you become a better troubleshooter and make you more efficient and effective in your current role as well as to prepare you for the questions you are likely to see on the certification exam.

CERTIFICATION OBJECTIVE 3.01

Diagnose and Resolve Issues Related to Automatic Private IP Addressing (APIPA)

Back in the days of Windows NT, a DHCP client that couldn't find a DHCP server wouldn't be able to connect to the network. One of the new features introduced in Windows 2000 DHCP client service and carried forward into Windows Server 2003 and Windows XP is Automatic Private IP Addressing (APIPA).

APIPA allows a Windows Server 2003 DHCP client that is not able to obtain an IP address from a DHCP server to automatically configure itself with an IP address on the 169.254.0.0/16 network. The benefit of this default setting over Windows NT 4.0 is that the user isn't presented with a TCP/IP error message and the DHCP client service continues to broadcast for an available DHCP server at regular five-minute intervals. This means that if a DHCP client comes online while the DHCP server is temporarily unavailable and is unable to obtain an IP address, five minutes later the DHCP client service will try again.

The one potential downside in using this default setting is that unless other network clients are configured with an IP address on the same network, the DHCP client will still not be able to communicate with other computers on the network while configured with an IP address on the 169.254.0.0/16 network. Microsoft's intent in designing and incorporating this feature was a good one, but it often led to problems in larger corporate networks. In smaller corporate networks, however, it was quite useful because it didn't require any TCP/IP configuration, and it still allowed all computers on a single subnet to communicate because they had APIPA addresses on the same subnet.

APIPA is a great feature for small, non-routed networks in which users don't want to bother with IP address configuration. With the original introduction of APIPA in Windows 2000, there was no graphical user interface (GUI) available that allowed you to disable APIPA; it had to be disabled by editing the registry. Although editing the registry to disable APIPA is no longer your only option, because you can now choose to use the *user configured* option, disabling APIPA through the registry still remains a valid option. To do this, use your registry editing tool to connect to the key **HKLM\System\CurrentControlSet\Services\Tcpip\Parameters\Interfaces\AdapterGUID**, where **AdapterGUID** is the globally unique identifier (GUID) specific to each adapter, and create a **REG_DWORD** data type named **IPAutoConfigurationEnabled** and configure it to use a data value of 0 to disable APIPA. This process must be repeated for each network adapter that you wish to disable APIPA for.

on the
() o b

To disable APIPA completely, you must edit the registry.

After Microsoft recognized the inherent problems associated with APIPA in larger multi-subnet environments, they have included a second option that, like APIPA, is available on the **Alternate Configuration** tab in the DHCP client's network properties shown in Figure 3-1 and known as the **User Configured** option.

The default alternative configuration setting is still APIPA in Windows Server 2003, but now you have the ability to change that to User configured. This means that if the DHCP client fails to obtain an IP address from DHCP, it will use its user-configured IP address, which as you can see in Figure 3-1 can include the IP address, subnet, gateway, and name resolution servers via multiple DNS and WINS server entries. Exercise 3-1 looks at how to configure this alternative configuration.

FIGURE 3-1

The Alternate
Configuration tab

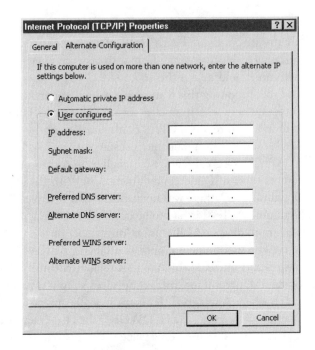

EXERCISE 3-1

Specifying an Alternative Configuration

This exercise will show you the steps involved in configuring an alternative IP address configuration for a DHCP client. This will allow the DHCP client to continue to operate with uninterrupted network connectivity if a DHCP server goes offline for an extended period of time, preventing the DHCP client from receiving or renewing an IP address.

1. Click **Start | Control Panel**. Right-click Network Connections and select **Open**.

2. Right-click the local area connection and select **Properties**.

3. In the **Local Area Connection Properties** dialog box, click **Internet Protocol (TCP/IP)**, and click **Properties**.

4. In the **Internet Protocol (TCP/IP) Properties** dialog box, select the **Alternate Configuration** tab, as shown in Figure 3-1, and select the radio button to the left of **User configured**. As you can see, the default setting is still APIPA, but this can now be changed through the GUI.

5. Enter an IP address, subnet mask, and optionally a default gateway, DNS and WINS server IP addresses, and click **OK**.

6. Click **Close** to close the local area connection Properties dialog box.

The one key difference that you must be aware of if you decide to use the user configured option over the APIPA default is that unlike APIPA, the DHCP client service does not continue to attempt to obtain an IP address dynamically every five minutes when the user-configured option is used. This means that if the client fails to obtain an IP address dynamically from DHCP, and configures itself with the user-configured IP address information, the DHCP client must either be recycled or you must take manual action to run **ipconfig /renew** to force a renewal.

<table>
<tr><td>ⓦ a t c h

A DHCP client configured to use the user-configured IP address option will not continue to attempt to obtain an IP address from a DHCP</td><td>*server. The DHCP client will have to either be rebooted or the ipconfig /renew command run on the client to force an IP address renewal.*</td></tr>
</table>

DHCP User Configured Options

Windows Server 2003 offers administrators a little more flexibility in how they configure DHCP clients if the client is not able to obtain an IP address. In Windows 2000, DHCP clients would automatically configure themselves with an APIPA address on the 169.254.x.y subnet, but now in Windows Server 2003 you have another option. In Windows Server 2003, you can now change the default APIPA setting to **User configured** and enter a static IP configuration that will be used when the DHCP client fails to obtain an IP address from a DHCP server.

This new option allows the administrator to preconfigure the DHCP client with a valid static IP, potentially the same IP the client had a reservation for on the DHCP server to allow the client to establish network connectivity even when its attempt to lease an IP address from DHCP fails. There are a couple important points to understand in using this new feature. First, the DHCP client service will not continue to attempt to lease an IP address every five minutes. Once the DHCP server is available, the client will have to be recycled or the **ipconfig /renew** command run to force an IP lease request. Second, if the alternative IP address conflicts with an existing IP address on the network when the client attempts to use it, the client will end up with an IP address of 0.0.0.0.

The new Alternate Configuration option that allows you to specify an alternative static IP address in the case of DHCP client failure is a great new feature but does require some planning in its use.

Now that you are familiar with the available options for DHCP clients that are not able to obtain an IP address, you can look into some of the reasons why this might be occurring.

There are a number of possible reasons why your DHCP clients are not able to obtain an IP address from a DHCP server, including

- The DHCP server is offline because of planned or unplanned maintenance.
- An intermediary network device such as a switch, router, or DHCP Relay Agent is offline, preventing the client from communicating with the DHCP server.
- The DHCP server is not authorized in Active Directory.
- The DHCP server does not have any activated scopes, or all the activated scopes do not have any IP addresses available.
- The DHCP client is a wireless client that is not able to authenticate to the wireless LAN (WLAN), thereby preventing it from obtaining an IP address.

In an effort to narrow down which of these potential problems is the true cause, run through some basic troubleshooting steps. First, log on to another DHCP client and determine if that client is also having problems obtaining an IP address from DHCP. This will help to identify whether the problem is isolated to only one computer or all DHCP client computers. If the problem appears to be occurring across multiple computers, then it might be a network device or DHCP server issue. Checking both of these would be logical next steps in the troubleshooting process.

To eliminate network devices such as routers and switches, configure one of the clients with a static IP address, and then open the command prompt and ping the remote DHCP server. If you receive a response, you can eliminate the network devices as the source of the problem. If a DHCP relay agent is configured on the local subnet to forward on DHCP traffic to the DHCP server, log on to the DHCP relay agent and confirm that the configuration is correct.

e x a m

ⓦatch

When you troubleshoot DHCP problems at the client, if the ipconfig */all command returns an IP address on the 169.254.0.0/16 network, check to ensure that the DHCP server is online and has IP addresses available within its scopes. Confirm that the DHCP server is authorized when required, and that the scopes are activated. Also check that other clients are able to connect with the DHCP server and lease an IP address.*

The next place to focus your attention is the DHCP server. Confirming that it is online and authorized if operating in an Active Directory environment and that its scopes are activated is a good place to begin. Next, confirm that the DHCP server service is bound to at least one network adapter and that there are IP addresses available in the DHCP scope. The system event log on the DHCP server should also be checked to help you identify any other server- or system-related errors that could be a reason for the problem.

Now that you are familiar with how to diagnose and resolve issues related to APIPA, you can shift your focus to diagnosing and resolving incorrect TCP/IP configurations.

CERTIFICATION OBJECTIVE 3.02

Diagnose and Resolve Issues Related to Incorrect TCP/IP Configuration

As you learned in Chapters 1 and 2, there are multiple ways to configure TCP/IP addressing for client computers, including automatic, dynamic, alternate, and manual configuration. Each of these different methods present the possibility of TCP/IP configuration errors resulting in network connectivity problems. This section is designed to help you learn how to diagnose and resolve these potential errors.

The first step in troubleshooting incorrect TCP/IP configurations is to identify what IP address, if any, the computer is configured with. This will act as a starting point in your troubleshooting efforts and provide some key information that you can use to continue the troubleshooting process. So how do you identify what IP address, if any, the client computer is currently configured to use? You use the **ipconfig** command at the command prompt, as discussed in Exercise 3-2.

EXERCISE 3-2

Using ipconfig

In this exercise, you will learn how to use the **ipconfig** command to identify a computer's current IP address configuration. This is a very useful first step in diagnosing IP configuration issues.

1. Click **Start** | **Run**, type **cmd**, and click **OK**.

2. In the command prompt window shown in the following illustration, type **ipconfig /all** and press ENTER.

```
C:\WINDOWS\system32\cmd.exe

Microsoft Windows [Version 5.2.3790]
(C) Copyright 1985-2003 Microsoft Corp.

C:\Documents and Settings\Administrator.WS03BASE2>ipconfig /all

Windows IP Configuration

        Host Name . . . . . . . . . . . . : WS03DC
        Primary Dns Suffix  . . . . . . . : corporate.mccaw.ca
        Node Type . . . . . . . . . . . . : Broadcast
        IP Routing Enabled. . . . . . . . : Yes
        WINS Proxy Enabled. . . . . . . . : Yes
        DNS Suffix Search List. . . . . . : corporate.mccaw.ca
                                            mccaw.ca

Ethernet adapter Local Area Connection:

        Connection-specific DNS Suffix  . : corporate.mccaw.ca
        Description . . . . . . . . . . . : Intel 21140-Based PCI Fast Ethernet Adapt
er (Generic)
        Physical Address. . . . . . . . . : 00-03-FF-32-C9-72
        DHCP Enabled. . . . . . . . . . . : No
        IP Address. . . . . . . . . . . . : 192.168.1.251
        Subnet Mask . . . . . . . . . . . : 255.255.255.0
        Default Gateway . . . . . . . . . : 192.168.1.1
        DNS Servers . . . . . . . . . . . : 192.168.1.250
                                            24.153.22.195

C:\Documents and Settings\Administrator.WS03BASE2>_
```

3. The results from the **ipconfig /all** command are displayed in the command prompt dialog box. Here you can identify the number of Ethernet adapters installed and configured within the computer and their specific configuration information. This is the information you can use to diagnose any problems. When you are finished in the command prompt, type **exit** and press ENTER.

As an alternative to **ipconfig /all**, TCP/IP configuration information can be viewed using the Status feature of a network connection. If you have configured each local area connection to **Show icon in notification area when connected**, you can right-click the network connection icon in the systray and select **Status**. If you have not configured the network connection icon to appear in the systray, you can open the Network Connections dialog box, right-click the local area connection, and select **Status**. Most administrators prefer the **ipconfig /all** command as it presents them with a wealth of information in a single command prompt window as opposed to having to move between different tabs in the GUI dialog boxes to locate all of the information you are looking for.

Now that you are familiar with how to identify your computer's IP address configuration, you can examine the information provided to better understand what it is we are looking for. You can see from the illustration in Exercise 3-2 that the results are displaying in two separate sections, the Windows IP Configuration section and the Ethernet adapter section.

on the *Some older Microsoft operating systems, such as Windows 95 and 98 use the*
Job *winipcfg command to identify the computer's IP configuration instead of ipconfig.*

In the Windows IP Configuration section, you can identify the computer's host name, primary DNS suffix, and WINS node type. In this example, the computer's host name is WS03DC, which is a computer in the corporate.mccaw.ca domain that uses a broadcast node type to resolve NetBIOS names. There are four node types to choose from, with broadcast being the default. The node type determines the order in which NetBIOS names are resolved. When you're troubleshooting an IP configuration, this is not the most critical piece of information, but it can be very useful when troubleshooting NetBIOS name resolution problems. Next, you find whether IP Routing and WINS Proxy are enabled, which they are in this example, and finally the DNS Suffix Search List. Like the node type, the DNS Suffix Search List is valuable information to have when troubleshooting DNS name resolution problems.

The Ethernet adapter section is where you should focus your attention while trying to diagnose IP configuration issues. In this section, you can find a wealth of diagnostic information, such as the description and Media Access Control (MAC) address of the NIC, whether the computer is configured to use DHCP, and the IP address, subnet, gateway and DNS information that the computer is configured to use.

The description information is particularly useful when the computer you are troubleshooting has more than one NIC, because it will allow you to correlate the IP configuration with the correct NIC. If the description is not enough to identify the NIC, the MAC address can be used, because each NIC has a unique MAC address. The DHCP Enabled section allows you to quickly identify whether this NIC is configured to use DHCP to obtain an IP address dynamically. In this example, it is set to **No**, which means that this NIC is manually configured. That rules out problems with the DHCP server, and allows you to focus your troubleshooting on the local computer.

on the *Remember that the DHCP client service is enabled or disabled independently*
Job *on each NIC in the computer, allowing you to have one NIC that obtains an*
IP address from a DHCP server while another NIC is statically configured.

Another interesting and important point to draw your attention to is the default configuration of the DHCP client service on computers running Windows Server 2003. Opening up the Services snap-in, shown in Figure 3-2, reveals something that at first glance might confuse a novice administrator. Look at the state of the DHCP Client service on the same computer that the **ipconfig /all** command was run on. The DHCP Client service is set to start automatically and is currently running. This can sometimes appear as contradictory to the results displayed from the **ipconfig /all** command. The reason for this has to do with DDNS. Even though the computer (WS03DC) is manually configured with an IP address, the DHCP client service is responsible for performing the dynamic update of the computer's DNS information with the DNS server even when it is not configured to obtain an IP address from a DHCP server.

The information found next within the Ethernet adapter section is the most important when diagnosing IP configuration issues, because this is where you find the IP address, subnet, gateway and DNS information that the client is configured to use. You should note the IP address, and ensure that this IP address is not being used by any other computer and, if DHCP is in use on the network, that this IP address is excluded from all DHCP scopes. Remember that IP addresses must be unique, and

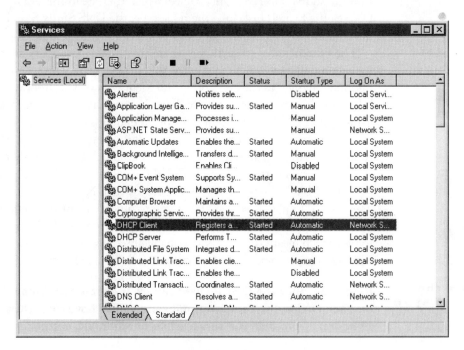

FIGURE 3-2

The DHCP client service

only one computer can use a single IP address. In this example, the client is configured to use the IP address 192.168.1.251 and the subnet 255.255.255.0, a Class C subnet mask. This means that this computer is able to communicate with computers on the same local subnet that have IP addresses that fall within the range of 192.168.1.1 through 192.168.1.254, with the exception of 192.168.1.251. This result set also tells you that the client is able to connect to other networks using the gateway located at 192.168.1.1. You also know the IP addresses of the two DNS servers that the computer is configured to use for DNS name resolution, one of which is located on the local subnet (192.168.1.250), and the other on a remote subnet (24.153.22.195).

Now that you know how to display a computer's IP configuration, how can you use that to diagnose incorrect TCP/IP configuration issues? The truth is there is no one specific answer to that question but rather more questions whose individual answers help in the diagnostic process. First, human error is a likely cause of TCP/IP configuration problems, and when you're dealing with manually configured IP addresses, you will commonly find typos in either the IP address or the subnet mask. Begin by confirming that each octet in both the IP address and subnet mask is correct. Entering multiple IP addresses can become mindless, repetitive work that can often lead to you entering **225** instead of **255** for one of the octets of the subnet mask or incorrectly entering an IP address. Also confirm that the gateway is on the same subnet as the IP address. If the problem you are troubleshooting is that the client cannot communicate with remote hosts or with its gateway, you have identified the problem. To further diagnose this issue, you can use the **ping** utility to test whether you can send an Internet Control Message Protocol (ICMP) request and receive a response from the remote host. This can be accomplished by typing the following command at the command prompt and pressing ENTER, where 192.168.2.50 is the IP address of the remote host shown in Figure 3-3, and where you are entering the command from the computer with IP address 192.168.1.250.

```
Ping 192.168.2.50
```

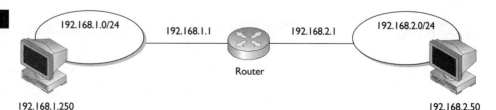

FIGURE 3-3

Testing connectivity

In this example, based on the current configuration, a response should be received, verifying that all communication is functioning correctly. What would the result be if the results of the **ipconfig** command on the client at IP address 192.168.1.250, shown in Figure 3-3, was as follows:

```
IP Address ....................: 192.168.1.250
Subnet Mask ...................: 255.255.252.0
Default Gateway ...............: 192.168.1.1
```

In this scenario, would the **ping** command fail or succeed in providing a response and why? It would fail, because the gateway address of 192.168.1.1 is not a valid IP address when using a 22-bit subnet mask of 255.255.252.0.

What would the result be if the **ipconfig /all** command returned the following results?

```
IP Address ....................: 192.168.1.250
Subnet Mask ...................: 255.255.255.0
Default Gateway ...............: 192.168.2.1
```

In this scenario, the **ping** command would also fail because the client's gateway address isn't valid for the network that the client is on, so all attempts to communicate with remote hosts would fail. The issue that can be somewhat confusing in this scenario is that the client would be able to communicate with all other computers on the local segment, which could lead you to believe that the problem was elsewhere if you only looked at the information superficially. Be sure to look at the IP configuration information carefully before jumping to any conclusions.

You probably won't be able to manually configure a client with a default gateway that is on a different subnet successfully. Even if you inadvertently enter an incorrect gateway IP address, or you enter an IP address on a different network segment, you will be presented with a warning dialog box as shown in Figure 3-4, which will bring this configuration error to your attention.

The following is a more complex network, shown in Figure 3-5, which consists of a number of different subnets connected by different routers. In this particular scenario,

FIGURE 3-4

Notification of
incorrect gateway

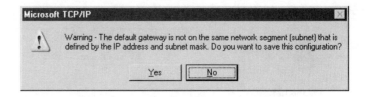

FIGURE 3-5 Routed network

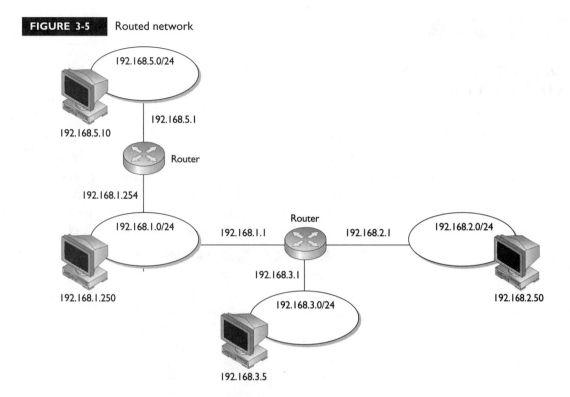

if you wanted to determine if there were any network problems between the clients with IP addresses 192.168.2.50 and 192.168.5.10, the fastest way to accomplish this would be to ping the remote computer. In this case, while logged on at 192.168.2.50, you could ping 192.168.5.10. If you receive a successful response, you can conclude that both routers and both clients were functioning, and correctly configured TCP/IP configurations.

One of the new features built into Windows Server 2003 is the IP conflict icon, shown in the illustration, that appears in the system tray when the operating system detects an IP conflict. This new feature helps to draw a user's attention to the problem and allows them to contact the appropriate IT administrative personnel to correct the issue. Exercise 3-3 explores how to use the IP conflict icon in the systray to resolve the IP conflict.

EXERCISE 3-3

Resolving IP Conflicts with the IP Conflict Icon

In this exercise you will learn how to resolve IP conflicts using the IP conflict icon in the systray.

1. Double-click the IP conflict icon in the systray to bring up the Local Area Connection Status dialog box shown in the following illustration. Notice how the Local Area Connection Status dialog box informs you that the IP address currently configured for use by the computer is invalid, and that as a result of the conflict, the computer has been given an IP address and subnet mask of 0.0.0.0.

2. Click the **Repair** button to perform a rudimentary repair operation; however, this is likely to fail. If it fails, click the **General** tab, and then click the **Properties** button.

3. In the **Local Area Connections** dialog box, select **Internet Protocol (TCP/IP)**, and click **Properties**.

4. In the **Internet Protocol (TCP/IP) properties** dialog box, enter a new IP address that is unique on the LAN, and click **OK**.

5. Click **Close** to close the Local Area Connections dialog box.

6. Click **Close** again to close the Local Area Connection Status dialog box. If the new IP address is unique, the red question mark over the network connection in the systray should disappear.

TCP/IP Troubleshooting Tools

There are many tools available within the Windows Server 2003 operating system to help you to diagnose and resolve TCP/IP configuration problems. In this section of the chapter you'll look at a number of these tools and explore when and where to use them.

ipconfig

The IP configuration tool included with Windows Server 2003 is known as **ipconfig**, and as you have learned earlier in this chapter, you can use this tool to provide you with the IP configuration for each NIC in the local computer. Earlier in this chapter we discussed using the **ipconfig** command with the **/all** switch, but there are a number of other switches to assist you in your troubleshooting efforts.

To learn about all of the switches and what each of them can offer you, enter the following command at the command prompt.

```
Ipconfig /?
```

In this section we will focus on the switches that can assist in troubleshooting TCP/IP configuration issues. One common problem that you are likely to run into when working with DHCP is the client being configured with APIPA, resulting in the client receiving an IP address on the 169.254.0.0/16 network, but having no network connectivity. One of the nice features of APIPA is that it continues to attempt to lease an IP address every five minutes, but if you want to force this renewal, you can use the following command.

```
Ipconfig /renew
```

The **/release** and **/renew** switches can be used together or you can simply use the **/renew** switch to force a renewal of the client's IP address with the DHCP server. This can be extremely useful when you have made changes to the scope options and the scope lease time is long, but you want clients to receive the updated settings. Forcing a renewal using the **ipconfig /renew** command will allow the existing DHCP clients to renew their leases and obtain the new scope settings. On multi-homed computers that have multiple NICs configured to obtain an IP address via DHCP, this command can be modified slightly to force a renewal for all adapters or for only specific adapters. To accomplish this, use the command **ipconfig /renew *Con***, which will renew all the DHCP leased IP addresses for all adapters that have "Con" in their names, such as "Local Area Connection 1."

Another common TCP/IP communication problem results from old, incorrect DNS name resolution information in the client's local DNS name cache. When the user of the computer attempts to connect to the DNS name of a remote computer, the DNS name is resolved to the wrong IP address, which can lead to a communication failure. If you think this might be the cause of the issue, and you would like to delete all of the entries in the DNS name cache, you can run the command **ipconfig /flushdns**.

ping

The **ping** utility allows you to test connectivity between two clients by sending ICMP requests and testing for ICMP responses. Pinging a remote host is a great way to test that TCP/IP is configured correctly on both the local and remote hosts, as well as all network devices in between.

One of the potential downsides to ping is that ICMP might be blocked at a firewall, preventing you from receiving a response from a remote host, and leading you to believe that either the remote host or a network device between you and the remote host is causing the problem. If you run into this, continue to use the **ping** command to ping each device that the TCP/IP packets must travel through to get to the remote host, starting with the devices farthest away from the client. In other words, using Figure 3-5 as an example, if you were pinging 192.168.5.10 from the host 192.168.2.50 and that failed, continue by pinging 192.168.1.254. If that fails, try to ping 192.168.2.1, and if that fails, attempt to ping a computer on your local subnet.

tracert

tracert is Microsoft tool comparable to **traceroute** in UNIX. **tracert** allows you to trace the route that your TCP/IP packets take. An example of **tracert** can be seen in Figure 3-6, where I have traced the route that packets take from a computer on my home network to www.yahoo.com. As you can see, there are a number of different routers and networks that my packets pass through on their way to www.yahoo.com, but eventually the connection is made. As you can see from Figure 3-6, **tracert** also displays a list of the interfaces of the near-side routers in the path that responded to the ICMP echo packets.

FIGURE 3-6   Troubleshooting with **tracert**

```
C:\WINDOWS\system32\cmd.exe                                              _ □ ×

C:\Documents and Settings\Administrator.WS03BASE2>tracert www.yahoo.com

Tracing route to www.yahoo.akadns.net [216.109.125.69]
over a maximum of 30 hops:

  1      1 ms    <1 ms    <1 ms   192.168.1.1
  2     53 ms    31 ms    30 ms   65.50.4.1
  3     28 ms    29 ms    27 ms   10.1.68.129
  4     28 ms    30 ms    29 ms   gw01-vlan965.etob.phub.net.cable.rogers.com [66.
185.93.145]
  5     28 ms    29 ms    29 ms   gw01.wlfdle.phub.net.cable.rogers.com [66.185.82
.97]
  6     31 ms    30 ms    27 ms   gw02.wlfdle.phub.net.cable.rogers.com [66.185.80
.134]
  7     44 ms    43 ms    43 ms   dcr1-so-4-2-0.NewYork.cw.net [206.24.207.97]
  8     51 ms    29 ms    50 ms   dcr2-loopback.Washington.cw.net [206.24.226.100]
  9     54 ms    55 ms    57 ms   bhr1-pos-10-0.Sterling1dc2.cw.net [206.24.238.16
6]
 10     58 ms    58 ms    56 ms   csr11-ve241.Sterling2dc3.cw.net [216.109.66.90]

 11     79 ms    54 ms    55 ms   216.109.84.162
 12     50 ms    49 ms    49 ms   v130.bas1-m.dcn.yahoo.com [216.109.120.142]
 13     55 ms    51 ms    53 ms   w16.www.dcn.yahoo.com [216.109.125.69]

Trace complete.

C:\Documents and Settings\Administrator.WS03BASE2>_
```

tracert is a useful troubleshooting tool to help you determine where on the network the TCP/IP packets stopped, and can be particularly useful in large, multi-segmented networks where multiple valid paths exist to get from the source to the destination.

on the
Job   *The* tracert *command included with Windows Server 2003 includes full support for both IPv4 and IPv6.*

pathping

Another TCP/IP route tracing tool that is similar to **tracert** is **pathping. pathping** is a combination of both **ping** and **tracert** that allows you to trace the route of TCP/IP datagrams from source to destination while also providing information about the degree of packet loss. The packet loss information can be useful in helping you determine what router or device along the way to the destination might be the cause of network problems. An example of the **pathping** command can be seen in Figure 3-7.

regedit

Although it is not usually a part of your standard TCP/IP troubleshooting toolkit, the registry editor **regedit** can be used to resolve TCP/IP configuration issues. From time

FIGURE 3-7

Using **pathping** to troubleshoot TCP/IP

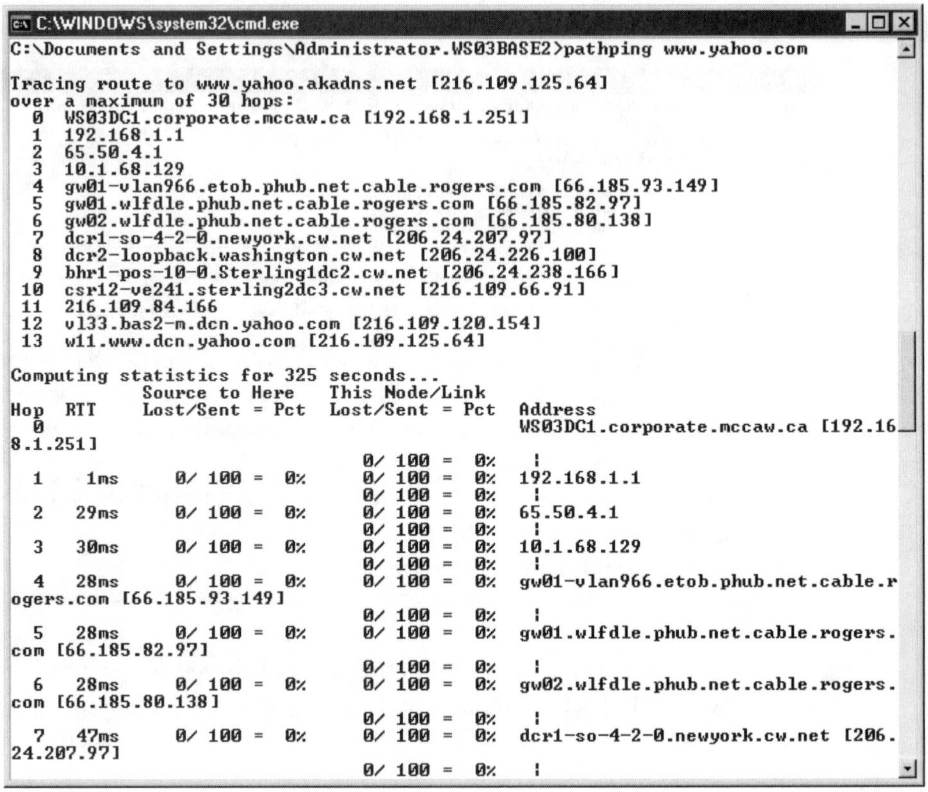

```
C:\WINDOWS\system32\cmd.exe                                              _ □ ×
C:\Documents and Settings\Administrator.WS03BASE2>pathping www.yahoo.com
Tracing route to www.yahoo.akadns.net [216.109.125.64]
over a maximum of 30 hops:
  0  WS03DC1.corporate.mccaw.ca [192.168.1.251]
  1  192.168.1.1
  2  65.50.4.1
  3  10.1.68.129
  4  gw01-vlan966.etob.phub.net.cable.rogers.com [66.185.93.149]
  5  gw01.wlfdle.phub.net.cable.rogers.com [66.185.82.97]
  6  gw02.wlfdle.phub.net.cable.rogers.com [66.185.80.138]
  7  dcr1-so-4-2-0.newyork.cw.net [206.24.207.97]
  8  dcr2-loopback.washington.cw.net [206.24.226.100]
  9  bhr1-pos-10-0.Sterling1dc2.cw.net [206.24.238.166]
 10  csr12-ve241.sterling2dc3.cw.net [216.109.66.91]
 11  216.109.84.166
 12  v133.bas2-m.dcn.yahoo.com [216.109.120.154]
 13  w11.www.dcn.yahoo.com [216.109.125.64]

Computing statistics for 325 seconds...
              Source to Here   This Node/Link
Hop  RTT    Lost/Sent = Pct   Lost/Sent = Pct  Address
 0                                               WS03DC1.corporate.mccaw.ca [192.16
8.1.251]
                                0/ 100 =  0%    |
  1    1ms     0/ 100 =  0%    0/ 100 =  0%    192.168.1.1
                                0/ 100 =  0%    |
  2   29ms     0/ 100 =  0%    0/ 100 =  0%    65.50.4.1
                                0/ 100 =  0%    |
  3   30ms     0/ 100 =  0%    0/ 100 =  0%    10.1.68.129
                                0/ 100 =  0%    |
  4   28ms     0/ 100 =  0%    0/ 100 =  0%    gw01-vlan966.etob.phub.net.cable.r
ogers.com [66.185.93.149]
                                0/ 100 =  0%    |
  5   28ms     0/ 100 =  0%    0/ 100 =  0%    gw01.wlfdle.phub.net.cable.rogers.
com [66.185.82.97]
                                0/ 100 =  0%    |
  6   28ms     0/ 100 =  0%    0/ 100 =  0%    gw02.wlfdle.phub.net.cable.rogers.
com [66.185.80.138]
                                0/ 100 =  0%    |
  7   47ms     0/ 100 =  0%    0/ 100 =  0%    dcr1-so-4-2-0.newyork.cw.net [206.
24.207.97]
                                0/ 100 =  0%    |
```

to time you are likely to run into an error message stating that "The registry subkey already exists." This could be a result of all the components not being properly removed when they were originally installed and then later removed. To correct this problem, you can use the registry editor to remove the lingering subkeys. TCP/IP settings are stored in a number of different registry keys, too many to list here, and beyond the scope of the certification exam. However, if you are interested in knowing the specific registry keys used by TCP/IP in Windows Server 2003, open **Help and Support** and run a search for "Troubleshooting: TCP/IP." Expanding the A *"The registry subkey already exists" message is displayed* entry will reveal all of the registry keys you want to know about.

Now that you have a good understanding of the many tools and techniques available to troubleshoot TCP/IP connectivity issues, take a look at some possible scenarios and their answers.

SCENARIO & SOLUTION

You are trying to test connectivity between a client and a remote host. What tools would best allow you to accomplish this?	**ping** and **tracert** are two tools that would allow you to test connectivity between a client and a remote host. Pinging the IP address of the remote client would tell you if all of the TCP/IP settings on all devices between and including the local and remote clients are correct. **tracert** would allow you to trace the route the packets take and determine bottlenecks along the route.
You would like to view all of the local TCP/IP configuration settings on a multi-homed server. What command would provide you with this information?	The **ipconfig /all** command provides you with a detailed list of the IP configuration settings for all adapters on the local computer.
The results of running **ipconfig /all** on the local computer show an IP address of 169.254.45.69 for one of your adapters. What can you surmise about this adapter?	This adapter is set to obtain an IP address from DHCP and has failed. The default alternate configuration option is set to APIPA, which has configured the computer with an IP address on the 169.254.*x.y* subnet.
Your troubleshooting has revealed that a DHCP client has failed to obtain an IP address via DHCP and has configured itself with a user-configured static IP address. How can you force a new DHCP IP address request?	Forcing a new DHCP IP address request or DHCPDISCOVER can be accomplished by running the **ipconfig /renew** command or by restarting the computer.

CERTIFICATION OBJECTIVE 3.03

Diagnose and Resolve Issues Related to DHCP Authorization

Before we dive into diagnosing and resolving issues related to DHCP server authorization, we'll begin with a review of the authorization process and requirements, because this knowledge can be very helpful during the troubleshooting process.

First, the authorization process for DHCP servers has dependencies. Windows Server 2003 allows you to select and configure one of three server types: domain controller, member server, or stand-alone server. A *domain controller (DC)* maintains a copy of the Active Directory database, and performs many roles, including authentication within a domain. A *member server* is a computer that is a member of a domain, but not a domain controller. Member servers maintain a local account database for local accounts and groups, but participate in the domain via a computer account in Active Directory. A *stand-alone server* is a computer configured as a member of a workgroup rather than a domain. For a computer running the DHCP server service to be authorized, it must be configured as either a domain controller or a member server. Stand-alone servers running DHCP cannot be authorized. Stand-alone servers running DHCP are configured to routinely attempt to detect authorized servers on the same subnet, and if they do, they automatically stop leasing IP addresses to DHCP clients.

Authorized Windows Server 2003 DHCP servers are configured to repeat the detection process every 60 minutes by default, and unauthorized DHCP servers repeat the detection process even more frequently, every 10 minutes by default. When DHCP auditing is enabled, you will see "Restarting rogue detection" entries reflecting this process in the audit log.

Let's complicate the authorization process a little by introducing multiple forests in the same physical location, which can often result after a corporate merger or acquisition. In a multi-forest environment like that displayed in Figure 3-8, a DHCP server exists and is authorized in a single domain within a single forest, in this case, the corp.solarsystem.com domain and forest. Once authorized, the DHCP server is able to lease IP addresses to all reachable clients, regardless of their domain or forest membership, and without requiring a cross-forest transitive trust between the forest root domains. Assuming that the routers in Figure 3-8 support the forwarding of DHCP and BOOTP traffic, all clients in both forests could be serviced by a single DHCP server. This assumes that a scope has been configured to support each possible subnet.

Authorizing a DHCP server within Active Directory requires membership in the Enterprise Admins group, and only servers running Windows 2000 Server or Windows

> **e x a m**
> **ⓦ a t c h**   *Stand-alone servers running DHCP automatically stop leasing IP addresses to DHCP clients if they detect an authorized DHCP server on their locall subnet.*

> **e x a m**
> **ⓦ a t c h**   *Once authorized in their own domain, DHCP servers in a multiple forest architecture are able to lease IP addresses to all reachable clients.*

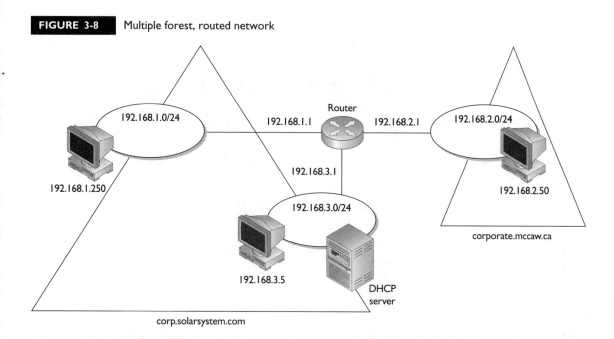

FIGURE 3-8 Multiple forest, routed network

Server 2003 support authorization. Exercise 3-4 looks at the steps involved in authorizing a DHCP server.

EXERCISE 3-4

Authorizing a DHCP Server

In this exercise, you will learn how to authorize a DHCP server and how to determine if a DHCP server is authorized.

1. In the DHCP snap-in, right-click the name of the DHCP server and select **Authorize**.

2. To identify the authorized DHCP servers in Active Directory, right-click DHCP and select **Manage authorized servers**. This will display the **Manage Authorized**

Server dialog box shown in the following illustration. Click the **Authorize** button, enter the name or IP address of the DHCP server you wish to authorize, and click OK.

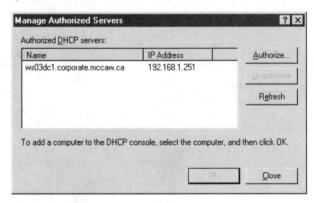

SCENARIO & SOLUTION

You have just upgraded your Windows NT 4.0 DHCP server to Windows Server 2003 and you would like to authorize the service. What group must you be a member of to accomplish this task?	DHCP server authorization requires that you be a member of the Enterprise Admins group, because the authorization is forest-wide.
Your organization has just finished the acquisition of another company. You are currently working with two Windows Server 2003 forests that are not currently connected by any trust relationships, but are on the same network. What must you do to allow the clients in the new company to use your DHCP server?	This is a trick question, because nothing is required so long as your existing DHCP server is already authorized, which it would be if it were leasing out IP addresses to existing clients. A DHCP server only requires authorization in a single forest to be able to lease out IP addresses to clients in different domains or forests.
Where can you look to determine if a DHCP server is authorized?	You can determine whether a DHCP server is authorized using a number of different tools and utilities, including **netsh**, the DHCP snap-in, and the DHCP audit log.

Be careful not to confuse the activation of scopes with the authorization of DHCP servers.

Once they are authorized, all DHCP servers listed in the DHCP snap-in appear with a green arrow pointing up, as opposed to unauthorized servers, which appear with a red arrow pointing down.

Now that you have a solid understanding of the DHCP authentication process, take a look at some different scenarios to test your knowledge.

CERTIFICATION OBJECTIVE 3.04

Verify DHCP Reservation Configuration

DHCP client reservations are a great way to help ensure that a specific client, identified by MAC address, always receives the same reserved IP address. The best way to verify that your IP address reservations are working is to create and test the reservation by running the **ipconfig /renew** command at the client. This forces the client computer to release and then renew its IP address, and it should obtain the reserved IP address from the scope of available IP addresses.

One important point to understand about DHCP reservations is that if the scope is almost depleted, and the only IP addresses available are reserved, the reservations will not be lost if another client sends a DHCPDISCOVER message to the DHCP server. In this case, the DHCP server will continue to hold the reserved IP addresses instead of providing the reserved address to the requesting client.

Also remember that reserving an IP address in a scope does not automatically force a client currently using that address to stop using it. You can run the **ipconfig /release** command on the client to force the client to release the existing IP address and obtain a new one, thereby freeing up the newly reserved address. Furthermore, reserving an IP address at the DHCP server does not force the new client for which the reservation is made to immediately move to that newly reserved IP address. For this to occur, the client must first issue a DHCP request message, which you can force with **ipconfig /renew**.

One of the keys to ensuring successful DHCP client reservations is having the right MAC address for the reservation. The Address Resolution Protocol (ARP) in conjunction with the **ping** command can be very handy in allowing you to determine the MAC address of a remote client when creating the DHCP address reservation. Exercise 3-5 examines how to use these two tools.

EXERCISE 3-5

Using ping and arp to Determine a Client's MAC Address

In this exercise you will learn how you can use both the **ping** and **arp** commands to determine a remote client's MAC address assisting you in the creation of a DHCP reservation for the client.

1. Open the command prompt, type **ping <IP address or name or remote host>**, and press ENTER.

2. Type **arp -a** and press ENTER. As you can seen in the following illustration, the **ping** command requires that the remote client's MAC address be resolved to its IP address, and this information is stored locally in the arp cache. The **arp -a** command can then be run to list the contents of the arp cache and display the IP address to MAC address mappings. Remember that when entering the MAC address into the DHCP reservation properties dialog box, do not enter the '-', only the numbers and letters without spaces.

```
C:\WINDOWS\system32\cmd.exe                                    _ □ ×

C:\Documents and Settings\Administrator.WS03BASE2>ping 192.168.1.50

Pinging 192.168.1.50 with 32 bytes of data:

Reply from 192.168.1.50: bytes=32 time=2ms TTL=128
Reply from 192.168.1.50: bytes=32 time<1ms TTL=128
Reply from 192.168.1.50: bytes=32 time<1ms TTL=128
Reply from 192.168.1.50: bytes=32 time<1ms TTL=128

Ping statistics for 192.168.1.50:
    Packets: Sent = 4, Received = 4, Lost = 0 (0% loss),
Approximate round trip times in milli-seconds:
    Minimum = 0ms, Maximum = 2ms, Average = 0ms

C:\Documents and Settings\Administrator.WS03BASE2>arp -a

Interface: 192.168.1.251 --- 0x2
  Internet Address      Physical Address      Type
  192.168.1.1           00-a0-cc-3b-c9-6d     dynamic
  192.168.1.50          00-a0-cc-3b-c9-72     dynamic

C:\Documents and Settings\Administrator.WS03BASE2>_
```

You can also verify DHCP client reservations with the **netsh** command. The **netsh** command sequence used to view a list of IP address reservations on a DHCP server with an IP address of 192.168.1.251 is shown in Figure 3-9. The key to successfully identifying the reserved IP information using **netsh** is to start by launching **netsh**,

---

FIGURE 3-9

Using **netsh** to view IP address reservations

```
C:\WINDOWS\system32\cmd.exe - netsh                          _ □ ×

C:\Documents and Settings\Administrator.WS03BASE2>netsh
netsh>dhcp
netsh dhcp>server \\192.168.1.251
netsh dhcp server>scope 192.168.1.0

Changed the current scope context to 192.168.1.0 scope.
netsh dhcp server scope>show reservedip

=================================================================
      Reservation Address  -     Unique ID
=================================================================

        192.168.1.10     -     00-50-3c-5f-6d-90-
        192.168.1.11     -     00-0c-50-9f-d4-98-
        192.168.1.12     -     00-c1-1d-20-c7-

No of ReservedIPs : 3 in the Scope : 192.168.1.0.

Command completed successfully.
netsh dhcp server scope>_
```

---

changing the context to **dhcp**, connecting to the server, then the scope, and then listing the IP reservations.

exam

ⓦatch

To change a reserved IP address for a current client, the existing address reservation for the client must first be removed and then a new reservation added. You can change any other information about a reserved client while keeping the reserved IP address.

CERTIFICATION OBJECTIVE 3.05

Examine the System Event Log and DHCP Server Audit Log Files to Find Related Events

Two excellent areas available to assist you in diagnosing problems with the DHCP server service are the system event log and the DHCP server audit logs. As you can see in Figure 3-10, you can filter the System Event Log to view only events with a source of DHCPServer. This allows you to quickly identify events specific to the DHCP Server service.

Enabling DHCP server auditing is another way to collect DHCP-related service information. Exercise 3-6 walks you through the process of enabling DHCP auditing.

FIGURE 3-10

Filtering the
System Event
Log for events
with source
DHCPServer

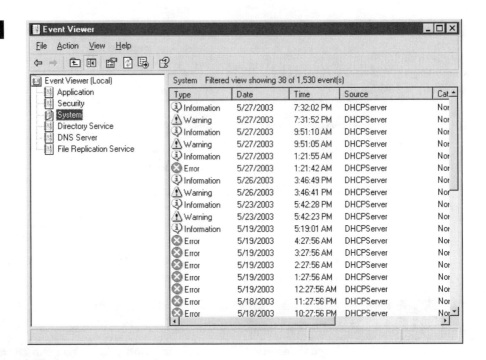

Enabling DHCP Auditing

In this exercise, you will enable DHCP auditing to allow you to collect more detailed information about the workings of the DHCP server service.

1. In the DHCP snap-in, right-click the DHCP server and select **Properties**.

2. On the **General** tab, select **Enable DHCP audit logging**.

3. Select the **Advanced** tab shown in the following illustration to specify the directory path where the audit log files will be created and saved, and then click **OK**. The default location is the **%windir%\System32\Dhcp** directory.

Now that auditing is enabled, if you begin to experience problems with the DHCP service, you can review the audit logs to help you diagnose the problem. Figure 3-11 shows you an example of part of a DHCP audit log. The first section of the log provides a listing of event codes, and the actual audit events can be found after this listing. This listing of event codes is intended to help you identify what the specific problem is. For example, if the DNS update failed with Event ID 31, this could indicate a communication problem between the DHCP server and DNS or a DNS configuration issue.

FIGURE 3-11

Viewing the
DHCP audit log

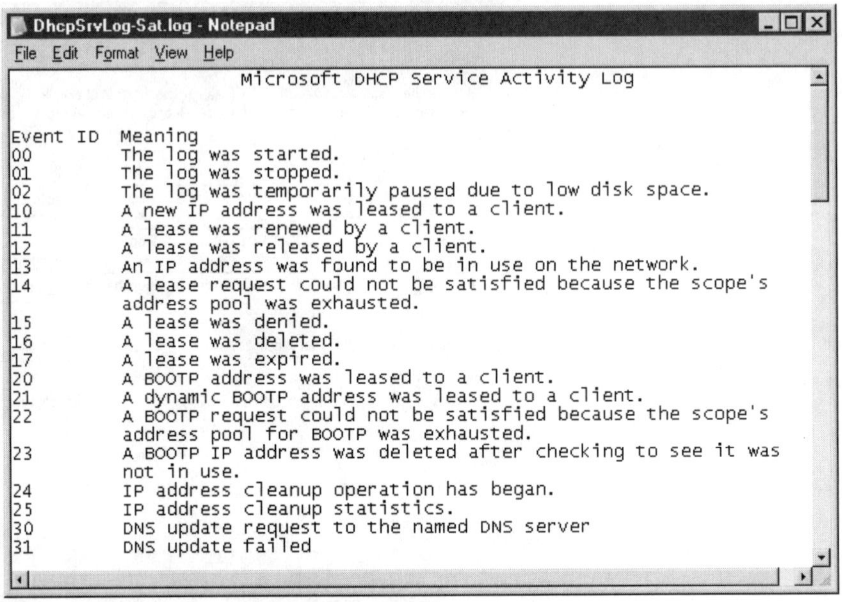

```
DhcpSrvLog-Sat.log - Notepad                                    _ □ ×
File  Edit  Format  View  Help
                    Microsoft DHCP Service Activity Log

Event ID  Meaning
00        The log was started.
01        The log was stopped.
02        The log was temporarily paused due to low disk space.
10        A new IP address was leased to a client.
11        A lease was renewed by a client.
12        A lease was released by a client.
13        An IP address was found to be in use on the network.
14        A lease request could not be satisfied because the scope's
          address pool was exhausted.
15        A lease was denied.
16        A lease was deleted.
17        A lease was expired.
20        A BOOTP address was leased to a client.
21        A dynamic BOOTP address was leased to a client.
22        A BOOTP request could not be satisfied because the scope's
          address pool for BOOTP was exhausted.
23        A BOOTP IP address was deleted after checking to see it was
          not in use.
24        IP address cleanup operation has began.
25        IP address cleanup statistics.
30        DNS update request to the named DNS server
31        DNS update failed
```

CERTIFICATION OBJECTIVE 3.06

Diagnose and Resolve Issues Related to Configuration of DHCP Server and Scope Options

You can diagnose and resolve issues related to the configuration of DHCP server and scope options in a number of ways and using a variety of tools. The first means that we will discuss to accomplish this is viewing your DHCP statistics.

Viewing the DHCP statistics for a given scope can quickly provide you with the total number of addresses in the scope, the number and percentage in use, and the number and percentage available. Viewing the DHCP server statistics shows you the start time of the DHCP server service and how long it has been up, and the number of each of the different types of DHCP messages such as discovers, offers, requests, acks, nacks, declines, and releases. It also provides you with the number of scopes configured on the server, the total addresses, and the number and percentage that are both in use and available.

When you diagnose DHCP using the DHCP server statistics, look at the uptime value, because this value should be a higher rather than lower number. If the service has been up for days, you can rule out service disruption as the cause of the problem. Next, look at the number of negative acknowledgements (nacks). A high number of nacks could indicate that your DHCP server is responding to IP address renewal requests from clients that normally lease their IP addresses from another DHCP server and the two DHCP servers aren't aware of one another's scopes. Clients usually receive a nack in response to a DHCPREQUEST if the DHCP server has since leased the current address to another client. This can happen when the lease duration is shortened but the client isn't aware of it yet, or if the DHCP server had its scope deleted and re-created, thereby losing its active lease data.

Also pay attention to the number of IP addresses available, because having a very small number or percentage available may also be a reason for problems. Exercise 3-7 walks you through the steps involved in configuring your DHCP server to automatically refresh its statistics.

<hr>

EXERCISE 3-7

Configuring and Viewing DHCP Statistics

This exercise will teach you how to configure your DHCP statistics to automatically refresh, and then how to display statistics for either your DHCP server or individual scopes, which can be useful when trying to diagnose problems with scopes and reservations.

1. In the DHCP snap-in, right-click the name of the DHCP server, and select **Properties**.

2. On the **General** tab, select **Automatically update statistics every**, specify the refresh frequency you desire in either hours or minutes, and click **OK**.

3. To display statistics for the server, right-click the DHCP server and select **Display Statistics**. To display statistics for the scope, right click the scope and

select **Display Statistics**. This illustration shows you the resulting statistics that are displayed for the scope.

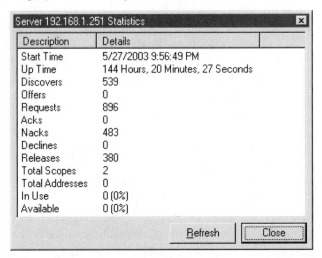

Description	Details
Start Time	5/27/2003 9:56:49 PM
Up Time	144 Hours, 20 Minutes, 27 Seconds
Discovers	539
Offers	0
Requests	896
Acks	0
Nacks	483
Declines	0
Releases	380
Total Scopes	2
Total Addresses	0
In Use	0 (0%)
Available	0 (0%)

Server 192.168.1.251 Statistics

Refresh   Close

CERTIFICATION OBJECTIVE 3.07

Verify That the DHCP Relay Agent Is Working Correctly

Verifying that the DHCP Relay Agent is working correctly is as simple as running the **ipconfg /release** and **ipconfig /renew** commands on a DHCP client that is located on a subnet with a DHCP relay agent, and not a DHCP server or router configured not to forward DHCP traffic. If the DHCP client is able to renew its IP address, you have verified that the DHCP relay agent is working.

If this simple test doesn't provide you with an IP address lease, open the RRAS snap-in on the DHCP Relay Agent, select **DHCP Relay Agent** in the IP Routing section, and view the listed interfaces and the statistics of the Relay Agent. In the list of interfaces, confirm that there is an interface that is connected to the local subnet that the client is also connected to, and then confirm that the relay mode for the interface is set to **enabled**. Last, right-click the DHCP Relay Agent and select **Properties**. On the **General** tab of the DHCP Relay Agent properties dialog box, ensure that one or more DHCP servers are listed.

In the DHCP Relay Agent interface statistics, look for both requests and replies being received when you run the **ipconfig /release** and **ipconfig /renew** commands on the DHCP client. If these statistics are not being updated when you release and renew your IP address, focus your troubleshooting on the client and its hardware configuration, and ensure that the network adapter is configured correctly and that there aren't any device problems identified in Device Manager. If this doesn't reveal anything, turn your attention to the networking devices between the DHCP client and the DHCP server. Also try to eliminate these intermediary devices by attempting to obtain an IP address lease from another client on the same segment as the client experiencing problems. If this second DHCP client is successful in obtaining a lease, you can rule out the intermediary devices and return your focus to the client experiencing problems.

CERTIFICATION OBJECTIVE 3.08

Verify Database Integrity

Verifying database integrity is another important component of the DHCP maintenance process. The DHCP database is a dynamic database whose contents change as DHCP clients are assigned or as they release their IP addresses. All of the configuration data for DHCP, such as the information about scopes, reservations, options, leases, lease durations, and exclusion ranges, is stored in the DHCP database. Therefore, the database must be available for the DHCP service to start. The DHCP database is stored by default in the **%systemroot%\system32\dhcp** directory, and it is automatically backed up every 60 minutes by default to the **%systemroot%\system32\dhcp\backup\jet\new** directory.

The DHCP database consists of a number of files, including **DHCP.mdb**, **DHCP.tmp**, **JET.log**, **JET*.log**, and **SYSTEM.mdb**. Table 3-1 describes the role each of the files plays.

Compacting the DHCP database is a process that compresses the database and removes any unused space. In Windows Server 2003, the DHCP server service compacts the database automatically while the service is running and the database is online, which reduces the need to manually compact the database using **jetpack**. Regularly

TABLE 3-1	Files That Make Up the DHCP Database

File	Description
DHCP.mdb	Database file that contains two tables: the name-to-IP-address mapping table and the IP address owner ID table.
DHCP.tmp	A temporary file that DHCP uses for temporary database information while the service is running.
JET.log, JET*.log	The transaction logs for the database. These logs can be used to recover data.
SYSTEM.mdb	A file used to store information about the structure of the database.

compacting the database helps to maintain a consistent level of performance. As the database grows by clients renewing or releasing their IP addresses over an extended period, the DHCP services performance can degrade.

The DHCP service is almost at the point of being self-managing because it also performs a consistency check of its database at startup and periodically thereafter to detect and correct any problems, but sometimes, even with these measures, the database can become corrupt or simply slower than normal. Manually compacting the database with the **jetpack** utility is an option that might correct these issues. Exercise 3-8 examines how to use **jetpack** to compact the DHCP database

EXERCISE 3-8

Compacting the DHCP Database with jetpack

In this exercise you will learn how to compact the DHCP server database using jetpack. You can use this process to attempt to correct a corrupt DHCP server database.

1. Click **Start | Administrative Tools**, and select Services.

2. In the **Services** dialog box, right-click the DHCP server service, and select **Stop**.

3. Open the command prompt and navigate to the **%systemroot%\system32\dhcp** directory.

4. Type **jetpack dhcp.mdb jetold**, where **jetold** is the name of a temporary database location that is used during the repair. Press ENTER.

5. In Services, right-click the DHCP server service and select **Start**.

Another option available to verify the database is to reconcile all of the scopes, a process that verifies the DHCP database values with DHCP registry values. Performing a reconciliation can be useful when you find that the database values aren't being displayed properly in the DHCP console, or after you have restored a DHCP database. One common issue that can occur after restoring the database on a server that had an older version of the same database running is that the scope and option information displays, but the active leases do not. Reconciling the database allows the client lease information from the registry to be populated to the DHCP database. Exercise 3-9 looks at how to reconcile a database.

EXERCISE 3-9

CertCam 3-9 ON THE CD

Reconciling the DHCP Database

This exercise will teach you how to reconcile the DHCP database to ensure that the information displayed in the DHCP snap-in is consistent with the information in both the registry and the database.

1. Open the DHCP snap-in.

2. To reconcile all scopes, right-click the name of the DHCP server, and select **Reconcile All Scopes**. To reconcile a single scope, right-click the name of scope and select **Reconcile**.

3. In the Reconcile dialog box, click **Verify**.

4. In the DHCP dialog box click **OK**.

5. Click **Cancel**.

on the
Job

After reconciling, the properties of individual clients shown in the list of active leases may have incorrect information displayed. This information inconsistency will correct itself upon lease renewal.

CERTIFICATION SUMMARY

In this chapter, you learned how to diagnose and resolve issues related to both DHCP and TCP/IP addressing. You have learned what to look for and how to resolve issues related to DHCP alternate configuration settings, such as APIPA and the user configured option. You also learned how to identify and correct issues related to incorrect IP address configuration and how the new IP conflict icon will help to alert you to an IP conflict.

This chapter also explored how to identify and resolve issues with DHCP server authorization, as well as where and how to authorize a DHCP server. Next you learned how to verify DHCP reservations and test to ensure that they are working correctly. We also discussed where to look for more detailed information on problems occurring with the DHCP service. This led to how to filter events from the source DHCP server in the System Event Log and how to enable DHCP server auditing.

Finally, you looked at how to diagnose and resolve issues with DHCP server and scope options as well as the DHCP relay agent and database integrity. All the information covered in this chapter relates to the troubleshooting of both DHCP and TCP/IP addressing, a key area in the certification exam.

✓ TWO-MINUTE DRILL

Diagnose and Resolve Issues Related to Automatic Private IP Addressing (APIPA)

❑ APIPA is one of two alternate configuration options available in Windows Server 2003, the other being the user configured option, which allows you to specify an alternative static IP address configuration.

❑ APIPA assigns a DHCP client an address on the 169.254.*x.y* network.

❑ APIPA is ideal for small, non-routed networks, because it does not assign a default gateway.

❑ APIPA can only be permanently disabled through a registry edit, but in Windows Server 2003, an alternative static IP address can be configured.

❑ APIPA will continue to attempt to locate a DHCP server every five minutes in an effort to obtain a valid leased IP address, but the user configured alternative static address does not.

Diagnose and Resolve Issues Related to Incorrect TCP/IP Configuration

❑ The **ipconfig /all** command can be used to identify the local IP configuration settings for all adapters installed on the local computer.

❑ Each adapter in the computer can be configured differently, allowing for one NIC to use DHCP to obtain an IP address while another NIC is statically configured.

❑ The DHCP client service is started and enabled on all computers running Windows 2000 or later, and is responsible for registering the client's name-to-IP-address mapping in DNS if DNS is configured to allow dynamic updates.

❑ A statically configured NIC must have both an IP address and subnet mask. To have access to other remote networks, it must also have a gateway address.

❑ **ping** can be used to test both a local and remote client's TCP/IP configuration. You can ping either the name or IP address, but to eliminate name resolution as a potential variable, ping the IP address.

❑ When you manually configure a NIC with static IP address settings and you accidentally enter an incorrect gateway, Windows Server 2003 will prompt you to the fact the gateway you entered is incorrect.

❑ When a statically configured computer identifies that another computer on the network is using the same IP address, the IP configuration icon in the systray shows an IP conflict icon.

Diagnose and Resolve Issues Related to DHCP Authorization

❑ DHCP servers are authorized, but DHCP scopes are activated.

❑ Only DHCP servers that are members of an Active Directory domain require authorization. In order to authorize a DHCP server, you must be a member of the Enterprise Admins group.

❑ Stand-alone DHCP servers cannot be authorized, because there is no directory service to store and manage the authorization. Stand-alone servers are configured to routinely attempt to detect authorized servers on the same subnet, and will stop leasing IP addresses if they detect one.

❑ Once authorized, DHCP servers are able to lease IP addresses to all reachable clients regardless of their domain or forest membership and without any cross-forest trusts.

Verify DHCP Reservation Configuration

❑ DHCP client reservations allow you to guarantee that particular clients, identified by MAC address, always obtain specific IP addresses from DHCP.

❑ Specific client options can be set for each client reservation to allow specific clients to receive unique option settings.

❑ Reserving an IP address in a scope does not automatically force a client currently using that address to stop using it. The **ipconfig /release** and **/renew** commands must be run on the client to allow the client to release and then obtain the new IP address.

❑ Client reservations require the client's MAC address, which can be obtained from a remote client by pinging that client and then running **arp -a** to obtain the MAC-to-IP-address mapping from the arp cache.

Examine the System Event Log and DHCP Server Audit Log Files to Find Related Events

❑ The System Event Log can be used to identify DHCP server–related messages by filtering on the source DHCPServer.

❑ DHCP auditing can be enabled or disabled in the properties of the DHCP server in the DHCP snap-in.

Diagnose and Resolve Issues Related to Configuration of DHCP Server and Scope Options

❑ DHCP server and scope statistics can be used to provide a quick look at what is happening on the DHCP server and report on the number of acks or nacks.

❑ It is important to ensure that scope options are configured and applied to the correct clients so that the clients receive gateway settings for their specific subnet.

Verify That the DHCP Relay Agent Is Working Correctly

❑ The DHCP relay agent can be tested by running the **ipconfig /renew** command from a remote DHCP client that is located on the same subnet as the DHCP relay agent.

❑ Ensure that the DHCP relay agent is configured to use at least one interface, and that the interface is connected to the same subnet as the DHCP clients. Also ensure that the DHCP relay agent is configured with the IP address of at least one DHCP server, and that it is able to connect to that server. Also confirm that the relay mode on the DHCP relay agent is set to Enabled.

Verify Database Integrity

❑ The DHCP database is located in the **%systemroot%\system32\dhcp** directory, and is automatically backed up every 60 minutes.

❑ **jetpack** can be used to manually compact the DHCP database, but Windows Server 2003 automatically compacts the database at regular intervals.

❑ The database can be reconciled after a DHCP database is restored or if you are finding that values in the DHCP snap-in aren't consistent, such as active leases not appearing.

SELF TEST

The following questions will help you measure your understanding of the material presented in this chapter. Read all the choices carefully, because there might be more than one correct answer. Choose all correct answers for each question.

Diagnose and Resolve Issues Related to Automatic Private IP Addressing (APIPA)

1. As the administrator of a small, single-subnet LAN, you are trying to decide on the IP configuration options that would best meet the needs of your particular network. Your network currently consists of 15 clients and two servers. One server, running Internet Connection Sharing (ICS) connects all clients to the Internet through a shared high-speed cable connection, and the other server acts as a file and print server. You do not currently have a DHCP server, and you do not want to statically configure each individual computer, but you do need them all to communicate with one another. Which of the following TCP/IP client settings would be best for your environment? (Choose all that apply.)

   A. Configure all the computers to obtain IP addresses automatically, and on the Alternate Configuration tab, select the APIPA option.

   B. Configure all the computers to obtain IP addresses automatically, and on the Alternate Configuration tab, select the user configured option.

   C. Configure all the computers to obtain IP addresses automatically, and select no alternate configurations.

   D. Configure all the computers statically with IP addresses and a subnet mask.

2. You are troubleshooting DHCP problems on a computer running Windows Server 2003. When you open the command prompt and type **ipconfig /all**, an automatically assigned IP address is returned. Which of the following IP addresses was returned?

   A. 172.16.35.64

   B. 192.168.1.1

   C. 129.145.34.62

   D. 169.254.1.60

Diagnose and Resolve Issues Related to Incorrect TCP/IP Configuration

3. You are the administrator of a small office network that has 25 client computers and four servers running Windows Server 2003. You have just installed Windows Server 2003 on a new fifth

server running Windows Server 2003 that has two NICs. You have configured one NIC to obtain an IP address through DHCP, and you have configured the other NIC statically. Shortly after making the network connection changes, you notice that one of the network icons in the systray has a red question mark over it, and network communications are only working on one of the two NICs. Which NIC is most likely having problems and what is the most likely cause of the problem?

- A. The dynamically configured NIC is most likely causing the problem. It probably is unable to find a DHCP server, and no alternate configuration has been defined.
- B. The dynamically configured NIC is most likely causing the problem. APIPA probably has configured an IP address that conflicts with another IP address already in use.
- C. The statically configured NIC is most likely causing the problem. The IP address entered is probably on the wrong subnet.
- D. The statically configured NIC is most likely causing the problem. The IP address entered probably conflicts with another IP address already in use.

4. You are the administrator of a number of servers running Windows Server 2003. You have taken one of the servers offline for testing, and configured it on the isolated, non-production network while you made and tested a number of configuration changes. Now that you are satisfied with the results of the tests, you have reconnected the server to the production network, but immediately after doing so you notice that the IP conflict icon appears in the systray. Which of the following is the most likely cause of this?

- A. The server has not been added to the authorized servers list, which has resulted in the Server service disabling the IP stack and displaying the IP address as in conflict.
- B. The DHCP client service is unable to obtain an IP address from a DHCP server.
- C. The DHCP client service is unable to obtain an IP address from a DHCP server, and APIPA has automatically configured the computer with an IP address, but the IP conflict icon remains until APIPA is able to obtain a valid leased address.
- D. The IP address configured on the server conflicts with an IP address already in use on the network.

5. You are the administrator for a number of computers running Windows Server 2003. You log on to one of your multi-homed servers to perform some regular maintenance and notice the IP conflict icon in the systray. You open the command prompt to troubleshoot the problem and type **ipconfig /all**. Figure 3-12 shows you the results. What is the most likely cause of the problem?

- A. The DHCP client service is unable to obtain an IP address from DHCP.
- B. The DHCP client service is unable to obtain an IP address from DHCP, and the IP address defined in the alternate configuration conflicts with another IP address on the network.

FIGURE 3-12

The results of **ipconfig /all**

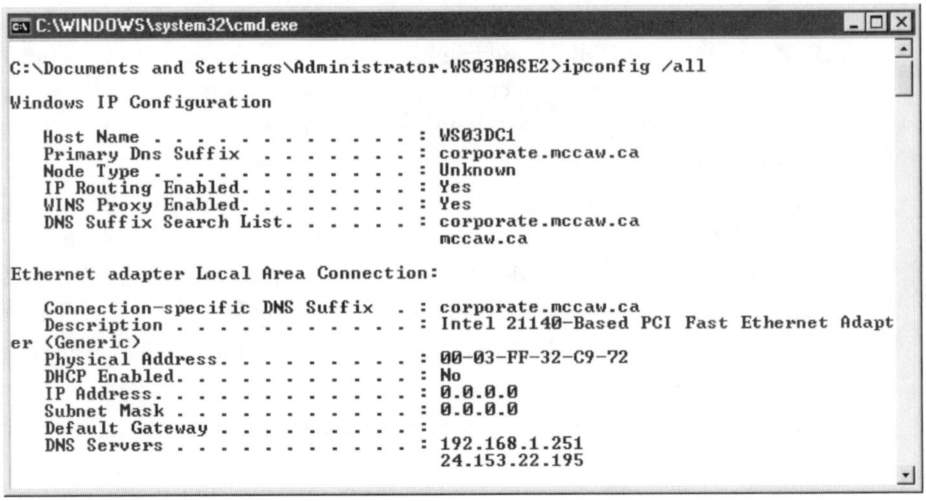

```
C:\WINDOWS\system32\cmd.exe                                        _ □ ×

C:\Documents and Settings\Administrator.WS03BASE2>ipconfig /all

Windows IP Configuration

        Host Name . . . . . . . . . . . : WS03DC1
        Primary Dns Suffix  . . . . . . : corporate.mccaw.ca
        Node Type . . . . . . . . . . . : Unknown
        IP Routing Enabled. . . . . . . : Yes
        WINS Proxy Enabled. . . . . . . : Yes
        DNS Suffix Search List. . . . . : corporate.mccaw.ca
                                          mccaw.ca

Ethernet adapter Local Area Connection:

        Connection-specific DNS Suffix  . : corporate.mccaw.ca
        Description . . . . . . . . . . : Intel 21140-Based PCI Fast Ethernet Adapt
er (Generic)
        Physical Address. . . . . . . . : 00-03-FF-32-C9-72
        DHCP Enabled. . . . . . . . . . : No
        IP Address. . . . . . . . . . . : 0.0.0.0
        Subnet Mask . . . . . . . . . . : 0.0.0.0
        Default Gateway . . . . . . . . :
        DNS Servers . . . . . . . . . . : 192.168.1.251
                                          24.153.22.195
```

    C. The statically configured IP address has an incorrect subnet mask.

    D. The statically configured IP address does not have a gateway address.

Diagnose and Resolve Issues Related to DHCP Authorization

  6. As one of the administrators in your organization, you have taken it upon yourself to study for the new Windows Server 2003 certification exams in an effort to obtain your MCSE. During your studying, you use the servers in the test lab to get some hands-on experience with the operating system. You are currently studying DHCP, and you have installed a DHCP server on a stand-alone server running in the lab network, which is configured with a completely isolated Active Directory forest that consists of one domain. No other DHCP server exists on the lab network. With the DHCP server service installed and a default scope created, you log on to a computer running Windows XP on the lab network, and change the TCP/IP settings to obtain an IP address via DHCP. At the command prompt you run the **ipconfig /renew** command, but you continually fail to receive an IP address. What is the most likely cause of the problem?

    A. The DHCP server is not authorized.

    B. The DHCP scope is not activated.

    C. The DHCP server is not a part of the Active Directory domain.

    D. The DHCP service requires Internet access and cannot exist on an isolated network.

  7. As an administrator in one of the child domains in your organization's global Active Directory forest, you have been trying to authorize a newly installed and configured DHCP server, but you have been unsuccessful. Which of the following best represents the reason why you are unsuccessful?

A. The authorization process can take a significant period of time in a large global Active Directory forest because of the time required to replicate.

B. The authorization process requires that you must be a member of the Schema Admins group.

C. The authorization process requires that you must be a member of the Enterprise Admins group.

D. The authorization process requires that an Application naming context must exist prior to the authorization.

8. As the administrator of your mixed Windows NT 4.0 and Windows Server 2003 domain, you are beginning the process of migrating your DHCP servers from Windows NT 4.0 to Windows Server 2003. Before the migration, you are concerned about authorization. You have currently upgraded the PDC to Windows Server 2003. The two DHCP servers are still currently running on a Windows NT 4.0 Server. Which of the following best represents the required configuration?

A. Authorize the Windows NT 4.0 DHCP servers in Active Directory.

B. Add the Windows NT 4.0 DHCP servers to the DNSUpdateProxy group.

C. Add the Windows NT 4.0 DHCP servers to the Pre Windows 2000 Compatible Access group.

D. Do nothing.

Verify DHCP Reservation Configuration

9. Which of the following commands can be used to identify the MAC address of a remote computer? (Choose all that apply.)

A. arp -a

B. netstat

C. ipconfig /all

D. ping

10. As the administrator of a medium size organization, you have just created a new IP address reservation for an existing DHCP client on the network to guarantee that client the same IP address. The client for which you created the IP address reservation is used as a print server by ten other client computers. You have logged on locally to verify that the client has obtained the reserved IP address, but you notice that it is still using its old IP address. Which of the following will resolve this?

A. Run the *arp -a* command.

B. Run the *netsh | dchp | server \\<dhcpservername> | force reservedip* command.

C. Run *ipconfig /release* followed by *ipconfig /renew*.

D. Run *ipconfig /refresh*.

Examine the System Event Log and DHCP Server Audit Log Files to Find Related Events

11. As the administrator of the DHCP services operating in your environment, you have enabled auditing to assist you in diagnosing some problems you have been experiencing lately. In which directory will you find the audit log files?

A. %windir%\system32\dhcp\backup\logs

B. %windir%\system32\dhcp\logs

C. %windir%\dhcp\backup\logs

D. %windir%\system32\dhcp

Diagnose and Resolve Issues Related to Configuration of DHCP Server and Scope Options

12. As the administrator of the DHCP services in your organization, you are responsible for diagnosing and troubleshooting DHCP-related problems. Your Active Directory infrastructure team made some changes over the weekend, and on Monday, a number of DHCP clients have been contacting you reporting that they are experiencing problems obtaining an IP address, and that they are not able to connect to the network. When you look at the DHCP server statistics, you notice that there are a significant number of nacks but no acks being sent out. Which of the following is the most likely cause of the problem?

A. The scope options are incorrectly defined.

B. There is no superscope.

C. The DHCP server isn't activated.

D. The DHCP server isn't authorized.

Verify That the DHCP Relay Agent Is Working Correctly

13. Which of the following commands run on a DHCP client on a remote subnet to the DHCP server will help you determine if the DHCP Relay Agent on the same subnet as the client is working correctly?

A. netsh dhcp testrelay

B. ipconfig /renew

C. On the Monitoring tab of the DHCP server properties dialog box, click Test.

D. nslookup \\dhcprelayagent

Verify Database Integrity

14. Which of the following tools can be used to compact your DHCP database?

    A. netsh

    B. jetpack

    C. DHCP snap-in

    D. compact

15. As the administrator of your network, you have noticed lately through some performance monitors you have configured that DHCP performance has been degrading. You recently purchased a new server, and you have restored the original DHCP database to the new server. After you start the DHCP service on the new server, which of the following steps should you perform?

    A. Run the **jetpack** utility.

    B. Enable DHCP auditing.

    C. Change the permissions on the DHCP folder.

    D. Reconcile the DHCP server.

LAB QUESTION

Because you are one of a number of consultants at a Microsoft Gold Partner, a new client has contacted you to help them troubleshoot and resolve TCP/IP connectivity issues they have been having after trying to implement and configure TCP/IP themselves.

The client had attempted to install and configure DHCP, create a single scope, and define scope options as well as client reservations. Your initial analysis has revealed that all of the clients in the organization are configured to obtain an IP address through DHCP. The results of the **ipconfig /all** command run on a number of clients has provided mixed results. Some clients returned IP addresses on the 169.254.0.0/16 network, and others returned static IP configurations on the 192.168.1.0/24 network. The clients with static configurations are able to function on the network and establish connections to remote computers, but the clients on the 169.254.0.0/16 network are only able to connect to one another. When you look at the DHCP server, you notice that there is a red arrow pointing down next to the scope named 192.168.0.1. Further investigation into the DHCP server reveals that the scope options are properly configured. What are some of the issues causing problems in your client's configuration?

SELF TEST ANSWERS

Diagnose and Resolve Issues Related to Automatic Private IP Addressing (APIPA)

1. ☑ **B.** The best TCP/IP configuration option for this environment is the option to configure all of the computers to obtain IP addresses automatically, and on the Alternate Configuration tab to select the user configured option. ICS automatically leases out IP addresses on the 192.168.0.0/24 subnet even if a DHCP server doesn't exist.

   ☒ **A** is incorrect because selecting the option to obtain an IP address automatically is correct, but not if used in conjunction with APIPA in this scenario because if the client ever failed to obtain an IP address, it would be configured with an IP on the 169.254.0.0/16 network, and it would not have a gateway to allow it to connect out to the Internet. **C** is incorrect because there is no option available to select not to use any alternate configurations. **D** is incorrect because statically configuring the IP addresses was to be avoided in this scenario.

2. ☑ **D.** APIPA assigned IP addresses are always on the 169.254.0.0/16 network, so the only valid IP address that could be returned from the **ipconfig /all** command is 169.254.1.60.

   ☒ **A, B**, and **C** are all incorrect because these addresses are not in the correct network.

Diagnose and Resolve Issues Related to Incorrect TCP/IP Configuration

3. ☑ **D.** The IP conflict icon will most likely appear for statically configured IP addresses, and denotes a conflict with another identical IP address on the network.

   ☒ **A** and **B** are incorrect because dynamically configured IP addresses are not likely to generate an IP address conflict. If a DHCP server is not available to lease an IP address or the scope has no more available IP addresses, then APIPA will automatically configure the computer with an IP address on the 169.254.0.0/16 network. **C** is incorrect because an IP address cannot be on the wrong subnet. A default gateway can be on a different subnet from the IP address, which will generate a warning, but it is the subnet that determines what network the computer is on.

4. ☑ **D.** The IP conflict icon appears when a computer attempts to use an IP address that is already in use on the network.

   ☒ **A** is incorrect because there is no requirement in Windows Server 2003 to add a server to an authorized servers list. Only DHCP servers running on Windows 2000 or Windows Server 2003 require authorization when running in an Active Directory domain. **B** and **C** are incorrect because the IP conflict icon doesn't appear when the DHCP client service is unable to obtain a leased IP address.

5. ☑   **B.** If the NIC is configured to obtain an IP address dynamically via DHCP but is unable, and the IP address defined in its alternate configuration conflicts with another IP address already in use on the network, the IP conflict icon will appear and the client will have an IP address of 0.0.0.0..

☒   **A** is incorrect because the IP conflict icon will not appear if and when the DHCP client service is unable to obtain an IP address from DHCP. **C** is incorrect because an incorrectly configured subnet mask will not cause the IP conflict message to appear. **D** is incorrect because a statically configured IP address without a gateway will not cause the IP conflict message to appear either.

Diagnose and Resolve Issues Related to DHCP Authorization

6. ☑   **B.** The DHCP scope must be activated before it can lease out IP addresses.

☒   **A** is incorrect because a stand-alone server running DHCP doesn't require authorization. **C** is incorrect because the DHCP server does not have to be a member of the Active Directory domain to lease out IP addresses to members of the domain. **D** is incorrect because the DHCP service does not require Internet access.

7. ☑   **C.** Authorizing a DHCP server requires that you must be a member of the Enterprise Admins group.

☒   **A** is incorrect because the speed of authorization isn't dependant on the size and scope of the Active Directory forest. **B** is incorrect because the authorization process does not require membership in the Schema Admins group. **D** is incorrect because the authorization process does not require an Application naming context exist.

8. ☑   **D.** No configuration is required for the DHCP servers running on Windows NT 4.0 DHCP servers. Only Windows 2000 and Windows Server 2003 DHCP servers require authorization.

☒   **A** is incorrect because Windows NT 4.0 DHCP servers do not require authorization. **B** and **C** are incorrect because the servers do not have to be added to any specific groups.

Verify DHCP Reservation Configuration

9. ☑   **A** and **D.** When used together, the **ping** and **arp -a** commands can identify the MAC address of a remote computer.

☒   **B** is incorrect because **netstat** is designed to allow you to display active TCP connections, and the ports on which the computer is listening as well as provide Ethernet statistics, the IP routing table, and statistics for both IPv4 and IPv6. **C** is incorrect because **ipconfig** is designed to allow you to display and refresh a local computer's IP configuration.

10. ☑ C. Running the **ipconfig /release** command followed by the **ipconfig /renew** on the client will result in the client obtaining the newly reserved IP address.

    ☒ A is incorrect because the **arp -a** command does not force an IP address renewal on the client. B is incorrect because the **netsh** command does not force an IP address renewal on the client. D is incorrect because there is **no /refresh** switch available for use with the **ipconfig** command.

Examine the System Event Log and DHCP Server Audit Log Files to Find Related Events

11. ☑ D. The default location for the DHCP audit logs is %windir%\system32\dhcp.

    ☒ A, B, and C are incorrect because none of these directory paths are the default location for the audit logs.

Diagnose and Resolve Issues Related to Configuration of DHCP Server and Scope Options

12. ☑ D. Nacks can be a result of the DHCP server not being authorized. If the Active Directory infrastructure team unauthorized the DHCP server over the weekend, this could be the cause of the problem.

    ☒ A is incorrect because an incorrectly defined scope option would not result in a nack. B is incorrect because a lack of a superscope would not result in a nack. C is incorrect because an unactivated scope would not result in a nack either.

Verify That the DHCP Relay Agent Is Working Correctly

13. ☑ B. Running the **ipconfig /renew** command on the DHCP client will allow you to test whether the DHCP Relay Agent is functioning. If you are able to renew the IP address, you can conclude that the Relay Agent is working properly.

    ☒ A is incorrect because the **netsh** command does not allow you to verify DHCP Relay Agent functionality. C is incorrect because the DHCP service does not include a Monitoring tab in the server's property dialog box. A Monitoring tab is found in DNS, but not DHCP. D is incorrect because **nslookup** is a DNS troubleshooting tool, not a DHCP tool.

Verify Database Integrity

14. ☑ B. jetpack is the utility that can be used to compact a DHCP database.

    ☒ A, C, and D. **netsh**, the DHCP snap-in, and compact.exe do not offer the ability to compact the DHCP database. Only jetpack provides this capability.

15. ☑ **D.** After a DHCP database is restored, it should be reconciled.

☒ **A** is incorrect because Windows Server 2003 automatically compacts the DHCP database, removing the requirement to perform the compacting operation manually. **B** and **C** are incorrect because enabling auditing and changing the permissions on the DHCP directory are optional steps that aren't required after restoring the database.

LAB ANSWER

There are a number of issues involved in the TCP/IP configuration problems. The diagnosis indicates that the DHCP server appears to be configured correctly, but the scope needs to be activated to successfully lease out IP addresses. Because the scope isn't activated, the DHCP clients are using their own alternate configuration settings to establish their IP address configurations.

The DHCP clients are receiving different IP addresses because of their different alternate configuration settings. In Windows Server 2003, you have two alternate configuration options: APIPA and user configured. Those with the default alternate configuration settings are receiving APIPA addresses on the 169.254.0.0/16 network, and are only able to communicate with one another because they are on the same subnet. The DHCP clients that are able to communicate with remote clients and access resources are configured to use the alternate user configured static IP address settings. These settings are what allow these clients to communicate with remote hosts because they provide gateway, DNS, and WINS server settings.

MICROSOFT® CERTIFIED SYSTEMS ENGINEER &
MICROSOFT® CERTIFIED SYSTEMS ADMINISTRATOR

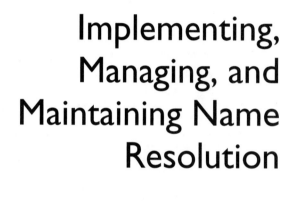

Part II

Implementing,
Managing, and
Maintaining Name
Resolution

MCSE/MCSA

MICROSOFT® CERTIFIED SYSTEMS ENGINEER &
MICROSOFT® CERTIFIED SYSTEMS ADMINISTRATOR

4

Implementing DNS

CERTIFICATION OBJECTIVES

T o pass the 70-291 certification exam, you must be very familiar with how to implement, manage, and maintain the Domain Name System (DNS). This chapter and the next two chapters will provide you with the knowledge you require to successfully prepare for the certification exam.

DNS is the de facto name resolution service on the Internet, and provides the underlying name resolution required to support Active Directory, Microsoft's Lightweight Directory Access Protocol (LDAP)–compliant directory service. The good news is that the fundamentals of DNS have not changed since Windows NT, because DNS is an open-based standard. What has changed are some of the tools and techniques used to implement, manage, and maintain the DNS service on a server running Windows Server 2003.

In this, the first of three chapters on DNS, you will learn how to install and configure the DNS service as well as how to configure server and zone options. This chapter will also introduce you to DNS forwarding, explain when DNS forwarding is useful, and show you how to configure DNS forwarding.

CERTIFICATION OBJECTIVE 4.01

Configure DNS Server Options

Before diving into the specifics of configuring the Domain Name System (DNS) server options, we'll spend a couple of minutes reviewing the basics of the DNS service and looking at the available and recommended ways to install the service.

DNS is a name resolution service that is used in TCP/IP networks that allows a user to locate computers using user-friendly Fully Qualified Domain Names (FQDNs). Computers prefer to communicate with one another by IP address on TCP/IP networks, but it is much easier for users to remember a name as opposed to an IP address, so DNS was designed to resolve the names to IP addresses for users. When a user enters a DNS name in an application such as a web browser, DNS can be configured on the client to resolve the name to its IP address. Other name resolution services also exist, such as the Windows Internet Name Service (WINS), but services such as WINS are often proprietary to a specific Independent Software Vendors (ISVs), like Microsoft in this case.

DNS is an open standard that is vendor-neutral and is supported across multiple vendor operating systems, and has become the standard name resolution service on the Internet. These days DNS is found in the majority of organizations, allowing both client computers and servers in those organizations to connect to and resolve names on the Internet.

Another reason you'll find DNS in a number of organizations is that DNS is the underlying and required name resolution service for Active Directory. Without DNS, Active Directory cannot function. One of the key changes that help to highlight this key dependency is the integration of the DNS service's installation during a domain controller promotion using **dcpromo**, something new to Windows Server 2003. The DNS service used to support Active Directory does not have to be run on the Windows platform, so even though using Microsoft's DNS service is recommended, it is not required. An alternative to Microsoft's DNS service is the Berkeley Internet Name Domain (BIND) service, generally found in heterogeneous computing environments running on UNIX or Linux servers. Regardless of the DNS implementation you select to use to support your Active Directory, the DNS service must support service resource (SRV) records, a component of DNS we will discuss later. The DNS service should also support the DNS dynamic update protocol (DDNS) and incremental zone transfer (IXFR). Although neither DDNS nor IXFR are required, they will go a long way in reducing DNS administration and bandwidth consumption. One last area that should be addressed before moving into the available options for installing DNS are the two types of queries used in DNS.

DNS Queries

DNS uses two types of queries to resolve names; recursive and iterative. *Iterative queries* request the best answer from a DNS server for a queried name. The DNS server that receives an iterative query checks its cache and the zones that it hosts for an answer, and even if the DNS server doesn't have a complete answer, it provides whatever partial answer it has. The DNS client then uses the partial answer (a referral to another DNS server) to identify the next DNS server to send its original query on to. An example of this is a DNS client querying a root DNS server for the FQDN srv1.corporate.mccaw.ca. In this case, the root DNS server's best answer may be the name of the DNS server that is authoritative for the .ca zone, so the client would again send it's FQDN query to the DNS server that is authoritative for the .ca zone. Typically, only DNS servers use iterative queries.

DNS clients generally use recursive queries that expect either a complete answer or an error code like "name does not exist" or "server failure." This does not preclude

DNS servers from also using recursive queries, however. A *recursive query* places the responsibility of resolving the query in the hands of the DNS server that receives the recursive query from the DNS client. Take for example a DNS client querying to resolve the FQDN srv1.corporate.mccaw.ca. The DNS client sends a recursive query to its preferred DNS server. This server, likely a local DNS server, checks its cache and the zones that it is authoritative for, but realizes, when it is unable to resolve the query itself, that it must send out an iterative query to the root DNS name server to assist it in finding an answer. The root DNS server responds to the iterative query with its best answer, which is the name of the .ca DNS server, and the local DNS server sends the same iterative query to the .ca DNS server in an attempt to resolve srv1.corporate.mccaw.ca. The .ca DNS server will respond with its best answer, the name of the DNS server authoritative for the mccaw.ca zone. Another iterative query is then sent to this DNS server and a response is provided that lists the name of the DNS server authoritative for the corporate.mccaw.ca zone. Finally, one last iterative query is sent to the DNS server authoritative for the corporate.mccaw.ca zone, and a response is received for the name to IP address mapping of the host srv1. The local DNS server then caches and forwards this resolved query back to the requesting client, as a response to the client's original recursive query. As you can see, the local DNS server that receives the recursive query is left to do all of the work.

Okay, now that you have a better grasp of some of the DNS fundamentals, let's take a look at the available DNS installation options.

Installing DNS

Setting up DNS in your network is not difficult, particularly in Windows Server 2003 with the new Manage Your Server wizard, which is now the recommended method for installing DNS. Don't be fooled, and try not to get turned off by the simplicity of the wizard interface. We encourage you to approach this wizard interface with an open mind. Although it is simplistic on the surface, the process that it is managing behind the scenes is much more sophisticated. The logic built into the wizard allows it to only install and enable the system services required by the service (DNS in this case) that you have chosen to install, thereby making the overall system much more secure, and the more secure a system is, the more reliable it is.

In general, when administrators are presented with a wizard, they feel as though the process they are about to embark on is not likely to be complex. When approaching the installation of DNS from only a point-and-click perspective, that assumption is likely true; however, the installation and configuration of DNS does require some careful planning to ensure that the solution you design meets the goals of the business and provides service availability within acceptable norms. Don't forget about those service level agreements (SLAs) or operating level agreements (OLAs) that are in place to measure your IT infrastructure's ongoing success.

Like many network services, you have a couple of options in how you can go about installing the DNS service. Like Windows 2000 Server, Windows Server 2003 allows the DNS service to be installed via the Add/Remove Windows Components feature found within Add or Remove Programs. Alternatively, you can insert the Windows Server 2003 CD and select to install Optional Windows Components, which will again allow you to install DNS via Add/Remove Windows Components. However, the recommended best practice for installing the DNS service on a computer running Windows Server 2003 is to use the Manage Your Server wizard, because the wizard will install and configure only the services required for the specific server role you select, in this case, DNS server. This provides you with a more secure, more locked-down server that in the end will also be more reliable. In addition to the Manage Your Server wizard, Service Pack 1 for Windows Server 2003, due out in December 2003, is expected to include the Security Configuration Wizard, which will provide administrators with a definitive list of the services required for each server role. This will allow you to further restrict security by applying a DNS server security template to the DNS server role you have configured. The Security Configuration Wizard will work in two different modes. In its simplest mode, the wizard will automatically identify the roles assigned to a server and inform the administrator and offer to disable any unnecessary services. In its more restrictive mode, the administrator will be able to instruct the wizard which roles should be assigned to a server, and the wizard will then disable all unnecessary services.

on the **job**

Service Pack 1 for Windows Server 2003, expected to be released in December 2003, will include the Security Configuration Wizard, which will allow you to apply preconfigured security templates based on a server's role.

EXERCISE 4-1

Installing DNS Using the Manage Your Server Wizard

In this exercise you will learn how to install DNS using the Manage Your Server wizard.

1. Click Start | Administrative Tools, and select Manage Your Server.

2. In the Manage Your Server dialog box shown here, click the **Add or remove a role** hyperlink.

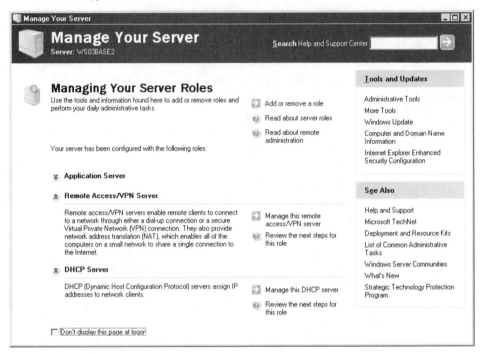

3. On the **Preliminary Steps** page of the Configure Your Server Wizard, click **Next**. The wizard will run a quick diagnostic check of the system's current configuration, and then present you with the **Server Role** page, which outlines the current role configuration.

4. On the **Server Role** page, select **DNS server** from the list of 11 roles as shown in the following illustration. Notice when you select the DNS server role, information appears with respect to that role on the right-hand side of that page allowing you to **Read about DNS servers** or **View the Configure Your Server log**. Click **Next**.

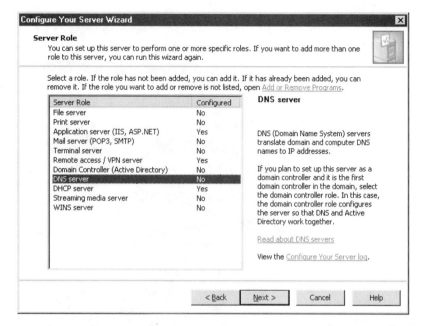

5. On the **Summary of Selections** page, confirm the selection you made, and read the options that will be executed based on that selection. Notice that if you only selected DNS server, a DNS server will be installed and then the Configure a DNS Server Wizard will run. Click **Next** and wait for the DNS service to install.

6. Once the DNS service is installed, you will be presented with the **Configure a DNS Server Wizard** dialog box. On the **Welcome** page, you can click the **DNS Checklists** button to reveal links to reference documentation that can assist in with the planning of your DNS infrastructure. Click **Next** to continue with the configuration.

7. On the **Select Configuration Action** page, shown in the following illustration, you have the choice of one of three options. The default option is to **Create a forward lookup zone**, and this is the option that you should select now. The second option is to **Create forward and reverse lookup zones**, and the third option allows you to **Configure root hints only**. Later in the chapter, in the

section titled "Configure DNS Zone Options," we will explain what each of these options means. Click **Next**.

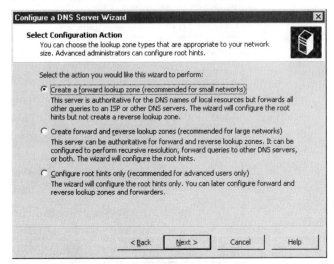

8. On the **Primary Server Location** page, shown here, leave the default option **This server maintains the zone** selected, and click **Next**. The other option on this page, **An ISP maintains the zone**, allows a corporate administrator to easily configure a secondary zone on a DNS server administered by the corporation to provide DNS server redundancy in conjunction with the ISPs DNS server.

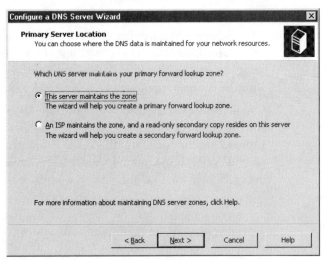

9. On the **Zone Name** page, enter the name of the zone. For example, if the domain is used to support an Active Directory domain named *corporate* in

the registered Internet domain namespace mccaw.ca, you would type the fully qualified domain name (FQDN) **corporate.mccaw.ca**, and click **Next**.

10. On the **Zone File** page, leave the default option **Create a new file with this file name** selected, and click **Next**. If you were moving an existing DNS zone from one DNS server to another, and you already had a DNS zone file, you would select the option **Use this existing file** and type the path to where the zone file is located. By default, all zone files are stored in the **%systemroot%\system32\dns** directory. Notice that the name of the file defaults to the FQDN that you specified on the Zone Name page, and has a **.dns** extension.

11. On the **Dynamic Update** page shown in the following illustration, you only have two of three options available. This is because you are installing the DNS service on a member server, not a domain controller (DC). On a DC, you would have also have the option to **Allow only secure dynamic updates**. The default option is **Do not allow dynamic updates**, but you can also select **Allow both nonsecure and secure dynamic updates**. Selecting to allow dynamic updates greatly simplifies administration, because clients that support DDNS are able to dynamically update their DNS-name-to-IP-address mapping information with DNS without any administrative intervention. Older legacy clients, such as Windows 95 and 98, which don't support dynamic updates, can also take advantage of this feature by integrating DHCP with DNS and having the DHCP server update the records on behalf of the legacy clients. Look to Chapter 3 to learn more about integrating DHCP with DNS. In this exercise, leave the default option and click **Next**.

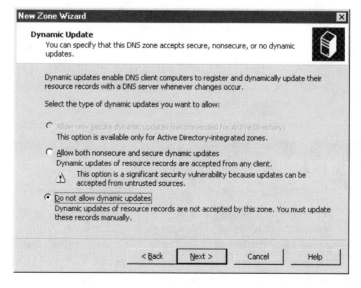

12. On the **Forwarders** page shown here, select whether you want to use forwarders, and if so, enter the IP address(es) of the DNS servers you wish to use as forwarders, and click **Next**. Configuring a forwarder on a DNS server allows requests for all domains that the DNS server is not authoritative for to be forwarded to a specific DNS server such as an internal DNS root server or the DNS server at the corporation's ISP. Windows Server 2003 also supports the use of conditional forwarders allowing you to forward queries ending in one domain name to one DNS server and queries for another domain name to another DNS server. We will explain the concept of forwarding in greater detail later in this chapter.

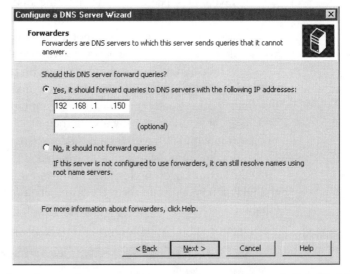

13. Confirm the configuration choices you have made, and click **Finish**.

14. In the **Configure Your Server Wizard** dialog box, click **Finish**. You have now successfully used the Configure Your Server Wizard to install and configure a DNS server.

If DNS is installed during the domain controller promotion process (dcpromo), a root zone is created. This makes the DNS server service think that it is a root Internet server, and therefore limits it from being configured to use forwarders or root hints. Best practices suggest that your DNS infrastructure be in place prior to installing Active Directory, but in some cases, such as a clean install at a new company, or for the creation of a pristine forest at an existing organization, this may not be the case.

Another option available in Windows Server 2003 for installing the DNS service is to select to have it installed automatically during the domain controller promotion (**dcpromo**) process.

Exercise 4-2 walks you through the domain controller promotion process to demonstrate the integrated DNS installation.

EXERCISE 4-2

CertCam 4-2 ON THE CD

Automating the Installation of DNS with dcpromo

In this exercise, you will learn how to select to automate the installation of the DNS service during the **dcpromo** process. This option can be used when installing your first Windows Server 2003 server in a new forest and domain on a network that doesn't currently use DNS.

1. Click **Start** | **Run**, type **dcpromo**, and click ENTER.

2. In the Active Directory Installation Wizard, on the **Welcome Page**, click **Next**.

3. On the **Operating System Compatibility** page shown here, click **Next**. What is important to note here is that the default security settings of Windows Server 2003 do not permit Windows 95 or Windows NT 4.0 with SP3 or earlier to log on to a domain controller running Windows Server 2003 or to access domain resources. However, this default functionality can be changed. The question you should ask yourself or your customer is "Do you want to degrade security to support these clients?" To learn the different ways to resolve this issue, click the **Compatibility Help** hyperlink.

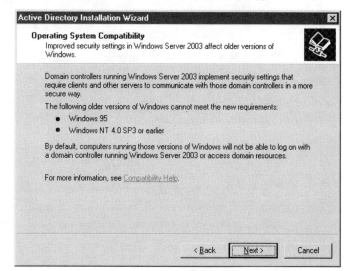

4. On the **Domain Controller Type** page, select either **Domain controller for a new domain** or **Additional domain controller for an existing domain**, and click **Next**. If you select the default option, **Domain controller for a new domain**, you will be sent to the **Create a New Domain** page, which is the option you should select in this exercise. If you select **Additional domain controller for an existing domain**, you will be taken to the **Network Credentials** page and asked to provide a user name, password, and domain of an account with sufficient privileges to install the Active Directory service on the computer.

5. On the **Create New Domain** page shown in the following illustration, select one of the three options **Domain in a new forest, Child domain in an existing domain tree**, or **Domain tree in an existing forest**, and click **Next**. In this exercise, select the default option **Domain in a new forest**.

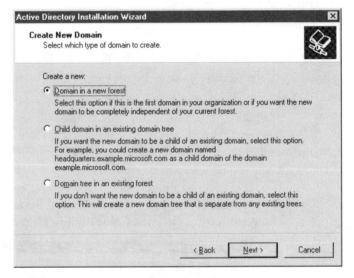

6. On the **New Domain Name** page, type the full DNS name for the new domain, and click **Next**.

7. On the **NetBIOS Domain Name** page, confirm the default name entered is correct and click **Next**. The NetBIOS domain name will always default to the child DNS domain name you specified on the New Domain Name page. For example, if you specified **corporate.mccaw.ca**, the NetBIOS domain name would default to **corporate**.

8. On the **Database and Log Folders** page, confirm or change the default directory paths, and click **Next**. It is not required, but highly recommended, to locate both the database and log folders on a partition or volume formatted with NTFS.

9. On the **Shared System Volume** page, confirm or change the default directory path, and click **Next**. Remember that the SYSVOL folder must be located on an NTFS formatted partition or volume.

10. New to the Windows Server 2003 **dcpromo** wizard is the **DNS Registration Diagnostics** page shown in the following illustration. This page is used to report any problems the wizard has detected from the DNS information you have supplied. If a problem is detected, as there is in this example, you are presented with three options. The default is **I have corrected the problem. Perform the DNS diagnostic test again**. The second option is the one that this exercise is designed to highlight, because it allows the wizard to **Install and configure the DNS server on this computer, and set this computer to use this DNS server as the preferred DNS server**. The last option, **I will correct the problem later by configuring DNS manually**, gives you the option of making the changes yourself. Select **Install and configure the DNS server on this computer, and set this computer to use this DNS server as the preferred DNS server**, and click **Next**.

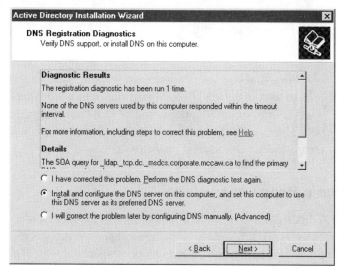

11. On the **Permissions** page, click **Next**.

12. Type and confirm a password on the **Directory Services Restore Mode Administration Password** page, and click **Next**.

13. Click **Next** on the **Summary** page, and when the promotion is complete, click **Finish**. One of the other new options you will notice during the promotion is that during the installation and configuration of DNS, you have the option to **Skip the DNS installation**.

INSIDE THE EXAM

New DNS Features in Windows Server 2003

There have been some noteworthy changes made to the DNS service in Windows Server 2003. DNS will be a major component in a number of the Windows Server 2003 certification exams.

New features in DNS include conditional forwarding, stub zones, and the ability to store Active Directory integrated zones within a new AD directory partition called the *application directory partition*.

Conditional forwarding allows you to configure a DNS server to forward to specific DNS servers based upon the domain name specified in the DNS query.

Stub zones provide you with a means of making DNS name query resolution more efficient while reducing the amount of required administration.

Members of the Domain Admins and Enterprise Admins groups are now able to create application directory partitions, which are capable of storing dynamic content such as DNS zone information, and provide you with great flexibility in designing your DNS replication topology.

Now that you are familiar with installing the DNS service, you can shift your focus to configuring DNS, which will include learning about how to configure DNS server options, zone options, and DNS forwarding.

The next area to turn your attention to is the configuration of the DNS server through the DNS server properties pages.

DNS Server Properties

In this section, you will learn about all of the DNS server options available in Windows Server 2003. You can modify the configuration of a specific DNS server with the different tabs found on the DNS server properties pages.

EXERCISE 4-3

Opening the DNS Snap-in

In this exercise, you will learn how to open the DNS snap-in. The DNS snap-in can be accessed a number of different ways. You can open a new MMC console and add individual snap-ins to it, or you can access it through either of the built-in **Computer Management** or **DNS** snap-ins, or by selecting **Manage Your Server**.

1. Click **Start | Administrative Tools**, and click **DNS**.
2. To access the properties of the DNS server, right-click the name of the DNS server, and select **Properties**.

Before you dive into the options on the different tabs in the DNS server properties, you'll notice the first change to the DNS snap-in as soon as you open the MMC. The Windows Server 2003 DNS snap-in includes an Event Viewer folder, which contains the DNS Events log. This lets you troubleshoot DNS issues from within the DNS snap-in, a nice management feature, again helping to make you more efficient in your administration. Another important point worth noting is that a command-line DNS administration tool named **dnscmd.exe** is available in the support\tools folder included on the Windows Server 2003 CD. The utility enables you to perform all of your DNS administration from the command line, as an alternative to using the GUI DNS MMC.

To access the DNS servers properties dialog box, open the DNS snap-in as explained in Exercise 4-3 and right-click the name of the DNS server and select properties. Also note the new options available on the context menu, such as **Launch nslookup** and **Export List**.

When the DNS server properties dialog box appears, you will see either seven or eight tabs. Seven tabs are displayed when the DNS service is running on a Windows Server 2003 member server, and an eighth tab, Security, appears when the DNS service is running on a Windows Server 2003 domain controller. Let's explore the configuration options available on each of these eight tabs.

Interfaces

The **Interfaces** tab, shown in Figure 4-1, allows you to define the interfaces that you want the DNS server service to listen on. This provides you with a granular level of control in your DNS server configuration by allowing you to define exactly what network interface cards (NICs) the DNS service is bound to.

Use the Interfaces tab when you want to isolate the DNS service to a specific subnet on a multi-homed server. This technique can be used in small, medium, and large companies. In smaller organizations, DNS may be used for internal DNS name resolution, providing support for Active Directory, but for Internet name resolution, external DNS servers at your ISP might be used. Another example of where this tab can be used in your configuration is in circumstances where your ISP does not permit

FIGURE 4-1

Specifying DNS
service bindings

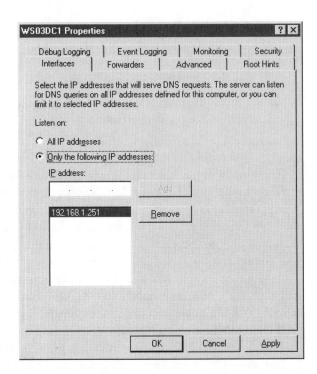

the operation of DNS servers on their network. In many smaller organizations or home-based businesses, you might require the DNS service be installed and running on the same server that runs network address translation (NAT), and that is connected to your ISP's network. Using the interfaces tab, you can select that only the internal interface be used to listen for DNS queries by selecting the **Only the following IP addresses** option on the Interfaces tab and then adding the IP address of the internal interface. This would allow the external interface to remain connected to the ISP's network and not violate your ISP connection agreement, because the DNS server service would not be bound to the interface used to establish your Internet connection.

Take a look at an example to make sure you have a complete understanding of this concept. Figure 4-2 shows a small corporate network that uses the 192.168.1.0/24 network as its LAN. A single computer, configured with two NICs, runs Windows Server 2003 and ISA Server. This computer is connected via NIC1 to the LAN, and via NIC2 to the ISP's network, and provides shared Internet access to all of the employees in the company. NIC1 is statically configured with an IP address of 192.168.1.251, and this address is the gateway address used by all computers on the LAN. NIC2 is configured to obtain an IP address dynamically from the ISP's DHCP server. The ISP agreement prevents you from running the DNS server service on NIC2, but you must run the DNS server service on the Windows Server 2003 computer. By using the Interfaces tab and

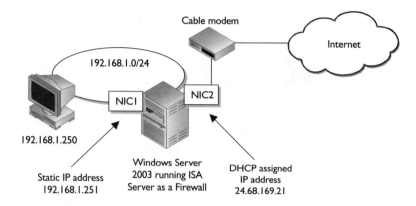

FIGURE 4-2

Defining DNS
server service
bindings

configuring **Only the following IP addresses** option and entering in the IP address
192.168.1.251 as shown in Figure 4-1, you can still run the DNS service without
violating your agreement with your ISP.

The default setting on the Interfaces tab is to listen on **All IP addresses**, which is
ideal for other architectures. It is quite common to have a single DNS server provide
name resolution services to clients on a variety of networks. A multi-homed DNS
server that is connected to multiple subnets will be configured by default to listen on

FIGURE 4-3

The Forwarders
tab

> **WS03DC1 Properties** ? ☒
>
> | Debug Logging | Event Logging | Monitoring | Security |
> | Interfaces | Forwarders | Advanced | Root Hints |
>
> Forwarders are servers that can resolve DNS queries not answered by this
> server. Forward queries for names in the following DNS domains.
>
> DNS do_main:
>
> All other DNS domains   New...
>
>   Remove
>
> To add a forwarder, select a DNS domain, type the forwarder's IP address
> below, and then click Add.
>
> Selected domain's forwarder IP address list:
>
> .   .   .   Add
>
>   Remove
>
>   Up
>
>   Down
>
> Number of seconds before forward queries time out: 5
>
> ☐ Do not use recursion for this domain
>
>   OK   Cancel   Apply

all of the subnets and provide name resolution services to clients on each of those networks, as well as to clients that connect through gateways on additional networks.

Forwarders

A *forwarder* is a DNS server on a network that other DNS servers are configured to use, and to whom they forward DNS queries for external DNS domain names that they are unable to resolve locally. Windows Server 2003 includes a new DNS feature known as *conditional forwarders*, which allow you to forward queries for specific domain names to specific DNS servers.

By default, the DNS server service included in Windows Server 2003 is configured to forward queries for **All other DNS domains** to an external DNS server listed on the **Forwarders** tab of the DNS server's properties. This default configuration is displayed in Figure 4-3.

Forwarders are discussed in more detail later in this chapter in the section titled "Configure DNS Forwarding."

Advanced

The **Advanced** tab of the DNS server properties shown in Figure 4-4 offers you a number of additional, advanced configuration options. At the top of the dialog box is the **Server version number**, which isn't configurable, but is included to allow you to quickly identify both the server version and the version of DNS running on the computer. As you can see from Figure 4-4, this screen shot was taken from a server running build 3790 and using DNS version 5.2.

Toward the bottom of the tab you have the ability to configure **Name Checking**. Multibyte UTF-8 is the default name checking method used in all Windows-based DNS services since Windows 2000, and is the preferred name checking method for all private DNS servers that do not provide name resolution on the Internet.

Internet host names were originally restricted to the character set specified in Request for Comments (RFC) 952 and 1123, which limited names to using uppercase and lowercase letters, the numerals 0 through 9, and hyphens (-). These RFCs also specified that the first character of the DNS name could be a numeral, and that names must be encoded using US-ASCII–based characters. At the international level, however, these requirements posed significant limitations, preventing extended character sets used for local naming standards. Support for UTF-8 is intended to help remove these limitations by expanding DNS character support beyond the RFC specification and providing enhanced default support for a Unicode transformation format. UTF-8 provides support for extended ASCII characters and translation of UCS-2, a 16-bit Unicode character set. Support for UTF-8 allows UTF-8 encoded

FIGURE 4-4

DNS server
properties
Advanced tab

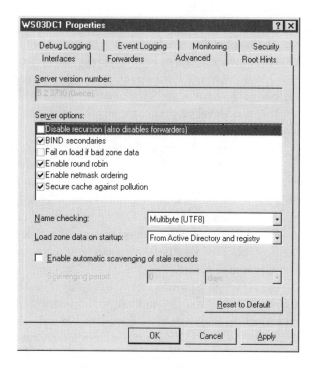

characters to be received, loaded and stored in the DNS zone database files and full
compatibility remains for traditional US-ASCII data encoding.

on the
Job

To learn more about the different name checking options available in
Windows Server 2003 DNS, look to _http://www.microsoft.com/technet/treeview_
/default.asp?url=/technet/prodtechnol/windowsserver2003/proddocs/standard
_/sag_DNS_und_UnicodeCharacterSupport.asp._

Another configurable option on the Advanced tab is the **Load zone data on**
startup option. By default, the DNS server loads data from both Active Directory
and the registry. The registry is simply a database repository for information about the
configuration of a computer, and acts as searchable repository for the operating system.
Other available options in the drop-down box include **From registry** and **From file**.
Leaving the default option **From Active Directory and registry** is the recommended
best practice in Active Directory environments, because it allows the local registry
data to be supplemented with zone data that is stored in Active Directory integrated
zones. Selecting the **From file** option requires that the file used be a text file named
Boot and that the Boot file be stored in the %systemroot%\system32\Dns directory.

The last of the options found on the Advanced tab includes the **Enable automatic scavenging of stale records** option. This option is not enabled by default, but can be enabled when you are working with primary zones. Aging and scavenging can be enabled either at the DNS server, as we are discussing here, or for selected zones. Enabling automatic scavenging of stale records at the server level determines the effect of zone-level properties for any Active Directory integrated zones that are loaded at the server.

Aging refers to the age of the resource record in the DNS zone database and uses the time-to-live (TTL) of the resource record to determine its age. Scavenging is the process that the DNS server can be configured to perform whereby it searches for old records whose TTLs have expired and deletes those records from the DNS zone. Scavenging helps to keep the DNS zone database accurate and up to date.

The default scavenging period of seven days is generally sufficient. However, it is configurable, so if your circumstances require a short or longer period, you can make the appropriate change.

The scavenging process can be manually initiated, or automated to occur at regular intervals. You can start manual scavenging by right-clicking the DNS server and selecting **Scavenge Stale Resource Records**. Automatic scavenging is also configured by right-clicking on the DNS server and selecting **Set Aging/Scavenging for All Zones**. With automatic scavenging, the default scavenging period is every 24 hours, and the minimum allowed value is every 60 minutes.

The **server options** section on the Advanced tab of the DNS server properties lets you set a number of advanced DNS configuration options, discussed in the following sections.

Disable recursion   The first option in the **Server options** section is one that we will discuss later in this chapter, the **Disable recursion** option. Enabling this option prevents you from using forwarders on the DNS server. By default, recursion is enabled for the DNS service.

BIND secondaries   Support for BIND secondaries is enabled by default in Windows Server 2003 DNS. By default, all Windows-based DNS servers use fast zone transfer format, which uses compression, and supports the transmission of multiple resource records (RRs) in each TCP message during a zone transfer. More recent versions of BIND, versions 4.9.4 and later, also support this format; however, if you are integrating with an older BIND version, having this option enabled will allow a Windows Server 2003 DNS server to transfer a zone using the slower, uncompressed transfer format. With the **BIND secondaries** option enabled, no fast transfers are made.

The Windows Server 2003 DNS development team has performed interoperability testing on the following versions of BIND: 4.9.7, 8.1.2, 8.2, and 9.1.0. If you are not integrating with legacy BIND implementations, consider disabling the BIND secondaries option.

Fail on load if bad zone data   By default, the Windows Server 2003 DNS service logs data errors, but ignores any incorrect data in the zone files and continues to load the zone. This default can be changed by enabling **Fail on load if bad zone data** so that if zone data is identified as incorrect, the zone will fail to load.

Enable round robin   Round-robin DNS is enabled by default, allowing the DNS server to rotate the list of resource records (RRs) when multiple RRs of the same type exist. Round-robin is a partial load-balancing mechanism that allows you to distribute network resource loads. I say *partial*, because round-robin isn't intelligent, like network load balancing (NLB), and will continue to resolve queries by providing name-to-IP-address mappings of servers that are currently unavailable.

This feature is designed to rotate in a round-robin fashion, meaning that if you have a list of three resource records that match a query, the first record is sent out in response to the first query, then the second record is sent out to the second query, followed by the third record to the third query. The fourth query is then sent the first IP in the list, and the process starts over. The problem with this method is that if the second server in the list is offline for whatever reason, its IP address is still sent out in response to the query. Therefore, by itself, round robin is not a complete load-balancing solution. What it does provide for is a simple way to load-balance client DNS requests for frequently queried multi-homed servers, such as web servers.

When round-robin is disabled, the order of the response to an incoming query is based on the static order of the RRs in the zone database file. Take a look at an example of using round-robin DNS to ensure you have a complete understanding of this feature.

A client sends a forward lookup-type query for a multi-homed server named www.mccaw.ca. The multi-homed host www has three IP addresses, and each IP address has a separate host (A) resource record in the mccaw.ca zone. These records appear in the following order:

```
www   IN A 10.0.0.100
www   IN A 10.0.0.101
www   IN A 10.0.0.102
```

In response to the first DNS client's query for www.mccaw.ca, the DNS server responds by sending the list in the same order listed in the preceeding. When a second DNS client send a query to resolve www.mccaw.ca, it receives the list with the IP address order of 10.0.0.101, 10.0.0.102, 10.0.0.100. If a third client were to query to resolve www.mccaw.ca it would receive the list with the IP address order of 10.0.0.102, 10.0.0.100, 10.0.0.101.

By default, DNS round-robin applies to all RR types; however, you can specify certain RR types be excluded in the round-robin rotation through a registry edit. To prevent specific RR types from being rotated by round-robin DNS, open **regedt32**, browse to the **HKEY_LOCAL_MACHINE\System\CurrentControlSet\Services\DNS \Parameters** key, and create a new string value called **DoNotRoundRobinTypes** (REG_SZ) with a string value that contains a list of RR type that you want to exclude. For example, if you wanted to prevent round-robin rotation for A, PTR, and SRV resource record types, the string value you enter would be **a ptr srv**. To restrict round-robin for all RR types, create a new REG_DWORD value called **RoundRobin** and set the data value to 0.

on the
job

For multi-homed names, local subnet priority supercedes the use of round-robin rotation, and when round-robin is enabled, it continues to be a secondary method used to sort multiple RRs returned in a listed answer.

Enable netmask ordering   In Windows Server 2003, the DNS service uses something known as *local subnet prioritizing*, aka netmask ordering, by default to give preference to IP addresses on the same network when a query resolves to a host name that is mapped to more than one IP address. The local subnet prioritizing feature requires that the client application attempt to connect to the host that is closest, which also usually means that the faster connection will be used, improving the end user's experience.

Here's an example of local subnet priority. A DNS client on the 10.0.0.1/24 subnet sends a query to a DNS server for a multi-homed server named File1. The DNS server determines that local subnet prioritization is required to order the query response by looking in the DNS zone to see if more than one A resource record matches the queried host name. If only a single A resource record exists or if the IP network address of the client doesn't match the IP network address of any one of the RRs, no prioritization is required. Because two A resource records exist, the DNS service determines which records match the requesting client's local subnet. Then the DNS service reorders the answer list so that A RRs that match the local subnet of the requesting client are moved to the top of the answer list, and then this reordered list is sent to the client.

Secure cache against pollution   By default, Windows Server 2003 DNS servers secure the DNS cache against pollution by using a secure response option, which prevents adding unrelated RRs that are included in a referral to their cache. The DNS server's cache plays a key role in improving the performance of referral answers by allowing a DNS server to return previously cached responses to new queries for the same name.

Enabling this feature allows the DNS service to decide whether or not to cache a referred name. The DNS server makes this determination by looking at whether or not the referral is part of the exact, related DNS domain name tree for which the original query was made. For example, if the original query was made for na.corporate.mccaw.ca, and a referral answer provided a record for a name not in the mccaw.ca domain name tree, that name would not be cached.

Root Hints

Windows Server 2003 DNS servers follow a specific resolution process when attempting to resolve a FQDN to an IP address. First, the DNS service queries its local cache, then it checks its zone records, it can be configured to then forward requests to forwarders, and finally it attempts resolution using its root servers. The root servers that a DNS server knows to use are configured on the **Root Hints** tab of the DNS server properties.

If DNS is installed during the domain controller promotion process (**dcpromo**), a root zone is created. The DNS service then thinks that the DNS server is a root Internet server, and as a root Internet server, it cannot be configured to use forwarders or root hints. Exercise 4-4 explains how to remove a root DNS zone.

EXERCISE 4-4

Removing a Root DNS Zone

In this exercise, you will learn how to remove a root DNS zone. You will have to do this if you have run **dcpromo** and selected to have DNS installed during the domain controller promotion process, and now you wish to use forwarders or root hints.

1. Click **Start** | **Administrative Tools**, and select **DNS**.

2. In the DNS snap-in, click the **+** to the left of the DNS server to expand the DNS server and reveal **Event Viewer**, **Forward Lookup Zones** and **Reverse Lookup Zones**.

3. Expand **Forward Lookup Zones**.

4. Right click the **.** representing the root DNS zone and click **Delete**.

The root hints are simply DNS data stored on a DNS server that identifies the authoritative DNS servers for the root zones of the DNS namespace. The root hints are stored in the file named **cache.dns**, which is located in the **%systemroot% \system32\dns directory**.

On the Root Hints tab shown in Figure 4-5, you can easily make changes to the root hints servers. Simply click **Add** to add a new root hints server or select an existing root hints entry, and click **Edit** to make changes. Select an existing entry and click **Remove** to delete an existing entry. A new option in Windows Server 2003 DNS also allows you to copy the **cache.dns** file from another DNS server by clicking **Copy from Server** and entering the IP address of the DNS server you want to copy the file from.

Debug Logging

The **Debug Logging** tab shown in Figure 4-6 is new to Windows Server 2003 DNS, and provides you with the ability to configure advanced logging to assist in troubleshooting DNS related problems. Debug logging is disabled by default. To enable debug logging, place a check mark in the box to the left of **Log packets for debugging**. To get useful debugging information in the log file, be sure to select a **Packet direction**, a **Transport**

FIGURE 4-5

Root Hints

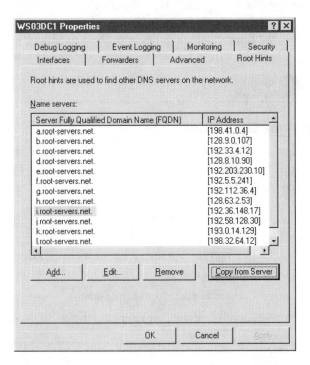

FIGURE 4-6

The Debug
Logging tab

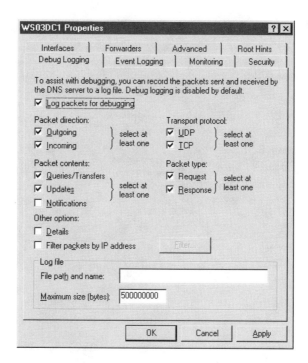

protocol, and one or more options, such as **Queries/Transfers**, **Request**, **Response**, **Updates**, or **Notification**. As you can see in Figure 4-6, you can also select to **Filter packets by IP address** and set the **File path and name** as well as the maximum size for the log. By default, **Dns.log** is the file located in **%windir%\system32\Dns** that contains debug logging information.

Event Logging

On the **Event Logging** tab, shown in Figure 4-7, you can configure the types of events that the DNS event log records. By default, the DNS event log, which is now included in the DNS snap-in, logs all events, but as you can see in Figure 4-7, the other options include **No events**, **Errors only**, and **Errors and warnings**.

Monitoring

The **Monitoring** tab, shown in Figure 4-8, provides you with the ability to test the DNS service by running either a simply query against the local DNS server or a reverse query against another DNS server. By enabling either of the test options, you can click **Test Now**, and manually force a test, or you can select to perform automatic testing at configurable intervals.

FIGURE 4-7

The Event
Logging tab

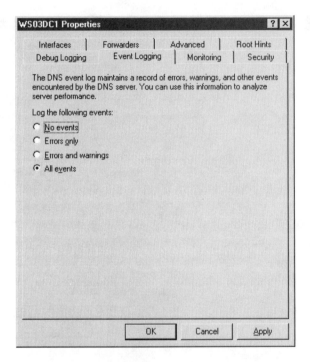

FIGURE 4-8

The Monitoring
tab

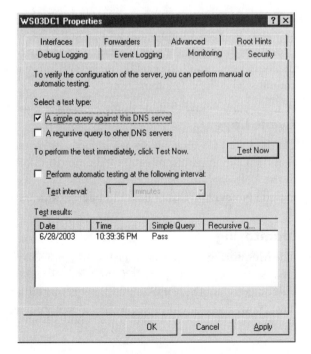

Security

The **Security** tab allows you to configure the access permissions for the DNS server. There are a few new features here worth mentioning, as they go a long way toward the goal of simplifying DNS administration. Clicking the Advanced button on the Security tab reveals the **Advanced Security Settings for Microsoft DNS** dialog box shown in Figure 4-9. The first thing to notice is the new tab at the top of this dialog box named **Effective Permissions**. Selecting the Effective Permissions tab allows you to select a user or group and have the operating system present you with that user's or group's effective permissions. This is a fabulous new improvement. A second nice addition can be seen in Figure 4-9 in the form of the **Default** button. If you ever want to revert to the default settings, you can do so by clicking the Default button.

At this point, you are familiar with all eight of the DNS server properties tabs and how to configure DNS server options. In the next section of this chapter we will explore the different types of zones available in the DNS service in Windows Server 2003, and how to configure these DNS zones.

FIGURE 4-9 Advanced Permissions

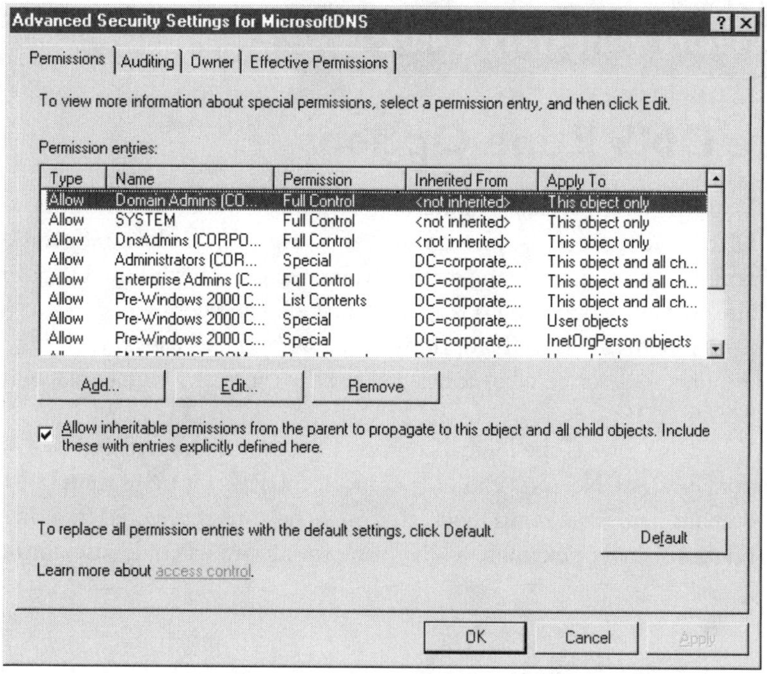

SCENARIO & SOLUTION

How can you configure a multi-homed DNS server to only listen on a single NIC?	In the DNS server properties, you can configure the NIC(s) that DNS is bound to on the Interfaces tab.
You have selected to have the DNS service installed during the **dcpromo** process. What default DNS configuration does that configure for you, and what limitations does it provide?	When the DNS service is installed through the **dcpromo** process, a root DNS server is installed. Forwarding is disabled on root DNS servers.
What other means are available in the DNS console to disable forwarding on the DNS server?	Selecting to **Disable recursion** on the Advanced tab of the DNS server properties will disable forwarding for the entire DNS server. Selecting to disable recursion at the bottom of the Forwarders tab allows you to disable forwarding for a specific conditional forwarding entry.
What two tools or utilities are available to administer the DNS service on a server running Windows Server 2003?	Both the DNS MMC and **dnscmd.exe** can be used to administer the DNS service.

CERTIFICATION OBJECTIVE 4.02

Configure DNS Zone Options

With the DNS service installed and a thorough understanding of how to configure the DNS server properties, you can shift your attention to the configuration of DNS zone options. Depending on the method you selected to install the DNS service, you may already have a Forward Lookup Zone installed and configured.

Before diving into the options available for DNS zones, we'll take a couple of minutes to describe what zones are and the types of zones available in Windows Server 2003.

A *DNS zone* is the logical container for the resource records for one or more domains. A DNS zone can only contain the RRs for more than one domain if the domain names are contiguous, that is, if they are connected by a direct parent-child relationship. For example a DNS zone for mccaw.ca could also contain the RRs for corporate.mccaw.ca because this namespace is contiguous, whereas the DNS zone for mccaw.ca could not contain the RRs for corporate.todaytoronto.com.

Allowing DNS namespaces to be divided up into zones, and having zone files maintained on DNS servers authoritative for those zones, provides DNS with scalability. Zone files can be stored in one of two ways in Windows Server 2003 DNS. They can be stored in a zone file, a text file named after the name of the zone and ending in **.dns** found in the **%systemroot%\system32\dns directory**; or they can be stored in the Active Directory database in the form of an Active Directory integrated zone. A DNS server is *authoritative* for a zone if it hosts the RRs for the names and addresses that the clients request in the zone file.

Zone Types

In the DNS service in Windows Server 2003 a zone can be *primary*, *secondary*, or a *stub* zone type, and each of these zone types can be either a *forward* or *reverse* lookup zone. Forward lookup zones provide name to IP address resolution where reverse lookup zones provide IP address to name resolution. Each of the different zone types, primary, secondary, or stub, can be configured as forward or reverse lookup depending on what you want to accomplish. Forward lookup zones are required for Active Directory name resolution where reverse lookup zones are optional. These different zone types allow you to design a DNS infrastructure that meets the needs of your business.

Primary Zones

A primary zone is the authoritative copy of the DNS zone. Resource records are created and modified in a primary zone. Think of a primary zone as being similar to a primary domain controller (PDC) in Windows NT 4.0. In a Windows NT 4.0 domain model, changes to the SAM database could only be made on the PDC, because the Windows NT 4.0 domain model used single-master replication. A primary DNS zone is similar in that new RRs can only be created on the DNS server hosting the primary zone, and are then replicated out to DNS servers hosting secondary zones through a process known as a *zone transfer*.

Normally, proper planning of your DNS infrastructure will result in the primary zone being located in the same physical location as the administrators who will manage and maintain your DNS infrastructure. Exercise 4-5 shows how to create a primary forward lookup zone.

Creating a Primary Forward Lookup Zone

In this exercise, you will learn how to create a primary forward lookup zone. Following the steps in this exercise will provide you with the knowledge required to establish the first DNS server in your planned DNS architecture.

1. Click **Start | Administrative Tools**, and select DNS.

2. In the DNS snap-in, expand the name of your DNS server.

3. Right click Forward Lookup Zones, and select **New Zone**.

4. The **New Zone Wizard** appears. On the **Welcome** page, click **Next**.

5. Notice on the **Zone Type** page, shown in the following illustration, that you have three zone type options, as discussed earlier. The default is a primary zone and the other two options are a secondary zone and a stub zone. Also notice at the bottom of the page that you have the option of storing the zone in the Active Directory. This option is only available when you create a zone on a domain controller, because member servers do not maintain a copy of the Active Directory database. Leave the defaults selected and click **Next**.

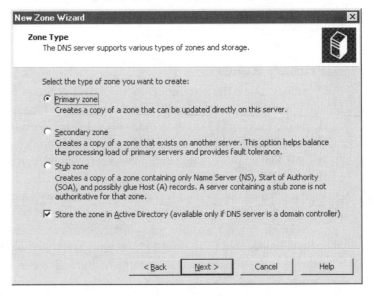

6. The next page in the Wizard, the **Active Directory Zone Replication Scope** page, shown in the following illustration, is new to Windows Server 2003. On this page, you can select how you want the zone data to be replicated. The default is **To all domain controllers in the Active Directory domain corporate.mccaw.ca**, the local domain. However, you can choose one of three additional options. The third option, **To all domain controllers specified in the scope of the following application directory partition**, will only be available if you have created an application directory partition previously using **ntdsutil**. However, you can also select **To all DNS servers in the Active Directory forest corporate.mccaw.ca** or **To all DNS servers in the Active Directory domain corporate.mccaw.ca**. Select the default option if you want to replicate the DNS information to DNS servers running Windows 2000 Server that are also configured as domain controllers. Click **Next**.

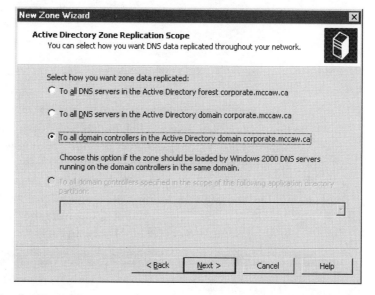

7. On the **Zone Name** page, type a name for the zone. The zone name should specify the portion of the DNS namespace for which the DNS server is authoritative. For example, if you have purchased a domain name called ggtopcoolbrands.com, and you are creating a primary forward lookup zone for this domain, you would type **ggtopcoolbrands.com**, and click **Next**.

8. On the **Dynamic Update** page, shown next, you can select the type of dynamic updates you want to allow. The default is **Allow only secure dynamic updates**,

and this is the recommended option for zones used for Active Directory. The other two options available to you include **Allow both nonsecure and secure dynamic updates** and **Do not allow dynamic updates**. Click **Next**.

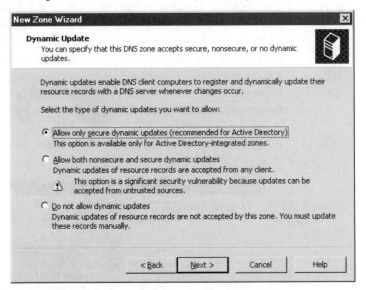

9. On the completion page, click **Finish**, and the new primary forward lookup zone will be created based upon the configuration you specified. Now if you expand **Forward Lookup Zones** in the DNS snap-in you will see the new primary forward lookup zone. Selecting the zone will reveal the two default entries, shown in the following illustration, that are created during the zone creation process. These two entries identify the Start of Authority (SOA) and the Name Server (NS) for the new primary zone.

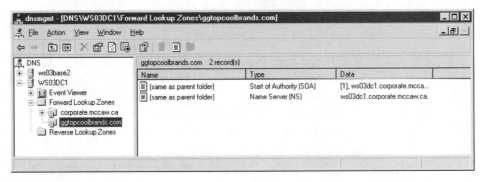

The use of primary zones dates back to the introduction of DNS, and zones are supported across different implantations of DNS. Their original single-master replication model can be limiting, however. As you learned in Exercise 4-5, if a primary zone is being created on a Windows 2000 Server or Windows Server 2003 domain controller, the primary zone can be configured to be Active Directory integrated. This option has a number of significant benefits. First, instead of storing the DNS zone information in a text file, it is stored in the Active Directory as an object, and therefore replicates as a part of Active Directory replication, meaning that zone transfers are no longer required. Also new to Windows Server 2003 Active Directory and DNS is the ability to configure the AD zone replication scope as shown in Exercise 4-5. You can now select from three different options of where you want the zone data to be replicated. The default selection is to replicate the zone data to all domain controllers in the Active Directory domain that the domain controller is a member of. This is the same location where the zone data was stored in Windows 2000 Server, the domain naming context. Remember that domain controllers separate Active Directory data into different *naming contexts* or *partitions*. In Windows 2000 Active Directory, domain controllers contained three partitions: domain, configuration, and schema partitions. Selecting the default option stores the DNS zone data in the domain partition, and this partition only replicates to other domain controllers within the domain.

e**x**a m
w a t c h
By default, only members of the Domain Admins and the Enterprise Admins groups can create a DNS application directory partition.

Windows Server 2003 Active Directory introduces a new naming context known as the *application partition*. The application partition provides the ability to store dynamic data, likely DNS RRs, that can change depending on the IP address leased to the client. It also lets you govern which domain controllers the application partition exists on. The application partition was introduced to enable administrators to be more granular in how they configure AD-integrated DNS, and where that information gets stored. One of the primary reasons the application partition was included in the Windows Server 2003 Active Directory was to address a major customer pain area. A number of large organizations have geographically dispersed offices. In some cases, these remote offices have local domain controllers that are members of the organization's single-domain forest. In Windows 2000, if you decided to integrate DNS with AD, that DNS zone information replicated to all DCs, and you had no control over which DCs it replicated to, which made granular control over replication traffic very difficult. The use of the application directory partition in Windows Server 2003 AD allows you to select where you want this DNS zone data object to replicate to, which brings us to the other two available options.

As shown in Exercise 4-5, the Active Directory Zone Replication Scope page allows you to select a fourth option, **To all domain controllers specified in the scope of the following application directory partition**. By default, this option is not enabled because an application directory partition must be created first. Creating an application directory partition is more of an Active Directory topic and not likely something you will see on the 70-291 certification exam, but it is important knowledge for you to have, so cover how to create an application directory partition in Exercise 4-6.

EXERCISE 4-6

Creating an Application Directory Partition

In this exercise, you will learn how to create an application directory partition that will be used to store AD integrated DNS zone data.

1. Log on to the domain as an ordinary user. Click **Start | Programs | Accessories**, and right-click **Command Prompt**. From the context menu, select **Runas**, select **The following user**, and enter the user name of an account that is a member of the Enterprise Admins group and a password for that account. Click **OK**.

2. The command prompt opens, running in the security context of the user with Domain Admin or Enterprise Admin permissions. Type **ntdsutil** and press ENTER.

3. Now, at the **ntdsutil** prompt, type **domain management** and press ENTER. This will allow you to execute domain management commands within the **ntdsutil** utility.

4. Type **connection** and press ENTER. This will put you into the connection context and allow you to select a domain controller that you wish to connect to.

5. Type **connect to server ws03dc1** and press ENTER, where ws03dc1 is the name of the domain controller you are connection to.

6. Type **quit** and press ENTER.

7. Type **create nc dc=appdns1,dc=corporate,dc=mccaw,dc=ca** and press ENTER.

8. Close the command prompt. Now within the DNS snap-in, right-click the DNS zone and select Properties. On the **General** tab, when you select to change the replication scope, on the **Active Directory Zone Replication Scope** page, the fourth option is available.

e x a m

ⓦ **a t c h**

If you are changing the storage of a DNS zone from the domain partition to an application directory partition in a Windows 2000 AD domain, the DC holding the Domain Naming Flexible

Single Master of Operations (FSMO) role also known as an Operations Master role must be transferred to the Windows Server 2003 DC for the DNS application directory partitions to exist.

Selecting to replicate the DNS zone data to all DNS servers in the AD forest allows for complete forest-wide replication to all DNS servers, as opposed to only domain-wide replication. This allows for the DNS zone data to be available on domain controllers outside of the original domain in a multi-domain forest, which can be useful when configuring corporate-wide name resolution. The other available option is to all DNS servers in the current AD domain, which means that if the DNS service isn't installed on one of five domain controllers, the one DC that is not running DNS will not receive the DNS zone data. This is ideal when the DC is located across a slow WAN connection and you haven't installed DNS on the DC, and therefore you don't need to use valuable WAN bandwidth to replicate DNS zone data that isn't required on the remote DC.

e x a m

ⓦ **a t c h**

Expect to know when to use the different zone configuration options based upon the goals you are trying to achieve.

Another benefit of AD integration is the ability to configure more restrictive permissions and further limit the computers that can dynamically update their DNS information to members of the domain.

o n t h e

Ⓙ **o b** *AD-integrated DNS zone data cannot be stored in Active Directory in Application Mode (ADAM). ADAM allows you to run AD as a service on a member server. To learn more about ADAM, search the Microsoft site for the ADAM white paper titled adam.doc.*

Secondary Zones

Secondary zones represent read-only copies of the DNS zone. This means that like the records found on a Windows NT 4.0 BDC, they can be read, but no changes can be made to them.

SCENARIO & SOLUTION

What is the default DNS zone replication scope in Windows Server 2003?	The **All DNS servers in the Active Directory domain** option is the default DNS zone replication scope option in Windows Server 2003. The replicates the zone data to all DNS servers running on DCs in the domain.
What DNS zone replication scope option should you select if you are running DNS on both Windows Server 2003 and Windows 2000 Servers?	The **All domain controllers in the Active Directory domain** option should be selected when running the DNS service on computers running both Windows 2000 and Windows Server 2003.
What DNS zone replication scope option requires that you manually create a new application directory partition? What tool or utility can you use to do this?	The **All domain controllers in a specified application directory partition** option requires that you first manually create an application directory partition. This can be done with the **ntdsutil** utility.
What is the last zone replication option available to you in Windows Server 2003, and where does it replicate to?	The **All DNS servers in the Active Directory forest** option replicates zone data to all DNS servers running on DCs in the forest.

To make changes, you must connect to the DNS server hosting the primary zone. For fault tolerance, it is very common to configure at least one secondary server, although for scalability, multiple secondary servers can be configured and geographically dispersed to provide local name resolution throughout an organization. Even though the RR information cannot be changed locally on DNS servers hosting secondary zones, the data can be used for name resolution by local clients.

Secondary zones are commonly found in networks that utilize primary zones. It is quite common to find a primary and multiple secondary zones hosted on UNIX BIND DNS implementations at larger organizations. Creating a secondary zone on a server running Windows Server 2003 allows the zone database file to be replicated to the Windows Server 2003 DNS server from the UNIX server hosting the primary zone. Exercise 4-7 walks you through the process of creating a secondary zone.

EXERCISE 4-7

CertCam 4-7 ON THE CD

Creating a Secondary Forward Lookup Zone

In this exercise, you will learn how to create a secondary forward lookup zone. Following the steps in this exercise will provide you with the knowledge required to establish redundancy in your standard DNS server architecture through the introduction of a DNS server that maintains a read-only copy (secondary zone) of your standard DNS zone file.

1. Click **Start | Administrative Tools**, and select **DNS**.

2. In the DNS snap-in, expand the name of your DNS server.

3. Right click Forward Lookup Zones, and select **New Zone**.

4. The **New Zone Wizard** appears. On the **Welcome** page, click **Next**.

5. Notice on the **Zone Type** page, shown earlier in Exercise 4-5, that you have three zone type options as discussed earlier. The default is to create a primary zone. Select **Secondary zone** and notice at the bottom of the page the option to storeing the zone in the Active Directory becomes grayed out. This is because you are not allowed to make configuration changes for a secondary zone, instead all configuration changes must be made to the properties of the primary zone and then replicated to the DNS servers hosting the secondary zones.

6. The next page in the wizard, the **Zone Name** page asks you to type in the name of the zone. Type in **corporate.mccaw.ca** and click **Next**. The zone name that you type should be the same zone name that exists on the DNS server hosting the primary zone.

7. On the **Master DNS** page enter the IP address of the DNS server hosting the primary DNS zone that you want the secondary zone to obtain zone information from.

8. Click **Finish**.

Stub Zones

Stub zones are new to Windows Server 2003. Stub zones are copies of a zone, but unlike secondary zones, which contain all of the records, a stub zone only contains the RRs that are necessary to identify the authoritative DNS server for that zone. These records include the SOA, NS, and select A records. The SOA and NS resource records are sometimes referred to as the *glue records*. Think of a stub zone as being similar to a hyperlink in the sense that it simply points to the DNS server that is authoritative for that zone. Exercise 4-8 explores the steps involved in creating a stub zone.

Creating a Stub Zone

This exercise will teach you how to create a stub zone. Stub zones can be used within an organization on to allow parent DNS servers to keep track of the DNS servers that are authoritative for child domains. This way, if a DNS client queries a parent DNS server for an address in a child domain, the parent DNS server can use the stub zone to identify which servers are authoritative.

1. In the DNS snap-in, expand the name of the DNS server, and right click **Forward Lookup Zones**.

2. Select **New Zone**, and on the **Welcome** page of the New Zone Wizard dialog box, click **Next**.

3. On the **Zone Type** page, shown earlier in Exercise 4-5, select **Stub zone** and click **Next**. Again, because the server I am using to take these screen shots is a domain controller, the option to store the zone information in the Active Directory is available. In this exercise, however I am going to uncheck that box because you are not always going to be configuring DNS on domain controllers.

4. On the **Zone Name** page, type the name of the zone and click **Next**. You can also click the Browse button to browse for the zone name. This helps to avoid typos.

5. On the **Zone File** page, confirm the information about the zone filename, and notice at the bottom of the dialog box that this file will be stored in the **%systemroot%\system32\dns** directory. Click **Next**.

6. On the **Master DNS Servers** page shown next, enter the IP address of the primary DNS server from which you want to copy the zone information, click **Add**, and click **Next**. You can enter more than one DNS server for redundancy in the event that the first DNS server in the list is unavailable.

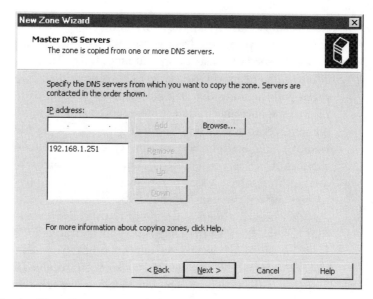

7. On the **Completion** page, click **Finish**.

Stub zones are ideal for use in environments where you want to configure local DNS clients to use a local DNS server for host name resolution for another DNS zone, but you don't want that DNS server to have to maintain a complete list of all of the other DNS zone's resource records. In a nutshell, stub zones help you to improve name resolution efficiency. Let's take a look at an example to clarify when and where to use stub zones. This example will use your existing knowledge of the two types of DNS queries, iterative and recursive.

To view a Microsoft webcast on stub zones and conditional forwarding, browse to *http://support.microsoft.com/default.aspx?scid=/servicedesks/webcasts /wc012103/wcblurb012103.asp.*

At the beginning of the chapter, we discussed the two types of queries used in DNS. We discussed how DNS clients generally use recursive queries and that recursive queries expect either a complete answer or an error code like "name does not exist" or "server failure." The key point here was that a *recursive query* places the responsibility of resolving the query in the hands of the DNS server that receives the recursive query from the DNS client. We used the example of a DNS client querying to resolve the FQDN srv1.corporate.mccaw.ca. The DNS client sends a recursive query to its preferred DNS server. This server, likely a local DNS server, checks its cache and the zones that it is authoritative for, but realizes, when it is unable to resolve the query itself, that it must send out an iterative query to the root DNS name server to assist it in finding an answer. The root DNS server responds to the iterative query with its best answer, which is the name of the .ca DNS server, and the local DNS server sends the same iterative query to the .ca DNS server in an attempt to resolve srv1.corporate.mccaw.ca. The .ca DNS server will respond with its best answer, the name of the DNS server authoritative for the mccaw.ca zone. Another iterative query is then sent to this DNS server and a response is provided that lists the name of the DNS server authoritative for the corporate.mccaw.ca zone. Finally, one last iterative query is sent to the DNS server authoritative for the corporate.mccaw.ca zone, and a response is received for the name to IP address mapping of the host srv1. The local DNS server then caches and forwards this resolved query back to the requesting client, as a response to the client's original recursive query.

This process puts all of the load on the local DNS server that receives the recursive query and this can be a significant amount of load, which in turn can slow down the response time to the client.

Stub zones can help make this name resolution process more efficient. Using this same scenario, imagine if the DNS client's local DNS server was authoritative for the mccaw.ca zone, and contained a stub zone for the corporate.mccaw.ca zone as shown in Figure 4-10. If this were the case, when the client sent its recursive query to its local DNS server, the local DNS server wouldn't have to go through the iterative query process and contact the root, and the .ca DNS servers, it would simply use the NS record of DNSSRV4 that it has in its zone file to send an iterative query to DNSSRV4, which is an authoritative DNS server for the corporate.mccaw.ca zone. This achieves a reduction in DNS traffic, and hopefully faster response times for the DNS clients. The other benefit here is that stub zones are updated automatically, so as authoritative name servers are added or removed in the delegated zone, these changes are automatically reflected in the stub zone.

The other benefit is that the local DNS server, DNSSRV1 in this example, does not have to maintain a complete copy of the corporate.mccaw.ca zone database file. It only has to maintain the SOA, NS, and glue A resource records for the authoritative DNS servers.

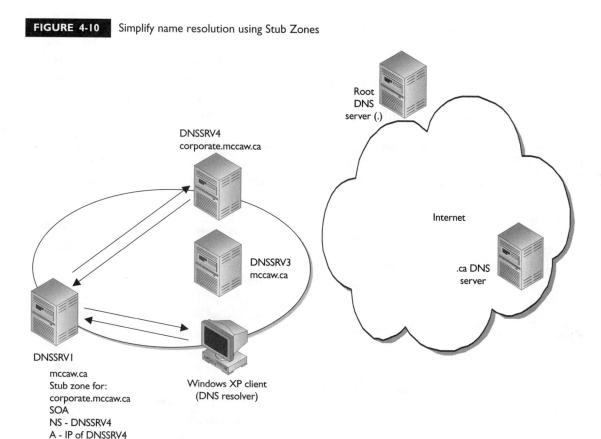

FIGURE 4-10   Simplify name resolution using Stub Zones

DNS stub zones are new to Windows Server 2003, and in addition to providing the benefits already mentioned, they have also been included to help reduce the amount of required administration. A common implementation issue that arose when using Windows 2000 DNS and zone delegation actually had a tendency to increase administration in order to ensure data consistency.

A very common Windows 2000 DNS architectural design includes a parent zone hosting a DNS namespace such as mccaw.ca, and delegating a child zone for the DNS namespace corporate.mccaw.ca to another DNS server. The DNS server hosting the child namespace is then configured to forward to the parent DNS server, or to use its own root hints to resolve names in the parent domain. This type of architecture allows the DNS server in the parent zone to know where to send queries for the child zone, and allows the child zone to know where to send queries for records in the parent zone. The issue that arises with this type of architecture, however, is that the delegation from the parent to the child must be updated every time a DNS server is added or removed from the child domain, because these delegation records are not dynamic. This then requires the parent zone's administrator to make the required changes, which conflicts with the goal of reducing administration.

on the
Job

To learn more about configuring delegations and the integration of Windows DNS with existing BIND implementations, search the Microsoft Knowledge Base for article Q255913 which discusses step by step how to configure delegation and forwarding.

Having said all of this, the use of delegation and forwarding is still a recommended solution with Windows Server 2003 DNS. Stub zones are not intended to replace delegations, but rather they have been added to enhance delegations. Stub zones work best in situations where delegations aren't effective by themselves, and where you need a way to minimize manual administration of changing NS resource records in the delegated domain. So far in these examples we have assumed that within a single organization you will be working with a single contiguous namespace, and this type of environment best suits the use of delegation and stub zones.

e x a m
w a t c h   *Know when and where to use either delegations and forwarding or stub zones.*

Organizations with non-contiguous or disjointed DNS namespaces are best suited to using conditional forwarders. Take for example the case of a corporate merger where one organization acquires another organization. The primary DNS namespace might be corporate.mccaw.ca, and the namespace of the acquired company corp.lind.ca. In this type of environment, it makes sense to use a conditional forwarder. One conditional forwarder can be created for corp.lind.ca on the DNS server that is authoritative for corporate.mccaw.ca, and a conditional forwarder for corporate.mccaw.ca can be created on the DNS server that is authoritative for the corp.lind.ca zone. This configuration will provide more efficient name resolution to clients in either domain looking to resolve names in the other zone.

So far in this chapter, you have learned how to install and configure DNS as well as how to create and configure DNS zone options. You now have the knowledge required to create and administer the DNS domain names in your organization. In the next section, you will learn how to use DNS forwarding to enhance and optimize your DNS infrastructure.

CERTIFICATION OBJECTIVE 4.03

Configure DNS Forwarding

Before you dive into the configuration of DNS forwarders, we'll spend a minute looking into the purpose of forwarders and then explore the name resolution process.

When a DNS server receives a query, it always attempts to resolve the query locally using its own zone files. In the case of a forward lookup query, a DNS resolver (a client operating system, like Windows XP, that is configured to use DNS) sends a query to the DNS server configured as its Preferred DNS server in its LAN connection properties. A forward lookup query is a request to resolve a FQDN to an IP address. For example, a DNS resolver might send a query to resolve www.mccaw.ca to an IP address. If you break this query down, the host name in the FQDN is www, and this host is found within the mccaw.ca domain, therefore the DNS query is really just looking for the IP address of the host www. That's essentially all that's happening when you type a URL into your web browser and press ENTER.

However, the DNS resolver's preferred DNS server is unable to resolve the query for whatever reason, possibly because the DNS server is not authoritative for the domain name requested. In other words, the preferred DNS server doesn't maintain the forward lookup zone files for the mccaw.ca domain, or it doesn't have the record cached from a previous lookup, then the DNS resolver's preferred DNS server must ask another DNS server to resolve the query. This is where DNS forwarders can be used. Here, DNS forwarders can allow you to designate specific DNS servers to use when resolving DNS domain names that are not local, such as names outside of your organization.

Figure 4-11 to help solidify this concept by reviewing the role of a DNS forwarder and the steps involved in the name resolution process. In this example, the Windows XP client is the DNS resolver, and it is configured to use the local DNS server as its preferred DNS server. The DNS resolver sends a recursive query to the local DNS server in an attempt to resolve the FQDN www.allmylifeIwantedto.com to an IP address. The local DNS server is authoritative only for the mccaw.ca domain, but it is configured to forward all requests for external domain names to the DNS server known in Figure 4-11 as Forwarder, so the local DNS server forwards the recursive query to the forwarder. The forwarder, which is also not authoritative for the allmylifeIwantedto .com domain, then sends out an iterative query to a root DNS server of the Internet in an attempt to discover an authoritative name server. The root DNS server responds in Step 4 with a partial answer that instructs the forwarder to ask the .com DNS server.

FIGURE 4-11 Name resolution process

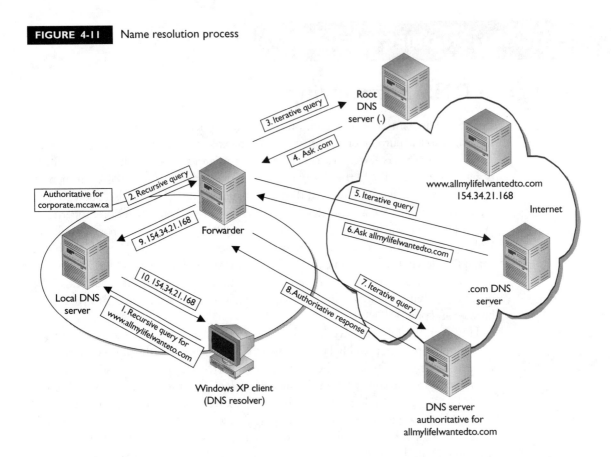

The forwarder then sends an iterative query to the .com DNS server, and the .com DNS server responds with a referral to the DNS server authoritative for the allmylifeIwantedto .com domain. The forwarder in Step 7 then sends out another iterative query to the DNS server authoritative for the allmylifeIwantedto.com domain, and receives the IP address for the host www in response to its query stating that the IP address is 154.34.21.168. The forwarder then caches the response locally in its DNS cache and replies to the local DNS server, which in turn caches the response and replies to the client. Thankfully all of this happens behind the scenes, otherwise just getting to one web site would be a dizzying process.

Windows Server 2003 DNS name servers can be configured to use forwarders in one of two modes: non-exclusive or exclusive. In non-exclusive mode, the default setting, the local name server that received the query can attempt to resolve the query on its own if the forwarder is unable to resolve the query.

In the example in Figure 4-11, if the forwarder was not able to resolve the query for www.allmylifeIwantedto.com, the local name server could attempt to resolve it on its own using its root hints. Normally, however, when forwarding is used, it is designed to allow for name resolution to be handled by one or a group of designated DNS servers as a way of limiting which DNS servers perform external name resolution. Therefore, using non-exclusive mode essentially goes against the original design goal. That said, non-exclusive mode also satisfies another criterion: availability. If your DNS forwarder is ever offline or unavailable, the local DNS server can attempt the resolution on its own, providing the DNS resolver with the answer it is looking for and keeping your end users happy. Once again, where there is a downside, there is often also an upside.

In exclusive mode, if the DNS forwarder is unable to resolve the query, the DNS client resolver receives a query failure message. To configure the DNS server in exclusive mode, place a check mark in the box to the left **Disable recursion** on the Advanced tab of the server properties dialog box. To disable recursion for an individual domain, place a check mark in the box to the left of **Do not use recursion for this domain** found at the bottom of the Forwarders tab while the domain in question is highlighted. Being able to disable recursion for individual domains is new to Windows Server 2003.

One of the issues associated with not using a forwarder is that all of your DNS servers send queries outside of your network based on their root hints, which can result in inefficient use of your Internet connection. Depending on your location and ISP connection agreement, it may be quite costly for companies that pay for bandwidth based on usage, and may be inefficient for networks with slow Internet connections as you lose the benefit of being able to resolve future identical queries from the forwarder's local DNS cache.

The goal of using a forwarder is to allow you to designate a specific DNS server or group of DNS servers to handle all external name resolution, thereby reducing Internet traffic. A DNS server configured as a forwarder will build up a large DNS cache of external DNS information over time from all of the DNS queries that it has resolved. This will allow the forwarder to resolve an increasingly larger percentage of future DNS queries using its cached DNS data, reducing the amount of ISP bandwidth used and increasing the response times for DNS clients.

To designate a DNS server as a forwarder, configure other DNS servers on the network to forward queries they cannot resolve locally to that DNS server. Exercise 4-9 will teach you the specific steps involved in configuring a DNS server to use a forwarder.

EXERCISE 4-9

Configuring a DNS Server to Use a Forwarder

This exercise will teach you how to configure a DNS server to use a forwarder. This can be useful if you want to have a single DNS server handle all external name resolution requests for internal DNS clients. In the example used earlier with Figure 4-11, the steps to follow would be performed on the local DNS server and the IP address you would be entering would be the IP address of the DNS server you want to use as the forwarder.

1. Click **Start | Programs | Administrative Tools**, and select **DNS**.

2. In the DNS snap-in, right-click the DNS server and select **Properties**.

3. In the section titled **Selected domain's forwarder IP address list**, type the IP address of the DNS server you want to use as the forwarder, and click **Add**.

4. If you are going to use multiple forwarders, also decide on the number of seconds you want the DNS server to wait for a response from one forwarder before trying another. Modify the default of five seconds in the text box to the right of **Number of seconds before forward queries time out**.

5. Last, decide whether you want to disable recursion for the domain. Placing a check mark in the box to the left of **Do not use recursion for this domain** configures the local DNS server to operate in exclusive mode. This means that the local DNS server will not attempt any further name resolution if the forwarders fail. Instead the local DNS server will return a failure message to the client.

When you use multiple forwarders, the default setting is for the DNS server to wait five seconds (by default) for a response from one forwarder IP address before trying another forwarder IP address, hence the importance of the Up and Down buttons on the Forwarders tab shown earlier in Figure 4-3. Make sure that the preferred forwarders are higher in the list than the other forwarders to allow them to be tried first.

If the DNS server exhausts all forwarders in the list without name resolution success, it will then attempt standard recursion, meaning that it will use its own root hints in an attempt to resolve the name, unless you have disabled recursion, placing the forwarder in exclusive mode.

Later in this chapter in the section titled "Disabling Forwarding," you will learn how to disable recursion on the DNS server as opposed to disabling recursion for individual forwarders. Disabling recursion on the DNS server completely prevents you from using forwarders on the server.

Forward-Only DNS Servers   Generally when you think of a DNS server, you likely think of a server that contains zone database files and is able to perform forward and possibly reverse lookup queries. Not all DNS servers are configured to maintain their own forward or reverse lookup zones, however, and yet they can still participate in the name resolution process. A DNS server can also be configured to not perform recursion after forwarders fail, meaning that if the server does not get a successful query response from any of the servers configured as forwarders, it returns a query failure. This type of DNS server configuration is referred to as a *forward-only DNS server*.

Forward-only DNS servers are ideal for scenarios where you don't want bandwidth consumed by DNS zone transfer traffic, but you do want to provide local name resolution through DNS. A forward-only DNS server builds up a DNS cache over time that allows it to resolve domain names that it has resolved previously by forwarding the query on to another specified DNS server.

Forward-only DNS servers differ from non-recursive DNS servers. Forward-only DNS servers build up a cache of the domain names that it resolves, and uses this cache in future attempts to resolve the same domain name. Non-recursive DNS servers do not retain a DNS cache, nor do they perform recursion. Both DNS server configurations will always attempt to resolve a query using their own authoritative data before using their forwarders.

Conditional Forwarding   Conditional forwarding is a feature that is new to the DNS service in Windows Server 2003. Conditional forwarders are rules created on DNS servers that are used to forward queries according to domain names. Conditional forwarders allow you to be more selective in the queries that are forwarded to a specific DNS server based on domain name, rather than having a DNS server forward all queries it cannot resolve locally to a forwarder. This new functionality greatly improves conventional forwarding by adding a name-based condition to the forwarding process.

A conditional forwarder consists of two components: a domain name that is used to establish the condition, and one or more IP addresses of DNS servers to forward domain-specific queries to.

The DNS name query resolution process is quite simple, but a few additional steps can be added when a conditional forwarder is configured. When a DNS client sends a query to a DNS server, the DNS server tries to resolve the name using its own zone data or from cached DNS information. If the DNS server is configured to forward for the domain name specified in the DNS query, the query is forwarded to the IP address of a forwarder that is associated with the domain name in the DNS server properties. An example of this can be seen in Figures 4-12 and 4-13, where two conditional forwarders exist, one for ngatedoorknob.com, and the other for mccaw.ca. When a query is received for a host in the ngatedoorknob.com domain, the request is forwarded to a DNS server at 207.169.54.22, as displayed in Figure 4-12. When a query is received for a host in the mccaw.ca domain, that request is forward to a DNS server at 204.153.221.95, as shown in Figure 4-13. If the DNS server has no forwarder listed for the name designated in the query, and no forwarder IP address has been added for **All other DNS domains**, the DNS server will try to resolve the query using standard recursion.

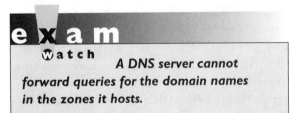

Conditional forwarders are ideal for organizations that want to improve name resolution between internal (private) DNS namespaces and can be particularly useful after a corporate merger. This technique can be implemented by configuring the DNS servers in one internal namespace to forward all queries

Conditional forwarder for ngatedoorknob .com

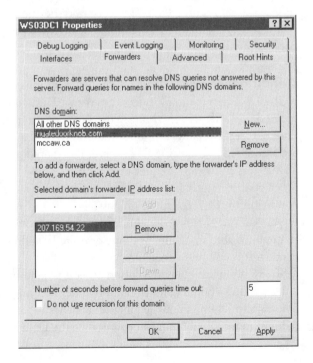

Conditional
forwarder
for mccaw.ca

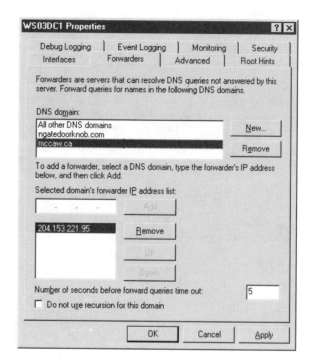

to the authoritative DNS servers in a second internal namespace, enabling streamlined name resolution between the two namespaces without performing recursion on the DNS namespace on the Internet. It also avoids having your DNS servers perform recursion to your internal root DNS server for different namespaces that exist within your organization.

One example of a situation where conditional forwarding can be used is shown in Figure 4-14, where you have a single Active Directory forest with two trees and six domains. Each domain contains multiple DNS servers that are authoritative for their own Active Directory domain namespaces. On the DNS server in the us.na.corporate .mccaw.ca domain, a conditional forwarder could be created for magwood.com that pointed to the IP address of one of the DNS name servers authoritative for the magwood .com domain. Another conditional forwarder could be created for the usa.magwood.com domain, pointing to the IP address of a DNS server authoritative for this domain. The same could be done for the eu.magwood.com domain. This would allow any query for hosts in any one of the three magwood domains to be forwarded to the DNS server authoritative for that domain.

What is not possible on a DNS server within the us.na.corporate.mccaw.ca domain that is authoritative for that domain is to create a forwarder for the us.na

FIGURE 4-14 An example of conditional forwarding

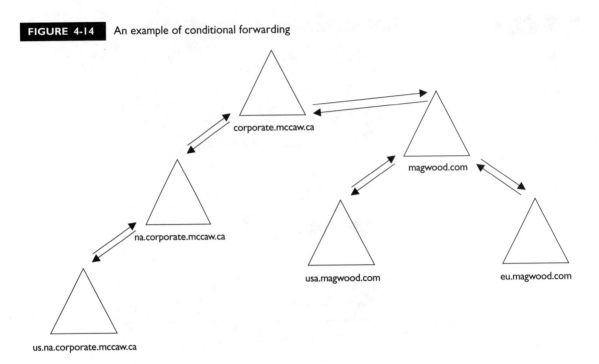

.corporate.mccaw.ca domain. A forwarder to the corporate.mccaw.ca domain or to the na.corporate.mccaw.ca domain could be created, but only if those DNS domains have been delegated to another DNS server.

The next question is this: What happens when a DNS server configured with multiple conditional forwarders receives a query for a domain name? In this case, the DNS server compares the domain name to its list of domain name conditions and uses the longest domain name condition, or the most specific condition, to determine the best match. For example, if the DNS server receives a query for mail.corporate.mccaw.ca, and a condition exists for both mccaw.ca and corporate.mccaw.ca, the DNS server would forward the query to the IP address associated with the corporate.mccaw.ca condition.

EXERCISE 4-10

Creating a Conditional Forwarder

This exercise will teach you how to configure a conditional forwarder, which allows you to have the DNS server forward based on domain names that you specify. In this exercise, the DNS server will forward all requests for computers in the texarabiahat .com domain to a DNS server at IP address 64.24.153.99.

1. Click **Start** | **Programs** | **Administrative Tools**, and select **DNS**.

2. In the DNS snap-in, right-click the DNS server, and select **Properties**.

3. Select the **Forwarders** tab, and under **DNS domain**, click **New**. Type **texarabiahat.com** in the **New Forwarder** dialog box shown here, and click **OK**. Remember that the domain you enter cannot be a domain that the DNS server is authoritative for.

4. With the texarabiahat.com domain selected, type the IP address (**64.24.153.99**) of the DNS server to use for the conditional forward in the section titled **Selected domain's forwarder IP address list**, and click **Add**, and then **OK**.

Disabling Forwarding   You can also disable forwarding at either the DNS server level or for individual domains. To perform this task, you must be a member

of the Administrators group on the local computer, or you must have been delegated the appropriate permissions. If the DNS server is a member of a domain, you must be a member of the Domain Admins group to perform this operation. Exercise 4-1 explains how to disable forwarding for the entire DNS server.

EXERCISE 4-11

Disabling Forwarding on a DNS Server

This exercise will teach you how to disable DNS forwarding for an entire server using the DNS snap-in.

1. Click **Start** | **Programs** | **Administrative Tools**, and then select **DNS**.

2. In the DNS snap-in, right-click the DNS server, and click **Properties**.

3. Select the **Advanced** tab, and in the **Server options** section, place a check mark next to **Disable recursion**, and click OK.

on the **Job**

If you disable Forwarding (recursion) on the DNS server, you will not be able to use forwarders on the same server.

Forwarding Best Practices

When you plan your DNS server forwarding architecture, keep the following best practices in mind to help you design the most efficient forwarding architecture.

- Keep things simple. This concept applies to your forwarder configuration as well. The less complicated it is, the easier it will be to maintain and administer.

- Use forwarders strategically to accomplish specific goals and improve performance such as for resolving offsite queries or sharing information between namespaces.

- Avoid chaining your forwarders. If you have a DNS server named DNSSRV1 configured to forward queries for corporate.mccaw.ca to DNSSRV2, do not configure DNSSRV2 to forward queries for corporate.mccaw.ca to DNSSRV3. Doing this would result in an inefficient name resolution process that could also result in errors if DNSSRV3 was ever accidentally configured to forward queries for corporate.mccaw.ca to DNSSRV1, which would result in a circular logic.

- Monitor the load on your forwarders. Recursive queries sent by forwarders to the Internet can require a significant amount of time to answer, and as the number of internal DNS servers using these forwarders increases, so too will Internet queries, which can result in performance degradation because of the substantial increase in network traffic. If network load becomes an issue, you can use more than one forwarder and distribute the load between forwarders.

■ When you configure your forwarders, avoid creating inefficient resolution. The DNS server will attempt to forward domain names according to the order in which they are configured in the DNS console. Always place a local DNS server higher in the forwarders list than a remote DNS server to ensure that the local server is always queried first, before the remote server. Always perform a regular, scheduled evaluation of your network's forwarding configuration to identify and resolve any inefficiencies.

CERTIFICATION SUMMARY

Setting up a DNS server typically involves installing the DNS service, followed by the configuration of DNS zones and the creation of DNS resource records for the hosts in your network to your DNS zones, and possibly the delegation of administration for these zones. Once all this is complete, the security settings should be applied to maintain the integrity of DNS zone data in the network.

In this chapter, you have learned about the different ways in which you can install the DNS service as well as how to configure DNS zone options and DNS forwarding. With respect to DNS forwarding, you learned about the new conditional forwarding functionality, a component that you should be very familiar with, in preparation for the certification exam.

✓ TWO-MINUTE DRILL

Configure DNS Server Options

❑ DNS can be installed through Add/Remove Windows Components, found within Add or Remove Programs in Control Panel.

❑ Best practices suggest using the Manage Your Server wizard to install DNS, because the wizard will only configure and enable the services required. During the installation of DNS using the Manage Your Server wizard, you are also prompted to configure a forward lookup zone.

❑ DNS can also be installed automatically during the **dcpromo** process. If this option is selected, a root zone is created, which prevents the DNS server from using forwarders or root hints.

❑ New to the **dcpromo** wizard is the DNS Registration Diagnostics page, which detects and alerts you to problems detected with the current DNS configuration during the domain controller promotion process and presents you with three options, one of which is to have the wizard install and configure DNS.

❑ DNS can be administered via a number of different tools, including the DNS MMC and **dnscmd**. **dnscmd** is installed with the Support Tools, which are found in the support\tools folder on the Windows Server 2003 CD. New to the DNS MMC in Windows Server 2003 is the DNS Event Log. **nslookup** can also be used for troubleshooting DNS related issues.

❑ The Interfaces tab can be used to limit the NICs that DNS is bound to.

❑ For multi-homed names, local subnet priority supercedes the use of round-robin rotation, but when round-robin is enabled, it continues to be the secondary method used to sort multiple RRs that are returned in a listed answer.

❑ A DNS server's root hints file is named **cache.dns**, and is stored in the **%systemroot%\system32\dns** directory. This file identifies the authoritative DNS server for the root zones of the DNS namespace. New to Windows Server 2003 is the ability from within the DNS MMC to select to **Copy from Server**, which allows you to copy the **cache.dns** file from another DNS server so that the customizations you make to the file only have to be made on one DNS server, and all the others can copy it from that one server.

❑ By default, the DNS event log records all DNS events.

Configure DNS Zone Options

❑ A DNS zone is the logical container for the resource records for one or more domains. The DNS service in Windows Server 2003 supports three types of zones; primary, secondary, and stub. Each of these three zone types can be either forward or reverse lookup.

❑ New to the DNS service in Windows Server 2003 is the ability to configure how you want the zone data to be replicated. You can choose to replicate it to all domain controllers in the domain, or to all DNS servers in the domain or to all DNS servers in the forest.

❑ The option to integrate the DNS zone in Active Directory is only available when installed the DNS service on a domain controller. AD-integrated DNS zones replicate during AD replication, and no longer require the use of zone transfers.

❑ AD integrated zones can be stored by default in the domain partition, or in Windows Server 2003 you can choose to store it in the Application Directory partition. AD-integrated DNS zone data cannot be stored in ADAM.

❑ The option to **Allow only secure dynamic update**s is only available on domain controllers running the DNS service

❑ Stub zones are copies of a zone that only contain SOA, NA, and select A resource records. Stub zones are not intended to replace forwarding, but rather make DNS more efficient in architectures that wouldn't benefit from forwarding.

❑ Conditional forwarders are ideal for making DNS more efficient within organizations that have non-contiguous DNS namespaces, such as organizations that have merged or acquired other companies and their associated networks.

❑ Stub zones allow DNS servers in parent zones to answer recursive queries that would have normally been referred to servers authoritative for the child domains.

❑ You must be a member of the Domain Admins or Enterprise Admins groups to create application directory partitions.

Configure DNS Forwarding

❑ By default, the DNS service in Windows Server 2003 forwards queries for all other DNS domains to the list of DNS servers you specify on the Forwarders tab.

❑ Windows Server 2003 also supports a new feature known as conditional forwarding. Conditional forwarding allows you to associate a specific domain or domains to be forwarded to a specific DNS server, providing you with more granularity in your administration and allowing DNS to be more efficient.

❑ A server with recursion disabled cannot use forwarders. Recursion can be disabled for the entire DNS server, or in Windows Server 2003, it can be disabled for individual domains on the Forwarding tab of the DNS server properties dialog box.

❑ DNS forwarding operates in one of two modes, exclusive or non-exclusive. In exclusive mode, if the DNS forwarder is unable to resolve the query, the DNS client resolver receives a query failure message. In non-exclusive mode, which is the default setting, the local DNS server will attempt to resolve the query itself if the forwarders are unable to resolve the query.

❑ The use of forwarders allows only designated DNS servers to resolve names on the Internet which optimizes the use of the DNS servers cache in responding to identical queries from different internal clients.

❑ A forward-only DNS server is different from a non-recursive DNS server because it builds up a cache. A non-recursive DNS server does not build up a DNS cache.

SELF TEST

The following questions will help you measure your understanding of the material presented in this chapter. Read the questions and answers carefully, because there might be more than one correct answer. Choose all correct answers for each question.

Configure DNS Server Options

1. As the administrator of your network, you are required to install and configure the DNS service on a computer running Windows Server 2003 in preparation for the migration from Windows NT 4.0 to Windows 2003. Your network contains client computers running Windows 95, Windows NT 4.0 Workstation, and Windows XP. Which of the following options can you use to install the DNS service? (Choose all that apply.)

    A. Use Add/Remove Programs.

    B. Insert the Windows Server 2003 CD and select to install Optional Windows Components.

    C. Use **dnscmd.exe**.

    D. Use the Manage Your Server wizard.

    E. Use the Security Configuration Wizard.

2. As the administrator of your network and the network services running within your organization, you continually try to implement and follow best practices in your daily administration. One of the tasks that you are planning is the installation of the DNS service on a server running Windows Server 2003. Which of the following options would you use to install the DNS service if you wanted to follow best practices?

    A. Install the DNS service through Add/Remove Windows Components in Add or Remove Programs.

    B. Install the DNS service using **dnscmd.exe**.

    C. Install the DNS service using **netsh**.

    D. Install the DNS service using the Manage Your Server wizard.

3. During the installation of the DNS service on a computer running Windows Server 2003, you are prompted with the Dynamic Updates page, but the option to use secure dynamic updates is grayed out and not available to you. Which of the following is the most likely cause of this?

    A. The computer on which you are installing DNS is not a member of an Active Directory domain.

    B. The account that you are using to install the DNS service is a member of the DNS Admins group, but not the local Administrators group on the server. Therefore, you do not have permission.

    C. The computer is not an Active Directory domain controller.

    D. Group policy has been enabled within the domain to prevent the use of dynamic updates.

4. As the network administrator for your organization, you have just completed the installation of your first Windows Server 2003 domain by upgrading an existing Windows NT 4.0 PDC. During the domain controller promotion process, you selected to have the wizard install the DNS service. You have logged on to the domain controller with your regular user account and have launched the DNS MMC using the **runas** command, and specifying the administrator account and password. You notice in the DNS MMC that you are unable to use forwarders. Which of the following best describes the reason for this?

    A. Allowing the **dcpromo** wizard to install DNS only allows stub zones to be created on that DNS server.

    B. Allowing the **dcpromo** wizard to install DNS creates an Active Directory–integrated, forward lookup zone. AD-integrated zones do not support the use of forwarders.

    C. Allowing the **dcpromo** wizard to install DNS creates an Active Directory–integrated, forward lookup zone, but the zone is not activated. The zone must be activated before you can make configuration changes.

    D. Allowing the **dcpromo** wizard to install DNS creates a root zone and prevents the use of forwarders.

5. Which of the following features is new to the Windows Server 2003 DNS MMC? (Choose all that apply.)

    A. The Debug Logging tab in the DNS server properties dialog box

    B. Selecting to launch **nslookup** from the context menu of the DNS server

    C. The forwarding tab in the DNS server properties dialog box

    D. The Event Viewer snap-in

6. You are the administrator of a small network that contains a single server running Windows Server 2003. This multi-homed server is configured as a domain controller, running DNS and DHCP, and also provides shared connectivity to the Internet for 21 local client computers via RRAS and NAT. The company uses a broadband Internet connection that doesn't permit server services on the ISP network. The local DNS zone used for AD resolution is corp.mccaw.ca. This zone contains a host address record for the company's local intranet web site, named www. Which of the following strategies would you use to limit DNS traffic to only the internal LAN?

    A. In the properties of the corp.mccaw.ca zone, select the Interfaces tab and only bind the DNS service to the internal NIC.

    B. In the properties of the DNS server, select the Interfaces tab and only bind the DNS service to the internal NIC.

C. In the properties of the DNS server, select the Forwarders tab and add the IP address of the ISP's DNS server.

D. In the properties of the DNS server, select the Forwarders tab, add the IP address of the ISP's DNS server, and at the bottom of the dialog box enable the option **Do not use recursion for this domain**.

7. You are the network administrator within your company. You have recently installed and configured DNS on a new server running Windows Server 2003. One of the configuration changes you made can be seen in Figure 4-15 on the Advanced tab of the DNS server properties. Here you have changed the default value for **Load zone data on startup** to **From file**. What is the name of the file that will be used to load the DNS data once this configuration change is applied?

A. hosts

B. cache.dns

C. root

D. boot

FIGURE 4-15

The Advanced tab of the DNS server's properties

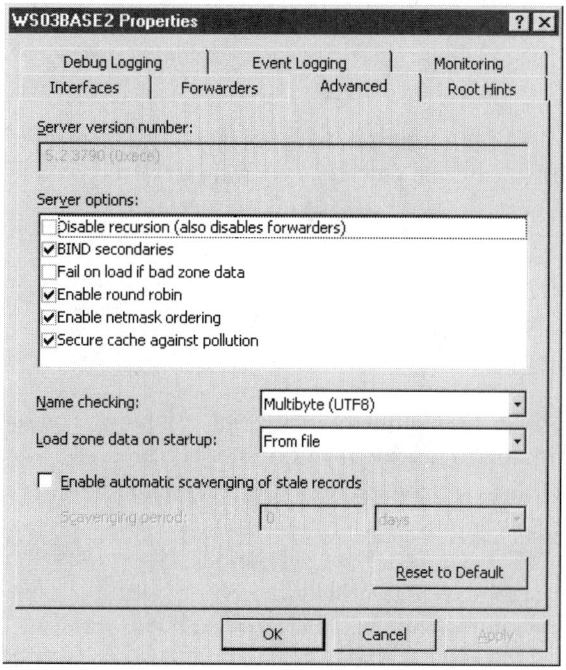

8. You are the administrator of the DNS infrastructure in your organization. You have just migrated your DNS servers from Windows NT 4.0 to Windows 2003. Looking at the Advanced tab of one of the DNS server's properties, shown in Figure 4-15, you would like to disable the option that prevents fast transfers from being made. Which option will you disable?

    A. **Recursion**

    B. **BIND secondaries**

    C. **Enable round robin**

    D. **Enable netmask ordering**

    E. **Secure cache against pollution**

9. You have just been hired as the network administrator for a medium-sized organization. One of your new responsibilities is the configuration and administration of DNS. The company has just recently migrated to the Windows Server 2003 platform on all of their servers. You are interested in optimizing name resolution within the network, and have been looking into the DNS resource records and DNS server properties. In the DNS resource records for the zone mccaw.ca, the zone used for name resolution in the DMZ network, you identified the following four entries listed in the following order:

    ```
    www    10.45.31.10
    www    10.45.31.20
    www    10.45.31.5
    www    10.45.31.30
    ```

    Looking at the DNS server properties, you have also noticed that DNS round-robin is not enabled. If eight external name queries were to be received by your DNS server, what response would the client who sent the seventh query receive?

    A. 10.45.31.10

    B. 10.45.31.20

    C. 10.45.31.5

    D. 10.45.31.30

10. You are the network administrator in your company. You have just completed the migration of your organization's network to Windows Server 2003. You are interested in optimizing name resolution within the network, and have been looking into the DNS resource records and DNS server properties on one of your multi-homed DNS servers that is attached to two separate subnets. The DNS server service is bound to both NICs. In the DNS resource records for the corp.mccaw.ca zone, you identified four entries with the same host name www, but different IP addresses listed in the following order in the DNS zone: 10.10.1.20, 10.10.2.10, 10.10.2.20,

and 10.10.1.10. Looking at the DNS server properties shown in Figure 4-15, which IP address will be the first returned to a client with an IP address of 10.10.2.100 that queries the DNS server for the host www?

A. 10.10.1.20

B. 10.10.2.10

C. 10.10.2.20

D. 10.10.1.10

11. As the senior network administrator in your organization, you are attempting to explain to a junior network administrator the DNS name resolution process used by the Windows Server 2003 DNS service. Place the following DNS name resolution steps in the proper order.

A. The DNS service checks its zone records.

B. The DNS service queries the first forwarder configured in its forwarder list.

C. The DNS service queries its local cache.

D. The DNS service queries a root server.

12. You are the network administrator for your company. You would like to begin collecting DNS debugging information using the Debug logging properties. In order to get useful information in your log, which of the following should you enable? (Choose all that apply.)

A. Packet direction

B. Packet type

C. Log packets for debugging

D. Packet size

E. Packet contents

F. Transport protocol

Configure DNS Zone Options

13. Which of the following zone types are supported in the DNS service in Windows Server 2003? (Choose all that apply.)

A. Primary

B. Reverse

C. Stub

D. Delegated

E. Secondary

14. You are the administrator of your organization's network. You have completed the planning for your DNS infrastructure and are in the midst of creating the first zone. Your organization is geographically dispersed across 15 different locations. Part of your mandate is to ensure that the DNS information is Active Directory integrated, but that you also keep unnecessary replication traffic to a minimum. Your organization's AD consists of a forest with a single domain. Not all domain controllers in your organization run the DNS service, but a number of member servers are configured with the DNS service. Which zone replication option will best meet your requirements?

    A. To all domain controllers in the Active Directory domain

    B. To all DNS servers in the Active Directory forest

    C. To all DNS servers in the Active Directory domain

    D. To all domain controllers specified in the scope of the following application directory partition

15. You are the network administrator in your organization. You are in the process of migrating your servers running Windows 2000 Server to Windows Server 2003. You would like to begin using some of the new functionality found within the DNS service running on Windows Server 2003 such as storing the DNS zone information in the application directory. What group must you be a member of in order to do this?

    A. Domain Admins

    B. Schema Admins

    C. Enterprise Admins

    D. Local administrators group on the DNS server

16. You are the network administrator for your organization. You have just installed Windows Server 2003 Standard Edition on a new server, and promoted the server using **dcpromo** to be an additional domain controller within your existing Windows 2000 Active Directory domain. After rebooting the new Windows Server 2003 domain controller, you open the DNS server properties dialog box in the DNS MMC and attempt to change the storage of the zone from the domain partition to an application directory partition, but you receive an error message. You are currently logged on with an account that is a member of the Enterprise Admins and Domain Admins groups. Which of the following actions will correct this problem?

    A. Transfer the Schema FSMO role from the Windows 2000 DC to the Windows Server 2003 DC.

    B. Transfer the Domain Naming FSMO role from the Windows 2000 DC to the Windows Server 2003 DC.

C. Transfer the PDC Emulator FSMO role from the Windows 2000 DC to the Windows Server 2003 DC.

D. Transfer the Infrastructure FSMO role from the Windows 2000 DC to the Windows Server 2003 DC.

17. You are the network administrator for your organization. You have just installed Windows Server 2003 Standard Edition on a new server and promoted the server using **dcpromo** to be an additional domain controller within your existing Windows 2000 Active Directory domain. Your current environment now consists of a single Windows Server 2003 DC, 21 Windows 2000 DCs, and two Windows 2000 member servers running DNS. Until now, the DNS zone data replicated via zone transfers, but you want to AD integrate DNS now. Which of the following options must you choose in the **Change Zone Replication Scope** dialog box to allow your Windows 2000 DNS servers to load an AD zone?

A. **All DNS servers in the AD forest**

B. **All DNS servers in the AD domain**

C. **All DCs in the AC domain**

D. **All DCs in a specified application directory partition**

Configure DNS Forwarding

18. You are the network administrator in your organization. You would like to configure a DNS server named Dnssrv1, which has a static IP address of 192.168.3.23 and that is authoritative for the corporate.mccaw.ca zone, to forward queries for the corp.allIwantedtodoinlife.com zone to another DNS server located at 10.10.1.2. Which of the following steps will you take to accomplish this? (Choose two. Each answer represents one part of the whole solution.)

A. On Dnssrv1, open the DNS MMC, and in the properties of the DNS server, select the **Forwarders** tab.

B. On Dnssrv1, open the DNS MMC, and in the properties of the corporate.mccaw.ca zone, select the **Forwarders** tab.

C. In the DNS domain section, click **New** and enter the domain name **corp.allIwantedtodoinlife .com**, and click **Add**. With this domain selected, enter the IP address **192.168.3.23** and click **Add**.

D. In the DNS domain section, click New and enter the domain name **corp.allIwantedtodoinlife .com**, and click Add. With this domain selected, enter the IP address **10.10.1.2** and click Add.

E. At the bottom of the Forwarders page, select **Do not use recursion for this domain**.

19. You are the network administrator for your organization. Your organization consists of a single AD domain name mccaw.ca and two sites, one in Toronto, Ontario, and the other in Overland Park, Kansas. You have configured a DNS server named DNSKS as a forward-only server in the Overland Park office. The Overland Park connects directly to the head office in Toronto through a secure VPN over the Internet. All name resolution to the Internet occurs on a server named DNS1 in Toronto. Place the following name resolution steps in the order in which they would occur when a client in the Overland Park office queries for a host on the Internet that has not been queried for before. Use only those steps that apply.

    A. DNSKS checks to see if it can answer the query authoritatively.

    B. DNS1 sends a series of iterative queries first to a root server, then to the DNS servers it gets referred to, until it finally finds the authoritative DNS server for the FQDN.

    C. The client sends the query to its preferred DNS server.

    D. DNSKS checks its local cache.

    E. DNSKS forwards the query to DNS1.

    F. The client checks its local DNS resolver cache for the name.

    G. DNSKS sends a series of iterative queries first to a root server, then to the DNS servers it gets referred to, until it finally finds the authoritative DNS server for the FQDN.

    H. DNS1 checks its local cache.

20. Which of the following best describes the difference between a forward-only DNS server and a non-recursive DNS server?

    A. A forward-only DNS server does not build up a cache relating to the domain name.

    B. A non-recursive DNS server does not build up a cache relating to the domain name.

    C. A forward-only DNS server does not perform recursion.

    D. A non-recursive DNS server is used only with conditional forwarding.

LAB QUESTION

You are the network administrator for your organization. Until recently, your Active Directory forest consisted of three domains in a single tree and forest. The company's network operations center (NOC) is located in Nashville, Tennessee, which is also the location of one of three corporate offices. The other two corporate offices are located in Brisbane, Australia and Berlin, Germany.

Your AD domain model contains a forest root domain named amer.mccaw.ca that contains two child domains asia.amer.mccaw.ca and euro.amer.mccaw.ca.

Your organization has just completed the acquisition of lind.ca, which has an existing AD forest of two domains. The forest root domain is etobicoke.lind.ca and the delegated child domain is sweden .etobicoke.ca. The Lind group of companies has offices in both Toronto and Stockholm. Both organizations' DNS servers run only on servers configured as domain controllers. Both organizations were also in the process of migrating to Windows Server 2003 before the corporate acquisition. You have just completed implementing the network architecture to facilitate communications between all offices in both organizations using secured VPNs between all facilities and now you must optimize the DNS infrastructure. Figure 4-16 displays the relevant parts of the corporate networks. DNSSRV1 and DNSSRV2 are both authoritative for the amer.mccaw.ca and mccaw.ca zones. DNSSRV3 and DNSSRV4 have been delegated authority for the euro.amer.mccaw.ca zone from DNSSRV1. DNSSRV5 and DNSSRV6 have been delegated authority for the asia.amer.mccaw. ca zones. All servers with an old number in their name are configured with primary forward lookup zones and all servers with an even number in their name are currently configured with secondary DNS zones. This is true for the servers in both the mccaw.ca and lind.ca domains. DNS1 and DNS2 are authoritative for the etobicoke.lind.ca and lind.ca zones. The sweden.etobicoke.lind.ca zone has been delegated to DNS3 and DNS4.

Use Figure 4-6 along with your newfound DNS knowledge to answer the following DNS planning and implementation questions.

1. Which server(s) would have delegated authority to the asia.amer.mccaw.ca zone?

2. How could you make name resolution more efficient between the two non-contiguous namespaces?

3. You have decided to change all of your zones from primary and secondary to Active Directory integrated. In doing this, you want to limit your DNS traffic to only the domain in which it is required. You also need to allow for some DNS servers currently running on Windows 2000 domain controllers. Which zone replication option will you select?

4. How could you use conditional forwarding to make your DNS name resolution more efficient?

5. Your organization is planning for significant growth over the next 12 months. In anticipation of this internal growth, you have decided to add four additional DNS servers for name resolution in the amer.mccaw.ca domain that will all be authoritative for that namespace. You would like to restrict external name resolution to only DNSSRV1 and DNSSRV2. How can you use the root hints to accomplish this on the four new DNS servers?

FIGURE 4-16 Lab question example

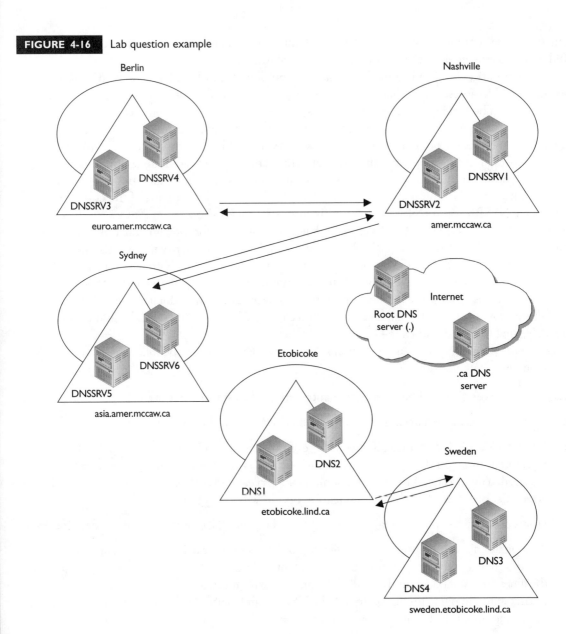

SELF TEST ANSWERS

Configure DNS Server Options

1. ☑ **A, B,** and **D.** The DNS service can be installed using Add or Remove Programs and the Add/Remove Windows Component option, or by inserting the Windows Server 2003 CD and selecting to install Optional Windows Components, or by using the Manage Your Server wizard.

   ☒ **C** and **E** are incorrect because the DNS service cannot be installed using dnscmd.exe or by using the Security Configuration Wizard. At this time, the Security Configuration Wizard has not been released so this could change upon release.

2. ☑ **D.** Using the Manage Your Server wizard to install the DNS service is the only option that adheres to best practices for the installation of DNS.

   ☒ **A** is incorrect because installing the DNS service through Add/Remove Windows Components in Add or Remove Programs is not the recommended best practice, although it will allow you to install the DNS service. **B** and **C** are incorrect because the DNS service cannot be installed using either **dnscmd.exe** or **netsh**.

3. ☑ **C.** The computer on which you are installing the DNS service must be an Active Directory domain controller for the option to use secure dynamic updates to be available.

   ☒ **A** is incorrect because the computer on which you are installing DNS must be not only a member of a domain but must also be an Active Directory domain controller in order to have the option of using secure dynamic updates. **B** is incorrect because permissions are not the issue in this question because if you have the permission to install DNS, you also have the permission to configure a zone on the DNS server. **D** is incorrect because Group Policy can be used to push out DNS dynamic update configuration settings to clients, but it cannot be used to prevent the installation of a DNS zone from using secure dynamic updates.

4. ☑ **D.** If DNS is installed by the **dcpromo** wizard, a root zone is created, which makes the DNS server think that it is a root Internet server, and therefore limits it from being configured to use forwarders or root hints.

   ☒ **A** is incorrect because using the **dcpromo** wizard to install DNS does not allow only stub zones to be created on that DNS server. **B** is incorrect because forwarding is configured in the properties of the DNS server, not in the zone properties. **C** is incorrect because DNS zones do not require activation. DHCP scopes require activation.

5. ☑ **A, B,** and **D.** New to the Windows Server 2003 DNS MMC are the Debug Logging tab, the ability to launch **nslookup** from the context menu of the DNS server, and the Event Viewer snap-in that allows you to view the DNS event log.

    ☒ **B** is incorrect because the forwarding tab in the DNS server properties dialog box is not new in Windows Server 2003.

6. ☑ **B.** The Interfaces tab in the properties of the DNS server can be used to selectively bind the DNS service to one or more NICs by selecting the option **Only the following IP addresses**. In this case, you would only want to bind DNS to the internal, private NIC to prevent this server service from operating on the ISP's network.

    ☒ **A** is incorrect because the Interfaces tab is only available in the DNS server properties, and is not an option in the zone properties. **C** and **D** are incorrect because the Forwarders tab does not include any options that allow you to limit specific network usage to individual networks.

7. ☑ **D.** When configured to **Load zone data on startup From file** as opposed to the default **From Active Directory and registry**, the file that will be used will be the boot file stored in **%systemroot%\system32\dns**.

    ☒ **A** is incorrect because the hosts file is a file that is stored locally on each DNS client and which can be used to enhance local name resolution. **B** is incorrect because **cache.dns** is the name of the file that stores the list of authoritative root name servers. **C** is incorrect because root is not a filename that is used by DNS.

8. ☑ **B.** With the **BIND secondaries** option enabled, no fast transfers will be made, so this option should be disabled.

    ☒ **A** is incorrect because disabling recursion will prevent the use of forwarders on the DNS server. **C** and **D** are incorrect because disabling round-robin or netmask ordering will not affect the use of fast zone transfers. **E** is incorrect because disabling the securing of the cache against pollution will not affect the use of fast zone transfers.

9. ☑ **A.** The client who sent in the seventh request would receive the IP address of 10.45.31.5 in response to its query. When round-robin is disabled, the order of the response to an incoming query is based on the static order of the RRs in the zone database file.

    ☒ **B, C,** and **D** are incorrect because of the way the resource records are entered in the DNS zone file. Only the IP address 10.45.31.5 would be returned to the client issuing the seventh query.

10. ☑ **B.** The IP address 10.10.2.10 will be returned first to the client. The reason the 10.10.1.20 address wouldn't be returned, even though it is listed first in the DNS zone, is that local subnet priority supercedes the use of round-robin.

☒   **A, C,** and **D** are incorrect because none of the remaining IP addresses would be returned first to the client because of the netmask ordering option being enabled in the properties.

11. ☑   **C, A, B, D.** The name resolution process used in resolving a FQDN to an IP address begins with the DNS server querying its local cache, followed by checking its zone records. Next, it queries the first forwarder configured in its forwarder list and continues down the list if name resolution isn't successful. As a last resort, the DNS server attempts to resolve the name using one of the root servers in its root hints.

12. ☑   **A, B, C, E,** and **F.** To collect useful debug logging information, log packets for debugging, packet direction, transport protocol, packet contents, and packet type should be enabled.
    ☒   **D** is incorrect because packet size isn't an option on the debug logging tab.

Configure DNS Zone Options

13. ☑   **A, C,** and **E.** Primary, stub, and secondary zones are the three types of zones supported in Windows Server 2003. Each of these three different types of zones can be either forward or reverse lookup.
    ☒   **B** and **D** are incorrect because reverse and delegated are not valid zone types in Windows Server 2003.

14. ☑   **B** and **C.** The best option in this situation is to select to replicate the zone information to either all DNS servers in the AD domain or all DNS servers in the AD forest, because they are one in the same.
    ☒   **A** is incorrect; because DNS runs on servers that are not configured as domain controllers, zone replication should be configured to go beyond only domain controllers. **D** is incorrect because the option to replicate the zone to all domain controllers specified in the scope of the following application directory partition is only available if the application directory partition has been created.

15. ☑   **A** and **C.** By default, only members of the Domain Admins or Enterprise Admins groups can create a DNS application directory partition.
    ☒   **B,** and **D** are incorrect.

16. ☑   **B.** If you are changing the storage of a DNS zone from the domain partition to an application directory partition in a Windows 2000 AD domain, the DC holding the Domain Naming FSMO role must be transferred to the Windows Server 2003 DC for the DNS application directory partitions to exist.
    ☒   **A, C,** and **D** are incorrect because the Domain Naming FSMO role is the only FSMO role that must reside on the Windows Server 2003 DC to allow the application directory partitions to be created.

17. ☑ **B.** To allow your Windows 2000 DNS servers to load an Active Directory zone, you must select the option **All DNS servers in the AD domain**.

    ☒ **A** is incorrect because selecting **All DNS servers in the AD forest** replicates the zone data to all DNS servers running on DCs in the AD forest. **C** is incorrect because selecting **All DCs in the AC domain** replicates zone data to all DNS servers running on DCs in the AD domain. **D** is incorrect because choosing **All DCs in a specified application directory partition** replicates zone data according to the replication scope of the specified application directory partition.

Configure DNS Forwarding

18. ☑ **A and D.** To successfully configure a conditional forwarder from Dnssrv1 to the DNS server that is authoritative for the corp.allIwantedtodoinlife.com domain, you would start by opening the DNS MMC, and in the properties of the DNS server, select the Forwarders tab. Then, in the DNS domain section, click New and enter the domain name corp.allIwantedtodoinlife.com, and click Add. With this domain selected, enter the IP address **10.10.1.2**, and click Add. This will configure Dnssrv1 to forward all queries for names within the corp.allIwantedtodoinlife.com to the authoritative DNS server located at 10.10.1.2.

    ☒ **B** is incorrect because DNS zone properties do not contain the Forwarders tab; this is only available in the properties of the DNS server. **C** is incorrect because to configure a conditional forwarder, you must enter the name of the domain and then the IP address of one or more DNS servers that you want queries for the specified domain to be directed to. **E** is incorrect because disabling recursion for the domain by itself does not allow you to configure a conditional forwarder.

19. ☑ **F, C, A, D, E, H, B.** The first step occurs on the client, which checks its local DNS resolver cache for the name. If the name isn't found within the local client's resolver cache, the client sends the query to its preferred DNS server. The client's preferred DNS server, DNSKS, checks to see if it can answer the query authoritatively. If it cannot, DNSKS then checks its local cache. If that doesn't result in an answer, DNSKS then forwards the query to DNS1, the DNS server it is configured to forward queries to. DNS1 checks its local cache, and then sends a series of iterative queries first to a root server, then to the DNS servers it gets referred to, until it finally finds the authoritative DNS server for the FQDN.

    ☒ **G** is incorrect.

20. ☑ **B.** A non-recursive DNS server does not build up a cache relating to the domain name nor does it perform recursion. A forward-only DNS server does build up a cache in attempts to resolve the domain name in the future, and can be configured to perform recursion.

    ☒ **A** is incorrect because a forward-only DNS server does build up a cache relating to the domain name. **C** is incorrect because a forward-only DNS server can perform recursion. **D** is incorrect because a non-recursive DNS server is not used only with conditional forwarding.

LAB ANSWER

1. DNSSRV1 would be the DNS server from which the delegation is created.

2. Conditional forwarders could be created on each of the DNS servers in the mccaw.ca domains that point to the lind.ca DNS servers. This would allow clients in the mccaw company to more efficiently resolve names in the lind.ca namespace. Conditional forwarders could also be created on each of the DNS servers in the lind.ca domains that point to the mccaw.ca DNS servers. This would allow clients in any of the lind.ca domains to more efficiently resolve names in all of the mccaw.ca zones.

3. For each zone, the option **To all domain controllers in the Active Directory domain <*domain name*>** should be selected. This will allow the zone to be loaded by DNS servers running on Windows 2000.

4. Conditional forwarding could be configured on each DNS server in Nashville, Berlin, and Sydney to forward all requests for names in the lind.ca namespace to both DNS1 and DNS2. Conditional forwarding could also be configured on all DNS servers in both Etobicoke and Sweden to forward all queries for names in the mccaw.ca namespace to DNSSRV1 or DNSSRV2.

5. Edit the root hints list either using the DNS MMC, or by editing the **cache.dns** file on one of the four new DNS servers. Delete all the existing entries and add only two new entries, one for DNSSRV1, and the other for DNSSRV2. On the remaining three new DNS servers open the DNS MMC, and select to copy the root hints from another server. Select the server from which you made the modifications.

5
Managing DNS

I n Chapter 4, you learned how to install the DNS service, and how to configure server and zones options, including DNS forwarding. This chapter focuses on issues related to managing DNS, including managing DNS zone settings, DNS record settings, and DNS server options.

Knowing how to manage the DNS service is critical for successful day-to-day administration. Because DNS is the underlying name resolution service required to support an Active Directory domain environment, you must be familiar with the tools and utilities available to manage the DNS service.

The many tools and utilities available to help you in your DNS administration include the DNS MMC, **dnscmd**, **dnslint**, **nslookup**, the Performance MMC, and the DNS event log. **dnscmd** and **dnslint** are two tools that are not installed by default with the installation of the Windows Server 2003 operating system, but both are included in the **\\Support\Tools** folder. Installing these support tools will be discussed in the next section.

CERTIFICATION OBJECTIVE 5.01

Manage DNS Server Options

Windows Server 2003 includes a number of enhanced command-line tools and utilities to make it easier for you to perform command-line–based administration. A number of these tools are included by default in the base operating system installation, but others must be installed separately, and can be found on either the Windows Server 2003 CD in the **Support\Tools** directory or on the Windows Server 2003 Resource Kit CD. Exercise 5-1 describes how to install the support tools.

EXERCISE 5-1

Installing Support Tools

This exercise will teach you how to install the support tools included on the Windows Server 2003 CD. These are an enhanced set of administration tools, including **dnscmd**, which we will look at in great detail in this chapter.

1. Insert the Windows Server 2003 CD in your CD-ROM drive, and open Windows Explorer.

2. In Windows Explorer, browse to your CD drive, and expand the Support folder. Then expand the Tools folder.

3. Right-click the file **suptools.msi**, and select **install**.

4. Click **Next** on the Welcome page.

5. Click **I Agree**, and click **Next** on the End User License Agreement page.

6. On the **User Information** page, enter your name and the name of your organization, and click **Next**.

7. On the **Destination Directory** page, either confirm the default file path or change the default file path, and click **Install Now**.

8. Once the installation is complete, click **Finish**.

Managing DNS server options includes a number of different areas that are discussed in this section. We will start with how to add multiple DNS servers to the DNS MMC to allow you to perform your GUI-based, multiple–DNS-server administration from a single console. Once you are familiar with the MMC interface, we will flip over to the command-line DNS administration tools, **dnscmd** and **dnslint**, and look at how these tools can be used to perform command-line–based administration. We will then continue on with a look at the available options for starting and stopping the DNS service. From there, we will shift focus to the different options available to you to update your DNS server data files. The last area that we will look at is how you can further optimize name server (NS) resource record registration.

DNS Administration Tools

There are four tools included on the Windows Server 2003 CD, two of which are installed with a default installation of the operating system and two that are included in the **Support\Tools** folder but not installed by default. This section will look at each of the available DNS administration tools, starting with the DNS MMC.

DNS MMC

The DNS MMC is the GUI tool that is installed by default during the installation of the Windows Server 2003 operating system, and can be found in the list of available MMCs under **Start | Administration Tools**. You can also open the DNS snap-in from within the **Manage Your Server Wizard**, or by opening an empty MMC console and adding the DNS snap-in. One additional way is by typing **dnsmgmt.msc** at the **Run** command.

Remember, regardless of the way in which you prefer to open the DNS administration console, that when you do open it, you should be logged on as an ordinary user, and use the **runas** command to launch and run the DNS MMC in the context of a user with administrative privileges. Exercise 5-2 demonstrates how to use the **runas** command to launch the DNS MMC and then how to add a DNS server to the DNS console.

EXERCISE 5-2

Using runas to Open the DNS MMC and Connect to a DNS Server

In this exercise you will learn how to use the **runas** command to open the DNS MMC and then add a remote DNS server to the console. Best practices suggest that you should always log on using an account without administrative privileges and use the **runas** command to run Administrative tools with administrative privileges.

1. Click **Start | Run**, type **runas /user:administrator %systemroot%\system32\ dnsmgmt.msc**, and press ENTER. Alternatively, you could also, right-click the DNS icon in Administrative Tools and select **Run as**.

2. The command prompt window opens, requesting the password for the account specified. Type the password for the account and press ENTER.

3. In the DNS MMC, right-click DNS, and select **Connect to DNS Server** from the context menu.

4. In the **Connect to DNS Server** dialog box, select **The following computer**, type the name of the remote DNS server in the text box, and click **OK**. This process can be repeated multiple times, allowing you to add numerous DNS servers into a single MMC snap-in and administer multiple servers from a single console.

dnscmd

The **dnscmd** utility allows you to administer DNS from the command line, and make changes to DNS server properties, zones, and resource records. The command-line switches included with **dnscmd** can work on the DNS server or the zone.

Some administrators prefer to work from the GUI, and others prefer to work from the command line, but regardless of your preference, you should familiarize yourself with the command-line tools as they can help you become a more efficient administrator by allowing you to automate a number of recurring manual tasks. Not to mention, you will be required to know them for the exam.

dnscmd is a great utility to help you modify DNS server settings remotely, particularly when the remote server is across a slow WAN link. It also allows you to create batch files that include **dnscmd**, and then copy these files over to the remote servers and execute them remotely. Automating recurring administrative tasks helps you to be more efficient. Take this one step further however and think about how you could incorporate command-line tools such as **dnscmd** into other applications such as Microsoft Operations Manager (MOM). For example, you could use **dnscmd** with the **/statistics** switch to capture and return information to the DNS administrator automatically when a DNS error occurs on a server monitored by MOM. This information could then be used by the DNS administrator to quickly identify and resolve the problem before it escalates into an issue that could potentially cause the DNS server to go into a distressed state.

on the Job

*dnscmd **provides more functionality than its predecessor tool** dnsstat. dnsstat* ***was included in different versions of the Windows NT Resource Kit.***

dnscmd is not installed during a default installation of the Windows Server 2003 operating system, and must be installed separately by installing the support tools found on the server CD in the **Support\Tools** directory and explained in Exercise 5-1. To successfully run **dnscmd**, you must be a member of the Administrators or Server Operators group on the DNS server that you wish to administer.

To access the **dnscmd** utility once you have installed the support tools, open a command prompt, type **dnscmd** and press ENTER. The following are a couple of examples of what you can do with **dnscmd**. If you are unfamiliar with the configuration of a specific DNS server, one of the first switches you might consider using is the **/info** switch, which returns a list of settings displayed in the DNS section of the registry, as shown in Figure 5-1. Figure 5-1 shows you a partial list of what is display when you run the command **dnscmd . /info**. Notice that the syntax uses a period (.). A period can be used in place of a computer name to indicate that you want to execute the command on the local computer. To execute this command against a remote computer, simply replace the period with the remote computer's name.

To see a complete picture of what is happening on a local DNS server, use the command **dnscmd . /statistics >c:\dnsstats.txt**. The results of this command are too extensive to capture in a single screen shot, but if you run the command as shown here, you will be able to pipe all of the information that would normally appear in the command prompt window to a file named **dnsstats.txt** on the C: drive. Alternatively, if you prefer to view the information on the screen, you could also use the **dnscmd . /statistics | more** command to pipe the output to the **more** utility. As in UNIX, **more**

FIGURE 5-1

dnscmd . /info

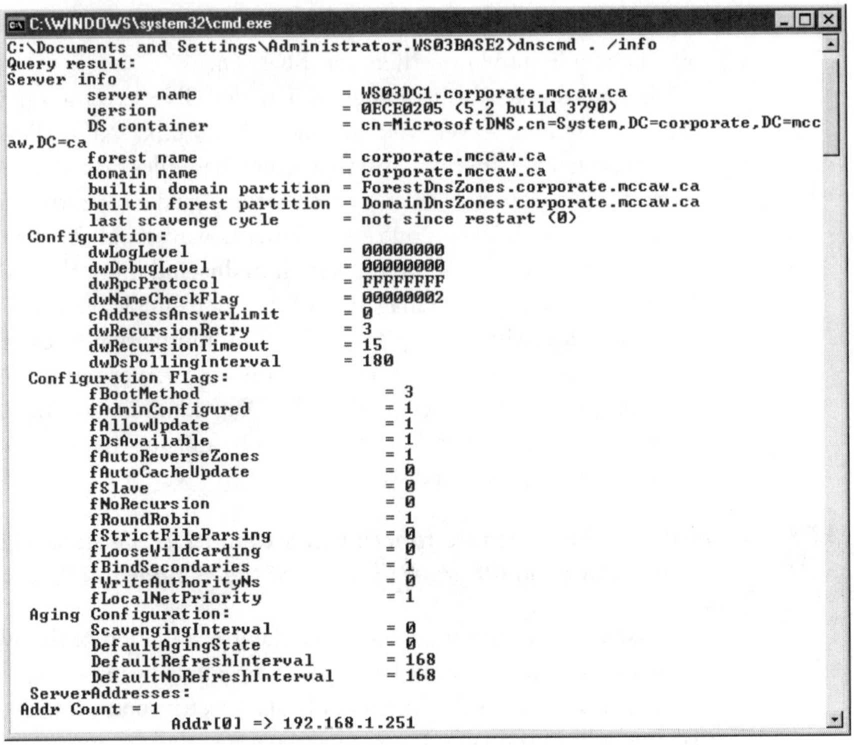

```
C:\WINDOWS\system32\cmd.exe                                               _ □ ×
C:\Documents and Settings\Administrator.WS03BASE2>dnscmd . /info
Query result:
Server info
        server name           = WS03DC1.corporate.mccaw.ca
        version               = 0ECE0205 (5.2 build 3790)
        DS container          = cn=MicrosoftDNS,cn=System,DC=corporate,DC=mcc
aw,DC=ca
        forest name           = corporate.mccaw.ca
        domain name           = corporate.mccaw.ca
        builtin domain partition = ForestDnsZones.corporate.mccaw.ca
        builtin forest partition = DomainDnsZones.corporate.mccaw.ca
        last scavenge cycle   = not since restart (0)
    Configuration:
        dwLogLevel            = 00000000
        dwDebugLevel          = 00000000
        dwRpcProtocol         = FFFFFFFF
        dwNameCheckFlag       = 00000002
        cAddressAnswerLimit   = 0
        dwRecursionRetry      = 3
        dwRecursionTimeout    = 15
        dwDsPollingInterval   = 180
    Configuration Flags:
        fBootMethod                 = 3
        fAdminConfigured            = 1
        fAllowUpdate                = 1
        fDsAvailable                = 1
        fAutoReverseZones           = 1
        fAutoCacheUpdate            = 0
        fSlave                      = 0
        fNoRecursion                = 0
        fRoundRobin                 = 1
        fStrictFileParsing          = 0
        fLooseWildcarding           = 0
        fBindSecondaries            = 1
        fWriteAuthorityNs           = 0
        fLocalNetPriority           = 1
    Aging Configuration:
        ScavengingInterval          = 0
        DefaultAgingState           = 0
        DefaultRefreshInterval      = 168
        DefaultNoRefreshInterval    = 168
    ServerAddresses:
Addr Count = 1
            Addr[0] => 192.168.1.251
```

allows you to use the SPACEBAR to advance a page at a time and ENTER to advance line by line. Either way, the information collected includes the following:

■ DNS server time statistics

■ Queries and responses, and types of queries

■ Master and secondary stats

■ WINS referrals

■ Dynamic updates by packet and internal

■ Security statistics

■ Directory service integration

■ Memory statistics

■ Timeout information

■ Database nodes

■ Records

■ Packet memory usage and **nbtstat** memory usage

■ Error, Cache, and Private stats

You can also configure forwarders by using **dnscmd** on a DNS server. To configure a forwarder for the **lind.ca** domain to use an authoritative DNS server at the IP address 24.37.89.154, type the following command: **dnscmd . /resetforwarders 24.37.89.154 /slave**. The **slave** parameter instructs the DNS server not to perform its own iterative queries. The **/resetforwarders** option is intended to be used on internal DNS servers that you want to send all of their unresolvable, external queries to a single DNS server that performs external name resolution.

The last command we will look at in this section, but by no means the last command available, allows you to reset the IP addresses that the DNS server listens on. By default, the DNS service listens on all IP addresses, but as you know from the discussion of the **Interfaces** tab in the DNS server properties in Chapter 4, this is configurable. To configure the DNS server to only listen on a single IP address of **192.168.1.251**, use the command **dnscmd . /resetlistenaddresses 192.168.1.251**.

Next we will turn our attention to the **dnslint** command. We will revisit **dnscmd** later in this chapter when we discuss the management of DNS zone settings.

dnslint

dnslint is a fairly new tool, originally released with Windows 2000, and now included with the support tools on the Windows Server 2003 CD. **dnslint** is designed to help you troubleshoot DNS issues by focusing in on one of three different areas, based upon the switch you use. You can use **dnslint** with the **/d** switch to diagnose lame delegation issues and other DNS related issues. The **/ql** switch lets you verify a user-defined set of DNS records on one or multiple DNS servers. In an Active Directory domain environment, the **/ad** switch can be used to verify DNS records and troubleshoot problems with Active Directory replication. Before we delve into these three areas in more detail, let's take a step back and review how DNS delegation works.

DNS Delegation   DNS divides namespaces into both *domains* and *zones*, which tends to confuse some people. The difference between a zone and a domain is subtle. Zones are used to store name information about one or more DNS domains, or a contiguous portion of a DNS domain namespace. For example, a zone could contain information about the **mccaw.ca**, **corporate.mccaw.ca**, and **amer.corporate.mccaw.ca** domains, as shown in Figure 5-2. The DNS server DNSROOT is the authoritative DNS server for the **.ca** namespace, while DNS1, DNS2, and DNS3 are all authoritative for the zone **mccaw.ca**, which includes all child and grandchild domains shown in the figure, such as **corporate.mccaw.ca** and **amer.corporate.mccaw.ca**. In this scenario,

FIGURE 5-2

DNS zones
and delegation

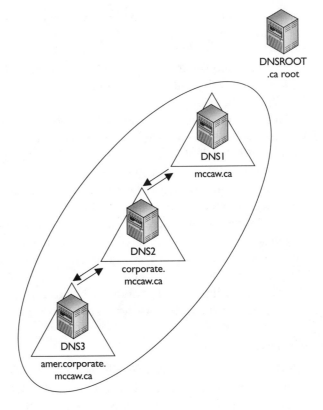

a single zone contains the resource records for three different domains that share a contiguous DNS namespace.

DNS servers are also known as *name servers* (NS). DNS servers store the zone database file, which contains all of the information about the zone, including its configuration information and the resource records within the zone. The DNS servers that store the DNS zone file are said to be *authoritative* for that zone, meaning that they are able to resolve queries for hosts within the zone. When a zone is first created, the first entry that is made within the DNS zone file is known as a start of authority (SOA) resource record. This SOA record is used to identify the primary DNS name server for the zone.

A domain, on the other hand, represents a specific DNS namespace such as **.ca**, **.com**, **.net**, **.au**, **.uk**, and so on. Child domains can exist in each root domain. For example, consider the **.ca** domain. The **.ca** domain contains all the resource records in **.ca** domain plus all the data in each of its child domains, such as **bc.ca**, **mb.ca**, and **on.ca**, where each child domain represents different provinces in Canada such as British Columbia, Manitoba, and Ontario. The difference between the **.ca** domain and the **.ca** zone is that the **.ca** zone contains only the data in the **.ca** domain. The reason for this is that authority for each of the child domains, **bc.ca**, **mb.ca**, and **on.ca**, is delegated to their respective DNS servers.

Look at Figure 5-2 again. The **mccaw.ca** zone consists of three domains, but only a single zone. If you wanted to separate the administration of these three domains for internal administration reasons, you could use delegation. On DNS1, in the **mccaw.ca** domain, you would create a new delegation for the **corporate.mccaw.ca** domain, and select DNS2 as the DNS server that would host the delegated zone. You could then connect to DNS2, and in the **corporate.mccaw.ca** domain, create a new delegation for the **amer.corporate.mccaw.ca** domain, and select DNS3 as the DNS server to host the domain. These changes would result in each of the three different domains having its own zone, but the parent zone of each respective child would know of its existence and would automatically be updated when additional DNS servers are added to the child zone.

There are a number of reasons to use delegation, some of which include

- To simplify the delegation of DNS management for a specific DNS domain to a given individual or group
- To improve the performance of DNS name resolution by distributing the load and maintenance of one large DNS zone database among multiple DNS name servers
- To achieve fault tolerance in your DNS architecture by distributing one large DNS zone database among multiple DNS name servers

Delegation enables you to assign responsibility or authority for a portion of the DNS namespace to a separate entity or other zone. When many large organizations planned their migration to Windows 2000 Active Directory, they commonly found a BIND DNS implementation that was being used to resolve the organization's Internet domain name. Because the DNS service running on Windows 2000 was the recommended name resolution service for Active Directory, it was common to delegate a new child domain to be used as the forest root domain for Active Directory. This allowed the existing BIND DNS implementation to coexist with the DNS service in Windows 2000 Server, but the DNS service on the Windows 2000 Server to handle the domain and zone for Active Directory. As you can see, delegation is the primary means by which DNS becomes a distributed, hierarchical namespace. Exercise 5-3 shows you how to create new delegations.

Creating New Delegations

In this exercise you will learn how to create a new delegation of a child domain. On a DNS server named **ws03dc.corporate.mccaw.ca**, you will create a new delegation for the **amer.corporate.mccaw.ca** domain, and select to host this new zone on a DNS server named **ws03base2.corporate.mccaw.ca**, which has an IP address of **192.168.1.250**.

1. In the DNS MMC, right-click the **corporate.mccaw.ca zone**, and select **New Delegation**.

2. On the **Welcome** page of the wizard, click **Next**.

3. On the **Delegated Domain Name** page, shown here, type **amer** in the **Delegated domain** box, and click **Next**.

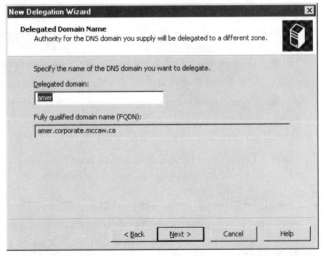

4. On the **Name Servers** page, click **Add**, and enter the FQDN of the DNS name server (**ws03base2.corporate.mccaw.ca**) that you want to host the delegated zone on. Click **Resolve**, and then click **OK**.

5. On the **Name Servers** page, click **Next**.

6. Click **Finish**. Notice that the DNS MMC, shown in the following illustration, now shows a new domain within the **corporate.mccaw.ca** zone. Note that the folder icon is slightly different from the others, and appears with a file appended

to it, indicating that it has been delegated. If you are also looking at the DNS MMC in color, the delegated folder appears gray instead of manila.

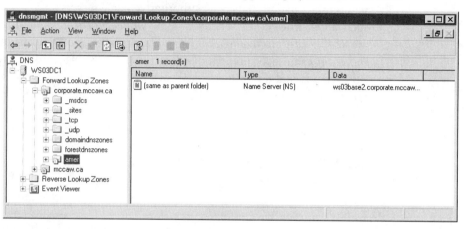

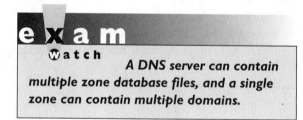

exam

ⓦatch   *A DNS server can contain multiple zone database files, and a single zone can contain multiple domains.*

As you can see in Exercise 5-3, a single DNS server is capable of hosting multiple zones and different zone types. Here you can see that **ws03dc** hosts both the **mccaw.ca** and the **corporate.mccaw.ca** zones. Another great example of this is a DNS server at an Internet service provider (ISP), which can contains hundreds of zones for different customers. That same DNS server could contain the primary zones for some domains and the secondary zones for other domains.

DNSLint: Diagnosing Lame Delegations   Now that you have an understanding of delegation, it's time to shift your attention back to how **dnslint** can help manage your servers. One way in which **dnslint** can be used is in diagnosing *lame delegations*. A lame delegation occurs when a subdomain, such as **amer.corporate.mccaw.ca**, has been delegated to a DNS server, such as **ws03base2**, and this DNS server doesn't exist. This may occur if the IP address that was used to create the original delegation (**192.168.1.250**) is no longer correct, or the zone has been removed from the DNS server, so it does not respond authoritatively to queries. The end result is that the query is not resolved, and the DNS client resolver receives an error. Lame delegation problems can be further compounded when other DNS issues are present.

Normally, diagnosing lame delegations on the Internet involves a number of steps and a significant amount of time. First, you must connect to **Internic.com** and use the **whois** utility to determine the authoritative name servers for a specific domain name, such as **Osborne.com**. Then, again using **whois**, you determine what the IP addresses are for the authoritative name servers. Next you can use **nslookup** to query each DNS server for each record type individually, such as A, NS, and MX records, as well as SRV records, and if you find additional authoritative DNS servers through **nslookup**, you must query all of these DNS servers as well. Once you have collected all of this information, you must then begin the tedious task of comparing your results from **nslookup** against what is on the DNS servers. This is where **dnslint** can help, because **dnslint** can perform all the steps in this process for you. By running the command **dnslint /d Osborne.com**, all of the preceding information will be provided for you seamlessly.

By default, **dnslint** does not check domains in a private namespace not registered with Internic, or domains two or more levels deep. To accomplish this, you will need to use the **/s** switch in a command like **dnslint /d corporate.mccaw.ca /s 192.168.1.251**. The **/s** switch is used to bypass using Internic and uses the IP address of the DNS server that you include after the **/s** switch. Regardless of which of the two commands you use, once **dnslint** has finished processing and collecting the information, it generates an HTML report named **dnslint.htm** and displays its findings. A sample report is shown here.

DNSLint Report
System Date: Fri Jul 18 16:20:52 2003
Command run:
dnslint /d mccaw.ca /s 192.168.1.251
Domain name tested:
  mccaw.ca
The following <u>2</u> DNS servers were identified as authoritative for the domain:

DNS server: User Specified DNS Server
IP Address: 192.168.1.251
UDP port 53 responding to queries: YES
TCP port 53 responding to queries: Not tested
Answering authoritatively for domain: Unknown

SOA record data from server:
Authoritative name server: ws03dc1.corporate.mccaw.ca
Hostmaster: hostmaster.corporate.mccaw.ca

Zone serial number: 1
Zone expires in: 1.00 day(s)
Refresh period: 900 seconds
Retry delay: 600 seconds
Default (minimum) TTL: 3600 seconds

Additional authoritative (NS) records from server:
ws03dc1.corporate.mccaw.ca 192.168.1.251

Mail Exchange (MX) records from server (preference/name/IP address):
None found

DNS server: ws03dc1.corporate.mccaw.ca
IP Address: 192.168.1.251
UDP port 53 responding to queries: YES
TCP port 53 responding to queries: Not tested
Answering authoritatively for domain: YES

SOA record data from server:
Authoritative name server: ws03dc1.corporate.mccaw.ca
Hostmaster: hostmaster.corporate.mccaw.ca
Zone serial number: 1
Zone expires in: 1.00 day(s)
Refresh period: 900 seconds
Retry delay: 600 seconds
Default (minimum) TTL: 3600 seconds

Additional authoritative (NS) records from server:
ws03dc1.corporate.mccaw.ca 192.168.1.251

Mail Exchange (MX) records from server (preference/name/IP address):
None found

Notes:
One or more DNS servers may not be authoritative for the domain

---

The **dnslint** report is also color-coded but in a black-and-white book this is difficult to see. The color-coding scheme uses yellow to indicate warnings, and red to indicate errors. In this report, there are no errors, but the Notes section does include a warning that is displayed in yellow.

dnslint includes some additional switches that can be used to provide more troubleshooting options. For example, the **/c** switch can be used to perform mail server connectivity tests. This switch instructs **dnslint** to attempt to connect to TCP ports 25, 110, and 143 for each mail server that **dnslint** identifies while processing. These ports are used by SMTP, POP3, and IMAP services, and **dnslint** will record whether or not it is able to successfully connect to these ports and what response it received once it connects. You can also specify which ports **dnslint** should verify by using a comma-separated list, such as **/c smtp,pop,imap**. In this scenario, **dnslint** can be used to troubleshoot mail server delivery problems.

Other available switches include the **/v** switch, which configures **dnslint.exe** to use verbose output to the screen, or the **/t** switch to create additional reports in a text file. The **/y** switch is used to confirm that you wish to overwrite old reports without prompting you. The **/y** and **/no_open** switches were included for use in batch files. The **/no_open** switch prevents the **.htm** report from opening once **dnslint** has completed processing. The last switch, **/test_tcp**, instructs **dnslint** to also test TCP port 53 on the DNS server, which isn't done by default but is one of the two ports used by DNS. **dnslint.exe** does automatically test UDP port 53.

on the **Job**

Exchange Server 2000 and the SMTP server in IIS 6.0 use TCP to query DNS, not UDP, because these servers send more data than UDP packets are capable of transmitting. Some DNS servers filter TCP port 53 out, and some are so overloaded they are unable to respond to all the TCP port 53 traffic because of the additional overhead of building and tearing down all the TCP sessions. Using dnslint *with the* /test_tcp *switch is an excellent way to test DNS server compatibility for use with Exchange 2000. Look to KB article 263237 for more information about this little-known fact.*

DNSLint: Diagnosing AD Replication   **dnslint** can also be used to test AD replication issues. As you know, DNS is the default name resolution service that supports Active Directory. When a domain controller wants to replicate with another domain controller, it uses DNS to locate another DC. The domain controller that wishes to replicate only knows the name of its replication partner, so it looks up the other DC's globally unique identifier (GUID) in the Active Directory. Once it finds the GUID, it then sends a recursive DNS query to the locally configured DNS server for the CNAME record that matches the GUID's name. The record name that it's looking for is **guid. _msdcs.<AD forest root domain>**. In the case of the **corporate.mccaw.ca** forest, you can see in Figure 5-3 that the GUID is **008714ab-f12e-47a6-8168-b3774a1545bd**.

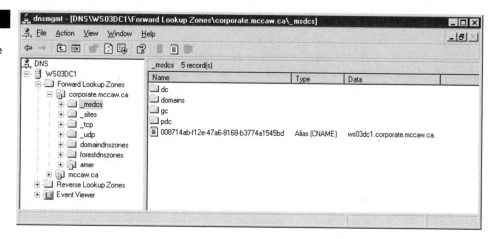

FIGURE 5-3

Determining the GUID of a DC

The response to the DC's query should be alias for the CNAME record, which would be the host name of the DC, **ws03dc1.corporate.mccaw.ca**, in this example. Now that the other DC's name is known, a query is sent out to resolve the name to an IP address required to connect to the other DC and replicate DNS data. You can use **dnslint** in an Active Directory environment to test and determine if DNS records used for AD forest replication can be resolved. An example of this is **dnslint /ad 192.168.1.251 /s 192.168.1.251**. In this example, the DNS server and domain controller are the same server. The IP address that follows the **/ad** switch specifies the LDAP server to query for all of the GUIDs in the entire AD forest. The IP address that follows the **/s** switch specifies the DNS server that is authoritative for the **_msdcs** zone, which is where the DNS records that we are interested in are registered by all DCs in the forest.

In this example, **dnslint** contacts the LDAP server specified by the **/ad** switch to find all the GUIDs for all the DCs in the entire forest. Then **dnslint.exe** queries the DNS server specified by the **/s** switch to resolve the names to IP addresses. This DNS server should be the server that is authoritative for the **_msdcs** zone. If the **_msdcs** zone has been delegated to another DNS server, **dnslint** can recognize this and query the DNS server that has been delegated authority. **dnslint** also attempts to discover other DNS servers that are authoritative for the root of the AD forest, and then queries these DNS servers for the CNAME records for the GUIDs found in AD.

dnslint also generates a report once it is done processing the information. By default, the results of this report will tell you if all of the DNS servers that are authoritative for the **_msdcs** zone have all of the GUID records that they should have, as shown in the sample report here.

DNSLint Report

System Date: Sat Jul 19 01:43:38 2003

Command run:

dnslint /ad 192.168.1.251 /s 192.168.1.251

Root of Active Directory Forest:

 corporate.mccaw.ca

Active Directory Forest Replication GUIDs Found:

DC: WS03DC1
GUID: 008714ab-f12e-47a6-8168-b3774a1545bd

Total GUIDs found: 1

The following 2 DNS servers were checked for records related to AD forest replication:

DNS server: User Specified DNS Server
IP Address: 192.168.1.251
UDP port 53 responding to queries: YES
TCP port 53 responding to queries: Not tested
Answering authoritatively for domain: YES

SOA record data from server:
Authoritative name server: ws03dc1.corporate.mccaw.ca
Hostmaster: hostmaster.corp.mccaw.ca
Zone serial number: 33
Zone expires in: 1.00 day(s)
Refresh period: 900 seconds

Retry delay: 600 seconds
Default (minimum) TTL: 3600 seconds

Additional authoritative (NS) records from server:
ws03dc1.corporate.mccaw.ca 192.168.1.251

Alias (CNAME) and glue (A) records for forest GUIDs from server:
CNAME: 008714ab-f12e-47a6-8168-b3774a1545bd._msdcs.corporate.mccaw.ca
Alias: ws03dc1.corporate.mccaw.ca
Glue: 192.168.1.251

Total number of CNAME records found on this server: 1
Total number of CNAME records missing on this server: 0
Total number of glue (A) records this server could not find: 0

DNS server: ws03dc1.corporate.mccaw.ca
IP Address: 192.168.1.251
UDP port 53 responding to queries: YES
TCP port 53 responding to queries: Not tested
Answering authoritatively for domain: YES

SOA record data from server:
Authoritative name server: ws03dc1.corporate.mccaw.ca
Hostmaster: hostmaster.corp.mccaw.ca
Zone serial number: 33
Zone expires in: 1.00 day(s)
Refresh period: 900 seconds
Retry delay: 600 seconds
Default (minimum) TTL: 3600 seconds

Additional authoritative (NS) records from server:
ws03dc1.corporate.mccaw.ca 192.168.1.251

Alias (CNAME) and glue (A) records for forest GUIDs from server:
CNAME: 008714ab-f12e-47a6-8168-b3774a1545bd._msdcs.corporate.mccaw.ca
Alias: ws03dc1.corporate.mccaw.ca
Glue: 192.168.1.251
Total number of CNAME records found on this server: 1
Total number of CNAME records missing on this server: 0
Total number of glue (A) records this server could not find: 0

In this example, all of the domain controllers were examined, but **dnslint** offers you the ability to be much more specific. For example, if you would rather focus on a single DC because that one DC is experiencing replication problems, that too is possible using a slightly different command such as **dnslint /ad /s localhost**. This command will use the local domain controller that you are executing the command on, and use the local domain controller's LDAP service to identify what GUIDs the local LDAP service knows about. Then **dnslint** will query the domain controller's locally configured DNS servers to determine what domain controllers the local DC knows about, and see if it can resolve all of those GUIDs to IP address. The report will then detail any domain controllers' GUID records the local server was unable to find. This will help you identify if DNS is the root cause of the AD replication issues.

dnslint: Diagnosing Missing Records   The third switch available with **dnslint.exe** is the **/ql** (query list) switch, which can help you determine or verify a set of DNS records and help you diagnose problems caused by missing record problems. This could be very useful in an Active Directory environment where you have a number of domain controllers that all register their SRV resource records with a DNS server. If a problem occurs that prevents this DNS registration, the DC will effectively be in distress. In this scenario, you can use **dnslint** to compare the current DNS records against the list of records you know should be there. In the case of domain controllers, you know that all of the records that must be created in DNS are stored in the **netlogon.dns** file on each domain controller. All the **netlogon.dns** files from all of your domain controllers could be combined into a text file and used by **dnslint**.

Another scenario where you could use **dnslint** is in a web farm environment where you have a number of web servers, and you receive a call indicating that clients cannot get to the web sites. Here, it would be nice to have a way to quickly go out to all of the DNS servers and verify that the IP addresses for the servers are properly registered with the DNS servers and that the resource records are properly configured. This will help eliminate a DNS configuration issue as the cause of the problem.

Another example of where **dnslint** can be used is to verify MX and A records for corporate email. Often, DNS name resolution is the cause of either incoming or outgoing mail problems.

Regardless of the scenario, you can use **dnslint** with the **/ql** switch and an input file to help diagnose the problem and identify any areas where DNS is having problems. The input file is simply a text file you create in Notepad that contains instructions telling **dnslint** what to do. This text file contains the IP address of one DNS server, and all the records you want to query from that DNS server. Here's an example:

```
DNSLint
[dns~server] 192.168.1.251
mccaw.ca,a,r
```

```
192.168.1.251,ptr,r
[dns~server] 24.38.94.56
lind.ca,cname,r
lind.ca,mx,r
_kerberos._tcp.dc._msdcs.lind.ca,srv,r
```

The file itself must start with the word **DNSLINT**. The second line is used to specify the IP address of the DNS server to send queries to, **192.168.1.251** in this example. The following lines indicate the queries that you want to have run in a comma-separated list. In this example, line 3 instructs **dnslint** to query the **mccaw.ca** domain for pointer (PTR) resource records and specifies to test for recursive queries. As you can see on line 4 in the example, you can specify multiple DNS servers, and the tests can be unique to each DNS server.

When **dnslint** parses through this file, it sends out queries to each server listed in the file, and then puts together a report in HTML. This helps you quickly verify if all the records on all of your servers are there, and can quickly alert you to missing resource records. Because most organizations assign static IP addresses to servers, imagine the value this tool could offer by helping you quickly identify if all of the records on one or more DNS servers that are used to support your organization's Active Directory.

Starting and Stopping the DNS Service

Knowing how to start and stop the DNS service is a fundamental part of system administration. It's a very easy task that can be accomplished a number of different ways.

Using the DNS MMC console, simply right-click the name of the DNS server and select **All Tasks** from the context menu. In the sub-context menu, select **Stop**. Notice that you can also pause and restart the service. Pausing the service allows any existing connections to drain but prevents any new connections from being established. Restarting the service lets you recycle that service, which can be useful if that one service is giving you problems.

Alternatively, at the command line, you can use the **net stop dns** command. This option lets you add the command to a batch file and automate its execution in the future. You could even use Task Scheduler to schedule the batch file to run on a recurring schedule. One of the issues that can come up when using the **net** command is that you don't know the name of the service that you wish to stop. To solve this issue, at the command prompt, run the **sc query >c:\services.txt** command to pipe the service names, their states, and a number of other service-specific parameters to a text file. Running this command without the **>c:\services.txt** component will display the results to the screen. A small section of the results can be seen in Figure 5-4.

To display the results for only the service you are interested in, such as DNS in this example, run the command **sc query dns**. The output from this command can be seen in Figure 5-5.

FIGURE 5-4

Results of
sc query

```
C:\WINDOWS\system32\cmd.exe                                               _□×

SERVICE_NAME: winmgmt
DISPLAY_NAME: Windows Management Instrumentation
        TYPE               : 20   WIN32_SHARE_PROCESS
        STATE              : 4    RUNNING
                                  (STOPPABLE, PAUSABLE, ACCEPTS_SHUTDOWN)
        WIN32_EXIT_CODE    : 0    (0x0)
        SERVICE_EXIT_CODE  : 0    (0x0)
        CHECKPOINT         : 0x0
        WAIT_HINT          : 0x0

SERVICE_NAME: wuauserv
DISPLAY_NAME: Automatic Updates
        TYPE               : 20   WIN32_SHARE_PROCESS
        STATE              : 4    RUNNING
                                  (STOPPABLE, NOT_PAUSABLE, ACCEPTS_SHUTDOWN)
        WIN32_EXIT_CODE    : 0    (0x0)
        SERVICE_EXIT_CODE  : 0    (0x0)
        CHECKPOINT         : 0x0
        WAIT_HINT          : 0x0

SERVICE_NAME: WZCSVC
DISPLAY_NAME: Wireless Configuration
        TYPE               : 20   WIN32_SHARE_PROCESS
        STATE              : 4    RUNNING
                                  (STOPPABLE, NOT_PAUSABLE, ACCEPTS_SHUTDOWN)
        WIN32_EXIT_CODE    : 0    (0x0)
        SERVICE_EXIT_CODE  : 0    (0x0)
        CHECKPOINT         : 0x0
        WAIT_HINT          : 0x0

C:\Documents and Settings\Administrator.WS03BASE2>sc query_
```

As you can see, we have a discussed a couple of options available to start and stop services but there are many more such as WMI, the **Net stop** command, **vbscript**, **jscript**, etc., too many to cover in this chapter. You should note that the tools and utilities that we have discussed in this section do not only apply to the DNS service, but can be used to perform the same operations on most services running on a Windows Server 2003 computer.

Updating Server Data Files

Another important DNS server administrative task to understand is how to update server data files. Manually updating DNS server data files for standard primary DNS zones causes the DNS server to immediately write its in-memory changes out to disk where the zone file is stored. By default, this is the **%windir%\system32\dns** directory. These

FIGURE 5-5

The results of
sc query dns

```
C:\WINDOWS\system32\cmd.exe                                               _□×

C:\Documents and Settings\Administrator.WS03BASE2>sc query dns

SERVICE_NAME: dns
        TYPE               : 10   WIN32_OWN_PROCESS
        STATE              : 4    RUNNING
                                  (STOPPABLE, PAUSABLE, ACCEPTS_SHUTDOWN)
        WIN32_EXIT_CODE    : 0    (0x0)
        SERVICE_EXIT_CODE  : 0    (0x0)
        CHECKPOINT         : 0x0
        WAIT_HINT          : 0x0

C:\Documents and Settings\Administrator.WS03BASE2>_
```

changes are normally stored in memory and only written to disk at predefined update intervals, or when the DNS server is shut down.

AD-integrated zones do not operate in the same way. To update the server data files for an AD-integrated zone, you must use the **dnscmd** utility. For example, if the name of your DNS server is DC1, and the name of the zone is **corporate.mccaw.ca**, you could use the command

```
Dnscmd DC1 /ZoneUpdateFromDs corporate.mccaw.ca
```

Exercise 5-4 demonstrates how to manually update server data files on a DNS server that is configured with a standard primary DNS zone, as well as a DNS server running on a domain controller with an Active Directory–integrated zone.

EXERCISE 5-4

Manually Updating Server Data Files

In this exercise you will learn how to manually update DNS server data files using the DNS MMC and **dnscmd**. Only **dnscmd** can be used to update DNS server data files that are Active Directory integrated.

1. Run the DNS MMC as a member of the Administrators group.

2. Right-click the name of the DNS server and select **Update Server Data Files**.

3. To update DNS server data files using **dnscmd** for Active Directory–integrated zones, open the command prompt and type **dnscmd** *servername* **/zoneupdatefromds** *zonename*, where *servername* is the name of the DNS server and *zonename* is the FQDN of the Active Directory–integrated zone.

Now that you are familiar with how to manually update server data files, we'll discuss restricting resource record registration for name servers.

Restricting NS Resource Record Registration

By default, any DNS server running on an Active Directory domain controller automatically adds NS resource records corresponding to itself when it loads a DNS zone. Exercise 5-5 teaches you how to change this default behavior.

By changing the registry to restrict the DNS server from registering NS resource records for authoritative zones, all existing NS resource records for the authoritative zones located on the DNS server are deleted automatically. Regardless of whether you have allowed or restricted the registering of NS resource records, the settings of these registry query responses sent to DNS clients from the authoritative DNS server will show that the responses are from an authoritative DNS server.

Restricting NS Resource Record Registration

In this exercise you will learn how to restrict name server resource record registration for Active Directory domain controllers.

1. Click **Start | Run**, type **regedt32**, and press ENTER.

2. In the **Registry Editor** dialog box, browse to the registry key **HKEY_LOCAL_MACHINE\SYSTEM\CurrentControlSet\Services\ DNS\Parameters**.

3. Select **Edit | New | DWORD Value** and enter **DisableNSRecordsAutoCreation** as the value name.

4. Double-click the new value and enter a value of **0x1** in the **Edit DWORD Value** dialog box, with **Hexadecimal** selected in the **Base** section of the dialog box. This creates a new local DNS server setting that applies to all DNS zones for which this DNS server is authoritative.

5. Close the **Registry Editor** and reboot the computer.

With the new knowledge you have about how to restrict NS record registration, you can now turn your attention to another important DNS concept that applies to both DNS server and DNS zone configuration: setting aging and scavenging properties.

Configuring Aging and Scavenging

Aging and scavenging of old DNS records is yet another DNS server administration task that you should be familiar with, although the configuration of aging and scavenging isn't limited to only the DNS server. The configuration of aging and scavenging must be set in both the DNS server properties as well as the individual zone properties for each of the zones included on your DNS server, though it must be set at the DNS server first before it can be effective at the zone level.

With the ability to use dynamic updates in Windows 2000 Server and Windows Server 2003, it is common, particularly in networks with mobile users, to find that resource records are automatically added, but are not automatically removed when the computers are removed from the network. To address this issue, the aging and scavenging settings can be configured on DNS servers and DNS zones running on computers running either Windows 2000 Server or Windows Server 2003.

In the DNS server properties, scavenging is configured on the **Advanced** tab, as shown in Figure 5-6. Enabling automatic scavenging allows for the scavenging of both manually and automatically created resource records. The caveat here is that manually created DNS records have a default time stamp of zero, which means they don't age. This is by design so that scavenging doesn't remove manual entries and force you to re-create these, thereby increasing the required amount of administration.

If you want certain manually created records to have a timestamp, you can create one for the specific record. This is discussed later in the chapter in the section titled "Manage DNS Zone Settings." Exercise 5-6 walks through the process of configuring scavenging at the DNS server.

FIGURE 5-6

Enabling
scavenging
for the DNS
server

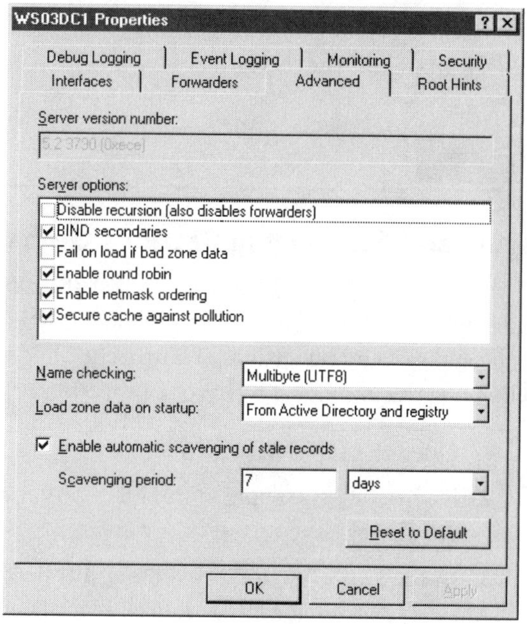

EXERCISE 5-6

Configuring Scavenging on a DNS Server

In this exercise, you will learn how to configure scavenging on a DNS server. This feature allows the DNS server to remove stale resource records from the DNS database on a scheduled basis, and help to reduce both the size of the DNS database and eliminate the potential for name resolution errors as a result of the presence of odd, outdated records.

1. Open the DNS MMC.

2. Right-click the name of the DNS server, and select **Properties**.

3. Select the **Advanced** tab, and select **Enable automatic scavenging of stale resource records**.

4. Click **OK**.

Now that you have enabled scavenging on the DNS server, you can also configure it individually for each DNS zone, or globally for all DNS zones on the server. By enabling aging and scavenging on the server, all future zones that are created inherit the DNS server's scavenging properties including the No-Refresh and Refresh intervals. Exercise 5-7 explains how to globally configure the settings and have them apply to all DNS zones on the server.

EXERCISE 5-7

Configuring Aging and Scavenging Settings Globally

In this exercise, you will learn how to set the global configuration for the aging and scavenging settings for all DNS zones on a DNS server. If you later wish to change the aging and scavenging settings of any of the DNS zones individually, you can do this by modifying the individual DNS zone properties.

1. Open the **DNS MMC**.

2. Right-click the name of the DNS server and select **Set Aging/Scavenging for All Zones**.

3. In the **Server Aging/Scavenging Properties** dialog box shown in Figure 5-7, select **Scavenge stale resource records** and configure the number of days for both the No-refresh and Refresh intervals. As you can see in Figure 5-7, the

FIGURE 5-7

Setting aging
and scavenging
properties

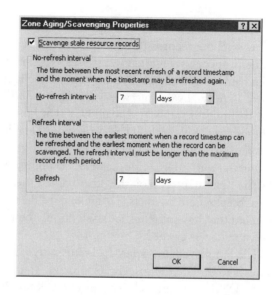

default for both settings is 7 days. When you change the default times, remember that the Refresh interval must be longer than the maximum record refresh time. Click **OK**.

4. The **Server Aging/Scavenging Confirmation** dialog box will appear as shown in Figure 5-8, allowing you to select to **Apply these settings to the existing Active Directory-integrated zones**. Click **OK**.

FIGURE 5-8

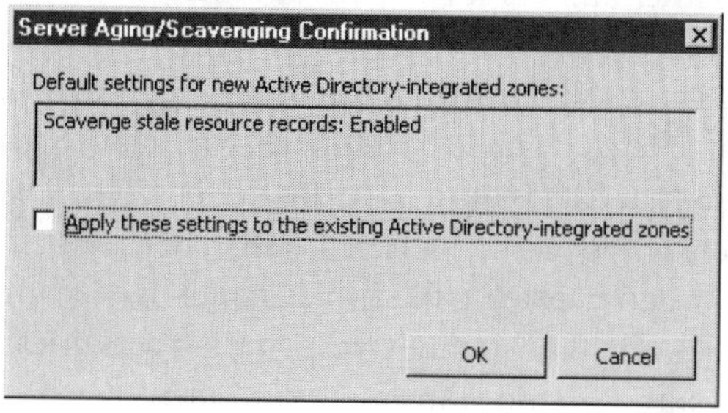

Confirming your
selections

The No-Refresh interval is the time period in which the DNS server does not allow resource records to refresh their timestamps. This interval is designed to reduce unnecessary replication traffic that can result from DNS clients refreshing their name and IP address information. DNS clients refresh their name and IP address every 24 hours, by default, which in turn modifies an attribute on the DNS record in AD that must be replicated to all DCs that host the DNS database. By not accepting refreshes for 7 days (default), unnecessary AD replication is greatly reduced. However, this setting does not prevent the DNS server from accepting updates that change the resource record information, such as a change to the client's IP address or name.

The Refresh interval on the other hand is the period during which the DNS server does accept refresh attempts. Therefore if the default settings of 7 days are not changed, a record that has not refreshed itself during the refresh interval will be scavenged 14 days after it was created.

The last scavenging-related administrative task you can perform across all DNS zones is to initiate the scavenging process. You do this by right-clicking on the name of the DNS server and selecting **Scavenge Stale Resource Records** from the context menu. Selecting this option presents you with a dialog box asking you to confirm that you wish to scavenge all stale resource records on the DNS server. Clicking **Yes** initiates the scavenging process and deletes all stale resource records.

With a solid understanding of the scavenging process under your belt, you'll next explore how to secure DNS.

Securing DNS

Another important component of server administration and managing server options is securing your DNS server. Like all initiatives, the first step in this process should include due diligence and planning. You should begin by deciding on the type of access your clients require, the tradeoffs you want to make between performance and security, and what data is most important to protect. Next you should familiarize yourself with some of the most common security issues related to DNS. The Windows Server 2003 Help and Support tool can be helpful in educating you to the common DNS security issues. The last step in your planning activities should include a study of your name resolution traffic, allowing you to identify which clients are querying which servers. Network Monitor is a tool included with Systems Management Server versions 2.0 and 2003, and can be used in promiscuous mode to sniff and capture packets on your network.

Now that you have decided on the type of access your clients require, you can begin the design and development of your security policy. Like security templates, DNS security policy can be broken down into three types: basic, mid-level and secure.

Basic DNS Security Policy

Implementing a basic DNS security policy does not require any additional configuration and is intended for networks in which you are not concerned about the integrity of your DNS data. These types of environments could include a private network with no external connectivity or isolated branch offices. A typical basic DNS security policy might consist of the following DNS settings:

- DNS servers configured to perform standard DNS resolution and configured with root hints that point to Internet root servers.
- DNS zones permitted to transfer to any server and the DNS service configured to listen on all IP addresses.
- The secure cache against pollution is disabled.
- Dynamic updates allowed for all DNS zones.

Mid-level DNS Security Policy

You can configure a mid-level DNS security policy on DNS servers running on member servers, which therefore doesn't require DNS zones to be stored in Active Directory. A mid-level DNS security policy might include the following settings:

- DNS servers are configured to use forwarders, and point to specific internal DNS servers, as exposure to the Internet is limited.
- DNS servers limit zone transfers to other name servers in the zone, and are configured to listen on specific IP addresses.
- The cache is secured against pollution, and secure dynamic updates are enabled for all zones.
- External DNS servers outside of your firewall are configured with Internet root hint servers, and all Internet name resolution is conducted using proxy servers.

Secure DNS Security Policy

The implementation of a secure DNS security policy is similar to that of a mid-level security policy, except that it is configured on DNS servers running on domain controllers with DNS zones stored in the Active Directory. A secure DNS security policy ensures that there is no DNS communication with the Internet, and might consist of the following settings:

- Internal DNS servers are configured as DNS roots, and all authority for DNS zones is internal because the DNS infrastructure within the organization has no Internet connectivity.

- DNS servers are configured with forwarders to use internal DNS server IP addresses, and are configured to limit zone transfers to specific IP addresses and listen on specified IP addresses.

- Secure cache against pollution is enabled, and secure dynamic update is configured for all DNS zones except top-level zones, which are configured not to allow any dynamic updates.

- The Discretionary Access Control List (DACL) on all DNS servers is configured to restrict administrative tasks to specific individuals, and all DNS zones are stored in AD.

- DACLs are also configured on all DNS resource records to allow only specific individuals to create, delete, or modify DNS data.

- The DNS registry keys found in HKEY_LOCAL_MACHINE\System\ CurrentControlSet\Services\DNS\ are secured.

- Recursion is disabled on DNS servers that do not respond to recursive queries from DNS clients and that are not configured to use forwarders.

Look to the following Technet article for more information on configuring different levels of DNS security: https://www.microsoft.com/technet/prodtechnol/ windowsserver2003/proddocs/datacenter/sag_DNS_imp_Security.asp.

CERTIFICATION OBJECTIVE 5.02

Manage DNS Zone Settings

The majority of the administrative tasks involved in managing DNS zone settings can be found in the property sheets of your DNS zone file. Right-clicking the DNS zone in the DNS MMC and selecting **Properties** will reveal the **DNS Zone Properties** dialog box. Within this dialog box, you will find six tabs if the DNS service is running on a domain controller, and five tabs if it is running on a member server. The sixth tab that doesn't appear when DNS is running on a member server is the **Security** tab. The five remaining tabs are **General**, **Start of Authority**, **Name Servers**, **WINS**, and **Zone Transfers**.

General Zone Properties

The **General** tab of the zone properties dialog box, shown in Figure 5-9, is where you can quickly identify and change the status of the zone. Normally, the zone's status will be **Running**. However as you can see to the right of the current status, you can pause the zone. Underneath the status, you can identify the zone type and replication scope, and to the right you can change both of these properties. Figure 5-9 shows the properties of a DNS zone that is Active Directory integrated and configured to replicate to all domain controllers in the Active Directory domain.

As you learned in Chapter 4, there are three different zone types to choose from: primary, secondary, and stub zones. The **Change Zone Type** dialog box shown in Figure 5-10 lets you select to store the zone information in the Active Directory but this option is only available if DNS is running on a domain controller. You shouldn't change the zone type without significant planning, including giving thought to the negative ramifications. For example, changing a zone from a secondary to a primary type can affect other zone activities, such as dynamic updates and zone transfers.

FIGURE 5-9

Zone properties
General tab

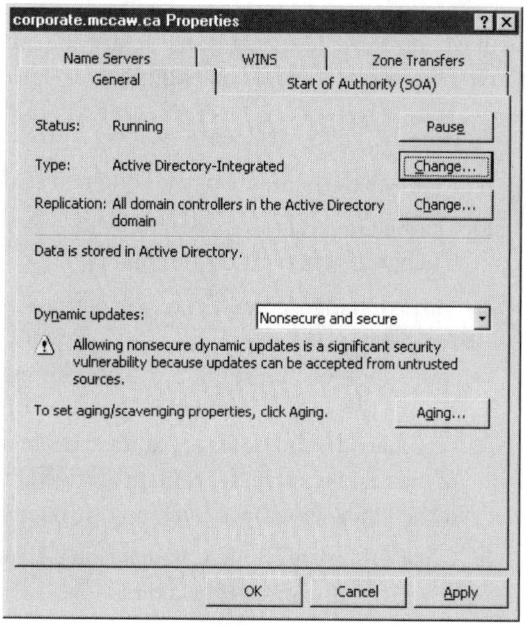

corporate.mccaw.ca Properties

| Name Servers | WINS | Zone Transfers |

General | Start of Authority (SOA)

Status: Running — Pause

Type: Active Directory-Integrated — Change...

Replication: All domain controllers in the Active Directory domain — Change...

Data is stored in Active Directory.

Dynamic updates: Nonsecure and secure

⚠ Allowing nonsecure dynamic updates is a significant security vulnerability because updates can be accepted from untrusted sources.

To set aging/scavenging properties, click Aging. — Aging...

OK   Cancel   Apply

FIGURE 5-10

Changing the
zone type

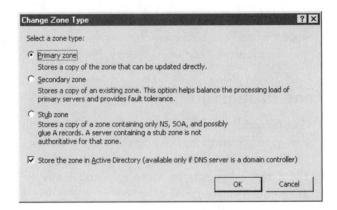

Changing a zone from primary to stub type is also not recommended because of the intended purpose of stub zones. Exercise 5-8 describes the steps involved in changing a zone type.

EXERCISE 5-8

Changing a Zone Type

This exercise is designed to teach you how to change a DNS zone type. This can be useful when you wish to change a primary and secondary DNS zone infrastructure to Active Directory integrated and eliminate the need for zone transfers.

1. Run the DNS MMC as a member of the Administrators group.

2. Right-click the name of the zone and select **Properties**.

3. On the **General** tab shown in Figure 5-9, note the current zone type, and click **Change** to the right of the zone type

4. In the **Change Zone Type** dialog box shown in Figure 5-10, select the zone type you would like to change to. If you choose either the **Secondary** or **Stub** zone types, you must enter the IP address of another DNS server that will be used as the source or master DNS server from which updated information will be obtained. Also note that at the bottom of this dialog box, you have the option of selecting to store the zone in Active Directory. This option is available only if the DNS server is a domain controller.

5. Click **OK** to close the **Change Zone Type** dialog, and click **OK** again to close the zone properties dialog box.

Modifying the zone replication scope is a new feature in Windows Server 2003, and described in Exercise 5-9. The DNS service in Windows Server 2000 introduced the ability to integrate the DNS zone file with Active Directory, making it an object that replicates with Active Directory replication, negating the need for zone transfers. This feature has been expanded in Windows Server 2003 to allow you to define the replication scope. This allows administrators to have more granular control over what servers receive the DNS zone object and better tune and optimize replication, which a lot of customers requested.

EXERCISE 5-9

MasterSim 5-9 ON THE CD

Changing a Zone File Replication Scope

This exercise will teach you how to change a zone file replication scope. This option is new to the DNS service in Windows Server 2003, and provides DNS administrators with much greater flexibility in selecting which servers they wish to have store DNS zone data.

1. Run the DNS MMC as a member of the Administrators group.

2. Right-click the name of the zone and select **Properties**.

3. On the **General** tab shown in Figure 5-9, note the current replication scope. The option to change the replication scope is only available if the DNS zone is Active Directory integrated. To change the scope, click **Change** to the right of **Replication Scope**.

4. This will display the **Change Zone Replication Scope** dialog box shown in the following illustration. Select the replication scope option you wish to use and click **OK** to close the **Change Zone Replication Scope** dialog. Click **OK** again to close the zone properties dialog box.

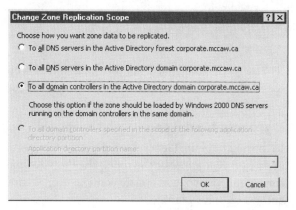

INSIDE THE EXAM

DNS Zone Replication

There are four zone replication scope options available in Windows Server 2003 DNS. The default option is set to allow replication of the zone to **All domain controllers in the Active Directory domain**. This option is the same as in Windows 2000, and is the recommended option to select if you want DNS servers running on Windows 2000 to load the DNS zone.

Another option in an environment where all DNS servers are running Windows Server 2003 is to select **All DNS servers in the Active Directory forest**. This allows the zone data to be replicated to all DNS servers running on domain controllers in the Active Directory forest. If you selecting this option, the DNS zone object information is no longer limited to only domain controllers in the domain, but can be made available to domain controllers throughout the forest. This option will increase replication traffic throughout the forest; take that into account when you plan your replication scope changes.

The third option is **All DNS servers in the Active Directory domain**, which replicates zone data to all domain controllers that are running the DNS service. This option is the default setting for AD-integrated zones running in an all-Windows Server 2003 environment. This option allows you to selectively replicate the DNS zone object within a single domain to only domain controllers running the DNS service, because these are generally the only DCs that require the information.

The last DNS zone replication scope option is **All domain controllers in a specified application directory partition**. This option is only available after you have created an application directory partition. You can do this with the **ntdsutil** utility, which was discussed in Chapter 4. Application partitions are new to Windows Server 2003 Active Directory.

Be very familiar with the different zone replication options, as the concept of zone replication is new to Windows Server 2003. You are likely to see a number of questions on the exam that test your understanding in this area.

When you plan your DNS zone replication scope, remember that the broader the scope, the more network traffic replication will generate.

Dynamic Updates

In the middle of the **General** tab of the zone properties dialog, you can see the dynamic update configuration for the zone. The drop-down box allows you to choose between three different dynamic update configuration settings: none, nonsecure and secure, and secure only.

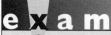

exam

ⓦ**a t c h**　　**AD-integrated zone data stored in an application directory partition is not replicated to the global catalog (GC) in the forest.**

DNS dynamic update (DDNS) allows DNS client computers to register with a DNS server and dynamically update their resource records as changes occur. This feature helps to reduce administration and make you more efficient. The potential downside, however, is that not all client operating systems support dynamic update. Only Windows 2000 and later operating systems natively support dynamic updates. One of the ways to get around this potential downside is to integrate DHCP with DNS and configure the DHCP server to perform the updates automatically on behalf of all client computers. Choosing this configuration option removes the requirement for DNS clients to support dynamic update, because it is all handled by the DHCP server.

exam

ⓦ**a t c h**　　**By default, Windows XP clients do not attempt dynamic update over a RAS or VPN connection. This**　　**default behavior can be changed, however, through the Windows XP client's advanced TCP/IP settings.**

Before you explore the various configuration options available within the zone's properties, you need to know how DNS dynamic updates work. Dynamic updates are usually triggered when either a DNS name or IP address changes. In this example, we will assume that a name change on a computer running Windows XP is what triggers the dynamic update. After a name change, through System properties, you are asked to reboot the computer, and as the computer restarts, the DHCP client service and the following steps are performed to update DNS. This happens regardless of whether the client computer is configured with a static IP address, or it obtains an IP address dynamically through DHCP.

First, the DHCP client service sends a SOA-type query using its new FQDN. The authoritative DNS server for the zone containing the client FQDN responds to the SOA query. The authoritative DNS server that responds will always be the primary server in the case of a standard primary zone. In the case of an AD-integrated zone, however, any DNS server loading the zone can respond, and will dynamically insert its own name as the primary server of the zone in the SOA query. Next, the DHCP client service attempts to contact the primary DNS server. Using the IP address of the authoritative DNS server, included in the SOA query response, the client sends a dynamic update request to the primary server. If this update request succeeds, the process concludes. If the update fails, the client sends an NS-type query for the zone name specified in the SOA record. Upon receiving a response to this query, the DNS

SCENARIO & SOLUTION

You would like to limit the replication of DNS related information to specific servers within your network. What type of DNS zone must be configured to accomplish this?	Only AD-integrated zones allow you to define a zone replication scope.
Which zone replication options would you select if you wanted to limit the replication of DNS zone information but required that it be available on servers outside of your domain?	To provide DNS zone information to servers outside of a single domain while still limiting it to only domain controllers, you could choose either **All DNS servers in the Active Directory forest** or **All domain controllers in a specified application directory partition.**
Describe the two ways that you can set up dynamic updates.	Dynamic updates can be configured to allow the DHCP clients to update their A and PTR information in DNS or to have the DHCP server update this information on their behalf.
When you are using AD integrated DNS zones, the configuration of which zone properties become less important?	When using AD integrated zones, the configuration of the zone transfers tab is less important because the DNS zone is now replicated with AD replication.

client sends an SOA-type query to the first DNS server listed in the SOA record. Once the SOA query is resolved, the DNS client then sends a dynamic update to the server identified in this last SOA query response.

From this point forward, dynamic updates are sent or refreshed every 7 days by default. Future updates will only generate zone changes or increase zone transfer traffic if names or addresses actually change. One other point to remember when discussing dynamic updates is that names are not removed from DNS zones if they become inactive or do not get updated unless you have configured scavenging.

Let's spend a minute to review some of the concepts and fundamentals that we have discussed thus far in the chapter.

Secure dynamic updates are only available with AD-integrated zones. When you use standard zone storage, dynamic updates are not available. Once you change a zone

e x a m

⬤ a t c h *Only AD-integrated zones can be configured to allow only secure dynamic updates. This feature isn't* *available on the Web Edition, because the Web Edition doesn't support being configured as a domain controller.*

to be Active Directory integrated on a computer running Windows Server 2003, the dynamic update setting defaults to **Only secure updates**. When the **Only secure updates** option has been selected, the DNS server will only accept a dynamic DNS update to authenticated computers that are members of the domain in which the DNS server is located. More extensive security settings can also be defined on the **Security** tab of the zone, where the DACLs are configured. Remember that this **Security** tab is only present on Active Directory–integrated zones and AD-integrated zones can only exist on domain controllers.

e x a m

watch
To enable DHCP servers to update DNS when the zone is configured for secure dynamic updates, the DHCP server computer accounts must be added to the DnsUpdateProxy group.

One problem that can arise with the use of secure dynamic updates is that they require that the owner of the resource record (the computer) be the only computer enabled to update that record. This can be an issue when you have configured DHCP to perform the DNS updates on behalf of the client computer. To resolve this problem, the DHCP server computer account must be added to the DnsUpdateProxy group.

Scavenging

At the bottom of the zone properties dialog box, you can configure the aging and scavenging properties for the zone by clicking the **Aging** button. Earlier in the chapter we discussed aging and scavenging as it related to the DNS server. In the DNS zone properties, you can configure unique aging and scavenging settings for the individual DNS zone. Exercise 5-10 will walk you through the steps involved in modifying an individual zone's aging and scavenging properties.

EXERCISE 5-10

Configuring Scavenging

This exercise explains how to enable and configure scavenging in the Windows Server 2003 DNS service to purge the DNS database of stale resource records.

1. Open the **DNS MMC**.
2. Expand the name of the **DNS server**. Expand **Forward Lookup Zones** and select the DNS zone that you want to configure scavenging for.
3. Right-click the name of the **DNS zone** and select **Properties**.

4. On the **General** tab, click the **Aging** button to open the **Zone Aging /
Scavenging Properties** dialog box.

5. Enable **Scavenge stale resource records**, and set the number of days you want
for the no-refresh interval and refresh. Click **OK**, and click **Yes** at the warning
message. Click **OK** again to close the zone properties dialog box.

SOA Zone Properties

The Start of Authority record is the first resource record created in a DNS zone file,
and is used to identify the primary DNS name server (NS) for the zone as well as the
e-mail address of the administrator that is responsible for the DNS zone. On the SOA
tab, shown in Figure 5-11, you are able to modify and manage all of this important DNS
zone information.

The information on the **Start of Authority** tab is particularly important for DNS
zone replication when you are working with zones that are not AD integrated. In
this case, the serial number is used to monitor and identify changes that are made to
the DNS zone file on the DNS server hosting the primary DNS forward lookup zone.

FIGURE 5-11

The **Start of
Authority** tab

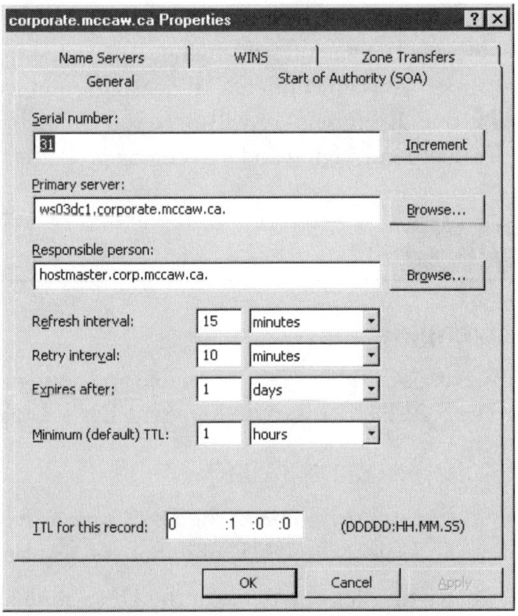

Selecting the **Increment** button allows you to manually increase the serial number and trigger a zone transfer to the DNS servers configured with secondary forward lookup zones.

The SOA tab also lets you change the primary server and the person identified as being responsible for the administration of the zone. You have also likely noticed that what appears to be an invalid e-mail address is listed in the responsible person text box. This is actually correct, because the @ symbol is replaced with a period on this property sheet.

On the SOA tab, the **Refresh interval** is 15 minutes by default. This is the amount of time that a secondary DNS server waits before requesting a copy of the SOA record from the primary DNS server. The secondary server looks at the serial number included in this record and compares it to its own to determine if a zone transfer from the primary DNS server is necessary.

The default retry interval of 10 minutes is the amount of time a secondary DNS server waits after a failed zone transfer before it tries again. A good rule of thumb is to keep the value of the retry interval smaller than the value of the refresh interval.

The default expiration interval of 24 hours is the amount of time a secondary DNS server waits after its last successful refresh before it stops responding to queries. In other words, if a secondary DNS server is unable to perform a refresh with its primary for a 24-hour period, after this time the secondary DNS server will stop responding to DNS queries because it assumes that its DNS zone data is out of date.

The last configuration setting on the SOA tab is the minimum time to live (TTL), which is 1 hour by default. This value defines the amount of time another DNS server may cache host records it receives from a query to this server.

As discussed earlier in this chapter, individual resource records can be configured with unique timestamps, and if this is the case, those individual timestamps override the minimum TTL configured in the SOA record.

Name Servers

The next tab in the DNS zone properties sheets is the **Name Servers** tab, shown in Figure 5-12. This tab is provided to allow you to add additional name servers. This list of name servers helps DNS clients locate other name servers that are also authoritative for the zone.

To add additional name servers, click the **Add** button in the lower-left corner. The **New Resource Record** dialog box appears, as shown in Figure 5-13. Enter the FQDN and IP address of the additional name server, click **Add**, and then click **OK**.

FIGURE 5-12

The **Name Servers** tab

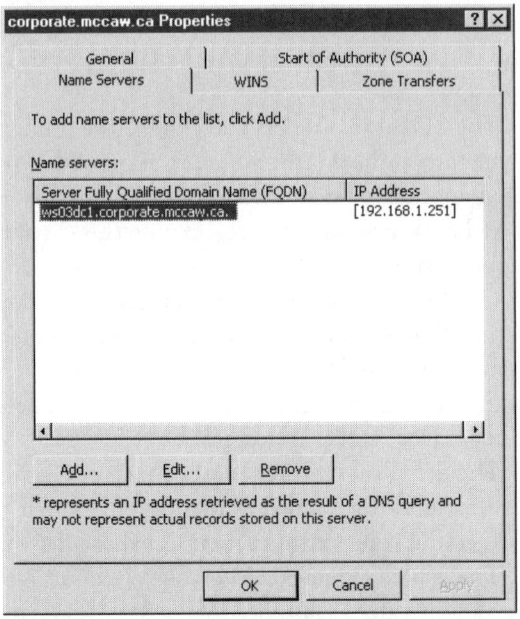

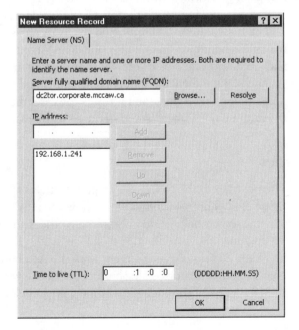

FIGURE 5-13

Adding a new name server

WINS

The **WINS** tab of the DNS zone property sheet allows you to integrate DNS name resolution with the Windows Internet Name Service (WINS) as a way of extending WINS support to non-WINS clients. DNS is a network service that the vast majority of operating systems natively support; however, WINS is proprietary name-resolution service that will fortunately be on its way out the door of most organizations over the next couple of years. Integrating WINS with DNS enables both WINS clients and non-WINS clients to use DNS as their primary means of name resolution, but also enables the DNS service to query WINS if DNS is unable to resolve the NetBIOS name that the client is looking for. This resolution process is displayed in Figure 5-14.

Only Windows 2000, 2003, and Windows NT 4.0 DNS servers support the nonstandard WINS lookup record.

The first step in the simplified name resolution process is for the DNS client to query its preferred DNS server. If that DNS server does not include a resource record for the name that is being queried for, the DNS server queries WINS. The WINS server then attempts to respond to the DNS server, and in turn the DNS server will respond to the DNS client. This configuration can be particularly useful in a mixed-client environment where not all Windows clients support dynamic DNS updates, and where the DHCP service hasn't been configured to perform the DNS updates on behalf of these clients. This will allow for the integration of DNS and WINS to provide a more effective name resolution policy.

The integration of WINS with DNS becomes a little more complicated when your network uses non-Windows DNS servers. If you administer in an environment that uses non-Windows DNS servers, recommended best practices from Microsoft suggest that you create a new DNS child domain and zone and delegate authority of the zone to a Windows Server 2003 DNS server. Figure 5-15 displays the DNS zone configuration on your network before the integration of WINS and DNS in the domain **mccaw.ca**, which is hosted by non-Windows DNS servers, which must remain authoritative.

FIGURE 5-14

WINS name resolution process

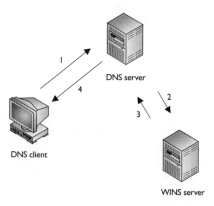

WINS and DNS
integration

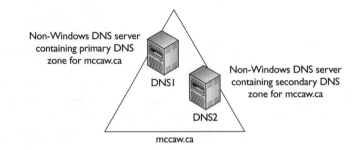

Following best practices from Microsoft, Figure 5-16 shows how to properly integrate WINS into this environment. This recommended approach involves creating a child DNS domain to which authority is then delegated for a new DNS zone configured on a Windows Server 2003 DNS server. This allows the non-Windows DNS server in the original DNS zone to remain authoritative for the **mccaw.ca** domain while enabling the integration of DNS and WINS in the new child domain. In this configuration, WINS client computers would register their name-to-IP-address mapping with the WINS server (**192.168.1.5**). All clients, WINS and non-WINS, would then be configured to use DNS as their primary means of name resolution, and should the DNS server fail to resolve the name resolution request, it would contact the WINS server to try and resolve the name. The DNS server would locate the WINS server through the WINS record created on the Windows Server 2003 DNS server. The Windows Server 2003 DNS server in the **wins.mccaw.ca** domain would also have to

Name resolution
with WINS-
integrated DNS

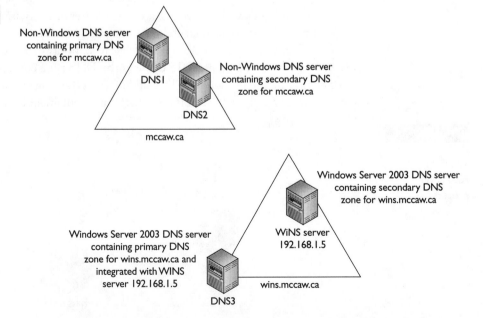

be configured to use WINS for forward lookup queries. The steps involved in configuring WINS integration are discussed in Exercise 5-11.

EXERCISE 5-11

Adding a WINS Record to a DNS Zone

In this exercise you will learn how to integrate WINS and DNS using the DNS MMC snap-in. This will allow you to configure a DNS server running on Windows NT 4.0, Windows 2000, or Windows Server 2003 with WINS to support integrated name resolution in a mixed client environment.

1. In the DNS MMC, expand the name of the DNS server, expand **Forward Lookup Zones**, right-click the name of the zone, and select **Properties**.

2. Select the **WINS** tab as shown here, and enable **Use WINS forward lookup**.

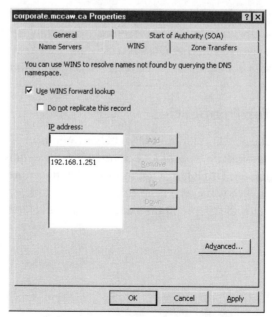

3. Enter the IP address of one or more WINS servers in the IP address box, and click **Add**.

4. In the lower-right corner of the **WINS** tab, click the **Advanced** button to reveal the **Advanced** dialog box shown here. Enter the values for **Cache time-out** and **Lookup time-out**. Click **OK** when you're finished.

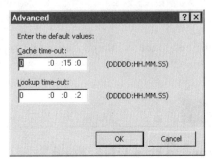

5. If your current DNS architecture includes any non-Windows DNS servers, enable **Do not replicate this record**, as WINS lookup records are non-standard DNS recourse records, unsupported on other DNS implementations. Click **OK**.

Zone Transfer Properties

The implementation of DNS in both Windows 2000 Server and Windows Server 2003 supports two types of zone transfers: full zone transfers (AXFR) and incremental zone transfers (IXFR). In a full zone transfer, the entire zone database file is transferred to all DNS name servers hosting standard secondary zones. Full zone transfers increase bandwidth consumption, and should be avoided across slow network connections.

Incremental zone transfers are the preferred choice for updating secondary zones, because only the changes that have occurred since the last update are transferred.

Support for Active Directory–integrated zones that do not use zone transfers but instead replicate as part of AD replication was introduced in Windows 2000 Server, and continued in Windows Server 2003. However, if you are faced with using standard primary and secondary zones, the configuration of the Name Servers and Zone Transfers tabs is important.

On the **Zone Transfers** tab shown in Figure 5-17, you can enable **Allow zone transfers** and select one of three options: **To any server, Only to servers listed on the Name Servers tab**, or **Only to the following servers**. Selecting the last option, **Only to the following servers**, requires that you manually enter the IP addresses of the DNS servers. The **Zone Transfers** tab is designed to allow you to configure more secure DNS settings and defaults to allow zone transfers to **Only to servers listed on the Name Servers tab**. If you are working with an Active Directory–integrated zone, you do not need to enable zone transfers, because the DNS database information will replicate as an object in Active Directory.

If you are using standard primary and secondary zones, you can also configure notification settings by selecting the **Notify** button on the **Zone Transfers** tab. The default setting is to automatically notify all of the servers listed on the **Name Servers**

FIGURE 5-17

Configuring Zone Transfer settings

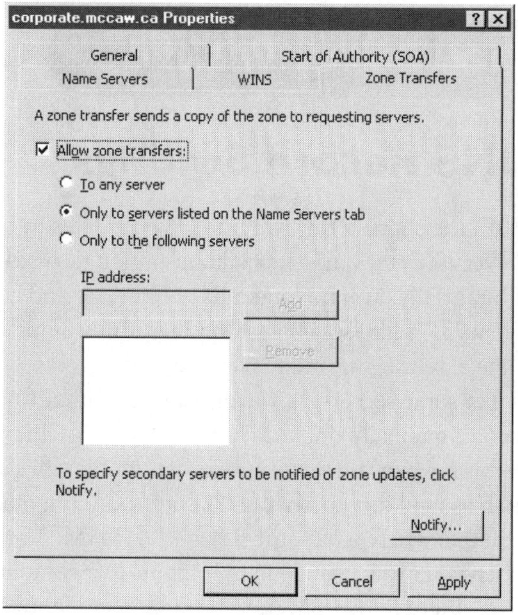

tab, but a second option of notifying only those servers that you specify by IP address is also available. This enables you to ensure that your zone databases are not transferred to any servers that you are unaware of, or to a rogue DNS server that has an NS resource record in the DNS database.

Both Windows 2000 Server and Windows Server 2003 support both full and incremental zone transfers. Older Windows operating systems, such as Windows NT 4.0, do not support incremental zone transfers. Therefore, DNS implementations that use both Windows NT 4.0 and Windows 2000 or 2003 must be configured to use only full zone transfers.

exam

watch

A Windows NT 4.0 DNS server configured with a secondary zone cannot ask for an incremental zone transfer. A Windows NT 4.0 DNS server configured with a primary zone cannot transfer partial information.

In this section, you have learned how to manage DNS zone settings. We'll wrap up this chapter with one last section on managing DNS record settings.

CERTIFICATION OBJECTIVE 5.03

Manage DNS Record Settings

With the support for dynamic DNS updates in both Windows 2000 and Windows Server 2003, the amount of administration required to manage DNS records has decreased substantially. You no longer have to create and change resource records manually as clients' IP addresses change, because this is handled by dynamic DNS updates and to some extent aging and scavenging.

For some servers, however, you still might find that you need to create resource records manually on an occasional basis to achieve a specific result. One great example of this is when you're using records that identify specific types of servers on the network, such as mail servers that use a corresponding mail exchange (MX) record. Another example where a canonical name (CNAME) or alias resource record can be useful is when you want a subdomain to point to a computer outside of your domain. This can be useful in allowing you to point a host record for **news.corporate.mccaw.ca** to your ISP's news server. As you can see in Figure 5-18, you can type in **news.ispserver.com** instead of an IP address.

FIGURE 5-18

Creating a
CNAME record

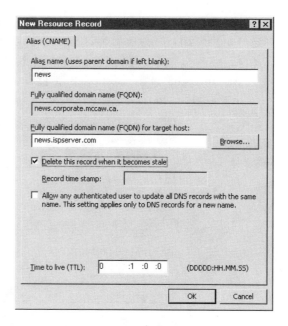

So what are some of the available resource record types that might require management? There are a number of different resource record types, but the most commonly found in forward lookup zones are host (A), alias (CNAME), mail exchange (MX), and service (SRV). In reverse lookup zones, you will find pointer (PTR) resource records.

Manually creating a new resource record is a straightforward process that is explained in Exercise 5-12.

EXERCISE 5-12

Manually Creating Resource Records

In this exercise, you will learn how to create a resource record manually in a DNS zone. This can be useful when you need to create resource records that are not created automatically via DDNS.

1. In the DNS MMC, expand the name of the DNS server, expand **Forward Lookup Zones**, and click the name of the DNS zone in which you wish to create a new resource record.

2. Right-click the name of the DNS zone and select one of either **New Host (A), New Alias (CNAME), New Mail Exchanger (MX)**, or **Other New Records**. In this case, select **Other New Records**.

3. In the **Resource Record Type** dialog box, select the type of resource record you wish to create, such as MX, and click **Create Record**.

4. In the **New Resource Record** dialog box shown in the following illustration, type the name of the host or child domain, if it is different from the FQDN displayed in the FQDN text box. This is generally left blank.

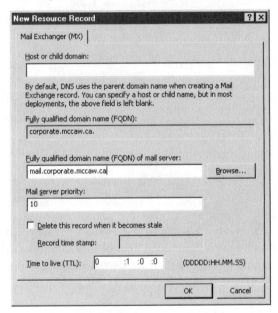

5. In the text box for the FQDN of the mail server, type the mail server's FQDN. Then either accept or modify the mail server priority, and click **OK** to dismiss the **New Resource Record** dialog.

6. Click **Done** to close the **Resource Record Type** dialog box.

Earlier in the chapter, during the discussion of enabling and configuring scavenging on the DNS server, we also mentioned that we would look at how to configure a timestamp for a manually created resource record. By default, manually created resource records have a timestamp of zero, meaning that they do not age. Exercise 5-13 demonstrates how to assign a timestamp to a manually created resource record.

EXERCISE 5-13

Configuring a Timestamp for a Manually Created Resource Record

In this exercise, you will configure a timestamp for a manually created resource record. This is only necessary if you want to allow a manually created record to be scavenged during the normal scavenging period.

1. In the DNS MMC, expand the name of the DNS server, expand **Forward Lookup Zones**, and select the zone that contains the manually created resource record that you want to configure with a timestamp.

2. Right-click the resource record, and select **Properties**. This will display the resource record properties dialog box, as shown in the following illustration. The additional properties seen here will only be displayed if you have enabled Advanced view. To enable Advanced view, click **Cancel**, right-click on the zone name, and select **View | Advanced**; then reopen the properties of the resource record. Alternatively, you can select the **View** menu in the MMC and select **Advanced**.

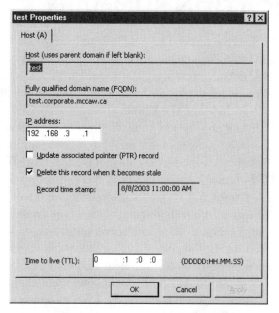

3. Select the option **Delete this record when it becomes stale**, set the TTL that you want the record to have, and click **OK**.

Because DNS is the de facto standard for name resolution on the Internet, and in most organizations, and with the potential for DNS host names and computer IP addresses to change, one other important component of managing DNS resource records is knowing how to delete a resource record. If a resource record becomes out of date and the client has not updated or removed the old record, this record will persist until the scavenging process removes it. If scavenging is enabled, this record could persist for an extended period of time and cause name resolution issues. To solve this problem, you can delete resource records from the DNS MMC console. Simply right-click the selected resource record and select **Delete** from the context menu. This will purge the record from within the DNS database and remove the corresponding name-to-IP-address mapping, hopefully resolving any name resolution issues once the change replicates to all other DNS servers.

In this section, you have learned how to create new resource records, configure the time stamp on existing resource records, and delete records. Managing DNS records isn't rocket science, but it does require an understanding of the various administrative interfaces available, as well as an understanding of DNS basics.

CERTIFICATION SUMMARY

In this chapter, you learned how to manage DNS server options, DNS zone settings, and DNS resource record settings. There are a number of administrative tools available to assist you in managing DNS, including the DNS MMC, **dnscmd**, and **dnslint**. As you learned, not all of these tools are installed by default, but can be found in the support tools included on the Windows Server 2003 CD.

In the first section on managing DNS server options, you learned that **dnscmd** is a command-line tool that enables you to administer DNS from the command line, or through automated scripts. **dnslint** is a tool that allows you to manage and troubleshoot DNS from the command line. You can use **dnslint** to diagnose and resolve lame delegations and AD replication issues, and to verify a set of DNS records. In the discussion about managing DNS server options, you also explored the use and configuration of aging and scavenging settings, and how to enable these on the DNS server. In the last part of this section, you learned how to secure DNS and the different components of basic, mid-level, and secure DNS security configurations.

The second section of the chapter focused on managing DNS zone settings, and looked at each of the tabs on the DNS zone properties dialog box, and how to configure the various settings.

The last section of this chapter focused on the management of DNS resource records, particularly how to create, delete, and configure timestamps.

Understanding how to manage DNS, and what tools can be used in various situations to perform administrative tasks is critical to be prepared for the certification exam. Be sure to run through the exercises in this chapter while sitting in front of a computer with Windows Server 2003 installed on it to ensure you are familiar with the administrative tasks and commands discussed throughout this chapter.

TWO-MINUTE DRILL

Manage DNS Server Options

❏ There are a number of tools available to administer and manage DNS from both the command line and GUI interface. These tools include the DNS MMC (**dnsmgmt.msc**), **dnscmd**, and **dnslint**.

❏ **dnscmd** and **dnslint** are not installed during the default installation of Windows Server 2003, but are included in the Support\Tools directory on the Windows CD-ROM.

❏ **dnslint** can be used to diagnose lame delegations and AD replication issues, and verify DNS server records.

❏ **dnscmd** must be used to update server data files stored in AD-integrated zones, whereas the DNS MMC can be used for standard zones.

❏ You can edit the registry to restrict name server registration.

❏ Aging and scavenging must first be enabled on the DNS server, and then at the individual zones. Scavenging is the process of removing stale records from the DNS database.

❏ There are three DNS server security configurations, basic, mid-level, and secure. Only high security configurations require that DNS be installed on a domain controller and that Active Directory–integrated DNS be used.

Manage DNS Zone Settings

❏ The zone type and zone replication types can be changed on the **General** tab of a DNS zone's properties dialog.

❏ A primary or secondary zone should not be changed to a stub zone. Changing a zone to be a stub zone requires that you enter the IP address of a master DNS server.

❏ There are three scope replication options for AD-integrated zones: **All domain controllers in the Active Directory domain**, **All DNS servers in the Active Directory forest**, and **All DNS servers in the Active Directory domain** (default).

❏ AD-integrated zone data stored in an application directory partition is not replicated to GCs.

❑ ADAM partitions cannot be used to store AD-integrated DNS data, and the Web Edition cannot be used to stored AD-integrated zones.

❑ Only AD-integrated zones support secure dynamic updates.

❑ To enable DHCP servers to update DNS when the zone is configured for secure dynamic updates, the DHCP server computer account must be added to the DnsUpdateProxy group.

❑ Only Windows NT 4.0, Windows 2000, and Windows Server 2003 DNS servers support WINS lookup records.

Manage DNS Record Settings

❑ You can manually create DNS resource records using either the DNS MMC or **dnscmd**.

❑ To view the timestamp value for individual resource records, select the **Advanced View** option in the DNS MMC.

❑ Old or stale DNS records can be manually deleted or left for the scavenging process to delete them. Ideally, old resource records should be removed as quickly as possible to prevent name resolution problems from occurring.

SELF TEST

The following questions will help you measure your understanding of the material presented in this chapter. Read the questions and answers carefully because there may be more than one correct answer. Choose all correct answers for each question.

Manage DNS Server Options

1. You are the network administrator in your company, and as such you are responsible for the administration and management of the company's internal DNS infrastructure. The company has approximately 3,500 employees located throughout its 15 worldwide offices. You have been monitoring the internal DNS infrastructure using the DNS management pack for Microsoft Operations Manager, and you have been alerted to problems relating to lame delegations. You would like to further troubleshoot lame delegations in the **corporate.mccaw.ca** domain. Which of the following utilities would allow you to accomplish this task?

   A. dnscmd.exe

   B. dnslint.exe

   C. dnsmgmt.msc

   D. nslookup.exe

2. You are the network administrator in your company, and you are attempting to explain the difference between DNS zones and DNS domains to a confused junior administrator. Which of the following statements best represents the truth about DNS zones and DNS domains? (Choose two.)

   A. A DNS server can contain multiple DNS zones.

   B. A DNS server can contain only a single DNS zone.

   C. A DNS zone can contain multiple contiguous DNS domains.

   D. A DNS zone can contain multiple non-contiguous DNS domains.

3. You are the network administrator in your company, and as such you are responsible for the administration and management of the company's internal DNS infrastructure. The company has approximately 6,500 employees located throughout its 15 worldwide offices. You have been monitoring the internal DNS infrastructure using the DNS management pack for Microsoft Operations Manager, and you have been alerted to problems relating to lame delegations. The internal DNS server that is the SOA for the domain **namer.corporate.mccaw.ca** has an IP address of 10.10.1.100. Which of the following commands will allow you to diagnose lame delegations?

   A. dnslint /d namer.corporate.mccaw.ca /s 10.10.1.100

   B. dnscmd /d namer.corporate.mccaw.ca /s 10.10.1.100

   C. dnslint /d namer /10.10.1.100

   D. dnscmd /d namer /10.10.1.100

4. You are the network administrator in your organization, and you are using **dnslint.exe** to troubleshoot Active Directory replication between domain controllers. To better help you troubleshoot AD replication, you want to list, in order, the replication steps that occur when DC1 wants to replicate to DC2 so that you can use this as a reference. Place the following name resolution steps in the correct order in which they occur during the Active Directory replication process.

   A. DC1 looks up DC2's GUID in the Active Directory.

   B. DC2 sends a heartbeat to DC1.

   C. DC1 sends a query to DC2 to resolve DC2's name to an IP address.

   D. DC1 sends an LDAP query to the configuration partition on a GC to locate DC2.

   E. DC1 sends a query to DNS to resolve DC2's name to an IP address.

   F. DC1 sends a recursive DNS query to its preferred DNS server for the CNAME record that matches the GUID.

5. You are the network administrator in your organization. You want to verify that all of the DNS SRV resource records that are found in **netlogon.dns** have been created in the DNS zone that supports your Active Directory domain, named **corporate.lind.ca**. Which of the following commands will you use to perform this verification?

   A. dnslint.exe /ql c:\input.txt

   B. dnscmd.exe /ql c:\input.txt

   C. dnslint.exe /query c:\input.txt corporate.lind.ca

   D. dnscmd.exe /query c:\input.txt corporate.lind.ca

6. You are the network administrator in your company. You have asked another administrator for a DNS management tool recommendation. Your colleague has recommended **dnslint.exe**. Which three areas will **dnslint.exe** allow you to manage and diagnose?

   A. Missing DNS resource records

   B. DNS zone configuration

   C. Lame delegations

   D. Active Directory authentication issues

   E. Active Directory replication issues

7. Which of the following DNS utilities is not installed during the default installation of the Windows Server 2003 operating system? (Select all that apply.)

   A. dnscmd.exe

   B. dnslint.exe

   C. dnsmgmt.msc

   D. nslookup.exe

8. You are the network administrator for your organization. You are trying to decide on the best DNS architecture for your organization. Which of the following represent valid reasons for choosing to create a DNS delegation?

   A. Your existing DNS infrastructure uses non-Windows DNS, and only Windows DNS supports Active Directory.

   B. Your existing DNS infrastructure uses Windows NT 4.0 DNS, and you want to integrate WINS.

   C. You wish to improve the performance of DNS name resolution.

   D. Your existing DNS infrastructure uses non-Windows DNS, and the DNS administration group does not want to enable dynamic update support on the existing zone.

Manage DNS Zone Settings

9. You are the network administrator within your organization, and you are responsible for administering DNS. You have just completed the migration from Windows NT 4.0 to Windows Server 2003 Active Directory, and you have a forest root domain and three child domains. Each child domain represents an old Windows NT 4.0 account domain. You have installed DNS on three domain controllers in each domain in the forest, and you have changed the domain and forest functional levels to Windows 2000 native. You perform all of your administration from a computer running Windows XP Professional that has all of the Windows Server 2003 administration tools installed locally. You open the DNS MMC and connect to the domain controller that was installed second in your forest. In the DNS MMC, you open the properties of the zone used for your forest and find that the option to configure your DNS replication scope is not available. Which of the following is most likely causing the problem?

   A. The domain controller you are connected to is not the schema operations master.

   B. The domain controller you are connected to is not the domain naming operations master.

   C. The zone has been migrated from Windows NT 4.0, and an update of the zone files has not occurred.

   D. The zone is not Active Directory integrated.

10. You are the network administrator in your organization. You are attempting to configure a DNS zone to support *Only secure dynamic updates*. You have installed the DNS service on a computer running Windows Server 2003 Web Edition. When you open the properties of the DNS zone, you are unable to change the zone type to AD integrated. Which of the following is the most likely cause of the problem?

    A. AD-integrated zones require that ADAM be installed on the Web Edition.

    B. AD must first be installed on the computer.

    C. The SMTP service must be installed locally as a component of IIS to allow for AD replication.

    D. The Web Edition doesn't support the AD domain controller role.

11. You are the network administrator in your organization, and as such, part of your responsibility is to manage and monitor DNS. You have just installed DNS on a second domain controller, and added the Active Directory–integrated zone named **corporate.mccaw.ca** that provides name resolution for your AD forest. Which one of the following zone transfer options will you find selected when you look at the properties of the DNS zone?

A. To any server

B. Only to servers listed on the Name Servers tab

C. Only to the following servers

D. To all domain controllers in the Active Directory domain corporate.mccaw.ca

12. You are the network administrator within your organization. You would like to bounce (restart) the DNS service from the command line. Which of the following commands will accomplish this? (Choose two. Each answer represents a partial solution.)

A. net restart dnsmgmt

B. net stop dns

C. sc stop dns

D. net start dns

E. sc start dns

13. You are the network administrator for your organization. You have configured your Windows Server 2003 DHCP server to perform dynamic updates for all client operating systems that obtain an IP from DHCP. You have also recently implemented a more secure DNS server policy that includes limiting the IP addresses that the DNS server can listen on, enabling only secure dynamic updates, and integrating the zone with Active Directory. You have noticed that client operating systems are no longer being dynamically updated by the DHCP server. Which of the following will correct this problem while maintaining a secure configuration?

A. Manually create a host resource record for the DHCP server in the DNS zone.

B. Manually create a DHCPSRV resource record in the DNS zone.

C. Add the DHCP server computer account to the DHCPUpdateProxy group.

D. Add the DHCP server computer account to the DNSUpdateProxy group.

Manage DNS Record Settings

14. You are the network administrator in your organization. You have just finished manually creating 10 resource records in your standard primary forward-lookup zone. You forgot during the creation of the records to configure above-average timestamps because these records should persist longer than others. When you open the properties of one of the records you just created, the option to configure a timestamp is not there. When you open the properties of the DNS zone, you verify that the dynamic update setting is set to allow both secure and non-secure dynamic updates. Which of the following best represents why you are unable to see and configure a timestamp?

    A. Timestamps only exist when the zone is AD integrated.

    B. The type of record you are viewing the properties of doesn't support timestamps.

    C. Timestamps cannot be configured when the dynamic update setting is set to allow both secure and non-secure updates.

    D. The Advanced view must be enabled.

15. You are the network administrator for your organization. While performing some regular DNS administrative tasks, you have noticed that there are old, manually created resource records in the DNS database that are no longer relevant. What is the most likely cause of this?

    A. You have not enabled scavenging on the DNS server.

    B. You have not set the No-Refresh and Refresh intervals.

    C. You have not assigned a timestamp to the manually created records.

    D. You have not deleted the old records as they became stale.

LAB QUESTION

You are the network administrator in your corporation. You are actively involved in implementing numerous changes to the company's existing DNS infrastructure. Your organization currently has a standard primary and secondary DNS architecture with the DNS service running on both domain controllers and member servers. Your new DNS design mandates that a secure DNS policy be implemented, and that name resolution issues due to incorrect DNS zone data must be minimized or eliminated completely. The new plan also calls for the DNS zone data to be stored only on Active Directory domain controllers. Your current Active Directory forest consists of three domains: a forest root domain and two child domains. The DNS zone information for the forest root domain must be available outside of the forest root domain, but you want to limit the DNS zone information for the two child domains to just the respective domains.

    1. Identify five key security-related settings that would be a part of a high-security DNS policy.

    2. What type of DNS zone is required to allow your new infrastructure to be implemented?

    3. What zone replication scope will you select for the forest root domain and two child domains?

    4. How will you address the issue of old, stale DNS data causing name resolution issues? What additional steps must you take for manually created resource records?

SELF TEST ANSWERS

Manage DNS Server Options

1. ☑ **B.** The **dnslint.exe** utility would be the best choice for troubleshooting lame delegation issues. Lame delegations occur when subdomains are delegated to DNS servers that no longer exist.

   ☒ **A** is incorrect because **dnscmd.exe** is a utility that allows you to administer DNS from the command line. **C** is incorrect because **dnsmgmt.msc** is a GUI alternative to **dnscmd.exe**. **D** is incorrect because **nslookup.exe** is designed to troubleshoot DNS issues.

2. ☑ **A and C.** A DNS server can contain multiple DNS zones, and a DNS zone can contain multiple contiguous DNS domains. This allows a DNS server to be the SOA for numerous DNS zones that contain one or more domains.

   ☒ **B** is incorrect because a DNS server can contain multiple zones. **D** is incorrect because a DNS zone cannot contain multiple non-contiguous DNS domains. A zone must contain contiguous DNS domains, such as **mccaw.ca** and **corporate.mccaw.ca**.

3. ☑ **A.** The correct command to use is **dnslint /d namer.corporate.mccaw.ca /s 10.10.1.100** because **dnslint** doesn't check domains two or more levels deep without the **/s** switch, which instructs **dnslint** to bypass Internic and use the DNS server specified by IP address after the **/s** switch.

   ☒ **B** is incorrect because **dnscmd** isn't designed to be used to check for lame delegations. **C** and **D** are incorrect because you must use the fully qualified domain name with **dnslint**.

4. ☑ **A, F, and E.** The first step in the name resolution process used in Active Directory replication is for the domain controller that wants to replicate (DC1) to look up its replication partner's (DC2's) GUID in the AD. Next, DC1 sends a recursive DNS query to its preferred DNS server for the CNAME record that matches the GUID. Finally DC1 sends a query to DNS to resolve DC2's name to an IP address.

   ☒ **B** is incorrect because there is no heartbeat in DNS or Active Directory. **C** is incorrect because in DNS name resolution, DNS clients query a DNS server, but DNS clients do not query other DNS clients. **D** is incorrect because no LDAP queries are sent to the configuration partition on a GC.

5. ☑ **A.** The **dnslint.exe /ql c:\input.txt** command can be used to run a query using the instructions in the **input.txt** file.

   ☒ **B, C, and D** are incorrect because none of these commands will produce the results you are looking for in the question.

6. ☑ **A, C,** and **E. dnslint** is designed to diagnose and manage three areas of DNS: detection of missing resource records, lame delegations, and AD replication issues.
   ☒ **B** is incorrect because **dnscmd** is designed to allow you to perform DNS administration. **D** is incorrect because DNS utilities as a whole are not designed to diagnose and manage Active Directory authentication issues.

7. ☑ **A** and **B.** Neither **dnscmd** nor **dnslint** is installed with the default installation of Windows Server 2003.
   ☒ **C** and **D** are incorrect because both **dnsmgmt.msc** and **nslookup** are installed during the default installation of Windows Server 2003.

8. ☑ **C** and **D.** There are a number of valid reasons to create a DNS delegation, but the two in this question are to improve performance by distributing the load and maintenance across multiple DNS servers, and to allow you to enable support in the child zone for features such as DNS dynamic updates without affecting the non-Windows DNS implementation.
   ☒ **A** is incorrect because there are a number of different versions of non-Windows DNS such as BIND that can support Active Directory. **B** is incorrect because Windows NT 4.0 DNS supports WINS resource records; only non-Windows DNS does not.

Manage DNS Zone Settings

9. ☑ **D.** The option to change the replication scope is only available if the DNS zone is Active Directory integrated.
   ☒ **A** and **B** are incorrect because you do not have to be connected to a domain controller that holds any of the operations master roles to change the DNS zone replication scope. **C** is incorrect because both new and migrated DNS scopes can have their DNS zone replication scope modified.

10. ☑ **D.** The Web Edition of the Windows Server 2003 operating system does not support the AD domain controller role, and AD integrated zones can only be configured on domain controllers. Furthermore, the option of *Only secure dynamic updates* is only available for AD-integrated zones.
    ☒ **A** is incorrect because AD-integrated zones cannot be stored in ADAM, nor can ADAM be installed on the Web Edition of the Windows Server 2003 operating system. **B** is incorrect because although it is true that AD must first be installed on the computer in order to AD-integrate a DNS zone, the Web Edition does not support the AD domain controller role. **C** is incorrect because the SMTP service is not a requirement for AD integration of a DNS zone.

11. ☑ **B.** The default zone transfer setting on DNS servers running on Windows Server 2003 is **Only to servers listed on the Name Servers tab**. This default option provides a great balance of both security and ease of administration.

☒   **A** is incorrect because the option **To any server** is too unsecure to be the default zone transfer setting. **C** is incorrect because the option **Only to the following servers** is restrictive but requires too much administration to be the default. **D** is incorrect because the option **To all domain controllers in the Active Directory domain corporate.mccaw.ca** is a zone replication option for AD-integrated zones but is not found on the **Zone Transfers** tab.

12.   ☑   **B** and **D**. The **net stop dns** and **net start dns** commands allow you to bounce the DNS service from the command line.
☒   **A, C,** and **E**. There is no **net restart** command or **sc stop** and **sc start** commands.

13.   ☑   **D**. To enable a DHCP server to perform dynamic updates in the DNS zone database when the zone is AD integrated and only secure updates are allowed, you must add the computer account of the DHCP server to the DHSUpdateProxy group.
☒   **A** is incorrect because manually creating a host resource record for the DHCP server in the DNS zone will not resolve the problem. **B** is incorrect because there is no DHCPSRV resource record type. **C** is incorrect because there is no group called DHCPUpdateProxy.

Manage DNS Record Settings

14.   ☑   **D**. The Advanced view must be enabled in order to view the timestamp information on an individual resource record.
☒   **A** and **B** are incorrect because timestamps can be created for resource records in all types of zones and for all types of records. **C** is incorrect because the dynamic update setting has no bearing on the timestamp configuration.

15.   ☑   **D**. Manually created resource records either must be deleted when they become stale or a timestamp must be assigned to them so that the scavenging process deletes them during its scheduled time. Manually created resource records have a default timestamp of zero which means that they don't age.
☒   **A** is incorrect because even if you enabled scavenging on the DNS server and the DNS zone, manually created records will only be scavenged if they have been configured with a timestamp. This is something that must be done manually. **B** is incorrect because the No Refresh and Refresh intervals do not need to be configured, because they default to 7 days if not configured. **C** is incorrect because manually assigning a timestamp to the manually created resource records is only part of a complete solution. Enabling scavenging on both the DNS server and DNS zone is the other part.

LAB ANSWER

1. Security-related settings that would be a part of a secure DNS policy include

   - Configure internal DNS servers as DNS roots.

   - Secure the cache against pollution.

   - Integrate the zone with Active Directory so that it is stored only on domain controllers, and use the DACL to limit access to perform administrative tasks to the appropriate groups.

   - Allow only secure dynamic updates.

   - Secure the registry keys found in HKEY_LOCAL_MACHINE\System\CurrentControlSet\Services\DNS\.

   - Disable recursion on the DNS servers that do not respond to recursive queries.

2. Only AD-integrated zones can be used to implement your new infrastructure, because only AD-integrated zones support only secure dynamic updates and the ability to limit zone replication.

3. For the forest root domain, select either **All domain controllers in a specified application directory partition** or **All DNS servers in the Active Directory forest** as the zone replication scope. Either of these selections require that the domain controllers running DNS be running Windows Server 2003, because Windows 2000 Server does not support the new application directory. For the two child domains, the zone replication scope option **All DNS servers in the Active Directory domain** would be ideal.

4. To reduce or eliminate name resolution issues caused by old, stale DNS records, enable aging and scavenging on both the DNS server and the DNS zone. For manually created resource records, create a timestamp for each record if you want these to be included in the scavenging process, because by default manually created resource records don't age.

MCSE/MCSA

MICROSOFT® CERTIFIED SYSTEMS ENGINEER &
MICROSOFT® CERTIFIED SYSTEMS ADMINISTRATOR

6

Maintaining DNS

I n this chapter we will focus exclusively on the tools available for monitoring DNS and how to use them. On the certification exam, you will be expected to know how to use tools like System Monitor, Event Viewer, Replication Monitor, DNS debug logs, dnslint, nslookup, and Microsoft Operations Manager (MOM) to monitor and diagnose DNS issues.

Over the last couple of years, Microsoft has dramatically increased its commitment to server and desktop management. In addition to a new release of SMS due out in the fall of 2003, we have also seen significant changes incorporated into Service Pack 1 for Microsoft Operations Manager. A future version of MOM is also expected to be released in 2004 and the management product development group's goal for MOM and SMS is to offer an integrated Microsoft System Center. The Microsoft System Center will be a suite of management services built on the underlying Windows manageability services and Dynamic Systems Architecture.

One of the fundamentals that has been learned by Microsoft's Operations Technology Group (OTG), as well as Microsoft Consulting Services (MCS), and many partners and customers is that monitoring is essential to long term system availability and overall system health. Many organizations that operate Microsoft applications and operating systems, particularly server operating systems in production environments, are beginning to realize the importance of monitoring these technologies. These companies are also finally starting to realize the benefits of monitoring, which include improved uptime and availability, better system reliability, improved security and overall improvements in process control and operational excellence, and more. Operations management is certainly not new to IT, but it is fairly new to the Microsoft landscape, and is an area where you will see a significant amount of focus and attention paid on an ongoing basis.

CERTIFICATION OBJECTIVE 6.01

Monitor DNS

Because DNS is the underlying name resolution service for Active Directory and the provider of name resolution services on the Internet, it has become a critical network service. Like any critical service or application, DNS must be routinely monitored to ensure that it is functioning correctly and within expected norms. DNS becomes even more important in organizations that are using Active Directory and Active Directory-integrated applications such as ISA Enterprise Edition, Exchange Server 2003, or SMS 2003. This chapter deals with only a single certification objective, but don't let that confuse you about the importance of monitoring DNS. In this chapter, we will look at all of the various tools available to monitor DNS, including tools not installed by default, but found in the support\tools folder on the Windows Server 2003 CD. We'll begin with a look at the DNS MMC and the options it has for monitoring and diagnosing DNS issues.

Using the DNS MMC to Monitor DNS

The DNS MMC includes a number of diagnostic and monitoring capabilities, including the ability to verify the DNS server's configuration by running a test manually or at a scheduled interval. The Monitoring tab in the DNS server properties, shown in Figure 6-1, lets you perform a *simple query* and or a *recursive query* to test the DNS server's configuration. Exercise 6-1 walks you through the steps involved in performing these tests.

FIGURE 6-1

Testing DNS using the options on the monitoring tab

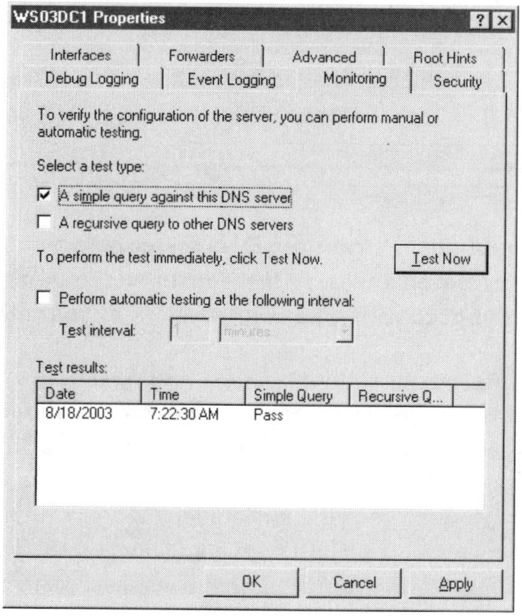

EXERCISE 6-1

Testing DNS Using the DNS MMC

In this exercise, you will learn how to test the configuration of a DNS server using the options available on the Monitoring tab of the DNS server properties in the DNS MMC. You should perform this type of test immediately after you have installed and configured DNS on a server to test that its configuration is functioning correctly, and then you should run this test again at scheduled intervals in the future. You can also run this test if you become aware of DNS problems to determine if the DNS server is operating successfully.

1. Open the **DNS MMC**.

2. Right-click the name of the DNS server and select **Refresh**.

3. Right-click the name of the DNS server and select **Properties**.

4. Select the **Monitoring** tab to reveal the property sheet shown in Figure 6-1 and place a check mark in the box to the left of **A simple query against this DNS server**.

5. Click the **Test Now** button.

6. Confirm that the results **Pass** the test in the **Test Results** section.

7. Click **OK** to close the DNS server properties dialog box.

8. Close the **DNS MMC**.

---

on the **Job**

You should Refresh the DNS server before running a test if you have just added or removed zones. In these instances you might receive incorrect results if you attempt to verify the configuration of your DNS server without first refreshing.

As you can see from the **Test results** section, the date and time of the test is listed, as are the results of either Pass or Fail. A **Pass** indicates that the DNS server's configuration is correct and functioning properly, and a **Fail** indicates something is not configured properly. It's common for the simple query to Pass and the recursive query to Fail. The simply query tests the forward lookup zones on the local server, whereas the recursive query tests the DNS servers configured on the **Root Hints** tab.

There are two common reasons why a recursive query fails. First, if the DNS server isn't able to access the DNS servers listed on the **Root Hints** tab, the recursive query will fail. Second, if the DNS server is able to access the DNS servers listed on the **Root Hints** tab, but the local domain isn't a registered domain name, the Root Hints servers won't know of the domain and the recursive query will also fail. This is common in organizations that have elected to use separate, isolated DNS domains to host the organization's internal DNS infrastructure used to support Active Directory. To allow the recursive query to achieve a Pass result, you can configure the **Root Hints** tab on each of the child DNS servers to include only the IP address of the internal root DNS server(s), and ensure that a root zone exists on the internal root DNS server. Figure 6-2 shows an example. Assume that NSINT1 is the internal root DNS server, and as such is configured with a root zone. The root hints and forwarding tabs on NSINT1 would not be configurable in the DNS property sheets. On the remaining DNS servers, the root hints could be configured with only the IP address and name mapping of NSINT1. When you view the monitoring tab on NSINT1, the option to perform a test recursive query will not be available. However, both the simple and recursive query tests would be available on all other DNS servers.

The one modification to the **Monitoring** tab that you might notice when you are working on a DNS server configured as a root server is that the option to perform a recursive query test is not available. This is the case when the server is a DNS root server as no recursion is required.

Diagnosing DNS Problems Using the DNS Debug Logs

The Debug Logging tab, shown in Figure 6-3, is another property sheet that lets you configure logging of DNS packets as a way to diagnose and debug issues you are experiencing with the DNS service. You can also use this tab to specify the name and

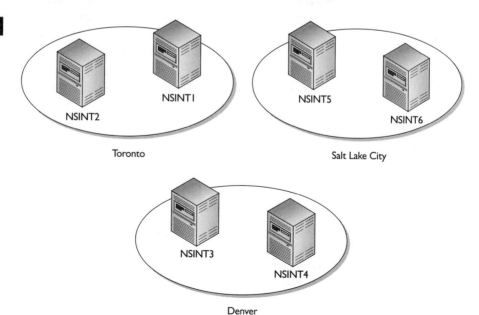

FIGURE 6-2

Differences between root and non-root DNS servers

NSINT1

NSINT2

Toronto

NSINT5

NSINT6

Salt Lake City

NSINT3

NSINT4

Denver

FIGURE 6-3

Configuring DNS
debug logging

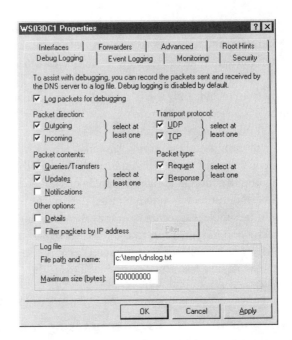

directory of the log file. You can see from Figure 6-3 that I have selected to name the file **dnslog.txt** and place it in the **c:\temp** directory. The default path for this file is **%windir%\system32\dns**, and the name of the log is **dns.log**.

If you open the log shortly after you enable logging, you can see the types of information contained in the file displayed next. The first part of the log file states the date and time that the log was created and then proceeds to provide a quick glossary of what the different character codes mean. After the glossary, you begin to see the statistics gathered in the log itself that can be used to diagnose and troubleshoot problems.

```
DNS Server log file creation at 8/18/2003 2:31:05 PM UTC
Log file wrap at 8/18/2003 7:55:42 AM
Message logging key:
    Field #   Information         Values
    -------   -----------         ------
       1      Remote IP
       2      Xid (hex)
       3      Query/Response      R = Response
                                  blank = Query
       4      Opcode              Q = Standard Query
                                  N = Notify
                                  U = Update
                                  ? = Unknown
       5      [ Flags (hex)
       6      Flags (char codes)  A = Authoritative Answer
                                  T = Truncated Response
                                  D = Recursion Desired
                                  R = Recursion Available
```

```
     7      ResponseCode ]
     8      Question Name

07:55:54 5D8 PACKET  UDP Rcv 192.168.1.251    55d4   Q [0001   D    NOERROR]
(5)_ldap(4)_tcp(4)corp(5)mccaw(2)ca(0)


07:55:54 5D8 PACKET  UDP Snd 192.168.1.251    55d4 R Q [8385 A DR NXDOMAIN]
(5)_ldap(4)_tcp(4)corp(5)mccaw(2)ca(0)


07:56:09 5D8 PACKET  UDP Rcv 192.168.1.251    b8d4   Q [0001   D    NOERROR]
(5)_ldap(4)_tcp(23)Default-First-Site-Name(6)_sites(4)corp(5)mccaw(2)ca(0)


07:56:09 5D8 PACKET  UDP Snd 192.168.1.251    b8d4 R Q [8385 A DR NXDOMAIN]
(5)_ldap(4)_tcp(23)Default-First-Site-Name(6)_sites(4)corp(5)mccaw(2)ca(0)


07:56:20 DD0 EVENT    The DNS server wrote version 1 of zone 1.168.192.in-addr.arpa to file
1.168.192.in-addr.arpa.dns.
07:56:21 5D8 PACKET  UDP Rcv 192.168.1.251    0cd5   Q [0001   D    NOERROR]
(9)corporate(5)mccaw(2)ca(0)


07:56:21 5D8 PACKET  UDP Snd 192.168.1.251    0cd5 R Q [8085 A DR  NOERROR]
(9)corporate(5)mccaw(2)ca(0)


07:56:21 5D8 PACKET  UDP Rcv 192.168.1.251    d1d2   U [0028         NOERROR]
(9)corporate(5)mccaw(2)ca(0)


07:56:21 514 PACKET  UDP Snd 192.168.1.251    d1d2 R U [00a8         NOERROR]
(9)corporate(5)mccaw(2)ca(0)


07:56:21 5D8 PACKET  UDP Rcv 192.168.1.251    69d3   Q [0001   D    NOERROR]
(2)gc(6)_msdcs(9)corporate(5)mccaw(2)ca(0)


07:56:21 5D8 PACKET  UDP Snd 192.168.1.251    69d3 R Q [8085 A DR  NOERROR]
(2)gc(6)_msdcs(9)corporate(5)mccaw(2)ca(0)


07:56:21 5D8 PACKET  UDP Rcv 192.168.1.251    25d1   U [0028         NOERROR]
(9)corporate(5)mccaw(2)ca(0)
```

Take a moment and analyze the following entry in the DNS debug log:

```
07:55:54 5D8 PACKET  UDP Snd 192.168.1.251    55d4 R Q [8385 A DR NXDOMAIN]
(5)_ldap(4)_tcp(4)corp(5)mccaw(2)ca(0)
```

From this entry, you can ascertain the following information:

- The event occurred at 7:55:54 A.M.

- A UDP packet was sent (Snd) from the DNS server to a remote client at the IP address (192.168.1.251). In this case, the remote client is the DNS server.

- It is a response (R) to a standard query (Q).

■ The response says that it is an authoritative answer (A), that recursion was desired (D), and that recursion was available (R).

■ The authoritative response was "Non-existent domain" (NXDOMAIN).

■ The query was for ldap.tcp.corp.mccaw.ca.

Now that you are familiar with how to use the **Monitoring** and **Debug Logging** tabs in the DNS MMC to diagnose, troubleshoot, and monitor DNS related issues, let's explore one last monitoring feature found in the GUI console, the DNS event log.

Diagnosing DNS Issues Using Event Viewer

In Windows Server 2003, the DNS event log can be found in a number of different MMC snap-ins. As in Windows 2000 Server, both the Event Viewer MMC and the Computer Management MMC display the DNS event log if the DNS server service is installed on the computer. New to Windows Server 2003 is the inclusion of the DNS event log in the DNS snap-in.

With this log, you can quickly identify all errors, warnings, and information events related to DNS. Simply double-click any event and the properties of that event will appear, as shown in Figure 6-4. As you can see from the event properties, you can quickly determine the date and time the event occurred, the type of event, the source (which in this case is DNS), the event ID, and the computer on which it occurred.

FIGURE 6-4

Opening a
DNS event

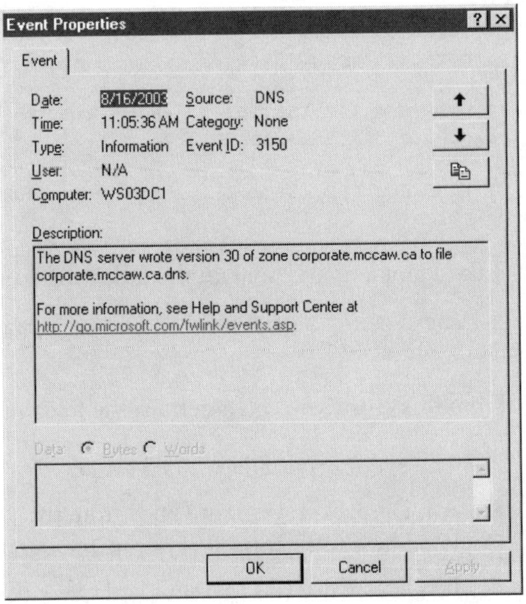

Event Properties

Event

Date: 8/16/2003   Source: DNS
Time: 11:05:36 AM   Category: None
Type: Information   Event ID: 3150
User: N/A
Computer: WS03DC1

Description:
The DNS server wrote version 30 of zone corporate.mccaw.ca to file corporate.mccaw.ca.dns.

For more information, see Help and Support Center at http://go.microsoft.com/fwlink/events.asp.

Data: ○ Bytes ○ Words

OK   Cancel   Apply

More detailed information can also often be found in the **Description** section as well as a link to the Help and Support Center at Microsoft's web site.

on the
()ob

Another great site to learn more about specific event IDs and how to resolve specific problems is www.eventid.net.

The DNS server event log is a great tool to assist in the monitoring of warnings and errors, but the amount of information that can be collected and stored in the log file can be overwhelming. To address this issue, you can create a filter to view only the types of events that are of interest to you. For example, you could create a filter that displays only warning and error events. Exercise 6-2 walks you through how to filter the records in the DNS event log.

EXERCISE 6-2

Filtering the DNS Event Log

In this exercise, you will learn how to filter the DNS event log to view only the events that you want to see. This will allow you to create a custom view of only warning and error events, allowing you to identify and deal with the most critical events.

1. Open the **DNS MMC** and expand the name of the DNS server.
2. Expand **Event Viewer**, right-click **DNS Events**, and select **Properties**.
3. Select the **Filter** tab, and in the **Event source** drop-down menu, select **DNS**.
4. Remove the check marks from the Event type **Information**.
5. Click OK.

In the properties of the DNS Events Properties shown in Figure 6-5 on the **General** tab, you will see that the default location for your DNS event log is **%windir%\system32\config** and the event log file is called **dnsevent.evt**. On this property sheet, you can also see the size of the event log file, when it was created, modified, and last accessed. You can also set the maximum log file size and what to do when the log reaches the maximum allocated size. Finally, you can clear the log on this property sheet.

Knowing how to view the DNS event log on a single computer is valuable knowledge, but in a large environment you will probably have more than one DNS server. The next logical question is, "How do I view the DNS logs on multiple computers?" Fortunately, the answer to this question is that like most tasks in Windows-based environments: you have a number of options.

Defining your
DNS event log
properties

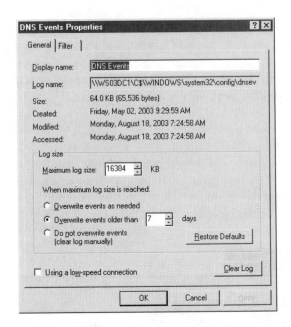

Viewing Multiple DNS Snap-ins in the MMC The first option is to create
a new MMC and add multiple Event Log, DNS, or Computer Management
snap-ins to the new MMC, and then change the focus of each of the snap-ins to look
at a specific computer. You can use the DNS snap-in to view the properties of the
DNS zones and quickly identify all of the DNS name servers in your environment.
You'll explore just how to accomplish this in Exercise 6-3.

EXERCISE 6-3

CertCam 6-3 ON THE CD

Adding Multiple DNS Consoles
to a New MMC

In this exercise, you will learn how to create a custom MMC console that contains
multiple DNS snap-ins, each focused on a different DNS server, allowing you to monitor
all the DNS servers in your organization.

1. Click **Start | Run**, type **mmc**, and press ENTER.

2. In the new, empty MMC console, select **File | Add/Remove snap-in**.

3. In the **Add/Remove Snap-in** dialog box, click **Add**.

4. Select the **DNS** snap-in, click **Add** three times, and click **Close**. Click **OK**.

5. All three of the DNS snap-ins will default to managing the local DNS server but this is what you are going to change. Right-click the second DNS snap-in listed in the MMC and select **Connect to DNS server**.

6. In the **Connect to DNS Server** dialog box shown in the following illustration, select **The following computer**, type the name of the remote DNS server in the text box, and click **OK**.

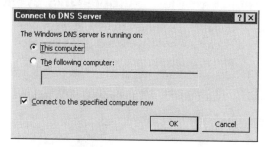

7. Repeat steps 5 and 6 for the third DNS snap-in listed in the MMC console. Now you have a single MMC console that allows you to view the local DNS server as well as two remote DNS servers.

The problem with this approach is that as your environment grows, so too does the number of snap-ins, and you are still faced with having to view multiple DNS event logs. The answer is EventCombMT, a GUI tool included in the version of the Windows Server 2003 Resource Kit available for download at the Microsoft web site, which is now free.

on the
job

You can download the Windows Server 2003 Resource Kit, both documentation and tools, from http://www.microsoft.com/windowsserver2003/techinfo/reskit/resourcekit.mspx.

Using EventCombMT EventCombMT is a resource kit utility that allows you to comb the events logs of multiple computers looking for events that match a very specific or very broad set of criteria. It is up to you to define the criteria, but the end result is that you can view all the event log information in either a text file or a **csv** file that is generated by EventCombMT for each system you comb, and that is stored by default in the **c:\temp** directory. You may be thinking that this doesn't solve your problem because now you have a collection of **csv** or text files. These files can be combined quickly to provide you with a single file that you can search, modify, or sort, and then store and reference at a later time. Exercise 6-4 walks you through how to use EventCombMT.

Using EventCombMT to View Multiple DNS Event Logs

In this exercise, you will learn how to use a Windows Server 2003 Resource Kit tool named EventCombMT to collect and view events from multiple DNS servers.

1. Download and install the Resource Kit tools using **rktools.msi**.

2. Click **Start | All Programs | Windows Resource Kit Tools**, and select **Command Shell**.

3. In the command shell dialog box, type **eventcombmt.exe**, and press ENTER.

4. Click **OK** in the information dialog box, if this is the first time you have launched EventCombMT.

5. In the EventCombMT dialog box, select the Options menu and configure the options you would like to enable. Notice that Cache SIDS, Auto Fail Unavailable Servers, and Cache DLLs are all selected by default. Select **Popup Warnings for Full Event Logs, Capture Event ID Statistics**, and **Write All Results to Database**.

6. Right-click in the **Select To Search** text box, and select **Add Single Server**. Type **ws03dc** and click **Add Server** and **Close**. To select all of the domain controllers in your domain, right-click the **Select To Search** text box and select **Get DCs in Domain**. Personally, I find the default output text file difficult to read and parse through, so I also like to select **Save Files As CSV Files**.

7. In the **Choose Log Files to search** section, select **DNS**, and deselect **System**.

8. In the **Event Types** section, select **Warning**.

9. As you can see from the options at the bottom of the **EventCombMT** dialog box shown in the following illustration, you can be very selective about the event IDs, source, and how far back you want to search. The other option is to enable **Get All Events With Above Criteria**. Once you have defined the criteria for your search, click **Search**.

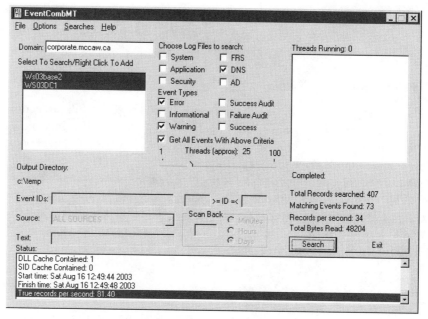

10. Click **Yes** to the dialog box that appears.

11. Once EventCombMT has combed the event logs of the systems you specified, it will open a Windows Explorer window to **c:\temp** and display the files that it generated.

With the results generated by EventCombMT in the **c:\temp** directory, you can quickly view the **csv** files with Excel, or combine the individual system files together and sort by the most common error. This will provide you with a comprehensive view of the DNS event logs across multiple computers in one file, and make it easier to diagnose and resolve the various errors and warnings.

EventCombMT also includes a number of built-in searches, one of which is included for DNS. The built-in DNS search scours the DNS event logs for DNS interface errors with an event ID of 4015, but as you have seen you can also create and save your own custom searches.

Knowing what the events are that are occurring across multiple DNS servers is one thing, but with that knowledge, wouldn't it be nice to have a tool that allows you to automate the response to specific events? Wouldn't it make you more efficient, if when a recurring DNS warning message appeared, you could have an automated response

---

INSIDE THE EXAM

DNS Monitoring Tools

Be sure that you understand the different tools and utilities available to monitor the DNS service. The exam will test your knowledge of the tools and require that you know the types of situations they are best used in. The exam is not likely to have a strong focus on monitoring DNS, but it is an area that completes the topic of DNS.

When approaching DNS monitoring and troubleshooting questions, remember that troubleshooting is a methodical process that is very similar to performing scientific research. When you conduct research studies, you first hypothesize about what you expect the results to be, define the variables, and then test your hypothesis. Troubleshooting is similar in the sense that you hypothesize what is likely causing the problem and then begin verifying configuration settings and performing tests, all the time eliminating what is working as the cause of the problem.

---

waiting to fire and resolve the issue? A tool that can do just that is Microsoft Operations Manager (MOM); in the next section, you'll take a look to see exactly what that application can provide.

Monitoring DNS Using Microsoft Operations Manager

A whole book could be dedicated to monitoring your Microsoft Windows operating systems, applications, and network services, but this section is designed to simply introduce you to the possibilities and give you a quick glimpse at what's possible with MOM.

Microsoft Operations Manager 2000 with Service Pack 1 is an operations management application that works in an agent and agent manager topology. The MOM server is the agent manager, and the MOM agents report back events, alerts, and performance data to the MOM server based on the rules that are installed on the agents. The software and hardware configuration of the MOM agents determines the rules that get pushed out to the client, and are dynamically adjusted every 24 hours to account for any configuration changes made to a MOM agent. This means that if the DNS server service is running on a server named server1, then as a MOM agent, server1 would receive the rules to monitor DNS. If DNS is removed from server1 two weeks later, at the regular 24 hour interval, which by default is 2:05 A.M., the rules for DNS would be removed.

The big selling feature of MOM is the rules included with the application that provide monitoring of services like DNS. The rules are logically organized into groups known as a *Management Packs*. Within the DNS Management Pack, there are over 170 default event rules that monitor DNS-related events. These default events, or customized events that you create, can be further configured with an automated response such as running a command, launching a script (VBScript or JScript), sending a notification via e-mail or to a pager, or updating a state variable. This automated response can be configured to occur on the MOM agent, your DNS server, and can automatically resolve the problem while at the same time alerting you via e-mail of the problem, and that corrective action was taken. If that isn't enough, each of the rules has significant knowledge included within them to better assist you in resolving the problem by providing potential causes and resolutions and live hyperlinks to the Microsoft Knowledge Base site if the information included in the rule doesn't solve the problem.

The other important point to remember about the rules within the Management Packs is that they are written by the product development groups at Microsoft that write the underlying technologies. Who better knows what to monitor than the people that wrote the code in the first place? Not to mention their knowledge about the cryptic debug log codes for services like DNS.

The end goal of any good operations management application is to make you more efficient in your daily administration by automatically responding to common events with known resolutions, and freeing up your time for other tasks.

You'll now take a look at a couple of the rules included in the DNS Management Pack. One rule that helps you to police DNS security is the "Zone transfer request for secondary specified zone refused by master server," which corresponds to event ID 6525. If this event occurs, the MOM agent service running on the DNS server will send a notification to the network administrators notification group (a group that is defined in MOM) to alert the members of this group to the potential threat of an attacker attempting to perform a zone transfer from an unauthorized DNS server.

Another rule that is automatically configured to send you a notification to alert you to a DNS server problem is "The DNS server could not initialize the remote procedure call (RPC) service," which corresponds to event ID 140. Having MOM notify you allows you to react quickly and solve trivial problems before they become more serious and take a server into a distressed state.

The DNS Management Pack included with MOM is also configured to collect and monitor performance-related information to help you establish a DNS performance baseline and perform long-term trend analysis, reporting, and planning. MOM uses the installed DNS PerfMon counters to collect this information on a scheduled basis as outlined in Table 6-1.

TABLE 6-1	Performance Monitor Counter	Schedule
MOM's Default DNS Performance Counters	DNS Process – % Processor Time	16 minutes
	DNS – Caching Memory	19 minutes
	DNS Process – Private Bytes	15 minutes
	DNS – Dynamic Update Written to Database/sec	21 minutes
	DNS – Total Query Received/sec	18 minutes
	DNS – Database Node Memory	20 minutes
	DNS – Dynamic Update Received/sec	17 minutes

As you can see, Microsoft Operations Manager is an operations management application that can be used to proactively monitor and respond to known issues using rules that are written by the respective product development groups at Microsoft. With the growth and adoption of Microsoft technologies within corporations, particularly in the server rooms where enterprise applications run, it is critical that these systems be monitored. Taking a proactive approach and monitoring these systems will lead to improved uptime, system availability and overall performance in both the short and long term.

on the *job*   *Download an evaluation copy of MOM with SP1 today from www.microsoft.com/mom.*

Having an environment with Microsoft Operations Manager available to assist you in diagnosing and then providing automated responses to known DNS issues as well as track and establish performance baselines is ideal, but not all organizations have implemented it yet. Thankfully, there are still some excellent tools included in the operating system out of the box to assist you in monitoring the performance of individual systems, such as System Monitor.

Monitoring DNS with System Monitor

As you have now seen, MOM can be used to monitor the performance of multiple servers running the DNS service. For environments without MOM, however, you can use built-in tools such as System Monitor. System Monitor can help you determine a performance baseline for your individual DNS servers, and use that baseline to monitor the performance of the DNS server over time. This can be useful in helping you determine performance degradation and alert you to potential performance issues before they become critical and take your system into distress.

The DNS counters that you decide to monitor are up to you and will be based upon the configuration of the DNS server. A good rule of thumb is to add at least one counter from each of the four key performance monitoring areas: network, disk, memory and CPU. In addition to these four areas, you should give some thought to the configuration of the DNS server and whether you are using AD-integrated zones or dynamic updates. If you are using AD-integrated zones, monitoring for zone transfer traffic isn't required, but if you are using dynamic updates, using counters such as **dynamic update rejected** might be appropriate. Likewise, if you have integrated WINS with DNS, then you might want to consider using counters like **WINS lookup received/sec** or **WINS response sent**.

Now that you have had a look at a number of DNS monitoring tools, take a minute to review what you have learned.

SCENARIO & SOLUTION

You would like to gather more in-depth information about what the DNS service is doing and the types of traffic it is receiving. What's the best way to accomplish this?	Enable DNS debug logging in the DNS property sheets. This will provide you with detailed information about incoming and outgoing packets and provide the contents of the packets for you to analyze.
You have noticed that no DNS events are being logged in your DNS event log on one of your DNS servers, but all other DNS servers are generating events. You run **nslookup** to test the DNS server, and you are able to receive a response. What's the likely cause of the problem?	DNS logging properties can be defined on the **Event Logging** page of the DNS server properties. It is likely that another administrator has selected the logging option **No events**, which is causing the problem. Change this setting to **All events** to begin collecting event information.
On the **Monitoring** tab, you have noticed that the option to perform a recursive query is not available. What is the most likely cause of this?	Recursive queries cannot be performed on root DNS servers. Check to see if the DNS server is configured as a root DNS server.
When you open **nslookup**, what is the first thing **nslookup** does before presenting you with a command prompt?	**nslookup** performs a reverse lookup on the IP address of the server that is running DNS. It is common for this reverse lookup to report an error if a PTR record doesn't exist for the DNS server.

Using Replication Monitor to Monitor DNS

With the ability to integrate DNS with Active Directory comes the requirement to monitor AD replication with tools such as Replication Monitor in order to achieve the goal of monitoring and troubleshooting DNS. Once a DNS zone is AD-integrated, it no longer replicates through zone transfers, but rather as an object in an AD partition. In Windows 2000 Server, AD-integrated DNS zones replicated in the domain partition, but now, in Windows Server 2003, you can store the DNS zone object in an application directory partition as well as the domain partition.

Active Directory Replication Monitor is a tool that is included in the support tools on the Windows Server 2003 CD. Exercise 6-5 explores how to use Replication Monitor to monitor AD replication and achieve the goal of monitoring DNS.

EXERCISE 6-5

Using Replication Monitor to Monitor AD Replication

In this exercise, you will learn how to use Replication Monitor, a tool included in the support tools on the Windows Server 2003 CD, to monitor AD replication. Monitoring AD replication allows you to ensure that AD-integrated DNS zones are also replicating properly as part of the AD.

1. Click **Start | Programs | Windows Support Tools**, and select **Command Prompt**.

2. In the Command Prompt, type **replmon** and press ENTER.

3. In Replication Monitor, right-click **Monitored Servers**, and select **Add Monitored Server**.

4. On the Add Monitored Server Wizard page click **Next**.

5. In the **Enter the name of the server to monitor explicitly** text box, type the name of a domain controller in your domain and click **Finish**.

6. To view the direct replication data for a specific partition such as the domain partition, expand the domain partition and select **Default-First-Site-Name\ <domain controller name>**. In the display pane, view the direct replication partner data as shown in the following illustration. Here you can see that the last replication attempt was successful and took place on 5/19/2003 at 0:03:41 A.M. Also notice the DC objects DomainDnsZones and ForestDnsZones for the DNS servers, which are a sure sign that you are looking at AD-integrated DNS.

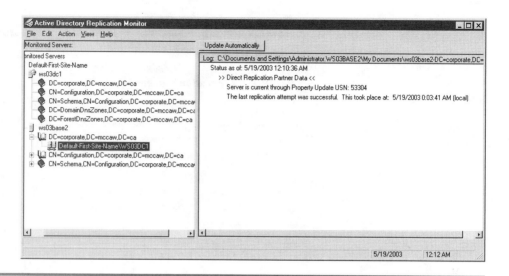

Replication Monitor is a great tool for diagnosing AD replication issues, and includes a number of excellent features including the ability to **Search Domain Controllers for Replication Errors**, and force synchronization with a specific replication partner by selecting **Synchronize with this Replication Partner**.

Replication Monitor also allows you to view the properties of a specific domain controller as you can see in Figure 6-6. This allows you to identify properties such as the GUID of the domain controller, the site it's a member of, and the name of the directory partition, as well as the transport used for replication and the date and time replication last succeeded. Even more important, you can see if replication has been failing, the number of failed attempts, the time replication was last attempted, and the reason for failure.

Diagnosing DNS Problems Using dnslint

In Chapter 5, we looked at how **dnslint**, a tool included in the support tools on the Windows Server 2003 CD, can help you to manage DNS, so this section should be more of a review. **dnslint** is designed to help you troubleshoot DNS issues by focusing in on one of three different areas based upon the switch you use. When you use **dnslint** is used with the **/d** switch, you can diagnose lame delegation issues and other DNS-related issues. With the **/ql** switch, **dnslint** can verify a user-defined set of DNS records on one or multiple DNS servers. In Active Directory environments, you can use the **/ad** switch to verify DNS records and troubleshoot problems with Active Directory replication, which can be useful when you're troubleshooting AD-integrated DNS zone replication problems.

Viewing a domain
controller's
properties using
Replication
Monitor

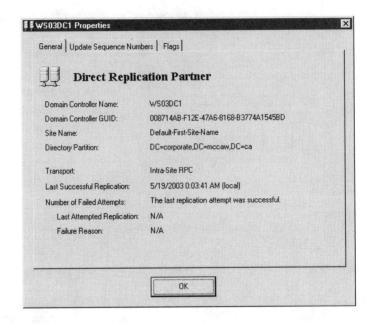

In this section, you'll take a look at how
dnslint.exe can be used to diagnose lame
delegations. A lame delegation occurs when
a subdomain such as amer.corporate.mccaw.ca,
has been delegated to a DNS server such as
ws03base2, and this DNS server doesn't exist
or its IP address has changed. To simulate this
scenario, I have created an Active Directory

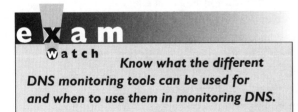

*Know what the different
DNS monitoring tools can be used for
and when to use them in monitoring DNS.*

domain with two domain controllers, ws03dc and ws03base2. ws03dc is also the GC
and holds all five Flexible Single Master of Operations (FSMO) roles, though that
isn't important for what you are about to test. The standard primary forward lookup
DNS zone exists on ws03dc, and a secondary forward lookup zone exists on ws03base2
for the zone corporate.mccaw.ca. ws03dc also contains a forward lookup root zone. A
new delegation for the child zone amer.corporate.mccaw.ca has been created on
ws03dc, with authority granted to ws03base2 at IP address 192.168.1.250. To
demonstrate how you can use **dnslint** to identify and diagnose lame delegations,
I have edited the NS record in the delegated zone for ws03base2 and changed the
IP address to 192.168.1.25, an incorrect IP address. Then, on ws03dc, run the
following command:

```
dnslint /d amer.corporate.mccaw.ca /s 192.168.1.251
```

As you can see from the results in the following report, dnslint has determined that one or more DNS server is not authoritative for the domain, one or more zone files may have expired, and the SOA record was unavailable or missing on one or more DNS servers.

DNSLint Report

System Date: Mon May 19 08:40:40 2003
Command run:
dnslint /d amer.corporate.mccaw.ca /s 192.168.1.251
Domain name tested:
amer.corporate.mccaw.ca

The following 1 DNS servers were identified as authoritative for the domain:

DNS server: User Specified DNS Server

IP Address: 192.168.1.251
UDP port 53 responding to queries: YES
TCP port 53 responding to queries: Not tested
Answering authoritatively for domain: NO
SOA record data from server:
Authoritative name server: Unknown
Hostmaster: Unknown
Zone serial number: Unknown
Zone expires in: Unknown
Refresh period: Unknown
Retry delay: Unknown
Default (minimum) TTL: Unknown

Notes:

One or more DNS servers is not authoritative for the domain
One or more zone files may have expired
SOA record data was unavailable and/or missing on one or more DNS servers

Normally, diagnosing lame delegations on the Internet involves the following steps:

1. Connect to **internic.com** and use the **whois** utility to determine the authoritative name servers for a specific domain name.

2. Use **whois** to determine what the IP addresses are for the authoritative name servers.

3. Use **nslookup** to query each DNS server for each record type individually such as A, NS, and MX records, as well as NS records. If you find additional authoritative DNS servers through **nslookup**, query all of those as well.

4. Compare your results from **nslookup** against what is on the DNS servers.

As you have now seen, this tedious and time-consuming process can now be completely automated for you using **dnslint**. Because, by default, **dnslint.exe** does not check domains in a private namespace not registered with Internic, or domains two or more levels deep, you had to modify the command slightly using the **/s** switch to specify the DNS server for **dnslint** to use, and after the **/d** switch you had to enter the fully qualified domain name **amer.corporate.mccaw.ca**.

You can also use **dnslint** to test AD replication issues. For a detailed example see the section on **dnslint** in Chapter 5. **dnslint** can also be used with the **/ql** (query list) switch, which can help you determine or verify a set of DNS records and help you diagnose problems caused by missing records. This switch was also explained in the section on **dnslint** in Chapter 5.

As you have seen, **dnslint** is an excellent tool that can assist you in monitoring and troubleshooting your DNS implementations, and save you a great deal of time in the process.

Troubleshooting DNS Using nslookup

nslookup.exe is a command-line utility designed to troubleshoot DNS issues by performing queries against DNS servers. The results, or lack of results, from your **nslookup** queries can be useful in diagnosing DNS-related problems. One common use for **nslookup** is querying a DNS server to determine if certain resource records exist, or if they have updated correctly after a zone transfer.

nslookup operates in two modes: interactive and non-interactive. In interactive mode, you can type in multiple commands at a command prompt and view the results. Non-interactive mode is designed to be used in batch files, or when you only want to run a single command. Exercise 6-6 looks at how to use **nslookup** to verify a zone delegation in interactive mode.

EXERCISE 6-6

Verifying a Zone Delegation with nslookup

In this exercise, you will learn how to use **nslookup** to verify a zone delegation. You should do this immediately after you create a new delegation to test and confirm that it is functioning correctly.

1. Click **Start | Run**, type **cmd**, and press ENTER.

2. At the command prompt, type **nslookup** *rootDNSserver IP address*, and press ENTER.

3. Type **nslookup** and press ENTER.

4. Type **set norecurse** and press ENTER.

5. Type **set q=NS** and press ENTER.

6. Type *FQDN of delegated domain* and press ENTER.

7. Note the results of the query as shown in the following illustration. All of the delegated DNS servers are returned in the response.

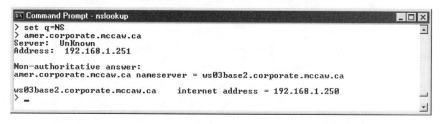

It is possible for no results to appear in the NS query response. If this happens, you can repeat Step 5, typing **set q=ns**, and then repeat Step 6, but use the FQDN of the parent DNS domain. If your original query used **amer.corporate.mccaw.ca**, the subsequent query should use **corporate.mccaw.ca**.

It is also possible for the NS query response to contain NS resource records but no A resource records. If this happens, type **set recurse** and query for the A resource records of the name servers listed in the results. If you are unable to find at least one valid IP address in the A resource record, your troubleshooting has found a broken delegation.

Executing *nslookup* ***queries does not require you to have administrative permissions.***

You can also use **nslookup** to help you verify WINS as the source for answering a DNS query. To test for a WINS forward lookup, use the following command:

```
Nslookup
Set debug
Set querytype=a
<FQDN of WINS host>
```

The FQDN of the WINS host is the fully qualified domain name of a WINS host such as **srv1.corporate.mccaw.ca**. In the response, pay particular attention to whether the server answers authoritatively or non-authoritatively, and what the time-to-live (TTL) value is. If the sever responded authoritatively, retype **set querytype=a** and **FQDN *of* WINS host**, and note if the TTL value was decremented in the second response. If the value decreased in the second response to an authoritatively answered query, you will know that the query answer was provided by a WINS server.

WINS lookups are handled uniquely in DNS, because an answer received back by a DNS server from a WINS server is cached like any other answer. However, it is also considered to be authoritative data. This means that WINS source data is returned to DNS clients as authoritative, but it ages while in the DNS names cache. This is what causes the changes in the TTL value, and helps you know that a WINS server provided the query answer.

You can also use **nslookup** to verify the DNS SRV resource records that are required to join an Active Directory domain. To view these, use the following command:

```
Nslookup
Set q=srv
_ldap._tcp.dc._msdcs.<ADdomainname>
```

Where the **<ADdomainname>** is the FQDN of your Active Directory domain. The results of this query should produce a list of all domain controllers in your Active Directory domain and their associated IP addresses. If the query fails to produce these results, focus your troubleshooting on dynamic updates or DNS server issues to diagnose the problem.

on the *job*

For more information on the switches that can be used with nslookup, *type* ? *at the* nslookup *prompt.*

CERTIFICATION SUMMARY

In this chapter, you have learned about the tools available to monitor and troubleshoot DNS. Monitoring DNS is critical to ongoing network operations within all enterprises. With DNS providing the underlying name resolution services for AD, and other directory-enabled applications' reliance on DNS, it must be monitored to alert you to issues before they affect your service level agreements.

The three primary tools available to monitor and maintain DNS are **nslookup**, **dnscmd**, and **dnslint**. You can also use other tools, including Microsoft Operations Manager, System Monitor, the DNS event log, and Active Directory Replication Monitor.

TWO-MINUTE DRILL

Monitor DNS

❑ The DNS MMC can be used to perform simple and recursive query tests, and enable DNS debug logging.

❑ The **Root Hints** tab is not configurable on a DNS root server, nor can a recursive query test be run.

❑ The DNS MMC now includes the DNS event log.

❑ EventCombMT is a Windows Server 2003 Resource Kit utility that can be used to comb the event logs on multiple systems for specific event IDs or specific types of events.

❑ **dnscmd**, **nslookup**, and **dnslint** are three utilities available to monitor DNS.

❑ System Monitor can be used to monitor DNS performance counters on one or more DNS servers, and help you to identify baseline system performance.

❑ Replication Monitor and other AD replication and troubleshooting tools can be used to monitor and troubleshoot AD integrated DNS zones.

SELF TEST

The following questions will help you measure your understanding of the material presented in this chapter. Read all the choices carefully because there may be more than one correct answer. Choose all correct answers for each question.

Monitor DNS

1. You are the network administrator in your company. One of your responsibilities is to manage and monitor DNS services. Which of the following tools can you use to monitor DNS? (Choose three.)

   A. nslookup

   B. netsh

   C. dnscmd

   D. dnslint

   E. netstat

   F. nbtstat

2. You are the network administrator in your organization. You have just completed the installation and configuration of both a forward and reverse lookup zone that will be used to support Active Directory. The forward lookup zone is called corporate.mccaw.ca, and the reverse lookup zone is for the 192.168.1.*x* subnet. You have also configured the DNS server to forward all DNS names for all other DNS domains to your ISP's DNS server at 207.76.143.22. The local DNS server is configured to use itself as the preferred DNS server, and is not currently configured to use an alternate DNS server. To test the DNS servers configuration, you open the DNS server properties dialog box. On the **Monitoring** tab, you select to perform both a simple and recursive query. The test results show the simple query passing and the recursive query failing. Which of the following steps must you take to resolve the problem?

   A. Configure the local DNS server's alternate DNS server IP address to be the IP address of the ISP's DNS server.

   B. Modify the Root Hints on the local DNS server to list only itself.

   C. Remove the forwarder.

   D. Add a root forward lookup zone.

3. You are the network administrator for your organization. You have just taken over responsibility for the DNS infrastructure that supports your organization's Active Directory. You are starting to familiarize yourself with the DNS topology and investigate the configurations of various DNS servers. When you open the properties of a DNS server named NSINT1, you notice that the

options on the **Forwarders** tab are all unavailable. Which of the following is the most likely cause of this?

A. The server is a DNS root server.

B. Forwarding is disabled at the forward lookup zone.

C. The **Root Hints** tab must be populated with name servers.

D. There are no local interfaces defined for the DNS server.

4. You are the network administrator in your organization. You are testing your DNS server's configuration using **nslookup**. You are performing these tests from the command prompt on the local, internal root DNS server. The IP address of this server is 192.168.1.251, and the TCP/IP properties of this server have 192.168.1.251 defined as the preferred DNS server. When you execute the **nslookup** command at the command prompt, you receive the following response.

```
C:\>nslookup
*** Can't find server name for address 192.168.1.251: Non-existent
domain
Default Server:  UnKnown
Address:  192.168.1.251
```

What is the most likely cause of this?

A. The DNS server doesn't have a reverse lookup zone.

B. The DNS server doesn't have a forward lookup zone.

C. The DNS server is configured as a root zone.

D. Forwarding has not been configured properly on the DNS server.

5. You are running **dcpromo.exe** on a member server running Windows Server 2003. DNS is installed locally and forwarding is configured to forward out to your ISP's DNS server. No zones currently exist in DNS on the local server, and the local TCP/IP properties show the preferred DNS server is pointing to the member server. During the domain controller promotion process, after entering the credentials required to add an additional DC to the domain, you receive the error message shown in the following illustration. Which of the following will resolve this problem and allow the **dcpromo** process to continue?

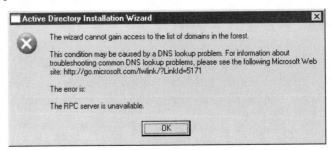

A. Change the preferred DNS server to be the ISP's DNS server.

B. Change the preferred DNS server to be the domain controller.

C. Add a reverse lookup zone to the DNS service running on the member server.

D. Integrate the DNS zone on the domain controller with Active Directory.

E. Run **ipconfig /registerdns** from the member server.

6. You are the network administrator for your organization. You have three DNS servers running Windows Server 2003 that host the DNS zone corporate.mccaw.ca. The internal root DNS server is DNINT1, and this server has an IP address of 192.168.1.10. You have also delegated a zone named amer.corporate.mccaw.ca to a DNS server named DNSINT5. The static IP address of DNSINT5 was changed recently, and you want to test that you have made the changes in all of the right places in DNS. Which of the following commands will allow you to do this?

A. **dnslint /d amer.corporate.mccaw.ca /s 192.168.1.10**

B. **dnslint /ql amer.corporate.mccaw.ca /s 192.168.1.10**

C. **dnslint /d corporate.mccaw.ca /s 192.168.1.10**

D. **dnslint /ql corporate.mccaw.ca /s 192.168.1.10**

7. You are the network administrator for your organization. You have three DNS servers running Windows Server 2003 that host the DNS zone corporate.mccaw.ca. The internal root DNS server is named NS1, and has an IP address of 192.168.1.45. You have also delegated a zone named amer.corporate.mccaw.ca to a DNS server named DNSINT5. The static IP address of DNSINT5 was changed recently. You want to ensure that all DNS records are up to date. Which of the following will best accomplish this goal? (Choose all that apply.)

A. On DNSINT5, run **ipconfig /registerdns**.

B. On DNSINT5, update the NS record in the delegated forward lookup zone amer.corporate. mccaw.ca.

C. On NS1, run **ipconfig /registerdns**.

D. On NS1, update the NS record in the forward lookup zone amer.corporate.mccaw.ca.

E. On NS1, update the NS record in the forward lookup zone corporate.mccaw.ca.

F. On DNSINT5, update the NS record in the forward lookup zone corporate.mccaw.ca.

8. You are the network administrator in your organization. You are testing your DNS server's configuration using **nslookup**. You are performing these tests from the command prompt on the local, internal root DNS server. The IP address of this server is 192.168.1.251, and the TCP/IP properties of this server have 192.168.1.251 defined as the preferred DNS server. You are testing trying to verify that your WINS server is answering a DNS query. To accomplish this you set the **querytype**=a and type the FQDN of a WINS host, and then repeat the process. Which of the following will indicate the response came from a WINS server?

A. If the TTL value of the second response is higher than the TTL of the first response, the answer came from a WINS server.

    B.   If the TTL value of the second response is lower than the TTL of the first response, the answer came from a WINS server.

    C.   If the TTL value of the second response is the same as the TTL of the first response, the answer came from a WINS server.

    D.   If the TTL value of the second response is zero, the answer came from a WINS server.

9. You are the network administrator in your organization. You have just completed the installation of the DNS server on a computer running Windows Server 2003. You have also configured two forward lookup zones. The first is an internal root zone, and the second is a standard secondary zone that uses the master DNS server IP address of 10.10.1.100. On the DNS server, you have also created a reverse lookup zone for the 10.10.1.x network. To test your DNS configuration, you use the **Monitoring** tab on the DNS properties dialog box. You run both a simple and recursive query and both fail. Which of the following is the most likely cause of the problem?

    A.   The reverse lookup zone is displayed as 1.10.10.in-addr.arpa in the DNS console, and should read 10.10.1.in-addr.arpa.

    B.   The root zone must be deleted, because root zones shouldn't exist on DNS servers with secondary zones.

    C.   A forwarder should be added to the DNS server.

    D.   A zone transfer should be performed for the secondary zone.

10. You are the network administrator in your organization. You have just enabled DNS debug logging in the DNS server property sheets, but you didn't specify a location for the log file. What is the default name and location where the file will be created?

    A.   **c:\windows\system32\dnslog.log**

    B.   **c:\windows\system32\dns\dnslog.log**

    C.   **c:\windows\system32\dns.log**

    D.   **c:\windows\system32\dns\dns.log**

11. In which of the following MMC snap-ins can you find the DNS event logs on a server running Windows Server 2003? (Choose all that apply.)

    A.   Computer Management

    B.   Event Viewer

    C.   Services

    D.   DNS

    E.   Performance Logs and Alerts

12. You are the network administrator in your organization. You are troubleshooting some DNS issues that are causing name resolution problems in your network. The DNS zone that is giving you problems is a standard primary zone with standard secondaries on three other DNS servers. You would like to open the zone files for the corporate.mccaw.ca zone on all four servers and compare the files for in discrepancies. Which of the following directory paths and filenames will you look for?

A. c:\windows\system32\dns\corporate.mccaw.ca.dns.log

B. c:\windows\system32\dns\corporate.mccaw.ca.dns.

C. c:\windows\system32\config\dns\corporate.mccaw.ca.dns.log

D. c:\windows\system32\config\dns\corporate.mccaw.ca.dns

13. You are the network administrator for your organization. You have noticed specific error messages recently within one of your DNS event logs, and you would like to identify how many other DNS servers are logging the same error, based on its event ID. Which utilities would you use to identify this?

A. **dnscmd**

B. Event Viewer

C. **nslookup**

D. EventCombMT

14. You are the network administrator for your organization. You have read about the command-line administration improvements made in Windows Server 2003. Part of your responsibility includes monitoring a worldwide DNS infrastructure that you recently migrated to run on computers running Windows Server 2003. You would like to start automating some of your routine DNS administrative tasks. When you open the command prompt and type **dnscmd** on a computer running Windows Server 2003, you receive the message that "'dnscmd' is not recognized as an internal or external command, operable program or batch file." Which of the following will resolve this problem?

A. Change the directory to **%windir%\system32** and rerun the command.

B. Change the directory to **%windir%\system32\dns** and rerun the command.

C. Use **regsvr32** to register **dnscmd.dll**.

D. Install the Windows Server 2003 support tools.

15. You are the network administrative in your organization. You are using **nslookup** to test the service records in your corporate DNS zone. You are currently logged on as an ordinary user running the command prompt as the Administrator, a member of Domain Admins. When you use **nslookup** to test the DNS server with the standard primary DNS zone, you receive responses to your queries without any problems. When you use **nslookup** to test any of your DNS servers that maintain standard secondary DNS zones, your queries fail. Which of the following will resolve this problem?

A. Enable "allow zone transfers" in the zone properties on your DNS servers that maintain the standard secondary zones.

B. Change the replication scope to not store any zone information in AD.

C. Confirm that all secondary DNS servers are listed on the zone's name servers tab.

D. Use the IP address of the DNS servers with the standard secondary zones, not their host names.

LAB QUESTION

You are the network administrator for your organization, and you are responsible for monitoring DNS. Your current DNS configuration consists of a server named DNSINT1 that hosts an internal root DNS zone, and an Active Directory-integrated forward lookup zone named corporate.mccaw.ca. DNSINT1 has an IP address of 10.10.1.100. DNSINT2 and DNSINT3 are also DNS servers that host copies of the corporate.mccaw.ca zone. A zone named amer.corporate.mccaw.ca has been delegated to DNSINT4, which has an IP address of 10.10.1.10. Your organization still has a number of Windows 95 and 98 clients, and you have not configured DHCP to provide dynamic DNS updates on behalf of these older clients. To manage name resolution for these older clients, you are using a single WINS server named WINS1. You have WINS-integrated your DNS zone corporate.mccaw.ca, but not the amer.corporate.mccaw.ca zone, because all of your older clients are in the corporate domain.

Provide detailed documentation on how you will use **nslookup** to verify the existence of the SRV resource records for the three DNS servers in the corporate.mccaw.ca zone, and how you will verify that the WINS1 is the source for answering a DNS query.

Document the **dnslint** commands you will use to determine if there are any lame delegations in either zone.

SELF TEST ANSWERS

Monitor DNS

1. ☑ **A, C,** and **D. nslookup, dnscmd,** and **dnslint** are all utilities that can be used to monitor DNS. You use **nslookup** to query for DNS resource records and troubleshoot DNS problems. **dnscmd** is a command-line utility that you can use to monitor and manage DNS. You can use **dnslint** to diagnose, monitor, and resolve DNS issues.
   ☒ **B** is incorrect because **netsh** is the net shell utility, and although it allows you to manage and monitor a number of different network configuration settings as well as network services, it is not designed to monitor DNS. **E** and **F** are incorrect because both **netstat** and **nbtstat** are NetBIOS utilities that allow you to manage and monitor NetBIOS, but not DNS.

2. ☑ **D.** In order for the recursive query to achieve a Pass, a root forward lookup zone must be created. If this was a child DNS server, modifying its Root Hints to point to the internal root DNS server would be sufficient.
   ☒ **A** is incorrect because although it is recommended, an alternate DNS server is not a requirement. **B** is incorrect because modifying the Root Hints on the local DNS server by itself is not enough to resolve the problem; a forward lookup root zone must be created. **C** is incorrect because forwarders are not configurable on root DNS servers.

3. ☑ **A.** Root DNS servers cannot be configured with forwarders.
   ☒ **B** is incorrect because forwarding is enabled and configured in the properties of the DNS server, not at the individual zones. **C** is incorrect because if the server is a root DNS server, the Root Hints are not configurable, and therefore it doesn't need to be populated with name servers. **D** is incorrect because the interface configuration will not affect the configuration of forwarders.

4. ☑ **A.** This error will appear when the DNS server doesn't have a reverse lookup zone created. Creating a reverse lookup zone and running **nslookup** again will allow the DNS server to perform reverse lookup using the server's IP address, and determine the DNS server's FQDN.
   ☒ **B** is incorrect because this error is related to the non-existence of a reverse lookup zone and has nothing to do with a forward lookup zone. **C** is incorrect because this error will appear regardless of whether a DNS server is configured with a root zone. **D** is incorrect because this error will occur regardless of whether forwarding has been enabled.

5. ☑ **B.** Changing the preferred DNS server to be the domain controller will allow the member server to find the domain controller and allow the **dcpromo** process to continue.
   ☒ **A** is incorrect because changing the preferred DNS server to be the ISP's DNS server will not solve this problem, as the ISP's DNS server will not be able to resolve the name of the domain controller. **C** is incorrect because adding a reverse lookup zone to the DNS service on the member server will not help. **D** and **E** are incorrect because integrating the DNS zone on the domain controller with Active Directory, or running **ipconfig /registerdns**, will not solve the problem.

6. ☑ **A.** The command **dnslint /d amer.corporate.mccaw.ca /s 192.168.1.10** would allow you to determine if there were any lame delegations.

   ☒ **B, C,** and **D** are incorrect. None of these commands would point you to lame delegations in the amer.corporate.mccaw.ca domain.

7. ☑ **A, B,** and **D.** Running **ipconfig /registerdns** on DNSINT5 will update the host and PTR resource record for DNSINT5. On DNSINT5, the NS record will also have to be updated in the amer.corporate.mccaw.ca zone and on NS1, the NS record in the forward lookup zone amer.corporate.mccaw.ca will have to be updated.

   ☒ **C** is incorrect because running **ipconfig /registerdns** on NS1 isn't required, as the IP address of NS1 has not changed. **E** and **F** are incorrect because DNSINT5 isn't a name server for the corporate.mccaw.ca zone, so its NS record does not need to be updated in that zone on NS1 or DNSINT5.

8. ☑ **B.** If the TTL value of the second response is lower than the TTL of the first response, the answer came from a WINS server. This is because this cached response ages while in the DNS name cache, where it would have been stored after the first response.

   ☒ **A, C,** and **D** are all incorrect. Only a lower TTL value indicates that the response came from a WINS server.

9. ☑ **D.** The most likely cause of both the forward and recursive query failing is improper configuration of the DNS zones, or a lack of zone records to answer the query. When the secondary zone was created, it is possible that there was a problem performing a zone transfer. Forcing a zone transfer and confirming receipt of the DNS resource records should resolve the issue.

   ☒ **A** is incorrect because the reverse lookup zone is displayed correctly. **B** is incorrect because root zones can happily co-exist with secondary zones on the same DNS server. **C** is incorrect because forwarders cannot be created on root DNS servers.

10. ☑ **D.** The default location for the DNS debug logging file is **c:\windows\system32\dns**, and the name of the file is **dns.log**.

    ☒ **A, B,** and **C** are incorrect, because none of these locations are the default, and dns.log is the name of the file.

11. ☑ **A, B,** and **D.** The DNS event logs can be viewed from the Computer Management, Event Viewer, and DNS MMCs.

    ☒ **C** and **E** are incorrect. The Services and Performance Logs and Alerts MMCs do not contain the DNS Event logs.

12. ☑ **B.** By default, zone database files are stored in the **c:\windows\system32\dns** directory and are named after the FQDN that they represent with **.dns** appended to the name. In this example, the zone database file would be called **corporate.mccaw.ca.dns**.

    ☒ **A, C,** and **D** are incorrect because none of these are the right path.

13. ☑ **B and D.** Both Event Viewer and EventCombMT would allow you to filter through multiple event logs on disparate systems to identify if the same errors were occurring across multiple systems.

☒ **A and C** are incorrect because **dnscmd** and **nslookup** and not designed to comb through DNS event logs on DNS servers.

14. ☑ **D. dnscmd.exe** is not installed by default during the installation of Windows Server 2003, but it can be easily added by installing the support tools.

☒ **A and B** are incorrect because changing the directory will not resolve the problem because the tool isn't installed. **C** is incorrect because there is no **.dll** registration required for this tool.

15. ☑ **A. nslookup** queries will fail against a secondary DNS server unless the **Allow Zone Transfers** option is enabled.

☒ **B** is incorrect because the replication scope option isn't available for standard primary and secondary zones. **C** is incorrect because confirming that all secondary DNS servers are listed on the zone's name servers tab won't solve the problem. **D** is incorrect because using the IP address of the DNS servers with the standard secondary zones instead of their host names won't solve the problem.

LAB ANSWER

You can use **nslookup** to verify the existence of the SRV resource records for all three DNS servers (DNSINT1, DNSINT2, and DNSINT3) in the corporate.mccaw.ca zone by running the following command:

```
Nslookup
Set q=srv
_ldap._tcp.dc._msdcs.corporate.mccaw.ca
```

To verify that WINS1 is the source for answering a DNS query, run the following command.

```
Nslookup
Set debug
Set querytype=a
Host.corporate.mccaw.ca
Set querytype=a
Host.corporate.mccaw.ca
```

If the TTL of the second response is lower than the TTL of the first response, you are able to confirm that WINS is providing the answer.

To determine if there are any lame delegations in the amer.corporate.mccaw.ca zone, use the command **dnslint /d amer.corporate.mccaw.ca /s 10.10.1.100**. To test for lame delegations in the parent domain, use the command **dnslint /d corporate.mccaw.ca /s 10.10.1.100**.

Part III

Implementing, Managing, and Maintaining Network Security

CHAPTERS

MCSE/MCSA

MICROSOFT® CERTIFIED SYSTEMS ENGINEER &
MICROSOFT® CERTIFIED SYSTEMS ADMINISTRATOR

7

Implement
Network Security

CERTIFICATION OBJECTIVES

As a system administrator, if you want to secure network traffic effectively, you need to understand network security issues, as well as the networking technologies that are used to build the networking environment. Security experts at Microsoft have assembled The Ten Immutable Laws of Security:

1. If a bad guy can persuade you to run his program on your computer, it's not your computer anymore.

2. If a bad guy can alter the operating system on your computer, it's not your computer anymore.

3. If a bad guy has unrestricted physical access to your computer, it's not your computer anymore.

4. If you allow a bad guy to upload programs to your web site, it's not your web site anymore.

5. Weak passwords trump strong security.

6. A machine is only as secure as the administrator is trustworthy.

7. Encrypted data is only as secure as the decryption key.

8. An out-of-date virus scanner is only marginally better than no virus scanner at all.

9. Absolute anonymity isn't practical, in real life or on the web.

10. Technology is not a panacea.

A number of these laws are addressed in the following three chapters. In this chapter you will learn how to implement security templates that are used to set common security baselines. Maintaining client software by patching in response to security bulletins issued by Microsoft is a common task for administrators. The Software Update Service is the tool that is used to administer the client operating system. In Chapter 8, you will look at the ongoing management of network security, and in Chapter 9, we will discuss the maintenance issues. You can count on network security issues being significant components of the certification exam.

We'll begin by looking at how to configure security templates and how to implement them.

CERTIFICATION OBJECTIVE 7.01

Implement Security Baseline Settings and Audit Security Settings by Using Security Templates

Security templates are collections of security settings that are stored as ordinary text files in an INF format in a text file. Windows Server 2003 comes with a number of predefined security templates that define an overall level of security settings. These baseline settings range from the basic workstation settings up to high security. The security templates are stored in the **%systemroot%\security\templates** folder, each with an **.inf** filename extension. Although you could edit the templates directly with Notepad or any other text editor, you don't need to. The tool for editing security templates is the Security Templates snap-in for MMC. The security templates are named according to the security level they provide, as listed in Table 7-1.

TABLE 7-1   The Security Templates

Template Name	Description
Compatible	This security template is designed for workstations. It removes all users from the Power Users group and relaxes some of the security settings for the Users group.
Hisecdc and Hisecws	These templates are used to configure a very secure domain. hisecdc is for a domain controller, and hisecws is for a workstation or member server. The settings from these templates include all the settings from the securedc and securews templates, and also require more security authentication, restrict security group membership, and require data signing and encryption in most network communication.
Rootsec	This security template holds the root file system permissions. You can use this template to reapply these root file system permissions should they be accidentally changed.
Securedc and Securews	These two security templates are designed to enhance the security settings that are the least likely to impact the usability of the computer. The secure template also restricts the use of the LAN Manager and NTLM authentication protocols.
Setup Security	The setup security template is created during the installation of the Windows Server 2003 and can thus vary from computer to computer based on the installation type. This template represents the default security settings that were applied during installation. These settings include the security settings for the root of the file system (see rootsec). Microsoft recommends that the setup security template is never applied through Group Policy because it is so large. Their recommendation is to apply parts of the template using the secedit.exe command-line tool.

on the **!** Job

Windows Server 2003 includes another set of hidden security templates that are used to restore the default NTFS permissions. These security templates are stored in the hidden %systemroot%\Inf folder. There are two templates — defltdc.inf, which is used on a domain controller (DC) and defltsv.inf, which is used on a member server.

The Setup Security template is created during the installation of Windows Server 2003 and will be individual to the installed server based on the installations type, clean or upgrade. After the installation is complete, the Local Computer Policy holds the security settings that are stored in the Setup Security template. Should you need to refer to the settings as they were set at installation, this template functions as the documentation, and works as the backup for the security settings so you can restore them in whole or in part at a later date.

The *Security Configuration Tool Set* is a group of tools that are used to implement and manage security templates:

- **secedit.exe** A command-line utility that performs the same tasks as the Security and Analysis snap-in. **secedit** is used when the tasks need to be run as scheduled tasks.
- **Security Configuration and Analysis snap-in** An MMC snap-in that is used to configure Windows Server 2003 security as well as analyze it.
- **Security Settings** An extension to the Group Policy snap-in that is used to configure local, domain, and OU security policies.
- **Security Templates snap-in** An MMC snap-in that is used to edit and create security template files.

The following sections detail how to work with these tools to implement Windows Server 2003 operating system security.

Security Templates Snap-in

The Security Templates Standalone snap-in is the MMC tool that is used to manage security templates. This section describes how to configure the snap-in and how to use it to create a new security template. In Figure 7-1 you can see what the snap-in looks

FIGURE 7-1	The Security Templates snap-in

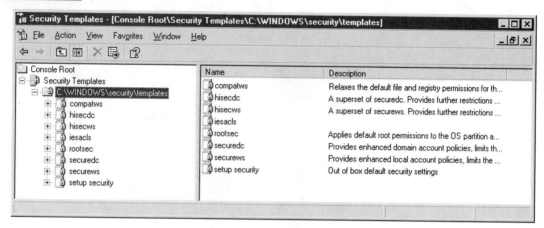

like after the Security Templates folder has been expanded. The templates are normally stored in *%systemroot%\Security\Templates*. Exercise 7-1 walks you through how to create a custom MMC with the Security Template snap-in.

EXERCISE 7-1

Creating a Microsoft Management Console with the Security Templates Snap-in

In this exercise, you will create a custom MMC console and add the Security Templates snap-in to this console.

1. Log in to your Windows Server 2003 as a user with administrative privileges.
2. Click **Start | Run**.
3. Type **mmc** in the Open text box. Click **OK**.
4. When the MMC opens, click **File | Add/Remove Snap-in**.
5. Click the **Add** button to show the **Add Standalone Snap-in** dialog box.

6. Scroll down the list to locate the **Security Templates** as seen in this illustration.

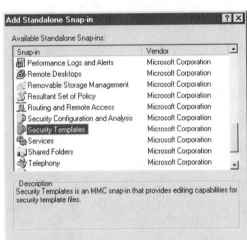

7. Click the **Add** button, followed by the **Close** button in the **Add Standalone Snap-in** dialog box to return to the **Add/Remove Snap-in** snap-in.

8. Click **OK** to return to the **MMC**.

9. Maximize the snap-in.

10. Click the **File | Save As** to save the custom console.

11. In the dialog box, type in the name as **Security Templates.mmc** and ensure that the location is set to **Administrative Tools** as in this illustration. Click **Save**.

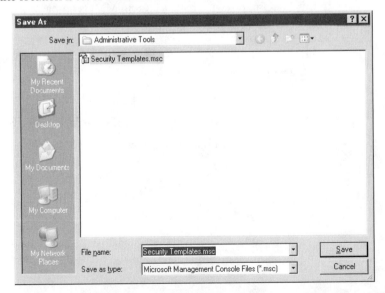

12. In the Security Templates MMC, click the plus sign to the left of Console Root to expand the node.

13. Expand the C:\Windows\Security\Templates node to view the security templates.

The result of this exercise is seen in Figure 7-1.

Creating a New Security Template

To create a new security template, start in the Security Templates snap-in by right-clicking the **C:\Windows\Security\Templates** node and choosing **New Template** from the context menu. You will be prompted for the name and description of the new security template. After you click OK, the new template is added to the list of templates in the Security Templates snap-in.

Once you have created the template you can modify the settings for the different areas that are governed by the template. Those areas are

- **Account Policies**   Defines the password policies, Account Lockout Policy, and Kerberos Policy.
- **Local Policies**   Defines the settings for Audit, User Rights, and Security Policies.
- **Event Log**   Defines the policies that control the use of the Event Log.
- **Restricted Groups**   Defines the membership of user groups that are considered sensitive.
- **System Services**   Startup and security permissions for system services.
- **Registry**   Defines the permissions for registry keys.
- **File System**   Defines permissions for folders and files.

In Exercise 7-2 you will create a new security template.

Once the new security template is created, you need to apply it. The templates are applied using the Security Configuration and Analysis snap-in as detailed in the next section.

Security Configuration and Analysis Snap-in

After the security template is configured to include the settings you want, you should apply the settings to you local computer. The tool you use to apply the security policy is Security Configuration and Analysis, an MMC snap-in that manages a database of the security settings that allows analysis of the differences between the current settings and the database. For more information on the analysis portion of the Security Configuration and Analysis snap-in, see Chapter 9.

The following exercise describes the steps to create and apply a custom security template.

EXERCISE 7-2

Creating and Applying a Security Template

In this exercise you will create a new security template and apply it to the local computer.

1. Open the Security Template MMC you created in Exercise 7-1 by clicking on **Start | All Programs | Administrative Tools | Security Templates**.

2. Expand the **Console Root** node.

3. Right-Click the **C:\Windows\Security\Templates** node, and choose **New Template** from the context menu.

4. Type a name for the security template, such as **MyTemplate**, and give it a short description, as you can see in this Illustration. Click **OK**.

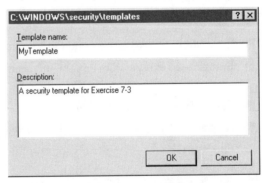

5. Expand **MyTemplate** to display the security sections.

6. Click **Password Policy** under **MyTemplate**.

7. Double-click the **Minimum Password Length** policy in the details pane.

8. Change the minimum password length to **6** as shown next. Click **OK**.

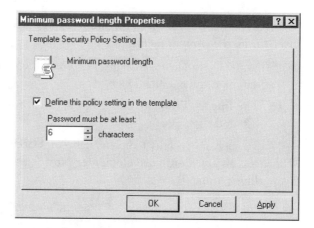

To apply the security template, you will add the Security Configuration and Analysis snap-in to the MMC.

9. Click **File | Add/Remove Snap-in**.

10. Click the **Add** button to show the **Add Standalone Snap-in** dialog box.

11. Scroll down the list to locate the **Security Configuration and Analysis** snap-in as seen in this Illustration.

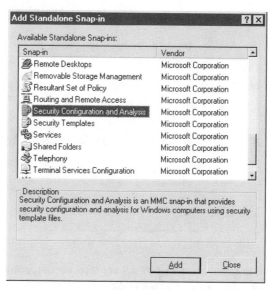

12. Click the **Add** button, followed by the **Close** button in the **Add Standalone Snap-in** dialog box to return to the **Add/Remove Snap-in** snap-in.

13. Click **OK** to return to the **MMC**.

14. Right-click **Security Configuration and Analysis**, and choose **Open Database** from the context menu.

15. In the **Open Database** dialog box enter the name **Exercise7-2** for the database name. Click **Open**.

16. The **Import Template** dialog box appears. Select **MyTemplate.inf** from the list, and click **Open**.

17. To apply the security template, right-click **Security Configuration and Analysis**, and choose **Configure Computer Now** from the context menu as seen in this Illustration.

18. Accept the default log file location in the **Configure System** dialog box by clicking **OK**.

19. You are returned to the **Security Configuration and Analysis** main display. Right-click **Security Configuration and Analysis** and choose **View Log File** from the context menu.

20. Review the log to see what steps were taken.

21. Test the password policy by trying to change your password to one shorter than six characters long.

In this exercise you created a security template and applied it to the local computer.

on the
ᴏo b

It is a good idea to put all related security snap-ins in one place. I have found that adding the Group Policy, Security Templates, and Security Configuration and Analysis snap-ins and saving the console to the Administrative Tools folder makes security issues easier to deal with.

You'll come back to the Security Configuration and Analysis snap-in in Chapter 9 when you look at the maintenance issues of security.

The secedit.exe Utility

The Security Configuration and Analysis snap-in is a nice interactive GUI-based tool for configuration and analysis, but when you need to script the tasks to be run at a scheduled time, or you want to work from the command line, you have the **secedit.exe** utility. Suppose you are administering a remote member server where the local administrators are making security changes on an ongoing basis. You could schedule **secedit.exe** to run on a schedule to analyze the current settings and apply the custom security template for that member server if the security settings change. In previous versions of Windows, **secedit** was used to force a refresh of group policies; in Windows Server 2003, this command (**secedit /refreshpolicy**) has been removed, and the functionality is now provided by the **gpupdate.exe** command.

To get a listing of the syntax for running **secedit.exe**, you can execute it from a command prompt with no parameters. The following is the syntax for the utility:

```
secedit [/configure | /analyze | /import | /export | /validate | /generaterollback]
```

The syntax differs depending on what main parameter is used. The syntax for the **/analyze** parameter is

```
secedit /analyze /db filename [/cfg filename ] [/overwrite] [/log filename] [/quiet]
```

The syntax for the **/configure** parameter is

```
secedit /configure /db filename [/cfg filename] [/overwrite][/areas area1 area2...] [/log filename] [/quiet]
```

The parameters are

- **/analyze** Used to compare the current configuration against a template.
- **/configure** Used to apply the settings from a template to the system.
- **/db** This is a required parameter. Specifies the path and name of the security database that holds the settings that will be applied (**/configure**) or that will be used for the analysis comparison.
- **/cfg** The path and security template filename to import into the security database.
- **/log** The path and file names of the log file.

- **/quiet** Suppresses output to the console screen; used when **secedit** is run as a scheduled task.

- **/verbose** Enables console output during operation; used to troubleshoot the execution of the **secedit** commands.

- **/overwrite** Used in conjunction with **/configure** to specify that the security template will overwrite rather than be added to the current settings on the server.

- **/area** Used in conjunction with **/configure** to specify specific security areas of the security template to apply.

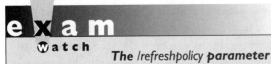

exam

⊕atch *The /refreshpolicy **parameter** is no longer used with secedit.exe; use gpupdate.exe **instead.***

Here are some examples of how to use **secedit.exe** in a couple of scenarios:

To analyze the current security settings against the **MyTemplate.inf** security template, with the result stored in the **MyTemplate.log** file, and the security database (**sdb**) is **MyTemplate.sdb**, use this command:

```
secedit /analyze /db MyTemp.sdb /cfg MyTemplate.inf /log MyTemplate.log
```

To apply the template settings, use this syntax:

```
secedit /configure /db MyTemp.sdb
```

If you apply the **/quiet** parameter, the output from the command will be suppressed.

CERTIFICATION OBJECTIVE 7.02

Implement the Principle of Least Privilege

The *principle of least privilege* is a security guideline that states that a user should have the minimum privileges necessary to perform a specific task. By limiting the privilege, the impact of a compromised user account is minimized. Under those circumstances when a user needs elevated privileges, he or she should use a tool such as **runas** to start the specific process. Administrators should use an account with restrictive permissions to perform their routine, nonadministrative tasks, and use an account with broader permissions only when performing specific administrative tasks where higher privileges are required.

EXERCISE 7-3

Running an Application with Administrative Privilege

In this exercise you will create a user account with no administrative privileges. While logged in under that account, you will run administrative tasks using the **runas** command. This exercise is designed to be executed on a member server.

To create a new user account, follow these steps:

1. Open Computer Management. Click Start | Administrative Tools | Computer Management.

2. Expand the Local Users and Groups node, and click the Users node.

3. Right-click the Users node, and choose New User from the context menu.

4. Fill in the information as shown in this illustration. Make sure the password is set to *password*.

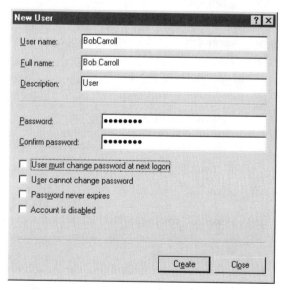

5. Click Create. Click Close.

To test the **runas** command, I have made the following assumptions:

- The administrator account uses a password of *password*.
- The user account is BobCarroll with a password of *password*.

6. Log off as Administrator.

7. Log on as BobCarroll.

8. Open the Local Security Policy MMC.

   Did it work? Did you find the MMC? You can find it under the Control Panel in Administrative Tools, but the result is the following error message.

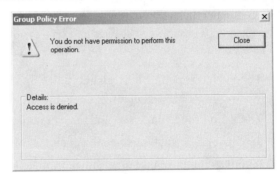

9. To run the MMC successfully, you will need to run the command as the Administrator.

10. Open a command window, click Start | Run, type in **cmd**, and click OK.

11. At the command prompt, enter the following command. Substitute your Windows Server 2003 computer name in place of *Jupiter* in this example:

```
C:\>runas /noprofile /user:Jupiter\administrator "%SystemRoot%\system32\secpol.msc
/s%SystemRoot%\system32\secpol.msc /s"
```

12. When prompted, enter the administrator password (*password*).

    Did it work? Now you should be able to perform the administrative task.

13. Log off as BobCarroll.

In this exercise you explored the **runas** command.

In addition to the command line **runas**, you also have the **Run as** option on the context menus available when you right-click most items in Administrative Tools. This is another way of executing administrative tools under the context of an administrator. If the **Run as** option is not visible for some items, hold down the left SHIFT key while right-clicking the program.

Software Restriction Policies

One of the issues that arise when you start to look at setting the least privilege for our systems is what software the user is allowed to run. The **Users** group is defined as "Users are prevented from making accidental or intentional system-wide changes. Thus, Users can run certified applications, but not most legacy applications." If you need tighter control over what applications can be executed, you can add a **Software Restriction Policy**.

The **Software Restriction Policy** sets rules on what software can be executed by anyone on the computer. In Exercise 7-4 you will implement the policy.

EXERCISE 7-4

Implementing a Software Restriction Policy

In this exercise you will use **Local Security Settings** MMC to configure a **Software Restriction Policies**.

1. Log on as administrator.

2. Click **Start | Administrative Tools | Local Security Settings** to open the **Local Security Settings** MMC.

3. Right-click **Software Restriction Policies**, and choose **New Software Restriction Policies** from the context menu. The result should look like this illustration.

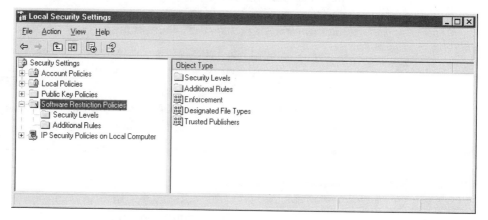

4. Double-click **Enforcement** in the right pane. The resulting Properties sheet looks like this illustration.

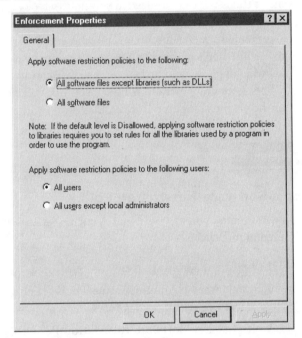

Select all software files if you want to have atomic control over exactly what files are allowed, including all Dynamic Link Libraries (DLLs). On this properties page, you can also specify that the policy applies to all users including the administrator, or exclude the administrator.

5. Under Designated File Types, you specify what is considered an executable. If you double-click the entry, you will find the predefined file types. You can add additional file types here.

6. Under Trusted Publishers, you can specify who will be able to select what publishers to trust, as well as what must be checked in order to trust a publisher.

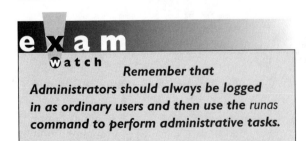

exam
⚔atch *Remember that Administrators should always be logged in as ordinary users and then use the* runas *command to perform administrative tasks.*

Now that you have a better idea of Security Templates, here are some possible scenario questions and their answers.

SCENARIO & SOLUTION

I want to compare the current security settings of a Windows Server 2003 with what it was set to when it was installed. What would I do?	You can use **secedit** to analyze the current security settings against the **Setup Security.int** security template. To do so, go to the **%systemroot%\security\templates** folder and run this command on the Windows Server 2003: **secedit /analyze /cfg Setup Security.inf /db Setup Security.sdb /log Setup Security.log /verbose**. Then you can review the log file for the differences.
Is there any reason why I shouldn't just apply the **Setup Security.inf** template through a Group Policy?	Yes. The **Setup Security.inf** template is the result after installation, and it is a very large file. Applying this template would take a very long time.
I applied the **hisecws.inf** security template, and I suspect that something happened with the Power Users group. What can I do?	The **hisec*.inf** security template restricts group membership and moves all members of the Power Users group to the Users group. You need to analyze what users really need Power User type privileges and then give only them those rights. Remember the principle of least privilege.

CERTIFICATION OBJECTIVE 7.03

Install and Configure Software Update Services

One of the sad truths of network administration is that your networks are the target of just about anyone who can put together a script and run it on your servers and workstations. This problem has been around for quite some time, but has increased since the summer of 2001. As an administrator, you need to ensure that any vulnerabilities with your server and workstation operating system software are patched as quickly as possible. This task has become much more convoluted since Code Red hit in 2001. At that time Windows administrators would install Service Packs if they provided more functionality or solved any specific problems, not because of security issues. At the time, Service Packs were scheduled releases that were not in response to security threats. Between Service Packs, Microsoft released patches that were available if you knew where to look, but these patches were mostly for operational fixes, not security. That situation changed dramatically when almost all Windows NT and Windows 2000 servers were affected by Code Red in 2001. The patch that would have stopped Code Red was released by Microsoft months before the attack, but because of the lackadaisical way administrators approached patches, over 350,000 hosts were affected in a 14-hour period. When Nimda hit the networks in the fall of 2001, similar numbers were seen, and again Microsoft had already released a patch that closed the security hole the worm exploited, almost a year prior.

The lesson from the summer and fall of 2001 is that network administration will never be the same. Microsoft's response to the security issues was to create a security web site **(http://www.microsoft.com/technet/security)** that is the portal for all security related issues and patches for all Microsoft operating systems. You should also subscribe to the security announcements from the same site, which will keep you up to date on current issues.

The traditional (before late 2001) method for managing patches was one of manual labor. The following steps show the process:

Manually collect information about the current patches by reading security announcements, monitoring the Security site, scanning other security sites, and communicating with other network administrators.

- Manually select the patches you need for you operating systems.
- Manually download the patches by connecting to download sites and manually gathering the patches one by one.
- Manually test the patches for all selected Operating Systems by keeping a selective test environment where the patches can be tested against your operating systems.
- Manually deploy the patches. Patches normally must be installed by a user that has administrative rights on the computer, leading to issues with security, because administrative accounts will be known by too many individuals.
- Start on the first step again in a perpetual loop.

One of the immutable laws of administration is that if the administration process requires more than one or two steps, it will probably not be performed as intended. Relying on the ability of an administrator to perform manual patch management is not realistic; relying on funding for a full-time administrator to perform patch management is not realistic; and relying on other administrators being able to fill in when the security administrator is on vacation is not realistic.

What is the solution? You need to patch our networks to ensure we do not open up the door to a bad guy, but the manual process is not realistic, so what to do? Microsoft has introduced a product that lets you streamline and automate major parts of the patch management: *Software Update Services (SUS)*. In the rest of this chapter we will look at how to install and manage SUS in a Windows 2003 domain.

Another product that is part of Microsoft's enterprise servers also has the ability to act as the Software Update Services. That is Systems Management Server (SMS) 2.0. SMS 2.0 together with the Systems Management Server Software Update Services Feature Pack expands the manageability of a large network. Table 7-2 contrasts SUS with SMSSUS Feature Pack.

TABLE 7-2	SUS and SMS Comparison	

Feature	SUS	SMSSUS Feature Pack
Content	Manual or automatic download of required updates	Automatic download of required updates.
Distribution	Scheduled synchronization of approved updates with other SUS servers.	Site to site distribution can be scheduled and is sensitive to the bandwidth of WAN links.
Installation	Manual or simple scheduling controlled by a Group Policy. Client's download is fault-tolerant and the installation can be scheduled as well.	Manual or advanced scheduling based on inventory, groups/organizational units, and sites.
Reports	Report through the Internet Information Services (IIS) logs.	Available through filtered reports that are built into the product.
Targeting	Targeting based on query.	Targeting based on inventory, groups/ organizational units, and sites.

The Software Update Service is a component of Microsoft's *Strategic Technology Protection Program (STPP)*. SUS can be installed on a Windows 2000 Server or a Windows Server 2003; it can be installed on a server that is part of an Active Directory (AD) network, or in a workgroup. Microsoft recommends that you install SUS in an AD network to enable you to manage the clients through Group Policy Objects (GPO). Some of the features SUS provides are

■ **Built-in security** Only administrators can use the administration web pages.

■ **Selective content approval** Administrators approve what clients can update.

■ **Content synchronization** Patches can be synchronized manually or on an automatic schedule.

■ **Server-to-server synchronization** Administrators can install multiple SUS servers to spread the load across the network.

■ **Update package hosting** Gives you a choice of where to keep the updates: locally or at the Microsoft update sites.

■ **Localization** Provides support for localized client operating systems.

■ **Remote administration** Allows administration through Internet Explorer 5.5 or higher.

■ **Logging** Lets you choose where to store the update logs.

- **JIT validation**   Enables Windows Update on the client to scan for needed updates that are available as configured by the administrator.
- **Background download**   Lets the client download the updates in the background without manual intervention.
- **Chained installation**   If multiple updates are to be installed, they are chained, minimizing the need for multiple reboots.

Software Update Services 1.0 Service Pack 1

The current version of SUS is version 1.0 Service Pack 1, and this is the version that is needed for Windows Server 2003. SUS 1.0 Service Pack 1 has introduced the following additions to the Automatic Update:

- **Rescheduled wait time**   This option lets Automatic Update reschedule the update for a fixed number of minutes in the future. This option allows for clients that were powered off to be updated without having to wait for the next scheduled event.
- **No automatic reboot with a logged on user**   This feature delays the restart after an update until there are no more users logged on to the server. If an administrator is logged on, he will be given the option to restart; non-administrators are only informed via a pop-up message that the computer needs to be restarted.
- **Restart popup message when new users log on**   If the computer needs to be restarted, any new user that logs on will get a pop-up message that the computer needs to be restarted.
- **Scheduled installs respects shut-down rights**   Users that do not have shut-down rights on the computer will receive pop-up messages that the computer needs to restart, but the Yes button is grayed out.

These features are configured through the registry of the server running Software Update Services. We will look at these settings in the management section later in this chapter. That is enough background, so now you can install SUS 1.0 Service Pack 1.

Installing Software Update Services Version 1.0 Service Pack 1

Software Update Services is available from the Microsoft download site at **http://www.microsoft.com/windows2000/windowsupdate/sus/**. It is not a part of the Windows Server 2003 CD. To install SUS, you need to have Internet Information Services (IIS) installed on the server, so first we will look at how to add IIS to the computer.

EXERCISE 7-5

Installing IIS

In this exercise you will learn how to install IIS on your Windows Server 2003 using the Manage Your Server wizard. Note that if you already have IIS installed, this exercise will fail.

1. Select **Start | Manage Your Server**, as shown in this illustration.

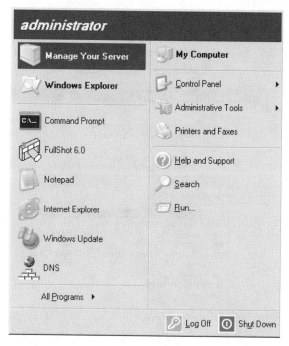

2. Verify that **IIS** is not installed by looking for the **Application Server** section as seen in this illustration. If it is present, skip to the end of this exercise.

≫ **Application Server**

Application servers provide the core technologies required to build, deploy and operate XML Web Services, Web applications, and distributed applications. Application server technologies include ASP.NET, COM+, and Internet Information Services (IIS).

➡ Manage this application server

② Read about application servers

② Read about Web Interface for Remote Administration of Web servers

② Review the next steps for this role

3. In **Manage Your Server**, click on the **Add or remove a role** link to open the wizard, as seen in this illustration.

 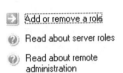

Managing Your Server Roles

Use the tools and information found here to add or remove roles and perform your daily administrative tasks.

Add or remove a role

Read about server roles

Read about remote administration

Your server has been configured with the following roles:

4. Click **Next**.

5. Select **Application Server (IIS, ASP.NET)** from the list of roles, as shown in this Illustration. Click **Next**.

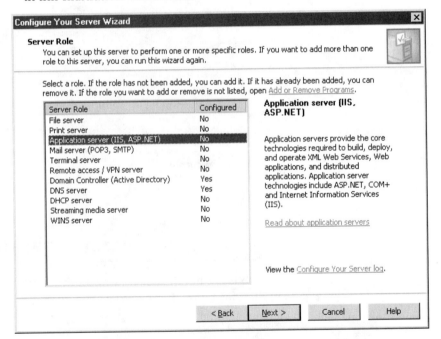

6. Select both **FrontPage Server Extensions** and **Enable ASP.NET**. Click **Next**.

7. Click **Next** to start the installation.

8. Insert the Windows Server 2003 CD in your CD drive when prompted. The installation will take a minute or two.

9. When the wizard is finished, click **Finish** to return to **Manage Your Server**.

10. Close **Manage Your Server**.

11. Click **Start** | **All Programs** | **Windows Update**. This will connect to the **Windows Update** site.

12. Click **Scan for updates**.

13. Install any available updates.

14. Close **Internet Explorer**.

---

e**x**a m

@atch

It is imperative that you install any patches to Windows Server 2003 before continuing the
installation. Installing IIS always involves the risk of opening security holes.

Now that your Windows Server 2003 is prepared for installation, you can proceed by reviewing the hardware requirements for SUS 1.0 Service Pack 1:

- Pentium III 700 MHz or higher processor
- 512 megabytes (MB) of RAM
- 50 megabyte (MB) for SUS
- Space for the update files. For example, to support 15,000 clients you will need 6GB of available hard disk space.

EXERCISE 7-6

CertCam 7-6 ON THE CD

Installing Software Update Services 1.0

In this exercise you will install Software Update Service on your Windows Server 2003.

1. Download SUS 1.0 Service Pack 1 from **http://www.microsoft.com/windows2000/windowsupdate/sus/**.

2. Save the downloaded file (**SUS10SP1.EXE**) in **C:\Temp**.

3. Click **Start** | **Run**, enter **C:\Temp\SUS10SP1.EXE**, and click **OK**.

4. Click **Next** to dismiss the welcome screen.

5. Read the **License Agreement** and select **I accept the terms of the License Agreement**. Click **Next**.

6. Click **Custom** to start the installation selection.

7. In the **Choose File Location** dialog box, specify where you want to install SUS (**C:\SUS** by default) and whether the update files are to be downloaded and stored locally or downloaded from Microsoft by the clients. Select **Save the updates to this local folder**, as seen in this illustration. Click **Next**.

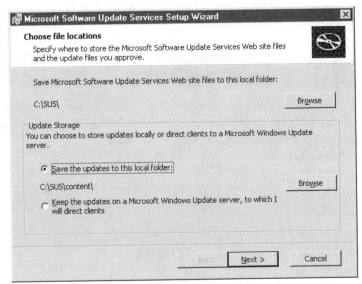

8. In the **Handling new versions of previously approved updates** dialog box, accept the default settings. Click **Next**.

9. In the **Ready to install** dialog box, make a note of the download URL. Click **Install**.

10. When the installation is complete, you are given the URL for the administration web site. Make a note of it, and click **Finish**. You are sent to the SUS Administration site in Internet Explorer.

11. Close the SUS Administration site.

After the Software Update Services are installed, you will need to configure the software to work with your environment.

on the **job**

I have found that installing SUS on a member server in the Active Directory domain gives me the most flexibility. Locating one SUS server in each site that has low bandwidth connections will also increase the functionality.

exam
ⓦatch
You can change all the installation options through the SUS Web Administration tool after the installation is complete.

Security enhancements in Windows Server 2003 can cause some problems when you want to access the SUS Web Administration page. You will need to make some configuration changes for Internet Explorer. Select **Tools | Internet Options**, and then select the **Security** tab. Select **Local Intranet** and click **Sites**, then add information to this dialog box as to what sites are considered local. Add **http://<computername>** to this list to make your local server name part of the intranet. You must restart Internet Explorer for the change to take effect.

Managing Software Update Services Version 1.0 Service Pack 1

Now that you have SUS installed, it is time to configure it to work on your network. All administration and configuration takes place by using the SUS Web Administration tools. You were given the URL to this web site in the last dialog box of the SUS installation. The URL follows the pattern **http://<servername>/SUSAdmin**, where <servername> is the name of the server SUS is installed on. If you are running an earlier version of Internet Explorer than 5.5, you will get an error page reminding you to upgrade your version of Internet Explorer. Figure 7-2 shows the interface of the SUS Web Administration tool.

Another way of starting the SUS Web Administration tool is to click Start | All Programs | Administrative Tools, and then choose Microsoft Software Update Services. To access the SUS Web Administration Tool, you must be a local administrator on the server where SUS is installed. This security measure ensures that only the administrator has access to the update setup.

Start configuring SUS by setting some options that are found under the **Set options** menu selection. When you click the link the following page will be displayed.

Set options

Set your Software Update Services options, and then click **Apply**.

Select a proxy server configuration:
○ Do not use a proxy server to access the Internet
◉ Use a proxy server to access the Internet
  ◉ Automatically detect proxy server settings
  ○ Use the following proxy server to access the Internet:
    Address: [   ] Port: [80]
    ☐ Use the following user credentials to access the proxy server:
    User: [   ] Password: [●●●●●●●●]
    ☐ Allow basic authentication when connecting to proxy server

FIGURE 7-2 Software Update Services Web Administration page

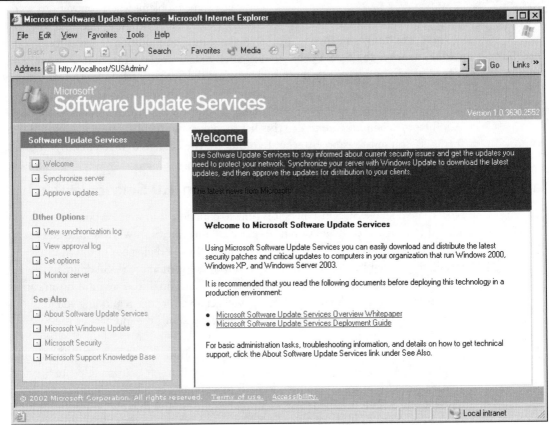

There are a number of areas to configure on this page, they will be handled in the following sections.

Proxy Settings

If your network is separated from the Internet by a proxy server, you need to configure the proxy server settings in the **Set options** page. If you are not using a proxy server, select **Do not use a proxy server to access the Internet**, otherwise select **Use a proxy server to access the Internet**.

The automatic proxy server detection allows your server to download the settings from the

---

e x a m

⚓ a t c h *If you are using* Internet Security and Acceleration Server *(ISA) that requires authentication, you need to enter the user name and the domain names in this format:* domain\user.

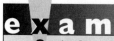

When you configure the **SUS server to** *Automatically detect proxy server settings,* **the server will also detect if there is no proxy server.**

proxy server without any additional configuration. If your proxy server does not allow automatic configuration, you need to enter information for the proxy server, including the name or port of the proxy server as well as the port number the proxy server is using. If your proxy server requires authentication, enter the user name and password. The option to use basic authentication translates into clear passwords being sent across the network. In the following illustration you can see how the proxy at the server Jupiter on port 8080 is configured to use the user name proxyJoe.

Select a proxy server configuration:

○ Do not use a proxy server to access the Internet

◉ Use a proxy server to access the Internet

    ○ Automatically detect proxy server settings

    ◉ Use the following proxy server to access the Internet:

        Address: |http://jupiter| Port: |8080|

        ☑ Use the following user credentials to access the proxy server:

        User: |proxyJoe| Password: |●●●●●●●●|

        ☐ Allow basic authentication when connecting to proxy server

Computer Name

As mentioned in Chapter 4, there are three methods a client can use to locate a network resource: DNS name, NetBIOS name, or IP address. The method to use depends of a number of factors, including what name servers are installed, and whether the network is routed. The IP address method will always work if TCP/IP is installed, and as TCP/IP is the standard protocol that is needed for Active Directory it is a forgone conclusion that TCP/IP is the network protocol. An example of how to specify an IP name is **http://10.0.0.251**.

Clients can find resources using the NetBIOS name if the client and resource are on the same subnet (not routed) and can use broadcasts, or if a Windows Internet Name Server (WINS) is installed on the network. NetBIOS names are the same as the computer name; for example, the server named Jupiter has a NetBIOS name of JUPITER. An example of how to specify a NetBIOS name is **http://jupiter**.

Domain Name Server (DNS) addresses are made up from a server and a domain name; such as **hare.nopcomp.com**. To use DNS names, the network must be configured with a DNS server. You know that there is a DNS server on the network if you are in an Active Directory domain. An example of how to specify a DNS name is **http:// jupiter.solsystemet.planet**.

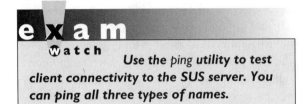

To configure the name clients will use to find the SUS server, enter the name in the **Server Name:** field of the **Specify the name your clients use to locate this update server,** as in the following illustration.

Specify the name your clients use to locate this update server:

Server name: jupiter.solsystemet.planet

If your clients cannot resolve a NetBIOS name (computername) you should change this to a DNS name (computername.domainname) or use the server's IP address.

Synchronization

In this section, you can determine where your SUS server will synchronize its content from. The choices allow you to use Microsoft's Windows Update servers, another SUS server, or a manually configured distribution point as the source of the content for this server. To configure synchronization with the Microsoft Update servers, select **Synchronize directly from the Microsoft Windows Update servers** under the **Select which server to synchronize content from** section.

To configure synchronization with a local SUS server or a manually configured content distribution point select **Synchronize from a local Software Update Services server.** Enter the name of the server using the NetBIOS name, DNS name, or IP address. For example, **http://servername.domain/.** The following Illustration shows how the synchronization is set to use the Microsoft Windows Update servers.

Select which server to synchronize content from:

○ Synchronize directly from the Microsoft Windows Update servers

○ Synchronize from a local Software Update Services server:

⬚

Type the name of the server. Example: CorpWU1

☐ Synchronize list of approved items updated from this location (replace mode)

Approval of New Updates

The way updated content is handled is set under the **Select how you want to handle new versions of previously approved updates:** section. When Microsoft releases new patches, they are made available on the Microsoft Windows Update servers, and you can download them to your SUS server to make available locally. During this synchronization, any content that is updated will be given the status **Updated** on the Approval page of the SUS Web Administration page. You set the options in this section to control how the updated material is handled for updates to packages that were already approved by the administrator, but had the content modified during synchronization.

There are two possible scenarios:

■ Automatically approve new versions of previously approved updates.

■ Do not automatically approve new versions of previously approved updates, I will manually approve these later.

Make your selection, depending on how deep you want to manage the update process.

Storage and Language

There are two different data types that are included in the synchronization between the Microsoft Windows Update servers and your SUS server: **metadata** and **packages**. Metadata is the fancy term used for data that describes data, or in the case of SUS, the dictionary objects that describe the packages and the platforms they apply to. The file that contains this information is named **Aucatalog1.cab** in the SUS download. The package contains the actual update.

The **Aucatalog1.cab** file is always downloaded during synchronization, but you have the choice of whether to download the packages. During the installation of SUS you are given the same option; this is where you can make the change after the installation.

If you have selected not to download the packages, they will be stored on the Microsoft Windows Update servers. Clients that run Automatic Updates will connect to your SUS server to determine the packages, and then download them from the Microsoft Windows Update servers. This option works very well when your network has a permanent connection to the Internet; you get an excellent load balance with the global Windows Update servers. You configure this option by selecting **Maintain the updates on a Microsoft Windows Update server**.

There are compelling reasons for maintaining your own storage of the packages, for example, if your connection to the Internet is slow, or not available from the production network. Keeping the updates stored locally also makes it possible to partition the content between multiple local SUS servers. Clients that run Automatic Updates connect to your SUS server to determine the approved packages and download them from the same server running SUS. You select this option by selecting **Save updates to a local folder**.

e x a m

ⓦ **a t c h** *If you remove a locale from the list of supported locales, any previously downloaded packages will stay on your server, but any client will only be able to access the selected locales.*

When you select to store the content locally, you also have the opportunity of selecting what locales to download by selecting the check boxes beside those locales you want.

EXERCISE 7-7

Configuring Software Update Services

In this exercise, you will configure the SUS server using the SUS Web Administration tool.

1. Ensure that you are logged in to the server as the local administrator.

2. Start the **SUS Web Administration** tool by clicking **Start | All Programs | Administration Tools | Microsoft Software Update Services**.

3. Click the **Set options** link in the menu on the left side of the page.

4. If you are not using a proxy server for your Internet access, select **Do not use a proxy server to access the Internet**. Go to Step 6.

5. If you are using a proxy server for Internet access, you need to enter that information first. Select **Use a proxy server to access the Internet**. Gather the proxy server information for your network and enter it in this table. Use this data to configure the proxy settings.

Option	Value
Proxy server address	
Proxy server port	
User name (if used)	
User password (if used)	

6. Verify that the server name that is configured is the name of your SUS server.

7. Select **Synchronize directly from the Microsoft Windows Update servers**.

8. Select **Do not automatically approve new versions of approved updates. I will manually approve these updates later**.

9. Ensure that **Maintain the updates on a Microsoft Windows Update server** is selected.

10. Click **Apply**. Click **OK** to acknowledge that you are sending information over the network.

Your SUS server is now configured, so you can start to look at synchronizing and approval of updates.

Synchronizing Content

After you have configured the SUS server, you need to synchronize with the Microsoft Windows Update servers or a local SUS server, depending on how you configured the SUS server. The synchronization will always download the metadata (**Aucontent.cab**) and optionally the packages, based on how the server was configured. There are two possible methods used to synchronize: manual and scheduled. In the following exercises you will see how to perform those actions.

EXERCISE 7-8

Manual Synchronization

In this exercise you will manually synchronize your SUS server.

1. Ensure you are logged in as the local administrator on your SUS server.

2. Open the SUS Web Administration tool. Click **Start | All Programs | Administration Tools | Microsoft Software Update Services**.

3. Click **Synchronize server** in the navigation bar.

4. Click **Synchronize Now**. When synchronization is complete, you will receive a pop-up message. When you click **OK**, you are taken to the Approval page.

EXERCISE 7-9

Configuring Automatic Synchronization

In this exercise, you will configure automatic synchronization of the SUS server.

1. Ensure you are logged in as the local administrator on your SUS server.

2. Open the SUS Web Administration tool. Click **Start** | **All Programs** | **Administration Tools** | **Microsoft Software Update Services**.

3. Click **Synchronize server** in the navigation bar.

4. Click Synchronization Schedule.

5. In the **Schedule Synchronization** dialog box, seen in the following illustration, set a schedule that synchronizes SUS every Monday at 2:00 A.M. Set the retry attempts should the synchronization fail to 5. Click **OK**.

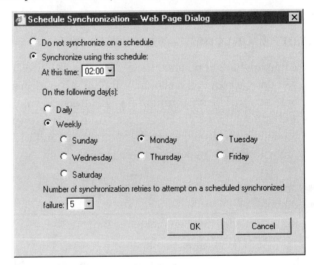

Approving Updates

After the you have synchronized SUS, you need to go through the updates and approve those that are going to be allowed on your network. The normal steps in this process would be to test the update to ensure it is stable with the mixture of software and hardware your network employs.

EXERCISE 7-10

Approving Updates

In this exercise you will approve some updates for use on your network.

1. Ensure you are logged in as the local administrator on your SUS server.

2. Open the SUS Web Administration tool. Click **Start** | **All Programs** | **Administration Tools** | **Microsoft Software Update Services**.

3. Click **Approve updates** in the navigation bar.

4. Locate and select **327696: Internet Information Services Security Roll-up Package**. Click the check box to the left of the update to approve it.

5. Click **Approve**.

6. You will be prompted that the list you are creating will overwrite any existing list. Click **YES**. Click **Accept** to accept the licensing agreement.

7. Click **OK**.

Once you have approved updates, you can always go back into the approval page to view the status of the updates. The status is displayed to the right of the update name. The status values are

- **New**   Indicates that this is a new update that has just been added to the catalog.
- **Approved**   Indicates that this update is approved for installation.
- **Not Approved**   Indicates that this update is not approved for installation.
- **Updated**   Indicates that this update has had its content changed.
- **Temporarily Unavailable**   Indicates that the package file is not available, or a dependency that is needed for installation is missing.

To get more information about an update, click the **Details** link under the update name. The information that is available includes the ***.cab** file, the locales each ***.cab** holds, the operating systems required, and a link to an optional **Read more** page.

Getting Status Information

There are two logs that are maintained for SUS: synchronization and approval logs. These logs are stored as XML files in folders that are only accessible to an administrator. The synchronization log is called **history-Sync.xml**, and is located in the folder **AutoUpdate\Administration** under the SUS website root. If SUS is installed in the default location, that translates to **C:\InetPub\WWWRoot \AutoUpdate\Administration**. The approval log is called **history-Approve.xml**, and is located in the same directory. Figure 7-3 shows how the **history-Approve.xml** file looks in Internet Explorer.

Now that you have SUS installed and configured, you need to look at how to configure the clients.

FIGURE 7-3 The **history-Approve.xml** file in Internet Explorer

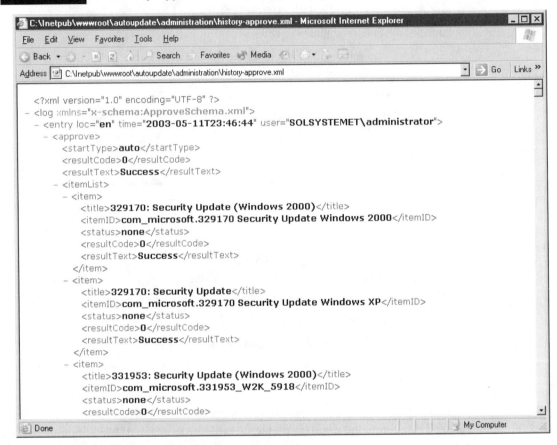

CERTIFICATION OBJECTIVE 7.04

Install and Configure Automatic Client Update Settings

Clients that want to use Software Update Services must be running the Automatic Updates client software that is available with SUS. The following operating systems can use Automatic Updates:

■ Windows 2000 Professional, Server, Advanced Server (Service Pack 2 or higher)

- Windows XP Professional
- Windows XP Home Edition
- Windows Server 2003, all versions

You can install the Automatic Update client on your client systems using any of the following methods:

- Install the Automatic Updates client using the Microsoft Installer (MSI) installation package
- Use the Microsoft Windows Update site
- Install Windows 2000 Service Pack 3
- Install Windows XP Service Pack 1
- Install Windows Server 2003

To access the MSI package for Automatic Update, you need to download it from the Microsoft download site. To go directly to the download page, use the URL **http://go.microsoft.com/fwlink/?LinkId=6930**. You will now install the Automatic Updates using the MSI setup.

INSIDE THE EXAM

Software Update Services

Because you now have to consider your networks as a battleground, you need to have support from the vendors to ensure that you have the best defenses against any type of attack. Microsoft has stepped out in the forefront to lead the way with an open update service, where it is easy to locate the latest updates and get information about vulnerabilities that have been found within existing software. Microsoft has built a very strong base for maintaining existing networks with the Software Update Services and the Automatic Update client.

One of the reasons behind the delay in getting Windows Server 2003 delivered was an exhaustive code review that was designed to find and repair any potential vulnerabilities before the product hit the street.

Because Microsoft has a vested interest in keeping administrators informed about updates and providing the means to intelligently manage your networks, you should not be surprised to find a number of questions on Software Update Services in the exam.

EXERCISE 7-11

Installing the Automatic Update Client

In this exercise you will install the Automatic Update client on a Windows XP Professional workstation.

1. Log into a Windows XP Professional workstation as a user with administrative rights.

2. Download the Automatic Update client (**WUAU22.msi**) from **http:// go.microsoft.com/fwlink/?LinkId=6930**. Save the file in **C:\Update**.

3. Click **Start | Run**, and enter **C:\Update\WUAU22.msi** as the command. Click **OK**.

4. The installation will proceed and end without any further messages.

5. Confirm that the installation succeeded by clicking **Start | Run**, and enter **%windir%\system32** as the command. Click **OK**.

6. Right-click **Wuaueng.dll**. Choose **Properties** from the context menu.

7. On the **Version** tab, confirm that the version number is 5.4.3630.2550 or higher.

To configure Automatic Update to use a server running SUS, you need to make registry changes to the client operating system by using a policy. Depending on your network environment, you will have a couple of choices of how to perform these registry changes:

■ Active Directory Group Policy
■ Windows NT 4 System Policy
■ Manual registry changes

To configure a Group Policy for Automatic Update, you need access to the **WUAU.adm** file. This administrative template contains the registry settings for Automatic Update. In the following exercise, you will configure a Group Policy and test it with a client.

EXERCISE 7-12

Configuring a Group Policy for Automatic Update

In this exercise, you will configure a Group Policy on your Windows Server 2003 domain controller that will be used by the Windows XP Professional workstations in your network.

1. Log in to your Windows Server 2003 as the domain administrator.

2. Click **Start | Run**.

3. Type **DSA.msc** to load the Active Directory Users and Computers snap-in.

4. Right click either the domain or Organizational Unit (OU) where you want to create the policy, and then click **Properties**.

5. Click the **Group Policy** tab.

6. Click **New**.

7. Type in **Automatic Updates** as the name of the policy. Click **Edit**.

8. Under **Computer Settings**, right-click **Administrative Templates**. Choose **Add/Remove Templates** from the context menu.

9. Verify that **wuau** is listed. If it is, go to step 13.

10. Click **Add**.

11. Enter the name of the Automatic Updates administrative template file: **%windir%\inf\WUAU.adm**.

12. Click **Open**.

13. Click **Close**.

14. Click **Computer Configuration**.

15. Expand **Administrative Templates**.

16. Expand **Windows Components**.

17. Click **Windows Update**. The policies you can set are shown in the right pane.

18. Double-click **Configure Automatic Updates** in the right pane.

19. Click **Enabled**.

20. Select **2 – Notify for download and notify for install** under **Configure automatic updating**.

21. Click **Next Setting**.

22. Click **Enabled**.

23. Enter the name of your SUS server in both of the text boxes. In my environment that is **http://jupiter**.

24. Click **Next Setting**.

25. In the **Reschedule Automatic Updates schedule installation** section, click **Enabled**.

26. Click **Next Setting**.

27. In the **No auto-restart for scheduled Automatic Updates Installation** section, click **Enabled**.

28. Click **OK**.

After you have applied the Group Policy, any computer that is in the domain will have the policy downloaded, and will start to use the SUS server. Given the settings from Exercise 7-12, the user logged in to a Windows XP Professional workstation will see the following after the computer has analyzed what updates are available.

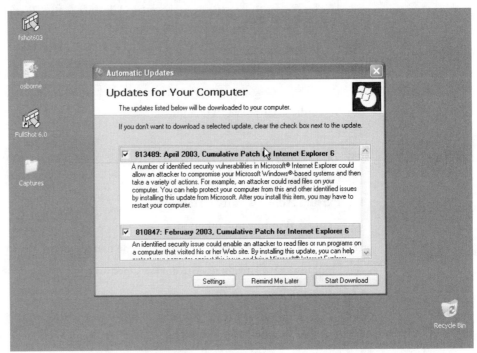

After you have started the download, it will run in the background with the Automatic Update icon displayed in the tray. You can hover over the icon to get information on how much has been downloaded. After the download is complete you will receive a message that all the files are downloaded and that installation can start. Your choices are to Install, request to be reminded later, or change the settings for Automatic Update as in this illustration.

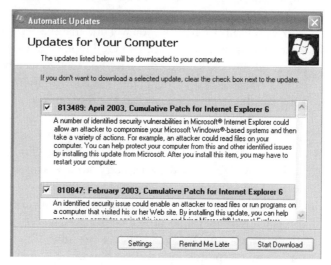

As soon as you select Install, the installation will take place, including any needed restarts. The system will only restart if you are the only user logged in and you have administrative rights to the computer.

Now that you have a better idea of Software Update Services, here are some possible scenario questions and their answers.

SCENARIO & SOLUTION

I want to use SUS on my network, but I do not have space on the server to keep all the updates. What are my options?	You can keep all the updates on the Microsoft Windows Update servers, letting your clients download from there when they need an update. You can also minimize the size of what you need to keep locally by only selecting the appropriate locales to download.
I have a number of Windows ME clients on my network; can I update them using SUS?	No. The Automatic Update client can only be installed on Windows 2000, Windows XP, and Windows Server 2003 computers.
Can I control the update process so the user can't decline the download and installation of the updates?	Yes. You can set the policy to automatically download the updates and install them on a schedule.

CERTIFICATION SUMMARY

The issue of network security is of paramount importance in Exam 70-291. Implementing network security by using security templates simplifies the process, and makes it possible to configure computers with the same security settings. When you work with security templates, you will find that the Security Configuration and Analysis stand-alone snap-in is an excellent GUI tool, but for scripted administration you will most likely use the **secedit** command-line tool. Remember that the **secedit** command can be scheduled to execute analysis or configuration actions. That way, you can automate the analysis of servers and workstations.

A major part of network security is ensuring that all computers connected to that network are running the latest updated operating system version. Software Update Services assists you in performing this task. The current version of SUS, 1.0 Service Pack 1, is available from the Microsoft download site, and can be installed on Windows Server 2003 either in an Active Directory domain or in a workgroup. Remember that SUS 1.0 Service Pack 1 can be installed on a domain controller. You administer SUS through a web site that is hosted by the SUS server and is only accessible to local administrators on the SUS server. Remember that the default security settings for Internet Explorer on Windows Server 2003 are such that you will not be able to connect to the SUS Web Administration site, and to enable access you need to add **http://<servername>** to the list of domains that are part of the local intranet.

✓ TWO-MINUTE DRILL

Implement Security Baseline Settings and Audit Security Settings by Using Security Templates

❑ Security Templates are managed through the Security Templates Standalone snap-in.

❑ Security templates are applied using the Security Configuration and Analysis stand alone snap-in, or by the **secedit** command-line tool.

❑ The Setup Security template is the backup of how security was configured during installation of Windows Server 2003.

❑ The **hisecdc** and **hisecws** security policies remove members from the Power Users group.

❑ You can audit security to verify that settings are in place.

❑ Restricted groups allow you to control security group membership through policies.

Implement the Principle of Least Privilege

❑ When you configure security, always limit access to exactly the level the user needs to perform the job, not more.

❑ Administrators should always be logged in using an ordinary user account, and should use **runas** to perform administration tasks.

Install and Configure Software Update Services

❑ To install Software Update Services, the server must have IIS installed.

❑ Before installing Software Update Services, the server must have the latest updates installed from the Microsoft Windows Update site.

❑ Administer Software Update Service using the SUS Web Administration site at **http://<*servername*>/SUSAdmin**.

❑ You can download all or part of the available updates to your local server; partial downloads are partitioned by locale.

❑ The catalog file is always downloaded even if the updates are kept on the Microsoft Windows Update servers.

❑ After synchronizing you need to test and approve the new updates.

Install and Configure Automatic Client Update Settings

❑ The Automatic Update client for Software Update Services is available as a download from the SUS web site.

❑ Configuration of Automatic Updates is through registry settings using a local policy, a GPO, or manual registry manipulations.

❑ The WUAU.adm administrative template must be added to have access to the registry entries.

SELF TEST

Implement Security Baseline Settings and Audit Security Settings by Using Security Templates

1. You are the administrator of your company's Windows Server 2003 network. You need to locate the physical file that represents the Security Template Research. What is the physical name of the Research Security Template?

   A. Research.sec

   B. Research.inf

   C. Research.tmp

   D. Research.stp

2. You are resolving security issues on a Windows Server 2003. You have found that the security settings for the c:\ file system are wrong. What security template would you use to restore the security settings for the c:\ file system?

   A. FileSystem.inf

   B. defltdc.inf

   C. Setup Security.inf

   D. root.inf

3. You are the administrator of your company's Windows Server 2003 network. You need to locate the physical file that represents the hisecdc security template. Where is the physical file that represents the hisecdc security template located?

   A. %systemroot%\inf

   B. %systemroot%\templates

   C. %systemroot%\security\templates

   D. %systemroot%\security\inf

4. What tools are used to edit security templates? (Choose all that apply.)

   A. Security Configuration and Analysis snap-in

   B. Active Directory Users and Computers

   C. **secedit** command-line utility

   D. Security Template snap-in

5. What tools are used to apply security templates? (Choose all that apply.)

   A. Security Configuration and Analysis snap-in

   B. Active Directory Users and Computers

   C. **secedit** command-line utility

   D. Security Template snap-in

6. You are a network administration consultant. You are currently working with a client who has noticed that some security settings have changed on their Windows Server 2003. You are asked to provide a report of all the security changes from a security template (BaseLine). What command line will produce such a report?

   A. **secedit /analyze /db BaseLine.sdb / cfg BaseLine.inf /log BaseLine.log /verbose**

   B. **secedit /report /db BaseLine.sdb / cfg BaseLine.inf /log BaseLine.log /verbose**

   C. **gpupdate /analyze /db BaseLine.sdb / cfg BaseLine.inf /log BaseLine.log /verbose**

   D. **gpupdate /report /db BaseLine.sdb / cfg BaseLine.inf /log BaseLine.log /verbose**

Implement the Principle of Least Privilege

7. What actions are against the principle of least privilege? (Choose all that apply.)

   A. Add the Domain User group to the local Power Users group.

   B. Give the Users group the right to shut down the server.

   C. Deny the Everyone group all access to all resources.

   D. Add your login account to the Administrators group.

Install and Configure Software Uupdate Services

8. Fingal Olsson, Senior Vice President of Information Technology, has asked you to detail for him what solutions are available for software update management. What solutions will you tell him about? (Choose all that apply.)

   A. System Management Server

   B. Microsoft Operations Manager

   C. Windows Server 2003

   D. Software Update Services

9. What Windows Server 2003 components *must* be installed before Software Update Services can be installed? (Choose all that apply.)

   A. A dedicated permanent Internet connection

   B. Terminal Services

   C. Active Directory

   D. Internet Information Services (IIS)

10. What tool do you use to administer Software Update Service?

   A. **susadmin** command-line utility

   B. SUS Web Administration

   C. SUS Administration extension snap-in

   D. Group Policy Editor

11. You are the administrator of your company's Windows Server 2003 network. You have configured Software Update Services on a local server, so that it keeps all update packages on the Microsoft Windows Update servers. When you monitor synchronization you find that some data is still transferred. What is transferred?

   A. There is a small amount of handshake between the systems; no file is actually transferred.

   B. The catalog (**SUScatalog1.xml**) is always downloaded.

   C. The catalog (**Aucatalog1.cab**) is always downloaded.

   D. The Software Update Services is updated at each synchronization event.

12. What format are the Software Update Services log files in?

   A. Access format (***.mdb**)

   B. NCSA common log format

   C. XML

   D. Microsoft IIS log file format

13. What logs are generated for Software Update Services? (Choose all that apply.)

   A. Performance log

   B. Approval log

   C. Client update log

   D. Synchronization log

Install and Configure Automatic Client Update Settings

14. You are the administrator of your company's Windows Server 2003 network. You are deploying Software Update Services on a server on this network. What operating systems are supported for the client? (Choose all that apply.)

    A. Windows XP Professional

    B. Windows 95 SR1

    C. Windows Server 2003

    D. Windows 98

    E. Windows 2000 Advanced Server

    F. Windows ME

15. You are the administrator for your company's Windows Server 2003 network. George Thusly, the Vice President of the Research and Development department, is working on the network using his laptop computer running Windows XP Professional. You have enabled Software Update Service and you have configured a Group Policy for all laptop computers to connect to the SUS server using the **http://jupiter** name. George calls you and tells you that the update has never worked, and he is very concerned that his computer is vulnerable. What must you do to solve the problem? (Choose all that apply.)

    A. Install a WINS server so the NetBIOS name can be resolved.

    B. Install the latest Automatic Update client software on the laptop.

    C. Refresh the policy on the laptop.

    D. Install Service Pack 1 on the laptop.

LAB QUESTION

You are the administrator for the Windows Server 2003 network in your company headquarters in Tallahassee, where your company employs a number of sales representatives that sell your products throughout the Americas. You have been given the task of building a solution for distributing software updates to the 325 Windows XP Professional workstations that have been installed with English, French, Spanish, or Portuguese versions of Windows XP Professional, seven Windows 2000 Advanced Servers, and three Windows Server 2003 systems. Your network connects to the Internet through a DSL that is rated at 584 Kbps and is protected by an ISA server. You have a server that can operate the software update solution. Your IT manager is concerned that untested updates will interfere with the sales operation, so you will need to test all patches before they are applied.

    Take an additional sheet of paper and build a checklist that lists the steps involved in implementing the solution.

SELF TEST ANSWERS

Implement Security Baseline Settings and Audit Security Settings by Using Security Templates

1. ☑ B. The Security Templates are stored in the text files that are in the INF format, and the correct filename is **Research.inf**.

☒ A, C and D are incorrect because .sec and .stp file extension are not used with any specific file format and .tmp is the standard for temporary files.

2. ☑ D. The root.inf security template is used to restore the root file system security settings.

☒ A is incorrect because **FileSystem.inf** is not a security template supplied with Windows Server 2003. B is incorrect because the **defltdc.inf** security template is used to restore default file system security settings, not the root settings. C is incorrect because the Setup Security template holds the security settings from when the computer was installed.

3. ☑ C. When a Windows Server 2003 is installed, it places the security templates in **%systemroot%\security\templates**, where **%systemroot%** defaults to **c:\windows**.

☒ A is incorrect because the **%systemroot%\inf** hidden directory is the repository for all the information files for the operating system, not security templates. B and D are incorrect because they both describe nonexistent folder locations.

4. ☑ D. The Security Templates snap-in is the tool used to edit and manage security templates.

☒ A is incorrect because the Security Configuration and Analysis snap-in is used to apply and analyze the security template, not to edit it. B is incorrect because this is the snap-in that is used to manage users and computers. C is incorrect because **secedit** is used to apply and analyze security templates.

5. ☑ A and C. The Security Configuration and Analysis snap-in and the **secedit** command-line utility are used to apply security templates.

☒ B is incorrect because this snap-in is used to manage users and computers. D is incorrect because the Security Templates snap-in is used to edit and manage security templates.

6. ☑ A. The **secedit** command with the **/analyze** parameter is the correct syntax.

☒ B is incorrect because **secedit** does not have a **/report** parameter. C and D are incorrect because **gpupdate** does not have those parameters.

Implement the Principle of Least Privilege

7. ☑ A, B and D. These outline steps that expand rights rather than removing them.

☒ C is incorrect because denying the Everyone group access will effectively make it impossible for anyone to access the server (doing this is not a good idea—I should know, I did it once to a DC).

Install and Configure Software Update Services

8. ☑ **A and D.** System Management Server 2.0 and Software Update Services are the two technologies that are available from Microsoft to solve the problem at hand.
☒ **B** is incorrect because MOM is used to manage the data, not the software. **C** is also incorrect because Windows Server 2003 is the operating system, not the software update solution.

9. ☑ **D.** The only item in the list that must be installed first is IIS.
☒ **A** is incorrect because even though it is nice, a permanent or even dedicated Internet connection is not a requirement. **B** is incorrect because Terminal Services has no connection with SUS. **C** is incorrect because AD is not required. It is nice to have so you can use Group Policy to configure your clients, but it is not a must.

10. ☑ **B.** SUS is managed through the SUS Web Administration site.
☒ **A and C** are incorrect because neither tool exists in the current version of SUS. **D** is incorrect because this is the tool for Group Policy, not for SUS.

11. ☑ **C.** The Aucatalog1.cab file is always downloaded at each synchronization event. It contains the catalog of update packages and the operating systems they apply to.
☒ **A** is incorrect because there is always a file transferred. **B** is incorrect because that is the wrong filename. **D** is incorrect because that is a good dream, but that is all it is right now.

12. ☑ **C.** XML has become the standard way of filing any data. XML documents can be opened as databases and analyzed using tools like Excel.
☒ **A, B, and D** are incorrect because none of these format are used.

Install and Configure Automatic Client Update Settings

13. ☑ **A, C and E.** The Automatic Update client will install on Windows 2000 Service Pack 2, Windows XP Professional Service Pack 1, Windows XP Home Edition Service Pack 1, and Windows Server 2003.
☒ **B, and D** are incorrect because those operating systems are not supported.

14. ☑ **B.** The most likely answer here is that the user is running an older non-supported Automatic Update client.
☒ **A** is incorrect because if WINS was an issue, the problem would have been reported from all users. **C** is incorrect because refreshing the policy will not start the update if the laptop is missing the proper version of the Automatic Update client. **D** is incorrect because Service Pack 1 does not include the latest version of the Automatic Update client.

15. ☑ **A.** Windows XP Home Edition is not part of the domain, so the Group Policy will not be applied. Manual editing of the registry is the only solution.

☒ **B** is incorrect because WINS is not the issue. **C** is incorrect because the client cannot receive Group Policies. **D** is incorrect because there is nothing in the question that indicates that there is a network problem.

LAB ANSWER

From the description of the environment, you can make certain decisions regarding the Software Update Services implementation. When you contrast the size of the Internet connection with the number of clients, it becomes apparent that the update packages should be stored locally. You know that you must support the English, French, Spanish, and Portuguese locales. You have also learned that you have an ISA server, which translates into a requirement to configure Software Update Services for that proxy. Here is the checklist for the implementation.

- ■ Inspect the assigned server.
- ■ Install IIS if it is not already installed.
- ■ Connect to the Microsoft Windows Update site to apply the latest updates.
- ■ Download Software Update Services.
- ■ Install Software Update Services.
- ■ Configure Software Update Services to include
  - ■ Proxy setting for the ISA server that connects to the Internet
  - ■ Specify the name of the Software Update Services server as **http://servername**.
  - ■ Synchronize directly from the Microsoft Windows Update servers.
  - ■ Do not automatically approve new versions of previously approved updates.
  - ■ Save the updates to a local folder.
  - ■ Change the list of locales to contain only English, French, Spanish, and Portuguese.
- ■ Synchronize.
- ■ Test and approve updates.
- ■ Roll out the latest Automatic Update client.
- ■ Create a Group Policy to apply Automatic Update.
- ■ Test.

MCSE/MCSA

MICROSOFT® CERTIFIED SYSTEMS ENGINEER &
MICROSOFT® CERTIFIED SYSTEMS ADMINISTRATOR

8

Manage Network Security

Ongoing monitoring and management makes up a major part of an administrator's involvement with network security. In this chapter, you will learn about IPSec and Kerberos, how to monitor them using the IPSec monitoring snap-in for the Microsoft Manage Console (MMC), and the Kerberos support tools you can use to keep tabs on the network.

CERTIFICATION OBJECTIVE 8.01

Monitor Network Protocol Security

Windows Server 2003 is the latest operating system from Microsoft that natively implements the Internet Protocol Security (IPSec) protocol. Unlike Secure Socket Layer (SSL), which is used for secure web site communication and is developed to work at a higher layer in the protocol stack, IPSec is implemented at the Network Layer and is therefore considered a Layer 3 (OSI layer) encryption technology.

This exam objective deals with monitoring network security, but before we start to look at the monitoring issues we need to define and configure IPSec so there is something to monitor. We will also delve into Kerberos and how to monitor it.

Network Protocols

The default Network Protocol used with Windows Server 2003 is TCP/IP. That protocol suite is covered in Chapter 1, so the following will be a quick refresher of that information.

Network protocols are said to be based on a reference model that defines the protocol in terms of layers. One of the most well known reference models is the Open Systems Interconnection (OSI) model that defines seven layers, as shown in Figure 8-1. This model defines the stages that network data passes through to get from source to destination; together, these layers are known as a *stack*. Each layer has a specific responsibility, defined here.

The following list summarizes the responsibilities for those layers:

1. **Physical Layer**   Controls the way unstructured bit-stream data is sent and received over the physical network.

2. **Data Link Layer**   Provides error-free data transfer between computers through the physical layer.

FIGURE 8-1

The OSI model

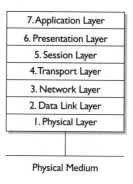

| 7. Application Layer |
| 6. Presentation Layer |
| 5. Session Layer |
| 4. Transport Layer |
| 3. Network Layer |
| 2. Data Link Layer |
| 1. Physical Layer |

Physical Medium

3. **Network Layer** Controls the physical path of the communication between computers based on the network conditions, routing, and other network factors.

4. **Transport Layer** Ensures that messages are received in the order they were sent, and that there is no duplication or loss of transmitted data.

5. **Session Layer** Establishes a communication session between processes running on different computers, supports message transfer of data.

6. **Presentation Layer** The data translator between the application's format and a common format that is used for the transfer over the network.

7. **Application Layer** Used by applications and users to access network services.

The OSI model is the reference model used when comparing protocols. It was introduced in 1978 by the International Standards Organization (ISO). TCP/IP, on the other hand was already an established protocol by that time, and was built around a four-layer reference model as can be seen in Figure 8-2.

The responsibilities for the four layers are as follows:

1. **Network Interface Layer** Manages how data is sent through the physical network. This layer deals with the hardware issues of the network.

FIGURE 8-2

The TCP/IP reference model

Application Layer		Telnet	FTP	SMTP	DNS	RIP	SNTP
Transport Layer		TCP		UDP	ICMP		ICMP
Internet Layer		IP			IPSEC		
Network Interface Layer		Ethernet	Frame Relay		Token Ring		ATM

TCP/IP Model   TCP/IP protocol suite

2. **Internet Layer**   Packages the data into IP datagrams that are sent across the network between computers. The IP datagram can be in clear text using the IP protocol, or secure using the IPSec protocol.

3. **Transport Layer**   Manages the session management between computers.

4. **Application Layer**   Defines the protocol for how host programs interface with the transport layers services.

The IPSec protocol is part of the Transport Layer (layer 3) in both the OSI and TCP/IP model. Now we will look at IPSec in more detail.

Understanding IPSec

The IPSec protocol is defined in a number of Request For Comments (RFC) documents, and RFC2401 is the central document as a mechanism to secure network traffic. The three areas that IPSec is responsible for are data integrity, confidentiality, and authentication at the Transport Layer (layer 3). The Microsoft implementation in Windows Server 2003 uses a Private/Public key structure matched with integrated automatic key management to ease implementation and management.

on the
Ⓙob

Public/private key technology is the basis for a large number of security schemes used in the Windows environment. It is based on the mathematics of prime numbers. Private keys are made from two very large prime numbers; the public key is the product of the two prime numbers in the public key. The time it would take to factor the public key to get to the original private key prime numbers far exceeds the time the information protected needs to be secret.

IPSec is designed as an end-to-end security system where trusts and security are established between a source and destination IP address. The IP address of the computer is not necessarily the principal endpoint of the communication. Rather, the system behind the IP address has the identity that is validated in the authentication process. Only the computers that are communicating must be aware of IPSec; it is transparent to the rest of the network. The only issue might be with firewalls and packet filters that need to know about the traffic to be able to pass it through to the other side of the network. Both computers that are configured for IPSec must have an IPSec policy that defines the rules for communication.

IPSec gives secure communications with a low cost of ownership, and is deployed in the network using these features:

■ Integrated with the Windows Server 2003 security framework.

- Active Directory (AD) centralizes the IPSec policy administration.
- IPSec is transparent to users and applications.
- Security configuration is flexible.
- Automatic key management.
- Automatic security negotiation.
- Public key infrastructure (PKI) support.
- Pre-shared key support through the Kerberos V5 protocol.

Some of the Internet standards that are supported by IPSec are DES, SHA, MD5, HMAC, 3DES, Diffie-Hellman technique, and the ISAKMP/Oakley (IKE) standard.

The content of the IPSec packets is not part of the exam, but you should be aware of them for better understanding of the monitoring tasks later in this chapter.

IPSec has two major components: the Authentication Header (AH) is used to verify the content, and the Encapsulating Security Payload (ESP) encrypts the data. AH adds additional binary data after the IP header of the network packet. This additional data does not make the traffic un-routable; routers treat the traffic as normal IP traffic. The ESP is associated with the encryption of the payload, but it can also be used for direct authentication.

You can use IPSec for end-to-end communications as well as for Virtual Private Network (VPN) security. In the end-to-end model, the traffic between two computers is secured, and either computer can communicate with other hosts with or without IPSec. When you use VPN security, the communication is going to be a higher burden for the server because all the traffic must be encrypted through the VPN tunnel. Let's install and configure IPSec.

Installing and Configuring IPSec

IPSec is provided as a service with Windows Server 2003 that is installed by default when Windows Server 2003 is installed. The configuration of IPSec is performed through IPSec Security Policies that define what network configuration should be used.

Implementing IPSec Security Policies

Now we'll discuss configuring IPSec by setting up a Security Policy. This task requires, at a minimum, two computers connected together with a hub or switch, the first computer running Windows Server 2003 configured as a domain controller, and the second computer running Windows XP Professional joined to the domain. In this scenario the Windows Server 2003 computer is called JUPITER and the Windows XP Professional computer is called MERCURY, the domain is called **solsystemet.planet**.

All the management is performed through a Microsoft Management Console that you will add a number of related snap-ins to.

EXERCISE 8-1

Setting Up an MMC for IPSec

In this exercise you will configure an MMC for use with IPSec configuration.

1. Log in to the Windows Server 2003 using an administrative account.

2. Click **Start | Run**.

3. At the **Run** dialog, type **mmc**. Click **OK**.

4. When the MMC opens, click **File | Add/Remove Snap-in**.

5. Click the **Add** button to show the **Add Standalone Snap-in** dialog.

6. Select **Computer Management** from the list, and click **Add**.

7. Select the **local computer**, and click **Finish**.

8. Select **Group Policy Object Editor** from the list, and click **Add**.

9. Click **Browse**, select **Default Domain Policy**, click **OK**, and click **Finish**.

10. Select **Computer Management** from the list, and click **Add**.

11. Select **Another Computer**, and click **Browse**.

12. Type the name of your workstation in the search dialog, click **OK**, and click **Finish**.

13. Select **IP Security Monitor**, and click **Add**.

14. Select **IP Security Policy Management**, and click **Add**.

15. In the **Select Computer or Domain** dialog, select **The Active Directory Domain of which this computer is a member**, and click **Finish**.

16. Select **IP Security Policy Management**, and click **Add**.

17. In the **Select Computer or Domain** dialog, select **Local Computer**, and click **Finish**.

18. Select **IP Security Policy Management**, and click **Add**.

19. Select **Another Computer**, and click **Browse**.

20. Type the name of your workstation in the search dialog, click **OK**, and click **Finish**.

21. Click **Close**, and then click **OK**.

22. Click **File** | **Save** in the MMC.

23. In the **Save As** dialog, give the console a meaningful name. I named my console **IP Security**.

Your console should look similar to the one in Figure 8-3.

Now that you have a console that you can manage the two computers from, you need to configure the IP Security Policy.

FIGURE 8-3

Creating the MMC for IP Security

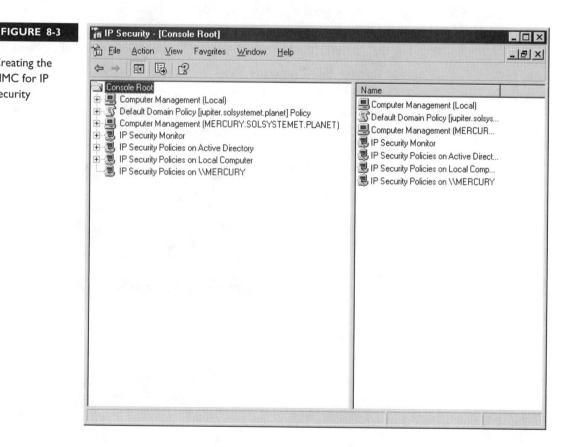

CertCam 8-2 ON THE CD

EXERCISE 8-2

Creating an IPSec Policy

The following steps will create and assign an IPSec Policy between the two computers in our network.

1. Log in to the Windows Server 2003 using an administrative logon name.

2. Open the **IP Security** MMC you created in Exercise 8-1.

3. In the left pane of the Console, right-click **IP Security on Local Machine**, and then click **Create IP Security Policy**. The **IP Security Policy Wizard** appears.

4. Click **Next** at the Welcome screen of the wizard.

5. Type your name for the new policy, and click **Next**. I used the default name **New IP Security Policy**.

6. Clear the **Activate the Default Response Rule** check box, and click **Next**.

7. Ensure that the **Edit Properties** check box is selected, which is the default, and click **Finish**.

8. In the **New IP Security Policy Properties** dialog, make sure the **Use Add Wizard** check box is selected (in the lower right corner), as shown in the following illustration. Click **Add** to start the **Security Rule Wizard**.

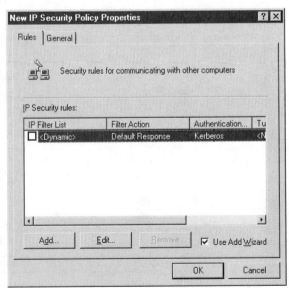

9. Click **Next** on the **Welcome** screen.

10. Select **This Rule Does Not Specify a Tunnel** (the default selection), and click **Next**.

11. Select the option for **All Network Connections** (the default selection), and click **Next**.

12. The next step is to specify the IP filter list, as shown in the following illustration. Click **Add** to start creating the filter.

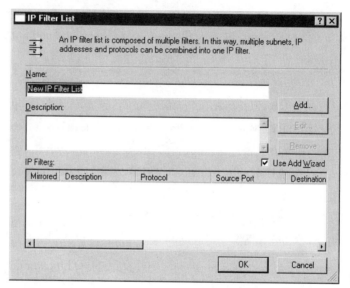

13. Enter a name for the **IP Filter List**; I used the default **New IP Filter List**. Make sure the **Use Add Wizard** is selected, and click **Add** to start the wizard.

14. Click **Next** on the **Welcome** screen.

15. Ensure that the **Mirrored** check box is selected, and click **Next**.

16. Use **My IP Address** as the source, and click **Next**.

17. Select **A Specific IP Address** for the destination, and enter the address of the workstation, as you can see in the following illustration. Click **Next**.

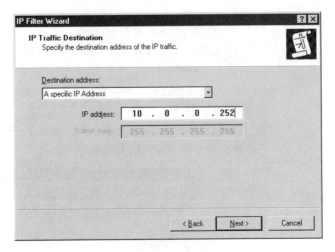

18. Select **Any** Protocol and click **Next**.

19. Make sure the **Edit Properties** check box is cleared, and click **Finish**. Click **OK**.

20. Select your new IP filter, and click **Next**.

21. In the **Security Rule Wizard**, ensure that the **Use Add Wizard** is selected, and click **Add**.

22. Click **Next** on the **Welcome** screen.

23. Give the **Filter Action** a name (I used the default name of **New Filter Action**), and click **Next**.

24. To set the behavior, select **Negotiate Security**, as seen in this illustration, and click **Next**.

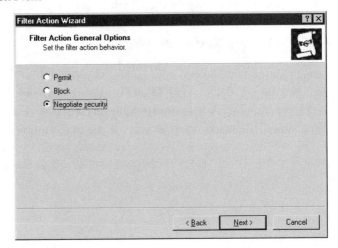

25. Select **Do not communicate with computers that do not support IPSec,** as shown in this illustration, and click **Next**.

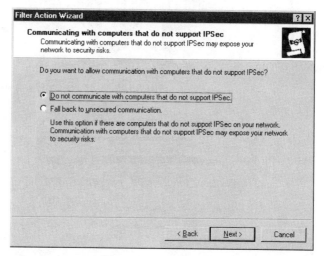

26. Set **IP Traffic Security** to **Integrity and Encryption**, and click **Next**.

27. Make sure the **Edit Properties** check box is cleared, and click **Finish**.

28. Select your new filter action, as shown in the illustration, and then click **Next**.

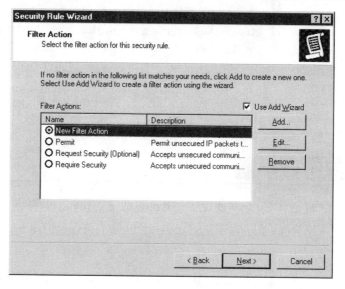

29. You will use a preshared key for this exercise. Enter it as shown in this illustration. Click **Next**. Make sure you remember the key; I have used the name of a most unlikely wizard, RINCEWIND.

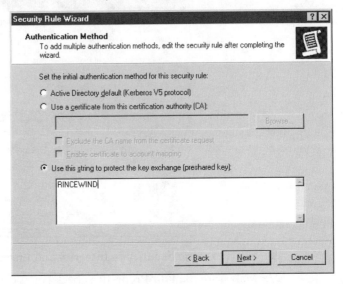

30. Clear the **Edit Properties** check box, and click **Finish**.

31. Select the **New IP Filter List**, and click **OK**.

32. Repeat these steps on the workstation. Remember that the destination IP for the workstation is the server.

After you configured IPSec on both the server and workstation, it is time to enable IPSec, and to test that it works.

EXERCISE 8-3

Assigning and Testing the IP Security Policy

Now you will assign and test the IPSec policy. Follow these step to do so.

1. Log in to the Windows Server 2003 using an administrative logon name.

2. Open the **IP Security** MMC you created in Exercise 8-1.

3. In the left pane of the MMC, select **IP Security Policies on \\MERCURY** (where MERCURY is the name of the workstation). There is now an extra policy that you built in Exercise 8-2.

4. Right-click the new policy, and then click **Assign** from the context menu. What happened? Did you get an error, as in this illustration?

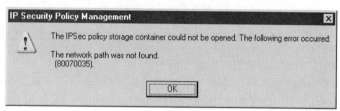

What is the problem? The issue here is that the workstation (MERCURY) has a policy that forces it to use IPSec when communicating with the server (JUPITER), so it is normal to get this error.

5. In the left pane of the MMC, select **IP Security Policies on Local Computer**. There is now an extra policy that you built in Exercise 8-2.

6. Right-click the new policy, and then click **Assign** from the context menu.

7. The status of the policy should change from **No** to **Yes** in the right pane of the MMC.

8. In the left pane of the MMC, select **IP Security Policies on \\MERCURY** (where MERCURY is the name of the workstation). Right click on the node and select **refresh** from the context menu. Now the policies are displayed.

9. Restart the workstation.

10. Open a command prompt on the Windows Server 2003. Ping the workstation, as in this example.

```
C:\>ping mercury.solsystemet.planet

Pinging MERCURY.solsystemet.planet [10.0.0.252] with 32 bytes of data:

Negotiating IP Security.
Negotiating IP Security.
Negotiating IP Security.
Reply from 10.0.0.252: bytes=32 time=2ms TTL=128

Ping statistics for 10.0.0.252:
    Packets: Sent = 4, Received = 1, Lost = 3 (75% loss),
Approximate round trip times in milli-seconds:
    Minimum = 2ms, Maximum = 2ms, Average = 2ms
```

11. As you can see, the IP Security is negotiated before you receive a successful ping.

12. Open the MMC and expand the IP Security Monitor node, then expand JUPITER, Main Mode, and select Security Associations. The resulting display is seen in this illustration, showing that there is an association between the two computers.

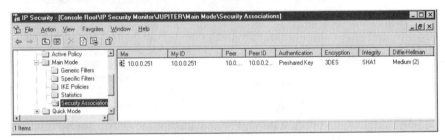

You will learn more about monitoring tasks later in this chapter.

Remember that IPSec is used to maintain the integrity and secrecy of data that is transported between **end-to-end systems providing transparency to the network. The data is only accessible to authenticated users.**

Now that you have a better idea of IPSec, here are some possible scenario questions and their answers.

SCENARIO & SOLUTION

What are the authentication methods that are supported by Internet Key Exchange (IKE)?	Public/private key signatures using Certificates, Kerberos V5, and preshared passwords.
What are IP filters responsible for?	IP filters determine what action to take for specific traffic, selecting IPSec or clear transport based on hosts and type of protocol.
What tool do I use to manage IP filters?	IP filters are managed through the IP Security Policy snap-in.

Why Monitoring?

The age-old question for administrators of any reasonably complex system has always been this: Why do I need to monitor this system? The answer to this question can be very philosophical, as well as leading to the Zen of administration. My reasons for monitoring are probably a bit more down-to-earth and reflect the engineering training I received almost 30 years ago. You monitor any system to ensure that you are aware of any changes that might represent future problems.

Monitoring consists of gathering data, using multiple tools that will ensure you have a baseline collection of measurements that you can compare against when you suspect the system might be going through some troubles. The methodology of monitoring is based on collecting information that describes what the system is doing when it's operating normally, and then you take samples that you compare against this standard.

In this section, you will learn about the tools for monitoring network security, which should allow you to develop your own methodology.

IPSec Explained

To understand the information that comes from the monitoring tools, you need to understand how IPSec connections are negotiated.

The peers that exchange data need to establish a security agreement, called a security association (SA). Both peers agree on how they are going to exchange and protect the information, as shown in the following illustration.

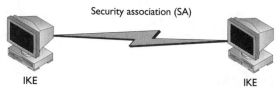

Security association (SA)

IKE   IKE

Each peer in this scheme is running the IPSec service, and has the Internet Key Exchange (IKE) component. The IKE is defined by the Internet Engineering Taskforce (IETF) as a standard method of security association and key exchange that

■ Provides centralizes SA management

■ Manages shared, secret keys used to secure the information

The central part of IPSec is the security association that is a combination of a negotiated key, security protocol, and security parameters index (SPI). These components work together to define the security that is used to keep the communication secure between the two computers (the endpoints). The SPI is a unique value that is used to differentiate the SA from any other SAs in existence on the receiving computer.

The negotiation for the secure channel is handled in two phases, main mode and quick mode.

Main Mode SA

During this first phase, the two computers establish a secure, authenticated channel that goes through the following steps to complete this negotiation:

1. Policy negotiation:
   - Encryption algorithm
   - Integrity algorithm
   - Diffie-Hellman group to be used
   - Authentication method

2. Diffie-Hellman exchange of public values. Only base information required by the Diffie-Hellman key determination algorithm is exchanged. Each computer generates the negotiated master key that is used for authentication.

3. Authentication. The authentication step is used to ensure that the two computers has authenticated the Diffie-Hellman key exchange to thwart a man-in-the middle attack.

Do not use Diffie-Hellman Group 1 (768 bits of keying material) for security reasons, always use Group 2048 (2048 bits).

Quick Mode SA　　During the quick mode, SAs are negotiated on behalf of the IPSec driver using these steps:

1. Policy negotiation:
   - IPSec protocol
   - Hash algorithm for integrity and authentication
   - Encryption algorithm.

2. Session key material is refreshed or exchanged.

3. SAs and keys, along with the SPI, are passed to the IPSec driver.

This second negotiation is protected by the main mode SA. The main mode provides identity protection; the quick mode protects the refreshing of key material.

Now you have seen the theory of IPSec, and you're ready to start working with the tools.

IPSec Monitoring Tools

As in any profession, there are special tools designed for the specific tasks of the job. One of the first things you learn is to use the right tool for the job. You must also learn about the tools and their use before using them. My son has been working in a warehouse while in high school, he had to take courses before he was allowed to drive the forklift, which is a dangerous tool. The same is true for network administration, where you have access to tools that could damage to the system if used wrong (I'm thinking of the registry editors here).

This discussion starts with the most common tool for administrators, the Event Viewer, followed by the IP Security Monitor and tools that are used to monitor Kerberos V5.

on the Job

The Event Viewer is the best tool that has come out of the Windows family of operating systems. The event system gives administrators as well as developers the ability to communicate status, warning, and errors to users and administrators.

Event Viewer

The Event Viewer is a graphical program that gives you access to event logs that are maintained by the Event Service. These Event logs are, at a minimum, the System, Application, and Security logs, but the list is expanded as additional components are added to the computer. The following list describes some of the logs:

- **System Log** Holds messages that are sent from the Operating System
- **Application Log** Receives messages from applications like Microsoft SQL Server 2000
- **Security Log** Used for security audits

Additional logs are added when necessary, like the Directory Service log, which is added when Active Directory is installed, or the DNS log that is installed when DNS is installed. Software developers can add additional logs for their products as needed.

IPSec messages are logged in the Security Log as audit messages. The following illustration shows one such message.

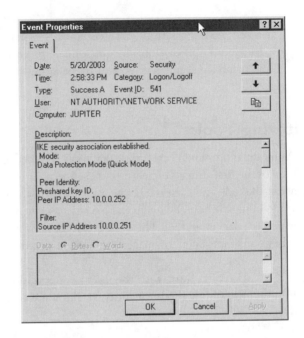

EXERCISE 8-4

Using the Event Viewer to View IPSec Messages

In this exercise you will learn how to use the Event Viewer to find and view IPSec messages.

1. Click **Start** | **Administrative Tools** | **Event Viewer**. This opens the Event Viewer, as shown in this illustration.

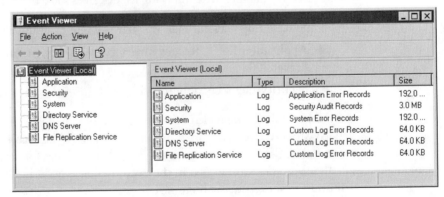

2. Click the Security log in the left pane to select it.

3. Set up a filter by selecting **View | Filter**.

4. Select **Security** as the **Event Source**.

5. Type in the **Event ID 541**, as shown in the following illustration. Click **OK**.

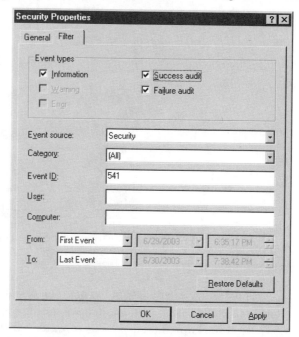

6. The resulting Event Viewer should look similar to the following illustration.

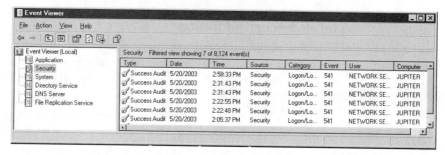

7. Double-click one of the events in the right pane to display the event information, as shown in the next illustration.

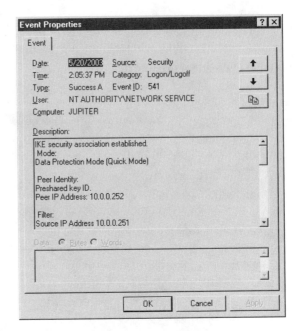

8. You can use the arrows to navigate between the messages.

The Event Viewer is one of the most important sources of information about usage, and one of the most powerful features of the filter is to only view the failure information. This lets you know if there are systems or users that are having problems, or even get an early warning that there might be something wrong with the security system.

The IP Security Monitor

The IP Security Monitor has a new look in Windows Server 2003. In Windows 2000, it was a stand-alone program, but it is now a snap-in for the Microsoft Management Console. The IP Security Monitor, or IPSecMon, provides information on the current policies, as well as statistics regarding the traffic using IPSec.

Before you can look at the content of the IP Security Monitor, you must create an MMC to hold it.

e x a m

ⓌatcH *Remember that IPSecMon is an MMC snap-in, not a stand-alone program that can be started from the Run dialog.*

EXERCISE 8-5

Creating an MMC for IP Security Monitor

In this exercise you will create a customized Microsoft Management Console and add the IP Security Monitor.

1. Log in to the Windows Server 2003 using an administrative account.

2. Click **Start** | **Run**.

3. At the **Run** dialog, type **mmc**. Click **OK**.

4. When the MMC opens, click **File** | **Add/Remove Snap-in**.

5. Click **Add**.

6. Select **IP Security Monitor**, and click **Add**.

7. Click **Close**, and then click **OK**.

8. Save the MMC.

The IP Security Monitor has three main areas where you can glean information about the configuration and workings of IPSec on your server. In the following illustration you can see the nodes, which hold the information that follows.

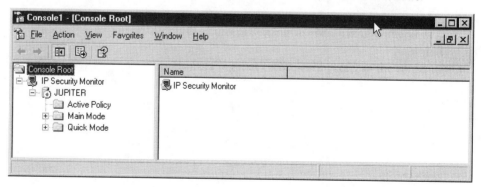

- **Active Policy**   Holds information about the current effective IPSec Policy, as shown in Figure 8-4.

- **Main Mode**   Lists the information for the Internet Key Exchange (IKE) for the server after Statistics has been selected, as shown in Figure 8-5.

- **Quick Mode**   Lists the information for the data exchange between the partners after Statistics has been selected, as shown in Figure 8-6.

FIGURE 8-4

Active Policy

Item	Description
✕ Policy Name	New IP Security Policy
✕ Policy Description	
✕ Policy Last Modified	5/20/2003 2:04:33 PM
✕ Policy Store	Local Store
✕ Policy Path	Not Applicable
✕ Organizational Unit	Not Applicable
✕ Group Policy Object Name	Not Applicable

FIGURE 8-5

Main mode
statistics

Parameters	Statistics	
✕ Active Acquire	1	
✕ Active Receive	0	
✕ Acquire Failures	0	
✕ Receive Failures	0	
✕ Send Failures	0	
✕ Acquire Heap Size	3	
✕ Receive Heap Size	2	
✕ Authentication Failures	0	
✕ Negotiation Failures	9	
✕ Invalid Cookies Received	0	
✕ Total Acquire	13	
✕ Total Get SPI	6	
✕ Key Additions	6	
✕ Key Updates	6	
✕ Get SPI Failures	0	
✕ Key Addition Failures	0	
✕ Key Update Failures	0	
✕ ISADB List Size	1	
✕ Connection List Size	0	
✕ IKE Main Mode	3	
✕ IKE Quick Mode	6	
✕ Soft Associations	0	
✕ Invalid Packets Received	0	

FIGURE 8-6

Quick mode
statistics

Parameters	Statistics	
✕ Active Security Associations	1	
✕ Offloaded Security Associations	0	
✕ Pending Key Operations	0	
✕ Key Additions	6	
✕ Key Deletions	5	
✕ Rekeys	2	
✕ Active Tunnels	0	
✕ Bad SPI Packets	0	
✕ Packets Not Decrypted	0	
✕ Packets Not Authenticated	0	
✕ Packets With Replay Detection	0	
✕ Confidential Bytes Sent	219815	
✕ Confidential Bytes Received	204554	
✕ Authenticated Bytes Sent	245432	
✕ Authenticated Bytes Received	230856	
✕ Transport Bytes Sent	242715	
✕ Transport Bytes Received	268072	
✕ Bytes Sent In Tunnels	0	
✕ Bytes Received In Tunnels	0	
✕ Offloaded Bytes Sent	0	
✕ Offloaded Bytes Received	0	

TABLE 8-1   Active Policy Items for a Computer

Policy Item	Description
Policy Name	The name of the active IPSec policy.
Policy Description	Description text that optionally can be added to the IPSec policy.
Policy Last Modified	The date and time that the active policy was last modified.
Policy Store	Where the active IPSec policy is stored; for computers, this is listed as **Local Store**.
Policy Path	This information is not displayed for computers; it only applies to domains.
Organizational Unit	This information is not displayed for computers; it only applies to domains.
Group Policy Object Name	This information is not displayed for computers; it only applies to domains.

Active Policy   The Active Policy node reports the current IPSec policy that is in effect on the domain, the local computer, or a remote computer. The information displayed for an Active Policy that is applied to a computer is summarized in Table 8-1.

The Active Policy node lists slightly different information when focused on the domain; these items are listed in Table 8-2.

The information listed under the Active Policy node documents the location and identity of the IPSec policy that has been applied to the domain, local computer, or remote computer. This is an excellent place to find out what policy is in effect.

exam

⩊atch   *You need to be a member of the Administrators group on the local or remote computer to get access to the Active Policy node.*

TABLE 8-2   Active Policy Items for a Domain

Policy Item	Description
Policy Name	The name of the active IPSec policy.
Description	Description text that optionally can be added to the IPSec policy.
Policy Last Modified	The date and time that the active policy was last modified.
Policy Store	Where the active IPSec policy is stored; for domains, this is listed as **Domain Store**.
Policy Path	The LDAP path to the active IPSec policy.
Organizational Unit	Documents the Organizational Unit (OU) that the IPSec policy is applied to.
Group Policy Object Name	Documents the Group Policy Object (GPO) that the IPSec policy is applied to.

Main Mode Statistics   The Main Mode node lists the Internet Key Exchange (IKE) information. There are a number of nodes under the Main Mode node that focus on different types of data. The Generic and Special Filter nodes list the IPSec filters that are in use, and you can find information about what security methods are available for the key exchange under the IKE Policy node. The Statistics node contains information about the IPSec statistics, as outlined in Table 8-3, and finally, the Security Associations node lists the current IPSec connections to this computer.

TABLE 8-3   Main Mode Statistics

Main Mode Statistic	Description
Active Acquire	The number of requests that are pending to start an IKE negotiation to get an SA between IPSec endpoints. This number includes any outstanding requests, as well as any queued requests. An *acquire* is a request to establish and SA between IPSec peers.
Active Receive	Reports how many received IKE messages are queued for processing.
Acquire Failures	The total number of outbound acquire requests that have failed since the IPSec service was started.
Receive Failures	The total number of errors in receiving IKE requests since the IPSec service was started.
Send Failures	The total number of errors in sending IKE messages since the IPSec service was started.
Acquire Heap Size	The number of entries in the Acquire Heap that stores successful requests to acquire an SA between IPSec peers.
Receive Heap Size	The number of incoming IKE messages in the Receive Heap.
Authentication Failures	The total number of identity authentication failures since the IPSec service was started. The types of identity authentication are Kerberos, certificate, and preshared key.
Negotiation Failures	The total number of negotiation failures since the IPSec service was last started. This number contains both main mode and quick mode numbers.
Invalid Cookies Received	The total number of cookies that did not match an active main mode SA since the IPSec service was last started. These cookies are used in IKE messages to identify the main mode SA that the message should be matched with.
Total Acquire	The total number of requests to start an SA that have been received since the IPSec service was last started
Total Get SPI	The total number of requests for a unique Security Parameters Index (SPI) from the IPSec driver since the IPSec service was last started.

TABLE 8-3	Main Mode Statistics *(continued)*

Main Mode Statistic	Description
Key Additions	The total number of outbound quick mode SAs that have been added to the IPSec driver since the IPSec service was last started.
Key Updates	The total number of inbound quick mode SAs that have been added to the IPSec driver since the IPSec service was last started.
Get SPI Failures	The total number of failed requests for a unique SPI that have been sent to the IPSec driver since the IPSec service was started.
Key Addition Failures	The total number of failed outbound quick mode SA addition requests that have been sent to the IPSec driver since the IPSec service was last started.
Key Update Failures	The total number of failed inbound quick mode SA addition requests that have been sent to the IPSec driver since the IPSec service was last started.
ISADB List Size	The number of main mode entries, including successful negotiations, negotiations in progress, and failed or expired negotiations that have not been purged yet.
Connection List Size	The current number of quick mode negotiations in progress.
IKE Main Mode	The number of successful SAs created during main mode negotiations since the IPSec service was started.
IKE Quick Mode	The number of successful SAs created during quick mode negotiations since the IPSec service was started.
Soft Associations	The total number of SAs formed with peers that have not responded to main mode negotiation attempts since the IPSec service was last started.
Invalid Packets Received	The total number of invalid IKE messages received since the IPSec service was started.

on the
ⓤob

*Soft Associations **are SAs between computers that did not respond to main mode negotiation attempts. If the IPSec policy allows communications with the computers that do not respond, a soft association is formed. Soft SAs are not secured by IPSec.***

e**x**a m
ⓦatch
The number of Send Failures typically increases for computers that establish SAs over temporary network connections, such as dial-up connections, virtual private network tunnels, and wireless connections.

INSIDE THE EXAM

IPSec Monitoring

On the exam you will have to know about the issues of monitoring the network for security and to keep a good watch on the IPSec statistics. You need to have a good understanding of what the statistics look like for a properly running network so that you can compare these numbers to the network when there are some issues. Specifically, the Main Mode (Phase I) statistics will give you information about the authentication portion of IPSec.

The Authentication Failure counter reports how many failed attempts there have been

for authentication. If you have problems communicating between peers, and the Authentication Failure number starts increasing, it usually means that there are mismatches in authentication method settings between the peers.

Remember the counters that tell the story: IKE Main Mode and ISADB List Size document how busy the server is, whereas Negotiation Failures and Authentication Failures reports the failures.

Quick Mode Statistics   Quick mode negotiates the security for the transfer of the data, as well as the refreshing of the keying material as needed. Table 8-4 lists the items that are part of the statistics you can gather about quick mode.

TABLE 8-4   Quick Mode Statistics Items

Quick Mode (IPSec) Statistic	Description
Active Security Associations	The number of active quick mode SAs.
Offloaded Security Associations	The number of active quick mode SAs that have been offloaded to network adapters that contain hardware for the IPSec cryptographic functions.
Pending Key Operations	The number of IPSec key exchanges that are in progress, but not completed.
Key Additions	The total number of keys for quick mode SA negotiations that have been added successfully since the last time the computer was restarted.
Key Deletions	The total number of keys for quick mode SAs that have been deleted successfully since the last time the computer was restarted.

TABLE 8-4   Quick Mode Statistics Items *(continued)*

Quick Mode (IPSec) Statistic	Description
Rekeys	The total number of successful rekey operations since the computer was last restarted.
Active Tunnels	The total number of active IPSec tunnels.
Bad SPI Packets	The total number of packets with incorrect SPI since the computer was last restarted.
Packets Not Decrypted	The total number of packets that have not been able to be deciphered since the computer was last restarted.
Packets Not Authenticated	The total number of packets where the data could not be verified because the integrity hash verification failed. This value is reset when the computer is restarted.
Packets With Replay Detection	The total number of packets containing an invalid sequence number since the computer was last restarted.
Confidential Bytes Sent	The total number of bytes sent using the Encapsulating Security Payload (ESP) protocol since the computer was last restarted.
Confidential Bytes Received	The total number of bytes received using the ESP protocol since the computer was last restarted.
Authenticated Bytes Sent	The total number of bytes sent using the Authentication Header (EH) or the ESP protocols since the computer was last restarted.
Authenticated Bytes Received	The total number of bytes received using the AH or ESP protocols since the computer was last restarted.
Transport Bytes Sent	The total number of bytes sent using the IPSec transport mode since the computer was last restarted.
Transport Bytes Received	The total number of bytes received using IPSec transport mode since the last time the computer was restarted.
Bytes Sent in Tunnels	The total number of bytes sent using the IPSec tunnel mode since the computer was last restarted.
Bytes Received in Tunnels	The total number of bytes received using IPSec tunnel mode since the last time the computer was restarted.
Offloaded Bytes Sent	The total number of bytes sent using IPSec hardware offload since the last time the computer was restarted.
Offloaded Bytes Received	The total number of bytes received using IPSec hardware offload since the last time the computer was restarted.

on the Job

If Bad SPI Packets is high, it means that the SPI is incorrect, which could be caused by the inbound SA having expired and a packet using the old SPI has recently arrived. This number is likely to increase if rekey intervals are short and there are a large number of SAs. A large number of packets with bad SPIs that are received within a short amount of time might indicate a packet spoofing attack.

Now that you have a better idea of the statistics that are available for IPSec, here are some possible scenario questions and their answers.

exam

watch   *If Packets With Replay Detection increases, this might indicate a network problem or replay attack.*

exam

watch   *If Packets Not Authenticated increases, this might indicate an IPSec packet spoofing or modification attack or packet corruption by network devices.*

SCENARIO & SOLUTION

What is the difference between authenticated bytes and transport bytes?	Transport bytes is the total number of bytes transmitted, whereas authenticated bytes only refers to those bytes that have been transmitted with authentication.
What are soft SAs?	Soft SAs are Security Associations between peers where one peer doesn't support IPSec, and the policy allows connection without IPSec. Soft SAs are not secured.
What is the difference between main mode and quick mode?	Main mode is the first phase in IPSec, when the key is negotiated. During this phase, the peers configure the channel. Quick mode deals with the transfer of data between the peers as well as the refreshment of the key matter.
Why are Diffie-Hellman Group 1 and 2 not considered secure?	These groups use a relatively short key length that can (and will) be broken. Always use the highest possible Diffie-Hellman group. Group 2048 is the currently highest bit length available.

Kerberos Monitoring Tools

Some interesting problems can occur when you use Kerberos V5 as the authentication method, and some of these can be very hard to solve. Fortunately, Microsoft has made a couple of tools available through the Windows Server 2003 Resource Kit that will help you find what Kerberos tickets (the keys) are currently issued. If you need a refresher on Kerberos see the next section.

One of these tools is the Kerberos Tray utility (**kerbtray.exe**) that resides in the Windows tray and gives you information about the tickets, as you can see in this illustration.

Using the **kerbtray** utility you can keep tabs on the tickets issued by Kerberos V5. The corresponding command-line utility is **klist.exe**. This utility takes one of three command-line switches: **tickets**, **tgt**, and **purge**. This is an example of the output from **klist** listing the cached tickets:

```
C:\ >klist tickets

Cached Tickets: (5)
    Server: krbtgt/SOLSYSTEMET.PLANET@SOLSYSTEMET.PLANET
        KerbTicket Encryption Type: RSADSI RC4-HMAC(NT)
        End Time: 5/25/2003 6:58:08
        Renew Time: 5/31/2003 20:58:08
```

```
Server: cifs/mercury.solsystemet.planet@SOLSYSTEMET.PLANET
    KerbTicket Encryption Type: RSADSI RC4-HMAC(NT)
    End Time: 5/25/2003 6:58:08
    Renew Time: 5/31/2003 20:58:08

Server: jupiter$@SOLSYSTEMET.PLANET
    KerbTicket Encryption Type: RSADSI RC4-HMAC(NT)
    End Time: 5/25/2003 6:58:08
    Renew Time: 5/31/2003 20:58:08

Server: ldap/jupiter.solsystemet.planet/solsystemet.planet@SOLSYSTEMET.PLANET
    KerbTicket Encryption Type: RSADSI RC4-HMAC(NT)
    End Time: 5/25/2003 6:58:08
    Renew Time: 5/31/2003 20:58:08

Server: host/jupiter.solsystemet.planet@SOLSYSTEMET.PLANET
    KerbTicket Encryption Type: RSADSI RC4-HMAC(NT)
    End Time: 5/25/2003 6:58:08
    Renew Time: 5/31/2003 20:58:08
```

To see the ticket-granting ticket (TGT) information, use the **tlist tgt** command resulting in this listing:

```
C:\ >klist tgt

Cached TGT:

ServiceName: krbtgt
TargetName: krbtgt
FullServiceName: administrator
DomainName: SOLSYSTEMET.PLANET
TargetDomainName: SOLSYSTEMET.PLANET
AltTargetDomainName: SOLSYSTEMET.PLANET
TicketFlags: 0x40e00000
KeyExpirationTime: 0/39/4 0:00:10776
StartTime: 5/24/2003 20:58:08
EndTime: 5/25/2003 6:58:08
RenewUntil: 5/31/2003 20:58:08
TimeSkew: 5/31/2003 20:58:08
```

e x a m

ⓦatch *Remember that the Kerberos utilities are part of the Resource Kit for Windows Server 2003.*

What Is Kerberos?   This section is a refresher on what Kerberos is and what it is used for. Windows Server 2003 uses Kerberos V5 as the authentication mechanism. Kerberos uses *tickets* to provide proof of the user's identity with regard to a requested service. These tickets are composed of encrypted data that includes the encrypted password. Kerberos acts as the trusted third party in authentication by providing the Key Distribution Center (KDC). KDC is running on all domain controllers as part of the Active Directory service where all the users' account information is stored (including passwords).

The steps of the Kerberos V5 authentication process are as follows:

1. The user (or system) on a computer authenticates to the KDC by using a password or even a smart card.

2. The KDC issues a special ticket known as the ticket-granting ticket (TGT) to the client. The client system uses the TGT to access the ticket-granting service (TGS), that is part of Kerberos V5 on the domain controller.

3. The TGS issues a service ticket to the client if the authentication succeeds.

4. The client uses this service ticket to gain access to the requested network resource.

What is so smart about the Kerberos V5 architecture is that there is no exchange of secrets to make it work. Kerberos is truly the trusted third party that can be relied on to consistently provide authentication services. The ticket-granting ticket is part of this magic . To see what happens, take a look at the following scenario that is taken from a different arena than the computer world.

Let me introduce the players:

■ **Mr. Kerberos**   Trusted Notary Public who can be trusted completely when it comes to certifying signatures. Otherwise, we do not know how trustworthy Mr. Kerberos is.

■ **Sven**   Intrepid Swedish adventurer who currently wants to have a coffee date with Nancy.

■ **Nancy**   Red-haired Irish gal who ignores all requests for coffee dates unless she knows the requester is bona fide.

■ **Mr. Simpson**   Unscrupulous Scottish rogue and penny-stock promoter who never managed to spell bona fide.

When Sven approaches Nancy asking if she wants to go to Moonpennies for a latte, she shakes her head and says that he must prove that he is bona fide. Sven then goes to see Mr. Kerberos to ask for help to prove that he is bona fide.

Mr. Kerberos hands Sven a piece of paper that contains, among other things, the signature of and stamp of Mr. Kerberos. Sven is requested to show this ticket-granting ticket whenever he returns to communicate with any of the players. Sven then sits down at the guest desk to fill out the request for a coffee date with Nancy. When he is done, he puts the request and the ticket-granting ticket in an envelope that he seals with his signature and seal. This envelope is then sent in to Mr. Kerberos.

Let us leave the story for a paragraph to see what has happened so far. Sven has asked for proof that he is bona fide (authenticated), Mr. Kerberos gives Sven a TGT (proof of identity of Mr. Kerberos), and Sven then assembles a request that he seals (encrypts) in such a way that Mr. Kerberos can verify that the TGT is intact and that Sven's identity is known.

Back to the story. Mr. Kerberos opens his ledger and verifies the signature and seal of Sven, and as he knows that Sven is bona fide, proceeds to put Sven's request together with the TGT into an envelope that can be verified by Nancy, should she get the envelope. Mr. Kerberos then gives this envelope to Sven. In the computer world, this would be the service ticket.

Sven takes the envelope he received and hands it to Nancy, who can verify that Mr. Kerberos has certified that Sven is bona fide (authenticated). Nancy and Sven then go to Moonpennies for a latte, thus proving that all stories end with coffee.

What a pretty story. Actually, that is the normal progression for the majority of authentication scenarios where a user is requesting access to a resource. I know you are wondering where Mr. Simpson would come into this, and this is his call to the stage.

There are times when someone manages to gain access to the service ticket and tries to gain access using it. Mr. Simpson manages to take the ticket from Sven when they both had lunch at the same greasy spoon on Hasting St. This is where some of the features of the clever devices that Mr. Kerberos has devised come into play. The final service ticket has time stamps that define when the ticket was created, and the expiration of the ticket. The way the ticket is encrypted using both Mr. Kerberos's and Sven's signature and seal makes it very unlikely that anyone can impersonate Sven. So when Mr. Simpson presents himself to Nancy, claiming to be Sven, Nancy can easily prove that he is not Sven, because the ticket does not fit the signatures of Sven and Mr. Kerberos.

I know that this is a lighthearted story about Kerberos and security, but those that know me are aware that coffee is an important part of my life, and it does describe what happens using everyday events.

CERTIFICATION SUMMARY

In this chapter you, have been introduced to IPSec and the tasks and tools involved in monitoring it. From the point of the 70-291 exam, what you need to know is that IPSec is configured using Policies that make use of IP filters to determine the type of traffic that is being used with IPSec. You also need to remember that the IPSec Monitor is now an MMC snap-in and that you use the IPSec Monitor to view the statistics for all the IPSec Security Associations for a particular computer. Also keep in mind that IPSec is peer-to-peer based on the computer, not the user.

TWO-MINUTE DRILL

Monitor Network Protocol Security

❑ Use preshared key material when the two peers are not part of Active Directory.

❑ Use Kerberos V5 keys if both peers are part of Active Directory.

❑ Avoid using Diffie-Hellman Group 1 and 2 key material; it is considered too easy to break.

❑ IPSec has two negotiation phases: Main Mode and Quick Mode.

    ❑ Main Mode handles authentication and key negotiation.

    ❑ Quick Mode handles the data and key refreshing.

❑ Use the IP Security Monitor snap-in to monitor IPSec.

❑ Use the IP Security Policy Manager snap-in to define and manage IPSec policies.

❑ Use the **kerbtray.exe** utility to find information about Kerberos V5 tickets.

❑ Use the **Klist.exe** command-line utility to capture information about the Kerberos V5 tickets and ticket-granting tickets, and to purge the ticket cache.

SELF TEST

Monitor Network Protocol Security

1. You are the administrator of your company's Windows Server 2003 network, and you are configuring IPSec for use on this network. When you use IPSec to authenticate data on your IP network, you can choose from a number of authentication methods. Which of the following authentication methods can be configured for use by IPSec? (Choose all that apply.)

A. Preshared keys

B. Kerberos V5 authentication

C. Microsoft Point-to Point Encryption (MPPE)

D. Certificate-based authentication

2. You are the network administrator for your company's Windows Server 2003 network. You have configured IPSec to use 3DES to encrypt data that is sent on a link between two Windows Server 2003 servers on you network. Data is flowing properly between the two servers, but when you look at the System Monitor on your systems, you find that the processor utilization remains close to 95 percent when the server is sending and receiving data over the network, and the actual throughput from your server is barely exceeding 20 Mbps on your 100 Mbps Ethernet network. What is the easiest way to resolve the servers slowness?

A. Subnet the network by adding an additional network interface card (NIC) to each server.

B. Add more memory to the server, and increase the size of the page file to be two times the size of physical memory.

C. Add an additional CPU to the server, and bind this CPU to the network subsystem.

D. Replace the network interface card (NIC) with one that can offload the IPSec processing to its own onboard processor.

3. You are the network administrator for your small law office. There are currently twenty users who share the same network, which is based on a Windows NT 4.0 domain. You have added a new Windows Server 2003 to this domain and you are in process of implementing secure and authenticated communication between the client database that is installed on the Windows Server 2003 computer and the Windows XP Professional workstations of the three criminal lawyers (CIU) in the office. This traffic must be secured and authenticated. What must you do to implement this requirement? (Choose all that apply. Each answer makes up one part of the full solution.)

A. You need to set up an L2TP tunnel between the client computers and the server.

B. You need to implement IPSec using a Group Policy Object for the CIU computers.

C. You need to promote the Windows Server 2003 to a DC in the domain.

D. You need to provide a digital certificate for the computers that will secure and authenticate communications.

E. You need to install new network interface cards (NICs) in the CIU computers that will offload encryption from the systems.

F. You need to configure local IPSec policies for the Windows Server 2003 and the CIU computers to use certificate-based authentication.

G. You need to provide a digital certificate for the lawyers that will secure and authenticate communications.

4. You are the network administrator for your small company's Windows Server 2003 network infrastructure. You have 200 workstations running Windows XP Professional and four Windows Server 2003 servers. You must install and configure IPSec to provide authentication security for the packets traveling over the network. You are not concerned about encrypting the data at this point because the majority of the traffic is e-mail based. How can you easily install and enable IPSec to provide security services on your company's workstations? (Choose all that apply.)

A. You can use the Group Policy console and define an IPSec security policy under the Computer Configuration settings. You can then apply this policy at the domain or OU level.

B. You can go to each computer and enable the IPSec security policy from the Local Machine Policies console.

C. You don't need to do anything to install IPSec—it's included in the operating system.

D. You can use the Group Policy console and define an IPSec security policy under the User Configuration settings. You can then apply this group policy to the site.

E. You need to install the IPSec service from the Network Connections applet in the Control Panel.

5. You have configured your network computers to use IPSec authentication and encryption when sending or receiving any data. What tool or utility on the workstation will allow you to verify the IPSec is working properly?

A. Network Monitor

B. Event Viewer

C. MMC with IPSec snap-in

D. IP Security Monitor

6. You are the network administrator for your company's Windows Server 2003 network. You have secured your Windows Server 2003 file servers with an IPSec security policy that requires that all communication be secure between client computers and the file server. Everything is working properly with your domain-based computers, but you have a Windows XP Professional computer

that is outside the domain and can't connect to one of the file shares on the server. You manually configured this workstation computer to use the preshared key for authentication. How can you check on the workstation computer to see what the problem might be?

- A. Use the IP Security Monitor to see if IPSec is functioning properly.
- B. Use Network Monitor to see if the packets are encrypted.
- C. Check the Event Viewer on the client that can't connect to see if the IPSec policy agent left any messages.
- D. Use the IP Security Policy Manager on the client that can't connect to monitor the connection traffic during main mode.

7. How can an administrator get information on what Kerberos tickets are in the ticket cache? (Choose all that apply.)

- A. The **kerbtray.exe** utility
- B. The **kerberos.exe** utility
- C. The Active Directory Users and Computers console
- D. The **klist.exe** utility

8. How can an administrator clear the Kerberos tickets that are in the ticket cache? (Choose all that apply.)

- A. The **kerbtray.exe** utility
- B. The **kerberos.exe** utility
- C. The Active Directory Users and Computers console
- D. The **klist.exe** utility

9. What layer is IPSec implemented in?

- A. Data Link Layer
- B. Network Layer
- C. Transport Layer
- D. Session Layer

10. What are the two major parts of IPSec? (Select two correct answers)

- A. The Authentication Header
- B. The Internet Protocol
- C. Encapsulating Security Payload
- D. Virtual Private Network

11. You are the network administrator for your company's Windows Server 2003 network. You are implementing IPSec between client computers that are running Windows XP Professional and a file server running Windows Server 2003. After you have implemented the security policy, you want to test the policy from the client. What command-line utility can be used to test the security policy?

    A. IPSecMon

    B. NSLOOKUP

    C. PING

    D. KCC

12. What are the authentication methods that are supported by Internet Key Exchange(IKE)? (Choose all that apply.)

    A. Kerberos

    B. ISAKMP/Oakley

    C. Certificates

    D. NTLM

    E. Preshared passwords

13. You have logged in to your workstation as the local administrator. Now you have started the IP Security Monitor snap-in and are trying to connect to the file server located in the server room. You are not successful in connecting. What can be done to rectify this problem?

    A. You must configure IPSec on your workstation.

    B. You must be logged in as the local administrator on the DC.

    C. You must be logged in as the local administrator on the file server.

    D. Go to the server room.

14. You are viewing the IPSec statistics for a file server you are the administrator of. You note that there are a large number of reported Soft Associations. What is the most likely reason for the large number of Soft Associations?

    A. There are computers on the network that do not respond to the main mode negotiation attempts.

    B. There are problems with the IPSec Diffie-Hellman Groups used in Main Mode negotiation.

    C. There are slow and intermittent wide area connections between the clients and the server.

    D. There are a number of peers with no IPSec hardware installed.

15. What is the meaning of the Authenticated Bytes Received counter in Quick Mode?

    A. Reports the total number of bytes received using IPSec transport mode since the last time the computer was restarted.

B. Reports the total number of bytes received using AH and ESP protocols since the last time the computer was restarted.

C. Reports the total number of bytes received using IPSec tunnel mode since the last time the computer was restarted.

LAB QUESTION

You are the network administrator for your company. You have just migrated from Windows NT 4.0 to Windows Server 2003. All of the file servers have been migrated, and about 90 percent of the desktop workstations and laptop computers have migrated to Windows XP Professional. The remaining computers are running Windows NT 4.0.

All your domain controllers have been migrated to Windows Server 2003 Active Directory, and you have configured Windows Server 2003 Certificate Services to be the certificate authority (CA) for your network.

You are using a private Class A address on your network and are using Network Address Translation (NAT) behind your firewall. Your network has a demilitarized zone that holds the public web and e-mail servers. You have four remote offices that connect to the corporate network over 192Kbps fractional T1 lines.

You would like to implement IPSec in your network. Please answer the following questions regarding this implementation.

1. Can you use IPSec to secure the network traffic between all of the client workstations and servers? If not, which ones will be unsupported? Can you implement IPSec with these computers on the network?

2. What role will the CA have in your IPSec implementation? Is it required for your IPSec implementation?

3. If you choose to configure an end-to-end IPSec from a user's computer in a remote office to the file servers in the corporate office, will NAT present a problem?

4. If you desire to implement IPSec to provide data integrity and authentication between your clients and server, is there any need to create elaborate custom IPSec security policies?

SELF TEST ANSWERS

Monitor Network Protocol Security

1. ☑ **A, B,** and **D.** IPSec can be configured to use preshared keys, Kerberos authentication, and certificate-based authentication. When you establish an IPSec security policy, Windows Server 2003 chooses Kerberos authentication by default. However, if you have installed and configured the Windows Server 2003 Certificate Service, you can choose to use certificate-based authentication. You can also choose this option if you have a digital certificate from a third-party certificate authority. Finally, you can choose to use a preshared key for authentication. This method is not recommended for production use, because it has the weakest security of the three methods.

   ☒ **C** is incorrect because MPPE is an encryption method that is used for Point-to-Point Tunneling Protocol VPNs.

2. ☑ **D.** The simplest way to effect a dramatic increase in speed for the server is to configure the IPSec/3DES encryption to take place on the network interface card (NIC). For this to work, you need to replace the existing NIC with one that can offload the processing of IPSec to itself. There are studies that have shown that when a server performs software encryption of data, especially 3DES, it slows the throughput to nearly 20 Mbps. However, if you offload that processing to a NIC, your throughput will increase to almost 70 Mbps while the processor utilization will drop from 90 percent to 65 percent.

   ☒ **A** is incorrect because the problem is not bandwidth related. **B** is incorrect because although more memory may improve the performance slightly, it will not have as much effect as a new NIC that offloads the IPSec processing. **C** is incorrect because, as with the memory, adding an extra CPU will not give the same benefits as changing the NIC.

3. ☑ **D** and **F.** The correct solution is to use IPSec with certificate-based authentication. To enable IPSec on the computers for the criminal lawyers, you need to make sure the computers have a valid digital certificate for the computer account. IPSec works on the computer level rather than the user level, and thus each computer requires a certificate.

   ☒ **A** is incorrect because you do not need to create a tunnel between the peers in order for IPSec to work properly. **B** is incorrect because you need an Active Directory domain in order to use Group Policy Objects, and this network is currently a Windows NT 4.0 domain. **C** is incorrect because promoting the Windows Server 2003 will create an Active Directory domain, and it will not help in this scenario. **E** is incorrect because adding a NIC will not configure the IPSec environment. **G** is incorrect because certificates must be for the computer not the user when used with IPSec.

4. ☑ **A** and **C.** IPSec is installed as part of the operating system, and does not have to be added in order to use it. The easiest way to enable IPSec on your workstations is to use the Group Policy console to configure an IPSec security policy. You then apply this group policy to either your domain or an OU.

☒   **B** is incorrect because although you can enable IPSec on the computers this way, you will be causing an administrative nightmare for yourself. Using a Group Policy is the easiest way to deploy this configuration. **D** is incorrect because IPSec security policy is not configured under the User Configuration settings in the Group Policy console. It is configured under the Computer Configuration settings. **E** is incorrect because the IPSec service is installed as part of the operating system.

5.   ☑   **D.** The IP Security Monitor snap-in will quickly allow you to see if IPSec is working properly on your workstation.
☒   **A** is incorrect because Network Monitor is not available for workstations (Windows XP Professional). **B** is incorrect because Event Viewer only shows limited information about certain IPSec-related events. **C** is incorrect because this is not a real snap-in.

6.   ☑   **C.** A quick way of determining the status of IPSec on a computer that is not functioning correctly is to examine the event logs. The IPSec policy agent will leave detailed messages regarding the status of the service. You use this information to resolve the problem.
☒   **A** is incorrect because you do not see any data in the IP Security Monitor when connections don't work properly. **B** is incorrect because you are not using encryption, and the network monitor is not installed on workstations. **D** is incorrect because the IP Security Policy Manager does not contain any connection information; it is used to configure security policies.

7.   ☑   **A and D.** These utilities display information about the Kerberos tickets.
☒   **B** is incorrect because there is no such utility. **C** is incorrect because Kerberos tickets are not displayed in that utility; it is used to manage Active Directory.

8.   ☑   **D.** The **klist.exe** utility is used to purge the Kerberos ticket cache by executing the **klist purge** command.
☒   **A** is incorrect because the **kerbtray** utility only displays information about the Kerberos tickest. **B** is incorrect because there is no such utility. **C** is incorrect because Kerberos tickets are not displayed in that utility; it is used to manage Active Directory.

9.   ☑   **B.** IPSec is implemented at the Network Layer, also known as Layer 3.
☒   **B, C** and **D** are incorrect because none of these layers are used for IPSec implementation.

10.   ☑   **A and C.** The Authentication Header (AH) and Encapsulating Security Payload (ESP) protocol are the two major components of IPSec.
☒   **B** is incorrect because the Internet Protocol is the base protocol of the TCP/IP suite of protocols, not a part of IPSec. **D** is incorrect because a VPN is what IPSec can be used to build.

11.   ☑   **C.** The best way to test the security policy is to ping the file server from the client. You will receive Negotiating IP Security messages until the two peers have finalized the negotiation phases. After that, you will see normal ping returns.
☒   **A** is incorrect because the IPSecMon utility is not available in Windows Server 2003. **B** is incorrect because NSLOOKUP is a tool for DNS diagnostics, not IPSec. **D** is incorrect because the KCC utility is used for Active Directory maintenance, not IPSec.

12. ☑ **A, C** and **E.** The authorization methods supported are Kerberos, certificates, and preshared passwords.
    ☒ **B** is incorrect because ISAKMP/Oakley is the algorithm used for security negotiations. **D** is incorrect because NTLM is the authentication method used by Windows for backward compatibility with older operating systems.

13. ☑ **C.** To get access to the statistics, you need to be logged in as the local administrator on the computer you are investigating. Strictly speaking, you need to be logged in as a member of the local administrators group.
    ☒ **A** is incorrect because there is no need for the parties that are connecting to have IPSec configured unless there is a security policy in place, and this question did not state anything about a policy. **B** is incorrect because there is no local administrator on the DC. **D** is incorrect because it is plain silly.

14. ☑ **A.** The most likely reason for a large number of soft SAs is that there are clients that don't respond to the main mode negotiation attempts.
    ☒ **B** is incoreect because the IPSec Diffie-Hellman Groups would not result in large numbers of SAs. **C** is incorrect because bad WAN links will not increase the number of SAs. **D** is incorrect because it is a figment of the imagination.

15. ☑ **B.** Authenticated traffic is the AH and ESP protocols only.
    ☒ **A** is incorrect because that counter would be Transport Bytes Received. **C** is incorrect because that counter would be Bytes Received in Tunnels.

LAB ANSWER

1. No, you cannot use IPSec to secure the communication between all of your clients and servers. The Windows NT 4.0 computers do not support IPSec. Your can implement IPSec on your network with the Windows NT 4.0 computers still in place; they just can't be part of the secure communication. You cannot implement the Secure Server Policy until all computers have been upgraded to Windows Server 2003 or Windows XP Professional.

2. Your CA can be used to provide certificates to your computers and users. The CA is not a required service in order to implement IPSec.

3. The way this network is configured, the NAT will not present a problem. Remote office users are connecting through the fractional T1 lines directly to the inside of your network, which means they are sharing the same private addressing scheme.

4. No, there is no need for anything elaborate if all you want to use is IPSec for data integrity and authentication. The default policies are more than adequate for this implementation.

9

Maintain Network Security

T he task at hand is to troubleshoot the connection problems that can occur when you are using IPSec and VPNs to connect remote clients to your network. In this chapter you will learn about the tools and information sources you can use to determine what the problem is and to resolve the connection problem.

CERTIFICATION OBJECTIVE 9.01

Troubleshoot Network Protocol Security

One of the best ways to learn about how a connection is configured is to analyze a successful connection. Setting up a remote connection using a recipe is one thing, but being able to troubleshoot a connection that does not work after the "canned" setup is what makes you a network administrator. In this section you will learn about the solution to a number of potential errors you might run into while configuring remote clients to server VPN connections.

Successful troubleshooting is based on knowledge and experience with the technology. You will learn about the sources of information you can use to learn about an established connection, which will allow you to confirm the settings that are in use.

Verify VPN Connection Options

After successfully establishing a connection, it is useful to see the options that are in effect for the connection. These options detail how the remote user connected, and what authentication and encryption methods the connection is using. You can find this information by right-clicking the VPN Connection icon located in the taskbar and clicking **Status**. The **Details** tab in the **Status** dialog box details this information, as shown in Figure 9-1.

The detailed information documents how this connection is configured: the remote access protocol that is used to establish the connection is PPP, TCP/IP is the transport protocol, and the most secure of the standard authentication methods (MS CHAP V2) was used. The data is encrypted through the channel using 128-bit MPPE and Microsoft Point-to-Point Compression (MPPC). By scrolling down the list, you will be able to glean additional information about the connection, including the IP address used for the VPN connection.

FIGURE 9-1

The VPN
connection
details

on the

Job

The strength of the encryption depends on your geographical location. Some locations in the world cannot use the same higher-strength encryption we have in North America. This is due to export restrictions on the technology behind the encryption.

This information gives you the ability to verify that the connection was established as intended. For example, if the design for the connection was to use L2TP, but you find that the Server type is PPTP, that gives you a place to start looking for additional information that will help you solve the problem.

If the connection failed, you will not be able to get the information from the connection. In that case, the first place to start looking in that case is in the System event log. The System event log contains error and warning messages regarding attempted VPN connections, and is an excellent location to get more information about the problem.

e x a m

Watch
Use the System log to learn more about the connection problem.

The System event log message in Figure 9-2 shows the warning message for the connection attempt. The message gives you information about why the L2TP connection failed, but the PPTP connection succeeded. The warning message states that the L2TP connection failed because there was no valid machine certificate for the IPSec encryption mechanism found for the client. The missing certificate prevented the establishment of L2TP.

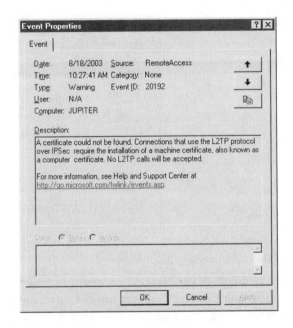

FIGURE 9-2

The warning message showing why the L2TP connection failed

Not Enough Available Ports

When it comes to misleading and obfuscated error messages, the prize must go to the message that Windows 2000 used when there were not enough available WAN ports. The message said that there was a modem problem, but you don't use a modem for this connection; it is performed over the network through a NIC. In Windows Server 2003, that message has become a bit more readable, but the message can still be misleading and steer you in the wrong direction. The most likely issue when you see the message in Figure 9-3 is that all the available L2TP and PPTP ports are in use. The remedy here is to increase the number of ports. The optimum number of ports should match the number needed during peak use of the remote service. The best way to gather this sort of information is to initially configure more ports than you need, and with logging configured, capture the port usage over time to establish the peak usage.

No Answer Errors

One common error you will probably run into is the one in Figure 9-3. This error is the result of not having any network connections, or the failure of the remote access server

FIGURE 9-3

FIGURE 9-3

No Answer

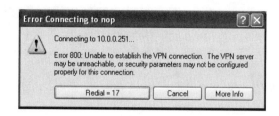

to successfully negotiate a connection with the client. The remote access server must have the L2TP and PPTP ports configured to accept incoming connection attempts. Selecting the **Remote Access Connections (Inbound Only)** option in the **Configure Device** dialog box, as shown in Figure 9-4, and configuring the number of needed ports should solve this problem. Each remote client requires one WAN Miniport for the connection.

The no answer problem can also be the result of a misconfigured RRAS server. Verify that the RRAS properties are set to enable the computer to be a router, as seen in Figure 9-5.

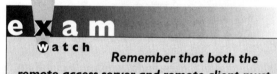

Remember that both the remote access server and remote client must have similar and compatible security configurations.

For incoming VPN connections to be allowed, the RRAS server must be configured. You can select either of the suboptions, **Local area network (LAN) routing only** or **LAN and demand-dial routing**. These two options will add the required WAN Miniports for L2TP and PPTP to be able to establish incoming VPN connections.

FIGURE 9-4

Configuring the PPTP WAN Miniport

FIGURE 9-5

RRAS server
configuration

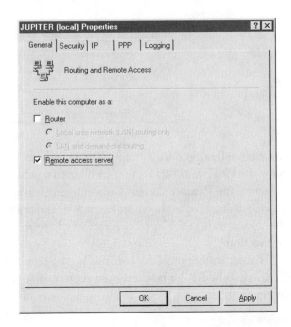

Authentication Protocol Problems

Problems with authentication protocols are generally the result of the remote VPN client and the VPN server being unable to agree on the authentication protocol to use. Both parties try to negotiate a common protocol that is as secure as possible. The default configuration is for both the VPN client and server to use MS-CHAP V2 first, followed by MS-CHAP, but if the defaults, have changed you will likely receive the error message seen in Figure 9-6, where Error 919 indicates the failure of the negotiation. The solution to this type of problem is to verify that the VPN client and server have the same settings. You do this by editing the authentication protocol properties on both the client and server to have at least one common authentication protocol.

There are other authentication-related problems that result in the refusal of the VPN server to authenticate the VPN client, and these are the permission-related problems. In order to establish a connection to a remote VPN server, the client must be granted **Allow dial-in** permission, or be granted that same permission through a remote access

FIGURE 9-6

Authentication
errors

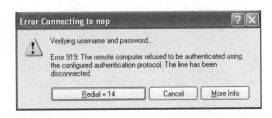

FIGURE 9-7

Permission
problem

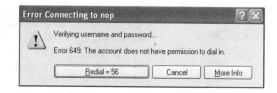

policy. If the dial-in permission is set to **Deny access** for the remote user account, the connection attempt will result in the error seen in Figure 9-7. To rectify this type of problem, you need to change the user's dial-in permission to **Allow access**, or to **Control access through remote access policy**, on the **Dial-in** tab of the user's **Property** dialog box, as seen in Figure 9-8.

When you select **Control access through remote access policy**, you also need to further verify the remote access policy to ensure the user will be able to connect.

on the
Job

Always verify that the user should have dial-in permission before enabling them.
Just because someone wants to dial in does not mean that they should.

A second way to solve the problem is to let the remote user authenticate the VPN connection using a user account that has dial-in permissions. When you click the

FIGURE 9-8

The Dial-in tab

FIGURE 9-9

Specifying a
different user
account to use
for the VPN
connection

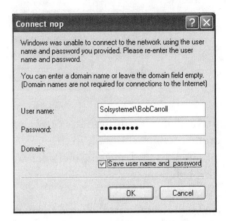

Redial button in the **Error Connecting Virtual Private Connection** dialog box, you
will be presented with the dialog box shown in Figure 9-9. If you enter the credentials
of an account that has dial-in permissions, the connection will succeed.

When you troubleshoot connection problems, you should enable additional logging.
The additional logging option is enabled through the properties dialog of the RRAS
server, as you can see in Figure 9-10. When you enable PPP logging, the log files are
stored in the **%windir%\tracing** folder. You should only use the additional logs for
troubleshooting, because adding them puts a load on the server that will lower its
ability to deal with user requests. For example, to learn more about errors related to
PPP, enable the logging option and view the PPP.LOG file in the **%windir%\tracing**
directory, as you can see in this excerpt from the PPP.LOG file:

```
[2516] 08-17 10:27:52:644:
[2516] 08-17 10:27:52:644: InsertInTimerQ called
portid=0,Id=2,Protocol=c223,EventType=0,fAuth=1
[2324] 08-17 10:27:52:844: Packet received (78 bytes) for hPort 129
[2516] 08-17 10:27:52:844: >PPP packet received at 08/17/2003 14:27:52:844
[2516] 08-17 10:27:52:844: >Protocol = CHAP, Type = Protocol specific, Length = 0x4e, Id =
0x2, Port = 129
[2516] 10:27:52:844: >C2 23 02 02 00 4C 31 C7 72 2D 14 3A 08 B8 E4 08  |.#...L1.r-.:....|
[2516] 10:27:52:844: >B0 E6 4F 9C 2E 10 A2 00 00 00 00 00 00 00 00 9C  |..O............|
[2516] 10:27:52:844: >66 93 81 31 65 A0 DD D5 72 2A E4 BD 84 BD 97 0F  |f..1e...r*......|
[2516] 10:27:52:844: >8A 88 0F B6 29 60 CC 00 53 6F 6C 73 79 73 74 65  |....)`..Solsyste|
[2516] 10:27:52:844: >6D 65 74 5C 42 6F 62 43 61 72 72 6F 6C 6C 00 00  |met\BobCarroll..|
[2516] 08-17 10:27:52:844:
[2516] 08-17 10:27:52:844: RemoveFromTimerQ called
portid=0,Id=2,Protocol=c223,EventType=0,fAuth=1
[2516] 08-17 10:27:53:184: <PPP packet sent at 08/17/2003 14:27:53:184
[2516] 08-17 10:27:53:184: <Protocol = CHAP, Type = Protocol specific, Length = 0x30, Id =
0x2, Port = 129
[2516] 10:27:53:184: <C2 23 03 02 00 2E 53 3D 37 46 45 35 38 44 34 37  |.#....S=7FE58D47|
```

```
[2516] 10:27:53:184: <43 38 32 31 42 37 42 35 42 41 46 41 37 38 37 41 |C821B7B5BAFA787A|
[2516] 10:27:53:184: <33 35 30 45 46 36 41 41 33 37 44 36 39 44 45 32 |350EF6AA37D69DE2|
[2516] 08-17 10:27:53:184:
[2516] 08-17 10:28:02:060: Encryption
[2516] 08-17 10:28:02:060: Strong encryption
[2516] 08-17 10:28:02:060: MPPE-Send/Recv-Keys set
[2516] 08-17 10:28:02:060: Auth Attribute Domain = SOLSYSTEMET
[2516] 08-17 10:28:02:060: Auth Attribute Idle Timeout Seconds = 0
[2516] 08-17 10:28:02:060: AuthAttribute MaxChannelsAllowed = -1
[2516] 08-17 10:28:02:060: FsmThisLayerUp called for protocol = c223, port = 129
[2516] 08-17 10:28:02:060: NotifyCaller(hPort=129, dwMsgId=17)
[2516] 08-17 10:28:02:060: Callback phase started
[2516] 08-17 10:28:02:060: CallbackPriv in CB = 1
[2516] 08-17 10:28:02:060: <PPP packet sent at 08/17/2003 14:28:02:060
[2516] 08-17 10:28:02:060: <Protocol = CBCP, Type = Protocol specific, Length = 0x8, Id =
0x1, Port = 129
[2516] 10:28:02:060: <C0 29 01 01 00 06 01 02 00 00 00 00 00 00 00 00 |.).............|
```

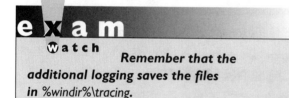

This short part of the log details the connection attempt by one user. In this exercise you will configure logging and locate entries in the PPP.LOG file.

FIGURE 9-10

Configuring
PPP logging

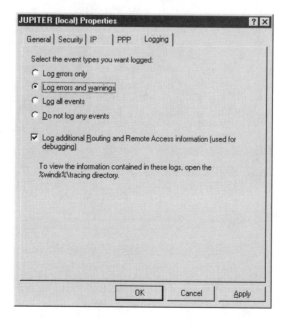

EXERCISE 9-1

Logging PPP Information

1. Log in to your server using your non-administrative account.

2. Click **Start | Control Panel**.

3. In the Control Panel, open **Administrative Tools**, right-click **Routing and Remote Access**, and select **Run as** from the context menu.

4. In the **Run As** dialog, select **The following user**, and type a user account and password that has administrative rights on the server. Click **OK**.

5. Right-click the RRAS server in the node tree, and select **Properties** from the context menu.

6. Open the **Logging** tab to configure logging.

7. Select **Log all events** and **Log additional Routing and Remote Access information**, as shown here:

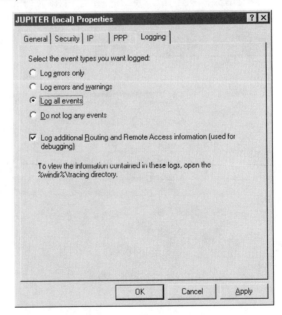

8. Click **OK** to save the configuration.

9. In order to have data in the logs you will need to connect and disconnect from a couple of clients. Make sure you misspell passwords, and start and stop the RRAS server a couple of times.

10. Open the **Event viewer** from Administrative tools.

11. Open the System logs and filter on **Remote Access**. Right-click **System** in the node tree, select **View** from the context menu, and click **Filter**.

12. Select **RemoteAccess** as the Event Source, as shown here:

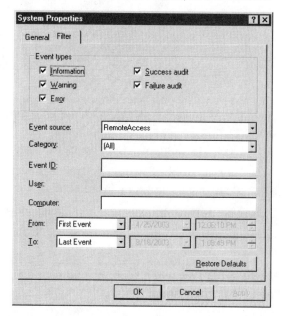

13. Click **OK** to display the events.

14. Review the events that were logged based on the usage of the system. The results should look something like the following illustration.

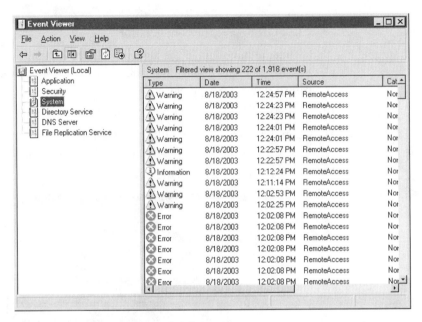

15. Open **My Computer** from the Start menu.

16. Navigate to the **%windir%\tracing** directory. Double-click the **PPP.LOG** file to open it in your editor.

17. Review the logging based on the usage of your system.

 Read the log files when there are no problems on the server, this way you know what the normal state is.

 Watch the amount of logging; it can easily overwhelm the server.

L2TP Connectivity Errors

When L2TP is initially configured, you may receive an error indicating that the connection attempt failed because the security negotiation timed out, as shown in Figure 9-11. This error stems from L2TP's reliance on IPSec, which is used for encryption and authentication. One of the steps that is commonly overlooked in the configuration of an L2TP VPN server is the installation of a machine certificate or the configuration of an IPSec policy that can be used to establish the L2TP connection. There are three options for authentication with IPSec; the default is Kerberos, and the other two options are

FIGURE 9-11

Missing certificate

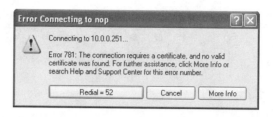

to use certificates or to use a preshared key. For the VPN server to be able to answer incoming requests for L2TP connections, it must have a configured IPSec policy. To solve the problem, you need to acquire and install a computer certificate from a Certificate Authority (CA). Both the Routing and Remote Access Server and the client computer require a computer certificate.

Now that you have a better idea of troubleshooting VPN connections, here are some possible scenario questions and their answers.

SCENARIO & SOLUTION

You are having problems with your RRAS server. You have determined that the Event Viewer probably will give more information about the functionality problem. What event log will you examine?	When Routing and Remote Access Service writes log messages into the event service, they are logged in the System log. Remember that RRAS is a service of Windows Server 2003, rather than an application. Therefore, the log messages are stored in the System log.
You have successfully configured and enabled Routing and Remote Access Service on your Windows Server 2003. After having configured a client and successfully connected to the RRAS server, you want to verify the parameters that are used by the connection. Where would you locate the parameters for a VPN connection?	The Details tab of the Connection's property dialog on the client will give you the effective parameters that are in use for the connection. To open the Connection property dialog, right-click the connection icon in the taskbar and select Status from the context menu.
What is the default encryption level that is used by MPPE to encrypt data that is sent through a PPTP VPN?	The default strength of MPPE encryption depends on your geographic location. It is currently 128-bit for most locations.
You have made configuration changes to the Routing and Remote Access Service on Windows Server 2003 in your office so you could learn about the settings and the impact of each. After you changed the properties on the General tab of the RRAS Properties dialog, you find that the Ports node has disappeared. How should the General tab be configured?	You set the type of service that the server should provide on the General tab of the RRAS Properties dialog. The two options: Router and LAN and Demand-dial Routing would return the Ports node and VPN functionality.

INSIDE THE EXAM

Certificates and VPNs

In order for a L2TP VPN connection to succeed, IPSec must be configured to authenticate. There are three ways IPSec can authenticated, and there are two ways to configure it.

- **Certificates** If you install a computer certificate on both the server and the clients, the negotiation will succeed, and there is no further configuration needed.

- **IPSec policy** As a second choice, you can configure an IPSec policy to determine how to authenticate the connection. The default is to use Kerberos, but certificates or preshared keys can be configured as well.

Remember that L2TP must have a configured IPSec authentication method to succeed.

CERTIFICATION SUMMARY

This chapter has taught you about how to troubleshoot VPN connectivity. The first step in any successful troubleshooting exercise starts with a good knowledge of the functioning system. Learn about connections from the Details tab of the Connection properties on the client as well as the settings of the Routing and Remote Access servers.

You explored the impact of misconfiguration, and saw some of the error messages that are designed to give you meaningful information. Last, you learned about additional logging, where the RRAS service stores information in log files. The location for these files is **%windir%\tracing**. The information stored in these log files is exhaustive and will sometimes seem to be overwhelming. Read the log files when there are no problems, getting yourself used to the content. That way, you will be prepared to analyze the log files when a problem does occur. Another topic visited in this chapter dealt with the computer certificates that are necessary for L2TP to use IPSec.

✓ TWO-MINUTE DRILL

Troubleshoot Network Protocol Security

❑ Checking the **Details** tab on the **Connection's Status** dialog gives you information that will help identify the characteristics of the connection. This includes the type and strength of encryption, compression, and the access protocol used.

❑ The default number of ports installed when Routing and Remote Access Service is configured and enabled varies depending on the server configuration you selected in the wizard. Monitor the number of ports used and modify them as needed. The port properties can be modified by editing the port's configuration by right-clicking the **Ports** node and selecting **Properties**.

❑ To successfully configure L2TP, the Windows Server 2003 requires a machine certificate to be installed so that IPSec negotiation will succeed.

❑ Logging of additional Routing and Remote Access information is enabled in the RRAS server's Properties dialog box, on the Logging tab.

❑ To get additional information about PPP for troubleshooting, you need to enable logging of additional RRAS information.

❑ The log files that are generated when additional Routing and Remote Access information logging is enabled are stored in **%windir%\tracing**.

❑ Remote clients and remote access servers must agree on an authentication protocol, and the remote user must have permission to dial in, in addition to being permitted access through an RAS policy.

❑ To permit incoming VPN connections, either LAN and Demand-dial Routing or the Remote Access Server option must be selected in the properties of the RRAS server.

❑ RRAS stores its event log messages in the System log, which is viewed through the Event Viewer.

SELF TEST

The following questions will help you measure your understanding of the material presented in this chapter. Read all the choices carefully, because there may be more than one correct answer. Choose all correct answers for each question.

Troubleshoot Network Protocol Security

1. You are the network administrator of your company's network. The network consists of 4 Windows Server 2003 servers, 280 Windows XP Professional workstations, and 500 Windows 2000 Professional workstations. 150 of the clients are notebook computers used by the sales and service department staff, which require access to the SQL server that is on the internal network. You have successfully implemented a Virtual Private Network using Routing and Remote Access Service on one of the Windows Server 2003 servers. When you tested the VPN installation, you connected successfully from both the Windows XP Professional and Windows 2000 Professional clients. Now you have been told that some, but not all, remote users receive an Error 649: The account does not have permission to dial in. You need to resolve this problem so that all clients that must dial in can do so. What steps would you take to solve this problem? (Choose all that apply. Each answer makes up a part of the solution.)

   A. Verify that **Permit Access** is selected on the **Dial-in** tab of the users; properties in Active Directory Users and Computers.

   B. Verify that the **Remote Access Policy** permits access.

   C. Verify that the **Permit Property** is set to yes for the RRAS server in the Routing and Remote Access console.

   D. Verify that **Control Access through Remote Access Policy** is selected on the **Dial-in** tab of the users properties in Active Directory Users and Computers.

2. You are the network administrator of your company's network. The network consists of 4 Windows Server 2003 servers, 280 Windows XP Professional workstations, and 500 Windows 2000 Professional workstations. 150 of the clients are notebook computers used by the sales and service department staff, which require access to the technical support database on a SQL server that is on the internal network. You have successfully implemented a Virtual Private Network using Routing and Remote Access Service on one of the Windows Server 2003 servers. When you tested the VPN installation, you connected successfully from both the Windows XP Professional and Windows 2000 Professional clients. When you deploy the VPN to the user community, you

find that they all receive an Error 781 informing the user about a missing certificate. What is the problem and how can it be resolved?

A. The Routing and Remote Access Server does not have a certificate, and needs to have one installed.

B. The client computers do not have a certificate and need to have one installed.

C. The remote users do not have a certificate, and need to have one installed.

D. The Routing and Remote Access Service does not have a certificate, and needs to have one installed.

3. You are the network administrator of your company's network. The network consists of 4 Windows Server 2003 servers, 280 Windows XP Professional workstations, and 500 Windows 2000 Professional workstations. 150 of the clients are notebook computers used by the sales and service department staff, which require access to the SQL server that is on the internal network. You have successfully implemented a Virtual Private Network using Routing and Remote Access Service on one of the Windows Server 2003 servers. When you tested the VPN installation, you connected successfully from both the Windows XP Professional and Windows 2000 Professional clients. Now you have been told that some remote users receive an Error 919: The remote computer refused to be authenticated using the configured authentication protocol. The line has been disconnected. You need to resolve this problem so that all clients that must dial in can do so. What steps would you take to solve this problem?

A. Verify that the clients are configured to use MS CHAP V2.

B. Verify that the Routing and Remote Access Server is configured to use EAP.

C. Verify that the Routing and Remote Access Server is configured to use MS CHAP V2.

D. Verify that the clients are configured to use EAP.

4. You are the network administrator of your company's network. The network consists of 4 Windows Server 2003 servers, 280 Windows XP Professional workstations, and 500 Windows 2000 Professional workstations. 150 of the clients are notebook computers used by the sales and service department staff, which require access to the SQL server on the internal server PLUTO, which is located in the Islington regional office. The network is seen in the following drawing. You have successfully implemented a Virtual Private Network using Routing and Remote Access Service on one JUPITER, which is located at the Long Branch office. When you tested the VPN installation, you connected successfully from both the Windows XP Professional and Windows 2000 Professional clients. Now you have been told that the remote users are unable to connect

to PLUTO and use the SQL application. You need to resolve this problem so that all remote clients have access to PLUTO. What step would you take to solve this problem?

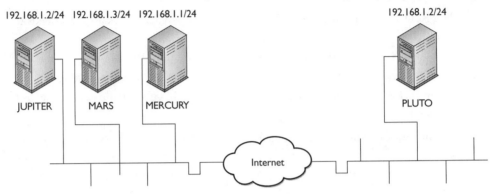

A. Change the IP address of JUPITER to 192.168.10.2/24.

B. Change the IP address of PLUTO to 192.168.10.2/24.

C. Verify the Routing and Remote Access servers properties to ensure IP routing is enabled

D. Verify that you can ping PLUTO from JUPITER.

5. You are the network administrator of your company's network. The network consists of 4 Windows Server 2003 servers, 280 Windows XP Professional workstations, and 500 Windows 2000 Professional workstations. 150 of the clients are notebook computers used by the sales and service department staff, which require access to the SQL server that is on the internal network. You have successfully implemented a Virtual Private Network using Routing and Remote Access Service on one of the Windows Server 2003 servers. When you tested the VPN installation, you connected successfully from both the Windows XP Professional and Windows 2000 Professional clients. Now you have been told that some remote users receive an Error 800: Unable to establish the VPN connection. After investigating the problem you have found that clients that connect in the morning are successful, whereas those that try the connection later in the day usually fail. There is no pattern to suggest that only some clients are affected; the problem seems to be random. You need to resolve this problem so that all clients that must dial in can do so. What is the next step you will take to solve this problem?

A. Turn on additional logging on the Routing and Remote Access Server to learn more about this problem. Log for 72 hours and then analyze the logs.

B. Open the Routing and Remote Access console, and verify that there are a minimum of 150 ports available.

C. Install Network Monitor, and capture the network traffic while a client attempts the connection.

D. Use System Monitor and capture all Network and Security counters.

6. You are the network administrator of your company's network. The network consists of 4 Windows Server 2003 servers, 280 Windows XP Professional workstations, and 500 Windows 2000 Professional workstations. 150 of the clients are notebook computers used by the sales and service department staff, which require access to the SQL server that is on the internal network. You have successfully implemented a Virtual Private Network using Routing and Remote Access Service on one of the Windows Server 2003 servers. When you tested the VPN installation, you connected successfully from both the Windows XP Professional and Windows 2000 Professional clients. Now you have been told that some remote users are having a problem establishing a VPN connection using PPTP. After investigating the problem, you have found that only some remote clients have a problem connecting. You have determined that you need to get more information about the PPTP connection attempt, and you need to enable PPP logging. You need to resolve this problem so that all clients that must dial in can do so. How do you enable PPP logging?

A. Enable additional Routing and Remote Access logging on the Logging tab of the Ports nodes properties dialog in the Routing and Remote Access console.

B. Enable additional PPP logging on the Logging tab of the Port nodes properties dialog in the Routing and Remote Access console.

C. Enable additional PPP logging on the Logging tab of the RRAS servers properties dialog in the Routing and Remote Access console.

D. Enable additional Routing and Remote Access logging on the Logging tab of the RRAS servers properties dialog in the Routing and Remote Access console.

7. Kung Karl, Vice President of IT, was just promoted from within the IT department to a new position. As a member of the IT department, Kung was not allowed to work from home, but as Vice President, Kung is now afforded that luxury. Kung has a Windows XP Professional client. Since his promotion, Kung has been having trouble accessing certain directories, but was too embarrassed to mention it to anyone in the networking department. When Kung works from home his first day, he discovers that not only can he not access certain directories within the network, he cannot even access the network. What is the problem and how can you resolve this issue? (Choose all that apply.)

A. Kung is using an incorrect user name and password. Have him use the correct name and password to access the network.

B. The RRAS server that Kung is dialing into is probably configured for EAP, and Kung is trying to use MS CHAP V2.

C. The RRAS server that Kung is dialing in to is not configured for Name Resolution. Add a local DNS server address to the RRAS server TCP/IP configuration.

D. Kung's account is probably still restricted from being used for dial-in. Change the dial-in permission to Allow dial-in or to control the permission using the remote policy.

8. You are the network administrator of your company's network. The network consists of 4 Windows Server 2003 servers, 280 Windows XP Professional workstations, and 500 Windows 2000 Professional workstations. 150 of the clients are notebook computers used by the sales and service department staff, which require access to the SQL server that is on the internal network. You have successfully implemented a Virtual Private Network using Routing and Remote Access Service on one of the Windows Server 2003 servers. When you tested the VPN installation, you connected successfully from both the Windows XP Professional and Windows 2000 Professional clients. You now want to document the effective configuration of the VPN connection. How will you find information about how a connection is configured?

   A. Open the **Status** dialog for the VPN connection and document the content of the **Details** tab.

   B. Open the **Property** dialog for the VPN connection and document the content of the **Status** tab.

   C. Open the **Status** dialog for the VPN connection and document the content of the **Connection** tab.

   D. Open the **Property** dialog for the VPN connection and document the content of the **Details** tab.

9. You are the network administrator of your company's network. The network consists of 4 Windows Server 2003 servers, 280 Windows XP Professional workstations, and 500 Windows 2000 Professional workstations. 150 of the clients are notebook computers used by the sales and service department staff, which require access to the SQL server that is on the internal network. You have successfully implemented a Virtual Private Network using Routing and Remote Access Service on one of the Windows Server 2003 servers. When you tested the VPN installation, you connected successfully from both the Windows XP Professional and Windows 2000 Professional clients. Now you have been told that some remote users are having problems establishing a VPN connection using PPTP. After investigating the problem, you have found that only some remote clients have problems connecting. You have determined that you need to get more information about the PPTP connection attempt, and you need to enable PPP logging. You successfully enable logging and you are now searching for the log files. Where is the PPP.LOG file stored?

   A. %windir%\tracing

   B. %systemroot%\tracings

   C. %windir%\system32\Logfiles

   D. %systemroot%\system32\Logfiles

10. You are the network administrator of your company's network. The network consists of 4 Windows Server 2003 servers, 280 Windows XP Professional workstations, and 500 Windows 2000 Professional workstations. 150 of the clients are notebook computers used by the sales and service department staff, which require access to the SQL server that is on the internal network. You have implemented a Virtual Private Network using Routing and Remote Access Service on one of the Windows Server 2003 servers. You have been experimenting with the configuration of the Routing and Remote Access Server. You need to make your RRAS server accept incoming PPTP connections, but you have not been able to get them to work. The properties of the

General tab of your RRAS server are shown in the following illustration. Based on the current configuration, why are your remote VPN connections over PPTP not working?

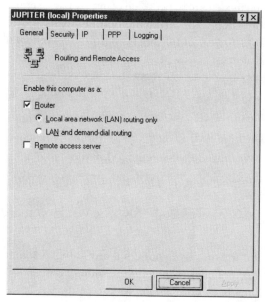

A. The PPTP ports are not configured to accept remote access connections.

B. The RRAS server will not route PPTP.

C. There are no PPTP ports installed.

D. MS CHAP V2 is disabled.

II. You are the network administrator of your company's network. The network consists of a single Active Directory domain. The network contains 10 Windows Server 2003 computers and 200 Windows XP Professional computers. A server named JUPITER has Routing and Remote Access installed, and is configured for incoming dial-up connections. Nine employees will be traveling to France. They need to be able to dial in to JUPITER while they are traveling. The employees will be using Windows XP Professional portable computers to dial in to the network. You need to ensure that the dial-in VPN connections on the portable computers are as secure as possible. Which three actions should you take? (Each correct answer presents part of the solution. Choose all that apply.)

A. Configure JUPITER to require EAP-CHAP authentication.

B. Configure JUPITER to require MS-CHAP v2 authentication.

C. Configure JUPITER to require L2TP connections for all dial-in users.

D. Configure JUPITER to require Microsoft Point-to-Point Encryption (MPPE) for all dial-in users.

E. Install a server encryption certificate on JUPITER and enable IPSec.

F. Install an encryption certificate on all client computers and enable IPSec.

12. You are the network administrator of your company's network. The network contains a Windows Server 2003 computer named JUPITER. JUPITER has Routing and Remote Access installed and has twelve 56 Kbps dial-up modems attached. The company has 25 employees who use Windows XP Professional portable computers to dial in to the network by using JUPITER. The 25 employees report that they are unable to connect to JUPITER. You discover that all the modems on JUPITER are being used by other dial-in users. You need to find additional information about the connections. How will you find additional information about the usage of the modems? (Choose all that apply.)

    A. View the Routing and Remote Access log in the Event Viewer, and filter on RemoteAccess.

    B. View the System log in the Event Viewer, and filter on RemoteAccess.

    C. View the logs in %windir%\tracing.

    D. View the logs in %systemroot%\system32\Logfiles.

    E. Enable logging on the **Logging** tab of the RRAS server's properties in the Routing and Remote Access console.

    F. Enable logging on the **General** tab of the RRAS server's properties in the Routing and Remote Access console.

13. You are the network administrator of your company's single-domain Windows Server 2003 network with Active Directory implemented. A Windows Server 2003 computer named JUPITER provides Routing and Remote Access services for incoming dial-up connections. Employees use JUPITER to connect to the office network while working out of the office. Employees working outside of the office use Windows XP Professional portable computers. You have created a remote access policy that will allow members of the Domain Users group to access JUPITER between 8:00 A.M. and 6:00 P.M. daily. You use smart cards for authentication. JUPITER is configured to use smart cards for authentication. You need to log the usage of JUPITER to build a baseline document to compare against if there are problems with the remote access service. What should you do? (Choose all that apply.)

    A. Enable logging on the **Logging** tab of the Routing and Remote Access Server's properties dialog.

    B. Archive the logging files from the %windir%\tracing **directory**.

    C. Archive the logging files from the %windir%\system32\Logfiles directory.

    D. Enable additional Routing and Remote Access logging on the **Logging** tab of the Routing and Remote Access Server's properties dialog.

    E. Enable PPP logging on the **Logging** tab of the Routing and Remote Access Server's properties dialog.

14. You are the network administrator of your company's single-domain Windows Server 2003 network with Active Directory implemented. The network consists of 21 Windows Server 2003 computers and 218 Windows XP Professional computers. A Windows Server 2003 computer named JUPITER has been configured with Routing and Remote Access services, and is configured to receive incoming dial-up connections. You purchase a new portable computer and install Windows XP Professional onto the computer. You name the computer GANYMEDE. You

attach two external modems to GANYMEDE. You create a VPN (PPTP) dial-up connection on GANYMEDE to connect to JUPITER. You configure the connection to use both modems on GANYMEDE and to use the Multilink protocol. You attempt to connect to JUPITER. You discover that only one of the modems connects to JUPITER. What is the first step you need to do to research this problem?

A. Enable PPP logging on JUPITER.

B. Enable PPP logging on GANYMEDE.

C. Enable additional Routing and Remote Access logging on JUPITER.

D. Enable additional Routing and Remote Access logging on GANYMEDE.

15. You are the network administrator of your company's network. The network consists of 4 Windows Server 2003 servers, 280 Windows XP Professional workstations, and 500 Windows 2000 Professional workstations. 150 of the clients are notebook computers used by the sales and service department staff, which require access to the SQL server that is on the internal network. You have successfully implemented a Virtual Private Network using Routing and Remote Access Service on one of the Windows Server 2003 servers. When you tested the VPN installation, you connected successfully from both the Windows XP Professional and Windows 2000 Professional clients. You would like to log some of the activity on a Routing and Remote Access services computer. You will need to audit all logon activity. What should you do?

A. Enable directory service access in the audit policy for the domain.

B. Enable audit logon events in the audit policy for the domain.

C. Enable audit account logon events in the audit policy for the domain.

D. On the Routing and Remote Access Server, enable logging of authentication requests within Remote Access Logging properties.

E. On the Routing and Remote Access Server, enable logging of accounting requests within Remote Access Logging properties.

16. You are the network administrator of your company's network. The network consists of 4 Windows Server 2003 servers, 280 Windows XP Professional workstations, and 500 Windows 2000 Professional workstations. 150 of the clients are notebook computers used by the sales and service department staff, which require access to the SQL server that is on the internal network. You have successfully implemented a Virtual Private Network using Routing and Remote Access Service on one of the Windows Server 2003 servers. When you tested the VPN installation, you connected successfully from both the Windows XP Professional and Windows 2000 Professional clients. Now your manager, Axel, has asked you to document the default authentication protocols used with the VPN. What protocols will you document? (Choose all that apply.)

A. CHAP

B. MS CHAP

C. MS CHAP V2

D. MS CHAP V3

17. You are the network administrator of your company's network. Kung Karl, Vice President of IT, was just promoted from within the IT department to his new position. As a member of the IT department, Kung was not allowed to work from home, but as Vice President, Kung is now afforded that luxury. Kung has a Windows XP Professional client. Since his promotion, Kung has been having trouble accessing certain directories; these problems have now been resolved. Kung has traveled to a remote site, and is attempting to connect to the remote access server to establish the connection. Kung is now receiving an error message that he needs a certificate. Needless to say, Kung is not amused. What is the problem, and how can you resolve this issue? (Choose all that apply.)

    A. Kung needs to reset his password.

    B. Kung needs a user certificate.

    C. Kung needs a computer certificate for his notebook computer.

    D. Kung needs to attend Remote Computing 101 at your training center; there are only finger problems here.

18. What is the first step to take in troubleshooting network protocol security?

    A. Log all available information about the problem.

    B. Interview the client who is experiencing the problem, reassure the client, and use that information to build a plan of attack.

    C. Learn how the system works when there are no problems, make sure you have sampled all the different log files, and that you know the system. Knowledge is power.

    D. Randomly select a starting point and make a small change to the environment, and then watch the result.

19. You are the network administrator of your company's network. The Vice President of your Management Information Systems & Organization (MIS&O) department is working from a remote client site for the week. The Vice President asked that you look over his laptop prior to his leaving for the customer site. He was very explicit that he did not want any troubles accessing the network remotely. His machine has been checked thoroughly and everything seems to be in working order. Once he arrives at the client site and attempts to connect using the client's LAN that is connected to the Internet, he receives an error message of Bad IP Address. The vice president promptly calls in to find out what the problem is. When you ask him to check his IP address, he informs you that his IP address is correct, as you can see in the following listing:

```
Physical Address. . . . . . . . . . : 00-03-FF-59-8B-7A
DHCP Enabled. . . . . . . . . . . . : No
IP Address. . . . . . . . . . . . . : 10.0.0.251
Subnet Mask . . . . . . . . . . . . : 255.255.255.0
Default Gateway . . . . . . . . . . : 10.0.0.2
DNS Servers . . . . . . . . . . . . : 10.0.0.251
                                      10.0.0.102
```

How do you learn more about this problem?

A. This is a client-side problem. Direct the Vice President to contact a support person at the client site.

B. Enable additional Routing and Remote Access logging, and direct the Vice President to repeatedly try to connect. Use the captured data to fix the problem.

C. Enable Authentication logging, and direct the Vice President to repeatedly try to connect. Use the data in the System log to solve the problem.

D. Start the Network Monitor and capture the connection attempts from the Vice President. Use the captured network traffic to solve the problem.

20. How many WAN Miniports are needed for each remote client?

A. 0

B. 1

C. 2

D. Variable

LAB QUESTION

You are the network administrator of your company's network. Kung Karl, Vice President of IT, was just promoted from within the IT department to his new position. As a member of the IT department, Kung was not allowed to work from home, but as Vice President, Kung is now afforded that luxury. Kung has a Windows XP Professional client. Since his promotion Kung has been having trouble accessing certain directories, as well as a problem with the computer certificate for his notebook computer. These problems have now been resolved. Kung has traveled to a remote site and has successfully established the connection. Kung is now ready to start the presentation and demonstration of your company's remote access service tracking application that incorporates a web-based application with Outlook and Excel. Kung has started his first demonstration when he receives an error message stating that the database server (PLUTO) is not found on the network. Kung turns off the LCD projector, begs forgiveness from the attendees, suggests a coffee break, and calls you for support. Kung is now very unhappy. What are the possible sources of these problems and how can you resolve them? Use the space on this page to detail a course of action to troubleshooting this problem.

SELF TEST ANSWERS

Troubleshoot Network Protocol Security

1. ☑ **B and D.** Based on the description of the problem and the erroneous answers, the only correct combination is to configure the user accounts to control access through the remote access policy, and then configure the remote access policy to allow the access.

   ☒ **A** is incorrect because the word in the dialog is to Allow access. **C** is incorrect because the access for individual accounts are not set in the Routing and Remote Access console.

2. ☑ **B.** For L2TP to use IPSec, both the Remote Access Server and the client computer require a computer certificate.

   ☒ **A** is incorrect because if the Routing and Remote Access Server is not accessible by any of the users it must be missing a computer certificate. **C** is incorrect because the certificate is for the computer, not the user. **D** is incorrect because the Routing and Remote Access Service does not need a certificate; it is the server (computer) that requires the certificate.

3. ☑ **C.** The default authentication protocols that the client and server will try are MS CHAP V2 and MS CHAP. When there is a failure of authentication with error 919, verify that the protocols are enabled on the server. As there is no mention of MS CHAP in the answers, **C** is the correct one.

   ☒ **A** is incorrect because the client cannot be configured to use one authentication method over another; the negotiation is driven by the server. **B** and **D** are incorrect because there is no mention in the question of the use of Extensible Authentication Protocol.

4. ☑ **C.** The indication in the question is that the Routing and Remote Access Server cannot route to the network for the clients.

   ☒ **A** and **B** are incorrect because this is not an IP addressing problem; the addresses given in the example will work. **D** is incorrect because the problem is with the routing between VPN clients and the network, not JUPITER and PLUTO.

5. ☑ **C.** With the pattern of access problems later in the day, the culprit is most likely a lack of ports. There should be a reasonable number of ports configured; in this case start with the same number of ports as remote computers. Then you can monitor the usage and remove ports that are not needed.

   ☒ **A** is incorrect because logging information for 72 hours will not solve the problem; it will only anger the clients. **C** is incorrect because gathering network traffic is not a very efficient way of determining the solution to this problem. **D** is incorrect because the counters listed will not help in determining the problem source.

6. ☑ **D.** The PPP logging is part of the additional logging that is configured on the **Logging** tab of the RRAS server's property dialog.

   ☒ **A** is incorrect because there is no Logging tab in the properties for the ports. **B** and **C** are incorrect because there are no PPP logging options in Windows Server 2003; it is now part of the additional logging.

7. ☑ **B and D.** These are the only answers that are relevant to the problem that Kung is experiencing. Verify that the authentication protocols are correct, and that the user account that Kung is using has been allowed dial-in permission.

   ☒ **A** is incorrect because Kung should know his user name and password since he uses it in the office daily. **C** is incorrect because the lack of DNS name resolution does not prevent remote access.

8. ☑ **A.** The **Details** tab of the **Status** dialog lists the effective configuration of the connection.

   ☒ **B, C,** and **D** are incorrect because they refer to combination of dialog boxes and property tabs that do not exist.

9. ☑ **A.** The directory is the **%windir%\tracing** directory; **%windir%** is the directory where the operating system is installed.

   ☒ **B** is incorrect because the tracings directory is wrong; **%systemroot%** refers to the same location as **%windir%**. **C** and **D** are incorrect because the directory structure is not where the files are stored.

10. ☑ **C.** To allow incoming VPN connections, one of the following two settings must be enabled: LAN and demand-dial routing or Remote access server for the ports setting to be added to the Routing and Remote Access Server. With the current setting, as seen in the **General** tab, no ports are installed.

    ☒ **A** is incorrect because there are no ports installed that can be configured, so the configuration of the ports is not of any consequence until the RRAS server is correctly configured. **B** is incorrect because there are no ports, and hence no connection, so routing is not an issue in this question. **D** is incorrect because there are no ports, so the authentication protocol is of no consequence.

11. ☑ **C, E,** and **F.** You enable IPSec and create certificates at both the server and the clients. Then you configure the server for L2TP. L2TP is required for IPSec.

    ☒ **A** is incorrect because there is a protocol EAP-CHAP, but Windows Server 2003 doesn't support it. Windows Server 2003 supports EAPTLS. **B** and **D** are incorrect because even though MS-CHAPV2 with MPPE encryption is also secure, it is the second-best solution.

12. ☑ **B and E.** Enabling logging will store the messages in the System log with a source of RemoteAccess.

    ☒ **A** is incorrect because the messages are viewed from the System log. **C** and **D** are incorrect because those directories are not used for the logging of port usage. **F** is incorrect because the **General** tab does not have any logging options.

13. ☑ **B and D.** The additional logs that are generated are stored in the **%windir%\tracing** directory. Remember to turn off the logging after you have gathered the baseline information.
    ☒ **A** is incorrect because logging in itself will store information for authentication, service start/stop, and so on in the System log. **C** is incorrect because this is the wrong directory for the log files. **E** is incorrect because there is no PPP logging in Windows Server 2003

14. ☑ **C.** To see what is happening with the connection, and the PPP negotiations you need to enable additional logging.
    ☒ **A and B** are incorrect. There is no PPP logging in Windows Server 2003. **D** is incorrect because the logging should be on the RAS server, not on the remote client.

15. ☑ **D.** Logons are authentication, so this is the right answer. Remember that the information is logged in the System log.
    ☒ **A, B,** and **C** are incorrect because the audit policy is not the correct place to enable this authentication logging task. **E** is incorrect because you want authentication, not accounting logging.

16. ☑ **B and C.** These are the default protocols; MS CHAP V2 will be tried first followed by MS CHAP.
    ☒ **A** is incorrect because CHAP is not one of the defaults. **D** is incorrect because there is no MS CHAP V3 authentication protocol.

17. ☑ **C.** In order for L2TP and IPSec to work, both the remote access server and the client computer need a computer certificate.
    ☒ **A** is incorrect because he has successfully logged in at the office, and even if the password was aged by now, he would only be prompted for a change. **B** is incorrect because the certificate is for Kung's computer. **D** is incorrect because even though it is tempting to blame the user, this is a time when the fault is with the configuration of the notebook.

18. ☑ **C.** The first step of any troubleshooting exercise takes place a long time before the problem is evident. Knowledge about the system and the architecture is what makes you an effective troubleshooter; there is absolutely no luck involved.
    ☒ **A, B,** and **D** are incorrect because they use techniques that invariably will frustrate the client and possibly delay the resolution of the problem.

19. ☑ **A.** The IP addresses are hard-coded (DHCP Enabled: NO), so they refer to some other network, not the one the computer is currently on. This should be resolved by the local network administrator of the client site.
    ☒ **B, C,** and **D** are incorrect because the problem is with the configuration of the notebook computer as demonstrated by the information from the Vice President. Any amount of logging on the RRAS server will only delay resolution of the problem.

20. ☑   **B.** Each remote client requires one WAN Miniport, either PPTP or L2TP depending on the VPN type.

☒   **A** is incorrect because every connection must have an end point. **C** is incorrect because there is no default multiport configuration. **D** is incorrect because there is no default multiport configuration.

LAB ANSWER

This is where you perform the career-check steps before you start. Based on the problems Kung has had so far at the remote client site, you can expect him to make a lot of noise when he gets back to the office.

The first step in this exercise is to ask Kung to open the **Status** dialog of the VPN connection and switch to the **Details** tab. Verify that all effective settings are what you expect. Your second step would be to try the same connection using your own credentials. If this succeeds, you know there is a permissions problem. You should then ask Kung to permit you to connect using his credentials. This is a way of getting closer to the problem, because you can work on a connection from your own computer rather than through a phone call. Just remember to keep Kung informed of what you are doing.

If you could not connect, the indication is that you have a routing problem between JUPITER and PLUTO. Log in interactively on JUPITER and try to access PLUTO. If this does not succeed, you then solve the connectivity problem. If the connection succeeds, you have a Routing and Remote Access Service routing issue.

Remember to keep the client informed as you go.

MICROSOFT® CERTIFIED SYSTEMS ENGINEER &
MICROSOFT® CERTIFIED SYSTEMS ADMINISTRATOR

Part IV

Implementing, Managing, and Maintaining Routing and Remote Access

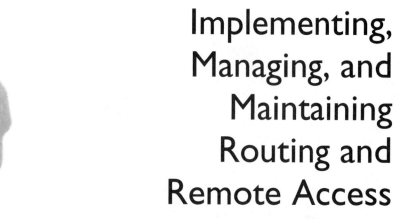

CHAPTERS

10

Implement Routing and Remote Access

Routing and Remote Access Service (RRAS) is the component of Windows Server 2003 that provides the services for remote connections between computers. The connections can be over dial-up networks (DUN), wide area networks (WAN), or a local area network (LAN). RRAS is installed when Windows Server 2003 is installed; to use it, you must enable and configure the service. In this chapter you will learn how to configure the clients for remote access and authentication using the different remote authentication protocols. In Chapter 11 you will learn about how to manage ports, filters, and routing. Chapter 12 provides the troubleshooting background you need to truly maintain a network.

CERTIFICATION OBJECTIVE 10.01

Configure Remote Access Authentication Protocols

Whenever a client connects to a server resource, the connection has two parts: the server that establishes the connections to remote clients, and the remote clients that initiate the connections. In this section we will explore the client-side connections that are available with Windows Server 2003—dial-up connections and virtual private network (VPN) connections, and the authentication protocols used. We will start by reviewing the remote access protocols supported by RRAS.

Remote Access Protocols

For the client to connect to the remote server, the two entities need to use a common remote access protocol. The concept of remote connection is shown in Figure 10-1.

The underlying LAN protocol is said to be *tunneled* through either the RAS protocol or the VPN. This way the connection and the client traffic are separated into two distinct parts. In almost all circumstances the LAN protocol will be TCP/IP, but there are choices regarding the RAS protocols.

Point to Point Protocol

Point to Point Protocol (PPP) is the replacement for SLIP (see later in this section), and is the default remote access protocol when clients are configured for remote access. PPP provides encryption of the authentication as well as compression of the headers and data during the transfer. Windows Server 2003 uses PPP to encapsulate the underlying

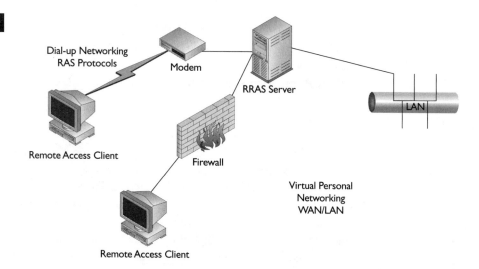

FIGURE 10-1

The types of remote client connection

Dial-up Networking RAS Protocols

Modem

RRAS Server

LAN

Remote Access Client

Firewall

Virtual Personal Networking WAN/LAN

Remote Access Client

LAN protocol (TCP/IP, NWLink, and NetBEUI) to permit any client access to the remote systems.

RAS

Remote Access Service (RAS) protocol is included for legacy support for those clients that only have access to RAS as their remote access protocol. RAS was introduced early in the life of the Microsoft operation systems; it was used to give remote access to users running MS-DOS, Windows 3.1, and Windows 3.11 for Workgroups. RAS is based on the Network Basic Input/Output (NetBIOS) environment relying on the point-to-point-not-routable nature of NetBIOS and the NetBEUI protocol.

SLIP

Serial Line Internet Protocol (SLIP) is one of the original remote access protocols that started under UNIX. SLIP is considered a legacy protocol and should only be used as the absolute last choice if no other Remote Access Protocols are available. Windows Server 2003 supports SLIP for outgoing connections only; RRAS does not support SLIP for incoming connections.

SLIP uses clear text authentication and does not provide compression of the network traffic. The original SLIP specification did not support dynamic TCP/IP configuration, resulting in static configurations.

ⓦatch **SLIP can only be configured for clients when the connection is using a modem for dial-up networking.**

AppleTalk Remote Access Protocol

Windows Server 2003 includes AppleTalk Remote Access Protocol (ARAP) to support Apple client's remote connections to environments running Windows Server 2003 and RRAS. Only Apple clients can connect remotely using ARAP.

DUN

Dial-up networking is the most common method of connecting a client computer to a remote network or server. Each day millions of connections are performed to connect clients to the Internet through their Internet Service Providers' (ISP's) access modems.

The term *dial-up networking* refers to the connection from the client to the remote server by means of the Public Switched Telephone Network (PSTN), or as it is sometimes called, Plain Old Telephone System (POTS). The client and the remote server are connected to the telephone network through modems that modulate the digital information from a computer into an analog signal and demodulate this analog signal back to the digital format.

Using DUN allows for connections from just about any phone line to the remote services of any type that supports one of the remote access protocols. Dial-up connections are initiated by the client, as described in Exercise 10-1, where you will configure a dial-up connection using PPP, and in Exercise 10-2 where you will change the connection to use SLIP.

EXERCISE 10-1

CertCam 10-1 ON THE CD

Configuring Dial-Up Connections on the Client

In this exercise, you will establish a dial-up connection in Windows Server 2003 that will use PPP to connect to a remote access server that connects to the Internet. The remote access server does not have to be a Windows Server 2003 computer running RRAS; it can be any remote access solution, including hardware-only RAS solutions and UNIX systems.

1. Click **Start** | **Connect To**, and click **Show all connections** to open the **Networks Connections** window.

2. Double-click the **New Connection Wizard** item to open the wizard. Click **Next** to start the wizard, as in this illustration:

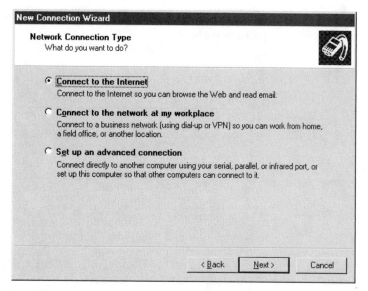

3. Select **Connect to the Internet** and click **Next** to display the following:

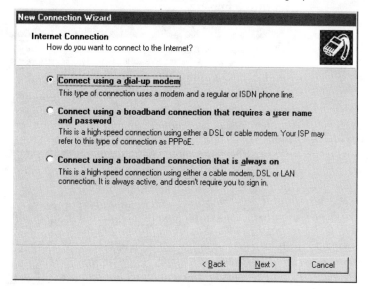

4. Select **Connect using a dial-up modem** and click **Next** to move to the next step of the wizard, as in this illustration:

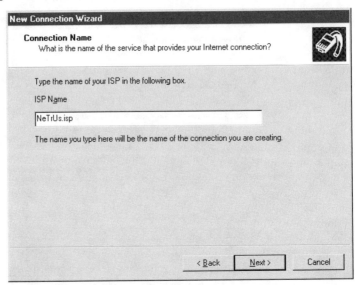

5. Type in the name of the ISP and click **Next**. I use the fictitious ISP **NeTrUs.isp** for this example.

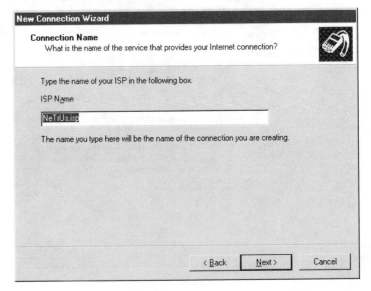

6. Enter the connection phone number for the ISP and click **Next**.

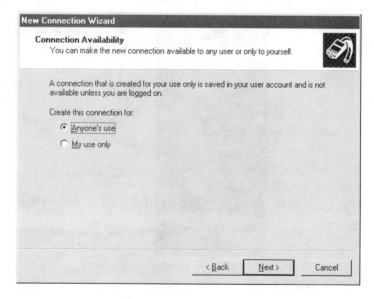

7. In the next step you need to decide who will be allowed to use this connection. Your choices are all users on the server, or only you. Select **Anyone's use** and click **Next**.

8. Enter the **User name** and **Password** for the connection and click **Next**. Note that the Internet Connection Firewall is enabled by default.

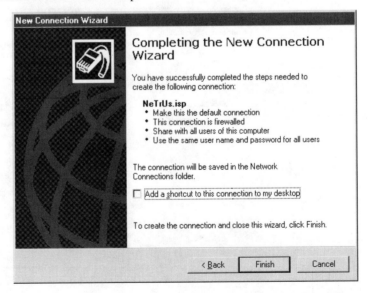

9. Click **Finish** to close the wizard. Note that you can create a shortcut to the connection on the desktop.

The default remote access protocol that is configured with the wizard is PPP. To change this to SLIP for use with UNIX servers, you need to manually change the settings for the connection as in Exercise 10-2.

on the
job

I have found that most modern implementations of UNIX support PPP, even if the version is older than the one used in Windows Server 2003. You should try PPP, and if there are problems between a UNIX implementation and Windows Server 2003 (or Windows XP Professional) you should disable the LCP extensions.

EXERCISE 10-2

Modifying the Connection to Use SLIP

1. Click **Start | Connect To**, and click on **Show all connections** to open the **Networks Connections** window.

2. Double-click the connection you created in Exercise 10-1 (NeTrUs.isp) to open the properties of the connection.

3. Click the **Network** tab of the **Property** dialog.

4. Select **SLIP: Unix Connection** as the type of dial-up server, as shown in this illustration:

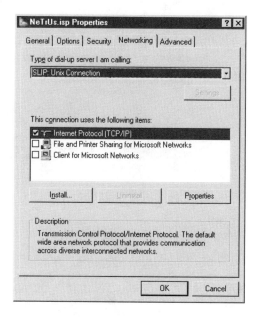

5. Click **OK**.

There is a second type of dial-up connection that does not make use of a modem or a network, which is the direct connection. The direct connection supports computer-to-computer connections using a serial or parallel cable, or an infrared connection. In Exercise 10-3 you will configure a direct connection. This type of connection is usually used to provide ad hoc connections between peers when there are no other networking options available.

EXERCISE 10-3

Configuring a Direct Connection to Another Computer

This exercise teaches you how to configure an infrared port to connect to a peer in an ad hoc fashion.

1. Click **Start | Connect To**, and click **Show all connections** to open the **Networks Connections** window.

2. Double-click the **New Connection Wizard** item to open the wizard. Click **Next** to start the wizard.

3. Select **Set up an advanced connection**, and click **Next**.

4. Select **Accept incoming connections**, and click **Next**.

5. In the **Devices for Incoming Connection** page, select all connection types and click **Next**, as shown in this illustration:

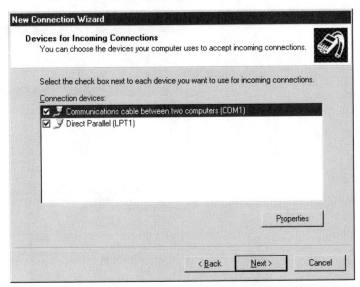

6. Select **Do not allow Virtual private connections** and click **Next**. You will configure a virtual private connection in a later exercise.

7. Next you need to select the user accounts that will be allowed to connect through this incoming connection. For the purpose of this exercise, select the **Administrator** account, as in this illustration. Click **Next**.

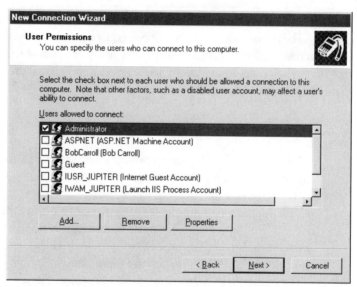

8. In the **Networking Software** selection, you must review the TCP/IP settings. You can give the connection a dedicated address or you can dynamically assign addresses to the connections from a Dynamic Host Configuration Protocol (DHCP) server. The caller can also request a specific TCP/IP address. Select the **Internet Protocol (TCP/IP)** option and click **Properties** to open this dialog:

9. Ensure that the there is a range of addresses assigned for the callers.

10. In this dialog you also control the access to the Local Area Network.

11. Click **OK** and then click **Next**.

12. Click **Finish** to complete the configuration of your connection.

The connections so far have been general in scope, and the security has been focused on the users' login credentials without any encryption of the payload. A very functional connection between a client and a server is the virtual private network (VPN), which we will delve into in the next section.

VPN

VPNs are networks that tunnel private payload through the public Internet in such a fashion that the traffic is virtually secure from snooping eyes. The architecture of a VPN can be seen in Figure 10-2.

VPN supports two protocols that are used to tunnel through any network: Point-to-Point Tunneling Protocol (PPTP) and Layer Two Tunneling Protocol (L2TP). The relationship between the WAN protocols (PPP), the tunneling protocols, and the payload (TCP/IP) is shown in Figure 10-3.

The bottommost protocol is the WAN protocol that carries the traffic between the peers in the connection, this is the Point-to-Point Protocol (PPP) connection between the client and the RRAS server. The middle layer represents the VPN protocol, and can be either PPTP or L2TP. This is the tunneling protocol that is used to encrypt the payload between the peers. The final layer is the payload, which represents the LAN protocol used for communication between the client and the server; this is TCP/IP in the case of Internet communication. The TCP/IP protocol encapsulates VPN data packets, which carry PPP, which encapsulates the data packets. This scheme provides data encryption, security checks, and validation at the point of transmission and reception, thus making the data more secure than if it had been transmitted using only TCP/IP. The TCP/IP protocol suite provides for guaranteed delivery of the data packets, but has no inherent method for securing the data. All transmissions are sent "clear," meaning anyone who has access to the network can capture the data as it is sent between the peers. TCP/IP is not considered secure for transmission over the Internet, so you use VPNs that tunnel traffic between the peers with no additional application changes. There are other possible ways of transmitting data securely between the peers, such as Secure Socket Layer (SSL), which is used to authenticate and encrypt the peers and the traffic between a web browser and web server.

FIGURE 10-2

The architecture
of a VPN

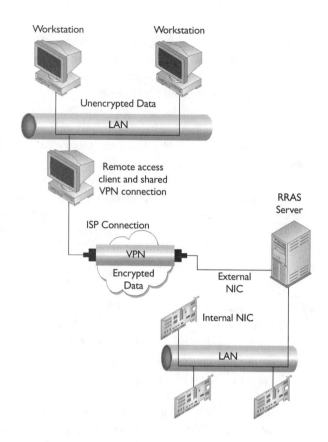

Point-to-Point Tunneling Protocol

PPTP is one of the supported VPN protocols for Windows Server 2003 environments. In fact, it has been supported since Windows NT 4.0, and is the main VPN protocol for use with older versions of the Windows operating systems. Windows 98, and NT 4.0 only support PPTP, so it is included for legacy support with these older operating systems.

FIGURE 10-3

The relationship
between the
protocols

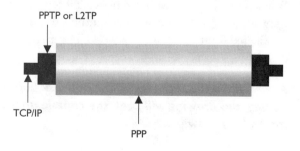

The benefits of PPTP include the widespread industry support from a large number of operating systems and hardware vendors. The security issues, however, are a drawback that will have you wanting to use L2TP whenever you have a chance.

The reason for the security issues with PPTP centers on the use of the Microsoft Point-to-Point Encryption (MPPE) as the built-in encryption provider that has a limited encryption facility. In addition, there is no header compression in PPTP, nor any authentication of the tunnel. As a result, PPTP uses more bandwidth than needed, and does not provide for endpoint authentication. Without endpoint authentication, there is no way for a client to verify that the server it has connected to is truly the desired server and not an impostor that has been added to the network. Impostor servers are commonly used by hackers to execute a man-in-the-middle attack that gives access to the clear data on the impostor server. Another potential drawback with PPTP is the reliance on IP-based networks, which prevents the use of the protocol over other types of networks.

Layer 2 Tunneling Protocol

L2TP provides higher security than PPTP, but it is a relative newcomer on the scene resulting in a weaker support from the industry. The weakness of PPTP has driven L2TP to become the tunneling protocol of choice for VPNs. L2TP was first included in Windows 2000, and is only supported in Windows Server 2003, Windows XP, and Windows 2000. The benefits of L2TP are that it supports header compression and tunnel authentication, and that it can operate over multiple, different networks. L2TP uses Internet Protocol Security (IPSec) for encryption and authentication. This results in a richer environment for configuration, including bandwidth control and tunnel authentication.

From the viewpoint of the VPN client, you have the ability of configuring the LAN and VPN protocols to use. But before we look at the client, we need to configure the server to act as an endpoint for a VPN.

For the following VPN exercises, you need to have access to a computer running Windows Server 2003 with two network interface cards (NICs) configured for different networks, and a client computer running Windows XP Professional with one NIC configured for the common network. The architecture of the network I used when developing this book can be seen in Figure 10-4.

on the
!
Ɵ o b
Always draw the topology of the network before you start implementing or testing, this drawing will keep the complexities in check. I use Visio to produce most of my drawings.

FIGURE 10-4

Network
architecture for
the exercises

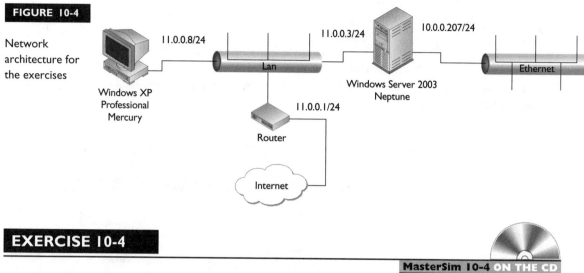

11.0.0.8/24

11.0.0.3/24

10.0.0.207/24

Lan

Ethernet

Windows XP
Professional
Mercury

Windows Server 2003
Neptune

11.0.0.1/24

Router

Internet

EXERCISE 10-4

MasterSim 10-4 ON THE CD

Configuring a VPN Server

In this exercise you will configure a Windows Server 2003 to be the VPN server for a
Virtual Private Network.

1. Click **Start | Administrative Tools | Routing and Remote Access** to open
   the **Routing and Remote Access** console window as shown in the following
   illustration:

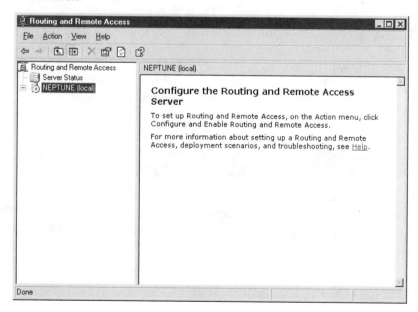

2. Right-click your server name in the left pane, and select **Configure and Enable Remote Access** from the context menu to start the **Routing and Remote Access Server Setup Wizard**. Click **Next** to start the wizard.

3. Select **Virtual Private Network (VPN) access and NAT** as the server type as shown in this illustration. Click **Next**.

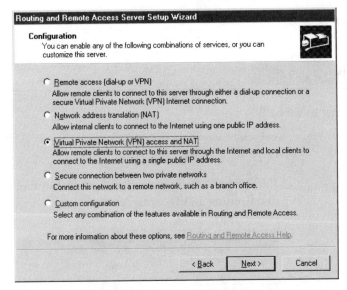

4. In the **VPN Connection** window, you need to select the network that connects to the Internet; select the Internet interface as shown in the next illustration. Click **Next**.

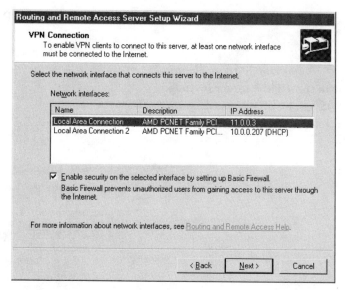

5. The VPN connection needs to have TCP/IP addresses assigned to it and the clients when they connect. The choices are to use a DHCP server or select a predefined range that is managed by RRAS. Select **From a specified range of addresses** as shown in this illustration, and then click **Next**.

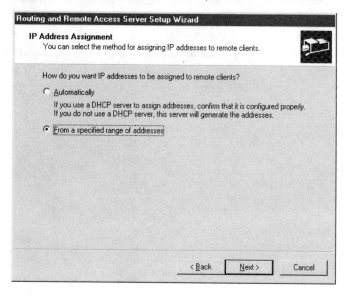

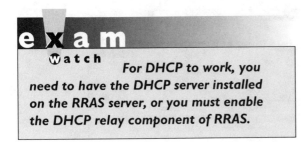

Watch *For DHCP to work, you need to have the DHCP server installed on the RRAS server, or you must enable the DHCP relay component of RRAS.*

6. In the **Address Range Assignments** dialog, click **New** and enter a range of addresses from 192.168.254.1 to 192.68.254.15 as in this illustration. Click **OK**.

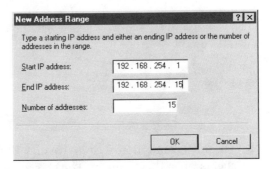

The resulting display should look like this illustration:

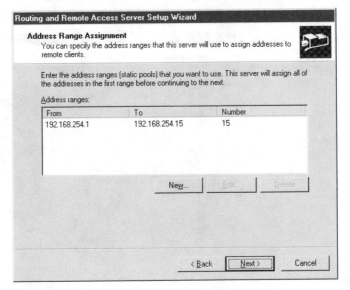

7. Click **Next** to make the decision regarding how to authenticate. Select **No, use Routing and Remote Access to authenticate connection requests**, as in this illustration. Click **Next**.

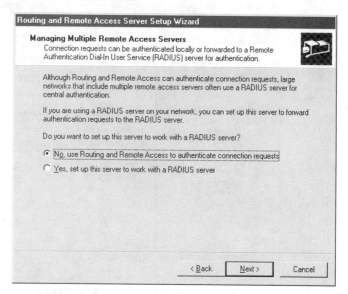

8. In the final dialog as seen here, click **Finish** to save the configuration and start RRAS.

9. After the wizard is finished, RRAS is started and can be seen in the **Routing and Remote Access** console, as in this illustration:

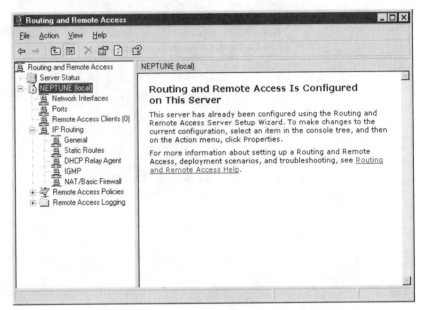

The next step is to configure the client to use this VPN server for access; this will be handled in Exercise 10-5.

The VPN server is configured for access from multiple clients; these clients must be configured to use the VPN in order to successfully connect and use the internal network that the RRAS is giving access to. When you configure the client, you need to know some information for the VPN server; in this exercise you referred to Figure 10-4 for that information.

INSIDE THE EXAM

RRAS and Automatic IP Assignment

When you configure RRAS to use DHCP, the remote access server must be able to reach a DCHP server to obtain the assigned addresses. This involves the ability to use the DHCP protocol, which is broadcast-based, and as such cannot pass through routers by default. Remember that the DHCP protocol has four types of packets that all must be delivered using a broadcast: DHCP discovery, DHCP offer, DHCP request, and DHCP acknowledgment.

Whenever a RRAS server starts, it requests a block of ten addresses from a DHCP server. If no DHCP server responds, the RRAS server will assign a block of addresses from the 169.254.0.0/16 Automatic Private IP Addresses (APIPA) network. This action is there to ensure that a DHCP client never finds itself without an IP address. The APIPA network is not routable, and any client that receives an address in that range (169.254.0.1 – 169.254.255.254) will not be able to access the internal network.

This behavior is perfectly normal if there is a failure with the DHCP server, but it is not what is expected when you want to use a functioning DHCP server that is on another network and cannot be reached by the broadcast DHCP packets. Under these circumstances, you need to configure a DHCP Relay Agent. As almost always when we deal with networking, there is more than one possible solution. The routers between the network with the RRAS server and the DHCP server can be updated to forward BOOTP traffic (DHCP packets). One client on the network where the RRAS server is connected can be configured to be a DHCP Relay Agent that will forward the DHCP traffic directly to the DHCP server. The RRAS server can be configured as a DHCP Relay Agent using the internal relay agent in the RRAS.

There is, however, a twist to this situation: if the remote client is Windows 98 or later, it will send a DHCP inform packet that must be routed to the DHCP server. This packet requests information about the DHCP server, the DNS and WINS server IP addresses, and the DNS domain name. The only way to ensure that this information reaches the client is to have the DHCP Relay Agent configured on the RRAS server.

Remember that if you do not receive the IP addresses you expect from the DHCP server, start looking at the network.

EXERCISE 10-5

Configuring a VPN Client

In this exercise you will configure a Windows XP Professional computer to be a client on the VPN you configured in Exercise 10-4.

1. Click **Start** | **Connect to**, and click **Show all connections** to open the **Network Connections** window, as shown in this illustration:

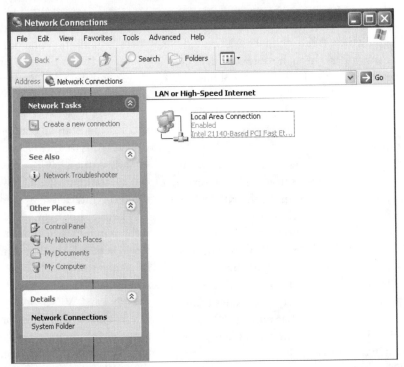

2. Click **Create a new connection** to open the connection wizard. Click **Next** to start the wizard.

3. Select **Connect to the network at my workplace** as shown in this illustration. Click **Next**.

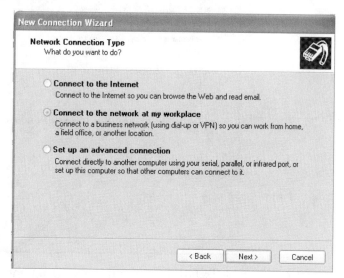

4. Select **Virtual Private Network connection**, and then click **Next**.

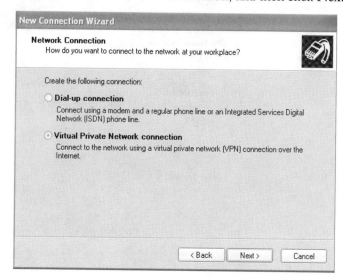

5. Enter a company name as in this illustration, and then click **Next**.

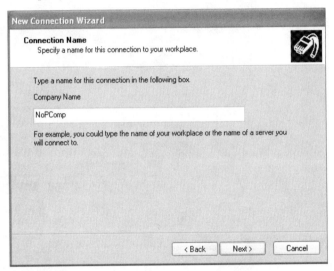

6. Enter the TCP/IP address of the server you want to connect to, as in this illustration, and then click **Next**.

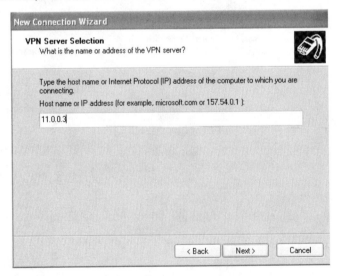

7. Select **My use only**, and click **Next**.

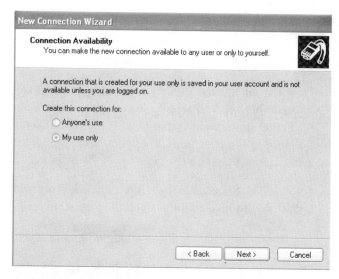

8. In the final dialog, click **Finish** to create the connection.

9. Click **Cancel** to dismiss the connection dialog for now.

Before we look at how to configure the protocols for the VPN channel, we should test what we have built so far in order to validate the exercises.

Testing the VPN

Now you will test the VPN by connecting to the server using the connection you just created, then you will access a shared folder on the server.

This exercise assumes that there is a shared folder on the server, which is called Neptune in the exercise. The name of the shared folder used is Captures, but the name is immaterial for the outcome of the exercise.

1. Click **Start** | **Connect To**, and click **NoPComp** on the Windows XP Professional client to open the **Connect NoPComp** dialog, as seen here:

2. Enter the **user name** as **Neptune\Administrator** and the **password** as **password**, and click **Connect**, as shown in this illustration:

3. After the connection is authenticated you will see a notification balloon telling you to click on it to see additional information about the connection. You can also use the connection icon in the tray to open the status dialog for the VPN connection.

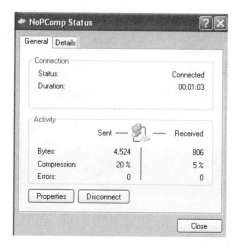

4. Click the **Details** tab to get more information about the VPN connection, as shown in this illustration. Click **Close** to dismiss the status dialog.

5. The next step in testing the VPN connection is to open the share on the server. Click **Start** | **Run** to open the **Run** dialog.

6. In the **Open** textbox, enter **\\Neptune\Captures**, as shown here, and click **OK**.

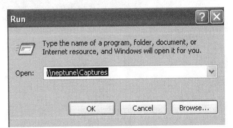

7. The result is that a folder opens based on the share on the VPN server.

Now that you have created a VPN using the default settings, we need to look deeper at the security settings for the VPN and what the default settings give you. This is the topic of the next section.

The Default VPN Settings

When you configure the RRAS side of the VPN, you have no choices as to the protocols used. RRAS will always attempt to use L2TP first and fall back to PPTP if that attempt fails. The client, on the other hand, configures the protocol and settings through the connection object. This object has some default settings that are important to know, because they are potentially not what you expect them to be. The following list shows the default settings for three of the tabs in the client-side connection properties.

Expect that your knowledge of the default VPN settings will be tested.

- **Security** Typical—requires secured password and data encryption. You need to select **Advanced** options to configure the protocols used.

- **Networking** Automatic VPN type. If both the server and the client support L2TP, that protocol will be used, but if there are no certificates installed, the client will fall back to PPTP.

- **Advanced** No Internet Firewall or no connection sharing configured.

EXERCISE 10-7

Customizing the VPN Client Settings

The properties of the client connection object are used to customize the VPN connection. In this exercise you will look at the options available when configuring a connection.

1. Click **Start** | **Connect to**. Right-click your VPN connection, and click **Properties** from the context menu.

2. The VPN connection's property dialog opens, as you can see in the following illustration. The property sheet has five tabs that configure different aspects of the VPN connection. On the **General** tab, you enter the IP address or the fully qualified domain name (FQDN) of the remote server, and you can configure a default connection to the Internet that will be dialed before the VPN connection is opened. This option is used when the client computer is connected to the Internet using a modem. The third item on the **General** tab is whether

to display an icon in the notification area when connected; this option is on by default.

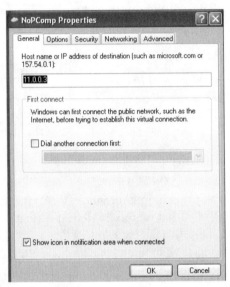

3. Select the **Options** tab, which displays the options regarding dialing and redialing. You can use these options to optimize how the user interacts with the connection while it is being dialed. The default is to show the progress of the connection and to prompt for security information, login name, password, certificate, smart card, and so on. Optionally, you can include the user's Windows domain in the security credentials. The redialing rules are used to ensure that the connection is re-established if it should drop, and that the connection is dropped if the link is idle for a specific length of time. This idle time option will save you a lot of money if the connection is billed by time, as most are.

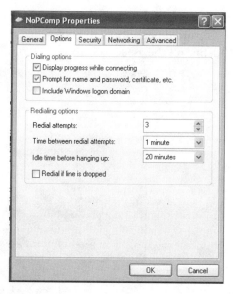

4. On the **Security** tab, you configure the security options for the connection to use typical or advanced settings. The typical settings are the default, and are shown in the following illustration. Your choices under the typical settings are to use secure passwords or a smart card, as well as automatically using your Windows logon credentials. Additionally you can require data encryption for the transport.

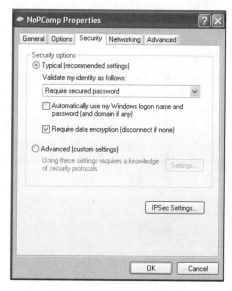

5. To configure the **Advanced** options, click the **Settings** button to display the **Advanced Security Settings** dialog, as shown in this illustration. You can define all the aspects of the connection from this dialog.

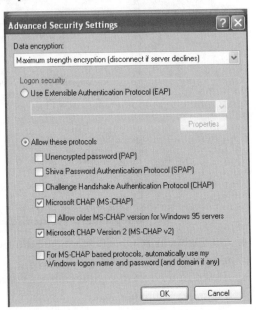

6. On the **Networking** tab, you select the VPN protocol that will be used for the connection. The default setting of **Automatic** allows the server and client to find the most secure protocol that is supported by both. The RRAS server will always try to use L2TP first and fall back to PPTP. If either protocol fails, the connection will also fail. The **Networking** tab also gives access to the networking components that are used by the connection. Each of the components can be configured. For example, the Internet Protocol (TCP/IP) component is used to configure the IP addressing that is used; the default is automatic addressing using DHCP. You can also turn off components by removing the check mark beside them. One possible component to remove is the File and Print Sharing for Microsoft Networks. You need this component only if the RRAS server needs access to files or printers defined on your computer.

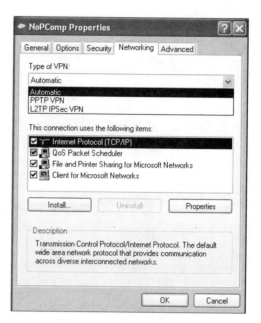

7. The **Properties** button on the **Networking** tab opens a dialog with three options. Two options are enabled by default, only **Negotiate multi-link for single-link connection** is cleared. The **Link Control Protocol (LCP) extensions** option is used to control how "smart" the client will be during the connection negotiation; clear the LCP option when the remote server is using older versions of the PPP software. The software compression option enables compression of the data through the driver as well as through the hardware; to use software compression you do not have to have hardware compression enabled. The **Multi-link for Single-link connections option** only works with Windows Server 2003 or Windows 2000 Server based RRAS and might improve multimedia transmission.

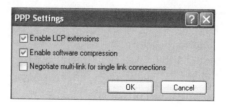

8. The **Advanced** tab gives you access to configure the Internet Connection Firewall (ICF) that is used to protect the client computer from unwanted connection attempts from the Internet. You also use this tab to configure Internet Connection Sharing (ICS). ICS functions as a central Internet connection for a local network. If you install ICS on a client computer, you only need one connection for a group of users. The connection will behave as you configure it; if you have specified that the connection is only for your use, the ICS will only function when you are logged in and connected. To make the ICS connection available at all times, you should configure the connection to be available to all users.

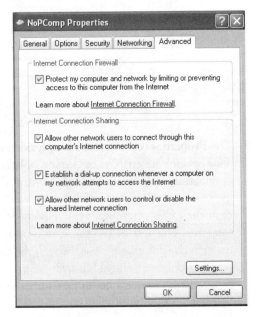

Now that you have a better idea of RRAS and VPN configuration, here are some possible scenario questions and their answers.

Now that you have learned about RRAS and VPN configuration, you need to expand into authentication of your clients.

SCENARIO & SOLUTION

You are the Network Administrator of your company's network that consists of twelve Windows XP Professional computers and three Windows Server 2003 computers. You have just added a second network interface card (NIC) to one of the Windows Server 2003 computers so that it can be connected both to the local network in the office and to the ADSL modem your ISP has installed at your premises. You must configure the Windows Server 2003 to share the Internet connection to all the other computers on the local network. Where in the Network Connection Wizard do you configure Internet Connection Sharing (ICS)?	The configuration of ICS is normally not performed using the Network Connection Wizard, even though there is an option to do so. Select the **Dial-up To the Internet** option on the **Network Connection Type** page to start the Internet Connection Wizard, which gives you the options to configure ICS.
You have configured a RRAS server to automatically use DHCP to assign addresses to the VPN clients. When you investigate the DHCP server, you find that as the RRAS service is started, a number of new leases are created, even though there are no clients connected. Why is this?	When RRAS is configured to use DHCP to automatically assign IP addresses to clients, it will request a block of ten addresses from DHCP as soon as RRAS starts. RRAS manages these addresses and will lease them in turn to the remote clients. In addition to the block of addresses that RRAS gets from DHCP for the clients, RRAS will also get a block of ten addresses for itself that are bound to the PPP adapter.
You have been asked to describe the benefits of using L2TP over PPTP. What are those benefits?	PPTP was the original tunneling protocol, and as such is lacking in some areas where L2TP excels. The most important benefit of using L2TP is the strengthened security L2TP offers. L2TP used IPSec to authenticate the end-points of the VPN to minimize the risk of a man-in-the-middle type attack. L2TP uses IPSec to encrypt the data transmitted as well. PPTP is only usable in a TCP/IP internetwork, whereas L2TP can be carried on a large number of dissimilar networks.
You are the network administrator for your company's remote access network. You have a number of RRAS servers installed for different roles. When you work with the RRAS servers, you have noted that there seems to be a difference between the different servers in how many VPN ports are configured. Why are there differences between the numbers of VPN ports for the different RRAS roles?	Depending on how RRAS is configured, the wizard will create different numbers of VPN ports. When RRAS is configured to be a VPN server, the wizard creates 128 PPTP and L2TP ports, reflecting the anticipated number of remote connections a VPN server would have. When RRAS is configured as a remote access server, the wizard only create five ports.
What are the remote access protocols that are supported when configuring client connections in Windows Server 2003?	There are four supported remote access protocols in Windows Server 2003: PPP, SLIP, Microsoft RAS, and ARAP. When you configure a client connection, you can use PPP, SLIP, and Microsoft RAS, but not ARAP, as your remote access protocol. When configuring RRAS you can use PPP, Microsoft RAS, or ARAP, but not SLIP, as the remote access protocol.

CERTIFICATION OBJECTIVE 10.02

Configure Internet Authentication Service (IAS) to Provide Authentication for Routing and Remote Access Clients

Secure authentication for remote access clients is a challenge for network administrators. This is especially true when the clients are from many different organizational units, where the directory information is spread out between many different directories and or platforms, and the clients can connect through multiple media access technologies, such as RRAS, WiFi, and VPN. One solution to this problem is to use Remote Authentication Dial-In User Service (RADIUS) servers to perform the authentication. RADIUS is a Internet Engineering Task Force (IETF) standard that is implemented on many different platforms.

Microsoft has implemented RADIUS in a product called Internet Authentication Service (IAS) that has been available since the RRAS product for Windows NT 4.0 (Windows NT 4.0 Option Pack). The current version comes as part of Windows Server 2003 Standard Edition, Windows Server 2003 Enterprise Edition, and Windows Server 2003 Datacenter Edition. The version of IAS that is shipped with Windows Server 2003 Standard Edition is limited to a maximum of 50 RADIUS clients and a maximum of two remote RADIUS server groups. The version that ships with the higher-end Windows Server 2003 versions has no such limitations. Figure 10-5 shows how IAS can be used as a RADIUS server where the directory information is located in an Active Directory domain.

IAS can also be configured as a RADIUS proxy, where the RADIUS servers can be implemented on any platform and the RADIUS authentication calls are forwarded from the client by the IAS proxy as shown in Figure 10-6.

Using IAS enables a uniform authentication environment irregardless of the connection methods or the equipment used. Different configurations can be configured for the following scenarios:

- Internet access
- Wireless access
- Dial-up or VPN remote access

- Public dial-up or wireless access
- Extranet access for business partners

IAS is installed as an additional Windows component as you will learn in the following exercise.

IAS as a RADIUS
server

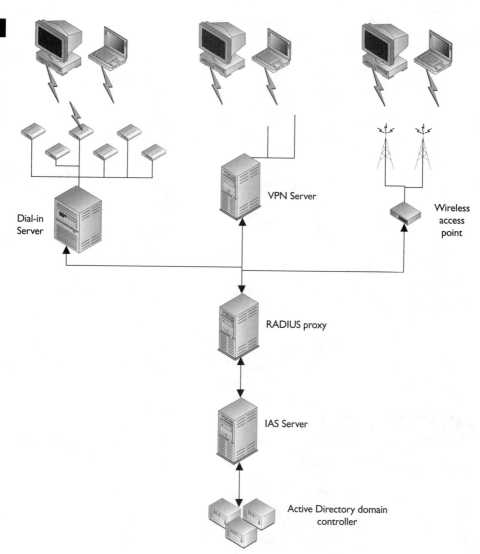

Dial-in
Server

VPN Server

Wireless
access
point

RADIUS proxy

IAS Server

Active Directory domain
controller

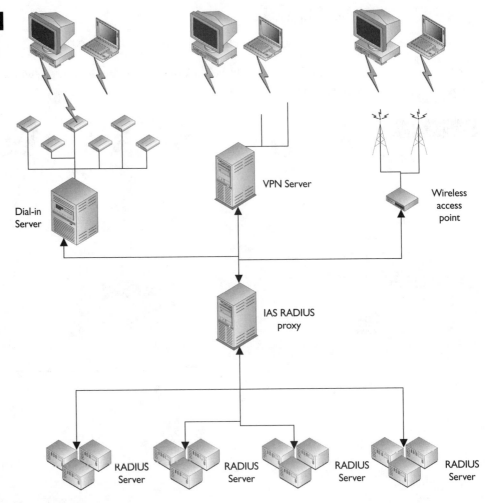

FIGURE 10-6

IAS as a RADIUS proxy

EXERCISE 10-8

Installing IAS

In this exercise you will install IAS.

1. Log into the domain controller where you want to install IAS; use an account that has administrative privileges.

2. Open **Add or Remove Programs** in the Control Panel.

3. Click **Add/Remove Windows Components**.

4. In the **Windows Components Wizard** dialog, click **Networking Services**, and then click **Details**.

5. In the **Networking Services** dialog, select **Internet Authentication Service**, as in this illustration, click **OK**, and then click **Next**.

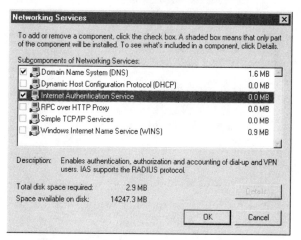

6. If you are prompted for the Windows Server 2003 CD, insert it to complete the installation.

7. After the installation is done, click **Finish** and then close the Add or Remove Programs application.

Once IAS is installed you will need to configure it before using IAS with RRAS. Exercises 10-9 and 10-10 are mutually exclusive—only one of them will succeed, as they both perform the same operation.

EXERCISE 10-9

Registering IAS Using the MMC

In this exercise, you will configure IAS for use.

1. Log into the domain controller where you want to install IAS, using an account that has administrative privileges.

2. Start the **Internet Authentication Service** console by clicking **Start** | **Administrative Tools** | **Internet Authentication Service**.

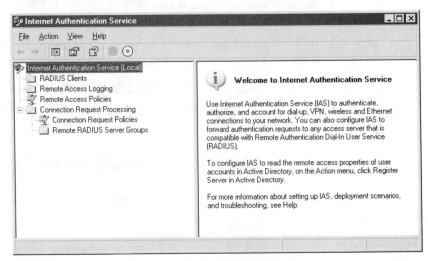

3. Right-click the **Internet Authentication Service** node, and then click **Register Server in Active Directory**.

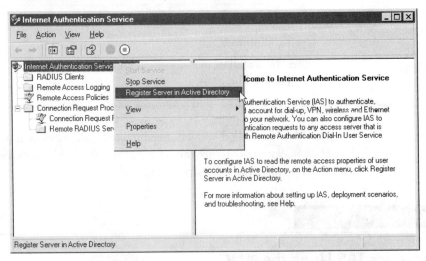

4. Click **OK** in the **Register Internet Authentication Service in Active Directory** dialog box.

Registering IAS in Active Directory using netsh

1. Log into the domain controller where you want to install IAS, using an account that has administrative privileges.

2. Open a command prompt.

3. At the command prompt, type

   ```
   netsh ras add registeredserver
   ```

4. The successful command returns the following:

   ```
   Registration completed successfully:
      Remote Access Server:  JUPITER
      Domain:                solsystemet.planet
   ```

5. Close the command prompt.

Now you will need to modify the user accounts that will be allowed access to the VPN through IAS authentication. You perform this task with Active Directory Users and Computers.

Configuring User Accounts

1. Log into the domain controller where you want to install IAS, using an account that has administrative privileges.

2. Open **Active Directory Users and Computers** by clicking **Start | Administrative Tools | Active Directory Users and Computers**.

3. Select the **Users** node in the object tree. Double-click the account you want to authorize in the **Users** pane.

4. Select the **Dial-in** tab of the user properties dialog. Select **Allow access**, and click **OK**.

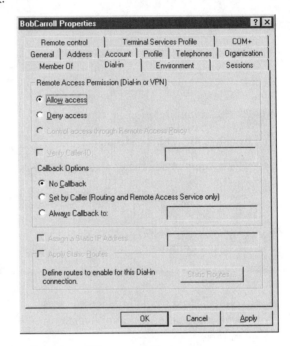

5. Close **Active Directory Users and Computers**.

In order for RRAS to be able to use the IAS server, you need to configure a RADIUS client.

Adding a RADIUS Client

1. Log into the domain controller where you want to install IAS, using an account that has administrative privileges.

2. Start the **Internet Authentication Service** console by clicking **Start | Administrative Tools | Internet Authentication Service**.

3. Right-click **RADIUS Clients**, and then click **New RADIUS Client**.

4. Specify a friendly name for the RADIUS client, and the FQDN or IP address of the RRAS server, as shown in this illustration:

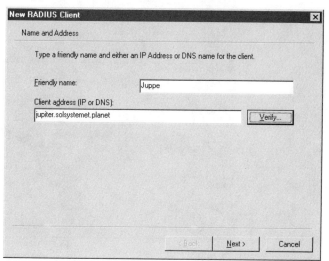

5. Click **Verify** to make sure the name is reachable. In the **Verify Client** dialog, click **Resolve**.

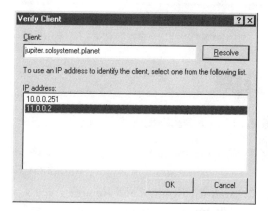

6. Select the IP address you want to use and click **OK**.

7. Click **Next**.

8. Select **RADIUS Standard** as the **Client-Vendor** type. Enter a shared secret to be used to validate the client. I used the password.

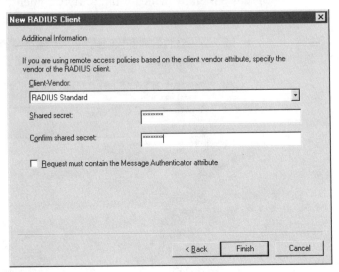

9. Click **Finish**.

10. Close the **Internet Authentication Service** MMC.

The final step is to enable RRAS to use the IAS server you just set up.

EXERCISE 10-13

Enabling RRAS to Use a RADIUS Server

1. Log into the domain controller where you want to install IAS, using an account that has administrative privileges.

2. Start the **Routing and Remote Access** console by clicking **Start | Administrative Tools | Routing and Remote Access**.

3. Right-click the server in the object tree, and click **Properties** in the context menu.

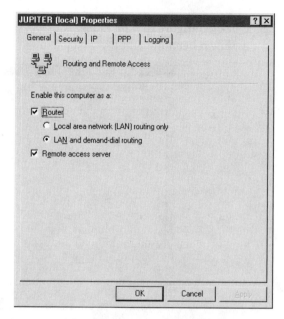

4. Select the **Security** tab in the Properties dialog. Select **RADIUS Authentication** as the Authentication provider, as shown in this illustration:

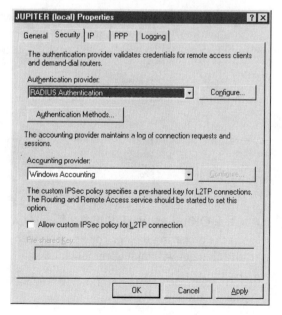

5. Click **Configure** to start adding RADIUS servers to the RRAS server, as shown here:

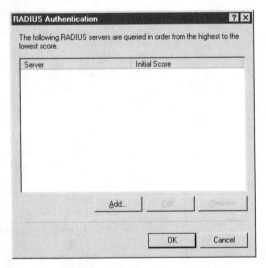

6. Click **Add**. Enter the FQDN of the IAS server defined earlier, click **Change** to enter the secret (password), and then click **OK**.

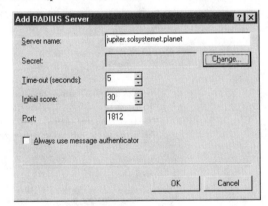

7. Click **OK** on the **RADIUS Authentication** dialog, and then click **OK** again on the properties dialog. You are reminded that RRAS must be restarted before the changes will take effect, click OK.

8. Right-click the RRAS server in the tree pane, select **All tasks** in the context menu, and click **Restart**.

9. Test the RRAS server using the client computer you configured earlier. When you are asked for the login name and password, use the account you defined above.

CERTIFICATION OBJECTIVE 10.03

Configure Routing and Remote Access Policies to Permit or Deny Access

So far, we have only discussed allowing dial-in access to the account that you want to use to dial in with. If that was the only mechanism available in controlling who may or may not access our remote access solution, you would have a poor environment. Fortunately the Windows Server 2003 RRAS has a very rich and atomic system that provides full control of who can access the server, when they can, and from what type of network the access must take place, just to mention some of the many combinations that are possible.

The authentication process uses combinations of remote access policies and profiles to produce the effective permission that will be used to determine whether to allow or deny the access attempt. The RRAS authentication process consists of two components that when combined determine the remote user's access. First, there is the user's dial-in permission, which is granted or denied by editing the user's properties in Active Directory. This is the same dial-in permission that has been used since Windows NT 4.0 and Windows 2000. The second part of the equation is an expanded version of the remote access policy that was introduced with Windows 2000. These remote access policies are broken down into three components that are always combined with the user's dial-in permission to determine whether to grant or deny remote access.

on the
job *I have found that the administration of multiple remote access servers that all need the same remote access policies is the one burden that will make the environment unstable after a period of time. One possible method that can be used to keep the remote access policies synchronized is to use the netsh command to retrieve the configuration from one "master" server and then apply these settings on other remote access servers. This method also acts as a version control of the remote access policies.*

Introduction to Remote Access Policies

Remote access policies are used to validate a number of the connection parameters before authorizing the connection. Some of the items validated are

- Dial-in permission
- Group membership
- Time of day
- Day of week
- Type of connection
- Authentication method
- Access client phone number or MAC address
- Access server identity

The validation of the connection results in either an authorized or a denied connection. If the connection is authorized, you can still restrict the connection based on the remote access policies. These connection restrictions include

- Maximum session time
- Idle timeout time
- Encryption strength
- IP packet filters

- IP address for PPP connections
- Static routes

These connection restrictions can be customized based on some of the other elements of the remote access policy, such as

- Time of day
- Authentication methods
- Identity of the access server
- Access client phone number or MAC address
- Group membership
- Type of connection

An example of this type of granular remote access policy would be a policy that specified different maximum session times for different types of connections (ADSL vs. POTS), or for members of different groups. As part of these restrictions, you can configure a remote access policy structure that takes into account whether the client is a business partner or an unauthenticated user, and set the resource and connection restrictions accordingly.

As mentioned in these lists, you can use group membership as a parameter to determine access authorization. You can also use the user name to grant authorization.

User Authorization

When you are managing remote access authorization based on the user, you have to grant or deny remote access for each individual user in the Active Directory if you are in a domain, or on the local RRAS server if you are in a workgroup. In addition to the access permission, you also need to create remote access policies to control the access. One possible configuration would be to create remote access policies for dial-in access as well as VPN access, and if applicable, for wireless access.

The decision tree when using user authorization follows this basic process, as shown in Figure 10-7.

The connection attempt must match all the conditions of at least one remote access policy to be granted access. Otherwise the connection is denied.

Group Authorization

If you are managing the remote connection authorization by using group membership, you set the remote access permission to **Control access through Remote Access Policy** on the user account in Active Directory. Then you create remote access policies that

FIGURE 10-7

User
authorization
process flow

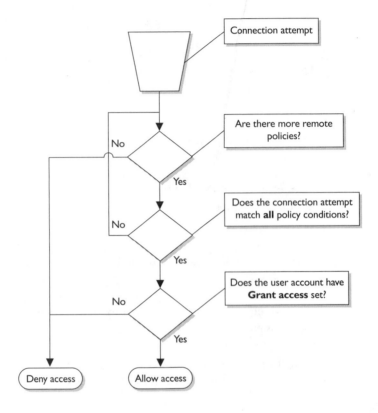

are based on different connection types and group memberships. For example, you should have one remote policy for VPN connections for all employees and a different remote access policy for customers.

The decision tree when using group authorization follows this basic process, as shown in Figure 10-8.

Remote Access Permissions on the User Object

The user object in Active Directory has an attribute that is used to grant or deny dial-in permissions. These permissions apply for any type of connection attempt: modem, WAN,

exam
⑆atch   *The Control access through Remote Access Policy **attribute of a user account is not available when the domain is in Windows 2000 mixed functional level.***   *You need to bring the domain up to Windows 2000 native functional level or Windows Server 2003 functional level to be able to use this option.*

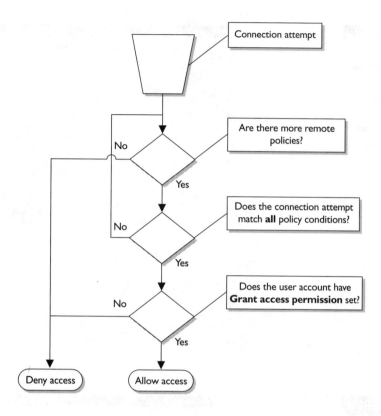

FIGURE 10-8

Group
authorization
process flow

LAN, wireless, and so on. Figure 10-9 depicts the **Dial-in** tab of the user's properties dialog when the domain is in Windows 2000 mixed functional level. Figure 10-10 shows the **Dial-in** tab of the user's properties dialog when the domain is in Windows 2000 native functional level or Windows Server 2003 functional level.

The three options for Remote Access Permission (Dial-in or VPN) are

- **Allow access**   The user is permitted to connect.
- **Deny access**   The user is not permitted to connect.
- **Control access through Remote Access Policy**   The remote access policy controls whether or not to allow the connection, and is used for group authorization. This option is not available if the domain is in Windows 2000 mixed mode.

The Callback Options controls how we want to use callbacks to manage our dial-in connections. The default is No Callback.

FIGURE 10-9

The **Dial-in** tab of the user's properties dialog, Windows 2000 mixed functional level

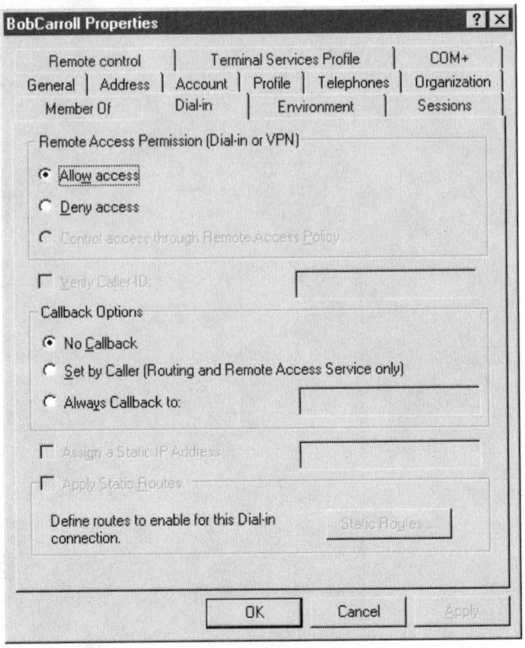

FIGURE 10-10

The **Dial-in** tab of the user's properties dialog, windows 2000 native functional level

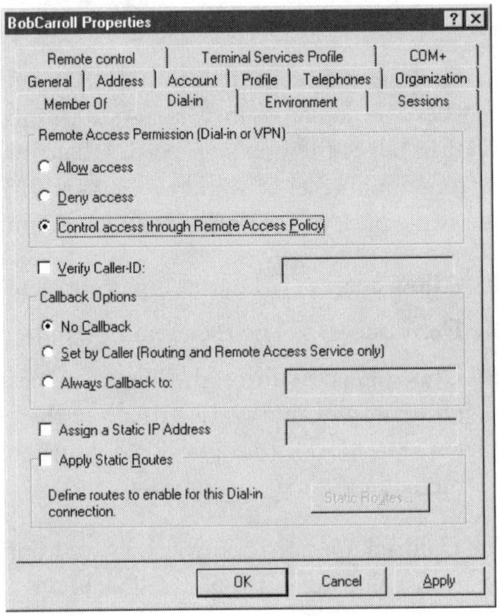

The Three Parts of a Remote Access Policy

Remote access policies are made up of three parts: conditions, permission, and profile settings. When you configure and enable Routing and Remote Access Service, two default remote access policies are created. The first policy specifies that the connection must be to a RRAS server, and the second makes the connections available 24/7. To view the remote access policies, you can use either the **Routing and Remote Access** console or the **Internet Authentication Service** console in the Remote Access Policies folder, as shown in Figure 10-11. You can view the details of the remote access policy by double-clicking the policy, as in Figure 10-12.

Conditions　　The conditions of the remote access policy are listed in the list box of the policy dialog; each remote access policy can have multiple conditions. The remote access policy seen in Figure 10-12 has only one condition, which specifies that users are required to connect between 00:00 on Sunday and 24:00 on the following Saturday, which results in a 24/7 condition.

Permissions　　There are two permissions you can set using the remote access policy: grant access and deny access. In the policy from Figure 10-12, the permission is set to deny access, which means that if the time is between 00:00 Sunday and 24:00 the following Saturday, access will be denied. The result of the default settings in the remote access policies and the user's dial-in permission is to always deny access.

Profile　　The third part of the remote access policy is the profile, which is configured by clicking the **Edit Profile** button. The resulting **Edit Dial-in Profile** dialog is shown in Figure 10-13.

FIGURE 10-11　　The remote access policies

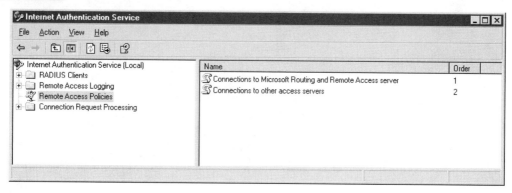

FIGURE 10-12

The parts
of a remote
access policy

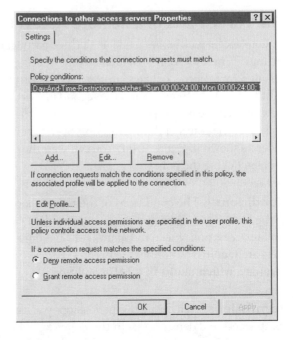

FIGURE 10-12

The parts
of a remote
access policy

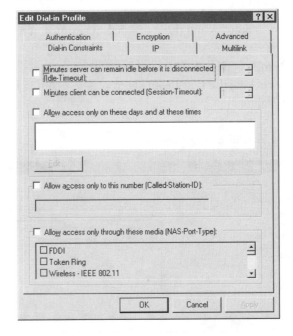

FIGURE 10-13

The **Edit Dial-in
Profile** dialog

The profile consists of six tabs that are used to configure:

- **Dial-in constraints**   Configures restrictions for the connection, such as idle time, dial-in media, and so on
- **IP**   Configures restrictions on the IP addressing, including whether to use DHCP or static addressing
- **Multilink**   Configures restrictions on the use of Multilink (combining the bandwidth of more than one device)
- **Authentication**   Configures restrictions on how the client must authenticate, including the protocols to use
- **Encryption**   Configures restrictions on what encryption levels are permissible for the connection
- **Advanced**   Configures additional connection attributes, such as RADIUS authenticated protocols

Now that you have looked at the components that make up remote access policies, you need to look at how to implement these policies.

Implementing Remote Access Policies

You might have wondered about where the remote access policies are stored, and it is a normal misconception that they are stored in Active Directory, but that isn't true. If you think about how the remote access policies are applied, against a particular connection through a particular RRAS server, it makes sense that the remote access policies are stored locally on the RRAS server itself, mainly because of the granularity that can be applied to the remote access policies. When you need to apply remote access policies across multiple RRAS servers, each server must be configured with the same policies, which poses an administrative problem. There are two solutions to this problem: store the policies in a text file using the **netsh** command, and then apply the policy on the rest of the servers using the same **netsh** command, or install and configure Internet Authentication Service (IAS), so that all RRAS servers using IAS can be configured centrally through this IAS server.

Next, you'll configure a remote access policy that will provide access to a security group in the domain.

EXERCISE 10-14

Create a Remote Access Policy

Suppose you are the network administrator for your company, and you need to grant the field sales staff VPN access to the internal network. The field sales staff are already members of the FIELDSALES security group. The following are the steps involved in creating the remote access policy.

1. Log into the domain controller where you want to install IAS, using an account that has administrative privileges.

2. Start the **Routing and Remote Access** console by clicking **Start | Administrative Tools | Routing and Remote Access**.

3. Right-click **Remote Access Policy**, and select **New Remote Access Policy** from the context menu.

4. In the **Add Remote Access Policy** dialog, enter a friendly name for the new remote access policy, and then click **Next**, as shown here:

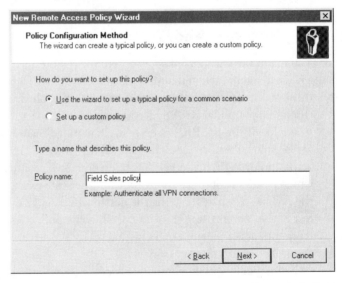

5. Select the **VPN** connection method, as shown next, and click **Next**.

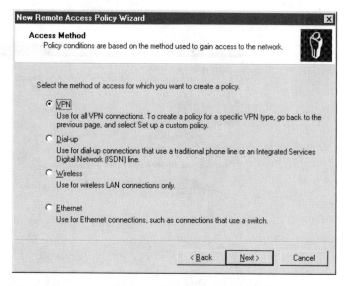

6. Select **Group** and click **Add** to add a group. In the **Select Group** dialog, enter the name of the group. Click **OK**.

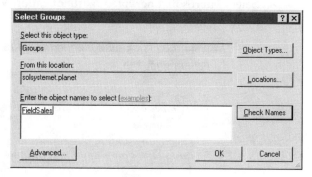

7. Click **Next**.

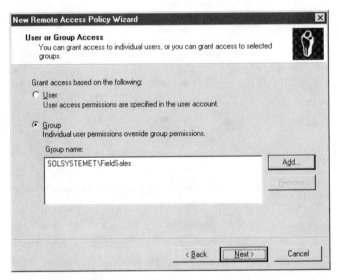

8. Select **Microsoft Encrypted Authentication Version 2 (MS-CHAPv2)**, as shown here. Click **Next**.

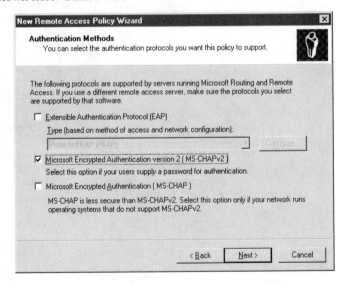

9. Leave the encryption levels at their defaults, and click **Next**.

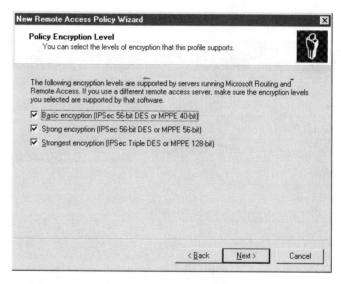

10. Click **Finish** to create the remote access policy.

11. Test the remote access policy by using one of the accounts in the FieldSales group.

Configuring a Remote Access Policy

Now that you have configured your first remote access policy, you need to look at the configuration of a that policy by adding conditions and modifying the remote access profile using the different options available. The first part of the remote access policy that is verified in the authentication process is the policy conditions. These policy conditions have been extended in the Windows Server 2003 version of RRAS. Table 10-1 lists the conditions that can be put on a policy. Single policies can have multiple conditions that are combined using a Boolean **and** operation.

| **TABLE 10-1** | Remote Access Policy Conditions |

Condition Attribute Name	Description
Authentication Type	The type of authentication that is being used by the access client
Called Station ID	The phone number of the network access server (NAS)
Calling Station ID	The phone number used by the caller
Client Friendly Name	The name of the RADIUS client that is requesting authentication
Client IP Address	The IP address of the RADIUS client
Client Vendor	The vendor of the network access server (NAS) that is requesting authentication
Day and Time Restrictions	The day of the week and the time of day of the connection attempt
Framed Protocol	The type of framing for incoming packets. Examples are PPP, SLIP, Frame Relay, and X.25
NAS Identifier	The name of the network access server (NAS)
NAS IP Address	The IP address of the NAS (the RADIUS client) that sent the message
NAS Port Type	The type of media that is used by the access client
Service Type	The type of service that is being requested
Tunnel Type	The type of tunnel that is being created by the requesting client
Windows Groups	The names of the groups to which the user or computer account that is attempting the connection belongs

The Remote Access Profile

Now that you have looked at the conditions, you need to look at the restrictions that are configured through the remote access profile. When you click the Edit Profile button in the remote access policy dialog, you open the **Edit Dial-in Profile** dialog, as seen in Figure 10-14. The **Edit Dial-in Profile** dialog has six tabs that we are going to examine in this section.

The options in the **Dial-in Constraints** tab are outlined in Table 10-2, and are seen in Figure 10-14.

The second tab in the **Edit Dial-in Profile** is the **IP** tab, as shown in Figure 10-15. This tab allows you to configure two settings: IP address assignment and IP packet

FIGURE 10-14

The **Edit Dial-In Profile** dialog open to the **Dial-in Constraint** tab

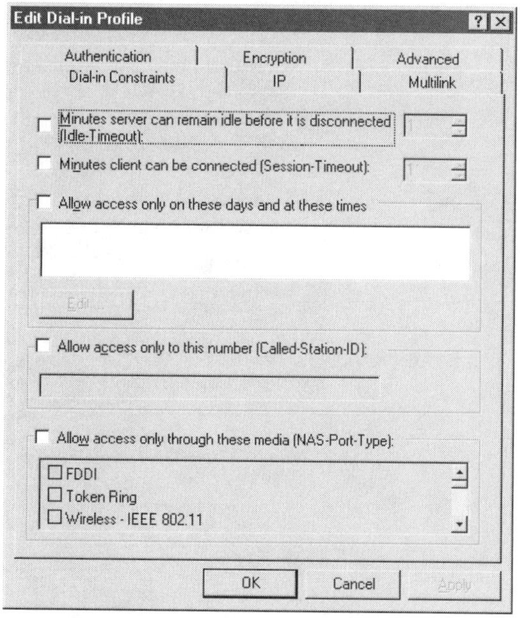

TABLE 10-2   Settings on the **Dial-in Constraint** Tab

Dial-in Constraint	Definition
Minutes server can remain idle before it is disconnected (Idle-Timeout)	The time that defines the number of minutes before an idle connection is closed.
Minutes client can be connected (Session-Timeout)	The maximum amount of time a client can stay connected in one session. Once the time has been reached, the session (connection) is closed.
Allow access only on these days and at these times	This setting has the same effect as the date and time condition, specifying the schedule that the connection is available for.
Allow access only to this number (Called-Station-ID)	Restricts what number the caller must be connecting from.
Allow access only through these media (NAS-Port-Type)	Allows you to limit the type of connection media that can be used to create the connection. For example to enable wireless access, you would enable the Wireless - IEEE 802.11 media, whereas others that can be used are ADSL, Ethernet, FDDI, X.25, and so on.

FIGURE 10-15

The **IP** tab

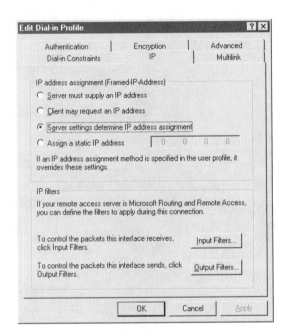

filters. The default IP address assignment policy is that the server determines the assignment; the other choices are

- **Server must supply an IP address**
- **Client may request an IP address**
- **Assign a static IP address**

The packet filter settings are definable both for incoming and for outgoing traffic, but are only effective during the remote connection that is governed by this remote access policy. When you configure an incoming (from client) packet filter, you will need to specify a destination network for the ports that are allowed. For more information on packet filtering see Chapter 11.

The **Multilink** tab, as seen in Figure 10-16, is used to configure both Multilink and Bandwidth Allocation Protocol (BAP) settings for the connection. Using Multilink enables users to use more than one device to connect to the remote access server, effectively adding the bandwidth together. Through the settings in the **Multilink** tab, you can control the maximum number of devices the client can use for the Multilink connection. BAP is used to make Multilink work more efficiently for those conditions where the incoming devices are in short supply. BAP monitors incoming Multilink connections, and drops underutilized connections based on the settings on the **Multilink** tab.

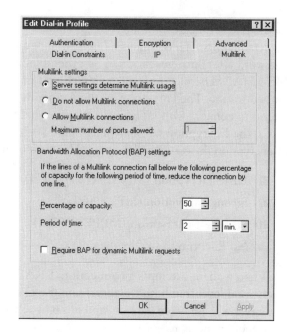

FIGURE 10-16

The **Multilink**
tab

The **Authentication** tab, seen in Figure 10-17 is where the Extensible Authentication Protocol (EAP) is configured. The EAP makes it possible to use such authentication

FIGURE 10-17

The
Authentication
tab

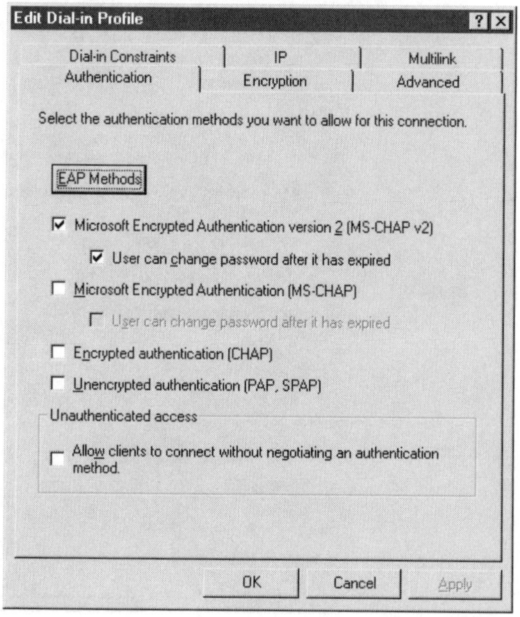

methods as certificates and smart cards. There is one authentication protocol enabled by default: MS-CHAP version 2, with the permission for the user to change the password after authentication. The other available authentication protocols are MS-CHAP version 1, encrypted CHAP, and unencrypted (clear text) PAP-SPAP authentication. The last option on the **Authentication** tab is whether or not to allow clients to connect without negotiating an authentication method.

On the **Encryption** tab, shown in Figure 10-18, you configure what strength of encryption the server will support. The choices are

- **Basic encryption (MPPE 40 bit)**
- **Strong encryption (MPPE 56 bit)**
- **Strongest encryption (MPPE 128 bit)**
- **No Encryption (off by default)**

When a client attempts a connection, RRAS tries to negotiate the strongest encryption level that both the server and the client can support. The default is that the server will use no encryption, and it is probably not a good idea to enable it except for troubleshooting reasons.

The **Advanced** tab, shown in Figure 10-19, is used to configure connection attributes. There are two default connection attributes that specify that the **Framed-Protocol** used for incoming connections must be PPP, and that the **Service-Type** must be Framed.

FIGURE 10-18

The **Encryption** tab

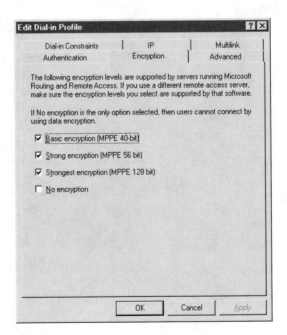

FIGURE 10-19

FIGURE 10-19

The **Advanced** tab

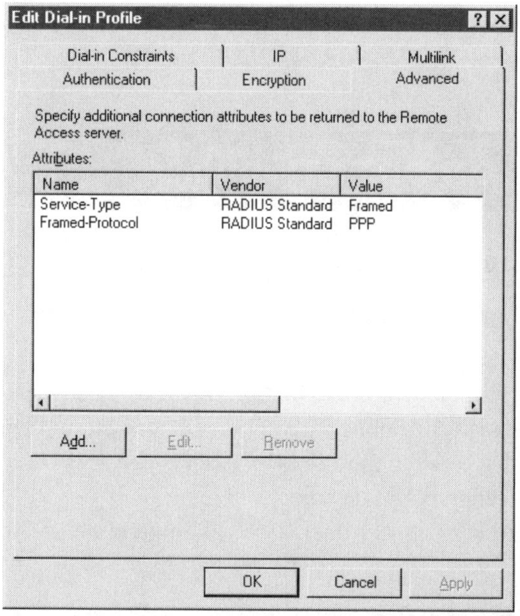

SCENARIO & SOLUTION

I have defined five remote access policies on one of my RRAS servers. When I install a second RRAS server, I do not see the new remote access policies. What went wrong with the installation?	Nothing went wrong with the installation; that is the behavior of remote access policies. The remote access policies are stored locally by the RRAS server and are not propagated. There are two possibilities for making the same policies active on multiple servers: if all RRAS servers use the same IAS server for authentication, you can manage the remote access policies from the IAS, or you can create a script of the RRAS configuration using the **netsh** command. This script can then be applied to additional RRAS servers using the **netsh** command.
The default remote access policy has been deleted from the RRAS server you are administering. What will you do?	The way to re-create the default policy is to create a new remote access policy with the following settings. Day-and-Time-Restriction—all days, all times. Deny remote access permission.
The domain I am administering is in Windows 2000 native functional level. I have just installed RRAS and I have created a new RRAS policy that is configured to deny access. The policy applies to all users. Some users, however, report that they can access the RRAS server and are allowed to connect. What could be causing this?	The most likely reason is that the users that can access the RRAS have their dial-in permission set to Grant access. This dial-in setting will override the remote access policy. In order to control the access through the remote access policy you need to set the users' dial-in permission to Control through the remote access policy.

There are many additional connection attributes that can be added based on vendor (3Com, Nortel, and so on) categories, as well as generic RADIUS attributes.

CERTIFICATION OBJECTIVE 10.04

Implement Secure Access Between Private Networks

One interesting configuration that uses VPNs is to connect offices with private networks through the public Internet, as you can see in Figure 10-20. In this architecture, the traffic between the offices travels through a VPN tunnel, and is terminated using a RRAS server on both sides. The configuration of the VPN can contain permanently connected Internet connections, as well as demand-dial connections.

Configuring a Secure Connection Between Two Private Networks

To configure the VPN between the private networks, you use the **Routing and Remote Access Setup Wizard** and select the **Secure connection between two private networks**, as in this illustration:

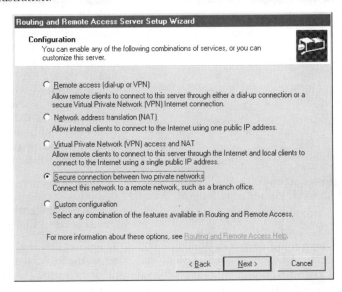

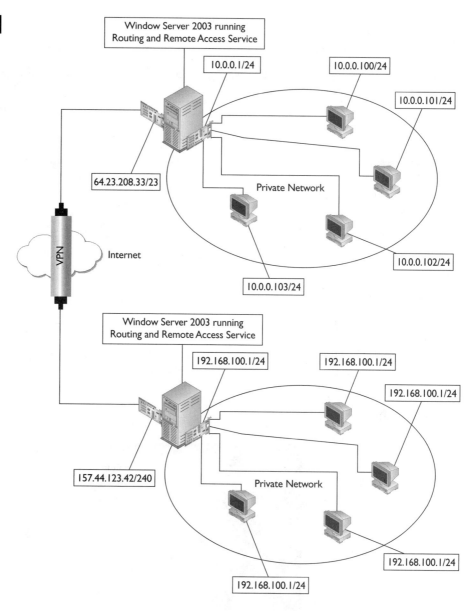

FIGURE 10-20

Secure
connection
between two
private networks

Under the **Demand Dial configuration,** you will determine whether or not to have a
permanent connection between the offices or connect (demand dial) when connections

are needed, or on a schedule. We will continue the permanent connection first, and will get back to the demand-dial configuration steps later in this section.

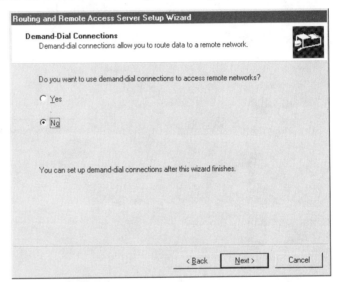

The last step is to review the configuration and click **Finish**. Note that there are two tasks mentioned on the summary page:

- Ensure that all interfaces have addresses.
- Install and set up routing protocols on each interface.

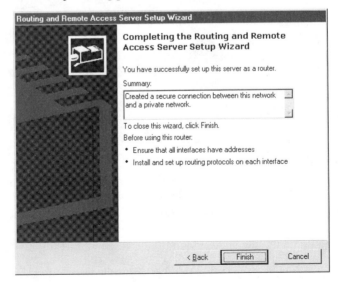

If you chose to use a demand-dial connection to the Internet, you will be presented with one more dialog where you need to determine the address scheme for the remote interface, as you can see in this illustration.

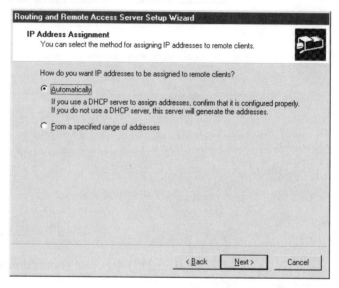

You have the selection of using DHCP or a manual range for the address assignment. In the summary page, you are informed that the Demand-Dial Interface Wizard will start after you have clicked on Finish.

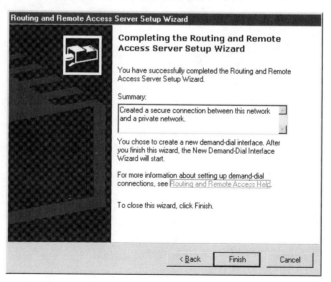

After the **Demand-Dial Interface Wizard** starts, you are asked to choose the name for the interface.

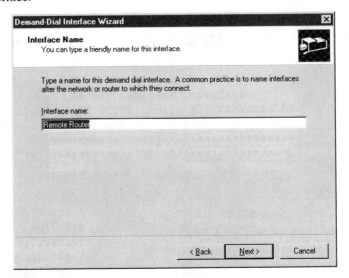

Then you will be prompted to select your connection method for the demand-dial interface. The choices are

■ Connect using a modem, ISDN adapter, or other physical device.

■ Connect using a virtual private network (VPN)

■ Connect using PPP over Ethernet (PPPoE)

Depending on your physical connection to your ISP, select the appropriate connection type.

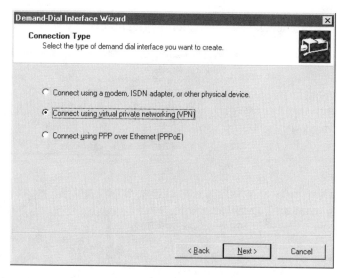

I selected to use a VPN for the demand-dial interface, so the next selection relates to the VPN configuration of a VPN protocol. The selections are

■ **Automatic**   Negotiate with the server to pick the most secure protocol that is available to both the server and the client.

■ **Point-to-Point-Tunneling-Protocol**   Demand the use of PPPTP.

■ **Layer 2 Tunneling Protocol**   Demand the use of L2TP

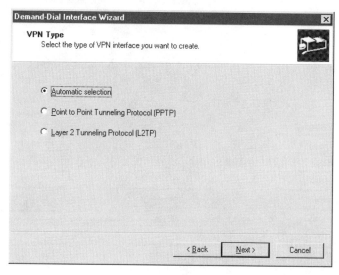

The next step is to identify the host that you are connecting to.

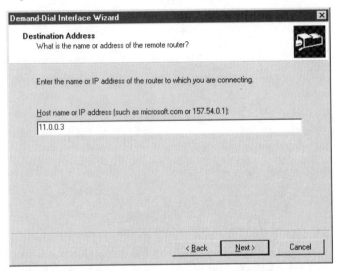

You want to leave the **Route IP Packets on this interface** setting enabled, and you also want to select the second option to add a user account that will be used by the remote router to connect back to you.

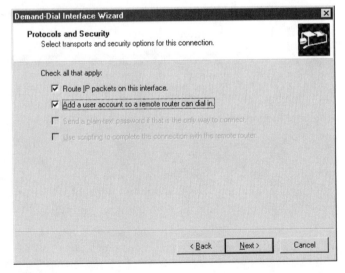

The static route sets the network addresses that are on the remote private network; you need to enter all network addresses that are present.

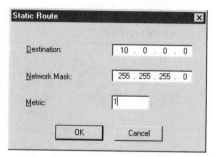

Once you have entered the static routes, they are listed in the following dialog.

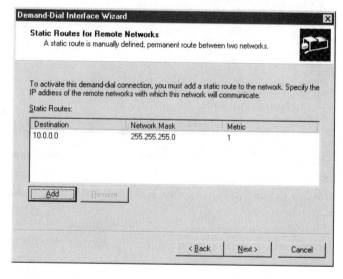

The dial-in credentials are configured to use the interface name of the router as the user name; you need to give that user name a strong password.

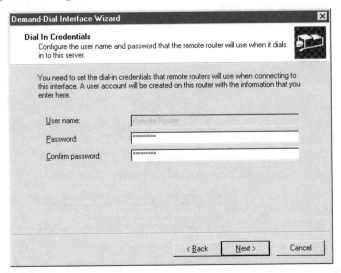

Then you will enter the credentials configured for the remote private network router.

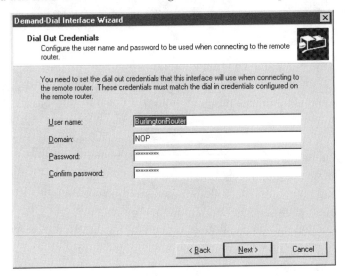

On the summary page, press **Finish** to complete the configuration of the demand-dial interface.

SCENARIO & SOLUTION

What is the static route for when I configure the router?	The static route is needed so that the router knows what networks can be reached through the tunnel. Without the static route, you would have to enable a routing protocol, which will add to the traffic and potentially lessen the security of the connection.
I have a small service office with five computers that need to connect through to out headquarters. The service office currently has an ADSL connection and a cable router installed for Internet sharing between the five computers. Can I use this environment to securely connect the service office to our Headquarters?	The answer is yes, with a modification. The cable router most likely does not have the capabilities needed to run the VPN protocols. What you would do is install a Windows Server 2003 with RRAS enabled to use PPPoE over the ADSL provider to connect to the Headquarters network. Unless you have an ISP that provides you a static IP for this type of connection, you will need to find and use the FQDN of the ADSL modem.

atch *Make sure there are known routes between the private networks, otherwise the connection will not work.*

As you can see, the information required here is very much the same information you would have supplied on a client to a VPN server, and that is exactly what you have set up. Once you have configured one side of the route, you need to perform the same tasks on the remote router to ensure that the two networks can exchange traffic through the private connection.

Now that you have a better idea of how to connect two private networks through the Internet, here are some possible scenario questions and their answers.

CERTIFICATION SUMMARY

This chapter has dealt with the aspects of the very important virtual private networks and how they are implemented, both as a means for mobile staff and business partners to access your internal network securely, and as a secure method of connecting private networks together using the public Internet.

You learned about the two tunneling protocols, PPTP and L2TP, and the different VPN connection protocols that can be configured, such as PPP, Microsoft RAS, and

ARAP. Remember that SLIP is only supported as an outgoing protocol, never as incoming to RRAS.

When you configured the VPN connection, you learned about the different methods of providing IP addresses to the remote clients: DHCP, or a static pool of addresses. Remember that if there is no DHCP server available when RRAS starts, it will configure APIPA from the 169.254.0.0/16 network, and that this network is not routable.

IAS was introduced as the Microsoft implementation of a RADIUS server; RADIUS is used to centralize the directory for remote access authentication. IAS can be used as a RADIUS server, or as a RADIUS proxy that makes it possible to use third-party RADIUS implementations to integrate multiple directory technologies for authentication.

You then learned about the remote access policy, with its three parts that combine to provide an atomic decision point as to whether the client will be allowed to connect to the RRAS server. The three parts are: conditions, permissions, and the profile. You learned that the dial-in permissions in Active Directory override the remote access policy unless the permission is set to be controlled by the policy. This permission is not available when the Windows Server 2003 domain is in Windows 2000 mixed functionality level, only in Windows 2000 native or Windows Server 2003 functionality level.

You learned about administration techniques for remote access policies by using the **netsh** command to copy RRAS configuration to a script and then apply that script to another RRAS server to effectively copy the configuration. A second technique was introduced that makes use of the IAS to centralize the management of the remote access policies.

TWO-MINUTE DRILL

Configure Remote Access Authentication Protocols

❑ Every remote access connection has two sides: the server side and the client side.

❑ Windows Server 2003 clients support PPP, Microsoft RAS, and SLIP as remote access protocols.

❑ Windows Server 2003 with RRAS installed as a remote access server supports PPP, Microsoft RAS, and ARAP for incoming connections.

❑ Windows Server 2003 supports two types of VPNs: L2TP and PPTP.

❑ L2TP is more secure than PPTP because it uses IPSec for the transport, resulting in authenticated endpoints of the connection as well as for encryption.

❑ IPSec requires certificates for RAS servers as well as for the client; L2TP is wrapped in the IPSec extended IP Packet.

❑ PPTP is more common because it is supported on more platforms.

❑ RRAS is installed by default under Windows Server 2003.

❑ RRAS must be configured and enabled before it can be used.

❑ RRAS can use a DHCP server to manage client IP addresses, or a static pool of addresses configured in the RRAS.

❑ If a DHCP server is not found when RRAS starts and addressing is set to automatic, RRAS will give the clients addresses from the APIPA network 169.254.0.0/16.

❑ If the DHCP server is not on the same network as the RRAS server, you need to configure the DHCP Relay Agent in RRAS.

❑ The DHCP Relay Agent is required to retrieve scope options for RRAS clients.

❑ RRAS grabs blocks of ten IP addresses at a time from the DHCP server. RRAS then manages these IP addresses as needed by its clients.

❑ All IP addresses obtained by RRAS from a DHCP server are released when the RRAS server shuts down.

Configure Internet Authentication Service (IAS) to Provide Authentication for Routing and Remote Access Clients

❑ RADIUS is used to allow centralized authentication of users that are connecting through different media, such as wireless, dial-up, and VPN.

❑ Microsoft has implemented RADIUS under the name IAS.

❑ IAS can be used as a RADIUS server.

❑ IAS can be used as a RADIUS proxy.

❑ Windows Server 2003 Standard Edition supports a maximum of 50 RADIUS clients and two RADIUS remote groups.

❑ Windows Server 2003 Enterprise Edition and Windows Server 2003 Datacenter Edition supports unlimited RADIUS clients and remote groups.

❑ IAS is installed through **Add/Remove Programs** in the Control Panel.

❑ IAS needs to be registered in Active Directory to enable the use of the Active Directory.

❑ IAS can be registered in Active Directory through the **Internet Authentication Service** console or through the netsh command-line utility.

❑ RADIUS clients are registered in IAS using the FQDN or IP address of the remote access server and a shared secret that is used for mutual authentication.

Configure Routing and Remote Access Policies to Permit or Deny Access

❑ Configure routing and remote access policies to permit or deny access

❑ Remote access policies consist of three parts: condition, permission, and profile.

❑ The default remote access policy is created when RRAS is configured and enabled.

❑ There must always be one remote access policy defined.

❑ Remote access policies are stored on the individual RRAS servers; there is no replication.

❑ Use **netsh** to copy the configuration from one RRAS server to another.

❑ Use IAS to centralize the administration of remote access policies.

❑ To be able to have the remote access policy determine whether to grant or deny the connection, the domain cannot be at the Windows 2000 mixed functionality level. The users' dial-in permissions must also be set to **Control Access Through Remote Access Policy**.

Implement Secure Access Between Private Networks

❑ RRAS can be configured to use a secure channel between two private networks.

❑ The VPN can be permanently connected or demand-dial.

❑ The connection to the public Internet can use permanent connections or modems.

SELF TEST

Configure Remote Access Authentication Protocols

1. You are the network administrator of your company's Windows Server 2003 network. You have just installed a Windows Server 2003 Standard Edition on the local network of your office, and then added an ADSL modem to the server and connected to your ISP for Internet connectivity. You want to let the rest of the users in your office use this connection to access the Internet. What do you need to do to enable this functionality? (Choose all that apply.)

    A. All of the users on the LAN must log on with your user name and password.

    B. All of the computers on the LAN must be on the same network, such as 10.1.1.0/24.

    C. All of the computers on the LAN must be on the same network, such as 169.254.0.0/160

    D. You must enable ICS and demand-dialing for the connection.

2. You are the network administrator of your company's Windows Server 2003 network. You have configured and enabled RRAS on a Windows Server 2003 on your network. The RRAS server is configured to automatically assign IP addresses from an internal DHCP server. You have configured the DHCP server to have a scope with 100 IP addresses to be used for your remote VPN users. All the 200 remote VPN users are from the Field Sales Department, and they will not be connected to the VPN at the same time. What feature will help you manage this situation to ensure the Field Sales users will always get a routable address when they connect?

    A. Configure the lease time on the DHCP scope to be 1 hour.

    B. Configure the lease time on the DHCP scope to be 72 hours.

    C. Let RRAS manage the IP address pool, which is the default.

    D. Configure RRAS to use a static pool of IP addresses that will be used when the 100 IP addresses in the DHCP scope are used up.

3. You are the network administrator of your company's Windows Server 2003 network. After configuring a dial-up connection to a UNIX server that supports an older version of PPP, you have been unable to connect using this connection. Which of these solution is most likely to resolve the problem?

    A. Configure the dial-up connection to use SLIP instead of PPP.

    B. Change the PPP settings for the connection by clearing the LCP option.

    C. Update the default router for the UNIX system to support BOOTP.

    D. Change the PPP settings for the connection by enabling the BOOTP protocol.

4. You are the network administrator of your company's Windows Server 2003 network. Your network consists of 279 Windows XP Professional notebook computers that all have wireless IEEE 802.11b built-in adapters. These notebook computers have been issued to the Field Service group, and are used both in the office as well as at customer sites where the Field Service representatives need to be able to access the company network in a secure manner. You have

investigated the customer network setup and have discovered that they have wireless coverage of all sites your Field Service staff will be working at. Your manager has asked you to investigate whether there is a feasible secure solution to this business problem. What will you tell your manager?

A. The solution is to configure a VPN between the customer's network and your network; then the Field Service staff can securely connect.

B. The solution is to configure a RRAS server as a VPN server and instruct all Field Service staff to connect to this VPN server.

C. There is no secure solution to this business problem.

D. The solution is to ask the customer to install RRAS to act as the VPN server for the Field Service staff..

5. You are the network administrator of your company's Windows Server 2003 network. You have installed RRAS on one of the Windows Server 2003 computers to provide secure VPN connections to your mobile sales force. You want RRAS to use a static pool of IP addresses for the clients, and you want to use the 10.10.1.0/24 network. However, addresses 10.10.1.1, 10.10.1.42, 10.10.1.129, and 10.10.1.254 must be excluded from the pool. Which steps will you take to accomplish this task? (Choose all that apply)

A. Add the IP address range 10.10.1.1 to 10.10.1.254.

B. Add the IP address range 10.10.1.2 to 10.10.1.253.

C. Add the IP address range 10.10.1.2 to 10.10.1.41.

D. Add the IP address range 10.10.1.130 to 10.10.1.253.

E. Add the IP address range 10.10.1.43 to 10.10.1.253.

F. Add the IP address range 10.10.1.130 to 10.10.1.254.

G. Add the IP address range 10.10.1.43 to 10.10.1.128

6. You are the network administrator of your company's Windows Server 2003 network. You have configured a Windows Server 2003 with an ADSL model to connect to your ISP. After you configured the connection, you successfully connected to the Internet through this connection. You also configured the connection to be shared on your LAN by enabling Internet Connection Sharing (ICS). Users report that they can access the Internet whenever you are logged in to the server, but if you are not logged in, the connection to the Internet fails. What is the problem and how can you resolve this issue with the least administrative effort? (Choose all that apply.)

A. Change the option for the connection to be available for all users.

B. Install RRAS and configure it to route the Internet traffic.

C. Change the authentication information for the connection by enabling the **Use this account name and password when anyone connects to the Internet from this computer** option.

D. Turn on the Internet Connection Firewall on the connection.

7. You are the network administrator of your company's Windows Server 2003 network. You have configured and enabled RRAS on a Windows Server 2003 on your network to provide VPN connections to mobile sales staff of your company. After you enable RRAS and configure a test client, you find that the connections are using PPTP, not L2TP, which is the written standard for all VPN connections in your company. You need to resolve the problem by enabling the use of L2TP. What steps will you perform to resolve the problem? (Choose all that apply.)

A. Obtain a computer certificate for the RRAS server and a computer certificate for the client computer from a CA.

B. Obtain a computer certificate for the RRAS server and a user certificate for the client computer from a CA

C. Install a computer certificate on the client computer.

D. Install a user certificate on the client computer.

E. Install a computer certificate on the RRAS server.

8. You are the network administrator of your company's Windows Server 2003 network. You are configuring your Windows XP Professional computer at home to connect to the RRAS server (NEPTUNE) at your office, which is the VPN server you installed earlier today. You tested the server while in the office and it functioned properly. Now you are going through the same steps on your home computer; you have configured the connection to connect to NEPTUNE. When you try to connect, you receive an error message that the server cannot be found. You then ping NEPTUNE and receive messages that the computer cannot be found. When you ping 157.33.45.21, the address of NEPTUNE, you get success responses. What is the most likely solution that will make it possible for you to connect to the office through the VPN? (Choose all that apply.)

A. Use the Distinguished Name of NEPTUNE rather than the NetBIOS name.

B. Use the IP address of NEPTUNE rather then the NetBIOS name.

C. Use the FQDN of NEPTUNE rather than the NetBIOS name.

D. Change NEPTUNE to \\NEPTUNE to use the NetBIOS name.

9. You are the network administrator of your company's Windows Server 2003 network. After configuring your Windows Server 2003 computer to connect to your ISP using all the default settings, and then sharing this connection with the ten users in your office, you find that there is a lot of activity on the Windows Server 2003 computer whenever it is connected to the Internet. What is the problem and how do we resolve the issue? (Choose all that apply.)

A. This is normal keep-alive traffic from the ISP.

B. Turn off File and Print Sharing on the connection; you are advertising your server to the ISP.

C. Reboot the server.

D. Turn on Internet Connection Firewall to block off all the ports.

10. You are the network administrator of your company's Windows Server 2003 network. Your manager has asked that you enumerate the tunneling protocols supported by RRAS. What are those tunneling protocols? (Choose all that apply.)

   A. PPTP

   B. PPPTP

   C. L2TP

   D. MS-CHAP Version 2

Configure Internet Authentication Service (IAS) to Provide Authentication for Routing and Remote Access Clients

11. You are the network administrator of your company's Windows Server 2003 network and need to explain what IAS is. What is IAS?

   A. The International Addressing Standard, used to specify IP addresses.

   B. A service that is used to access RRAS servers securely.

   C. A service that runs on a UNIX server to provide authentication in a mixed network.

   D. A service that implements the IETF standard for RADIUS and RADIUS proxy.

12. You are the network administrator of your company's Windows Server 2003 network. Where is IAS installed from?.

   A. From the Microsoft Windows Server 2003 web site

   B. From the IAS folder on the Windows Server 2003 CD

   C. From the Windows Server 2003 CD through Add/Remove Programs

   D. From the Routing and Remote Access Service CD using the RRAS installer

Configure Routing and Remote Access Policies to Permit or Deny Access

13. You are the network administrator of your company's Windows Server 2003 network. You have just configured and enabled RRAS on a Windows Server 2003 Enterprise Edition domain controller on your network. You start **Active Directory Users and Computers** and open the properties for your own user account, and then open the **Dial-in** tab. You notice that the choice to have the remote access policy control access is grayed out. You need to be able to make the selection to have the remote access policy control access to the RAS server. What step must you take to enable the **Control access through Remote Access Policy**? (Choose all that apply.)

   A. Log in using an account in the RRAS Admin Universal Group.

   B. Update the schema of the forest to enable the **Control access through Remote Access Policy** option.

C. Increase the domain's functional level to native.

D. There is no remote access policy created yet; you must create one.

14. You are the network administrator of your company's Windows Server 2003 network. You are configuring the remote access policies to control connections that are originating on Ethernet segments that are connected to the Internet through a router as well as clients that are using wireless connectivity through an auditorium. The policy for the auditorium must be very restrictive because it is a public area. Most clients that connect through the network also use the auditorium. How can you configure this environment?

A. Create multiple remote access policies tied to the individual users.

B. Set different profiles for the different remote access policies.

C. Create multiple remote access policies that are tied to security groups.

Implement Secure Access Between Private Networks

15. You are the network administrator of your company's Windows Server 2003 network. You are configuring a secure connection between two of your company's offices, Mimico and Whitby. The Mimico office is connected through a permanent high-speed DSL connection to the Internet with a fixed IP address of 69.12.42.42 (NEPTUNE.masiw.com), and the Whitby office is connected through a dynamic cable modem that changes its IP address every three hours (CD345612.wht.east.networkRus.to). The RRAS server in Whitby is called SERVER1, and the one in Mimico is called SERVER2. How will you configure the connection between the two offices? (Choose all that apply.)

A. Configure SERVER1 to connect to CD345612.wht.east.networkRus.to.

B. Configure SERVER2 to connect to CD345612.wht.east.networkRus.to.

C. Configure SERVER1 to connect to NEPTUNE.masiw.com.

D. Configure SERVER2 to connect to NEPTUNE.masiw.com.

E. Configure SERVER1 to use demand-dial.

F. Configure SERVER2 to use demand-dial.

G. Configure SERVER1 to use a permanent connection.

H. Configure SERVER2 to use a permanent connection.

LAB QUESTION

You are the network administrator for a company that sells fasteners to the trades as well as the public. Last week, your company merged with another fastening company. Your management has decided that to streamline the ordering of products and sharing of resources between the two companies, you will connect the two networks with a VPN and route traffic between them. You have been given the task of configuring the network so that the published goal of full connectivity with the maximum security is meet. The following illustration shows the architecture of the networks. Your task is to write the proper role against each computer and assign the correct IP addressing to make the architecture work.

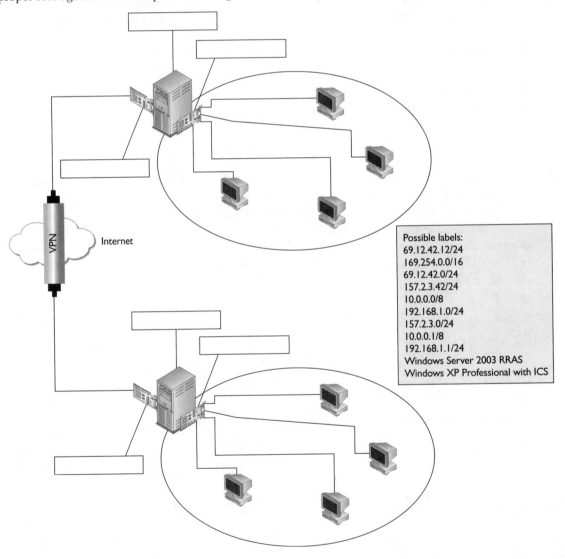

Possible labels:
69.12.42.12/24
169.254.0.0/16
69.12.42.0/24
157.2.3.42/24
10.0.0.0/8
192.168.1.0/24
157.2.3.0/24
10.0.0.1/8
192.168.1.1/24
Windows Server 2003 RRAS
Windows XP Professional with ICS

SELF TEST ANSWERS

Configure Remote Access Authentication Protocols

1. ☑ **B, and D.** The local network must use a common routable network, and ICS must be enabled. You also need to enable demand-dialing for the router.
   ☒ **A** is incorrect because that would only lower the security, but not make the connection available remotely. **C** is incorrect because 169.254.0.0/16 is not routable.

2. ☑ **C.** RRAS obtains blocks of ten IP addresses at a time from the DHCP server, and then these address are managed by RRAS.
   ☒ **A, B, and D** are incorrect because the IP addresses are managed by RRAS.

3. ☑ **B.** Older versions of PPP will have problems with the LCP extensions. By disabling them, you ensure backward compatibility.
   ☒ **A** is incorrect because SLIP is not a choice when disabling LCP extensions will work. **C and D** are incorrect because BOOTP has no impact on PPP.

4. ☑ **B.** The customers' network does not have to change to let your Field Service staff connect to the VPN server.
   ☒ **A** is incorrect because this type of network-to-network configuration would also enable the customer to gain access to the internal network, which is not secure. **C** is incorrect because there is definitely a secure solution in B. **D** is incorrect because it is not the customer network that needs to be available, and this solution would be the wrong way around.

5. ☑ **C, D, and G.** You need to enable three ranges of addresses to cover the requirements, 10.10.1.2–10.10.1.41, 10.10.1.43–10.10.1.128, and 10.10.1.130–10.10.1.253.
   ☒ **A** is incorrect because that is the whole network including the excluded addresses. **B** is incorrect because that is the address range including 10.10.1.129, which should be excluded. **E** is incorrect because that range also includes the 10.10.1.129 address, which should be excluded. **F** is incorrect because that range includes the excluded 10.10.1.254 address.

6. ☑ **A and C.** Making the connection available to all users and setting the authentication to use the same name for all connections will make the connection available to the users on the network.
   ☒ **B** is incorrect because that is not the least administrative effort, even though it would work. **D** is incorrect because the use of ICF has no effect on the sharing of the connection.

7. ☑ **A, C, and D.** There must be computer certificates installed with the server and the client computers.
   ☒ **B and D** are incorrect because the certificates must be for the computer, not the user.

8. ☑ **B and C.** The NetBIOS name cannot be resolved over the Internet, so you must use the FQDN or the IP address of the server.
   ☒ **A** is incorrect because the DN is an Active Directory term and not applicable. **D** is incorrect because using a UNC will not make the NetBIOS name resolution work any better.

9. ☑ **B** and **D**. The problem here is that the default is to leave File and Printer sharing on, even though it probably will not be needed. The default is to not enable ICF, so turning ICF on will further drop the traffic.

   ☒ **A** is incorrect because there is no keep-alive traffic. **C** is incorrect because rebooting is not always the solution to baffling problems.

10. ☑ **A** and **C**. RRAS supports PPTP and L2TP tunneling protocols only.

    ☒ **B** is incorrect because this protocol is just my mistyping, and **D** is incorrect because this protocol is not a tunneling protocol; it is used for authentication.

Configure Internet Authentication Service (IAS) to Provide Authentication for Routing and Remote Access Clients

11. ☑ **D**. IAS is the Microsoft implementation of the standard RADIUS server, which can be installed either as a RADIUS server or as a RADIUS proxy.

    ☒ **A**, **B**, and **C** are incorrect because these answers are just figments of my imagination.

12. ☑ **C**. IAS is installed using the Add/Remove Programs application from the Windows Server 2003 CD.

    ☒ **A** is incorrect because IAS is not available from the web site. **B** is incorrect because there is no IAS folder on the Windows Server 2003 CD, and **D** is incorrect because an IAS is installed through Add/Remove Programs.

Configure Routing and Remote Access Policies to Permit or Deny Access

13. ☑ **C**. The **Control access through Remote Access Policy** is only available in Windows 2000 native functional level or Windows Server 2003 functional level.

    ☒ **A** is incorrect because there is no such group, **B** is incorrect because a schema update will not enable the use of this attribute, and **D** is incorrect because there must always be at least one remote access policy.

14. ☑ **B**. By creating different remote access policies with different profiles restricted by the media type, you will be able to manage this requirement.

    ☒ **A** and **B** are incorrect because the users need access using both media types.

Implement Secure Access Between Private Networks

15. ☑ **A**, **D**, and **F**. Use the FQDN and configure Whitby (SERVER2) to demand-dial. This allows you to work with the dynamic connection in the Whitby office.

    ☒ **B**, **C**, **E**, **G**, and **H** are incorrect because using these settings the servers would connect to themselves and the Whitby office would have connectivity problems.

LAB ANSWER

The following illustration shows the solution to the lab question.

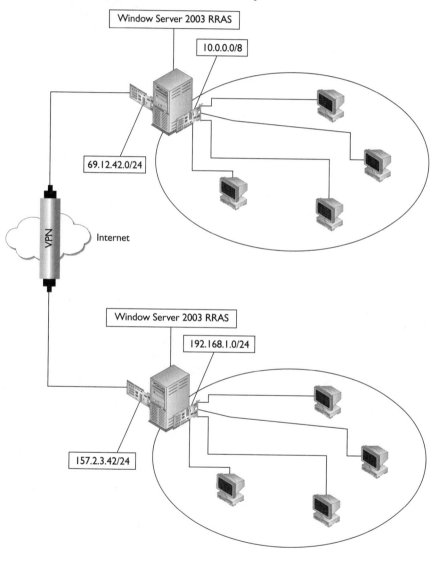

11

Manage Routing and Remote Access

CERTIFICATION OBJECTIVES

Once you have configured and enabled Routing and Remote Access Service, you still need to address a number of additional issues to make sure RRAS is operating in the fashion it was designed to. In this chapter, you will meet with such varied items as port filters and routing protocols. In the end you will have worked with and seen the configuration and management of a routed environment. The topics in this chapter cover the management of packet filters, RRAS routing, devices and ports, routing protocols, routing tables, routing ports, and RRAS clients routing.

CERTIFICATION OBJECTIVE 11.01

Manage Remote Access

Managing the Routing and Remote Access Service (RRAS) is one of the major parts of a Network Administrator. Although connecting remote clients to a RRAS server is not a tricky business, connecting through the RRAS server to other LANs can be a bigger task. This is where you need to manage routing between the remote client and the LAN. Routing in RRAS includes the routing interfaces, devices, ports, and protocols. In this section you will be introduced to all of them so you will be ready for the RRAS routing questions in the 70-291 exam. Before you get into the RRAS routing issues, you need to understand the topic of port filtering, so that's where you'll start.

Managing Packet Filters

Packet filters are esoteric items that are designed to keep your brain spinning as you try to remember the different ports and what they are used for. Rest assured, this is one of those areas of networking where everyone starts with a slightly bewildered and confused face. In this section we will take you through what ports are and what they are used for, as well as the most important ones to remember for the exam. After the theory about the ports, you will learn how to define packet filters that will help you manage the traffic of your VPN servers as well as basic routing management. Before you get in too deep, you need to learn what a port is and how it relates to a packet.

TCP/IP Ports

The TCP/IP port is defined as an end-point of a communications link. This means the port acts as the address within a computer that is defined to receive the traffic for a specific program. You could compare a computer that has a TCP/IP address (say 192.168.1.200) with an office building that also has an address (say 42 George St. Mimico, ON, M8V 3Q2). This office building has thirteen floors with a total of 1,500 workers. This comparison is valid because both objects (computer and office building) can be uniquely defined by the address. Imagine that Bob the delivery man is entering the office building to deliver a packet addressed to John Smith, 42 George St., Mimico, ON, M8V 3Q2. Here is the process Bob follows:

- Start on the thirteenth floor.
- Ask every person if he is John Smith.
- Continue until all persons on the floor have been asked, or John Smith has been found.
- Go to the floor below.
- Continue until John Smith is found.

As you will realize, this process will successfully keep Bob employed in going through every floor of the building socializing with the staff while searching for the recipient. The computer equivalent process for this process is that all communication is sent to the address of the computer, and the computer will have to open every packet that arrives to find what process is to receive the communication. This will result in a very inefficiently operating computer.

The solution in both cases is to add one piece of information to the address. In the case of the office building, you can add a cubicle number, for example, John Smith, Cubicle 12-42, 42 George St., Mimico, ON, M8V 3Q2. This way Bob can go directly to the twelfth floor and locate cubicle 42 to deliver the packet. In the case of the computer, a 16-bit number is added to the address that indicates the recipient program you want to communicate with, for example, 192.168.1.200:25. Adding the number 25 at the end of the address is saying "connect to the computer 192.168.1.200 on port 25."

There are a total of 65,535 ports available for each of the two TCP/IP transfer protocols: UDP and TCP. These port numbers are separated into three distinct groups: well-known ports, registered ports, and dynamic (private) ports. These groups are managed by the Internet Assigned Numbers Authority (IANA) and depending on the grouping certain rules apply. The ports are governed by a Request For Comment RFC1700. To learn more about the ports and their rules you can find the current version of the RFC at **ftp://ftp.isi.edu/in-notes/rfc1700.txt**. The various groups are listed here:

- **Well-known ports**   Ports between 1 and 1024. These ports are assigned by IANA.
- **Registered ports**   Ports between 1024 and 49151. These ports are listed by IANA.

■ **Dynamic (private) ports**   Ports between 49152 and 65535. IANA does not manage these ports.

The well-known ports are used by specific services that are common between computer systems, and these ports can usually only be used by system processes (services) that are running under System or Administrator privileges. Some of the well-known ports are used for system connections that are connected for long periods; others are used as contact ports for unknown partners that need a known point to start the communication and continue on a dynamic port for the rest of the session.

The registered ports are maintained in a list by IANA. These ports are usable by most users. These ports are registered by vendors to ensure that collisions don't occur between applications. The dynamic or private ports are free for use, but there are possible collisions when two or more applications try to use the same port.

To learn more about the ports and their usage you might want to read up on the assignments on the IANA web site at **http://www.iana.org/assignments/port-numbers**. Microsoft lists the usage of ports in the Windows family of products in the Knowledge Base article 150543. Table 11-1 provides a summary of the most common ports.

on the job   *To quickly find a Q article from the Microsoft Knowledgebase you need to type the article number (150543 in this case) into the address box of your browser and press ENTER. The default behavior of Internet Explorer is to open a search page listing the location of the article as the first entry.*

Make sure you know the ports used for SMTP, POP3, and Telnet.

The key to packet filtering is to allow only the type of traffic that the server should respond to and ignore any other. This is one of the basic tenets of network security: permit only needed traffic on the network. RRAS in Windows Server 2003 works together with the TCP/IP protocols that are included with the operating system to control the permitted traffic, as well as customizing the port that is used for VPN connections.

Port Filtering

The default setting for the TCP/IP protocols in Windows Server 2003 is to allow all ports for both TCP and UDP. If the server is designed to work only as a web server on ports 80 (HTTP) and 443 (HTTPS), you would limit the network interface to allow only those two ports. As mentioned in Table 11-1, these are TCP ports, and there are no UDP ports needed for these two protocols.

TABLE 11-1	Function	TCP Port	UDP Port
Port Usage	Browsing		137, 138
	DHCP Lease		67, 68
	DHCP Manager	135	
	Directory Replication	139	138
	DNS Administration	135	
	DNS Resolution		53
	Echo	7	7
	Event Viewer	139	
	File Sharing	139	
	FTP	21	21
	HTTP	80	
	HTTPS	443	
	IMAP	135	
	IMAP (SSL)	993	
	Kerberos	88	88
	LDAP (AD)	389	
	LDAP (SSL)	636	
	LDAP Global Catalog	3268	
	NetBIOS	139	137, 138
	NNTP	119	
	NNTP (SSL)	563	
	Performance Monitor	139	
	POP3	110	
	POP3 (SSL)	995	
	PPTP	1723 IP protocol: 47 (GRE)	
	SMTP	25	
	Telnet	23	23

The basic port filtering takes place within the network properties of the interface. You open these properties from the Network Connections application in the Control Panel, as shown in Figure 11-1.

Double-click the connection that you want to configure (Local Area Connection). The status for the connection is displayed. Click **Properties** to display the **Local Area Connection Properties,** as in Figure 11-2.

To configure port filters, select **Internet Protocol (TCP/IP)** in the dialog box and click **Properties** to open the **Internet Protocol (TCP/IP) Properties,** as shown in Figure 11-3.

Click the **Advanced** button to open the **Advanced TCP/IP Settings** dialog. Port filtering is located on the **Options** tab, as shown in Figure 11-4.

The default settings are that all protocols are permitted; that is, all ports and IP protocols are set to **Permit All.** Changing any of these settings will effectively control what ports are allowed on all adapters installed in the server.

In the following exercise, you will configure the port filter on your server.

The port filters are used to list only the allowed ports.

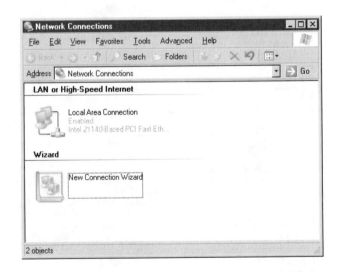

FIGURE 11-1

Network
Connections
application

FIGURE 11-2

Local Area
Connection
Properties

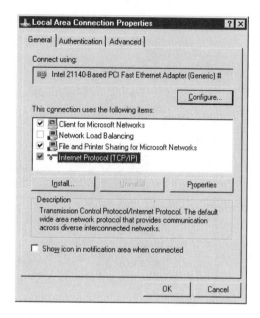

FIGURE 11-3

The TCP/IP
Properties

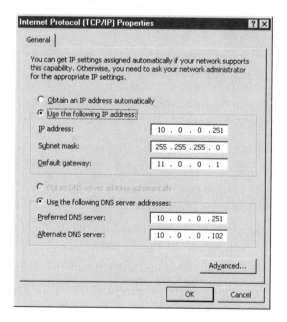

FIGURE 11-4

FIGURE 11-4

The Options tab

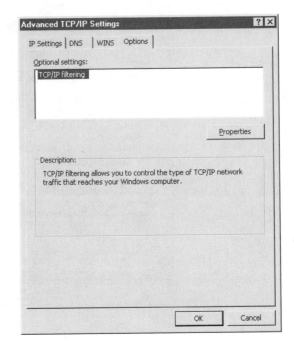

CertCam 11-1 ON THE CD

EXERCISE 11-1

Configuring Port Filters

In this exercise you will configure the port filter of a Windows Server 2003 to permit only port 80 (HTTP). You will test this setting in a following exercise.

1. Open the properties for your network connection by clicking **Start | Control Panel | Network Connections | Local Area Connection**.

2. Click **Internet Protocol (TCP/IP)** in the **Local Area Connection Properties** dialog. Click **Properties**.

3. Click **Advanced** in the **Internet Protocol (TCP/IP) Properties** dialog to open the Advanced TCP/IP Settings.

4. Click the **Options** tab to display the TCP/IP options for the connection.

5. Click **TCP/IP filtering** and then click **Properties** to display the following illustration:

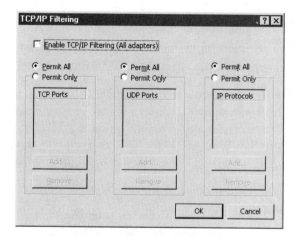

6. To block access to all ports except 80, click **Permit Only** for the TCP, UDP and IP Protocol settings. Click **Add** under the TCP settings, enter **80** as the port number, and click **OK**. The resulting settings should be like this:

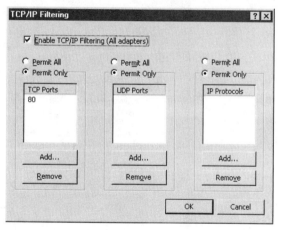

7. Click **OK** four times, and click **Yes** when prompted to reboot.

The result of this port filter setting is that the server now only responds to HTTP requests, you will test this in the next exercise.

EXERCISE 11-2

Observing Port Filtering in Action

For this exercise we assume there are two computers connected on the same network. The first computer is running Windows Server 2003 and has IIS, FTP, and SMTP installed. The second computer is running Windows XP Professional and will act as the client. The Windows Server 2003 has a port filter that only permits port 80, as configured in Exercise 11-1.

1. Log on to the client computer.

2. Open Internet Explorer, enter the address of the Windows Server 2003 in the address bar, and press ENTER. The result should look like the following illustration.

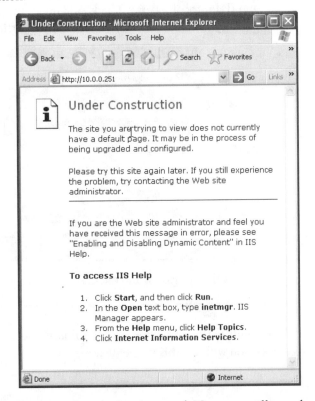

The HTTP protocol worked as expected. Next you will test the FTP protocol.

3. Open a command prompt on the client computer and enter the following command:

```
ftp 10.0.0.251
```

The result should be

```
C:\>ftp 10.0.0.251
> ftp: connect :Unknown error number
ftp> quit
C:\>
```

The FTP port is blocked. Exit from the ftp tool using the **quit** command.

4. Use the **ping** command to test the communication to the server.

```
C:>ping 10.0.0.251
```

The result may surprise you. The **ping** command works and returns the following:

```
C:\>ping 10.0.0.251
Pinging 10.0.0.251 with 32 bytes of data:

Reply from 10.0.0.251: bytes=32 time=1ms TTL=128
Reply from 10.0.0.251: bytes=32 time=3ms TTL=128
Reply from 10.0.0.251: bytes=32 time=1ms TTL=128
Reply from 10.0.0.251: bytes=32 time=7ms TTL=128

Ping statistics for 10.0.0.251:
    Packets: Sent = 4, Received = 4, Lost = 0 (0% loss),
Approximate round trip times in milli-seconds:
    Minimum = 1ms, Maximum = 7ms, Average = 3ms
```

5. You have now tested the port filter.

The reason the **ping** command worked even though port 7 had not been allowed is that the port filter implemented does not filter out Internet Management Control Protocol (ICMP) traffic.

Configuring PPTP and L2TP Filtering

You can configure VPN connections using two possible architectures: the VPN server can be connected directly to the Internet, in front of the firewall, or you can connect the VPN server behind the firewall, either on the local network or in the DMZ. The two possible architectures are seen in Figure 11-5.

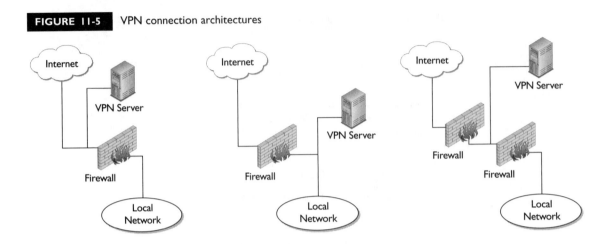

FIGURE 11-5 VPN connection architectures

The first choice, where the VPN server is directly exposed to the Internet, is the least secure because the VPN server has no additional protection from attack. The second architecture offers additional security protection for the VPN server, and so this architecture is the most popular. The issue is that the VPN traffic must be allowed through the firewall, and the protocols and ports differ between PPTP and L2TP.

For PPTP traffic you have to allow IP protocol 47, the Genetic Routing Encapsulation (GRE); and TCP port 1723, which is used for the tunnel creation, maintenance, and termination. For a discussion of TCP/IP, see Chapter 1.

For L2TP traffic, you need to enable IPSec traffic to pass through the firewall. The two important parts of IPSec are the Encapsulated Security Protocol (ESP), which uses IP protocol 50, and the Authentication Header (AH), which uses IP protocol 51, so you need to enable both those protocols. You also need to enable UDP port 500 for security negotiation.

on the
ⓘob

ESP encrypts the data traffic between two computers, AH does not encrypt the data. AH is used to ensure the data is not modified during transport.

When you know the parties that are going to communicate over a VPN, you can further tighten the security by specifying that only those computers using either PPTP or L2TP are permitted to communicate. The configuration is particularly useful when you are connecting two servers via a VPN where you know the IP address of each server.

In addition to the packet filtering provided by the firewall, the VPN server has additional port filtering. You use the RRAS snap-in to specify incoming and outgoing packet filters. Exercise 11-3 teaches you how to configure VPN server packet filters.

EXERCISE 11-3

Configuring PPTP and L2TP Packet Filters

In this exercise, assume that you have two local networks in Montego Bay and Ocho Rios. You will configure the RRAS servers by adding an additional layer of security through packet filters. The network is shown in the following illustration.

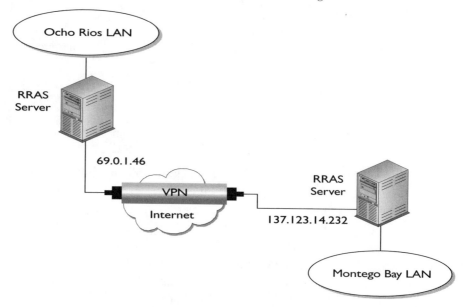

1. Start with the RRAS server in Montego Bay. Open the RRAS snap-in, by clicking **Start | Administrative Tools**, and selecting **Routing and Remote Access**.

2. In the RRAS snap-in, expand the RRAS server and the IP Routing folder.
   Click **General**, right-click the external interface, and click **Properties**. This
   will open the external network adapter's Properties dialog box, shown here:

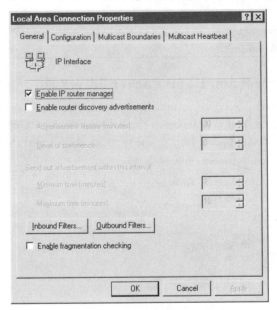

3. To define input filters, click the **Inbound Filters** button, and then click **New**
   to open the **Add IP Filter** dialog and define the filter.

4. Start by defining the PPTP filter. Select the **Destination Network** check
   box, and enter the IP address of the external NIC of the local VPN server
   (you are in Montego Bay, so that is **137.123.14.232**). Then enter a subnet
   mask of **255.255.255.255**. In the **Protocol** drop-down box, select **TCP** with
   a Source port of **1723**. The dialog should now look like the following illustration.
   Click **OK** to define the filter.

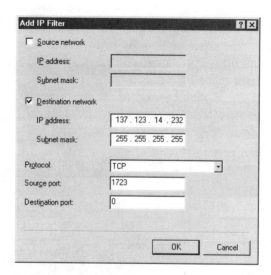

5. Click **New** again in the **Inbound Filters** dialog. In the **Add IP Filter** dialog, select **Other** from the **Protocol** drop-down control, enter **47** as the protocol number, and click **OK**. This step will allow GRE through, which is needed by PPTP.

6. Click **New** again in the **Inbound Filters** dialog. Select the **Destination Network** check box, enter the IP address of the external NIC of the local VPN server (you are in Montego Bay, so that is **137.123.14.232**). Enter a subnet mask of **255.255.255.255**. In the **Protocol** drop-down box, select **TCP** with a Destination port of **1723**. Click **OK** to define the filter. This step created an outbound filter for PPTP. So far all required filters for PPTP have been created.

7. To define the L2TP filter, click **New** in the **Inbound Filters** dialog, select the **Destination Network** check box, enter the IP address of the external NIC of the local VPN server (**137.123.14.232**). Enter a subnet mask of **255.255.255.255**. In the **Protocol** drop-down box, select **UDP** with a Source port of **500**, and a Destination port of **500**. Click **OK** to define the filter for ISAKMP, which will enable IPSec negotiation.

8. Click **New** again in the **Inbound Filters** dialog. select the **Destination Network** check box, enter the IP address of the external NIC of the local VPN server (**137.123.14.232**). Enter a subnet mask of **255.255.255.255**. In the Protocol drop-down box, select **UDP** with a Source port of **1701**, and a Destination port of **1701**. Click **OK** to define the filter for L2TP.

9. In the **Inbound Filters** dialog, select **Drop all packets except those that meet the criteria below,** as shown in the following illustration. Click **OK**.

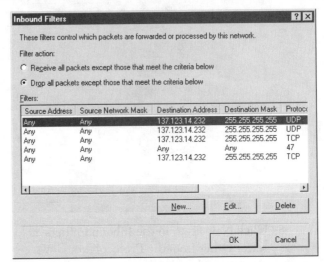

This concludes the creation of Inbound Filters, next you need to create the Outbound Filters.

10. Create the filters in Table 11-2 using the **Outbound Filters** dialog.

TABLE 11-2 Properties for Outbound Filters

Filter	1	2	3	4	5
Source Address	Any	137.123.14.232	137.123.14.232	137.123.14.232	137.123.14.232
Source Network Mask	Any	255.255.255.255	255.255.255.255	255.255.255.255	255.255.255.255
Destination Address	Any	Any	Any	Any	Any
Destination Network Mask	Any	Any	Any	Any	Any
Protocol	47	TCP	TCP	UDP	UDP
Source Port	Any	1723	Any	500	1701
Destination port	Any	Any	1723	500	1701
Explanation	GRE	PPTP Inbound	PPTP Outbound	ISAKMP	L2TP

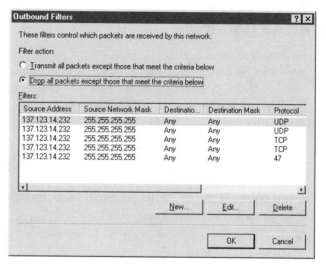

11. This finalizes the configuration of the Montego Bay server. The same steps need to be performed on the Ocho Rios server to make the filter functional.

w a t c h *Remember that the well-known ports for HTTP and HTTPS are 80 and 443, respectively.*

Now that you have a better idea of TCP/IP ports and port filtering, here are some possible scenario questions and their answers.

SCENARIO & SOLUTION

What ports must be allowed for L2TP to be permitted through a firewall?	IPSec uses UDP port 500 and IP protocol 50 and/or 51. L2TP uses UDP port 1701. These must be permitted to allow L2TP through the firewall.
What ports must be allowed for PPTP to be permitted through a firewall?	PPTP uses TCP port 1723 and IP protocol 47 (GRE). These must be permitted to allow PPTP through the firewall.
What port is used for SSL on a web server?	SSL uses the HTTPS protocol. This protocol makes use of the well-known TCP port 443. HTTP uses TCP port 80.

Managing RRAS Routing

Routing and Remote Access uses a group of routing interfaces, devices, and ports that represent the physical network equipment. *Routing interfaces* are the logical or physical network interface that packets are forwarded through. *Routing devices* are either hardware or software that are used to establish physical or logical point-to-point connections. *Routing ports* are the communication channels that support a single point-to-point connection.

In this section you will learn about these objects and how to manage them.

Managing Routing and Remote Access Routing Interfaces

The server that has Routing and Remote Access Service enabled uses a routing interface to forward unicast and multicast IP packets as well as AppleTalk packets. Under RRAS there are two types of routing interfaces:

- **LAN interfaces**   A LAN interface is a physical interface that is normally a LAN connection that uses one of the local area networking technologies, such as Ethernet. Because it is a physical interface, the routing interface reflects the installed NIC. Some Wide Area Network (WAN) adapters are also represented as a LAN interface; this is true for Frame Relay virtual circuits that are represented as LAN interfaces. A LAN interface is always connected and available, and a LAN interface does not require authentication to become active.

- **Demand-dial interfaces**   Demand-dial interfaces represent a point-to-point connection, and are logical interfaces. The point-to-point connection can be a fixed connection (physical) through two connected routers, or a connection through two modems that use analog telephone lines, or a logical connection through routers connected together over a VPN through the public Internet. Demand-dial connections are either established when needed (on-demand), or are connected and stay connected (persistent). Demand-dial interfaces normally require authentication prior to connecting, and the equipment used is either a device or a port.

Routing interfaces are managed through the RRAS snap-in in an MMC, as you can see in Figure 11-6.

The routing interfaces that you see are the default interfaces for a server with two physical network adapters connected to separate networks. The Loopback routing interface represents the 127.0.0.1 IP address, and the Internal interface represents the

FIGURE 11-6 Routing Interfaces in the RRAS snap-in

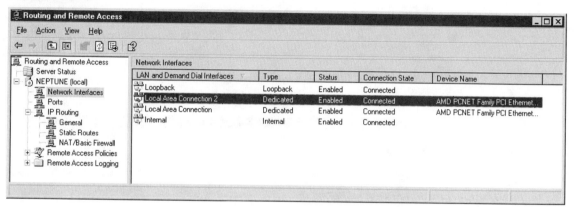

FIGURE 11-6   Routing Interfaces in the RRAS snap-in

RRAS internal interface. You manage the interfaces through the Network Connections application in the Control Panel.

Demand-dial interfaces are the only possible addition, and indeed it is the only management item for routing interfaces.

To add a new demand-dial interface, right-click the **Network Interfaces** node under the RRAS server and select **Add Demand-dial Interface** from the context menu. The resulting Demand-Dial Interface Wizard will help you configure the interface. After you click **Next** to go past the welcome screen of the Demand-Dial Interface Wizard, you will need to give the interface a name; make this name descriptive.

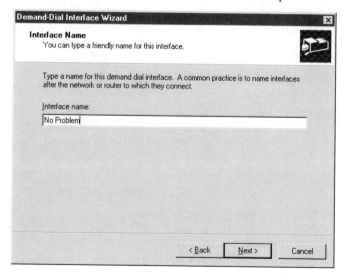

There are three choices for connection between your RRAS server and the remote router, as shown in the following illustration:

■ Modem connection, which includes ISDN adapters, cable modems, or other physical devices.

■ Virtual Private Network (VPN)

■ Point-to-Point Protocol (PPP) over Ethernet (PPPoE)

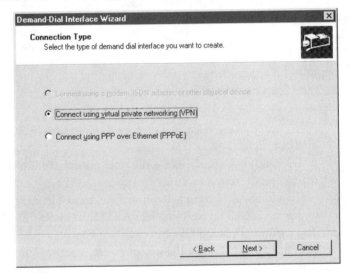

Select VPN as the type of connection, and click **Next** to get to make the **VPN type** selection. There are three options, as shown in the following illustration:

■ Automatic selection

■ Point-to-Point Tunneling Protocol (PPTP)

■ Layer 2 Tunneling Protocol (L2TP)

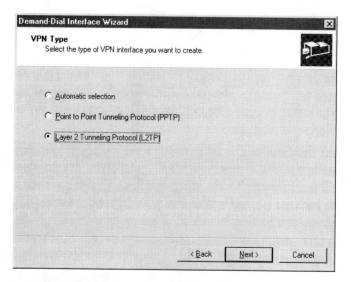

Select **Layer 2 Tunneling Protocol**, and click **Next**.

On the **Destination Address** page, you need to supply the FQDN or IP address of the remote router that we will connect to, as shown here.

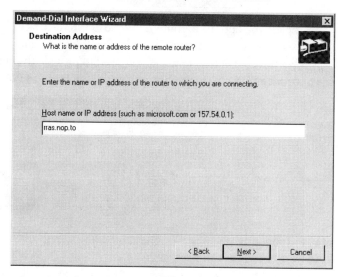

The remote router is here known as rras.nop.to. Click **Next**.

The wizard now requests options for protocols and security. You will notice that the selections for sending plain text passwords are grayed out; this is because you selected L2TP on an earlier screen.

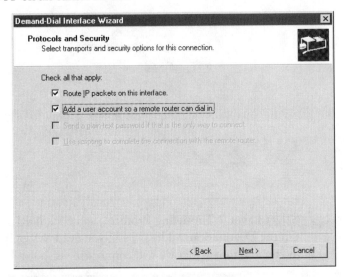

Select the options to route IP over this interface as well as to have the wizard create an account to be able to authenticate to the remote router, and click **Next**.

For the connection to work, you need to provide the address of the remote TCP/IP network as a route on the **Static Routes for Remote Networks** page, as shown here.

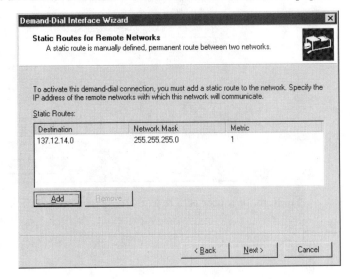

The remote network in this case is 137.12.14.0/24. Click **Add**, enter the information for the remote network, and click **OK**, as shown in the following illustration.

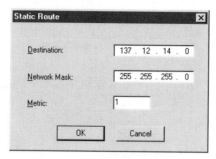

Back on the **Static Routes** page, click **Next**.

On the **Dial In Credentials** page, you are prompted for the authentication credential for the interface, as shown in the following illustration. This is the information the administrator of the remote router needs to supply to be able to connect to this RRAS server.

Provide the local authentication information and click **Next**.

On the **Dial Out Credentials** page, you are prompted for the authentication information for the remote router, as shown in the following illustration.

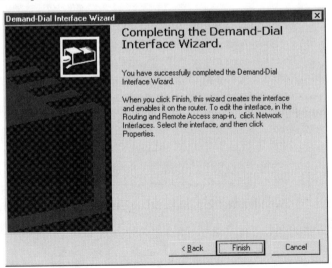

The connections to the remote router are secured using this account. After you enter the information, click **Next**. On the next page, shown in the following illustration, click Finish to complete the configuration of the demand-dial interface. As is seen here.

As you can see in Figure 11-7, the demand-dial interface is configured and enabled, but disconnected. To make the new demand-interface available, you need to manage the interface and configure the availability and the rules for how and when to connect.

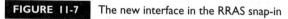

FIGURE 11-7 The new interface in the RRAS snap-in

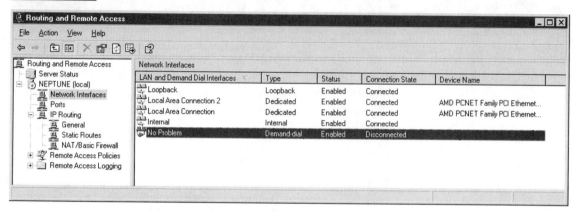

Managing Devices and Ports

A *port* is the channel of a device that supports a single point-to-point connection. *Devices* are the physical hardware or software that make ports available that demand-dial and remote access connections can use for point-to-point connections.

Devices can be physical hardware, like modems or ISDN adapters, or they can be virtual, like a VPN that provides connections. Some devices support single ports, for example, a modem, or multiple ports, such as a modem bank.

Devices and ports are viewed through the Ports node in RRAS snap-in as seen in Figure 11-8.

FIGURE 11-8 The Ports node in the RRAS snap-in

SCENARIO & SOLUTION

What are ports?	A port is a the channel of a device that supports a single point-to-point connection.
How do I add an demand-dial interface?	Demand-dial interfaces are added through the Demand-dial Interface Wizard. The wizard is started from the RRAS snap-in.
What are interfaces?	The routing interfaces represent the network interface cards installed on the server as well as any demand-dial interfaces and the Loopback interface.
Where do I configure interfaces?	Interfaces are configured through the RRAS snap-in; they are enumerated in the Network Interfaces node under the RRAS server name.

Now that you have a better idea of the parts of RRAS routing, here are some possible scenario questions and their answers.

CERTIFICATION OBJECTIVE 11.02

Manage TCP/IP Routing

The other side of the Routing and Remote Access Service is the Routing that is used to turn your Windows Server 2003 into a network router. Routing is the process of forwarding packets between subnets so that they reach the intended recipient. Figure 11-9 shows how routers work together to move data from Network 1 to Network 2. The arrows represent a couple of the possible paths the data transmission can take. In order to see how TCP/IP routing operates we need to examine the Open Systems Interconnection (OSI) and the Department of Defense (DoD) network models.

The Network Models

When network protocols are developed, they are described using a layered model that describes how the data flows between the network and the application. When you look at the TCP/IP suite of protocols, you need to examine the OSI and DoD models.

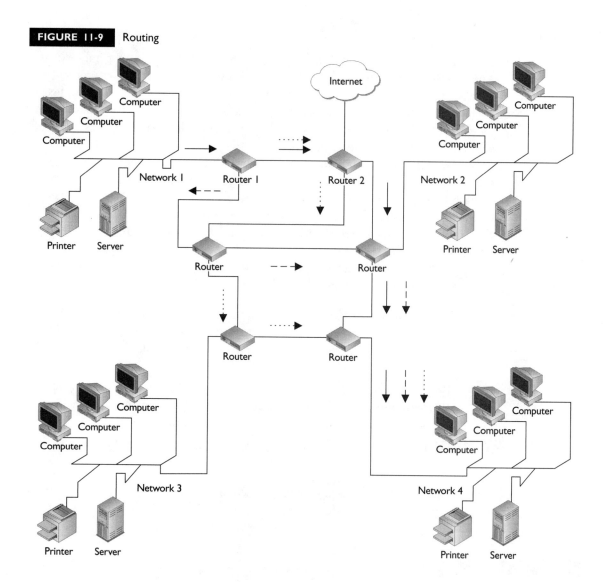

FIGURE 11-9   Routing

Examining the OSI Model

Every modern network protocol starts by being described using the Open Systems
Interconnection (OSI) model. We could spend a whole chapter on the OSI model, but
for the purpose of routing, we will only look at the parts that are used for packets to
travel between networks.

The OSI model, shown in Figure 11-10, was developed by the International Standards Organization (ISO) in 1977 to promote multivendor interoperability. As a reference model, the OSI model does not specify any communications protocols. Instead it provides guidelines for communication tasks. It divides the complex communications process into smaller, more simple, subtasks. This way, the issues become more manageable, and each subtask can be optimized individually. The design of the OSI model was arrived at through some of the object-oriented techniques that developers use todayencapsulation and abstraction. This way, the model, and any implementations can be—maintained without having to redesign the entire model.

Each layer is assigned a specific task. Also, each layer provides services to the layer directly above it, and uses the services of the layer directly below it. For example, the network layer uses the services from the data link layer, and provides services to the transport layer.

In the context of routing, it is important to explain the services provided by the first three layers of the OSI model:

■ The Physical layer (layer 1) provides the physical connection between a computer system and the network wiring. It specifies cable pin assignments, voltage levels for the signals on the wire, and so on. The data unit at this level is the bit.

■ The Data Link layer (layer 2) provides the packaging and unpackaging of data for transmission. The data unit at this layer is called a frame. A frame represents the data structure much like a database record.

■ The Network layer (layer 3) provides routing of data through the network. The data unit at this layer is called a datagram.

The OSI model describes a network protocol in a very elegant way. The TCP/IP protocol suite, however, was developed mostly before the inception of the OSI model. The TCP/IP suite was based on what is known as the DoD model.

The OSI model

Layer	
7	Application
6	Presentation
5	Session
4	Transport
3	Network
2	Data Link
1	Physical

Examining the DoD Model

When the United States Department of Defense (DoD) defined their own networking model in the mid-1960s, the OSI model was not even thought of yet. The DoD model defines four layers and is simpler than the OSI model. Figure 11-11 shows the mapping between the OSI model and the DoD model.

Although the DoD model predates the OSI model by some ten years, you can still compare the two.

- The Process/Application layer in the DoD model maps to the top three layers of the OSI model.

- The Host-to-Host layer, also known as the Transport layer in the DoD model, maps to OSI's Transport layer.

- The DoD Internet layer corresponds to the Network layer in the OSI model.

- The Network access layer in the DoD model maps to the bottom two layers in the OSI model.

Each layer is associated with one or more protocols that specify how certain networking functions behave. The Internet/Network layer protocols for the TCP/IP suite are discussed later in this chapter. Next we'll examine the devices associated with the first two layers in the OSI model—Physical, Data Link, and Network.

Internetworking Devices

At the base of all TCP/IP routing is the routing table, which contains routing information maintained by the network stack and the routing protocols. This routing table is one of the most frequently accessed structures in the TCP/IP stack—on a busy host this can be hundreds of accesses per second. The command-line utility **netstat** is used to

Comparison between the OSI and DoD models

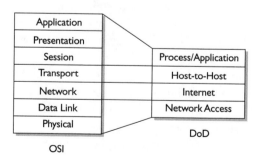

view the content of the routing table. The following is the output from executing the **netstat –r** command:

```
C:\>netstat -r

IPv4 Route Table
===========================================================================
Interface List
0x1 ......................... MS TCP Loopback interface
0x2 ...00 50 56 40 32 13 ...... AMD PCNET Family PCI Ethernet Adapter #2
0x3 ...00 50 56 40 32 12 ...... AMD PCNET Family PCI Ethernet Adapter #3
===========================================================================
===========================================================================
Active Routes:
Network Destination        Netmask          Gateway       Interface  Metric
        0.0.0.0          0.0.0.0         10.0.0.2      10.0.0.203      30
       10.0.0.0    255.255.255.0       10.0.0.203      10.0.0.203      30
     10.0.0.203  255.255.255.255        127.0.0.1       127.0.0.1      30
   10.255.255.255  255.255.255.255     10.0.0.203      10.0.0.203      30
       11.0.0.0    255.255.255.0        11.0.0.3        11.0.0.3       30
       11.0.0.3  255.255.255.255        127.0.0.1       127.0.0.1      30
   11.255.255.255  255.255.255.255      11.0.0.3        11.0.0.3       30
      127.0.0.0        255.0.0.0        127.0.0.1       127.0.0.1       1
      224.0.0.0        240.0.0.0       10.0.0.203      10.0.0.203      30
      224.0.0.0        240.0.0.0        11.0.0.3        11.0.0.3       30
  255.255.255.255  255.255.255.255     10.0.0.203      10.0.0.203       1
  255.255.255.255  255.255.255.255      11.0.0.3        11.0.0.3        1
Default Gateway:        10.0.0.2
===========================================================================
Persistent Routes:
  None
C:\>
```

Each entry in the table contains a *destination* and a *gateway* (sometimes referred to as a *router*) address pair. For a given destination address, the router address indicates that host to which an IP datagram should be forwarded in order to reach the destination. The *interface* entry is used to determine which NIC is used, and the *metric* indicates the number of hops between the router and the destination.

When you build an internetwork, there are a number of devices that you can use, and they all work on different layers in the reference model. We are focusing on the router in this chapter.

A router can determine the best route between two or more networks. A router has access to the network (software) address information, which means it operates at the network layer of the OSI model as seen in Figure 11-12. Because it needs to access the network address information, it is very protocol-specific. When a router encounters a datagram with a protocol it does not support, the datagram is dropped.

There are additional network devices such as bridges, repeaters, and switches, just to mention a few; the use of these devices falls outside the scope of this chapter.

The entry that lists the destination 0.0.0.0 with a mask of 0.0.0.0 is the default route that the router will use if there is no explicit route for a destination.

on the **()ob** *The original name for the device that is now called a router was gateway, because it was the gateway to the rest of the network. The term gateway is used interchangeably with router, as you saw in the routing table listing. Be aware of this naming issue.*

The Routing Table and How to Build It

The routing table is central to how the routing is managed, as you saw in the previous section. The router can learn about the possible routes through static entries in the table, or the table can be dynamically built and maintained using routing protocols.

Initially, a router only know knows those networks (subnets) that it is directly connected to. The router learns about other networks by two means: static routes and routing protocols.

A *static route* is a path in a router's routing table that is manually configured by a network administrator. For each destination (network or host), the network administrator configures the next hop router and the cost associated with the route. The routing information never changes, hence the term *static route*, even if part of the network path becomes unavailable.

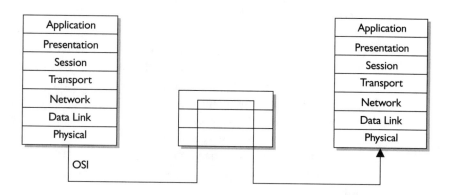

FIGURE 11-12

A router in reference to the OSI model

Static routing has significant drawbacks because the network's routing topology is defined and entered by the network administrator, which can lead to errors in the definition of the routes. These errors can be as simple as typing errors, or the inability of the routing to change as the network changes. Static routes can be useful, however, when used in conjunction with dynamic routing protocols. You can use static routes to define backup routes as well as to configure those routing segments where you want the traffic to follow a particular path at all times. For example, you could use a static route on a particular segment to force all traffic to use a high-bandwidth link at all times.

Dynamic routes are configured while the network is operational, and the routers communicate between each other the knowledge of networks they can reach. This communication is performed using one or more of the routing protocols. The most common protocols are:

- Routing Information Protocol (RIP)
- Open Shortest Path First (OSPF)
- Interior Gateway Routing Protocol (IGRP)
- Internet Control Message Protocol (ICMP)

These routing protocols are broken down into two distinct classifications: interior routing protocols and exterior routing protocols.

Interior routing protocols, sometimes called Interior Gateway Protocols (IGPs), are generally used within a private network to dynamically determine the best route to each network.

Exterior routing protocols are used to exchange routing information between autonomous systems (a fancy word to describe systems that share the same routing protocol, that is, a private network).

The routing protocol can use one of two algorithms when determining routes, cost of the path, and so on. These are classified as either *link state routing protocols* or *distance-vector routing protocols*.

Distance-Vector Routing Protocols   Each router that uses a distance-vector routing protocol keeps a routing table that describes its world, the router's view of the network. As an example, shown in Figure 11-13, Router A sees that Networks 1 and 2 are one hop away (connected directly), whereas Network 3 is two hops away. Router 2, however, sees Network 2 and 3 as one hop away, and Network 1 as two hops away. The routers have different views of the same network.

Each router receives routing information from the routers that are directly connected to it. The router adds one hop to the route (the router's own cost), and passes the

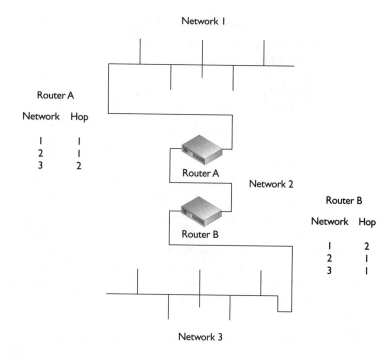

FIGURE 11-13

A sample
network

updated information to the next router in the line. The distance-vector routing protocol uses "used" or "secondhand" information from its direct neighborhood.

The route that the router selects is based on the cost, or *metric*, of the route. The metric used depends on the protocol. One of the drawbacks of the distance-vector routing protocol is that routers send the entire routing table for each update. To keep the routing tables current, the information is broadcast on a regular schedule.

Routing Information Protocol (RIP) is the best known and most widely used of the distance-vector routing protocols.

The advantages of distance-vector based routing protocol are

- Simpler
- Easy to configure

The disadvantages of distance-vector based routing protocols are

- Large routing tables
- High network traffic overhead
- Does not scale
- High convergence time

Link State Routing Protocol Link state routing protocols are the alternative to distance-vector routing protocols. Using the link state routing protocol, a router calculates a hierarchal view, a *tree*, of the entire network, with itself as the root, as shown in Figure 11-14.

Router C builds a network view based on the route information it receives directly from the other routers. In link state, each router distributes information about its directly connected networks and their associated metrics only.

The routers only include the best path gleaned from the metric to the other routers. When a router detects changes in the state of its direct links, the router distributes (broadcasts) the change to all routers through a process known as *flooding*. Flooding updates every router's routing table because it only sends state change information (hence the name *link state*).

These flooding packets are generally very small, and are sent infrequently, so the impact on the bandwidth of the links is small.

Windows Server 2003 Routing and Remote Access service supports the Open Shortest Path First (OSPF) protocol, the best known and widely used link state routing protocol.

FIGURE 11-14 The network as seen by router C using link state routing protocols

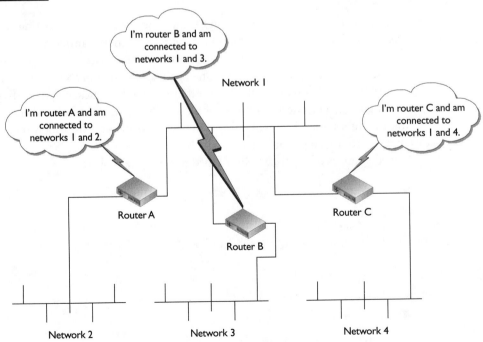

Advantages of link state based routing protocols are

- Smaller routing table
- Low network overhead
- Ability to scale
- Lower convergence time

Disadvantages of link state based routing protocols are

- Complex
- More difficult to configure
- Resource intensive

Now that you have looked at the theory, you can look at the individual routing protocols.

Routing Information Protocol (RIP)   The Routing Information Protocol (RIP v1) is documented in RFC 1508/1388, and has been available since 1988. It is a distance-vector routing protocol that sends its routing updates on a fixed schedule of every 30 seconds. If a route is learned through a RIP update message, and then subsequent update messages do not refresh this route within 180 seconds, the route is assumed to be unreachable and is removed from the routing table.

RIP v1 is one of the most widely used routing protocol today, mostly because it is easy to implement. In most cases the network administrator only needs to enable RIP. The protocol has some serious drawbacks, however.

- Based on Internet classes
- Broadcast RIP announcement
- Subnet mask not announced with the route
- No protection from rogue RIP routers
- Limited size network, hop count of 16 is unreachable
- Slow convergence when the network topology changes

Version 2 of RIP (RIP v2) is defined in RFC 1723, and is designed to solve some of the problems with RIP v1. You might ask why we need a second version of the RIP protocol when there are better routing protocols such as OSPF. RIP has the following advantages over OSPF:

- Easy to implement
- Simple to use on small to medium-size network

The changes between RIP v1 and RIP v2 are

- **Multicast RIP announcements**   Rather than broadcast announcements, RIP v2 uses the IP multicast address of 224.0.0.9.
- **Subnet masks**   The RIP v2 announcements also contain the network mask along with the network ID.
- **Authentication**   Incoming RIP announcements can be authenticated to solve the problem of rogue routers.

Open Shortest Path First (OSPF)   The Open Shortest Path First (OSPF) protocol is a link state routing protocol that was introduced in 1989 as defined in RFC 2328. OSPF is designed for exchanging routing information within a large or very large single autonomous system; therefore, it is designed as an Interior Gateway Protocol (IGP). One of the most appealing advantages of OSPF is its efficiency: OSPF requires very little network bandwidth even in very large networks. The disadvantage of OSPF is its complexity: OSPF implementations must be planned, and are more complicated to administer. The algorithm used to calculate the routes in the routing table is Shortest Path First (SPF). This algorithm produces the shortest route (based on cost) between the router and the networks of the internetwork. SPF-calculated routes are always loop-free.

OSPF routers do not exchange routing table entries like RIP routers; rather, they maintain a view (map) of the network that is updated after any changes to the network topology. This view is called the *link state database*, and is synchronized among all the OSPF routers. The routes in the routing table are calculated from the link state database.

OSPF has the following features:

- Fast convergence
- Loop-free routes
- Scalable
- Network mask is advertised with the network ID

- Authentication support
- Support for external routes

Internet Control Message Protocol (ICMP)   Sometimes, even if you have not configured dynamic routing on an IP router, routes can be automatically added to your routing table by the Internet Control Message Protocol (ICMP). ICMP was first introduced in 1980 in RFC 792/1256. Its function is to be an error-reporting and diagnostic utility used by routers and hosts to communicate the status of the connection. ICMP is always part of any TCP/IP implementation, and Windows Server 2003 is no exception, and it is enabled by default with no configuration. The messages of ICMP provide route redirection, among other things. *Route redirection* means that if your host sends a packet to a router that knows of a shorter path to your destination, the router sends a redirect message to your host, informing it of the shorter route.

In RFC 1256 a *router discovery* feature was added to ICMP; this router discovery is not a routing protocol, but a way of identifying routers in the neighborhood. When a router starts up, it sends a router discovery request asking any routers to identify themselves. This request is sent using the 244.0.0.2 multicast address, or as a broadcast if the interface does not support multicast. Only routers that are directly connected to the local network will respond to the request.

ICMP can make you routers act as if you have a dynamic routing protocol installed.

Managing TCP/IP Routing Protocols

You manage routing through the Routing and Remote Access service snap-in. In the following exercises you will learn how to perform the actions to add and remove the routing protocols.

EXERCISE 11-4

Adding a IP RIP Version 1 Routing Protocol

1. Open the **Routing and Remote Access** snap-in.

2. In the console tree, expand the computer node, followed by the IP Routing node, and then click **General**, as shown in the following illustration.

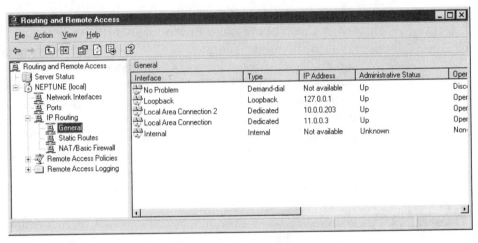

3. Right-click **General**, and click **New Routing Protocol** in the context menu. The **New Routing Protocol** dialog appears, as shown here:

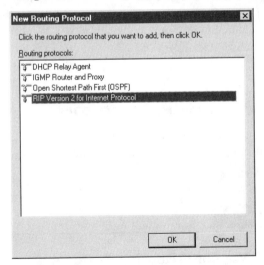

4. Click **RIP Version 2 for Internet Protocol**, and then click **OK**.

5. Now you need to configure the protocol by adding Routing Interfaces to it. Click the **RIP** node in the console tree.

6. Right-click **RIP**, and select **New Interface** in the context menu.

7. Select **Local Area Connection**, and click **OK**.

8. Change the **Outgoing Packet Protocol** to **RIP version 1 broadcast**, and click **OK**, as shown here:

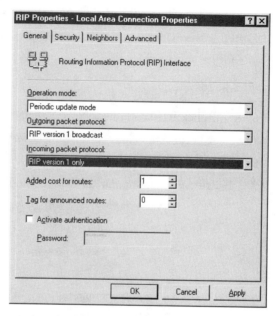

9. Repeat steps 5 though 8 for all the interfaces installed on the server.

This completes the installation of a RIP Version 1 IP Routing protocol. To configure RIP version 2 routing protocol see Exercise 11-5.

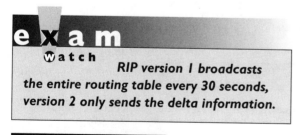

The routing protocol that was configured in Exercise 11-4 (RIP version 1) is probably the simplest protocol of them all, but it uses a lot of network bandwidth. RIP version 2 is a better choice, and that is the protocol you will configure in the next exercise.

watch
RIP version 1 broadcasts the entire routing table every 30 seconds, version 2 only sends the delta information.

EXERCISE 11-5

Deploying RIP Version 2 Routing Protocol

In this exercise, you will add RIP version 2 to the RRAS router.

1. Open the **Routing and Remote Access** snap-in.

2. In the console tree, expand the computer node, followed by the IP Routing node, and click **General**.

3. Right-click **General**, and click **New Routing Protocol** in the context menu.

4. In the **New Routing Protocol** dialog, click **RIP Version 2 for Internet Protocol**, and then click **OK**

5. Now you need to configure the protocol by adding Routing Interfaces to it. Click the **RIP** node in the console tree.

6. Right-click **RIP**, and select **New Interface** in the context menu.

7. Select **Local Area Connection**, and click **OK**.

8. Change the **Outgoing Packet Protocol** to **RIP version 2 broadcast**.

9. Change the **Incoming Packet Protocol** to **RIP version 2 only**, as shown here:

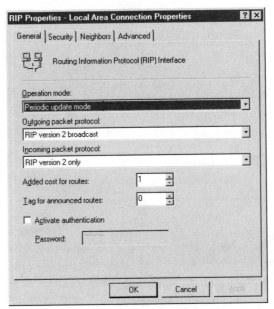

10. Click the **Security** tab and verify that the **Action** is to accept all incoming routes, as shown here:

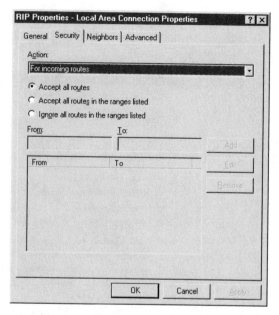

11. Click the **Neighbors** tab, and enter any static routers that are neighbors, as shown here:

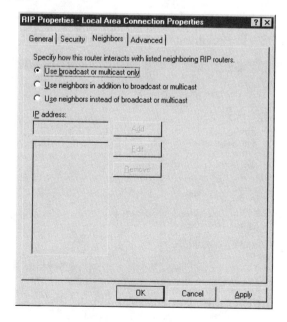

12. Click the **Advanced** tab and review the default settings. Note that the default Periodic announcement interval is 30 seconds, as shown in the following illustration. Click **OK**.

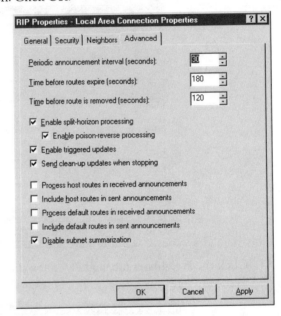

13. The resulting view of the Routing and Remote Access snap-in is shown here:

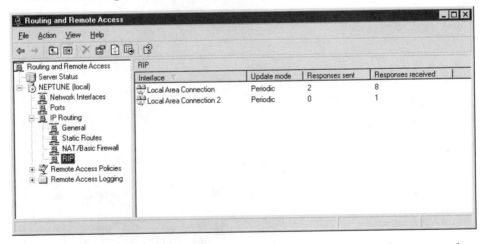

14. Confirm the routes by following these steps. Open a command prompt and issue the **netstat –r** command.

15. Note the routes that are found through other routers on your network. The following illustration is from my test lab.

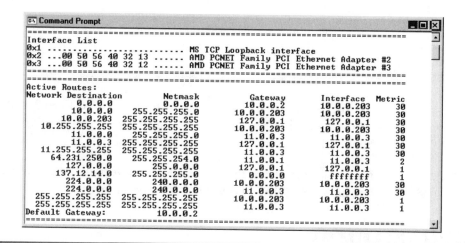

There are times when a router needs to be stripped down, and you need to remove routing protocols. The following exercise takes you through removing the RIP protocol from RRAS.

EXERCISE 11-6

Removing an IP RIP Routing Protocol

1. Open the **Routing and Remote Access** service snap-in.

2. In the console tree, expand the computer node, followed by the IP Routing node, and click the **RIP** routing protocol, as shown here:

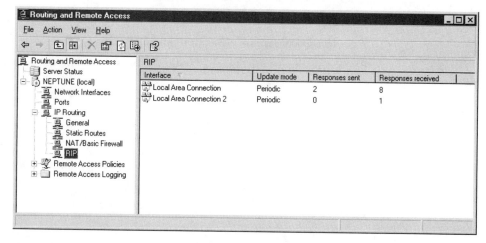

3. Right-click the RIP routing protocol, and click **Delete** in the context menu.

4. Click **Yes** to delete the RIP routing protocol.

Now you have seen how to work with RIP, versions 1 and 2, which is a distance-vector protocol. We will now go through how to enable and configure the Open Shortest Path First routing protocol with RRAS.

Make sure the entire routing environment is planned before you start implementing OSPF in a production environment.

EXERCISE 11-7

Adding an IP OSPF Routing Protocol

In this exercise, you will install and configure OSPF Routing Protocol with RRAS.

1. Open the **Routing and Remote Access** snap-in.

2. In the console tree, expand the computer node, followed by the IP Routing node, and click **General**.

3. Right-click **General**, and click **New Routing Protocol** in the context menu.

4. In the **New Routing Protocol** dialog, click **Open Shortest Path First (OSPF)**, and then click **OK**.

5. Now you need to configure the protocol by adding Routing Interfaces to it. Click the **OSPF** node in the console tree.

6. Right-click **OSPF**, and select **New Interface** in the context menu.

7. Select **Local Area Connection**, and click **OK**.

8. Accept the defaults for the General tab, as shown here:

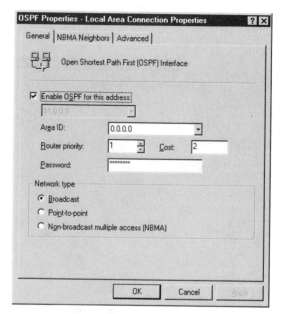

9. Click the **NBMA Neighbors** tab and manage any Non-broadcast Multiple Access (NBMA) routers. Note that this tab is disabled unless you select **Non-broadcast Multiple Access (NBMA)** on the **General** tab.

10. Click the **Advanced** tab and review the default settings, shown in the following illustration. Click **OK**.

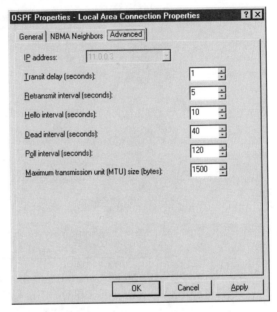

11. Repeat steps 6 through 10 for other interfaces.

12. The resulting view of the Routing and Remote Access snap-in is shown here:

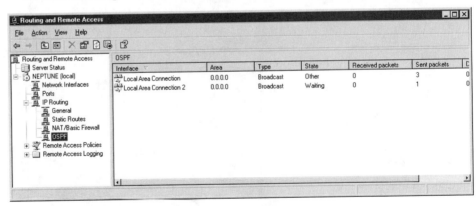

13. Confirm the routes by following these steps. Open a command prompt and issue the **netstat –r** command.

14. Note the routes that are found through other routers on your network. The following illustration is from my test lab.

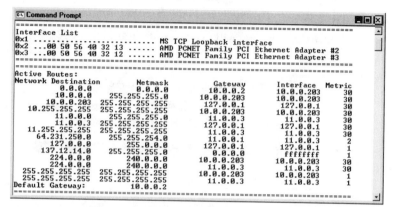

EXERCISE 11-8

Removing an IP OSPF Routing Protocol

1. Open the **Routing and Remote Access** service snap-in
2. In the console tree, click the **OSPF** routing protocol
3. Right-click the OSPF routing protocol, and click **Delete** in the context menu.
4. Click **Yes** to delete the OSPF protocol.

Managing TCP/IP Routing Tables

The router keeps the information it needs to make decisions about how to route packets in the routing table. This table can be populated with known routes either *automatically*, using dynamic routing protocols, or *statically*, using static routing entries. In this section you will learn how to add static routes to the routing table using both the RRAS snap-in and the **route** command-line utility.

EXERCISE 11-9

MasterSim 11-9 ON THE CD

Adding a Static Route Using the RRAS Snap-in

In this exercise you will manage static routes in a RRAS environment using the RRAS snap-in.

1. Open the **Routing and Remote Access** snap-in.

2. In the console tree, expand the computer node, followed by the IP Routing node, and click **Static Routes**, as shown here:

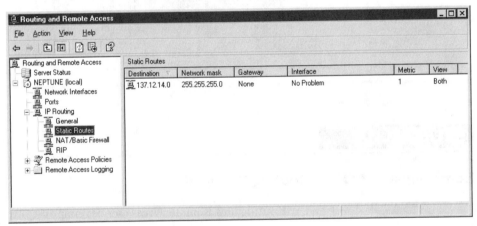

3. Right-click **Static Routes**, and select **New Static Route** from the context menu. The **Static Route** dialog appears, as shown here:

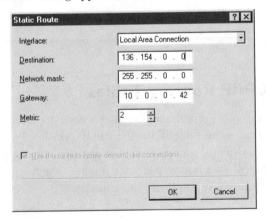

4. Select the interface that the static route is accessible through.

5. Specify the destination address, network mask, gateway address, and metric.

6. Click **OK** to accept the static route.

Adding a Static Route Using the route Utility

In this exercise you will manage static routes in an RRAS environment using the **route** command-line utility.

1. Open a command prompt.

2. Enter the following command to add a static route to the 157.0.0.0/8 network through the 11.0.0.12 router with a metric of 3.

   ```
   C:\ >route ADD 157.0.0.0 MASK 255.0.0.0 11.0.0.12 METRIC 3
   ```

3. To view the routes continue with Exercise 11-11.

There are times when you will need to verify the entries in the routing table. In the following exercise you will learn how to print the routing table using either the RRAS snap-in, the **route** command utility, or the **netstat** command utility.

Printing the Routing Table

In this exercise you will print the routing table using both the RRAS snap-in and command-line utilities.

1. Open the **Routing and Remote Access** snap-in.

2. In the console tree, expand the computer node, followed by the IP Routing node, and click **Static Routes**.

3. Right-click **Static Routes**, and select **Show IP Routing Table** from the context menu. The Routing Table window appears, as shown in the following illustration.

NEPTUNE - IP Routing Table					
Destination	Network mask	Gateway	Interface	Metric	Protocol
0.0.0.0	0.0.0.0	10.0.0.2	Local Area Connection 2	30	Network management
10.0.0.0	255.255.255.0	11.0.0.1	Local Area Connection 2	4	RIP
10.0.0.0	255.255.255.0	10.0.0.203	Local Area Connection 2	30	Local
10.0.0.203	255.255.255.255	127.0.0.1	Loopback	30	Local
10.255.255.255	255.255.255.255	10.0.0.203	Local Area Connection 2	30	Local
11.0.0.0	255.255.255.0	10.0.0.2	Local Area Connection 2	4	RIP
11.0.0.0	255.255.255.0	11.0.0.3	Local Area Connection	30	Local
11.0.0.3	255.255.255.255	127.0.0.1	Loopback	30	Local
11.255.255.255	255.255.255.255	11.0.0.3	Local Area Connection	30	Local
64.231.250.0	255.255.254.0	11.0.0.1	Local Area Connection	2	RIP
65.50.128.0	255.255.248.0	10.0.0.2	Local Area Connection	2	RIP
127.0.0.0	255.0.0.0	127.0.0.1	Loopback	1	Local
127.0.0.1	255.255.255.255	127.0.0.1	Loopback	1	Local
137.12.14.0	255.255.255.0	0.0.0.0	No Problem	1	Static
137.12.14.0	255.255.255.0	11.0.0.1	Local Area Connection 2	4	RIP
157.0.0.0	255.0.0.0	10.0.0.2	Local Area Connection 2	4	RIP
157.0.0.0	255.0.0.0	11.0.0.12	Local Area Connection	3	Network management
224.0.0.0	240.0.0.0	11.0.0.3	Local Area Connection	30	Local
224.0.0.0	240.0.0.0	10.0.0.203	Local Area Connection 2	30	Local
255.255.255.255	255.255.255.255	11.0.0.3	Local Area Connection	1	Local
255.255.255.255	255.255.255.255	10.0.0.203	Local Area Connection 2	1	Local

4. To view the routing table using command-line utilities, first open a command prompt.

5. Enter **route PRINT** and press ENTER. The routing table appears, as shown in the following illustration.

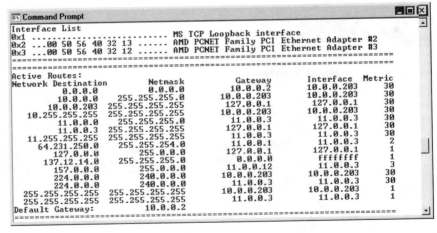

6. A second command that you used in previous chapters is the **netstat** command. When you use **netstat** with the **–r** flag (**netstat –r**), it produces the same routing table.

Now that you have a better idea of routing protocols, here are some possible scenario questions and their answers.

SCENARIO & SOLUTION

What is a gateway?	The term *gateway* has been part of the TCP/IP vocabulary since the early days when the device that connected a network to the backbone internet was a gateway that translated between the protocols and provided the connectivity. This is what you call a *router* today. You will see the terms used interchangeably when working with TCP/IP. Be careful to read any questions that use the term *gateway* to ensure from the context that a router is referred to, and not a device that translates between different protocols.
Why is RIP version 1 considered bad?	RIP v1 is a distance-vector routing protocol where every router sends its entire routing table to every network segment every 30 seconds.
Why is RIP version 2 considered better than RIP version 1?	RIP v2 still sends information to every network segment, but the information only contains the changed information since the last transmission. RIP v2 can also use Multicast to lessen the load on the network. RIP v2 also supports secure connections to solve the problem of rogue routers.
Why is it important to plan an OSPF installation?	OSPF allows you to break your network into manageable subnets and to treat the groups of routers as one entity. Control of the transmission of information between these groups of routers can be optimized for the best performance and security. In order to make the OSPF environment work efficiently, you must properly plan and design the routing environment before it is implemented.

CERTIFICATION SUMMARY

In this chapter you have learned about how to manage Remote Access, and especially TCP/IP packets and packet filtering. Remember which ports are used for specific protocols, and how to filter them, for this is information that surely will be tested in the 70-291 exam. In the second part of this chapter you learned about how to implement and manage RRAS routing. The scenarios used were demand-dial routing, as well as TCP/IP routing. You learned about the routing protocols that are used for routers to learn about the network and how to route traffic between different parts. Remember that RIP 2 is the preferred routing protocol, and that OSPF must be carefully planned before implementation.

✓ TWO-MINUTE DRILL

Manage Remote Access

❑ When your RRAS server is deployed behind a firewall, the firewall must have packet filters configured to allow access.

❑ For L2TP (IPSec) to be allowed through a firewall, UDP port 500 and IP protocol 50 and/or 51 as well as UDP 1701 must be permitted on the firewall.

❑ When you configure packet filters on the RRAS server, configure them on the external network adapter.

❑ For PPTP to be allowed through the firewall, TCP port 1723 and IP protocol 47 (GRE) must be permitted through the firewall.

❑ For HTTP and HTTPS to be allowed, TCP ports 80 and 443 must be permitted.

❑ Input and output filters for the VPN server must have UDP ports 500 and 1701 permitted.

Manage TCP/IP Routing

❑ Routing interfaces are either LAN or demand-dial interfaces.

❑ RRAS supports three types of connections for routing connections: modem, VPN, and PPoE.

❑ Routing ports are used to define point-to-point connections.

❑ The OSI model is known as a reference model because it describes a theoretical network protocol.

❑ Use either **netstat –r** or **route PRINT** to print the routing table.

❑ In TCP/IP, the terms *gateway* and *router* are used interchangeably.

❑ Static routing uses manually entered routes that rarely change.

❑ Dynamic routings are automatically entered in the routing table and reflect the current, dynamic state of the network.

❑ Windows Server 2003 supports RIP (v1 and v2), OSPF, and IGRP as routing protocols.

❑ RIP version 1 sends the entire routing table to all segments every 30 seconds.

❑ RIP version 2 supports incremental route transmissions, as well as inclusion of the network mask.

❑ Distance-vector routing protocols (such as RIP) are broadcast-based, where each router is aware of its immediate neighborhood and sends this information at scheduled intervals to all nearby routers.

❑ Routers that use link state routing protocols calculate a hierarchal view of the entire network where the router is the root of the tree.

SELF TEST

Manage Remote Access

1. You are the network administration for your company's corporate network. You have configured RRAS as a VPN server that allows a PPTP connection to be established with another remoter VPN server at IP address 136.1.34.42. The IP address of the local RRAS server's external network adapter is 136.5.34.43. You would like to configure inbound packet filters on the local VPN server that only allow PPTP through the firewall. Which of the following input filters will you need? (Choose all that apply.)

   A. Create a filter with destination address 136.5.34.43 and destination network mask 255.255.255.255 that uses protocol 47.

   B. Create a filter with destination address 136.5.34.43 and destination network mask 255.255.255.255 that uses protocol TCP and source port 1723.

   C. Create a filter with destination address 136.5.34.43 and destination network mask 255.255.255.255 that uses protocol TCP and destination port 1723.

   D. Create a filter with destination address 136.5.34.43 and source network mask 255.255.255.255 that uses protocol TCP and source port 1723.

   E. Create a filter with destination address 136.5.34.43 and source network mask 255.255.255.255 that uses protocol TCP and destination port 1723.

2. You are the network administration for your company's corporate network. You have installed and configured an RRAS server as a VPN server. It is located behind your corporate firewall, and you need to enable external user's VPN access to the RRAS server. Which of the following steps must you perform to give external VPN access to your RRAS server using L2TP? (Choose all correct answers.)

   A. Configure the firewall to open UDP port 1701.
   B. Configure the firewall to open TCP port 1723.
   C. Configure the firewall to open UDP port 500.
   D. Configure the firewall to open TCP port 500.
   E. Configure the firewall to allow IP protocol 17 to go through.
   F. Configure the firewall to allow IP protocol 47 to go through.
   G. Configure the firewall to allow IP protocol 50 to go through.
   H. Configure the firewall to allow IP protocol 51 to go through.

3. You are the network administration for your company's intranet. You recently deployed a RRAS server that provides secure routing (VPN) between a branch office and headquarters. The remote users located at the branch office need to get access to a Microsoft SQL Server that

is located behind the firewall at headquarters. What changes do you need to perform on the firewall to allow access to the Microsoft SQL Server?

A. Configure the firewall to allow TCP port 1733.

B. Configure the firewall to allow UDP port 1733.

C. Configure the firewall to allow IP protocol 1733.

D. No action needed.

4. You are the network administration for your company's corporate network. You need to configure a port filter to allow access from a POP3 application to a mail server on your network. Some users are using SSL for security when accessing the server. What ports must you enable? (Choose all that apply.)

A. TCP port 25

B. TCP port 110

C. TCP port 23

D. TCP port 995

5. You are the network administration for your company's intranet. You have configured a port filter that allows the following ports: TCP 80, TCP 443, and TCP 1733. Which of the following applications will work with these port settings? (Choose all that apply.)

A. Web browser using any HTTP connection.

B. Web browser using any HTTPS connection.

C. Web browser using any FTP connection.

D. The **ping** command.

6. How many TCP ports can be used?

A. 1024

B. 50,000

C. 65,535

7. You are the network administration for your company's intranet. You have been asked by your manager, John Liang, who is responsible for the assignment of the TCP/IP port numbers?

A. World Wide Web Consortium (W3C)

B. International Standards Organization (ISO)

C. United Nations (UN)

D. Internet Assigned Numbers Authority (IANA)

E. Internet Engineering Group (IEG)

F. European Computer Manufacturers Association (ECMA)

Manage TCP/IP Routing

8. You are the network administration for your company's corporate network, and you need to describe the routing layer in the DoD model. Which layer in the DoD networking model is responsible for routing?

- **A.** Layer 1: Network Access
- **B.** Layer 2: Internet
- **C.** Layer 3: Host-to-host
- **D.** Layer 4: Process/Application

9. You are the network administration for your company's corporate network, and you need to describe the routing layer in the OSI model. What layer in the DoD networking model is responsible for routing?

- **A.** Layer 1: Physical
- **B.** Layer 2: Data Link
- **C.** Layer 3: Network
- **D.** Layer 4: Transport
- **E.** Layer 5: Session
- **F.** Layer 6: Presentation
- **G.** Layer 7: Application

10. What tools are used to read the routing table of RRAS as installed on Windows Server 2003? (Choose all that apply.)

- **A.** The **net** command
- **B.** The **netstat** command
- **C.** The **routingtbl** command
- **D.** The **route** command
- **E.** The RRAS snap-in
- **F.** The Routing snap-in

11. You are reading the routing table output from the **netstat –r** command. You have noticed an entry that lists the destination as 0.0.0.0 and the mask as 0.0.0.0. What does this entry mean?

- **A.** It is the entry that will be used for all traffic that exceeds 15 hops.
- **B.** It is the default route for all packets that do not have an explicit route in the table.
- **C.** It is the entry that will be used for all traffic with CRC errors.
- **D.** It is an erroneous entry; it will be ignored by the router.

12. You are the network administrator for your company's corporate network. The network is depicted in the following illustration. What routing strategy should you select? (Choose the best answer.)

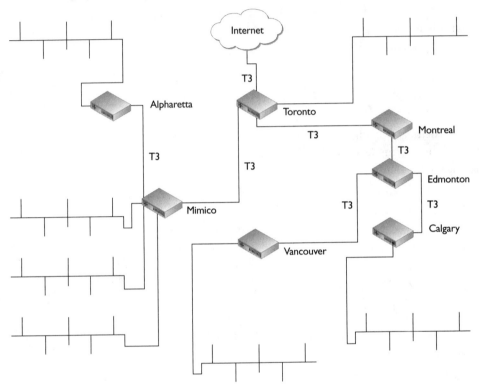

A. RIP version 1
B. RIP version 2
C. OSPF
D. Static routes

13. You are the network administrator for your company's corporate network. The network is depicted in the following illustration. What routing strategy should you select? (Choose the best answer.)

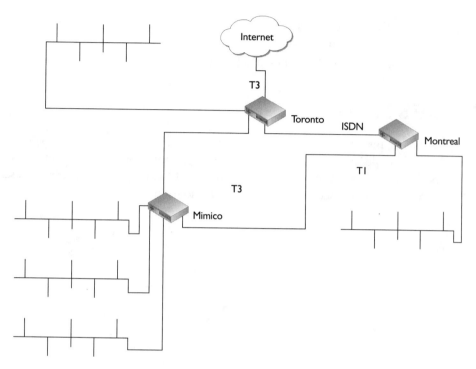

A. RIP version 1
B. RIP version 2
C. OSPF
D. Static routes

14. You are the network administrator for your company's corporate network. You have been asked to make a presentation about RIP version 2 to your management. What multicast address used by RIP version 2 will you describe to your management?

A. 224.0.0.9
B. 127.1.1.1
C. 226.0.0.9
D. 127.0.0.9.

15. You are the network administrator for your company's corporate network. You have been asked to make a presentation about RIP version 1 to your management. What is a rogue router?

A. A rogue router is a router that is overworked (from the French word for red).

B. A rogue router is a router that is not part of the network, but is advertising routes to try to redirect traffic to a clandestine network.

C. A rogue router is a router that no longer can route the traffic sent to it because one of the network segments has gone down.

D. A rogue router is a router that echoes back all traffic sent to it, causing a network storm.

LAB QUESTION

You are the network administrator for your company's corporate network. Your company is headquartered in Mimico, ON, with a sales office in Islington, ON, and a regional office in Montreal, PQ. Your company has located a service office in downtown Toronto, ON, where your Internet presence is hosted. The corporate network is seen in the following illustration.

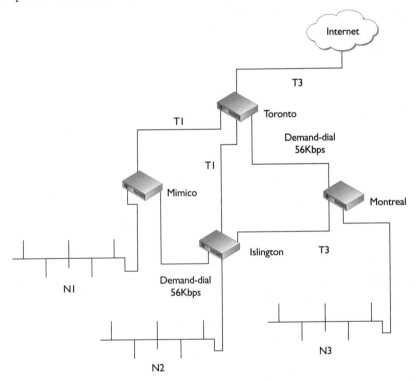

You need to design the routing for your network, ensuring that you have the most manageable network structure possible. Currently, you have installed four Windows Server 2003 computers with RRAS; these servers will be used as the routers in the four locations (Mimico, Islington, Toronto, and Montreal). What routing strategy will you use to ensure your network is routed in the most efficient manner?

SELF TEST ANSWERS

Manage Remote Access

1. ☑ **A, B,** and **C.** These filter settings enable IP protocol 47 and TCP port 1723 both for inbound as for outbound traffic. These are the requirements for PPTP.

☒ **D** and **E** are incorrect. Source addresses are used when configuring outbound filters, but source addresses are not used to configure inbound filters. The external IP address of the RRAS server on the local computer is the destination IP address for all inbound traffic.

2. ☑ **A, C, G,** and **H.** L2TP uses UDP port 500 and 1701 for IPSec as well as IP protocol 50 or 51. These settings will enable L2TP traffic through..

☒ **B** is incorrect because TCP port 1723 is the port for PPTP not L2TP. **D** is incorrect TCP port 500 is not used by L2TP. **E** and **F** are incorrect because IP protocol 17 is not used by L2TP and IP protocol 47 is used by PPTP.

3. ☑ **D.** The traffic over the VPN is encapsulated, and the individual ports that the application needs do not need to be enabled on the firewall.

☒ **A, B,** and **C** are incorrect because the VPN carries the connections to the Microsoft SQL server, so the firewall does not need to be configured for this traffic.

4. ☑ **B** and **D.** POP3 use TCP port 110 and POP3(SSL) uses port 995.

☒ **A** is incorrect because TCP port 25 is used for SMTP. **C** is incorrect because TCP port 23 is used for Telnet.

5. ☑ **A, B,** and **D.** Port 80 is for the HTTP protocol, port 443 is for the HTTPS protocol, and the port command uses ICMP, is not blocked by the filter action.

☒ **C** is incorrect because FTP uses port 21, and that port was not in the list.

6. ☑ **C.** The port number is an unsigned 32-bit number with a maximum of 65,535.

☒ **A** and **B** are incorrect because they define numbers that are not the maximum for a 32-bit number.

7. ☑ **D.** IANA is the responsible body.

☒ **A, B, C, E,** and **F** are incorrect because, entertaining as it could be to have the UN debate the port number assignments, none of these bodies have any authority over the number assignments.

Manage TCP/IP Routing

8. ☑ **B.** Layer 2 in the DoD model, the Internet layer, is responsible for routing.
    ☒ **A** is incorrect because Layer 1, the Network Access Layer, is responsible for the physical connection. **C** is incorrect because Layer 3, the Host-to-Host layer, is responsible for session control. **D** is incorrect because Layer 4, Process/Application Layer, is responsible for the application.

9. ☑ **C** is correct. Layer 3, the Network layer, is responsible for routing.
    ☒ **A, B, D, E, F,** and **G** are incorrect because none of these layers (physical, data link, transport, session, presentation, or application) are responsible for routing.

10. ☑ **B, D,** and **E.** The **netstat** and **route** command-line utilities as well as the RRAS snap-in, can be used to print the routing table.
    ☒ **A** is incorrect because the **net** command is used to manage network connections not routing. **C** and **F** are incorrect because there are no such commands.

11. ☑ **B.** This is the entry that indicates the default route that the router will use when there is no explicit route.
    ☒ **A, C,** and **D** are incorrect because these answers are all patently silly.

12. ☑ **B.** RIP version 2 is the correct answer because the high bandwidth between all sites makes RIP version 2 the better choice because RIP version 2 requires less management and has fewer maintenance issues. This network is small enough to use RIP version 2.
    ☒ **A** is incorrect because the broadcast traffic is not needed when you can use RIP version 2. **C** is incorrect because OSPF is more involved to plan and deploy. **D** is incorrect because RIP version 2 will provide the dynamic routes needed, and there is no need to manage slow versus fast links in this network.

13. ☑ **D.** In this environment where there are slow links mixed with fast ones it is more advantageous to use static routes to force the traffic over the faster links and only use the ISDN link as a fall-back connection.
    ☒ **A, B,** and **C** are incorrect because dynamic routing is not the answer for this small network with some slower links. Incidentally, RIP version 1 is never the right answer.

14. ☑ **A.** 224.0.0.9 is the correct address.
    ☒ **B, C,** and **D** are incorrect because these addresses are all wrong.

15. ☑ **B.** A rogue router is a device that advertises its routes in an environment where the router does not belong. This is one of the many problems with RIP version 1.
    ☒ **A, C,** and **D** are incorrect because they do not describe what the term *rogue router* means; some of these answers could work, though.

LAB ANSWER

The problem with this network is that there are a mixture of high-bandwidth links (T1 and T3) with two demand-dial 56Kbps links. Your routing decision must ensure that these demand-dial links are never used unless there are problems with the high-speed links.

The most efficient strategy here is to use static routes to force the traffic to use the high-speed links, and set up the demand-dial links as backup by setting the metrics to higher numbers.

TABLE 11-3	From	To	Metric
	Mimico	Toronto	1
The Static Routes	Mimico	Islington	10
	Islington	Toronto	1
	Islington	Montreal	1
	Islington	Mimico	10
	Montreal	Islington	1
	Montreal	Toronto	10
	Toronto	Mimico	1
	Toronto	Islington	1
	Toronto	Montreal	10

MCSE/MCSA

MICROSOFT® CERTIFIED SYSTEMS ENGINEER &
MICROSOFT® CERTIFIED SYSTEMS ADMINISTRATOR

12

Maintain Routing and Remote Access

CERTIFICATION OBJECTIVES

I n this chapter, you will be introduced to troubleshooting VPNs and remote access. Some of these problems are related to the configuration of the Routing and Remote Access Service, but most are the result of problems that are outside of the RRAS server. For example, a bad routing table in a router can have profound effects on the router's ability to communicate across the network between computers. This problem will impact the VPN, but it is an external problem. In this chapter, you will use all the skills you have learned in this book to successfully resolve these problems.

It has been stated many times before, but it is so important it bears stating again: the success of a troubleshooting exercise depends on the prior knowledge and expertise of the person performing the troubleshooting. For the 70-291 exam, you will find these skills being used in questions that present a large amount of information, which require you to extract the relevant pieces in order to understand the question and answer it correctly. That is what this chapter is about: we will look at the issues you will meet when maintaining a Routing and Remote Access Service environment.

The topics in this chapter are troubleshooting VPN and remote access, as well as gaining access to resources on subnets beyond the RRAS server. We will also look at the issues that arise when you use RRAS as a router-to-router VPN, as well as demand-dial issues.

CERTIFICATION OBJECTIVE 12.01

Diagnose and Resolve Issues Related to Remote Access VPNs

The remote access VPN is the architecture that lets your remote clients connect over a VPN using a dial-in connection through an Internet Service Provider (ISP), or through a LAN that is connected to the Internet through a router and possibly a firewall, as shown in Figure 12-1. The issues that come up with these types of VPNs are that the client's environment is a changing map, where you have very little if any control over how the client computer is configured at the time of the connection. There are a couple of common problems that come up on a rather frequent basis: bad IP configuration of the client computer, and bad protocol configuration of the VPN. We looked at the protocol issues in Chapter 9, but will revisit some of the issues here as well.

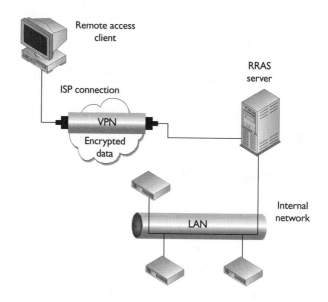

FIGURE 12-1

Remote client
connection
over a VPN

The process of connecting a client to your internal network via a VPN starts with the client computer successfully connecting to the local network and acquiring a valid TCP/IP configuration from a DHCP server, or by manually configuring the TCP/IP protocol. If the remote client does not have a valid TCP/IP configuration, there is little chance that a connection can be established.

e x a m

ⓦ a t c h *Always suspect the TCP/IP configuration when you deal with remote client issues; it is a good place to start.*

Once the TCP/IP configuration is established, and the user starts the connection attempt, the remote computer needs to resolve the name of the Remote Access server using either the FQDN or the IP address of the server. This is another potential problem area—the TCP/IP configuration for the remote client must have a valid DNS server configured, and the Remote Access server must have a proper address record in a DNS zone that can be queried from a public site.

on the

ⓙ o b *If you want to avoid the DNS issues you can configure the remote client to use the IP address rather than the FQDN.*

Once the remote computer has resolved the address of the Remote Access server, it can start the connection negotiation. Depending on the type of VPN, there are other pitfalls, as you saw in Chapter 9. If the VPN uses L2TP, the traffic is carried using IPSec, and IPSec requires a means of mutual authentication. The common solution for the VPN is to install computer certificates on the Remote Access server and all the remote client computers that will connect. If you use PPTP, this issue does not occur.

Even if the client has connected successfully, there are still areas that can give you grief, as you will see in the next section, which deals with access to local resources.

Remote Access Client and TCP/IP

TCP/IP is the network protocol that is used for all VPN. The configuration of TCP/IP is probably the most common problem you will encounter with remote access. The following is meant to be a review of TCP/IP rather than an exhaustive treatment.

A TCP/IP Review

TCP/IP is a suite of protocols used to communicate between computers (called hosts). Each host has a unique 32-bit host address that is used to find the host on the IP network. For example, my notebook currently uses the following address: 00001010000000000000000011001001. I only use that format of the address when I have severe routing problems, mostly the address is represented as four octets separated with a period (.). The equivalent is 10.0.0.201. That is so much easier to remember, but I defy anyone to remember more than a handful of IP addresses.

Each IP address is usually given together with a second piece of information: the *network mask*. The network mask is a string of ones (1) and zeros (0) that identify the subnet that the host is on. The host itself uses this information to determine what traffic is local, and does not need to be forwarded to a router, and what traffic is remote, and must go through a router to another subnet. Network masks are written either in an octet (class) format as 255.255.255.0, or as a classless format as the number of bits that are part of the network. The classless notation is part of the IP address as in this example 10.0.0.201/24, which indicates that the network is 24 bits.

For a host to communicate with remote (routed) hosts, it must have an entry for a router to use. This is either the *default gateway* or a static entry in the routing table of the host. If there is no route, there will be no communication.

This is where DNS comes in. DNS is used as the white pages of the network; it translates between a human-readable name like polkagris.nopcomp.com and the numeric address 10.0.0.201. The human-readable address is called the *Fully Qualified Domain Name* (*FQDN*) and is preferred as the means of locating a host on the network.

The parts of TCP/IP addressing so far are

- IP address
- Network mask
- Default gateway
- DNS

These entries are mandatory for a client to be able to establish the TCP/IP communication with any other host. The most common method of ensuring that mobile computers are properly configured is to use a Dynamic Host Configuration Protocol (DHCP) server to configure the computer when it is attached to the network. The easiest method of learning about the TCP/IP configuration is to use the command-line utility **ipconfig** with the **/all** switch, as shown in this listing.

```
C:\ >ipconfig/all
Windows IP Configuration
   Host Name . . . . . . . . . . . . : POLKAGRIS
   Primary Dns Suffix  . . . . . . . : nopcomp.com
   Node Type . . . . . . . . . . . . : Hybrid
   IP Routing Enabled. . . . . . . . : No
   WINS Proxy Enabled. . . . . . . . : No
   DNS Suffix Search List. . . . . . : nopcomp.com
Ethernet adapter Local Area Connection:
   Connection-specific DNS Suffix  . : nopTo.com
   Description . . . . . . . . . . . : Intel(R) PRO/100 VE Network Connection
   Physical Address. . . . . . . . . : 08-00-46-5C-8B-7A
Dhcp Enabled. . . . . . . . . . . : Yes
Autoconfiguration Enabled . . . . : Yes
   IP Address. . . . . . . . . . . . : 10.0.0.201
   Subnet Mask . . . . . . . . . . . : 255.255.255.0
   Default Gateway . . . . . . . . . : 10.0.0.2
   DHCP Server . . . . . . . . . . . : 10.0.0.2
   DNS Servers . . . . . . . . . . . : 192.168.22.67
                                       192.168.22.195
                                       192.168.22.67
   Lease Obtained. . . . . . . . . . : Wednesday, August 20, 2003 9:43:22 AM
   Lease Expires . . . . . . . . . . : Thursday, August 21, 2003 9:43:22 AM
C:\>
```

The important information here is that the client is automatically configured by DHCP, as you can see in the two highlighted lines in the printout. When you're troubleshooting remotely, make it a habit to ask the remote user to open a command prompt and print the TCP/IP configuration, and read it back to you.

There is one more issue with TCP/IP and the Windows environment, and that is the Windows Internet Naming Server (WINS). WINS is used to resolve NetBIOS computer names to IP addresses. For example, my workstation has the NetBIOS name POLKAGRIS. If you have configured the VPN to connect using a NetBIOS name, the client must have an available and configured WINS server, or a configured LMHOSTS file with the entry for your Remote Access server.

on the
ö o b

Always determine what type of name is entered for the Remote Access server: FQDN, NetBIOS, or IP address.

This has been a very fast review of TCP/IP with a focus on remote access VPNs.

EXERCISE 12-1

CertCam 12-1 ON THE CD

Determining the TCP/IP Configuration

In this exercise you will find the TCP/IP configuration of your workstation.

1. Log on to your workstation using a normal user account.

2. Click on **Start | Run** to open the **Run** dialog box.

3. Type **cmd** into the **Open** textbox and click **OK** to open the command prompt.

4. At the command prompt, type **ipconfig** to see a summary display of the TCP/IP configuration:

```
C:\>ipconfig
Windows IP Configuration
Ethernet adapter Local Area Connection:
        Connection-specific DNS Suffix  . : nopTo.com
        IP Address. . . . . . . . . . . . : 10.0.0.201
        Subnet Mask . . . . . . . . . . . : 255.255.255.0
        Default Gateway . . . . . . . . . : 10.0.0.2
C:\>
```

You might see additional network interfaces listed, depending on your workstation's configuration. Note that there is no information about the method of configuration nor about DNS configuration.

5. Type **ipconfig /all** at the command prompt to get a full listing of the configuration:

```
C:\ >ipconfig/all
Windows IP Configuration
    Host Name . . . . . . . . . . . . : POLKAGRIS
    Primary Dns Suffix . . . . . . . : nopcomp.com
    Node Type . . . . . . . . . . . . : Hybrid
    IP Routing Enabled. . . . . . . . : No
    WINS Proxy Enabled. . . . . . . . : No
    DNS Suffix Search List. . . . . . : nopcomp.com
Ethernet adapter Local Area Connection:
    Connection-specific DNS Suffix  . : nopTo.com
    Description . . . . . . . . . . . : Intel(R) PRO/100 VE Network Connection
    Physical Address. . . . . . . . . : 08-00-46-5C-8B-7A
    Dhcp Enabled. . . . . . . . . . . : Yes
    Autoconfiguration Enabled . . . . : Yes
    IP Address. . . . . . . . . . . . : 10.0.0.201
    Subnet Mask . . . . . . . . . . . : 255.255.255.0
    Default Gateway . . . . . . . . . : 10.0.0.2
    DHCP Server . . . . . . . . . . . : 10.0.0.2
    DNS Servers . . . . . . . . . . . : 192.168.22.67
                                        192.168.22.195
                                        192.168.22.67
    Lease Obtained. . . . . . . . . . : Wednesday, August 20, 2003 9:43:22 AM
    Lease Expires . . . . . . . . . . : Thursday, August 21, 2003 9:43:22 AM
C:\>
```

In this listing you see all the information about the client's TCP/IP configuration.

The ipconfig *utility has a number of uses, but it is the fastest way of getting information about the TCP/IP configuration of servers and workstations alike.*

Client Troubleshooting

There is a logical methodology to use when troubleshooting remote client VPN issues. These steps are in many cases identical to troubleshooting TCP/IP connectivity issues. The tools you will use are **ipconfig, ping, tracert,** and **nslookup**. These tools are used in many places throughout this book and are documented in Chapter 14.

When a remote access VPN client calls in to report a failure to connect to the VPN, you normally start with one step: make sure that the client computer is connected to the network at the site where he is located. You will be surprised how many times the client and the network administrator have been troubleshooting a computer that is not connected to the network. Verify that the client computer has a valid IP address for the network it is connected to by using **ipconfig /all** to print the configuration.

Once you have confirmed the TCP/IP configuration, you need to verify that the remote client can exchange packets with the Remote Access server; use the **ping** command for this verification. The host you ping is the one that is configured in the VPN configuration of the client. For example if the VPN is configured to connect to remote.nopcomp.com, issue the command **ping remote.nopcomp.com**. If this fails with no replies, ping the IP address of the Remote Access server to verify that the network actually routes the traffic correctly.

If you can ping the Remote Access server using the FQDN, you've verified the DNS and routing configuration. If you can only ping the IP address, you've verified the routing, but you know that the DNS configuration is bad. Or you have a routing problem to the DNS server.

To resolve a DNS problem, you need to verify that the DNS sever that the client computer is using (according to the documentation you gleaned from the **ipconfig** utility) is functional. The tools to use are **nslookup** and **ping**. For more information about troubleshooting DNS issues, see Chapter 6.

To resolve routing problems, you use tools like **tracert**, **ping**, **pathping**, and **route**. We will look at the routing issues later in this chapter, and the Internet issues in Chapter 14.

If everything is working from a network point of view, you need to verify the VPN connection properties as well as the user account properties. The problem may be protocol-related if there is nothing wrong with the network, but it is very unusual for a protocol issue to show up as a network problem. The only real possibility is that the client receives an Error 678: The remote computer did not respond.

The TCP/IP configuration we have looked at so far is used for the remote client to gain access to the Remote Access server. Once connected, the VPN will be using its own TCP/IP configuration that includes the same settings that you saw here. The critical information that the Remote Access server must configure for the client is a DNS server and a default gateway. If these are not configured, the remote client won't be able to use any resources outside of the Remote Access server, as we will explore in the next section.

Now that you have a better idea of remote access VPN issues, here are some possible scenario questions and their answers.

SCENARIO & SOLUTION

What happens if one of my remote clients hard-codes the IP configuration for use on our internal network, and he then travels to Cleveland and tries to connect to our VPN through the hotel high-speed network?	The real problem is that the client configuration is static for one subnet internally to your organization. The hotel's ISP will not be able to use DHCP to configure the hard-coded configuration, resulting in no communication.
Why does the remote client need a correct DNS server configured?	In order to be able to resolve the FQDN of the Remote Access server into an IP address to connect to, the remote client must have access to a configured DNS server.
Do we really need a DNS server configured?	No, you don't need a DNS server, but without one, you will have to configure your remote clients with IP addresses for the Remote Access server, or install and maintain Hosts files on all your remote clients. In either case the administrative burden is very high.
The remote client is using the IP address 10.0.0.201/24 and is configured to use 11.0.0.1 as the default gateway. Will that work?	No. The two addresses are on different subnets, so traffic to the default gateway will be seen as remote. This leads to a spiral where no traffic is ever routed.

CERTIFICATION OBJECTIVE 12.02

Diagnose and Resolve User Access to Resources Beyond the Remote Access Server

Once the remote client has connected to the Remote Access server through the VPN, the potential problems are not over. To gain access to resources on the internal network, the RRAS server must route the traffic for the client. This section will look at some of these problems, using the network shown in Figure 12-2.

The remote clients connect to MERCURY, which is the Remote Access server, located at the Mimico site. The resources that are needed for the remote clients are located in two different sites: Long Branch is connected via a VPN, and Islington, which is at the same campus as Mimico, is connected with a router.

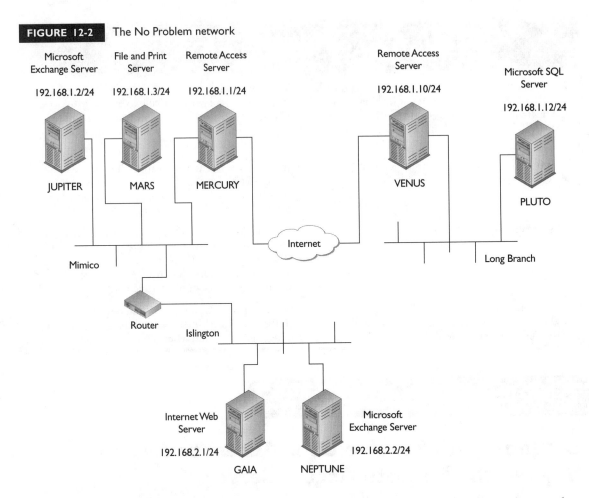

FIGURE 12-2 The No Problem network

When the client connects, it needs to be given access to the internal network through MERCURY. The client connection must be configured with a default gateway and DNS for name resolution. There are two methods that can be used to configure the IP addresses that are given to the remote client: either the Remote Access server uses a DHCP server that is configured for the scope, or the RRAS server uses a static range of addresses for the remote clients. The DNS configuration is the configuration of the Remote Access server, and the default gateway is set to the connection.

As you can see in Figure 12-2, if MERCURY does not have a proper configuration for DNS and routes for both the Long Branch and Islington sites, there would not be any access at all. You control this using the IP tab of the Routing and Remote Access Server's property dialog from the RRAS console, as you can see in Figure 12-3.

FIGURE 12-3

The IP tab

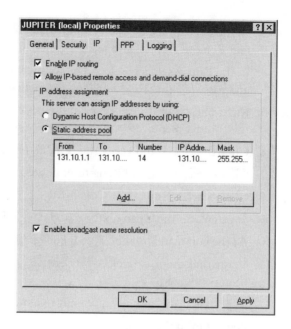

There are some important settings on this tab:

- **Enable IP routing**   Clearing this tab will prevent any routing beyond the Remote Access server. To enable routing, this option must be on.
- **Enable broadcast name resolution**   Enabling this option allows clients to resolve host names on the local network segment without the use of DNS or WINS.

If you do not want routing, clear the **Enable IP routing** option, and no routing will take place. In the case of the sample network, routing is needed for the clients to reach the needed resources. A properly configured DNS or WINS entry in the TCP/IP configuration is also needed because GAIA and NEPTUNE are on a different network.

EXERCISE 12-2

Verifying Routing and Remote Access Service Settings

In this exercise you will verify the settings for routing for VPN clients.

1. Log in to your server using your non-administrative account.

2. Click **Start | Control Panel**.

3. In the Control Panel, open **Administrative Tools**, right-click **Routing and Remote Access**, and select **Run As** from the context menu.

4. In the **Run As** dialog, select **The following user** and type a user account and password that has administrative rights on the server. Click **OK**.

5. Right-click your RRAS server in the node tree, and select **Properties** from the context menu.

6. Click the **IP** tab and verify that **Enable IP routing** is turned on.

7. Close the Routing and Remote Access console.

8. Click **Start | Run**.

9. Type **cmd** in the **Open** textbox, and click **OK**.

10. At the command prompt, type **ipconfig /all**.

11. Verify that there are DNS server entries, and that the default router has been configured.

12. Type **exit** at the command prompt to close the window.

13. Log out from the session.

Now that you have a better idea of resource access beyond the RRAS server, here are some possible scenario questions and their answers.

SCENARIO & SOLUTION

Why would I enable broadcast name resolution for my VPN server?	If you only want to make the local segment available, with the least amount of management, use broadcast name resolution. Remember to make sure there is no DNS or WINS defined for the clients on the VPN for this method to work as planned.
I don't have a DHCP server on my network. What are my choices for configuring the clients?	You can configure a static range of IP addresses that are used for remote clients when they connect to the VPN server.
How do I totally block access beyond the VPN server for all remote clients?	The way to totally stop routing through the VPN server is to turn off the Enable IP routing option on the IP tab of the servers properties.

CERTIFICATION OBJECTIVE 12.03

Troubleshoot Demand-dial Routing

When you connect routers using demand-dial connections, you open up a different set of problems. The most common ones are

- Failure of the on-demand connection to connect automatically
- Failure to make the demand-dial connection
- Failure to reach resources beyond the calling or answering router
- Failure of the autostatic updates

In the following sections I will detail how to troubleshoot these problems.

Failure of the On-demand Connection to Connect Automatically

When the on-demand connection fails, there are a couple of items to consider on the Routing and Remote Access Service server that is configured to use a demand-dial connection. The first item to investigate is to make sure the proper static route exists and is configured to use the proper demand-dial interface. You confirm the static route from the **Static Routes** node in the Routing and Remote Access console. Open the properties for the static route to ensure it is configured to use the designated on-demand interface, as seen in Figure 12-4. Verify that the option **Use this route to initiate demand-dial connections** is selected.

The demand-dial interface might be disabled, and will not be used. You can see the status of the network interfaces in Figure 12-5. To enable the demand-dial interface, right-click the demand-dial interface in the **Network Interfaces** node in Routing and Remote Access console and select **Enable** from the context menu.

When the demand-dial interface is configured, it is given a schedule of operation that dictates when it is allowed to connect. One possible issue is that the schedule prohibits the connection at this time. To verify the schedule, open the **Dial-out hours** dialog from the context menu of the demand-dial interface, as seen in Figure 12-6.

One final trouble area is that the filters for the demand-dial interface on the calling router may be set to prevent the connection attempt. Verify the filter settings in the **Set IP demand-dial Filters** dialog from the context menu of the demand-dial interface.

FIGURE 12-4

Verifying the
static route

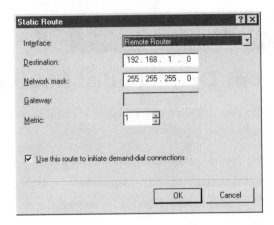

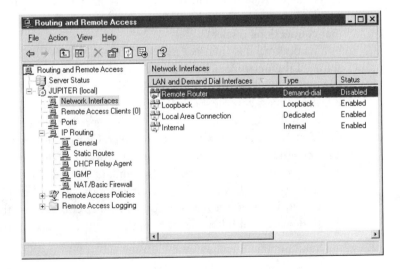

Always look for information
in the question that indicates that the
interface can connect automatically
if it is designed to do so.

In Figure 12-7 you can see that all traffic is
allowed except from the 10.0.0.0/24 network
to the 66.23.0.0/16 network.

These are the first items to look for when
the demand-dial connection fails to connect
automatically.

FIGURE 12-5

Network
Interface status

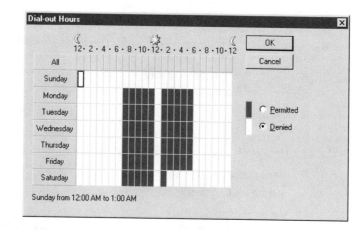

FIGURE 12-6

The demand-dial
interface schedule

Failure to Make the Demand-dial Connection

The largest numbers of problems are normally centered on the failure of the demand-dial
connection to succeed, even if all the settings for the static route, schedule, and filters

FIGURE 12-7

Demand-dial
filters

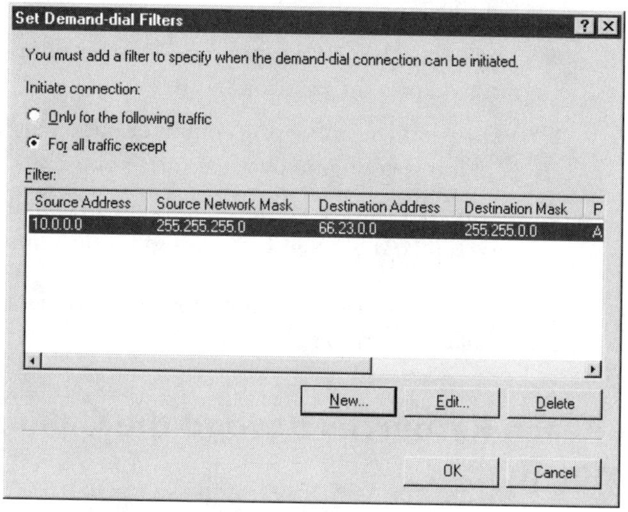

are correct. In this category we need to verify a number of items from the profound to the esoteric. In the following list you see the items to verify.

- Verify that the calling and answering computers are running the Routing and Remote Access Service, and that it is started.
- Verify that both the calling and answering computer have routing enabled.
- Verify that the dial-up ports used on both the calling (outbound) and answering (inbound) computers are configured to allow demand-dial routing.
- Verify that the dial-up ports used by the demand-dial interface on both the calling and answering computer are free and not used by other applications.
- Verify that the calling and answering computers have at least one common authentication method through remote access policies.
- Verify that the calling computer is using the correct domain, and that the name and password are correct for the answering computer.
- Verify that the password is 14 characters or less in length if the authentication used is MS CHAP with 40-bit MPPE encryption.
- Verify that the user account used by the calling computer has not been disabled or locked out.
- Verify that the user account used by the calling computer has been configured not to expire the password.
- Verify that the answering computer has enough free addresses in the address pool if it is configured with a static pool.
- Verify that the answering computer can communicate with the RADIUS server, if RADIUS authentication is selected.

This is a long list of verifications for those problems that will face you when the demand-dial connection fail to connect.

Failure to Reach Resources Beyond the Calling or Answering Router

Even after the connection has been established there are potential problems that will keep you, as the network administrator, reaching for the bottle of Milk of Magnesia. I am talking about the stubborn router that never shows the resources that are on the local segments beyond the demand-dial router. Here again is a checklist of verifications that will help you solve the problem.

■ Verify that the demand-dial connection isn't viewed as a remote access connection if it is a two-way initiated demand-dial connection.

The answering router determines that the calling router truly is a router by matching the credentials of the caller with the name of the demand-dial interface. To view how the connection was finalized use the Routing and Remote Access console. If the caller connected as a router, the port shows a status of Active and the demand-dial interface shows Connected. If the caller connected as a remote access client, the connection shows up under the Remote Access Clients node.

Two-way initiated connections can be started by either router, which means that the two routers must be given a mirror configuration of the other. For example, if you have two routers, R1 and R2, where the demand-dial interface of R1 is named MIMICO and the interface of R2 is named ISLINGTON, you would need to perform the following configuration of credentials:

■ R1 logs in to R2 using ISLINGTON as the user name.

■ R2 logs in to R1 using MIMICO as the user name.

■ Verify that the correct static routes are configured on the calling router and that the answering router has the proper routing protocols configured so the routes are advertised when the demand-dial route is established.

■ Verify that the routes are created on both sides of the connection to support exchange of traffic in both directions. There is no default route for demand-dial connections; these routes must be configured on both sides of the connection so traffic can be exchanged.

■ Verify that there are routes configured on any other routers on both sides of the connection to support the demand-dial route.

■ Verify that there are no filters on the demand-dial interfaces that block the desired traffic.

■ Verify that there are no packet filters configured on the answering router that block the desired traffic.

exam
ⓦatch   *Remember that there are*
no default routes when you use demand-dial
routes. You must create the routes explicitly
as static routes.

When you lay out the traffic over a demand-dial router, you must always know what traffic should and should not cross the route. One reason for the demand-dial route is that there is no business need for a permanent connection, so there is normally filtering designed into the demand-dial interfaces.

The process of exchanging routes between the calling and answering router is called *autostatic updates*. To configure autostatic updates, you add the demand-dial interface to the RIP routing protocol with the operation mode set to **Auto-static update mode**, and the outgoing packet protocol set to RIP version 2 multicast. Figure 12-8 shows how this is configured.

Troubleshooting Tools

If a demand-dial interface experiences a problem connecting, it records the reason why the connection failed. This reason is available as part of the data about the demand-dial interface. To check the reason for a demand-dial connection failure, you need to open the Routing and Remote Access console and right-click the demand-dial interface to

FIGURE 12-8

Enabling
autostatic mode

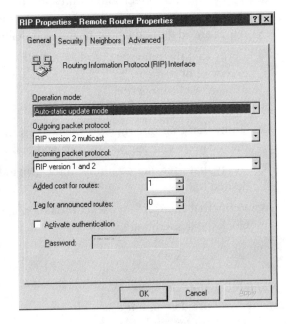

display the context menu. Click **Unreachability Reason** to display a popup with the reason of the failure. Figure 12-9 shows where the menu option is located, and Figure 12-10 shows a sample reason.

There are a number of reasons why the demand-dial interface is left in an unreachable state, including a lack of ports for the demand-dial interface, RRAS is paused, the demand-dial interface is disabled, or the schedule prevents the connection.

There are a couple of tools available when you troubleshoot the failure of demand-dial routing. You can use event logging on the answering router to capture what went wrong. To configure logging, select **Log all events** from the **Logging** tab of the property dialog of the answering router. Try the connection and view the log entries in the Event Viewer in the System log. Remember to return the log setting to normal after you have solved the problem.

Windows Accounting and Logging is selected from the **Remote Access Logging** node in the Routing and Remote Access console. You can configure the logging to track the usage of demand-dial and remote access as well as authentication attempts. These log files are stored in the **%systemroot%\system32\logfiles** folder.

If you need to investigate the traffic sent between demand-dial routers during connection establishment and data transfers, you can use the Network Monitor that

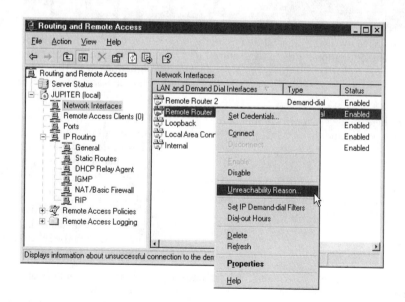

FIGURE 12-10

The
Unreachability
reason dialog

comes as a part of Windows Server 2003. The Network Monitor tool cannot interpret and decode the encrypted portions of the traffic, however. Finally, if you need very detailed information for the connection attempt you can enable tracing. Tracing is enabled on the **Logging** tab of the RRAS server Properties dialog by enabling **Additional Routing and Remote Access information**. Tracing should only be enabled for short periods for troubleshooting a particular problem. The output logs are stored in the **%eindir%\tracing** directory.

Now that you have a better idea of troubleshooting demand-dial routing, here are some possible scenario questions and their answers.

SCENARIO & SOLUTION

Why do I have to use the demand-dial interface name as authentication for the calling router?	The signal to the answering router that it is another router calling is that the user name used for authentication is the same as the name of the demand-dial interface. Any other user name is interpreted as being a remote access client.
Why is there no default route when I connect between two demand-dial routers?	Demand-dial routers do not have a default route. Rather, all traffic that is to traverse the connection must be defined using static routes. This is to ensure the demand-dial router, which is usually low bandwidth, only carries the desired traffic.
There is a schedule for the demand-dial router. Why should I use this schedule?	The schedule is used to focus the traffic across a link to certain times of the day to minimize the cost of the link. The demand-dial router is only allowed to connect during the scheduled times. The default schedule is every hour of every day.
Why must I configure a static route for a demand-dial connection?	Demand-dial connections will not start a connection attempt, except when traffic is directly addressed to the interface. This is the role of the static route for on-demand connections.

CERTIFICATION OBJECTIVE 12.04

Troubleshoot Router-to-Router VPNs

When you have enabled two Windows Server 2003 computers to link two sites using a router-to-router VPN, there are a number of trouble spots that potentially will create problems for the operation of your network. Some of these issues and their resolution are similar to the other routing configurations you have seen in this chapter, but some are VPN-specific issues that are similar to those experienced by remote access clients connecting over a VPN.

In this section we will list the items to verify when you troubleshoot router-to-router VPN problems.

- Verify that both the routers are running the Routing and Remote Access Service, and that it is started.

- Verify that the Local and remote routing (LAN and WAN router) is enabled on both of the routers to ensure that routing takes place, as shown here:

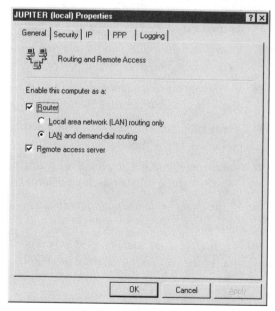

■ Verify that the PPTP or L2TP ports are configured for inbound and outbound demand-dial connections, as shown here:

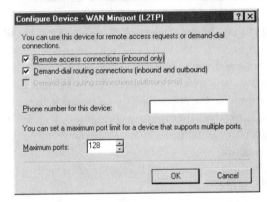

■ Verify that there are enough ports (PPTP or L2TP) for the connection. If not, increase the number of available ports.

■ Verify that both the calling and answering router support the same tunneling protocol. Ensure there are enough PPTP or L2TP ports available.

■ Verify that the calling and answering routers have a common authentication method based on a remote access policy.

■ Verify that the calling and answering routers have a common encryption method based on a remote access policy.

■ Verify that the user account used to establish the connection has the correct dial-in and access permissions.

■ Verify that the remote access policy settings are not in conflict with the properties of the router.

■ Verify that the answering router can authenticate the user name and credentials that the calling router uses for authentication.

■ Verify that the answering router has enough addresses if it is using a static IP address pool.

■ Verify that static routes are added on both sides of the connection to ensure that traffic can be routed over the VPN.

- Verify that autostatic mode is enabled, and that RIP version 2 multicast is configured for both VPN interfaces.

- Verify that the account used for authentication is the one configured for the remote interface. The user name is the name of the interface; if another user name is used, the connection will be interpreted as a remote access client.

Now that you have a better idea of troubleshooting router-to-router VPNs, here are some possible scenario questions and their answers.

SCENARIO & SOLUTION

Why do RIP interfaces have to be marked as autostatic when used with router-to-router VPNs?	The method used to announce the static routes of one router to the other in a router-to-router VPN is to use RIP V2 multicast, and to use the autostatic method to ensure that both routers know the networks on either side. If autostatic is not used, you will be unable to access resources beyond the router.
Why would I use the Network Monitor?	The Network Monitor is the tool used to capture network traffic, and then to analyze the traffic to troubleshoot at the lowest level of networking. The value of using the Network Monitor is that all traffic is available and can be seen in the context of the connection; analyzing the output from Network Monitor is a complicated task that requires experience to master.
What are my options for addressing between routers in a router-to-router VPN?	The answering router must have the ability to give the calling router an address. There are two ways of handing out the addresses: use an external DHCP server, or define a pool of static addresses that are used by the router. In either case, there must be enough free addresses so the calling router is guaranteed it will get an address.

CERTIFICATION SUMMARY

In this chapter you learned about the issues related to troubleshooting connections between remote access clients and servers as well as between routers that make up a VPN between sites in your network. As a network administrator, you will use this knowledge to benefit in your daily work, as well as for the 70-291 exam.

From this chapter emerged a common thread when troubleshooting VPN connectivity: the two parties to the connection must use the same protocols, and have initial TCP/IP connectivity to connect. If you work with on-demand routers, you need to ensure that the router will be triggered by the traffic you want to use by configuring a static route as well as verifying the schedule for the connection.

Remember that a router that connects to another router needs to authenticate using the name of the remote router's demand-dial interface to ensure the connection is interpreted as a router-to-router connection. If the connection shows up under the Remote Access Client node, there is something wrong with the authentication.

✓ TWO-MINUTE DRILL

Diagnose and Resolve Issues Related to Remote Access VPNs

❏ Verify the initial TCP/IP configuration using the **ipconfig** utility.

❏ Remember that the default gateway must be on the same subnet as the client.

❏ To find a remote access server by name, there must be a configured name resolution solution, by having a DNS entry that can be connected to.

❏ Use the **ping** utility to verify that you can communicate with the remote host.

❏ Use DHCP to configure mobile clients.

Diagnose and Resolve User Access to Resources Beyond the Remote Access Server

❏ Verify that IP routing is enabled on the answering router.

❏ Enable broadcast name resolution to have routing to the local subnet of the answering router.

❏ Enable the appropriate routing protocols to provide access to the routed network.

❏ To block access to any resources beyond the answering router, you need to disable IP routing and broadcast name resolution.

Troubleshoot Demand-dial Routing

❏ Verify that the routers are enabled and that RRAS is running on both routers.

❏ Verify that the schedule allows connections at the times you need the connections.

❏ Verify that the traffic is allowed with no filters enabled for the desired networks.

❏ Verify that there are free ports for the connection.

❏ Verify that the routers are configured to connect using the demand-dial interface name of the remote router.

❏ Verify that the account used for authentication has not expired or been locked out.

Troubleshoot Router-to-Router VPNs

❑ Verify that the static routes are configured for both sides.

❑ Verify that autostatic and RIP V2 multicast is configured for proper routing across the route.

❑ Verify that there are no filters or port rules that limit the traffic.

❑ Verify that the planned traffic can transverse the route.

❑ Use the **Unreachable reason** from the context menu of the demand-dial interface to get a report on why the connection was not made.

❑ Enable logging to learn more about the problem.

❑ Enable tracing to get an exhaustive set of logs to see all aspects of the connection.

❑ Verify that the ports are configured as inbound and outbound demand-dial connections.

SELF TEST

Diagnose and Resolve Issues Related to Remote Access VPNs

1. What tool do you use to learn about how a computer is configured to use TCP/IP?

   A. net

   B. winipconfig

   C. ipconfig

   D. tracert

2. You are the network administrator for your company's network, which consists of six Windows Server 2003 computers and 85 Windows XP Professional computers. 35 of the client workstations are mobile and connect to the network through a remote access server running Routing and Remote Access Service on one of the Windows Server 2003 computers. Des is one of the users who uses his computer remotely. Today Des has called you to inform you that he gets an error message when he tries to connect to the remote access server from a client's location. You ask Des to run the **ipconfig /all** command and report the information to you. The following is the pertinent information:

   ```
   Ethernet adapter Local Area Connection:
      Connection-specific DNS Suffix  . : Nopcomp.com
      Description . . . . . . . . . . . : Intel(R) PRO/100 VE Network Connection
      Physical Address. . . . . . . . . : 08-00-46-5C-8B-7A
      Dhcp Enabled. . . . . . . . . . . : Yes
      Autoconfiguration Enabled . . . . : Yes
      IP Address. . . . . . . . . . . . : 10.0.0.201
      Subnet Mask . . . . . . . . . . . : 255.255.255.0
      Default Gateway . . . . . . . . . : 10.0.1.2
      DHCP Server . . . . . . . . . . . : 10.0.0.22
      DNS Servers . . . . . . . . . . . : 45.153.22.67
      Lease Obtained. . . . . . . . . . : Friday, August 22, 2003 10:57:10 AM
      Lease Expires . . . . . . . . . . : Saturday, August 23, 2003 10:57:10 AM
   ```

   What is the solution to the connection error?

   A. The address of the default gateway is on the wrong network, the DHCP server has the wrong configuration, or Des's computer has a hard-coded default gateway.

   B. Des's computer does not have a valid IP address. Configure his computer to use DHCP or enter an IP address.

   C. The DNS address is not correct.

   D. The subnet mask is incorrect for the configuration.

3. You are the network administrator for your company's network, which consists of six Windows Server 2003 computers and 85 Windows XP Professional computers. 35 of the client workstations are mobile and connect to the network through a remote access server running Routing and Remote Access Service on one of the Windows Server 2003 computers. Des is one of the users who uses his computer remotely. Today Des has called you to inform you that he gets an error message when he tries to connect to the remote access server from a client's location. You ask Des to run the **ipconfig /all** command and report the information to you. The following is the pertinent information:

```
Ethernet adapter Local Area Connection:
    Connection-specific DNS Suffix   . : Nopcomp.com
    Description . . . . . . . . . . . : Intel(R) PRO/100 VE Network Connection
    Physical Address. . . . . . . . . : 08-00-46-5C-8B-7A
    Dhcp Enabled. . . . . . . . . . . : Yes
    Autoconfiguration Enabled . . . . : Yes
    IP Address. . . . . . . . . . . . : 169.254.0.201
    Subnet Mask . . . . . . . . . . . : 255.255.0.0
    Default Gateway . . . . . . . . . : 10.0.1.2
    DHCP Server . . . . . . . . . . . : 10.0.0.22
    DNS Servers . . . . . . . . . . . : 45.153.22.67
    Lease Obtained. . . . . . . . . . : Friday, August 22, 2003 10:57:10 AM
    Lease Expires . . . . . . . . . . : Saturday, August 23, 2003 10:57:10 AM
```

What is the solution to the connection error?

A. The address of the default gateway is on the wrong network, the DHCP server has the wrong configuration, or Des's computer has a hard-coded default gateway.

B. Des's computer does not have a valid IP address. Configure his computer to use DHCP or enter an IP address.

C. The DNS address is not correct.

D. The subnet mask is incorrect for the configuration.

4. You are the network administrator for your company's network, which consists of six Windows Server 2003 computers and 85 Windows XP Professional computers. 35 of the client workstations are mobile and connect to the network through a remote access server running Routing and Remote Access Service on one of the Windows Server 2003 computers. Des is one of the users who uses his computer remotely. Today Des has called you to inform you that he gets an error message when he tries to connect to the remote access server from a client's location. You ask Des to run the **ipconfig /all** command and report the information to you. The following is the pertinent information.

```
Ethernet adapter Local Area Connection:
   Connection-specific DNS Suffix  . : Nopcomp.com
   Description . . . . . . . . . . . : Intel(R) PRO/100 VE Network Connection
   Physical Address. . . . . . . . . : 08-00-46-5C-8B-7A
   Dhcp Enabled. . . . . . . . . . . : Yes
   Autoconfiguration Enabled . . . . : Yes
   IP Address. . . . . . . . . . . . : 10.0.0.201
   Subnet Mask . . . . . . . . . . . : 255.254.255.0
   Default Gateway . . . . . . . . . : 10.0.0.2
   DHCP Server . . . . . . . . . . . : 10.0.0.22
   DNsS Servers . . . . . . . . . . . : 45.153.22.67
   Lease Obtained. . . . . . . . . . : Friday, August 22, 2003 10:57:10 AM
   Lease Expires . . . . . . . . . . : Saturday, August 23, 2003 10:57:10 AM
```

What is the solution to the connection error?

A. The address of the default gateway is on the wrong network, the DHCP server has the wrong configuration, or Des's computer has a hard-coded default gateway.

B. Des's computer does not have a valid IP address. Configure his computer to use DHCP or enter an IP address.

C. The DNS address is not correct.

D. The subnet mask is incorrect for the configuration.

5. What utility can you use in troubleshooting the cause of an unreachable host? (Choose all that apply.)

A. ping

B. tracert

C. nslookup

D. arp

Diagnose and Resolve User Access to Resources Beyond the Remote Access Server

6. You are the network administrator for your company's network, which consists of six Windows Server 2003 computers and 85 Windows XP Professional computers. 35 of the client workstations are mobile and connect to the network through a remote access server running Routing and Remote Access Service on one of the Windows Server 2003 computers. Des is one of the users who uses his computer remotely. Today Des has called you to inform you that after he has established the connection to the remote access server, he is unable to reach resources on the internal network. You look at the configuration of the RRAS server, as seen in this illustration:

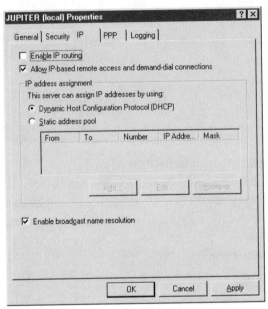

What is the solution to Des's resource problem?

A. Enable IP routing to give access to resources beyond the remote access server.

B. Clear the use of broadcast name resolution to give access to resources beyond the remote access server.

C. Add additional addresses into the static address pool to give access to resources beyond the remote access server.

D. This dialog box does not indicate an error. Enable tracing and ask Des to access the resource again so you can get a log file of the attempt to solve the problem.

7. You are the network administrator for your company's network, which consists of six Windows Server 2003 computers and 85 Windows XP Professional computers. 35 of the client workstations are mobile and connect to the network through a remote access server running Routing and Remote Access Service on one of the Windows Server 2003 computers. You have a written a security policy that states that no remote access client shall have access to resources beyond the remote access server. How will you implement this security policy? (Choose all that apply.)

A. Disable IP routing on the IP tab of the properties for the RRAS server.

B. Disable IP routing by removing the RIP protocol from the RRAS server.

C. Disable broadcast name resolution on the IP tab of the properties for the RRAS server.

D. Enable the IP routing sink on the Advanced IP tab of the properties for the RRAS server.

Troubleshoot Demand-dial Routing

8. You are the network administrator for your company's network, which consists of six Windows Server 2003 computers and 85 Windows XP Professional computers. Your company operates two sites that are connected with on-demand routers implemented with Windows Server 2003 computers running Routing and Remote Access Service. You have been having problems establishing the route between the two routers. The following illustration is from the answering router:

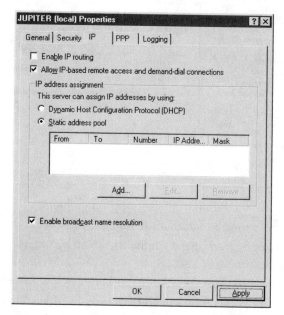

What is the solution to the connection problem?

A. Enable RIP V2 multicast to make the connection work.

B. Disable broadcast name resolution to make the connection work.

C. Enable IP routing to make the connection work.

D. Add addresses to the static address pool.

9. You are the network administrator for your company's network, which consists of six Windows Server 2003 computers and 85 Windows XP Professional computers. Your company operates two sites that are connected with on-demand routers implemented with two Windows Server 2003 computers running Routing and Remote Access Service, ServerA and ServerB. ServerA calls ServerB to establish the route. You have been having problems with the route between ServerA and ServerB. The connection seems to succeed, but the routers do not route the traffic as expected. The following illustration is from the answering router:

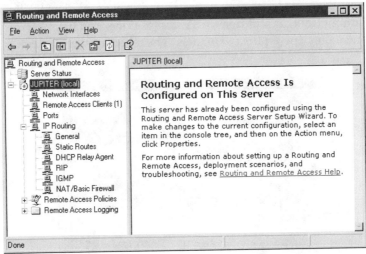

What is the most likely solution to the connection problem?

A. ServerB is using the wrong user account to authenticate on ServerA.

B. Add the user account ServerB uses to authenticate on ServerA to the RouteAdmin local security group on ServerA.

C. ServerA is using the wrong user account to authenticate on ServerB.

D. Add the user account ServerA uses to authenticate on ServerB to the RouteAdmin local security group on ServerB.

10. You are the network administrator for your company's network, which consists of six Windows Server 2003 computers and 85 Windows XP Professional computers. Your company operates two sites that are connected with on-demand routers implemented with two Windows Server 2003 computers running Routing and Remote Access Service, ServerA and ServerB. ServerA calls ServerB to establish the route. You have been having problems with the route between

ServerA and ServerB. The connection seems to succeed but the routers do not route the traffic as expected. The following output is from the answering router.

```
C:\>net start
...
        Print Spooler
        Protected Storage
        Remote Procedure Call (RPC)
        Remote Registry
        Secondary Logon
        Security Accounts Manager
        Server
        Shell Hardware Detection
        Simple Mail Transfer Protocol (SMTP)
        Software Update Services Synchronization Service
        System Event Notification
        Task Scheduler
        TCP/IP NetBIOS Helper
        Telephony
        Terminal Services
        Windows Remote Access Service
        Windows Management Instrumentation
        Windows Time
        Wireless Configuration
        Workstation

The command completed successfully.
```

What action need you take to establish the connection between ServerA and ServerB?

A. Stop and restart the Routing and Remote Access Service on ServerA by issuing the command **net stop remoteaccess**, followed by **net start remoteaccess**.

B. Stop and restart the Routing and Remote Access Service on ServerB by issuing the command **net stop remoteaccess**, followed by **net start remoteaccess**.

C. Start the Routing and Remote Access Service on ServerA by issuing the command **net start remoteaccess**.

D. Start the Routing and Remote Access Service on ServerB by issuing the command **net start remoteaccess**.

11. You are the network administrator for your company's network, which consists of six Windows Server 2003 computers and 85 Windows XP Professional computers. Your company operates two sites that are connected with on-demand routers implemented with two Windows Server 2003

computers running Routing and Remote Access Service, ServerA and ServerB. ServerA calls ServerB to establish the route. You have been having problems with the route between ServerA and ServerB. The connection does not succeed, and the routers do not route the traffic as expected. The following illustration is from the account properties authentication account for ServerB:

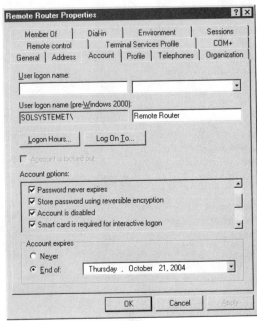

What is the solution to the connection problem?

A. The account has expired; change the expiration date.

B. The account needs a new password; reset the password.

C. The account is disabled; clear the disabled control.

D. The account's smart card has expired; renew the smart card.

12. You are the network administrator for your company's network, which consists of six Windows Server 2003 computers and 85 Windows XP Professional computers. Your company operates two sites that are connected with on-demand routers implemented with two Windows Server 2003 computers running Routing and Remote Access Service, ServerA and ServerB. ServerA calls

ServerB to establish the route. You have been having problems with the route between ServerA and ServerB. The connection seems to succeed, but the routers do not route the traffic as expected. You investigate the RIP configuration to see what the problem might be. The following illustration is from the answering router:

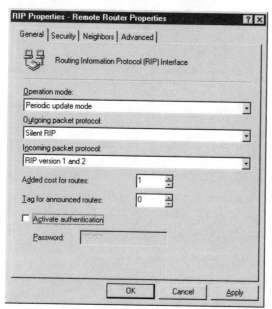

What is the solution to this routing problem? (Choose all that apply)

A. Change the Operations mode to autostatic.

B. Change the Outgoing packet protocol to RIP version 1 broadcast.

C. Change the Outgoing packet protocol to RIP version 2 muilticast.

Troubleshoot Router-to-Router VPNs

13. You are the network administrator for your company's network, which consists of six Windows Server 2003 computers and 85 Windows XP Professional computers. Your company operates two sites that are connected with on-demand routers implemented with two Windows Server 2003 computers running Routing and Remote Access Service, ServerA and ServerB. ServerA calls ServerB to establish the route. You have been having problems with the route between ServerA and ServerB. The connection does not succeed and the routers do not route the traffic as expected. The following illustration is from the calling router:

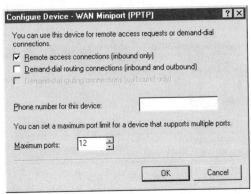

What is the most likely problem preventing routing from taking place?

A. The ports are only for incoming traffic; no outgoing connections are available.

B. Add more ports; there must be at least 128 ports configured.

C. Enter a phone number on the port to ensure callback works.

D. The problem is with the router, not the ports.

14. You are the network administrator for your company's network, which consists of six Windows Server 2003 computers and 85 Windows XP Professional computers. Your company operates two sites that are connected with on-demand routers implemented with two Windows Server 2003 computers running Routing and Remote Access Service, ServerA and ServerB. ServerA calls ServerB to establish the route. The Network Interface on ServerA is named RRASRouter, and on ServerB it is named RemoteInterface. You have been having problems with the route between the ServerA and ServerB. The connection does not succeed and the routers do not route the traffic as expected. The following illustration is from the calling router:

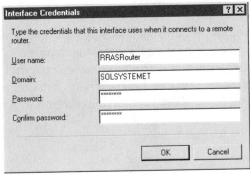

What must you do to successfully connect between ServerA and ServerB?

A. Change the account name to RemoteInterface.

B. Change the account name to Administrator.

C. Create an account named RemoteInterfaceUser and use this account.

15. You are the network administrator for your company's network, which consists of six Windows Server 2003 computers and 85 Windows XP Professional computers. Your company operates two sites that are connected with on-demand routers implemented with two Windows Server 2003 computers running Routing and Remote Access Service, ServerA and ServerB. ServerA calls ServerB to establish the route. The Network Interface on ServerA is named RRASRouter, and on ServerB it is named RemoteInterface. You have been having problems with the route between ServerA and ServerB. The connection does not succeed, and the routers do not route the traffic as expected. The following illustration shows the properties of the user account used to authenticate to ServerB:

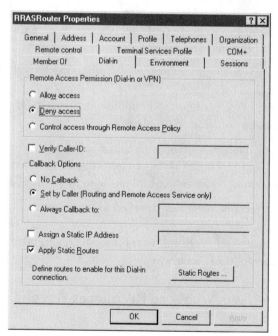

What can be done to rectify this problem?

A. Enter a static IP address for the user.

B. Disable the callback.

C. Remove the static routes.

D. Allow dial-in.

SELF TEST ANSWERS

Diagnose and Resolve Issues Related to Remote Access VPNs

1. ☑ **C.** Using the **ipconfig** command-line tool with the **/all** option gives a comprehensive report on how TCP/IP is configured.

   ☒ **A** is incorrect because the **net** command is used on the application level, to map drives, and to start and stop services, but not for TCP/IP. **B** is incorrect because there is no command with that name in Windows Server 2003. **D** is incorrect because **tracert** is used to verify the route, not the configuration.

2. ☑ **A.** The default gateway must be on the same subnet as the computer. In this case the gateway is remote to the computer. This problem can be on the DHCP server, or as part of a hard-coded gateway on the computer.

   ☒ **B** is incorrect because the IP address is correct as given. **C** is incorrect because there is no evidence in the information to indicate that the DNS entry is incorrect. **D** is incorrect because there is no evidence that the subnet mask is incorrect.

3. ☑ **B.** This IP address was automatically generated when the DHCP server could not be contacted; this address is not routable.

   ☒ **A, C,** and **D** are incorrect because the IP address is not routable, and that is the underlying problem that is causing the connection problem.

4. ☑ **D.** The subnet mask cannot contain zeros in the middle. This mask is given as 1111 1111 1111 1110 1111 1111 0000 0000, resulting in a broken mask.

   ☒ **A, B,** and **C** are incorrect because the broken subnet mask prevents any communication.

5. ☑ **A, B,** and **C. ping, tracert, nslookup** are used to test connectivity, routing, and name resolution.

   ☒ **D** is incorrect because Address Resolution Protocol (ARP) is a data link layer protocol used to map IP addresses to MAC addresses.

Diagnose and Resolve User Access to Resources Beyond the Remote Access Server

6. ☑ **A.** The problem here is that routing is disabled. This effectively makes it impossible to reach resources beyond the local network of the Remote Access server.

   ☒ **B** is incorrect because broadcast name resolution controls a method of accessing the local network. **C** is incorrect because the static address pool has nothing to do with remote resource access. **D** is incorrect because the dialog box indicates that the IP routing is disabled.

7. ☑ **A and C.** These are the only answers that address removing access to the networks beyond the Remote Access server.

☒   **B** is incorrect because removing RIP will not disable access. **D** is incorrect because even though it sounds good, there is no such option.

Troubleshoot Demand-dial Routing

8. ☑   **D.** Based on the dialog box, there are no addresses for the calling router. To use static address pools, there must be entries in the table.
☒   **A, B,** and **C** are incorrect because they do not address the problem of missing IP addresses.

9. ☑   **C.** This is a best guess as to the problem, but with one remote access client listed in the dialog, you should suspect that the user account used for the calling router to authenticate is wrong.
☒   **A** is incorrect because the authentication is the other way around; ServerA authenticates to ServerB. **B** and **D** are incorrect because the connection ended up as a remote access client connection, thus there is a user name problem.

10. ☑   **D.** The Routing and Remote Access Service is not started on ServerB. To start it you can use the long name or the short service name, **remoteaccess**.
☒   **A** and **B** are incorrect because the service is not started, so restarting it makes no sense. **C** is incorrect because the service must be started on ServerB, not on ServerA.

11. ☑   **C.** This account is disabled, and that is why you cannot connect.
☒   **A** is incorrect because the account has not expired. **B** is incorrect because the password is set to never expire. **D** is incorrect because smart cards never expire.

12. ☑   **A** and **C.** The rules for RIP configuration for router-to-router routing are to use autostatic mode and RIP v2 multicast.
☒   **B** is incorrect because the RIP v1 broadcast protocol will not produce the expected results.

Troubleshoot Router-to-Router VPNs

13. ☑   **A.** No ports are configured for outgoing connections, and as this is on the calling router, there will never be a successful connection.
☒   **B** is incorrect because there is no such rule, and there are no outgoing connections. **C** is incorrect because without outgoing ports, there will never be a chance to get a callback. **D** is incorrect because the problem is with the ports.

14. ☑   **A.** The user account must be the same as the demand-dial interface name of the called router.
☒   **B** and **C** are incorrect because using any other user name than the name of the remote demand-dial interface will result in a remote access client connection, not a router connection.

15. ☑   **D.** The user account must have dial-in permissions in order for usage to be allowed. Set it either to Allow or to control through remote access policy.
☒   **A, B,** and **C** are incorrect because neither is a problem when the connection is attempted if the account does not have dial-in permissions.

Part V

Maintaining a Network Infrastructure

13

Monitor
the Network
Infrastructure

There is a common misconception that once the remote access service is configured and put into production the work is over, but that's not the case. This is where the real work of the network administrator starts. This chapter will present the tasks involved in managing the remote access server as well as monitoring the network. One of the tools available is the ability to log access, and you will learn how to configure and monitor logging on an access server using the tools available.

CERTIFICATION OBJECTIVE 13.01

Manage and Monitor Network Traffic

In the course of your administrative duties, you may perform more monitoring than any other task. We will start this section with the tasks involved in bringing down a remote access production system, and how you communicate with the users.

Managing Network Access

When you install and configure the Routing and Remote Access service on a single Windows Server 2003 machine, you have unfortunately built a system that has a flaw. If that one RRAS server goes down, whether because of maintenance or an accident, the result is the same. The system is unavailable to the users, and the help desk calls will start coming in fast and furious. The solution is to have a second server that can be used to take the load when the production server is down for any reason. Figure 13-1 shows the recommended configuration of a network access system that can handle a single system failure.

The following are the recommended steps to take when you have to bring down the production server for maintenance.

1. Configure a replacement server that will act as the remote access server.

2. Schedule the downtime to take place during the slowest time of the business. Remember that the server may get heavy load outside of the core business hours if staff access the network while traveling.

3. Communicate with the clients to inform them that you are going to perform maintenance; be sure to include the time of and expected length

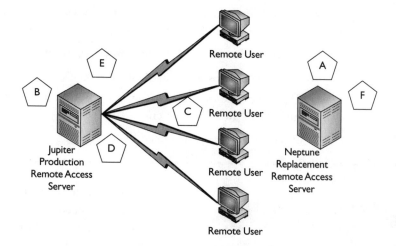

FIGURE 13-1

Recommended
configuration
for RRAS

of the maintenance. Ensure that any changes are communicated as the
maintenance period approaches.

4. At the appointed time for the maintenance, disconnect any connected clients
   using the **Routing and Remote Access** console. Send a message to the users
   before disconnecting them.

5. Stop the Routing and Remote Access service.

6. Start the replacement server.

In Exercises 13-1 and 13-2, you will learn how to send messages to individual users,
as well as to all connected users. Then we will disconnect any remaining users and
stop the Routing and Remote Access service.

EXERCISE 13-1

Sending a Message to an Individual Remote Access Client

In this exercise, you will learn how to send a message to an individual connected
remote access client.

1. Log in to your server using your non-administrative account.

2. Click **Start | Control Panel**.

3. In the Control Panel, open **Administrative Tools**, right-click **Routing and
   Remote Access**, and select **Run As** from the context menu.

4. In the **Run As** dialog, select **The following user**, and type a user account and password that has administrative rights on the server. Click **OK**.

5. Open the **Routing and Remote Access** console from Administrative Tools.

6. Click **Remote Access Clients** in the tree.

7. Right-click the user name you want to send a message to, and click **Send message** in the context menu.

8. Enter the message, and click **OK** to send it.

<table>
<tr><td>**watch**

Always work using a normal user account and use the Run as **functionality when you need extra rights to perform a task.**</td><td>Sending messages to individual users is fine when you need to deal with single issues, but sometimes you need to let every user know about a network issue.</td></tr>
</table>

EXERCISE 13-2

Sending a Message to All Connected Remote Access Clients

In this exercise, you will send a message to all connected remote access clients.

1. Log in to your server using your non-administrative account.

2. Click **Start | Control Panel**.

3. In the Control Panel, open **Administrative Tools**, right-click **Routing and Remote Access**, and select **Run as** from the context menu.

4. In the **Run As** dialog, select **The following user**, and type a user account and password that has administrative rights on the server. Click **OK**.

5. Open the **Routing and Remote Access** console from Administrative Tools.

6. Click **Remote Access Clients** in the tree.

7. Right-click **Remote Access Clients** in the tree, click **Send to All** in the context menu.

8. Enter the message, and click **OK** to send it.

Once you have communicated with the connected remote access clients, you can disconnect them from the server.

EXERCISE 13-3

Disconnecting Connected Remote Access Clients

In this exercise you will disconnect connected remote access clients.

1. Log in to your server using your non-administrative account.

2. Click **Start | Control Panel**.

3. In the Control Panel, open **Administrative Tools**, right-click **Routing and Remote Access**, and select **Run As** from the context menu.

4. In the **Run As** dialog, select **The following user**, and type a user account and password that has administrative rights on the server. Click **OK**.

5. Open the **Routing and Remote Access** console from Administrative Tools.

6. Click **Remote Access Clients** in the tree.

7. Right-click the user you want to disconnect, and click **Disconnect** in the context menu.

8. Verify that the user has been disconnected.

After all users are disconnected, you need to stop the remote access service, and there are a couple of possible approaches to this task. You can use the **Routing and Remote Access** console, or the **Services** application in Administration Tools, or the **net** command. Using the **Routing and Remote Access** console, you right-click the server and select **All tasks | Stop** from the context menu, as shown in Figure 13-2. To start the server again, you right-click the server again and select **All Tasks | Start**.

To start the Services application, click **Start | Administrative Tools**, and select **Services**. Select **Routing and Remote Access** in the list, right-click it, and click **Stop** from the context menu, as shown in Figure 13-3. To start the service, right-click the service and select **Start**.

The third method is to use the **net** command to manage the Routing and Remote Access service. You will learn how to perform this task in Exercise 13-4.

FIGURE 13-2

Stopping the
server from
the **Routing and
Remote Access**
console

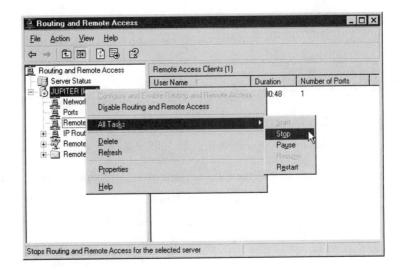

FIGURE 13-3 Stopping the server from the **Services** application

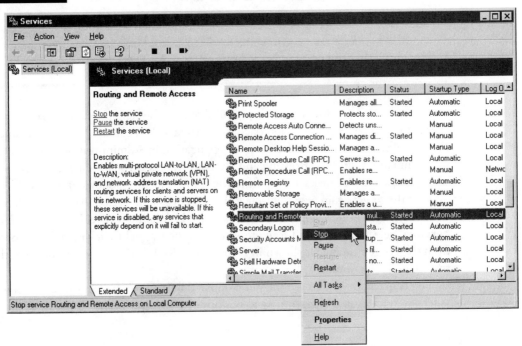

EXERCISE 13-4

Starting and Stopping the Routing and Remote Access Service

The command prompt has again become one of the tools used to manage Windows Server 2003. In this exercise you will use one of the early command-line tools that have been part of the Microsoft environment for some time, the **net** command.

1. Log in to your server using your non-administrative account.

2. Click **Start | Run**.

3. In the **Run** dialog enter **cmd** as the command, and click **OK**.

4. Enter **runas /user:*solsystemet*/administrator cmd**, and press ENTER. (Substitute your domain name for *solsystemet*.

5. Enter the password when prompted. A new copy of the command prompt will open, as shown here:

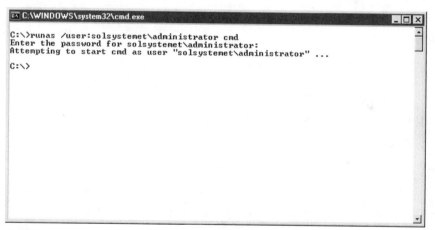

```
C:\>runas /user:solsystemet\administrator cmd
Enter the password for solsystemet\administrator:
Attempting to start cmd as user "solsystemet\administrator" ...

C:\>
```

6. At the new command prompt, enter the following command to stop Routing and Remote Access: **net stop remoteaccess**.

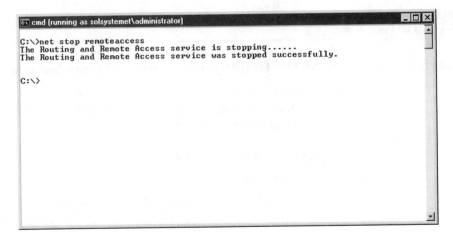

7. To start the service again, enter **net start remoteaccess**.

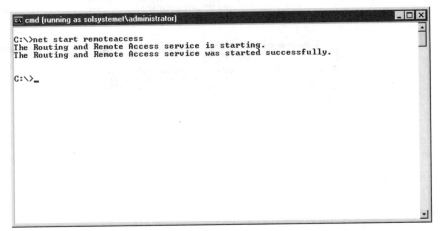

8. To verify that the service is running, enter **net start**.

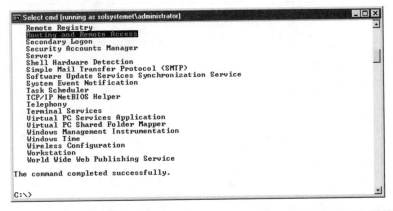

SCENARIO & SOLUTION

How do I plan for my RRAS server being down for any reason?	The most cost effective solution is the one recommended by Microsoft. In this solution you configure a second server that will be used when the RRAS server is down.
How do I send a message to all connected Remote Access clients?	You can send messages to all connected remote access clients, or to individual clients with the **Routing and Remote Access** console. Right-click the **Remote Access Clients** node and select **Send to all** to send a message to every connected remote access client. To send individual messages, select the individual client in the **Remote Access Client** node, right-click, and select **Send message**.
How do I disconnect remote access clients if I need to shut down the Remote Access server?	Right-click the individual remote access client inside the **Remote Access Clients** node, and select **Disconnect** from the context menu.
How do I stop and start the Routing and Remote Access service?	There are a couple of ways to perform this task. You can use the **net** command: **net stop remoteaccess** will stop the service and **net start remoteaccess** will start it. Second, you can use the Services application from the Administrative Tools folder to start and stop the service. You can also control the RRAS service from the **Routing and Remote Access** console.

Now that you have a better idea of managing the network access environment, look at some possible scenario questions and their answers above.

CERTIFICATION OBJECTIVE 13.02

Configure Logging on a Network Access Server

Logging is the process of keeping information about what has happened on the remote access server, with regard to how the service is used. In this section you will learn about how to configure logging using the event log, local authentication log, and RADIUS authentication logging.

Event Logging

Event logging is used to keep a record of server errors, warnings, and other related information in the system event log. You enable and configure event logging for the Routing and Remote Access service on the **Event Logging** tab of the **Properties** dialog for the remote access server, as shown in Figure 13-4.

By configuring event logging, you can enable logging of so many different events that the server can be totally bogged down with the logging activity and start having performance issues with serving the remote clients.

There is also an option on the **Logging** tab that enables you to log additional information (also known as Tracing), which should only be used for troubleshooting access problems. When you enable **Log additional Routing and Remote Access information**, a large number of logs will be created in the **%systemroot%\Tracing** directory.

on the 　 **job** 　 *Tracing adds a significant load to the server and should only be used for troubleshooting access problems.*

Authentication and Accounting Logging

The process of collecting information about the connection process is called Authentication and Accounting Logging. The items that are logged can be defined when you enable

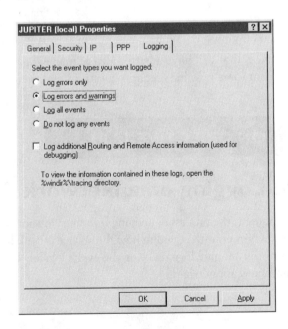

FIGURE 13-4

Enabling logging for the remote access server

the logging on the **Security** tab of the RRAS server properties. The logs themselves are stored in the **%systemroot%\System32\LogFiles** directory of the server. When you enable Authentication and Accounting Logging using the RADIUS accounting provider, you specify the format of the storage from two choices: Internet Authentication Service (IAS) or a database-compatible format. The choice of format is determined by what tools you will use to analyze the data. IAS and RRAS can be configured to save the log file in a central database so all information is available from one source.

Here are some properties you should consider when configuring logging:

- The type of information to log
    - Accounting information
        - Accounting on
        - Accounting off
    - Authentication requests
        - Authentication request
        - Authentication accepts and rejects
    - Periodic status
- Where the logs are stored
- The log file format
    - IAS format
    - Database-compatible
- How often new logs are started and when the logs are recycled
    - Daily
    - Weekly
    - Monthly
    - Never
    - When the log exceeds a preset size
    - Delete old files when the disk is full

You must consider how valuable these logs are when your system has been under attack and you need to detect the attack as well as investigate where it came from.

Depending on the type of environment you work in you might be forced to maintain these logs forever.

on the job

Do not forget to back up the log directory.

EXERCISE 13-5

Enabling Windows Accounting

In this exercise you will configure Routing and Remote Access to use Windows to keep accounting information.

1. Log in to your server using your non-administrative account.

2. Click **Start | Control Panel**.

3. In the Control Panel, open **Administrative Tools**, right-click **Routing and Remote Access**, and select **Run as** from the context menu.

4. In the **Run As** dialog, select **The following user**, and type a user account and password that has administrative rights on the server. Click **OK**.

5. Right-click your server in the tree, and click **Properties** in the context menu.

6. Select the **Security** tab.

7. In the **Accounting provider** drop-down, select **Windows Accounting**, as shown in the following illustration, and then click **OK**.

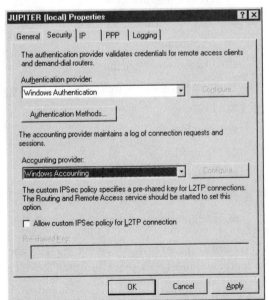

Accounting can also be based on a RADIUS server. Exercise 13-6 shows how that is configured.

EXERCISE 13-6

Enabling RADIUS Accounting

1. Log in to your server using your non-administrative account.

2. Click **Start | Control Panel**.

3. In the Control Panel, open **Administrative Tools**, right-click **Routing and Remote Access**, and select **Run as** from the context menu.

4. In the **Run As** dialog, select **The following user**, and type a user account and password that has administrative rights on the server. Click **OK**.

5. Right-click your server in the tree, and click **Properties** in the context menu.

6. Select the **Security** tab.

7. In the **Accounting provider** drop-down, select **RADIUS Accounting**, and then click **Configure**.

8. In the **RADIUS Accounting** dialog, click **Add**.

9. In the **Add RADIUS Server** dialog, shown here, in the **Server name** field, type the name of the RADIUS server. Then click **Change**.

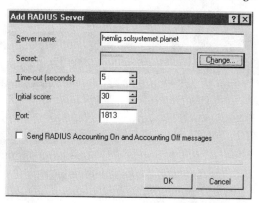

10. In the **Change Secret** dialog, type the secret in the **New secret** field, and again in the **Confirm new secret** field. Click **OK**.

11. Click **OK** in the **RADIUS Accounting** dialog, shown here:

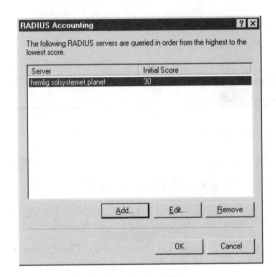

12. In the **RRAS Properties** dialog, click **OK.**

In addition to the logging that can be configured through the server properties, you can also collect detailed information about specific connection types: PPP, L2TP/IPSec (audit), and L2TP/IPSec (Oakley). These logs are enabled in different areas of Windows Server 2003. The details can be found in Table 13-1.

TABLE 13-1   Connection-Specific Logging

Connection Type	Log File Name	Description	Enabled By	Managed Through
PPP	PPP log	Logs the functions and control messages during a PPP connection	**Routing and Remote Access** console, server properties. On the **Logging** tab, enable logging.	Log is stored in **%systemroot%\tracing**
L2TP/IPSec	Audit log	Logs IPSec events	Using the **netsh ipsec** command utility as well as registry changes.	Event Viewer
L2TP/IPSec	Oakley log	Logs Internet Key Exchange Main and Quick Mode negotiations	Enabled in the registry by setting **HKEY_LOCAL_MACHINE \System \CurrentControlSet \Services\PolicyAgent\Oakley \EnableLogging DWORD** to a value of **1.**	Event Viewer

EXERCISE 13-7

Configuring Oakley Logging

The usual warnings about making changes to the registry apply to this exercise; there is always the chance that a change to the registry could result in an unwanted feature.

1. Log in to your server using your non-administrative account.

2. Click **Start | Run**.

3. In the **Run As** dialog, enter **cmd** as the command, and click **OK**.

4. Enter **runas /user:*solsystemet*/administrator regedt32** and press ENTER. Substitute your domain name for *solsystemet*.

5. Enter the password when prompted. The **Registry Editor** will open.

6. Navigate the registry to **HKEY_LOCAL_MACHINE\System\ CurrentControlSet\Services\PolicyAgent\Oakley**, as shown here:

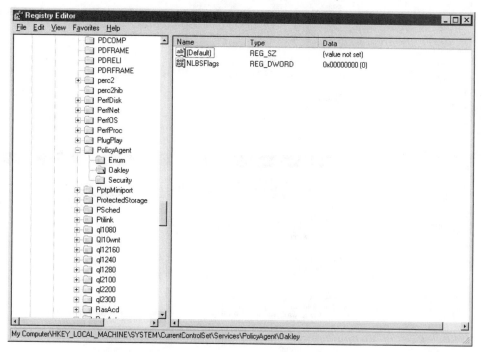

7. Right-click **Oakley,** and select **New | DWORD value** from the context menu.

8. Change the name of the DWORD to **EnableLogging**.

9. Double-click **EnableLogging** to open the **Edit DWORD Value** dialog.

10. Change the value to **1**, as shown here. Click **OK**.

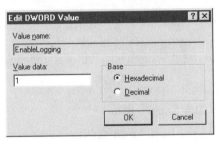

11. Close the registry editor.

12. Enter **runas /user:*solsystemet*/administrator cmd**, and press ENTER. Substitute your domain name for *solsystemet*.

13. Enter the password when prompted. A new copy of the command prompt will open.

14. Stop Routing and Remote Access and IPSec by entering the following commands:

```
net stop remoteaccess
net stop policyagent
```

15. Restart the service by using these commands:

```
net start policyagent
net start remoteaccess
```

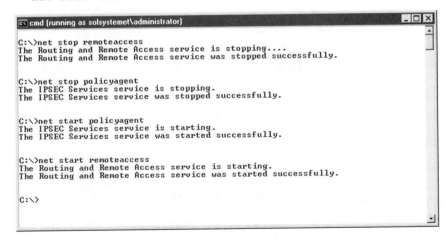

SCENARIO & SOLUTION

Where do I find the PPP log after I have enabled it?	The PPP log is located in the **%systemroot%\Tracing** directory.
I need to enable logging for L2TP/IPSec. Where do I do that?	There are two logs that can be enabled, and they use different methods. The Audit Log is enabled using the **netsh ipsec** command. The Oakley log is enabled by editing the registry.
Is it true I have to reboot the Windows Server 2003 server after enabling Oakley logging?	No, you do not have to reboot the server, but you must stop and start IPSec and RRAS. You can do this by issuing the following commands: **net stop remoteaccess** **net stop policyagent** **net start policyagent** **net start remoteaccess**

CERTIFICATION OBJECTIVE 13.03

Collect and Monitor Network Access Data

You need to monitor your server's performance to acquire data that you'll use to continuously evaluate the workload of the server and the impact of the workload on the system's performance. Monitoring also enables you to keep tabs on the changes and trends in workload over time, as well as tracking usage over time to plan for future needs.

Monitoring the network while testing configuration changes will give you valuable information about the feasibility of the configuration change. Another use of monitoring is to use the information as a troubleshooting tool when you need to isolate those components that are having problems.

The final use of monitoring is its use as a tool to identify bottlenecks in the system. These components need to be optimized to function better in the production system.

The tools used to collect network access data are

- **System Monitor**   Lets you view real-time performance data targeted at the role of the server.
- **Performance Logs and Alerts**   Captures performance data for later analysis.
- **Wireless Monitor**   Logs details about wireless network access points and clients.

System Monitor

You start the System Monitor by clicking **Administrative Tools | Performance** (this name is a throwback to Windows NT 4.0, where the tool was called Performance Monitor). Figure 13-5 shows the default view of the System Monitor with the counters that the Microsoft engineers thought would be most helpful. You'll need to make changes to these counters to glean information about your network.

The information displayed in the System Monitor can be customized by selecting counters from objects in the operating system as you will see in Exercise 13-8. Objects are items in the server such as the Network while counters are items that are part of that object such as TCP packets/seconds. There are a large number of objects available for monitoring; depending on what the focus of the monitoring is, you will need to select a proper selection of objects. The most common objects that are monitored are

- **Memory** One of the most important resources, this counter gives information about the memory subsystem regarding the use of real versus virtual memory, and how often swapping takes place.

- **Processor** Provides information on how the processor or processors are functioning.

- **Network** Reports on the behavior of the network segment the server is connected to, as well as the NIC.

- **Disk** Reports on how the disk subsystem is used and its performance.

These four objects will allow you to measure the most important aspects of the server. In addition there are other objects that will enhance your remote access monitoring:

- **IAS Authentication Server** Contains counters that are used to monitor incoming and outgoing authentication requests.

- **IAS Authentication Client** Counters for the IAS client.

- **RAS Port** Contains counters with information about individual remote access ports.

- **RAS Total** Counters for the entire remote access service.

Chart view of the Systems Monitor lets you add individual counters that are part of the objects. To add counters, click the + button in the toolbar to open the **Add**

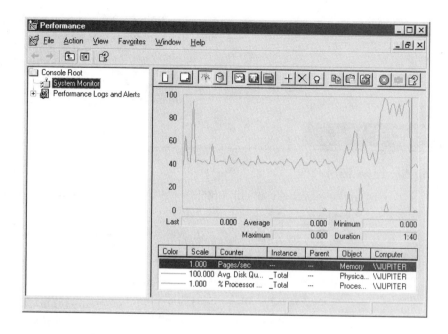

FIGURE 13-5

The default view of the System Monitor

Counters dialog, as shown in Figure 13-6. When you change the Object, the different counters are displayed. To find information about a counter, click the **Explain** button, as shown in Figure 13-7.

FIGURE 13-6

The **Add Counters** dialog

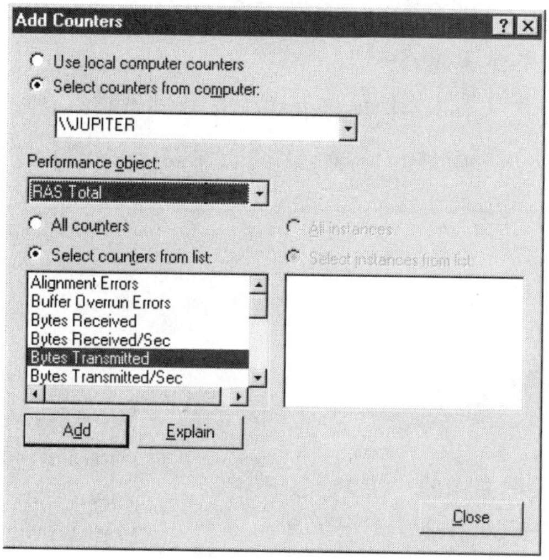

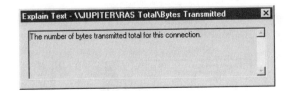

FIGURE 13-7

Explaining
a counter

EXERCISE 13-8

Using System Monitor

In this exercise, you will configure the System Monitor to gather information about the server.

1. Log in to your server using your non-administrative account.

2. Click **Start | Control Panel**.

3. In the Control Panel, open **Administrative Tools**, right-click **Performance**, and select **Run As** from the context menu.

4. In the **Run As** dialog, select **The following user**, and type a user account and password that has administrative rights on the server. Click **OK**. The System Monitor opens.

5. Click the **+** button on the toolbar to open the **Add Counters** dialog.

6. Select **RAS Total** from the **Performance objects** drop-down.

7. Select **Bytes received** under **Select counters from list**.

8. Click **Add**.

9. Click **Close** to return to System Monitor.

10. Save the customized System Monitor by clicking **File | Save As**.

Wireless Monitor

exam

ⓌⓐⓉⓒⒽ *Use the Wireless Monitor to monitor wireless access points.*

To monitor wireless traffic, you need to add the Wireless Monitor snap-in to your management console. You can use this snap-in to monitor the wireless access points and users that make use of your wireless network.

INSIDE THE EXAM

Wireless Networks

Be prepared to answer questions that refer to wireless networks in the 70-291 exam. This technology is new since the last round of exams, so the exam writers have used the term *wireless* to its best. When you see questions that use wireless networking you need to remember only one thing: the only difference between wired and wireless networking is in monitoring.

The Wireless Monitor gives you the ability to keep an eye on wireless access points and measure how the wireless network functions.

CERTIFICATION SUMMARY

In this chapter, you were introduced to the topics that deal with the work that takes place after the remote access solution has been set up. We focused on the logging of information from different parts of the Routing and Remote Access Service.

One often-overlooked issue is what will happen if the existing RRAS server goes down. We investigated the recommendations from Microsoft on how to create an environment where you can switch servers almost seamlessly.

Another area you looked at was how to collect access data, and where you can find that information within Windows Server 2003.

TWO-MINUTE DRILL

Manage and Monitor Network Traffic

❏ Have a stand-by solution for when the RRAS server becomes unavailable.

❏ Send messages to all connected remote access clients to inform them about network problems.

❏ Disconnect individual remote access clients if they do not respond to messages to disconnect themselves.

❏ Never log in directly using an Administrator account. Log in as a normal user and use the **Run as** facility to become an Administrator for that program only.

Configure Logging on a Network Access Server

❏ Event logging stores errors, warnings, and information messages from Routing and Remote Access Service in the event log.

❏ If you enable additional information logging, you must monitor the server for load. This type of logging is only for troubleshooting, and should only be used for short periods.

❏ Authentication and Accounting logging stores the logs in **%systemroot%\ System32\LogFiles** by default.

❏ Authentication and Accounting logging can be stored in IAS or database-compatible formats.

❏ Authentication and Accounting logging can be centrally stored using a database server or a RADIUS (IAS) server.

❏ To log the PPP protocol, enable the PPP log.

❏ To log L2TP/IPSec, you have access to two logs: the Audit and the Oakley logs.

Collect and Monitor Network Access Data

❏ Tools to use to collect and monitor network access include the System Monitor, Performance Logs and Alerts, and the Wireless Monitor.

❏ Common counter are Memory, Processor, Network, Disk, RAS Total.

SELF TEST

Manage and Monitor Network Traffic

1. You are the network administrator of your company's network. Your current task is to disconnect all remote access clients that are connecting into the network through the JUPITER server. After you have sent a message to all remote access clients to disconnect from JUPITER and connect through NEPTUNE instead, you need to disconnect those users that have not done so already. What tool and procedure would you use?

   A. Use the **Routing and Remote Access** console. Individually disconnect each remote client from the **Remote Access Clients** node by selecting each remote access client individually, right-clicking on the entry, and then selecting **Disconnect** from the context menu.

   B. Use the **Routing and Remote Access** console. Disconnect all remote clients from the **Remote Access Clients** node by right-clicking the **Remote Access Clients** node, and selecting **Disconnect All** from the context menu.

   C. Disconnect all remote access clients by executing the **netsh rras disconnect:all** command-line utility.

   D. Use the RRAS application in the Control Panel. Highlight all remote access clients on the **Connected** tab, and click the **Disconnect** button.

2. You are the network administrator of your company's network. You are currently preparing to turn off the PLUTO Windows Server 2003 Routing and Remote Access server. What tool and method do you use to send messages to all connected remote access clients in the most efficient manner?

   A. Use the **Routing and Remote Access** console. Individually send a message to each remote client from the **Remote Access Clients** node by selecting each remote access client individually, right-clicking the entry, and then selecting **Send Message** from the context menu.

   B. Use the **Routing and Remote Access** console, send a message to all remote clients from the **Remote Access Clients** node by right-clicking the **Remote Access Clients** node and selecting **Send Message** from the context menu.

   C. Disconnect all remote access clients by executing the **net send PLUTO\ALL** command-line utility.

   D. Use the **Message** application in the Control Panel, highlight all remote access clients on the **Connected tab**, and click the **Send Message** button.

3. You are the network administrator of your company's network. Today you are instructing a new employee in the proper use of the **Routing and Remote Access** console. What is the recommended way of starting the RRAS console?

   A. Log on as the Administrator and then start the RRAS console.

    B. Log on with a special RRAS administration account that has the permissions to start the RRAS console.

    C. Log on as a regular user, and start the RRAS console using the **Run As** feature, by right-clicking the shortcut from the **Administrative Tools** menu.

    D. Log on as a regular user, start a command prompt, issue the **runas /user:solsystemet /administrator cmd** command to start a new command prompt with administrative permissions, and start the RRAS console from the **Administrative Tools** menu.

4. You are the network administrator of your company's network. The IT department has published a new intranet web site to answer frequently asked questions arising from the recent rollout of RRAS as the corporate portal for remote users who connect through both dial-up and Internet connections. You need to document the procedure you will follow when the RRAS server must be brought down for maintenance. In this document, you are now explaining how connected remote clients will be notified that the RRAS server will be off-line, and how you will disconnect those remote access clients that do not disconnect within the time limit. What steps are correct for this description? (Choose all that apply.)

    A. Send a message to each individual remote access client.

    B. Send a message to all remote access clients.

    C. Disconnect each individually connected remote access client.

    D. Disconnect all connected remote access clients.

5. You are the network administrator of your company's network. You are currently documenting how to stop the RRAS service on your Windows Server 2003. What are the possible ways of stopping the RRAS service? (Choose all that apply.)

    A. Use the **net stop remoteaccess** command.

    B. Use the **net stop rras** command.

    C. Use the **Services** application from **Administrative Tools**.

    D. Use the **Routing and Remote Access** console.

    E. Use the RRAS application in the Control Panel.

6. You are the network administrator of your company's network. You need to verify that RRAS has been successfully started on your Windows Server 2003. What methods are correct for verifying that RRAS is successfully started? (Choose all that apply.)

    A. Issue the **net start** command and verify that "remoteaccess" is in the list of running services.

    B. Issue the **net start** command and verify that "Routing and Remote Access" is in the list of running services.

    C. Start the **Services** application, and verify that "Routing and Remote Access" is running.

    D. Start the MMC and add the Session snap-in, which will display running services.

Configure Logging on a Network Access Server

7. You are the network administrator of your company's network. Greg Paull, Senior Vice President of Sales, was just promoted from within the sales department to his new position. As a member of the sales team, Greg was not allowed to work from home, but as Sr. Vice President, Greg is now afforded that luxury. Greg has a Windows XP Professional client. Since his promotion, Greg has been having trouble accessing certain directories, but was too embarrassed to mention it to anyone in the networking department. When Greg works from home his first day, he discovers that not only can he not access certain directories within the network, he cannot even access the network. What tools would you use to learn more about Greg's connectivity problem? (Choose all that apply.)

   A. Scan the event log for entries regarding Greg's connection attempts.

   B. Scan the Authentication and Accounting logs in **%systemroot%\System32\LogFiles** for entries regarding Greg's connection attempts.

   C. Scan the Authentication and Accounting logs in **%systemroot%\Tracing** for entries regarding Greg's connection attempts.

   D. View Greg's connection attempt in the **Routing and Remote Access** console under **Remote Access Clients**.

8. You are the network administrator of your company's network. You have been asked by one of your fellow network administrators where the event log for Routing and Remote Access Service is enabled on Windows Server 2003. How do you respond?

   A. On the **General** tab of the **Properties** dialog for the remote access server in the **Routing and Remote Access** console.

   B. On the **Event** tab of the **Properties** dialog for the remote access server in the **Routing and Remote Access** console.

   C. On the **Security** tab of the **Properties** dialog for the remote access server in the **Routing and Remote Access** console.

   D. On the **Logging** tab of the **Properties** dialog for the remote access server in the **Routing and Remote Access** console.

9. You are the network administrator of your company's network. You are currently reviewing the logging options available for the Authentication and Accounting logs. What formats can the Authentication and Accounting logs be stored in? (Choose all that apply.)

   A. W3C log format

   B. IAS format

   C. Microsoft SQL Server format

   D. Database-compatible format

10. You are the network administrator of your company's network. You are looking for the information related to Authentication and Accounting. Where are the logs stored by default? (Choose all that apply.)

    A. %systemroot%\System32\Logs

    B. %systemroot%\System32\LogFiles

    C. %systemroot%\Tracing

    D. %systemroot%\Tracing\Logs

    E. Event Viewer

11. You are the network administrator of your company's network. You need to give one of your fellow network administrators instructions on where to enable PPP logging on the Windows Server 2003 that has Routing and Remote Access Service enabled. Where is PPP logging enabled?

    A. By adding **HKEY_LOCAL_MACHINE\System\CurrentControlSet\Services\PPP\ EnableLogging** as a **DWORD** with a value of **1**.

    B. On the **Logging** tab of the **Properties** dialog for the remote access server in the **Routing and Remote Access** console.

    C. On the **Logging** tab of the **Properties** dialog for the **PPP** node in the **Routing and Remote Access** console.

    D. By issuing the **netsh ppp log:on** command.

12. You are the network administrator of your company's network. You need to give one of your fellow network administrators instructions on where to enable Oakley logging on the Windows Server 2003 that has Routing and Remote Access Service enabled. Where is Oakley logging enabled?

    A. By adding **HKEY_LOCAL_MACHINE\System\CurrentControlSet\Services\ PolicyAgent\Oakley\EnableLogging** as a **DWORD** with a value of **1**.

    B. On the **Logging** tab of the **Properties** dialog for the remote access server in the **Routing and Remote Access** console.

    C. On the **Logging** tab of the **Properties** dialog for the **IPSec** node in the **Routing and Remote Access** console.

    D. By issuing the **netsh ipsec log:on** command.

13. You are the network administrator of your company's network. You need to locate the PPP logs for the Routing and Remote Access Service enabled on the Windows Server 2003 JUPITER. Where are the PPP logs located?

    A. %systemroot%\System32\Logs

    B. %systemroot%\System32\LogFiles

    C. %systemroot%\Tracing

    D. %systemroot%\Tracing\Logs

    E. Event Viewer

14. You are the network administrator of your company's network. You need to locate the Audit logs for the Routing and Remote Access Service enabled on the Windows Server 2003 JUPITER. Where are the Audit logs located?

A. %systemroot%\System32\Logs

B. %systemroot%\System32\LogFiles

C. %systemroot%\Tracing

D. %systemroot%\Tracing\Logs

E. Event Viewer

15. You are the network administrator of your company's network. You need to locate the Oakley logs for the Routing and Remote Access Service enabled on the Windows Server 2003 JUPITER. Where are the Oakley logs located?

A. %systemroot%\System32\Logs

B. %systemroot%\System32\LogFiles

C. %systemroot%\Tracing

D. %systemroot%\Tracing\Logs

E. Event Viewer

16. You are the network administrator of your company's network. You need to configure centralized Authentication and Account logging. What options are available for centralized logging? (Choose all that apply)

A. Shared file folder

B. IAS server

C. .NET Framework XML file

D. Microsoft SQL Server

17. You are the network administrator of your company's network. You have just configured Oakley logging on the Windows Server 2003 server that is enabled with Routing and Remote Access Service. To complete the configuration you need to perform some special tasks. What are those tasks? (Choose all that apply.)

A. Execute **net stop policyagent**.

B. Execute **net stop oakley**.

C. Execute **net stop remoteaccess**.

D. Execute **net stop rras**.

E. Execute **net start policyagent**.

F. Execute **net start oakley**.

G. Execute **net start remoteaccess**.

H. Execute **net start rras**.

Collect and Monitor Network Access Data

18. You are the network administrator of your company's network. You recently configured and enabled Routing and Remote Access Service on one of the Windows Server 2003 servers at your location. The server's name is PLUTO, and is designed to give remote access to the corporate network for clients from the Customer Care Division. Some of the end users in the Customer Care Division complain of not being able to access the network consistently, and that when they do get access, the speed is very low. You need to diagnose the problem, and you are looking at what tools are available for gathering information about the PLUTO server. What are the available tools for performance monitoring with Windows Server 2003? (Choose all that apply.)

    A. Performance Monitor

    B. Wireless Monitor

    C. System Monitor

    D. The **netsh perf** command

19. You are the network administrator of your company's network. You recently configured and enabled Routing and Remote Access Service on one of the Windows Server 2003 servers at your location. The server's name is PLUTO, and is designed to give remote access to the corporate network for clients from the Customer Care Division. Some of the end users in the Customer Care Division complain of not being able to access the network consistently, and that when they do get access, the speed is very low. You need to diagnose the problem, and you have decided to use System Monitor to gather information about the PLUTO server. What is the default view the System Monitor opens in?

    A. Wireless Monitor.

    B. Performance Logs and Alerts.

    C. There is no default; System Monitor opens in the view that was last used.

    D. Chart view.

20. You are the network administrator of your company's network. You recently configured and enabled Routing and Remote Access Service on one of the Windows Server 2003 servers at your location. The server's name is PLUTO, and is designed to give remote access to the corporate network for clients from the Customer Care Division. Some of the end users in the Customer Care Division complain of not being able to access the network consistently, and that when they do get access the speed is very low. You need to diagnose the problem, and you have decided to use System Monitor to gather information about the PLUTO server. You now need to determine what objects and counters should be added to System Monitor. What are the most common objects that should be added? (Choose all that apply.)

    A. Memory

    B. Processor

C. IO

D. Processes

E. Disk

F. Mutexes

G. RAS Total

H. RAS Port

LAB QUESTION

You are the network administrator for you company's network in Indiana. Stephen is your Manager, and he is very concerned that the remote access solution that was put in about six months ago will fail. Currently 80 of your field staff use the Windows Server 2003 Routing and Remote Access Sertvice solution.

Stephen is worried that his busy schedule will be interrupted if the remote access server has to be shut down for any reason. For this reason, Stephen has scheduled a meeting with you so he can tell you about his concerns. This meeting has now been rescheduled five times because Stephen is so busy. You know that the topic of the meeting is to be disaster and business continuation issues with the remote access server.

Because you are a proactive network administrator, you opt for the option of preparing a solution before the much-delayed meeting actually takes place.

You need to provide a step-by-step proposal that documents the process of replacing the existing remote access server with a second server. You can be sure that funding will be available for extra hardware because of the worry Stephen feels.

Put the steps in Table 13-2. If you need more space, use a separate sheet of paper.

TABLE 13-2   The Remote Access Lab

Step	Description

SELF TEST ANSWERS

Manage and Monitor Network Traffic

1. ☑ **A.** You can only disconnect individual clients through the **Routing and Remote Access** console.

    ☒ **B** is incorrect because the **Routing and Remote Access** consol does not have this functionality. **C** is incorrect because the **netsh** command does not have the functionality. **D** is incorrect because there is no RRAS application.

2. ☑ **B** is correct because the **Routing and Remote Access** console gives you the ability to send messages to all connected remote access clients.

    ☒ **A** is incorrect because you can send messages to all users in one step. **B** is incorrect because without an IP address the manager would not be able to log on to the network. **C** is incorrect because the **net** command does not have that functionality. **D** is incorrect because there is no Message application.

3. ☑ **C.** The recommended administration model is to log in as a regular user and then run applications that need administrative rights by using the **Run As** feature.

    ☒ **A** is incorrect because this answer goes against the current security recommendations. **B** is incorrect because there is no RRAS administration account. **D** is incorrect because starting a command prompt as an administrator does not transfer any administrative rights to other programs that are not started from the command prompt.

4. ☑ **B and C.** By communicating with all connected users they will be able to save any work and disconnect themselves. After a time, you should disconnect all remaining remote clients that are still connected.

    ☒ **A** is incorrect because you can send one message to all users in one operation. **D** is incorrect because there is no option to disconnect all users in one operation.

5. ☑ **A, C, and D.** These answers describe commands that correctly stop the Routing and Remote Access Service.

    ☒ **B** is incorrect because the service name is **remoteaccess**. **E** is incorrect because there is no RRAS application.

6. ☑ **A and C.** The **net start** command will list all running services; the name for the Routing and Remote Access Service is **remoteaccess**. The **Services** application lists the same information in a window.

    ☒ **B** is incorrect because the name is **remoteaccess**. **D** is incorrect because there is no such snap-in, however enticing it sounds.

Configure Logging on a Network Access Server

7. ☑ **B.** The logs for Authentication and Accounting will assist you in learning more about failed logins.
☒ **A** is incorrect because the event log will not list failed logins. **C** is incorrect because that is not the correct path for the Authentication and Accounting logs. **D** is incorrect because the **Routing and Remote Access** console will only list successful connections.

8. ☑ **D.** The **Logging** tab of **Routing and Remote Access** console is where the logging is enabled.
☒ **A** and **B** are incorrect because neither of those tabs are used to configure logging. **C** is incorrect because there is no Security tab.

9. ☑ **B** and **D.** The logs can be stored in either the IAS or database-compatible formats.
☒ **A** is incorrect because the W3C format is not an option. **C** is incorrect because that is not an option.

10. ☑ **B.** The logs are stored in the LogFiles directory of System32. This is the normal location for the majority of log files in Windows Server 2003.
☒ **A** is incorrect because that is not the default location. **C** is incorrect because that is the location for the PPP log. **D** is incorrect because there is no such location. **E** is incorrect because the Event Viewer is not used for these logs.

11. ☑ **B.** Selecting logging on the **Logging** tab turns on the PPP logs.
☒ **A** is incorrect because that registry key will not make any difference to anything. **C** is incorrect because that setting does not exist. **D** is incorrect because the **netsh** command does not have that capability.

12. ☑ **A.** Oakley logging is enabled by editing the registry.
☒ **B, C,** and **D** are incorrect because none of these commands can be used to enable Oakley logging.

13. ☑ **C.** This is the default location of the PPP logs under Windows Server 2003.
☒ **A, B,** and **D** are incorrect because none of these locations are the default for PPP logging. **E** is incorrect because you cannot view the PPP logs with Event Viewer.

14. ☑ **E.** You view the Audit logs through the Event Viewer.
☒ **A, B, C,** and **D** are incorrect because the Audit logs are stored with the event logs and viewed with the Event Viewer.

15. ☑ **E.** You view the Oakley logs through the Event Viewer.
☒ **A, B, C,** and **D** are incorrect because the Oakley logs are stored with the event logs and viewed with the Event Viewer.

16. ☑ **B** and **D.** You can store the logs in an IAS (RADIUS) server or using the Microsoft SQL Server.

☒ **A** and **C** are incorrect because neither is an option. The XML option sounds very interesting, but it is not available.

17. ☑ **A, C, E,** and **G.** You need to stop and start **ipsec** and Routing and Remote Access Service; the correct names are **policyagent** and **remoteaccess**.

☒ **B, D, F,** and **H** are incorrect because there are no services by that name.

Collect and Monitor Network Access Data

18. ☑ **B** and **C.** The Wireless Monitor gives you information about wireless access points and routers, and the System Monitor is the tool you use to measure the performance of a Windows Server 2003 server.

☒ **A** is incorrect because that is the Windows NT name for the tool; it is now called System Monitor. **D** is incorrect because the **netsh** command does not have that functionality.

19. ☑ **D.** The System Monitor always starts in the Chart view.

☒ **A, B,** and **C** are incorrect because the System Monitor always starts in the Chart View.

20. ☑ **A, B, E,** and **G.** These are the most important objects to measure when you are looking for performance bottlenecks like this one.

☒ **C** is incorrect because there is no IO object. **D** is incorrect because the process object is used to measure a particular program, but in this case you are interested in the server. **F** is incorrect because, interesting as they are, Mutexes as objects are not going to give you any help in this case. **H** is incorrect because you use RAS port object to monitor a specific port, but you are interested in the server as a whole.

LAB ANSWER

The solution to this question is to configure a second Windows Server 2003 that is configured identically to the server that is to be replaced, as shown in Figure 13-8. The steps you need to take are listed in Table 13-3.

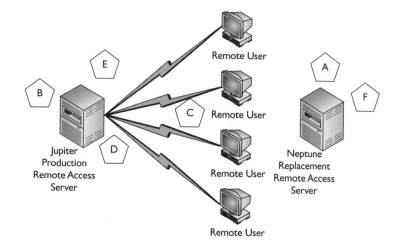

FIGURE 13-8

The architecture
for RRAS
replacement

TABLE 13-3   The Solution

Step	Description
A	Configure a replacement server that will act as the remote access server.
B	Schedule the downtime to take place during the slowest time of the business. Remember that the server might get heavy load outside of the core business hours if staff access the network while traveling.
C	Communicate with the clients to inform them that you are going to perform maintenance; be sure to include the time of and expected length of the maintenance. Ensure that any changes are communicated as the maintenance period approaches.
D	At the appointed time for the maintenance, disconnect any connected clients using the **Routing and Remote Access** console. Send a message to the users before disconnecting them.
E	Stop the Routing and Remote Access Service.
F	Start the replacement server.

14

Troubleshoot the Network Infrastructure

I n this, the last chapter of the book, you will learn about troubleshooting Internet connectivity, as well as issues with Windows Server 2003 services, and how to manage services using the recovery options. The Internet connectivity issue can be one of those heart-pounding situations that can make a problem into something quite scary or a chance to show your mettle and shine, which is what you want to prepare for.

With an understanding of Internet connectivity under your belt, you will shift gears and turn your attention to diagnosing and resolving problems related to service dependencies. In the last two sections of this chapter, you will learn how to use a variety of different tools to identify services and the processes they are running within, how to end nonresponsive processes, and how to configure service recovery options.

You'll begin with a look a what's involved in diagnosing Internet connectivity issues.

CERTIFICATION OBJECTIVE 14.01

Troubleshoot Connectivity to the Internet

I still remember the first time I faced an Internet connectivity problem. It was at least two weeks after I had successfully connected the company I was working for to the Internet. In the early days of the Internet the big issue was to ensure that e-mail was exchanged between us and our customers. The previous connection to the Internet had been through a mail router located at our U.S. partner in New Jersey, but now we had our own ISDN connection to a local ISP in Toronto, we were routing our own e-mail, delivery was almost instantaneous, and it had been almost two weeks since I had it configured and put into production.

That morning was memorable in that I had no idea what was going to happen. In two weeks, our e-mail clients had gotten accustomed to instantaneous e-mail delivery and replies. I met one of our clients in the cafeteria as I was filling my coffee mug; she asked if there was something wrong with the e-mail system, because it was so slow. The same question was posed by a number of clients I met on my way to my desk. As I reached my desk, I found the help desk manager waiting for me. The help desk was swamped with e-mail related calls, and she wanted to know what to tell our clients. As far as I was concerned, this was going to be an easy repair. What can go wrong with a simple connection to the Internet after all?

At the end of the day I had solved the problem, not by brilliant troubleshooting or by superior knowledge of the process. No, I found the hard way that if you do not have all the tools and knowledge at your fingertips before you have a problem, it will take much longer to learn under fire. I solved it, with the help of our other administrators, with the help of our limited knowledge of routed TCP/IP (this was in 1995), and some knowledge I had of the UNIX tools I had used five years before.

The problem was simple to see: no e-mail was delivered to the Internet, the queue was filled, no e-mail was received from the Internet, and it was bounced into the out queue by the e-mail system. So it was an e-mail problem, right? How wrong I was.

The solution was equally simple, once found: repair the DNS zone that was missing a trailing . (dot) for one record. This rendered DNS nonfunctional, so the e-mail system could not deliver any messages or verify the sender for any message.

The tools I used were **ping**, **tracert**, **nslookup**, telnet (yes it is a troubleshooting tool as well), and a healthy dose of humility that I found would help. As it turned out, this problem would show up from time to time because the DNS administrator would forget the trailing . (dot); this was in the days before **dnslint**.

on the *Learn the use of all the command-line tools so that you are versed in their use.*
Job *That way you can focus on the problem, rather than on the tool.*

The moral of this story is that knowledge is power, and that there are a small number of tools to know that will help you locate the source of the problem. In this section, you will look at your old friends **ping**, **tracert**, **nslookup**, as well as a newcomer, the **pathping** utility.

INSIDE THE EXAM

TCP/IP Troubleshooting

The most important step to take when troubleshooting Internet connectivity issues is to take small steps. You also need to make sure that you know what the result of a particular test means. When you ping a remote host using its FQDN and it fails, you need to make sure to determine if it is the failure of the network or the name resolution. Ping the DNS server; if you

get an answer, use **nslookup** to see what the DNS server answers. Only then can you determine that the problem is routing or DNS.

It is easy to be blinded by the sheer volume of information, but if you take small steps, the information becomes manageable. Remember to focus on only one step at a time, moving steadily toward the resolution of the problem.

The Routing Tools

The routing tools are used to verify connectivity, as well as how a particular connection is routed across the Internet. indeed, these tools are used to troubleshoot any network that you need to get more information about. The way you use the tools depends on the symptoms of the problem. If you need to verify that a particular host is reachable (and that it can reach you in return) you use the **ping** command. If you need to verify that the route used is the one you have designed, you use the **tracert** command. If you want a report about the quality of the network, you use the **pathping** command.

ping

The **ping** command is designed to help verify IP connectivity; it is one of the main tools used to troubleshoot a network. The **ping** command sends an ICMP echo request to a host, and then waits for the reply from the host. This verifies that two hosts can communicate. You can use the **ping** command with the FQDN of the host, or with the IP address if you don't need to test name resolution.

Table 14-1 lists the options for the **ping** command.

For example, to test the connectivity to the host **www.osborne.com**, enter the following command:

```
C:\>ping www.osborne.com
Pinging www.osborne.com [198.45.24.162] with 32 bytes of data:

Reply from 198.45.24.162: bytes=32 time=43ms TTL=238
Reply from 198.45.24.162: bytes=32 time=42ms TTL=238
Reply from 198.45.24.162: bytes=32 time=43ms TTL=238
Reply from 198.45.24.162: bytes=32 time=70ms TTL=238

Ping statistics for 198.45.24.162:
    Packets: Sent = 4, Received = 4, Lost = 0 (0% loss),
Approximate round trip times in milli-seconds:
    Minimum = 42ms, Maximum = 70ms, Average = 49ms
```

To perform reverse name resolution, use the **–a** option:

```
C:\>ping -a 198.45.24.162
Pinging www.osborne.com [198.45.24.162] with 32 bytes of data:

Reply from 198.45.24.162: bytes=32 time=43ms TTL=238
...
```

| TABLE 14-1 | **ping** Options |

Option	Description
–t	Continually sends ICMP echo packets; use CTRL-BREAK to interrupt.
–a	Requests reverse name resolution from an IP address to an FQDN.
–n *Count*	Specifies the number of ICMP echo requests to send; the default is four.
–l *Size*	Specifies the size in bytes of the data fields in the ICMP echo request; the default is 32 bytes. Used to test fragmentation issues.
–f	Sends the ICMP echo request with the **Don't fragment** flag set to **1** in the header.
–i *TTL*	Specifies the Time-To-Live (TTL) for the ICMP echo request; the default is the default TTL of the host.
–v *TOS*	Specifies the Type Of Service (TOS) of the ICMP echo request.
–r *Count*	Specifies the number of hops to account for in the path taken by the ICMP echo packet.
–s *Count*	Specifies the Internet Timestamp option for the ICMP echo request.
–j *HostList*	Specifies the use of the Loose Source Route option in the IP header.
–k *HostList*	Specifies the use of the Strict Source Route option in the IP header.
–w *Timeout*	Specifies the time to wait for a reply to the ICMP echo request; the default is 4,000 ms.
–R	Specifies that the round-trip path is traced (IPv6 only).
–4	Specifies that IPV4 is used.
–6	Specifies that IPv6 is used.
TargetName	Specifies the name or address of the host to ping.
–?	Gets help at the command prompt.

If you cannot resolve the name of the host to an IP address, try to ping the IP address direct. If that succeeds you have connectivity, if it fails you need to go about the troubleshooting in logical steps. The recommended steps are

1. Ping the local computer using the special address **127.0.0.1**, or the host name **localhost**:

```
ping 127.0.0.1
```

2. If that step succeeds, ping the IP address of the local host. For example, if the IP address of the local host is **10.0.0.201**:

```
ping 10.0.0.201
```

These two steps verified that the local installation of TCP/IP is functional. The next step will verify that you can communicate with the local subnet.

3. Ping the default gateway for the local subnet. For example, if the router is at **10.0.0.2**:

```
ping 10.0.0.2
```

If this step succeeds, you have proof that your local subnet is functional.

4. Ping a remote host. For example if you know that there is a host at **198.45.24.162**:

```
ping 198.45.24.162
```

After these four steps, you have validated the infrastructure of the Internet connection.

5. Finally, ping the remote host using a FQDN to validate the DNS installation:

```
ping www.osborne.com
```

If you follow this methodology, you will, in the end, have repaired any connectivity issues.

a t c h   *The ping command tests both the path to the remote host as well as the path back to your server.*

EXERCISE 14-1

CertCam 14-1 ON THE CD

Using ping to Troubleshoot an Internet Connection

In this exercise, you will work on your Windows Server 2003. This exercise is designed for you to test the TCP/IP configuration to reach the web server at **www.osborne.com**.

1. Log in to your Windows Server 2003 machine.

2. Click **Start | Run**. Type **cmd** in the **Open** textbox and click **OK**.

3. At the command prompt, type **ipconfig /all** to document the TCP/IP configuration. Write the information into the following table.

Information	Data
Local IP address	
Default gateway	
DNS server	
Remote host	www.osborne.com 198.45.24.162

4. To find the current address of the remote host issue the following command-line command:

   C:\> nslookup www.osborne.com

5. Ping the loopback address of the local server:

   ping 127.0.0.1

   Did it succeed? If so, continue with Step 5.

6. Ping the local IP address. Did it succeed? If so, continue with Step 6.

7. Ping the remote host using the IP address. Did it succeed? If so, continue with Step 7.

8. Ping the remote host using the FQDN. Did it succeed? If so, your Internet connection is functioning.

tracert

When you are troubleshooting Internet connectivity, you will often find that the local subnet is functioning, but when you ping the remote host, you experience problems. The first step is to try a different remote host, preferably in a different geographic area, to allow you to determine how widespread the problem is. Once you have determined that you have a routing problem somewhere between you and the remote host, you can use the **tracert** (trace route) utility to determine where the offending router is located, so you can repair it if it is on your network, or notify the ISP if it is on theirs.

The **tracert** utility uses the IP TTL and error messages from ICMP to determine the route from one host to another. I have found that tracert is a tool I run when things are working, so I have a documented "normal" route. Then when things do go wrong, I can compare to see what is likely the problem.

The **tracert** utility prints out a list of addresses of the near side of the routers as well as the minimum, average, and maximum round-trip time for each router. For example, the following traces the route to **www.osborne.com**:

```
C:\>tracert www.osborne.com -d

Tracing route to www.osborne.com [198.45.24.162]
over a maximum of 30 hops:

  1    10 ms     9 ms    14 ms   64.230.254.110
  2     8 ms     9 ms     8 ms   64.230.245.130
  3     7 ms     7 ms     6 ms   206.108.107.217
  4    10 ms     9 ms    10 ms   206.108.107.230
  5     9 ms    10 ms    16 ms   209.58.25.69
  6    22 ms    24 ms    19 ms   64.86.80.221
  7    22 ms    21 ms    22 ms   66.110.8.130
  8    23 ms    23 ms    23 ms   207.45.198.74
  9    31 ms    23 ms    23 ms   152.63.22.230
 10    32 ms    24 ms    19 ms   152.63.23.129
 11    33 ms    33 ms     8 ms   152.63.0.177
 12    33 ms    33 ms    12 ms   152.63.67.122
 13    34 ms    33 ms    38 ms   152.63.66.93
 14    40 ms    37 ms    49 ms   157.130.101.102
 15    40 ms    38 ms    39 ms   64.22.197.23
 16    61 ms    64 ms    65 ms   64.22.197.50
 17    42 ms    32 ms    41 ms   64.22.208.90
 18    41 ms    35 ms    52 ms   198.45.24.244
 19    43 ms    36 ms    44 ms   198.45.24.162
Trace complete.
```

The **–d** option suppresses DNS lookup of the name of the router. Any "Request timed out messages" indicate that those routers did not return a reply, so they are invisible to the **tracert** utility.

The command-line options for **tracert** are listed in Table 14-2.

TABLE 14-2	tracert Options

Option	Description
–d	Suppresses reverse name resolution from an IP address to an FQDN.
–h *MaximumHops*	Specifies the maximum number of hops to trace; the default is 30.
–j *HostList*	Specifies the use of the Loose Source Route option in the IP header.
–w *Timeout*	Specifies the time to wait for a reply to the ICMP echo request; the default is 4,000 ms.
–R	Specifies that the round-trip path is traced (IPv6 only).
–S	Specifies the source address to use (IPv6 only).
–4	Specifies that IPV4 is used.
–6	Specifies that IPv6 is used.
TargetName	Specifies the name or address of the host to ping.
–?	Gets help at the command prompt.

w a t c h   *The last router listed in a trace with problems is usually the router with problems.*

When you use the **tracert** utility, you often find that the last router that is listed is the router that is having problems communicating. That is the router that becomes the prime suspect.

EXERCISE 14-2

Using the tracert Utility

In this exercise, you will trace the routers between your server and the web server at **www.osborne.com**.

1. Log in to your Windows Server 2003 machine.

2. Click **Start | Run**, enter **cmd** in the **Open** textbox, and click **OK**.

3. Enter **tracert www.osborne.com** at the command prompt.

4. Analyze the returned data. How many hops? How slow is the slowest link?

pathping

The **pathping** utility is used to get reports about the network conditions. The report contains information about the latency and traffic loss between routers. The utility is called **pathping** because it sends multiple ICMP echo request messages to each of the routers it finds along the route to the remote host. The utility uses the return messages and the timing of the messages to calculate the latency and packet loss.

The first part of the **pathping** utility performs a function similar to the **tracert** utility to identify the routers. It then analyses each of the routers to produce the statistics.

The command options for **pathping** are listed in Table 14-3.

TABLE 14-3   **pathping** Options

Option	Description
–n	Suppresses reverse name resolution from an IP address to an FQDN.
–h *MaximumHops*	Specifies the maximum number of hops to trace; the default is 30.
–g *HostList*	Specifies the use of the **Loose Source Route** option in the IP header.
–p *Period*	Specifies the period to wait between pings to the routers; the default is 250 ms.
–q *NumQueries*	Configures how many pings are sent to each router; the default is 100.
–w *Timeout*	Specifies the time to wait for a reply to the ICMP echo request; the default is 3,000 ms.
–i *IPAddress*	Specifies the source address to use.
–4	Specifies that IPV4 is used.
–6	Specifies that IPv6 is used.
TargetName	Specifies the name or address of the host to ping.
–?	Is used to get help at the command prompt.

For example the following is a run that uses **pathping** on **www.osborne.com**:

```
C:\>pathping www.osborne.com -n

Tracing route to www.osborne.com [198.45.24.162]
over a maximum of 30 hops:
   0  10.0.0.251
   1  64.230.254.110
   2  64.230.245.130
   3  206.108.107.217
   4  206.108.107.230
   5  209.58.25.69
   6  64.86.80.221
   7  66.110.8.130
   8  207.45.198.74
   9  152.63.22.230
  10  152.63.23.129
  11  152.63.0.177
  12  152.63.67.122
  13  152.63.66.93
  14  157.130.101.102
  15  64.22.197.23
  16  64.22.197.50
  17  64.22.208.90
  18  198.45.24.244
  19  198.45.24.162

Computing statistics for 475 seconds...
                  Source to Here   This Node/Link
Hop  RTT      Lost/Sent = Pct   Lost/Sent = Pct  Address
  0                                               10.0.0.251
                                  0/ 100 =  0%    |
  1   10ms     0/ 100 =  0%      0/ 100 =  0%  64.230.254.110
                                  0/ 100 =  0%    |
  2    9ms     0/ 100 =  0%      0/ 100 =  0%  64.230.245.130
                                  0/ 100 =  0%    |
  3    9ms     1/ 100 =  1%      1/ 100 =  1%  206.108.107.217
                                  0/ 100 =  0%    |
  4   10ms     0/ 100 =  0%      0/ 100 =  0%  206.108.107.230
                                  0/ 100 =  0%    |
  5   10ms     0/ 100 =  0%      0/ 100 =  0%  209.58.25.69
                                  0/ 100 =  0%    |
  6   19ms     0/ 100 =  0%      0/ 100 =  0%  64.86.80.221
                                  0/ 100 =  0%    |
  7   19ms     0/ 100 =  0%      0/ 100 =  0%  66.110.8.130
```

```
                                               0/ 100 =  0%    |
   8    18ms     0/ 100 =  0%    0/ 100 =  0%  207.45.198.74
                                 0/ 100 =  0%    |
   9    18ms     0/ 100 =  0%    0/ 100 =  0%  152.63.22.230
                                 0/ 100 =  0%    |
  10    19ms     0/ 100 =  0%    0/ 100 =  0%  152.63.23.129
                                 0/ 100 =  0%    |
  11    25ms     0/ 100 =  0%    0/ 100 =  0%  152.63.0.177
                                 0/ 100 =  0%    |
  12    25ms     0/ 100 =  0%    0/ 100 =  0%  152.63.67.122
                                 0/ 100 =  0%    |
  13    26ms     0/ 100 =  0%    0/ 100 =  0%  152.63.66.93
                                 0/ 100 =  0%    |
  14    39ms     0/ 100 =  0%    0/ 100 =  0%  157.130.101.102
                                 0/ 100 =  0%    |
  15    43ms     0/ 100 =  0%    0/ 100 =  0%  64.22.197.23
                                 0/ 100 =  0%    |
  16    34ms     0/ 100 =  0%    0/ 100 =  0%  64.22.197.50
                                 0/ 100 =  0%    |
  17    35ms     0/ 100 =  0%    0/ 100 =  0%  64.22.208.90
                                 0/ 100 =  0%    |
  18    33ms     0/ 100 =  0%    0/ 100 =  0%  198.45.24.244
                                 1/ 100 =  1%    |
  19    35ms     1/ 100 =  1%    0/ 100 =  0%  198.45.24.162
Trace complete.
```

The information gathered is very useful when it comes to diagnose defective routes on the network. By having a documented **pathping** run from when the network was functioning correctly, you can compare the information at a later date when there are problems. This way you will be able to pinpoint the problem area faster.

w a t c h *Remember that the pathping **utility reports statistics regarding latency and packet loss per link.***

nslookup

As my story earlier in this chapter showed, there are other problems with the Internet connection than TCP/IP problems. DNS is probably the largest area of addressing problems, especially when a large amount of manual maintenance is performed on the zone files. The network administrator must have an intimate knowledge of how the DNS structure is designed, and where the DNS servers are located. For example, the DNS service I use for my company has DNS servers located on a number of continents to ensure that massive service outages would not affect the service levels. The way you test that DNS servers function properly has already been detailed in Chapter 6, so I will only look at some issues of using **nslookup** to verify the data.

nslookup

nslookup is the utility you use to query a DNS server, and to verify that the data is correctly delivered from a client's point of view. The **nslookup** program can be executed in two modes: command-line and interactive. You use the **nslookup** utility in the command-line mode when you need to look up one address, and in interactive mode to enter more than a couple of queries, or when you need to set options on how the DNS queries are to be processed.

The following is an example of using **nslookup** in command-line mode to query for the addresses of **www.microsoft.com**:

```
C:\>nslookup www.microsoft.com
Server:   dns.nopcomp.com
Address:  66.153.22.67

Non-authoritative answer:
Name:    a562.cd.akamai.net
Addresses:  81.52.249.54, 81.52.249.95, 81.52.249.71, 81.52.249.63
Aliases:  www.microsoft.com, www.microsoft.com.edgesuite.net
C:\>
```

The control is returned directly to the command prompt after the command, whereas when you use the interactive mode, you are presented with a prompt from the **nslookup** utility direct. In this example you can see how I query for the mail exchangers (the fancy name for e-mail servers) for a couple of domains:

```
C:\>nslookup
Default Server:  dns.nopcomp.com
Address:  66.153.22.67

> set type=MX
> microsoft.com
Server:  dns.wlfdle.rnc.net.cable.rogers.com
Address:  24.153.22.67

microsoft.com    MX preference = 10, mail exchanger = maila.microsoft.com
microsoft.com    MX preference = 10, mail exchanger = mailb.microsoft.com
microsoft.com    MX preference = 10, mail exchanger = mailc.microsoft.com
maila.microsoft.com    internet address = 131.107.3.124
maila.microsoft.com    internet address = 131.107.3.125
```

```
mailb.microsoft.com          internet address = 131.107.3.123
mailb.microsoft.com          internet address = 131.107.3.122
mailc.microsoft.com          internet address = 131.107.3.121
mailc.microsoft.com          internet address = 131.107.3.126
> osborne.com
Server:  dns.nopcomp.com
Address:  66.153.22.67

osborne.com      MX preference = 0, mail exchanger = mail.eppg.com
osborne.com      nameserver = NS1.MHEDU.com
osborne.com      nameserver = NS2.MHEDU.com
NS1.MHEDU.com    internet address = 198.45.24.13
NS2.MHEDU.com    internet address = 198.45.24.14
> exit
C:\>
```

Using the **set type** command to request the MX (mail exchange) records, you use **nslookup** to test how a particular domain is represented by a DNS server. To focus your query on a particular DNS server, use the **set server** command.

Now that you have a better idea of troubleshooting Internet connectivity, here are some possible scenario questions and their answers.

SCENARIO & SOLUTION

How do I determine if my connectivity problem to the Internet is a routing or a name resolution problem?	When you ping a FQDN and it does not resolve, you are faced with the possibility that the problem is a DNS one. Ping the remote host using its IP address; if that succeeds, you probably have a DNS problem. Ping the DNS server by IP address, and use the **nslookup** utility to verify the data of the DNS server.
What is the time in ms listed in the output from the **pathping www.osborne.com –n** command?	That is the average latency for the router based on the 100 ICMP echo requests that were sent to each router.
How do I find addresses and FQDNs for remote hosts on the Internet that I can use for testing?	The DNS **root** servers are a family of servers that will always be online and are well known. If you can not find any other servers that are in your organization, look them up in the root hints section of DNS.
Can I use **tracert** to test name resolution as well?	Yes, you can, that is the default setting of **tracert**. It will perform a reverse lookup for each router. This is sometimes very slow, and you are probably better off using the **–d** option to suppress the reverse lookup.

Diagnose and Resolve Issues Related to Service Dependency

In this section we will look at the administrative tasks involved in diagnosing and resolving issues related to service dependency. We will also examine a number of tools that can be used to perform the diagnostics, such as the **Services** snap-in, Task Manager, Service Controller (**sc.exe**), Tasklist, and Taskkill. We'll start this discussion by describing what a service is, and what services provide in Windows Server 2003.

A *service* is a process or set of processes that add functionality to Windows Server 2003 by providing support to other programs. The default installation of Windows Server 2003 provides a set of core services, all of which can be seen in Task Manager on the **Processes** tab, shown in Figure 14-1.

FIGURE 14-1

List of services shown in Task Manager

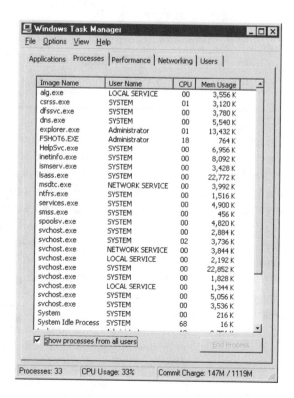

Although Task Manager allows you to identify what services or processes are running on a given computer, it can't provide you with a list of service dependencies, which is very important to know. One quick approach to resolving a problem on a server is to end the process that is hung or that appears to be negatively affecting performance from within Task Manager. However, before you end a process in this manner, you should identify all other dependent services so that you are aware of the full effect ending the process will have on the computer. Exercise 14-3 describes the process of ending a task using Task Manager.

EXERCISE 14-3

Ending a Process Using Task Manager

In this exercise you will learn how to end a task using Task Manager. This can be useful when an application or process goes into a "not responding" state, and you want to end that process to restore full functionality to the computer.

1. Press CTRL-ALT-DELETE.

2. In the **Windows Security** dialog box, click **Task Manager**.

3. In the **Windows Task Manager** window, select the **Processes** tab.

4. Select the affected process, and click **End Process**.

Ending a process is the easy part, as you can see. The difficult part can be identifying which process represents the non-responding applications. For some applications, primarily foreground and notification area applications, this isn't a complicated issue at all, because they are listed on the **Applications** tab in Task Manager. For server services, however, identifying the process that a service is running in is more involved, and can be accomplished using a utility such as Tasklist.

An example of a foreground applications is Microsoft Word 2003, which when running can be seen as on the **Application** tab in Task Manager. A more involved job is to identify which of the multiple **svchost.exe** processes the Background Intelligent Transfer Service (BITS) runs within. This is where Tasklist can be used with the **tasklist.exe /SVC** command.

Now that you are familiar with how to end a process, you need to begin to answer some of the tougher questions, such as how you can associate applications or services with specific processes, and how you can identify service dependencies for a specific service.

Start by answering the easy question first: how to identify service dependencies. Like many tasks in a Windows environment, you have a number of options to achieve this goal. Two tools are available to allow us to accomplish this task. The first is the **Services** MMC (**services.msc**) and the second is **sc.exe**. Exercise 14-4 walks you through the steps involved in using the **Services** MMC to identify a service's dependencies.

EXERCISE 14-4

Identifying Service Dependencies Using the Services MMC

In this exercise, you will learn how to identify a service's dependencies using the **Services** MMC.

1. Click **Start | Administrative Tools | Services**.

2. In the **Services** MMC, right-click the service that you wish to view the services for, and select **Properties**.

3. In the service properties dialog box, select the **Dependencies** tab.

4. On the **Dependencies** tab, shown in the following illustration, you can see the services that this particular service depends on, as well the services that are dependent on this particular service.

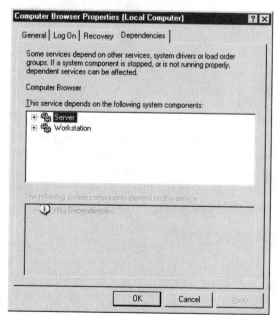

This same task can also be accomplished using **sc.exe**, as shown in Exercise 14-5.

EXERCISE 14-5

Using sc.exe to View Service Dependencies

In this exercise you will learn how to identify service dependencies using **sc.exe**.

1. Click **Start** | **Run**.

2. Type **cmd** and press ENTER.

3. To identify the dependencies for the alerter service, at the command prompt, type **sc qc alerter** and press ENTER.

4. This will return the results shown in the following illustration, enabling you to identify the dependencies of the alerter service.

```
C:\WINDOWS\system32\cmd.exe

C:\Documents and Settings\Administrator.WS03BASE2>sc qc alerter
[SC] QueryServiceConfig SUCCESS

SERVICE_NAME: alerter
        TYPE               : 20  WIN32_SHARE_PROCESS
        START_TYPE         : 2   AUTO_START
        ERROR_CONTROL      : 1   NORMAL
        BINARY_PATH_NAME   : C:\WINDOWS\system32\svchost.exe -k LocalService
        LOAD_ORDER_GROUP   :
        TAG                : 0
        DISPLAY_NAME       : Alerter
        DEPENDENCIES       : LanmanWorkstation
        SERVICE_START_NAME : NT AUTHORITY\LocalService

C:\Documents and Settings\Administrator.WS03BASE2>_
```

Now you can address the issue of how you can associate applications or services with specific processes. One tool that we can use to do this is Tasklist (**tasklist.exe**), which can be used to display a list of applications, services, and their respective Process IDs (PIDs). This tool can be used to display this information on either the local computer or a remote computer. To determine which services are running within a given process on the local computer, simply execute the following command at the command prompt.

```
Tasklist /SVC
```

Figure 14-2 shows the results of this command. You can see that with the **services.exe** process, both the Event Log and the Plug and Play services are running. Therefore, ending the services.exe process would stop the Eventlog and Plug and Play services. The output of Tasklist also allows you to identify the PID associated with a specific process. This can be used to cross-reference the process listed in the Tasklist output

FIGURE 14-2

Identifying the
services running
within a process

```
C:\WINDOWS\system32\cmd.exe                                                    _ □ x
C:\Documents and Settings\Administrator.WS03BASE2>tasklist /SVC

Image Name                    PID Services
========================= ====== =============================================
System Idle Process             0 N/A
System                          4 N/A
smss.exe                      308 N/A
csrss.exe                     356 N/A
winlogon.exe                  380 N/A
services.exe                  424 Eventlog, PlugPlay
lsass.exe                     436 HTTPFilter, kdc, Netlogon, PolicyAgent,
                                  ProtectedStorage, SamSs
svchost.exe                   616 RpcSs
svchost.exe                   668 TermService
svchost.exe                   808 Dhcp, Dnscache
svchost.exe                   824 LmHosts
svchost.exe                   852 BITS, Browser, CryptSvc, dmserver,
                                  EventSystem, helpsvc, lanmanserver,
                                  lanmanworkstation, Netman, Nla, RasMan,
                                  RemoteAccess, Schedule, seclogon, SENS,
                                  ShellHWDetection, W32Time, winmgmt,
                                  wuauserv, WZCSVC
spoolsv.exe                  1092 Spooler
msdtc.exe                    1124 MSDTC
vpcsrvc.exe                  1184 1-vpcsrvc
dfssvc.exe                   1208 Dfs
dns.exe                      1248 DNS
svchost.exe                  1300 ERSvc
inetinfo.exe                 1352 IISADMIN
ismserv.exe                  1368 IsmServ
ntfrs.exe                    1404 NtFrs
svchost.exe                  1524 RemoteRegistry
UPCMap.exe                   1548 UPCMap
tcpsvcs.exe                  1588 DHCPServer
svchost.exe                  1824 W3SVC
alg.exe                      2112 ALG
wmiprvse.exe                 2132 N/A
svchost.exe                  2212 TapiSrv
explorer.exe                 2808 N/A
HelpCtr.exe                  3132 N/A
HelpSvc.exe                  3224 N/A
HelpHost.exe                 3284 N/A
cmd.exe                      1324 N/A
wmiprvse.exe                 1576 N/A
tasklist.exe                 2104 N/A

C:\Documents and Settings\Administrator.WS03BASE2>
```

with the list of processes in Task Manager to ensure that you end the correct task.
As you can see, there are often multiple instances of the same task, running different
services. The best example of this is the **svchost.exe** process, which is listed a number
of different times in the Tasklist output.

The PID column is not displayed by default in Windows Task Manager, but you
can add it quite easily using the **View | Select Columns** menu option in Windows
Task Manager.

Tasklist can also be used to identify processes that are in different process states
such as "not responding," which can allow you to quickly identify and then end
these processes. To identify all processes that are in a "not responding" state, use the
following command.

```
Tasklist /FI "status eq not responding"
```

Figure 14-3 shows the results of this command run on the local computer. As you
can see from the output, the process name, its PID, and its current memory usage are
displayed.

FIGURE 14-3

Identifying
processes
that are not
responding
using Tasklist

```
C:\WINDOWS\system32\cmd.exe                                              _ □ ×
C:\Documents and Settings\Administrator.WS03BASE2>tasklist /FI "status eq Not re
sponding

Image Name                    PID Session Name        Session#    Mem Usage
========================= ====== ================ =========== ============
HelpHost.exe                 3284 Console                    0       5,444 K

C:\Documents and Settings\Administrator.WS03BASE2>
```

If you don't want to have to switch back and forth between the command prompt where you are identifying processes and the GUI Task Manager where you are familiar with ending processes, you can also use Taskkill at the command prompt to end a process. Suppose you want to end the unresponsive process **helphost.exe** with the PID 3284. You would execute the following command:

```
Taskkill /PID 3284
```

The result of this command is the successful termination of the process with PID 3284, as shown in Figure 14-4.

For more information on services and their dependencies, perform a search on google.com ***for*** Win2kservices.doc ***or browse to*** http://www.microsoft.com/windows2000/ docs/win2kservices.doc. ***There will likely be an updated white paper on Windows Server 2003 services, so keep your eyes open for that as well.***

CERTIFICATION OBJECTIVE 14.03

Use Service Recovery Options to Diagnose and Resolve Service-Related Issues

The Services MMC is one of the first and most logical places to start when confronted with the task of using service recovery options to diagnose and resolve service-related issues. There are two views in the **Services** MMC in Windows Server 2003 denoted by the two tabs at the bottom of the console: **Standard** and **Extended**.

FIGURE 14-4

Killing a process
with Taskkill

```
C:\WINDOWS\system32\cmd.exe                                              _ □ ×
C:\Documents and Settings\Administrator.WS03BASE2>taskkill /PID 3284
SUCCESS: Sent termination signal to the process with PID 3284.

C:\Documents and Settings\Administrator.WS03BASE2>_
```

The Extended view is the default, and offers you additional information in the form of a description of the service and the ability to start, stop, pause, or restart the service through a hyperlink, depending on the service and its current state. Take the World Wide Web Publishing Service for example. Figure 14-5 shows the extended view in the services snap-in with the World Wide Web Publishing Service highlighted. Here you can see a brief description of the service, and you have the ability to stop, pause, or restart it as it is currently running.

Double-clicking a specific service in the **Services** MMC or right-clicking on a service and selecting **Properties** will display the respective service's properties dialog box and present you with four different tabs.

On the **General** tab, shown in Figure 14-6, you can identify the service name, its display name, description, the path to the executable, startup type, and any startup parameters, and you have the ability to start, stop, pause, or restart the service.

Every service in Windows Server 2003 has three startup states: disabled, manual, and automatic. Disabled services are installed but not currently running. To start a disabled service, the startup type must first be changed to **Manual** or **Automatic**. Services with a manual state are installed, but will only start when called by another application, service, or by a user with administrative privileges. Services that are set to automatic are started by the operating system at initialization, after device drivers are loaded.

FIGURE 14-5   The Extended view in the Services MMC

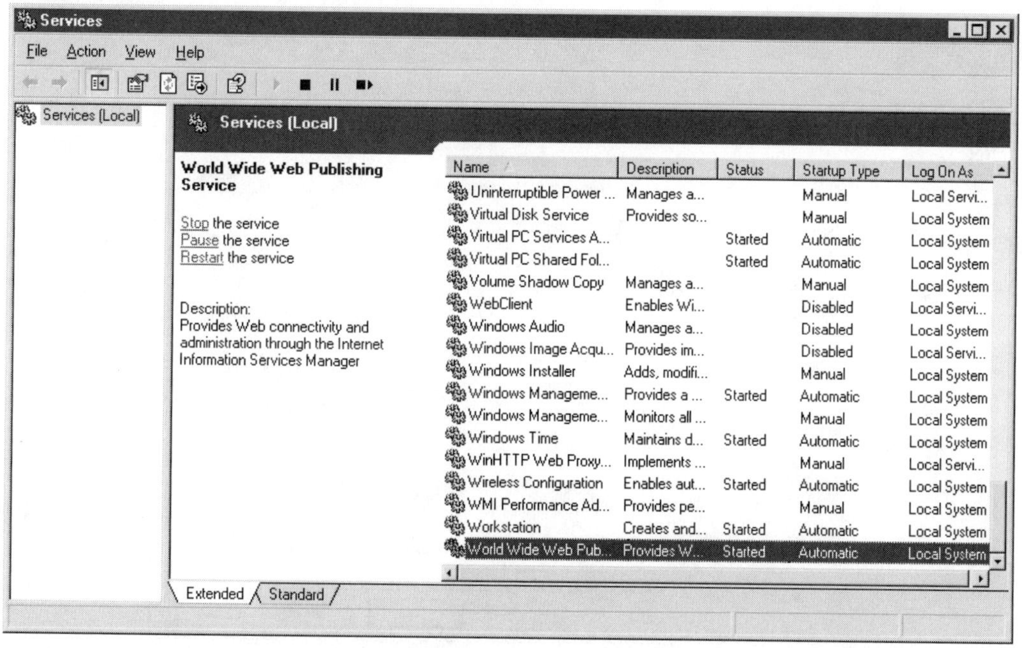

FIGURE 14-6

General service
properties

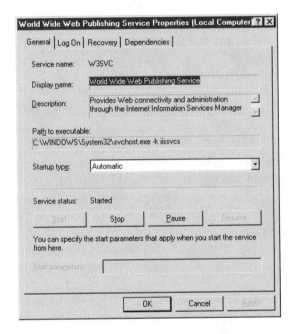

On the **Log On** tab shown in Figure 14-7, you can configure the account that is used
by the service to log on. In the majority of cases, this will be a local system account,
but in other application-specific circumstances, such as with SQL Server, you may
decide to create your own service account on the local computer or in the domain,

FIGURE 14-7

Log On service
properties

assign the account the required rights and permissions, and use this account for the service. You can also use the **Log On** tab to enable or disable a service within a specific hardware profile.

It isn't as likely that you will have hardware profiles on your production servers, because profiles are for mobile computers like notebooks, but it is possible. In the case of a notebook, you can create both a docked and an undocked hardware profile. Then, within **Services**, disable all the services that you don't want or need while the notebook computer is undocked to optimize resource usage.

The third tab in the service properties dialog box is the **Recovery** tab shown in Figure 14-8. On the **Recovery** tab, you can configure responses to service failures. This can be useful in automating the administrative task of restarting a service should it stop unexpectedly. From the failure response drop-down dialog boxes, you are given four options:

- **Take no action**
- **Restart the service**
- **Run a Program**
- **Restart the Computer**

You can also configure individual responses to the first failure, second failure, and subsequent failures allowing you to elevate the level of response with each repeated service failure. Exercise 14-6 walks you through the process of configuring recovery options.

FIGURE 14-8

Service **Recovery** tab

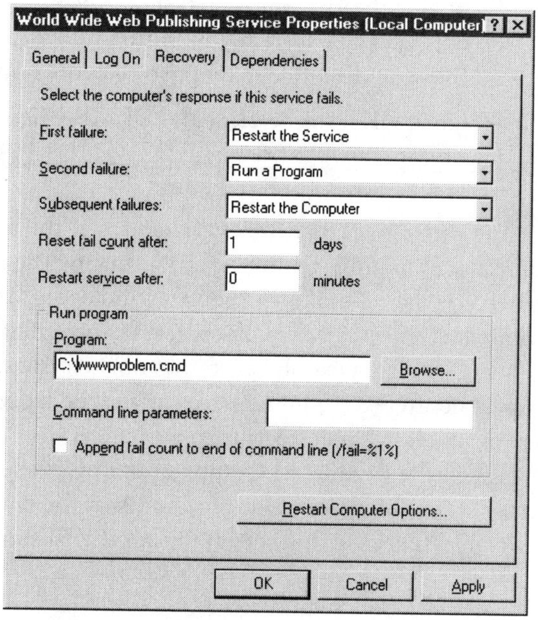

EXERCISE 14-6

Configuring Service Recovery Options

In this exercise, you will learn how to configure individual service recovery options. This will provide you the ability to escalate the severity of response with each additional service failure. In this exercise, you will configure a service restart as the response to the first failure, execute a command in response to the second failure, and finally restart the entire system on subsequent failures.

1. Click **Start | All Programs | Administrative Tools | Services**.

2. Double-click the **DHCP Client** service.

3. Select the **Recovery** tab.

4. In the **First Response** drop-down box, select **Restart the Service**.

5. In the **Second Response** drop-down box, click **Run a Program**. In the **Program** text box, type **c:\scripts\DHCPClientproblem.cmd**. I have written this command file to send a notification by e-mail to alert you to the service problem and to use the **net start** command to attempt to start the DHCP client service.

6. In the **Subsequent failures** drop-down box, select **Restart the Computer**.

7. Click the **Restart Computer Options** button.

8. Change the **Restart computer after** counter to **4** minutes.

9. Enable the **Before restart, send this message to computers on the network** option. Type **SystemX is shutting down in 4 minutes. Please save all open files and disconnect all existing connections** and click **OK**.

10. Click **OK** again to close the **DHCP Client Properties** dialog box.

You can also use the **Recovery** tab to set the reset failure count and specify a duration in minutes to wait before restarting the service. The latter can be useful when you have a number of services and applications running on a server with limited resources, and you know from experience that certain services have a tendency to fail, possibly on startup due to system resource unavailability at the time, but after 4 or 5 minutes, restarting the failed services when system resources are available again corrects the problem.

When the Restart the Computer option is selected as one of the recovery options, the **Restart Computer Options** button at the bottom of the **Recovery** tab becomes available. Clicking this button reveals the **Restart Computer Options** dialog box

FIGURE 14-9

Computer restart
options

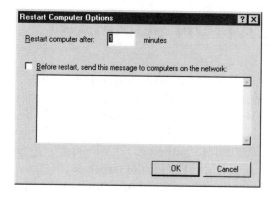

shown in Figure 14-9, where you can configure both the time prior to the system shutdown and a text message that will be sent using the messenger service to all of the computers on the network, alerting them to the system's pending shutdown.

The **Dependencies** tab shown in Figure 14-10 is the last of the four tabs in the service properties. On this tab, you are provided with a list of services that the current service depends on and a list of services that are dependent on this service. In the example shown in Figure 14-10, you can see that the World Wide Web Publishing Service depends on three other services: HTTP SSL, IIS Admin Service, and Remote Procedure Call (RPC).

FIGURE 14-10

Service
dependencies

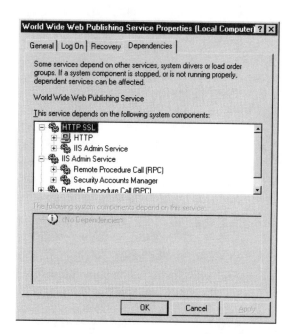

CERTIFICATION SUMMARY

In this chapter, you have been exposed to the tools used to troubleshoot Internet connectivity issues. The tools introduced are centered around the use of **ping** to zero in on the problem spot, and **tracert** to find the router that possibly has problems routing the traffic. You were also introduced to the methodology of how to determine where the problem is located.

The utilities **pathping** and **nslookup** were used to glean further information about the network and DNS configurations.

When diagnosing and resolving service dependency issues, you have learned how to use utilities such as the **Services** MMC, Tasklist, Taskkill, and Service Controller to manage, monitor, and maintain services. You also learned how to identify what services are running within a given process, and how to end a process when required.

In the last section, you learned about service recovery options and how to define these to allow automated responses to be taken to first, second, and subsequent service failures. You also learned how to configure the properties of a service using the **Services** MMC, and how to obtain a rich set of valuable service-related information from tools like Service Controller and Tasklist. This information will be very helpful when you are confronted with a computer running Windows Server 2003 that is experiencing service-related problems.

✓ TWO-MINUTE DRILL

Troubleshoot Connectivity to the Internet

❑ Use **ping** to test communication with a remote host.

❑ Use **ping** with the IP address of the host to test just the network.

❑ Use **ping** with the FQDN of the host to test name resolution.

❑ Use **tracert** to locate the router that is experiencing problems.

❑ Use **pathping** to gather latency and packet loss statistics about the network.

❑ Use **nslookup** to test a DNS server, to ensure the correct data is returned to the client.

Diagnose and Resolve Issues Related to Service Dependency

❑ Services provide support for other programs.

❑ Task Manager, **Services** MMC, and Service Controller are utilities that can be used to monitor and maintain services.

❑ Both the **Services** MMC and Service Controller can be used to identify a service's dependencies and the services that the service in question is dependent on.

❑ Task Manager can be used to quickly end processes that are hung, or nonresponding applications.

❑ When multiple instances of the same service are running on a computer, the PID for the process can be used to determine the process that a specific service is running in.

Use Service Recovery Options to Diagnose and Resolve Service-Related Issues

❑ Service recovery options allow you to restart a service, run a command, or reboot the entire computer after a service failure, providing you with a way to automate administrative actions to service failures.

❑ The properties of a service reveal a great deal of information about the service, including the path to the service's executable, command parameters, the account used by the service to log on, recovery options, and dependencies,

SELF TEST

The following questions will help you measure your understanding of the material presented in this chapter. Read the questions and answers carefully, because there may be more than one correct answer. Choose all correct answers for each question.

Troubleshoot Connectivity to the Internet

1. Name resolution is handled by DNS. What tool would you use most often to test DNS? (Choose all that apply.)

   A. nslookup

   B. ping

   C. net

   D. dnslint

2. You are the network administrator for your company's network. You are currently troubleshooting a problem for one of your sites, which connects to the Internet through an ISDN connection to their local ISP. They report that they cannot reach **off.nop.to**, which is located at the IP address **10.0.42.42**. What is the first step you will take?

   A. Use **nslookup** to verify the DNS entry for the remote host **off.nop.to**.

   B. Ping **off.nop.to** in order to ascertain if the problem is network related or DNS related.

   C. Ping the DNS server to see if it is online.

   D. Use **pathping off.nop.to** to find the broken router.

3. You are the network administrator for your company's network. You are currently troubleshooting a problem for one of your sites, which connects to the Internet through an ISDN connection to their local ISP. They report that they cannot reach **off.nop.to**, which is located at the IP address **10.0.42.42**. You have determined that the **ping off.nop.to** command fails. What is the next step you will take?

   A. Use **nslookup** to verify the DNS entry for the remote host **off.nop.to**.

   B. Ping the default gateway in order to ascertain if the problem is on the local network.

   C. Ping the DNS server to see if it is online.

   D. Ping **10.0.42.42** in order to ascertain if the problem is network related or DNS related.

4. You are the network administrator for your company's network. You are currently troubleshooting a problem for one of your sites, which connects to the Internet through an ISDN connection

to their local ISP. They report that they cannot reach **off.nop.to**, which is located at the IP address **10.0.42.42**. You have determined that the **ping off.nop.to** command fails, but **ping 10.0.42.42** succeeds. What is the next step you will take?

A. Use **nslookup** to verify the DNS entry for the remote host **off.nop.to**.

B. Use the **tracert 10.0.42.42** command to ascertain where the problem is located.

C. Ping the DNS server to see if it is online.

D. Use the **tracert** utility to investigate the route to the DNS server.

5. You are the network administrator for your company's network. You are currently troubleshooting a problem for one of your sites, which connects to the Internet through an ISDN connection to their local ISP. They report that they cannot reach **off.nop.to**, which is located at the IP address **10.0.42.42**. You have determined that the **ping off.nop.to** command fails, but **ping 10.0.42.42** succeeds. When you ping the IP address of the DNS server, the command succeeds. What is the next step you will take?

A. Use **nslookup** to verify the DNS entry for the remote host **off.nop.to**.

B. Use the **tracert 10.0.42.42** command to ascertain where the problem is located.

C. Ping the default gateway to see if it is online.

D. Use the **tracert** utility to investigate the route to the DNS server.

6. You are the network administrator for your company's network. You are currently troubleshooting a problem for one of your sites, which connects to the Internet through an ISDN connection to their local ISP. They report that they cannot reach **off.nop.to**, which is located at the IP address **10.0.42.42**. You have determined that the **ping off.nop.to** command fails, as does the **ping 10.0.42.42** command. What is the next step you will take?

A. Use **tracert 10.0.42.42** to ascertain where the problem is located.

B. Use **tracert off.nop.to** to ascertain where the problem is located.

C. Use **nslookup 10.0.42.42** to find the broken router.

D. Use **nslookup off.nop.to** to find the broken router.

7. What utility can be used in troubleshooting the cause of an unreachable host? (Choose all that apply.)

A. **ping**

B. **tracert**

C. **nslookup**

D. **arp**

Diagnose and Resolve Issues Related to Service Dependency

8. You are the network administrator in your organization. You are researching tools available to troubleshoot service-related problems. You would like to be able to pipe all service-related information on a computer running Windows Server 2003 out to a text file so that you can print the document and work from a hardcopy. Which of the following tools will allow you to accomplish this? (Choose all that apply.)

    A. Windows Task Manager

    B. Service Principal

    C. Service Controller

    D. Tasklist

9. You are the network administrator in your organization. You have decided to use Tasklist to identify all of the processes running on a local computer running Windows Server 2003. You would also like to know what services are running within each of the processes. Which of the following commands will display this information?

    A. **tasklist /SVC /FO LIST**

    B. **tasklist /FI services**

    C. **tasklist /PID**

    D. **tasklist /SVC /FO TEXT**

10. You are the network administrator in your company. You recently installed an application on one of your computers running Windows Server 2003. After the installation, one of the services that the application depends on began functioning irregularly and often entered a hung state. The dependant service is not directly related to the application, and you are unsure of which process the service runs in, so you used Tasklist to identify the process. Unfortunately, there are multiple instances of the process running on the local computer. Which of the following will allow you to identify the correct process in Task Manager and end that task?

    A. Using Tasklist, highlight the identified process and launch Windows Task Manager. This will open **Windows Task Manager** and highlight the affected process.

    B. Simply open **Windows Task Manager** and select the **Processes** tab. The affected process will be listed as not responding.

    C. In **Windows Task Manager**, change the display options to filter and display only hung processes.

    D. In **Windows Task Manager**, change the display options to add the PID column.

11. You are the network administrator in your organization. You are planning on implementing a very restrictive security policy on one of your computers running Windows Server 2003, which will include disabling all unnecessary services for the server's role as a domain controller. You want to avoid disabling services that other services depend on. Which of the following tools will allow you to view service dependencies?

A. Dependents

B. **sc**

C. **services.msi**

D. Control Panel

12. You are the network administrator in your company. Your organization uses a number of contract consultants who have accounts on your network, but those accounts are supposed to have limited rights. One of the file and application servers in the HR department is always supposed to be off-limits to consultants and most employees as well, except for those who work in the HR department. While performing some regular service on the computer, you noticed an abnormal amount of system activity. You would like to quickly view all of the processes running on the computer and see which users are associated with which processes. Which of the following will allow you to accomplish this?

A. Open Windows Task Manager and select the **Users** tab.

B. Open the **Services** MMC and select the **Log On** tab.

C. Open the **Services** MMC and select **View | Advanced | Show all users**.

D. Open Windows Task Manager and select to show processes from all users on the **Processes** tab.

Use Service Recovery Options to Diagnose and Resolve Service-Related Issues

13. You are the network administrator within your company. One of your computers running Windows Server 2003 is experiencing service startup problems during initialization. The hardware configuration of the system doesn't appear to be sufficient to provide enough system resources to all services starting up during boot up, and this leads to one or more of the same services failing upon startup. Normally, when this occurs during business hours, you manually start the services, but a new patch management security policy now dictates that all servers be remotely shut down and restarted every night at 12:05 A.M., and a script has been written to accomplish this task. The difficultly now is that these services remain in a failed state until you arrive in the morning to restart them. Which of the following actions can you take to resolve and automate the solution to this ongoing problem?

A. In Windows Task Manager, right-click the process in which the services run and select **Set Priority | High**.

B. In Windows Task Manager, right-click the process in which the services run and select **Set Priority | Realtime**.

C. In the **Services** MMC, right-click the service, and on the **Dependencies** tab, disable all applications that depend on this service.

D. In the **Services** MMC, right-click the service, and on the **Recovery** tab, set the first failure action to restart the service, and change the **restart service after** value to **3** minutes.

14. You are the network administrator for your company. Your new corporate security policy mandates that all accounts, including service accounts, must have their passwords changed every 37 days. To comply with this policy, you have changed the passwords for all of the service accounts in Active Directory using Active Directory Users and Computers, because all of your service accounts are domain accounts. As soon as this task is complete, you begin noticing service failures on a number of servers throughout your network. What can you do to correct this problem and still abide by the corporate security policy?

    A. Change the passwords back to the original password in Active Directory Users and Computers.

    B. Make the same password change to the local system account on each of the servers.

    C. Make the same password change to the local computer service account on each of the servers.

    D. Make the same password change in the services' properties.

15. You are the network administrator in your organization. You have configured your notebook to run Windows Server 2003 so that you could take it home and familiarize yourself with the operating system. When the notebook is at the office, you connect to the LAN using your docking station, but at home, you use a wireless NIC. The office currently doesn't have any wireless access, and you would like to disable the services related to your wireless NIC while at the office. Which of the following will allow you to accomplish this in the most efficient manner? (Choose all that apply.)

    A. Using the Services MMC, disable the wireless service for the office hardware profile.

    B. Using the Services MMC, configure the wireless service to use a local computer account.

    C. Create a new hardware profile for home use.

    D. Create a local computer account as opposed to one in Active Directory to be used for the wireless service.

LAB QUESTION

You are the network administrator for your organization. You are putting together some documentation on the configuration of your servers, and you would like to include the services that are running and the processes that they are running in. You would also like to document all of the service accounts that are being used by the various services. Finally, you would like to configure service restart options for all of the services to restart the service at the first failure and to send a net send message to the administrator upon the second failure. Document the steps you would take to accomplish these tasks.

SELF TEST ANSWERS

Troubleshoot Connectivity to the Internet

1. ☑ **A and B. nslookup** is the main test utility, but **ping** is also commonly used to test name resolution and connectivity in one step.

   ☒ **C** is incorrect because the **net** command is used to configure resources in Windows. **D** is incorrect because **dnslint** is used to test the quality of the DNS zone files, not that DNS returns correct data.

2. ☑ **B.** Always start by using the **ping** utility to determine if the problem is name-resolution or DNS related.

   ☒ **A** is incorrect because there is nothing indicating that the DNS server is at fault. **C** is incorrect because there is nothing to indicate that you are having a DNS problem. **D** is incorrect because there is nothing indicating that you have a bad route.

3. ☑ **D.** If the **ping** command fails with the FQDN of the remote host, try pinging the IP address of the host.

   ☒ **A** is incorrect because there is no firm indication that the problem is with DNS yet. **B** is incorrect because that would be the first step to take. **C** is incorrect because there is no firm indication it is a DNS problem yet.

4. ☑ **C.** After determining that the problem is with name resolution, you should ping the DNS server to see if it is online.

   ☒ **A** is incorrect because you still do not know if the DNS server is online. **B** is incorrect because you already know that the problem is not a network problem. **D** is incorrect because you still do not know if the DNS server is online.

5. ☑ **A.** Use the **nslookup** utility to verify the data for the **off.nop.to** server.

   ☒ **B** is incorrect because you already know the problem is with DNS. **C and D** are incorrect because you know the DNS server is answering.

6. ☑ **A.** The correct step here is to find out where the traffic is stopped. Alternatively, you could have used the IP address of the DNS server for this step.

   ☒ **B** is incorrect because name resolution does not work. **C and D** are incorrect because the problem is network related, not DNS related.

7. ☑ **A, B, and C. ping, tracert,** and **nslookup** are used to test connectivity, routing, and name resolution.

   ☒ **D** is incorrect because Address Resolution Protocol (ARP) is a Data Link layer protocol used to map IP addresses to MAC addresses.

Diagnose and Resolve Issues Related to Service Dependency

8. ☑   **C and D.** Only the Service Controller and Tasklist utilities will allow you to pipe all of the service-related information from the local computer out to a text file.
    ☒   **A** is incorrect because Windows Task Manager will not allow you to pipe out service-related information to a file. **B** is incorrect because Service Principle is not a tool that is used to manage services.

9. ☑   **A.** Only the command **tasklist /SVC /FO LIST** will display a list of processes that are running on the local computer and the services that are running within each process.
    ☒   **B, C,** and **D** are incorrect as none of these commands will result in the processes on the local machine being listed, nor will they show the services that are running within each process.

10. ☑   **D.** Adding the PID column to Windows Task Manager will allow you to identify the affected process by its PID in both utilities, thereby guaranteeing that you end the correct process.
    ☒   **A** is incorrect because highlighting the affected process in Tasklist and launching Windows Task Manager will not identify the affected process. **B** is incorrect because hung processes are not identified in Windows Task Manager as not responding on the **Processes** tab, only on the **Applications** tab are nonresponding applications identified this way. **C** is incorrect because there are no display options in Windows Task Manager that filter for only hung processes.

11. ☑   **B.** Only the Service Controller (**sc.exe**) will allow you to view service dependencies. Alternatively, you could also view service dependencies using the **Services** MMC, but the extension for that is **.msc**, not **.msi**.
    ☒   **A and C** are incorrect because **Dependents** and **services.msi** are not utilities included in the Windows Server 2003 operating system. **D** is incorrect because you could access administrative tools and the **Services** or **Computer Management** MMC through Control Panel, but Control Panel alone doesn't allow you to view service dependencies.

12. ☑   **D.** To view the processes used by all users on a computer, open Windows Task Manager and select to show processes from all users on the **Processes** tab.
    ☒   **A** is incorrect because the **Users** tab shows you the users that are currently logged on or connected to the computer, but it does not show you the processes that they are using. **B** is incorrect because the **Log On** tab in the **Services** MMC shows you the account used by the service to log on. **C** is incorrect because the **Services** MMC has a series of four tabs: General, Log On, Recovery, and **Dependencies**, but it doesn't have a View menu option.

Use Service Recovery Options to Diagnose and Resolve Service-Related Issues

13. ☑   **D.** In the **Services** MMC, right-click the service, and on the **Recovery** tab, set the first failure action to restart the service, and change the **restart service after** value to **3 minutes**. This will allow the computer to restart the failed service after three minutes, when more system resources should be available to start the service.

☒ **A** and **B** are incorrect because changing the service priority will not configure the service to restart. **C** is incorrect because in the **Services** MMC, you are not able to disable dependent services on the **Dependencies** tab.

14. ☑ **D.** Once the service account passwords have been changed in Active Directory Users and Computers, they must also be changed in the services' properties, which can be done through the **Services** MMC.

☒ **A** is incorrect because changing the passwords back to the original password in Active Directory Users and Computers will solve the problem, but will not abide by the corporate security policy. **B** is incorrect because the password of the local system account does not need to be changed for the services to run effectively because the services are using domain service accounts. **C** is incorrect because domain service accounts are being used, so there shouldn't be any local service accounts to worry about.

15. ☑ **A** and **C.** To disable the wireless service on the local computer while connected at the office, you could create a new hardware profile for use at home. This way the default profile will be used when at the office by disabling the wireless service in the default profile.

☒ **B** and **D** are incorrect because using the **Services** MMC to configure the wireless service to use a local computer account would not disable the wireless service while at the office.

LAB ANSWER

To identify the services that are running on your servers, you could use the Service Controller utility, the **Services** MMC, or Tasklist to list and document the services. You can identify the processes that the services are running in using Tasklist.

To use Tasklist to determine the services that are running, and the processes that they are running in, type the following command:

```
Tasklist /SVC /FO LIST
```

The results of this command can them be cut and pasted into a text document and saved as part of your documentation.

To document all of the service accounts that are being used by the various services, you could use the **Services** MMC and manually view the **Log On** tab in the properties of each service that is using a specific service account. You can quickly and easily determine which service is using a service account by looking at the **Log On** As column in the **Services** MMC.

To configure service restart options for all of the services to restart the service at the first failure and to send a **net send** message to the administrator upon the second failure, you could again use the **Services** MMC, open the properties of each service and make the required changes on the **Recovery** tab.

Glossary

A record Same as a host record or address record; uniquely identifies a single host within the namespace.

Access Control Entry (ACE) A single entry in an access control list (ACL).

Access Control List (ACL) The means by which an administrator controls access to resources, by granting permissions to specific users and security groups. Found on the **Security** tab of an object's **Properties** dialog box.

account lockout A policy that automatically disables an account after a specified number of failed logon attempts.

account policy A set of rules for how passwords must be defined and authenticated.

ACE *See* Access Control Entry.

ACL *See* Access Control List.

Active Directory A directory of resources available on a Windows Server 2003 network.

AD *See* Active Directory.

Address Resolution Protocol (ARP) The TCP/IP protocol used in resolving IP addresses to hardware addresses.

Address Transfer (AXFR) The original method of zone replication used by DNS, in which the entire zone database is replicated to secondary name servers.

API *See* Application Programming Interface.

APIPA *See* Automatic Private IP Addressing

Application Programming Interface (API) A set of routines that application programs can access to request and carry out lower-level services.

ARP   *See* Address Resolution Protocol.

Asynchronous Transfer Mode (ATM)   A network communications mode designed to carry data, voice, and video.

ATM   *See* Asynchronous Transfer Mode.

attribute   A characteristic or individual setting within an object. For example, a file has a Read-Only attribute that can be set on or off.

audit   To track network activities by users.

audit policy   A policy that defines the events to be tracked and maintained in a log.

authentication   The process by which a network validates a user's logon information.

authentication protocol   The method used by a client to authenticate to a service; these protocols can send the data in clear text, or encrypt the data using a number of encryption schemes.

Automatic Private IP Addressing (APIPA)   A method of ensuring that a computer is given an IP address even though there is no DHCP server available on the network. The APIPA address is non-routable.

AXFR   *See* Address Transfer.

bandwidth   The speed at which data can move through a connection, usually measured in bits per second (bps). For example, a 56 Kbps connection can move up to 56,000 bits per second.

BOOTP   Bootstrap Protocol. Originally a means of allowing clients to boot from a server computer, and a precursor to DHCP.

BOOTP forwarding   A means of allowing broadcast messages to get across a router.

bridgehead server   The point of contact between two sites, used for Active Directory replication.

broadcast   A message sent to all hosts in a local area network when the specific address of the desired host is not known.

built-in groups   The default security groups found in Windows Server 2003 and Windows XP Professional that assign rights and permissions to groups based on common job functions.

CA   *See* Certificate Authority.

certificate   Information used for authentication and secure data exchange.

Certificate Authority (CA)   An issuer of security certificates used for secure HTTP (SSL) connections.

certificate services   Software services that provide smart card authentication, secure web-based authentication, secure e-mail, and more.

child object   An object that resides within some higher-level object of the same type, such as a subfolder within a parent folder.

client   A computer or program that connects to and interacts with a server computer or program.

CNAME record   Canonical name; a DNS resource record that provides alternative names for an existing resource.

computer account   Similar to a user account, but uniquely identifies a specific computer, rather than a person, in the domain.

connectionless protocol   A type of protocol that transmits messages without first establishing an open connection between the source and destination. IP and UDP are both connectionless protocols.

connection-oriented protocol   A type of protocol that requires a stable connection to be set up between two machines before transmitting data. TCP is a connection-oriented protocol.

console tree   The left pane of the Microsoft Management Console (MMC).

container   An object, such as a folder, that is capable of storing more objects.

DACL   *See* Discretionary Access Control List.

datagram   A single unit of data transported across network lines.

DC   *See* domain controller.

DDNS   *See* Dynamic DNS.

default gateway   The address to which all requests for resources outside the local network are sent.

default groups   Predefined security groups that have predetermined rights and permissions.

delegation   The ability to assign a task, or portion of a task, to a specific user or group.

Dfs   *See* Distributed File System

DHCP   *See* Dynamic Host Configuration Protocol.

DHCP client   Any computer that is capable of obtaining its IP information automatically from a DHCP server.

DHCP Relay Agent   A component that sends DHCP traffic between network segments that are not connected with routers that support BOOTP Forwards.

DHCP scope   A range of IP addresses that a DHCP server is allowed to assign to clients.

DHCP server   Any Windows Server 2003 computer set up to assign IP information to DHCP clients.

directory service   A database containing information about resources available on the network.

Discretionary Access Control List (DACL)   The portion of an object's security descriptor that allows or denies permissions to specific users and groups.

Distinguished Name (DN)   The name that uniquely identifies an object by its relative distinguished name plus the names of container objects and domains. Every Active Directory object has a distinguished name.

Distributed File System (Dfs)   A means of organizing shares from multiple computers into a logical structure that the user can access without knowing the physical locations of the shared folders.

distribution group   A group used solely for e-mail or application distributions, but not for security.

DN   *See* Distinguished name.

DNS   *See* Domain Name System.

domain   A collection of computers that share a common Active Directory database and are contained within a single security boundary.

domain controller (DC)   Any computer running Windows Server 2003, Windows 2000, or Windows NT Server that is used for authentication and stores the Active Directory database, or the security accounts database (SAM), in the case of Windows NT 4.0.

domain local group   A security or distribution group that is local to the domain and can contain universal groups, global groups, other domain local groups from the same domain, as well as accounts from any domain in the domain tree or forest.

domain name   A name that uniquely identifies a domain, for example, microsoft.com or osborne.com.

Domain Name System (DNS)   The distributed hierarchical namespace used on the Internet and most other TCP/IP networks.

dynamic disk   A physical disk that provides more flexibility than a basic disk in creating volumes. Dynamic disks support mirror volumes, spanned volumes, and stripe sets.

Dynamic DNS (DDNS)   A system that provides clients with dynamically assigned IP addresses to register their names directly in the DNS server database.

Dynamic Host Configuration Protocol (DHCP)   A means whereby clients can obtain TCP/IP settings, including IP address, subnet mask, default gateway address, and more, from a server.

dynamic routing   General term for routing protocols, such as Routing Information Protocol (RIP) and Open Shortest Path First (OSPF), that allow routers to automatically build their own routing tables.

encryption   The process of protecting data by making it indecipherable to unauthorized persons.

Ethernet card   *See* network interface card.

Event Viewer   An administrative tool used for viewing system, security, and other events that occur on the system.

FAT   *See* File Allocation Table.

fault tolerance The ability of a computer or operating system to continue to function normally when a hardware error occurs.

File Allocation Table (FAT) The file system originally used in DOS and 16-bit versions of Windows; doesn't provide the ACLs found in NTFS.

File Replication Service (FRS) The service that provides multimaster file replication for Active Directory and Dfs file synchronization.

File Transfer Protocol (FTP) A standardized protocol for exchanging files in a TCP/IP network.

firewall Hardware or software designed to prevent unauthorized access to a private network.

folder redirection A group policy extension that allows you to redirect users' Application Data, Desktop, My Documents, or Start Menu folders.

forest The term for all the items in an Active Directory database. A forest can contain multiple domains and multiple domain trees.

forward lookup The DNS query process in which a DNS name is resolved to an IP address.

FQDN *See* Fully Qualified Domain Name.

FRS *See* File Replication Service.

FTP *See* File Transfer Protocol.

Fully Qualified Domain Name (FQDN) The complete name of a host, including the domain to which it belongs. For example, Server01.certifiable.local.

gateway Another term for *router*, as well as the term used to describe any service that allows two disparate networks to communicate.

global catalog A domain controller that contains a partial replica of an Active Directory database.

global catalog server   A Microsoft Windows Server 2003 domain controller that holds a copy of the global catalog for the entire forest.

global group   A security group that can store user accounts from its own domain, but can be used to set rights and permissions to objects inside, and outside, the domain.

globally unique identifier (GUID)   A 128-bit number that is guaranteed to be unique, and is assigned to objects when they are created. Renaming an object does not change its GUID.

GPO   *See* Group Policy Object.

group   The generic term for a security group or distribution group.

group policy   A collection of policy settings that can be applied to multiple computers or users, then filtered to apply only to selected security groups.

Group Policy Object (GPO)   A collection of group policy settings stored as a single object to be linked to Active Directory domains, sites, or OUs.

GUID   *See* globally unique identifier.

home folder   A user's personal folder(s), such as the My Documents folder.

hop   The unit of measure describing the act of crossing a router.

host   Any computer or other device that is connected to a network. Each host has a host name that uniquely identifies it on the network.

host name   The name of a specific host on a network; can be the same as the computer name.

host record   A DNS resource record that identifies a single host within the namespace.

HOSTS file   An ASCII text file used in some TCP/IP networks to store host names to IP address mappings. A precursor to modern DNS.

HTTP   *See* Hypertext Transfer Protocol.

Hypertext Transfer Protocol (HTTP)   The protocol used by the World Wide Web.

IANA   *See* Internet Assigned Numbers Authority.

IAS   *See* Internet Authentication Service.

ICMP   *See* Internet Control Message Protocol.

IETF   *See* Internet Engineering Task Force.

IGMP   *See* Internet Group Management Protocol.

IIS   *See* Internet Information Service.

IMAP   *See* Internet Message Access Protocol.

in-addr.arpa domain   A top-level domain used for reverse mapping of IP addresses to domain names.

incremental zone transfer (IXFR)   A method of replicating DNS zone data across name servers, where only information that has been changed is transferred.

internet (lowercase i)   Any two or more subnets connected together to allow internetworking between them.

Internet (uppercase I)   The global TCP/IP network that offers the World Wide Web and other well-known services.

Internet Assigned Numbers Authority (IANA)   The agency responsible for assigning unique IP addresses to Internet hosts.

Internet Authentication Service (IAS)   A feature of Windows NT version 4.0 and later that extends the operating system's network authentication capabilities. Internet Authentication Service implements the Remote Authentication Dial-In

User Service (RADIUS). IAS is used to provide centralized authentication for users connecting through many different connection points.

Internet Control Message Protocol (ICMP)   A network layer protocol that carries administrative messages. Used by utilities such as **ping**.

Internet Engineering Task Force (IETF)   The large open community of engineers responsible for the operation and evolution of Internet standards.

Internet Group Management Protocol (IGMP)   A protocol used to manage multicast transmissions.

Internet Information Service (IIS)   The server software included with Windows Server 2003 editions.

Internet Message Access Protocol (IMAP)   A protocol that, like POP, allows e-mail clients to communicate with mail servers.

Internet Protocol (IP)   The network layer of TCP/IP responsible for end-to-end communications.

internetwork   A group of interconnected subnets, local area networks, or wide area networks.

intersite replication   Active Directory replication that takes place across two AD sites.

intranet   A private network that uses the same TCP/IP protocols used by the Internet.

intrasite   A web site that is accessible to the local network, but not to the public at large.

intrasite replication   Active Directory replication among domain controllers within an AD site.

IP   *See* Internet Protocol.

IP address   An address that uniquely represents a host on a TCP/IP network, usually expressed in dotted quad format, such as 192.168.0.1.

IP Security Protocol (IPSec)   A set of TCP/IP protocols designed for encrypted communications between computers that share a public key.

IPSec   *See* IP Security Protocol.

IXFR   *See* Incremental Zone Transfer.

Kerberos   The authentication protocol used to provide secure network access.

L2TP   *See* Layer 2 Tunneling Protocol.

LAN   *See* Local Area Network.

Layer 2 Tunneling Protocol (L2TP)   A protocol that allows computers to set up secure tunnels across ATM, Frame Relay, and X.25 media.

LDAP   *See* Lightweight Directory Access Protocol.

Lightweight Directory Access Protocol (LDAP)   The protocol used by Active Directory, based on standards defined in RFC 2251.

LMHOSTS file   An ASCII text file originally used in LAN Manager networks to resolve NetBIOS names to IP addresses.

load balancing   A means of distributing the workload of a server program across multiple computers.

Local Area Network (LAN)   A network that connects an office, usually high speed.

local group   A security group that defines rights and permissions that apply to the local computer.

Microsoft Management Console (MMC)   A generic tool used to display the various administrative tools, such as Active Directory Users and Groups, Internet Services Manager, and more.

mixed mode   A Windows Server 2003 network where the domain controllers are Windows Server 2003 based as well as Windows 2000 Server based. The Active Directory Domains and Trusts or Active Directory users and computers snap-in allows you to switch from mixed mode to native mode.

MMC   *See* Microsoft Management Console.

modem   A device that translates digital signals into analog for transmission over an analog network.

multimaster replication   A replication method in which any domain controller can accept changes and replicate those changes to any other domain controller.

name resolution   The process of converting a name, like www.microsoft.com, to a numeric address, like 207.46.197.100.

namespace   A hierarchical naming system, such as that used by DNS.

NAT   *See* Network Address Translation.

native mode   A Windows Server 2003 network where all domain controllers are Windows Server 2003 based. The Active Directory Domains and Trusts snap-in allows you to switch from mixed mode to native mode.

NetBEUI   A transport protocol used in some earlier versions of the Windows operating system, now replaced by TCP/IP.

NetBIOS   An application programming interface that can be used to enable communications within MS-DOS, LAN Manager, and OS/2 networks.

Network Address Translation (NAT)   A technique that allows clients with unregistered, private IP addresses to access resources on the Internet.

network interface card (NIC) The hardware that allows a computer to connect to and interact with a network. Also called an Ethernet card.

Network Monitor A tool supplied with Windows Server 2003 used to capture and analyze network traffic.

NIC *See* network interface card.

nslookup A command-line tool used to query a DNS server to troubleshoot DNS configuration issues.

NT File System (NTFS) The preferred file system used in Windows Server 2003 to provide large volumes and control access to individual files and folders.

NTFS *See* NT File System.

object Any entity that can be created, named, and treated as a unit.

organizational unit (OU) A container within Active Directory into which you can place computer accounts, user accounts, and other network resources so you can manage them as a unit.

OU *See* organizational unit.

owner The person who controls permissions that define who can access a folder or other object.

packet The largest unit of data that can be transmitted across a network at one time.

packet filter A software filter that allows or disallows traffic through a router, based on the type of packet. Can be controlled by port or protocol of the packet.

packet switching The type of network communications found on the Internet where messages are broken down into packets, transmitted across a network, and reassembled into proper order at the destination computer.

pathping   A command-line tool used to report on the route between two hosts as well as the latency of the network segments of that route.

parent object   The container for another object. For example, My Documents is the parent to any subfolders that exist within the My Documents folder.

partition   A portion of a physical disk defined to appear as a physically separate disk.

permissions inheritance   The process where the permissions assigned to an object are automatically applied to child objects.

ping   The name of a command, but also used as a verb. For example to "ping server01" means to enter the command **ping server01**. The **ping** command sends a message to another computer and gives you information whether the two computers can reach other.

PKI   *See* public key infrastructure.

pointer (PTR) record   A DNS resource record used in a reverse lookup zone to provide reverse IP-address-to-name resolution.

policy   A collection of desktop settings and security settings.

port   A number that represents a specific connection point in an IP address. For example, HTTP uses port 80 as the default.

primary master   A DNS server that acts as the only server capable of accepting changes.

private key   The secure half of a public/private key that is used on the server side, used in asymmetric encryption for secure communications.

proxy server   A server that sits between clients and "real" servers that the clients interact with. Clients make requests to the proxy server, which in turn contacts the real server and passes the information back to the client.

public key The public half of a private/public key pair that may be distributed to clients. Data encrypted by the public key can only be decrypted by the appropriate private key.

public key infrastructure (PKI) The generic term used to describe the standards and rules that regulate the use of certificates and private/public key pairs.

publish To make visible in Active Directory, or to make available for installation as when publishing an application to users.

query A request for information.

RADIUS *See* Remote Authentication Dial-In User Service.

refresh interval Generally used to describe the timeframe in which a client can update its information, or request updates from another computer.

Remote Access Policy A set of conditions and parameters for the connection that defines the constraints that will be imposed on the connection.

Remote Authentication Dial-In User Service (RADIUS) A popular standard used for maintaining and managing remote user authentication and validation. The new Routing and Remote Access Service (RRAS) can operate as a RADIUS client. This allows RAS clients and dial-up routers to be authenticated against a RADIUS server.

replication The act of copying data from one computer to other computers to keep their current data stores in sync.

Request for Comments (RFC) The main method of communication used by the Internet Engineering Task Force (IETF). Internet standards are defined in the RFCs at **www.ietf.org**.

reservation A specific IP address that is maintained by DHCP for a specific client based on the unique network ID of the network card.

resolver Any DNS client that is capable of accessing a DNS name server to convert a host name to an IP address.

resource record (RR)   A record contained within a DNS zone database file to identify a single resource within the namespace.

reverse lookup   A DNS query where an IP address is resolved to a host name, rather than vice versa.

RFC   *See* Request for Comments.

right   Permissions that apply to the system as a whole, as opposed to a single folder or file. For example, "Log on Locally" would be considered a right rather than a permission.

RIP   *See* Routing Information Protocol.

roaming user profile   A user profile that is stored on a server and downloaded to a computer when a user logs on. Allows a user to have the same settings and home folder regardless of which computer he or she logs on to.

root domain   The domain at the top of a DNS hierarchy, represented by a period (.) or a blank space.

router   A device or computer that can route packets between two or more separate subnets or networks.

Routing and Remote Access Service (RRAS)   A Windows service that provides for remote access to the network over a number of connection media, and also provides for routing of network traffic.

Routing Information Protocol (RIP)   A dynamic routing protocol that allows users to build and maintain their own routing tables.

routing interface   A software component that provides routing access to the network.

routing table   A list of network destinations and the routers and interfaces required to reach them, stored in every TCP/IP network.

RR   *See* resource record.

RRAS *See* Routing and Remote Access Service.

schema The structure of an Active Directory database, describing object classes, the type of objects that can be created, and the attributes associated with each object class.

second-level domain A specific entity within a top-level domain. For example, *microsoft.com* is a second-level domain name, where *com* is the top-level name.

secondary master In non-Active Directory DNS zones, the read-only copy of the zone database file that is replicated from the primary name server.

Secure Sockets Layer (SSL) A security protocol used to create secure web sites, where all transmissions are encrypted.

security group A group with a stored set of rights and permissions. User accounts can be made members of the group and will inherit those rights and permissions.

security identifier (SID) A number that uniquely identifies user, group, and computer accounts that are created when the object is created, and never changes.

security log A log file that tracks security events when auditing is enabled, and can be viewed through Event Viewer.

security template A collection of security settings stored in a text file (**.inf**) that can be imported into a Group Policy Object.

server A computer or program that provides a service on a network. For example, a web server serves web pages to clients that request them.

service pack A software update distributed as a package on CD, or made available as an Internet download.

share (Verb)to make available to other computers in a network; (noun) a shared resource.

shared resource A file, folder, printer, program, or data that is accessible from multiple computers in a network.

SID   *See* security identifier.

Simple Mail Transfer Protocol (SMTP)   A TCP/IP protocol generally used to carry messages between servers.

Simple Network Management Protocol (SNMP)   A TCP/IP protocol used to carry information about the status of resources within the network.

single-master replication   A replication technique where only one computer is capable of accepting changes, and then replicates those changes to other servers.

site   In Active Directory, a collection of computers, subnets, or both connected by fast, reliable network connections.

site link   A link across two Active Directory sites used for replicating AD data between the sites.

site link bridge   Three or more Active Directory sites sharing the same transport for replication.

SMTP   *See* Simple Mail Transfer Protocol.

snap-in   A tool used within the Microsoft Management Console, usually for administrative purposes.

SNMP   *See* Simple Network Management Protocol.

SOA record   *See* Start of Authority record.

Software Update Service (SUS)   A Windows service that provides administrative management over software patch management.

SRV record   A DNS service resource record used to register and identify TCP/IP services that are available in the zone.

SSL   *See* Secure Sockets Layer.

stand-alone server   A Windows Server 2003 computer that does not participate in the domain and has its own local list of valid user accounts and security groups.

Start of Authority (SOA) record   Used to identify the namespace over which a DNS name server has authority, as well as other general information such as the replication schedule.

static route   A route contained within a routing table that was added manually and doesn't change.

subdomain   A child domain, a domain that is contained within a parent of the same name. For example, thisnet.mydomain.com would be a subdomain of mydomain.com.

subnet   A group of computers that share the same network address and can communicate with one another by broadcasting.

subnet mask   A TCP/IP parameter that identifies which bits in an IP address identify the network, and which bits identify the specific host.

SUS   *See* Software Update Service.

SYSVOL   A shared folder containing a server's copy of a domain's public files.

T-1   A dedicated leased-line connection with a bandwidth of 1.544 Mbps.

TCP   *See* Transmission Control Protocol.

tracert   A command-line tool that provides information on the route traffic takes between two hosts.

Transmission Control Protocol (TCP)   The connection-oriented protocol used in TCP/IP, usually to deliver large bodies of information, such as files.

trust relationship   A link between two domains where a user's security credentials used to log on to one domain automatically pass through and authenticate the user on the other domain.

tunnel   A secure network link through which encapsulated, encrypted data can be transmitted to maintain privacy.

UDP   *See* User Datagram Protocol.

UNC   *See* Universal Naming Convention.

Uniform Resource Locator (URL)   The address that provides access to a specific resource. For example, **http://www.osborne.com** is the URL for the Osborne/McGraw-Hill web site.

universal group   A security or distribution group that can be used anywhere in a domain tree or forest.

Universal Naming Convention (UNC)   A simple naming scheme in which a resource is identified by server name and specific name, as in Server01 SharedDocs (a shared folder on a computer named Server01).

URL   *See* Uniform Resource Locator.

user account   A collection of information that uniquely identifies a single person who is allowed to log on to the network.

User Datagram Protocol (UDP)   A stateless protocol in TCP/IP that transfers data without waiting for acknowledgment of packets received.

Virtual Private Network (VPN)   A network that connects two entities through an encrypted channel. Can be used to connect a single host to a network, or to connect networks together. The VPN usually uses the public Internet for the connection.

volume   A storage medium that is formatted as a file system (such as NTFS) and appears as a drive (such as C:).

VPN   *See* Virtual Private Network.

WAN   *See* wide area network.

well-connected   Connected with high-speed, reliable networking hardware, such as Ethernet.

well-known port   TCP/IP port numbers that have been assigned by IANA. Examples include port 80 (World Wide Web) and port 21 (FTP).

wide area network (WAN)   A network that spans a large geographical area.

Windows Internet Naming Service (WINS)   A service that provides centralized registration of NetBIOS clients, and provides NetBIOS name-to-IP-address resolution.

WINS   *See* Windows Internet Naming Service.

zone   In DNS, the namespace over which a DNS name server has authority.

zone database file   The database in which host-name-to-IP-address mappings are stored in a DNS zone.

zone transfer   The act of replicating a database zone file across multiple name servers.

INDEX

INTERNATIONAL CONTACT INFORMATION

AUSTRALIA
McGraw-Hill Book Company
Australia Pty. Ltd.
TEL +61-2-9900-1800
FAX +61-2-9878-8881
http://www.mcgraw-hill.com.au
books-it_sydney@mcgraw-hill.com

CANADA
McGraw-Hill Ryerson Ltd.
TEL +905-430-5000
FAX +905-430-5020
http://www.mcgraw-hill.ca

GREECE, MIDDLE EAST, & AFRICA
(Excluding South Africa)
McGraw-Hill Hellas
TEL +30-210-6560-990
TEL +30-210-6560-993
TEL +30-210-6560-994
FAX +30-210-6545-525

MEXICO (Also serving Latin America)
McGraw-Hill Interamericana Editores
S.A. de C.V.
TEL +525-1500-5108
FAX +525-117-1589
http://www.mcgraw-hill.com.mx
carlos_ruiz@mcgraw-hill.com

SINGAPORE (Serving Asia)
McGraw-Hill Book Company
TEL +65-6863-1580
FAX +65-6862-3354
http://www.mcgraw-hill.com.sg
mghasia@mcgraw-hill.com

SOUTH AFRICA
McGraw-Hill South Africa
TEL +27-11-622-7512
FAX +27-11-622-9045
robyn_swanepoel@mcgraw-hill.com

SPAIN
McGraw-Hill/
Interamericana de España, S.A.U.
TEL +34-91-180-3000
FAX +34-91-372-8513
http://www.mcgraw-hill.es
professional@mcgraw-hill.es

UNITED KINGDOM, NORTHERN,
EASTERN, & CENTRAL EUROPE
McGraw-Hill Education Europe
TEL +44-1-628-502500
FAX +44-1-628-770224
http://www.mcgraw-hill.co.uk
emea_queries@mcgraw-hill.com

ALL OTHER INQUIRIES Contact:
McGraw-Hill/Osborne
TEL +1-510-420-7700
FAX +1-510-420-7703
http://www.osborne.com
omg_international@mcgraw-hill.com

Sound Off!

Visit us at **www.osborne.com/bookregistration** and let us know what you thought of this book. While you're online you'll have the opportunity to register for newsletters and special offers from McGraw-Hill/Osborne.

We want to hear from you!

Sneak Peek

Visit us today at **www.betabooks.com** and see what's coming from McGraw-Hill/Osborne tomorrow!

Based on the successful software paradigm, Bet@Books™ allows computing professionals to view partial and sometimes complete text versions of selected titles online. Bet@Books™ viewing is free, invites comments and feedback, and allows you to "test drive" books in progress on the subjects that interest you the most.

Get certified...
in a flash!

CardDeck
EXAM PREPARATION **FLASH CARDS**

Available for Windows & Pocket PC!

Study anytime, anywhere
on your laptop or
Pocket PC!

O Leverage proven flash-card study methods!

O Dramatically increase memory retention!

O Create your own custom card sets!

O Add images & media to reinforce key concepts!

Inside the enclosed CD:

- **Card Deck for Windows**
- **Card Deck CE for Pocket PC**
- **Over 100 sample cards covering all exam topics!**

Pocket PC

*Visit us online for more
great IT certification card sets
based on McGraw-Hill/Osborne publications.*

2003 ezflashcards, LLC.

Prepare

Get the books that show you not only what—but *how*—to study